HISTORY OF
THE DIOCESE OF CLEVELAND

→≫ · ≪←

His Holiness Pope Pius XII

To Our Venerable Brother
Edward Francis Hoban
Bishop of the Diocese of Cleveland
PIUS PP. XII
Venerable Brother,
Health and Apostolic Benediction.

Having learned with paternal gratification of the celebrations which are to mark the centenary of the erection of the Diocese of Cleveland, We gladly extend to you, Venerable Brother, Our very cordial felicitations on this blessed and joyous occasion.

Under God's Providence and by His divine favor the salutary work of the upbuilding of the Church has gone on steadily and unceasingly down through the course of a hundred years. The many churches, religious houses, schools and charitable institutions, are the material monuments testifying to its flourishing growth, to the devoted labours of zealous pastors, priests and people, and to the generous sacrifices which they readily made to provide for the religious, moral and social needs of the rapidly increasing Catholic community. The vital force underlying that wonderful growth has been none other than that divine life of faith, hope and charity which, under God, has taken such deep roots in the hearts of the people of Cleveland and which finds such a fair and noble expression in the growing numbers of young men and women who, year after year, like perennial flowers blossoming forth in the garden of the Church, devote their lives to the service of God, and to that of their fellow-man in God.

In their apostolic work for the establishment and extension of the Church, which is the mystical Body of Christ, many priests from your Diocese have gone, with ready will and selfless devotion, to the far foreign fields of the missions, while others labour in the same sacred cause, and with equally generous zeal, nearer home. From their numbers some have been raised to the fulness of the sacred priesthood and, under Our Jurisdiction, share Our pastoral solicitude for the Church of God in the dioceses committed to their care. Among these We recall with special gratification Our Beloved Son, Edward Cardinal Mooney, whose zealous labours for the Church, and for the recognition of Catholic social principles in public life, have made him worthy to be honoured with the Cardinalitial dignity. We rejoice with you, Venerable Brother, in this blessed fruitfulness which has been productive of so much good for souls and which redounds, under God, to the honour of the Church in Cleveland.

It is by reason of this intensive and extensive growth that, on two occasions within the past hundred years, the Holy See has deemed it opportune to erect new dioceses from out of the territory which was originally subject to the jurisdiction of the Bishop of Cleveland. On this solemn occasion, it is your joy and your privilege as Bishop of the Diocese from which such thriving ecclesiastical life has radiated, to offer heartfelt and public thanks to God for the many and great blessings of the past hundred years.

It is particularly fitting that the solemn ceremony of the dedication of your newly enlarged Cathedral, the mother church of the Diocese, should form the center, as it were, of your centenary celebrations, for in this historic event the generous aspirations of your predecessors in the pastoral office, and of the devoted priests and faithful of past generations, find their fulfillment, and the accumulated labours of the past are merged with the beneficent activity of the present, to the praise and glory of God. What has especially consoled Us is that, with truly pastoral solicitude, you have instituted a general mission throughout the Diocese in preparation for this solemn event. In this observance of spiritual renewal and of rededication of the temple of God in mens' hearts, We see the most salutary expression of your humble thanksgiving to God for blessings received. We hear from grateful hearts the hymn of praise "give glory to God for He is good, for His mercy endureth forever" (i. Paral. v. 13); and We are confirmed in hope that, in the years ahead, the faithful of the Diocese of Cleveland, loyal to the laws of God and of His Church, staunch in their devotion to their pastors, jealous of the sacred traditions of Catholic home life, watchful for the truly Catholic education and upbringing of the children with whom God has blessed them, will hand on to future generations the sacred heritage of the faith, pure and undefiled.

The ceremony of the dedication of your Cathedral, so expressive of the primacy of God in the public and private life of the faithful, finds its due complement in the solemn blessing of those other institutions which you have the honour to dedicate, and which have as their object the fulfillment of the divine precept of fraternal charity. We have come to know the all-embracing and Christ-like nature of that charity; for frequently in the past We have had gracious tokens of your devoted assistance and of your filial interest in Our works of merciful relief and, on this joyous occasion, with a largeness of heart such as becomes the pastoral office, you, Venerable Brother, have made Us, on behalf of your people, a munificent offering whereby the suffering members of Christ in many lands will be made sharers of your joy, and will realize that they are not forgotten by their fellow-members in His mystical Body. In that same spirit of charity you and the members of your beloved flock, have come generously to the assistance of the war-shattered Diocese of Boulogne-sur-Mer, thus remembering the praise of gratitude to God for the gift of faith by graciously honouring the memory of him who, as the first Bishop of the Diocese of Cleveland, was the guardian of the purity of that faith.

From Our paternal heart, greatly comforted and consoled by the magnificent charity of which the Diocese of Cleveland has given such abundant proof, We extend to you, Venerable Brother, the expression of Our deep and appreciative gratitude. On "this day which the Lord has made" (Psl. xciv. 24) We rejoice with you and with the members of your beloved flock, and We earnestly pray that God may ever prosper the "faith and labour and charity" (1. Thessal. 1.3) of the Church in Cleveland. In pledge of that divine assistance We gladly impart to you, Venerable Brother, to your devoted priests and religious, and to your faithful people, Our paternal Apostolic Benediction.

Given at the Vatican on the twenty-second day of April, in the year of Our Lord nineteen hundred and forty-eight, and in the tenth year of Our Pontificate.

Pius PP. XII

His Excellency Archbishop Edward Francis Hoban

HISTORY OF THE DIOCESE OF CLEVELAND

Origin and Growth (1847-1952)

BY

MICHAEL J. HYNES
PH.D., D.SC. HIST. (*Louvain*)

1953

DIOCESE OF CLEVELAND

1027 SUPERIOR AVENUE, CLEVELAND, OHIO

First Edition

Nihil obstat

ANTHONY N. FUERST

Censor Librorum

Imprimatur

† EDWARD F. HOBAN

Archbishop: Bishop of Cleveland

Cleveland JULY 23, 1952

DESIGNED AND PRODUCED BY THE WORLD PUBLISHING COMPANY

CLEVELAND, OHIO

FOREWORD

With a deep sense of gratitude to God, and with grateful recognition of the painstaking and scholarly work of the author of this volume, we present the history of one hundred years of Catholicity in the Diocese of Cleveland.

The progress of the Church and the spread of God's kingdom on earth is of extreme interest and concern to every Catholic worthy of the name. It is the unfolding of the Divine Plan and the fulfillment of Christ's promise to His Apostles when He sent them into the world with the assurance of His support and guidance even to the end of time.

The history of Christ's Church in this diocese parallels the history of the settlement and development of the land itself. Catholics were among the first settlers; Catholics helped to clear the forests and cultivate the land; Catholics were here to develop commerce and industry and to people the cities. The Church here is no exotic plant; it is a sturdy tree, deep-rooted in the soil. It has grown with the growth and has bloomed with the development of the commonwealth. Inured to its climate, braving its storms and invigorated by them, it has yielded abundantly the fruits of religion and sanctification. Protected by those guarantees of liberty contained in the first instrument of government in these parts and afterwards incorporated into the constitution of the State, the Church here did not have to pass through a period of violent persecution such as she endured in other parts of this nation. Annoyance there was, at times, and discrimination, but not because of persecutory laws.

The progress of the Christian Faith here has contributed inestimably to the stability and perpetuity of good government. The Catholic Church is the friend of law and order, the upholder of legitimate authority, the stern opponent of anarchy as well as of oppression; by her conservative spirit, she is an element of strength to the nation, inculcating respect for constituted authority and for the laws framed to promote the welfare and happiness of the community.

Knowing the difficulties bred by national rivalries, Cleveland's bishops have always insisted that clergy and people, no matter from what country they came, should be thoroughly identified with the land in which their lot was cast, and should study its laws and political constitution and be in harmony with its spirit and become as soon as possible assimilated to the social body in all things pertaining to the domain of civil life. The first Catholics, poor and despised, have grown

to be a mighty host in the community, filling high positions of trust
in business, in the professions, and in the government; in times of war,
they have contributed their generous share to the forces which protect
our country; at much cost to themselves, they have educated their children in the fear and love of God, the basis for true patriotism and true
citizenship.

Three flourishing dioceses now occupy the territory assigned by
Pope Pius IX to the spiritual care of Bishop Rappe in 1847. More than
a thousand priests are required to minister to the hundreds of thousands of Catholics who have succeeded the little flock then cared for
by less than a score. Great churches have supplanted the log-cabin
chapels. In the present Diocese of Cleveland alone, nearly 75,000 pupils
are enrolled in the elementary and high schools; there are three colleges, a university, and dozens of institutions and agencies which
dispense every form of Christian charity.

In the Providence of God, this progress has been due to the happy
and cordial cooperation of bishops, priests, and people. The bishops,
as is their divinely appointed task, laid the foundations and supervised
the erection of the superstructure. They recruited the members of
the clergy and filled the ranks of the teachers in the schools. It has
been their work to consolidate and expand whatever had been done
by their predecessors; to vindicate the right of the Church to carry
out her divine mission to spread the Kingdom of God; to introduce
and maintain ecclesiastical discipline; to reprove, to exhort, and to
lead the flock to live always in accord with the laws of God and man.
The devoted priests, diocesan and religious, under the direction of
the bishops have been ever ready to consecrate to the service of their
people their time and talents, making every sacrifice of human ambition and human love. The noble women in the religious communities
have given their all to the education of a Christian generation, to the
relief of every kind of human suffering and need, and to perpetual
prayer to the hidden majesty of Christ in the Eucharist for the salvation of all men. The equally devoted, self-sacrificing, generous, and
intelligent laity, truly the joy and crown of the diocese, have appreciated all these ministrations and have responded with the outpouring
of reverence and filial love and devotion, and with the offering of their
substance without which these great works of the Church would be
impossible. Sacred and tender ties of charity have ever bound the pastor
to his spiritual children; and by that interdependence, mutual affection
and confidence have been quickened and fostered.

While, with mingled feelings of joy and gratitude and hope, we
recall the wonderful things God has wrought in this diocese through
His servants who have gone before us, and while we pay humble
homage to the fructifying influence of the Holy Spirit working within
it all for the progress of the Church, we also feel the profound sense
of responsibility that devolves upon us of this generation to emulate
the virtues of our fathers in the Faith, to tread zealously and loyally

in their footsteps, and to widen the field opened by their apostolic labors. History records the accomplishments of the past, but it also sets the pace for the future. To want courage or to lack zeal now would be reprehensible; the past would be a reproach to us, if we were to fail to carry on the pious works of those who have preceded us. God uses human instruments; and we must all regard ourselves as included among the providential agents whom He has chosen for the fulfillment of His decrees. We have entered into an inheritance that we may cultivate it and increase it.

If Bishop Rappe and a tiny band of priests and people accomplished so much with so little at their disposal, much more indeed will be expected of us with multiplied numbers and resources. We must leave behind us monuments of faith and good works to which posterity will be able to point with pride when the next mile-stone in the history of the diocese is reached.

Pope Pius IX founded our diocese; Pope Pius XII has blessed it at the century mark; may God ratify this blessing by giving it an increase of strength and holiness and good works for His eternal glory.

† EDWARD F. HOBAN

Archbishop: Bishop of Cleveland

PREFACE

THIS work is the result of a commission by the Most Reverend
Archbishop Edward F. Hoban, sixth Bishop of Cleveland, who desired to commemorate the one hundred years existence of his diocese
in the permanent record of the sacrifices, the struggles and the untiring efforts of our fathers in the Faith for the maintenance and growth
of Christ's kingdom on earth. Whenever possible the record is based
upon original archival sources. Naturally the later history depends
principally upon printed documents and newspaper accounts which
have been controlled by personal observation. Most of the material
for the period of Bishop Rappe is to be found at Notre Dame University in the National Catholic Archives which were made available
by the kindness of the Reverend Doctor Thomas T. McAvoy, C.S.C.,
to whom we are indebted also for many helpful suggestions. The
few but valuable Rappe letters in the Baltimore Cathedral Archives
were placed at our disposal by Archbishop Francis P. Keough. From
the archives of the Archdiocese of Cincinnati, Brother Paul O'Brien
of the Brothers of Mary was able to transcribe and to send us many
pertinent letters. According to their rules the Roman Archives are not
open to the public except for material at least one hundred years old.
Nevertheless, Monsignor John Krol, vice-chancellor, who visited the
Eternal City with Archbishop Hoban, was able to obtain much valuable information. Monsignor Vincent Balmat, the chancellor, has been
very kind and helpful in making accessible all the material in the Cleveland Archives which are at the present time being catalogued and
calendared. There is little for the Rappe administration in them but the
completeness of the material for the succeeding administrations made
it unnecessary to search elsewhere. Monsignor George Houck meticulously preserved all incoming correspondence and conscientiously kept
copies of all outgoing letters during the more than thirty years that
he was chancellor. The latter are bound in solid volumes arranged
chronologically.

Many letters concerning the Diocese of Cleveland have been edited
in the *Life and Letters of Bishop McQuaid* by the Reverend Doctor
Frederick Zwierlein. The letters of Archbishop Purcell of Cincinnati
which were concerned with the visitation of the Church in these
parts and appeared in the *Catholic Telegraph* of that city were reprinted by Monsignor Houck in the history mentioned below. These

and the files of the *Catholic Universe* and of the later *Catholic Universe-Bulletin* of Cleveland which go back to 1874 have been well used. The officials of the Western Reserve Historical Society Library deserve special thanks for their courtesy in making available the files of Cleveland's earlier newspapers and the digest of much of their content in the *Annals of Cleveland* which was compiled by the W.P.A. writers.

Monsignor Houck, mentioned above, in 1887 published the first general history of the diocese which went through four editions and was also printed in German. It was later amplified into a large two-volume work under the title *History of Catholicity in Northern Ohio and the Diocese of Cleveland, 1749–1900*, published by him and Michael W. Carr in 1903. These volumes contain summary sketches of the missionaries and the bishops and short chronological accounts of the three administrations, brief sketches of all the parishes composed by the various pastors with cuts of the old and newer churches, short auto-biographies of most of the then living priests with their pictures and notices of nearly all the deceased priests, religious and secular, who had served in the diocese up to 1900. Much valuable material was found here. Monsignor Houck has given an almost complete case history of the so-called troubles, sporadic manifestations of "trustee-ism" and other problems which occurred in the development of the new diocese. These in their proper perspective have lost much of their seeming importance and for that reason they have not been allowed to distort the positive picture of Catholic life which flourished in spite of them. In 1942 the Ohio State University and the Cleveland Chancery sponsored the printing of the *Parishes of the Catholic Church in the Diocese of Cleveland* which had been prepared by the Ohio Historical Records Survey Project of the Work Projects Administration. It includes the parishes in the present Diocese of Youngstown and is valuable for the information it gives about the extent and location of the individual records. Another source of information were the answers furnished by the pastors to the questionnaires sent out by the Chancery. We wish to express sincere gratitude to the Fathers for their kindness.

It has been difficult to compress the great mass of material into one volume. For that reason very few quotations are made and the history of the single parishes and of the priests who have labored in them must be a project for the future. But a sincere attempt has been made to give a general view of the administration of the six successive bishops who have governed the diocese, this being a natural division of the growth of the Church in a particular locality: each bishop while guiding the diocese in its normal development along recognized lines, nevertheless, in the solution of particular problems and in the fulfillment of particular needs gives a personal and individual tone to the work of the Church. An attempt has been made, however, to avoid unnecessary repetitions.

It would be impossible to enumerate the names of all those to whom the author is indebted for valuable suggestions and actual help. Gratitude must be expressed, however, to Doctor Carl Wittke for permission to use the *History of the State of Ohio* of which he is chief editor, to Doctor John H. Lamotte for like permission in regard to his *History of the Archdiocese of Cincinnati*, and to Monsignor George Whitehead for assistance in expediting the printing of this volume. We wish also to recognize the courtesies extended by Cleveland's local newspapers, the *Plain Dealer*, the *News*, the *Press*, and especially the *Catholic Universe-Bulletin*.

⫸ CONTENTS ⫷

Contents

⇛ LIST OF ILLUSTRATIONS ⇚

HISTORY OF
THE DIOCESE OF CLEVELAND

⫸ · ⫷

THE OHIO COUNTRY

FOLLOWING THE RECOMMENDATIONS OF THE bishops at the Sixth Provincial Council of Baltimore, Pope Pius IX on April 23, 1847, formally and officially separated some 15,000 square miles in northern Ohio from the jurisdiction of the Bishop of Cincinnati and established them as the territory of the new Diocese of Cleveland. The area of this diocese has since been reduced to about one-quarter of its original size, by the erection of the Diocese of Toledo in 1910 and of the Diocese of Youngstown in 1943. Despite the fact that as now constituted it occupies less than ten per cent of the total area of Ohio, it will be of interest for a better understanding of its history to recall briefly the principal happenings in the development of the State from a primitive wilderness into one of the most important commonwealths in the nation.[1]

The Ohio Country, as it was called, was first part of the old Northwest Territory, which comprised all the land west of the Allegheny Mountains to the Mississippi River and north of the Ohio River. Later it was limited to the area bounded by the Ohio and the Allegheny Rivers on the east and the south, by Lake Erie and the Maumee River valley on the north, and by the Miami and the Auglaize Rivers on the west. With minor boundary adjustments, it was admitted into the Union as a sovereign State in 1803, according to the provisions of the Northwest Ordinance under which it had been governed for the sixteen preceding years.

Ohio received its name from the river at its southern border. The French called the Ohio the Beautiful River. Three-fourths of the State is a gently rolling country, the highest elevation 1,550 feet, the average 500 to 1,000 feet above sea level. Great sheets of ice at one time covered most of it and as they receded they smoothed out the many deep, sharp ridges and deposited great drifts of fertile soil. The dam-

[1] This introductory narrative is based upon several works, which include the 6-volume *History of the State of Ohio*, a publication of the Ohio State Archeological and Historical Society under the general editorship of Carl Wittke, Columbus, 1941–1942; *Lake Erie*, by Harlan Hatcher, Indianapolis, 1945; *History of the Archdiocese of Cincinnati*, by John Lamotte, Cincinnati, 1921; *The Right Reverend Edward Dominic Fenwick, O.P.*, by Victor F. O'Daniel, O.P., Washington, 1921; *History of the Roman Catholic Church in the United States*, by Thomas O'Gorman, New York, 1900.

ming of the rivers created temporary lakes, especially in the north, which when they retreated left in their wake sandy beaches, sand pits, and bogs. In the northwestern section these swampy marshes were later drained to become rich farmlands. Lake Erie as it receded left behind it three long parallel sand beaches, natural highways, the pioneer ridge roads readily recognizable even today.

A low ridge of hills enters Ohio from the east near the line between Ashtabula and Trumbull Counties and extends west by south into Indiana, making a divide or watershed which sends the drainage to the Ohio River or to Lake Erie. Hiram, Ravenna, Akron, Medina, Ashland, Mansfield, and Marion are on or near this ridge. President Garfield put it graphically when he remarked that a little bird standing on a barn near one of these towns could by a flutter of its wings cast a drop of rain into the Gulf of Mexico or the Gulf of St. Lawrence.

The Ashtabula, Grand, Cuyahoga, Black, Vermilion, Huron, Sandusky, and Maumee Rivers drain the northern section of the State into Lake Erie. Short portages between their headwaters and the many rivers and creeks which empty into the Ohio River on the south afforded excellent north-south means of communication despite the heavy forests. In this way continuous journeys could be made on the Grand-Mahoning, the Miami-Maumee, the Sandusky-Scioto, the Cuyahoga-Tuscarawas-Muskingum Rivers. These waterways of the Indians served the trappers, the traders, the soldiers, and settlers of later times. They mark the route of turnpikes, canals, railroads, and modern highways. Indian trails through the woods also helped to open the interior to explorers and traders. Of these, the most important in the Ohio Country ran from Fort Pitt (Pittsburgh) to Detroit. It followed the watershed from the mouth of the Beaver River in Pennsylvania to the Muskingum River, which it crossed and then ran by way of Wooster and Fort Sandusky to Detroit. There were numerous others, including the one along the southern shore of Lake Erie which marked the path for later highways and railroads.

The soil of the greater part of Ohio was rich and supported abundant vegetation, great forests and grassy meadows. Wild life was very plentiful. It included foxes, black bears, deer, beavers, and buffaloes and some 300 species of birds. The rivers were alive with fish of many varieties. Considerable deposits of coal were to be discovered later, especially in the southeastern section. The oil wells were gradually exhausted but the natural gas wells are still productive. Great beds of clay and shale furnished the basis for the important ceramic industry. Limestone and sandstone quarries are numerous, especially in the northern part. Flint beds furnished the Indians with their weapons.

Not much is known of the earliest inhabitants. These nameless aborigines, probably the ancestors of what we know as American Indians, left behind them great earthen mounds, excellently preserved, which are to be found in many parts of the State. They served some social purpose, monuments to the dead or earthworks for defense. The only native Ohio Indian tribe seems to have been the Eries, called "Cats" by the French, who lived along the southern shore of Lake Erie. Traces of them are to be found in the lower courses of streams emptying into the lake, particularly in the Cuyahoga River Valley. In the year 1655, as recorded in the *Jesuit Relations,* the powerful and fierce Iroquois, called the Five Nations, swept westward into this territory. They killed or captured most of the Eries, the others were driven west to the Mississippi River. The Ohio Country, thereafter, was claimed by the Iroquois as their own hunting ground, and all others were rigorously excluded from it for half a century.

When, however, the arrival of European settlers along the Atlantic Coast engaged the attention of the Iroquois, some of the scattered tribes returned. The Miamis were again to be found on the shores of Lake Michigan and along the banks of the Miami River in Ohio. About 1750 the Delawares settled in the upper Muskingum Valley and then later along the Sandusky River in the present Wyandot County. A few of them were converted by the Moravian missionaries. The Ottawas migrated from the country north of Lake Erie to settle in the Ohio county named after them. The Wyandots, composed of remnants of the Huron and other tribes north of the lakes who had survived the Iroquois conquest, established themselves on the southern shore of Lake Erie, some opposite Detroit, others in the region of Sandusky Bay and in the lower valley of the Maumee River. Extending their influence to the south, they became the dominant tribe in Ohio, especially in the valley of the Scioto River. Other tribes, including the Mingoes and the Shawnees in the southern section, made a total of about 15,000 Indians in the State at the middle of the eighteenth century.

The first white men to enter the Ohio Country were French explorers, traders, and missioners from Canada who had already discovered the territory farther north and west. The northern route, the first one used by them, was traced by the brave high-minded soldier and navigator, Samuel de Champlain, in 1615. From Quebec it followed the St. Lawrence River then the Ottawa River, Lake Nipissing, and the French River to Georgian Bay and Lake Huron. The way was open, then, to Lake Superior, Lake Michigan, and the rivers not far beyond, which emptied into the Mississippi. Jesuits and Franciscans accompanied the explorers into that country. The other more southerly route led to the discovery of the Ohio Country. It extended from the St. Lawrence River through Lake Ontario, past Niagara Falls, to Lake Erie and Lake Huron. Known to the French as early as 1632, it was considered very dangerous because of the difficult portage around the great falls and, particularly, because of the control exercised by the hostile Iroquois who destroyed a flourishing Huron mission in 1649.

When a temporary peace had been arranged with these fierce warriors, the intrepid Frenchman, René Robert Cavalier de La Salle, hearing from friendly Indians of the great river which flowed westward to the Gulf of Mexico, decided to find it. Included in the party which left Montreal on July 6, 1669, were the Sulpicians, Fathers Dollier de Casson and René de Bréhant de Galinée.[2] On the portage between Lake Ontario and Lake Erie they encountered Louis Jolliet, the Canadian explorer, on his way back to Montreal. His account of the Ottawa Indians induced the Sulpicians to part company with La Salle and to make their perilous way along the northern shore of Lake Erie to the mouth of the Detroit River. Their return journey to Montreal was made over the better-known northern route.

La Salle and the rest of the party continued southward and, despite the scantiness of the records, modern historians are convinced that he discovered the Allegheny River (thought then to be the Ohio) and went down the great stream to the falls of the Ohio at Louisville, Kentucky, before he returned to Canada. The French Government for some reason or other failed to develop this more direct route to the Mississippi Valley, preferring the one which used Lake Erie and the Maumee and Wabash Rivers. Against great odds, La Salle established navigation through Lake Erie to the upper lakes. In August, 1679, he launched the 45-ton Griffin, the first sailing vessel on Lake Erie, at a point near the French fort at Niagara, and in a three-day journey brought it to Detroit.

[2] James H. Coyne, tr. and ed., *The Journey of René de Bréhant de Galinée,* Toronto, 1903; *Papers and Records of the Ontario Historical Society,* IV, part 1. In the first volume of the *History of the State of Ohio,* previously mentioned, the journey of Galinée is incorrectly placed along the southern shore of Lake Erie.

2

THE FIRST MISSIONARIES

THE CLAIMS OF THE FRENCH TO SOVEREIGNTY remained unchallenged until venturesome colonists from Virginia, Carolina, and Pennsylvania established English trading posts in the Ohio Country. In 1748 prominent Virginians organized the Ohio Company to trade with the Indian trappers and hunters, and to cut the French line of communication between Canada and Louisiana. Soon trading centers appeared all over what is now the State of Ohio, as far north as Fort Sandusky near the bay of that name on Lake Erie. As justification the new claimants alleged that their original colonial charters gave them title to all the land west of the colonies to the other sea, and that in any case the land belonged to the Iroquois who were English subjects.

Conflict between the two interests was almost inevitable, and the European wars between England and France had their counterpart in America for the control of the Ohio Country. Chosen to reassert the French claim, the courageous Céleron de Blainville, who was previously commandant at Detroit, came from Canada with a company of 250 men in June, 1749. On the banks of the Allegheny River at the present city of Warren, Pennsylvania, and at the mouth of each important tributary of the Ohio River—the last one on the banks of the Great Miami—he buried a leaden plate proclaiming the renewed possession by the King of France of the Ohio and of all the rivers discharging into it and the lands through which they flowed. He compelled the English traders whom he met to leave and after his five-month absence returned to Canada. The celebrated Jesuit mathematician, Joseph Pierre de Bonnecamps, accompanied Céleron and drew the first good map of the State of Ohio, which was published with his account of the journey. He was undoubtedly the first priest to offer Holy Mass in the southern part of the State.

The English were forced to abandon their trading post at Sandusky and the French erected a small fort at the upper end of the bay. Here then, a group of Wyandot (Huron) Indians from the Detroit district made their homes. In 1749 Father Pierre Potier, S.J., the authority on the language of the Hurons, visited them and presumably celebrated Mass for them. According to the well-known historian, John Gilmary Shea, Armand de La Richardie, another Jesuit from Detroit, built a rough chapel for them in 1751.[1] Father Potier was the last of the old Jesuit missionaries of the West, and when he died in 1758 the Indians had to make the long journey to Detroit to receive the sacraments. Early English Protestant settlers have testified to the strong attachment of these Wyandots to the Catholic Church. The silver crucifixes given them by the missionaries were carefully treasured. Four such crosses, 5 by 2½ inches, engraved with a mysterious "C.A.," were discovered in the debris of an old Indian graveyard on the Sandusky waterfront which was exposed in the flood of 1856; others were found at Fremont and Port Clinton.[2] Deprived of priests, however, many fell away from the Faith.

The French domination, however, was not to last. It came to an end in 1758 when the English under General Forbes, with the help of the Indians who had been persuaded to change their allegiance, captured Fort Duquesne, at the site of the present Pittsburgh, and forced the French back to Detroit. A few years later, by the terms of the Treaty of Paris (1763), France ceded to the Crown of England, Canada and all the territory east of the Mississippi except New Orleans. However, the Indians in Pontiac's Conspiracy captured all the western forts except Detroit and Fort Pitt, but by the end of 1764 the bulk of them had submitted to English rule.

Ten years later the English Government, to neutralize the claims of the seaboard colonies, passed the Quebec Act which provided that the territory north and west of the Ohio River was subjected immediately to the government of Quebec in Canada. The new law extended to the western country the same guarantees for the liberty of the Catholic religion and worship which had been made to the Canadians in the Treaty of Paris. The English Protestant colonists along the Atlantic saw themselves cut off from these rich western lands. The American Continental Congress made official protest against such religious liberty for Catholics as arbitrary and dangerous. This measure of common justice was put forward by the colonists as one reason for breaking with the mother country. Yet, at the very same time, the Congress sent a deputation which included Father John Carroll, the future first Bishop of Baltimore, to ask the aid and cooperation of the Catholic Canadians (unsuccessfully as it turned out) in the impending War of Independence.

After the Revolution and another Treaty of Paris (1783) acknowledging the independence of the American Colonies, the English were determined to hold Detroit and the forts in the North which controlled the Great Lakes and the Wabash Valley. The Indians were systematically stirred up against the American settlers in the Ohio Country and were it not for the supply of military equipment brought up the

[1] George F. Houck, *History of Catholicity in Northern Ohio and the Diocese of Cleveland, 1749 to 1900*, 2 vols., Cleveland, 1903, I, 3–6. Cf. Lamotte, *Op. cit.*, 11.
[2] Sr. M. Austin Irick, R.S.M., *Early Catholicity in the Sandusky Region prior to 1847*, unpublished dissertation, Notre Dame University, 1939; *Catholic Universe* (abbreviated hereafter as *C.U.*) Jan. 30, 1879; Nov. 3, 1881.

Mississippi from Spanish New Orleans the West might well have been lost. The Indian raids aroused the frontiersmen and in retaliation they wiped out a Christian colony of Indians who had been converted by the Moravian missionaries. Several expeditions sent against the tribes were unsuccessful. It was not until 1794 that General Anthony Wayne, the Revolutionary War hero, crushed them in the Battle of Fallen Timbers (near Defiance). Convinced finally that their English allies had deserted them, the Indians agreed in the Treaty of Grenville, August 3, 1795, to give up all the country except for a small strip of land running west from the Cuyahoga River. This pacification made possible the settlement of what was to be known as the Western Reserve (and west of it) with comparative safety from Indian disturbance. The British, however, still maintained possession of Michigan and the forts along the southern shore of Lake Erie, and gave them up only in Jay's Treaty of 1796.

During the time of this occupation the last priest from the Archdiocese of Quebec and the first English-speaking priest in Ohio exercised the ministry not only in the garrison but also among the Indians around Sandusky. This priest was Father Edmund Burke, later (in 1818) Titular Bishop of Sion and Vicar Apostolic of Nova Scotia. Born in Ireland in 1753, he was teaching in the seminary in Quebec in 1786. When the Jesuits were forced to abandon their western missions he was inspired with the desire to take their place. Through Archbishop Troy of Dublin the matter was brought to the attention of Cardinal Antonelli of the Congregation of the Propaganda and as a result, in 1794, Bishop Hubert of Quebec appointed the same Father Burke Administrator of Upper Canada. Father Burke had conceived plans meanwhile for a Prefecture of the Indian Territory, independent of the jurisdiction of the Bishops of Quebec, Baltimore, and New Orleans. The British encouraged him in his work, anxious to avail themselves of his influence with the Catholic Indians. He distributed corn to them, around the present Toledo and farther west, and found them to be well disposed, though he characterized all the Indians as heathens. There must have been some Catholics among them, however, for he described his post as "the last and most distant parish inhabited by Catholics on the earth." In general there existed "neither law nor justice nor subjection" and he never saw a man "either Indian or Canadian without his gun in his hand and his knife at his breast." In such rough surroundings he did what he could. He offered the Holy Sacrifice in his cabin near the fort erected by the British on the Maumee River, later called Fort Meigs, the site of the present Perrysburg. When the English troops were withdrawn, Father Burke left (probably in the spring of 1796) for Halifax in Nova Scotia, where he died in 1820.[3]

All the other priests in the region which is now Ohio, Illinois, Indiana, and Michigan were also recalled by the Bishop of Quebec and the spiritual care of the whole Northwest Territory devolved upon Bishop

[3] Shea's letter to Houck, in Houck, *Op. cit., loc. cit.*

Carroll of Baltimore. He had no one to send until the Sulpicians, newly
arrived refugees from the French Revolution, offered themselves for
the work. Several of them became pioneer bishops. Father Levadoux
and Father Gabriel Richard, the only priest ever to sit in Congress and
who died a victim of his devotion to the plague-stricken, labored in and
around Detroit; Father John Dilhet served in the area from Sandusky
in Ohio to the St. Joseph River at the head of Lake Michigan, and as
far south as Fort Wayne, among the "fast decaying descendants of
former Canadians and of Catholic Indians."

3

EARLY SETTLEMENTS

LTHOUGH THE SOVEREIGNTY OF THE UNITED
States over the Ohio Country had been vindicated,
the problem of its government still remained. This was
solved when it was agreed finally that the Northwest
would be disposed of for the common benefit of all the
States and that the States eventually to be formed out of it would become coequal members of the Federal Union. Virginia in her act of
cession reserved certain tracts of land in southern Ohio to satisfy the
bounties promised her soldiers in the Revolutionary War. Congress,
also, made some reservations for that purpose and for the support of
schools. One proposition to set aside a section in each township for the
support of religion was not adopted. Connecticut in her act of cession,
September 13, 1786, retained ownership of a strip of land extending
120 miles west of the Pennsylvania line between 41 degrees north latitude and Lake Erie, which became known as the Western Reserve.

For the establishment and preservation of law and order in these
Federal lands, the "Ordinance for the Temporary Government of the
Territory of the United States Northwest of the Ohio River" was
adopted by Congress in 1787. Five articles, constituting a bill of rights,
guaranteed religious freedom, the right of *habeas corpus*, and trial by
jury. Slavery and involuntary servitude were abolished in the whole
Territory. Article Three has often been quoted as a statement of the
policy imposed upon the new country: "Religion, morality, and knowledge being necessary for a good government and the happiness of
mankind, schools and the means of education shall forever be encouraged." These provisions were incorporated in the Constitution of the
State of Ohio, when it was recognized as a sovereign State in 1803, the
first one formed out of the original Northwest Territory.

Several years before Ohio was admitted into the Union permanent
settlements had been made. Veterans of the War of Independence came
with their families to claim their bounties. Liberal terms, cheap prices,
and free land offered to the first arrivals by the speculative land companies attracted many more. Two main routes brought them from the
East: the Forbes Road from Philadelphia through Lancaster, Carlisle,
and Bedford to Pittsburgh; the Cumberland Road from Maryland and
Virginia to Wheeling on the Ohio River. Adventuresome frontiersmen

from neighboring States hewed out new homes for themselves in the Ohio forests. The first organized settlement was made at Marietta, and it became the seat of the territorial government. By the end of 1788, 132 men and their families lived there under the protecting guns of Fort Harmon. Another group in the same year established themselves at what is now Cincinnati. The newly appointed Governor called upon the new settlers to make Christmas a day of thanksgiving to God.

In 1790 the first Catholic settlement was made at Gallipolis, some distance down the Ohio from Marietta, by a group of disillusioned Frenchmen. In the disturbed times of the French Revolution these people—a few physicians and army officers, coachmakers, gilders, and barbers—misled by the glowing and exaggerated terms of the advertisements bought worthless land warrants from the French Scioto Land Company. Discovering the fraud when they arrived in Virginia, most of them nevertheless went on to Ohio and took up residence in the log cabins prepared for them. Their inexperience, famine, and Indian attacks induced a few of them to seek a home in neighboring States, but about 300 remained.

At least one priest came out from France with them. He was the Benedictine, Father Peter Joseph Didier, who had been appointed Prefect Apostolic for the colony, with instructions to communicate with Bishop Carroll, then recognized as having spiritual authority over the whole country. An attempt in France to have a bishop consecrated for them failed. Apparently discouraged with his charges, Father Didier left them and went farther on, to labor around St. Louis, where he died in 1799. Father Stephen Badin, the first secular priest ordained in the United States, and his companion, Father Barriéres, visited the colony on their way to Kentucky in 1793. High Mass was sung in the garrison and forty children were baptized. When Father Badin called there again about fifteen years later, he found "still a spark of faith there" and he saw some hope for the Church in the Irish families in the vicinity. At a later period Archbishop Purcell described the place as "pretty much a blank on the Catholic map of Ohio," although he, too, found some consolation in the presence of a few fervent German Catholic families. It was a long time before a Catholic church building was erected in the town.[1]

Not until the power of the Indians had been broken by General Anthony Wayne in the north, was the way opened for the settlement of the Western Reserve in the northeastern section of Ohio by immigrants from New England, New York, and Pennsylvania. The New Connecticut, as it was also known, was disposed of exclusively for the benefit of the mother-state. In 1792 500,000 acres in the western section of the Reserve (the present Erie and Huron Counties) were given to the inhabitants of the Connecticut coast towns which had suffered from the British attacks in the Revolutionary War. Called "Firelands" or "Sufferers Lands," they were not opened to settlers until the extinction

[1] *Lamotte, Op. cit.,* p. 13.

of the Indian claims some time later. The Connecticut Land Company, a purely speculative organization, bought the remaining lands for $1,200,000, a sum which was used as an endowment for the schools of Connecticut.

One of the officers of the company, Moses Cleaveland, a veteran of the war and a prosperous, shrewd, and courageous lawyer, led a group of fifty-two persons, including two prospective settlers and their wives, to Ohio to inspect the purchase. A few of the party remained behind, near the mouth of the Conneaut River, to survey the lands along the eastern border. The others, with Cleaveland, reached the mouth of the Cuyahoga River on July 22, 1796. The precipitous bluffs overhanging the river afforded good protection for the three cabins which were erected as a nucleus for a permanent settlement. The Cuyahoga River, which had already been recognized by George Washington and Benjamin Franklin for its strategic importance, was navigable fifteen miles for larger ships and sixty miles for smaller craft. A short portage then led to the head of the Tuscarawas River. Prior to the settlement started by Cleaveland the French had a trading post in 1755 at Tinker's Creek (Bedford) up the Cuyahoga, and in 1786 the Moravian Delaware Indians found a temporary resting-place at this point. During the English occupation small cabins had been erected on or near the same site.

Cleaveland and his engineers divided a square-mile section at the mouth of the Cuyahoga into 220 city lots with the two principal streets, Superior and Ontario, crossing at right angles; and they marked off the basis for future surveys before returning home, leaving after them the first English settlers at Conneaut and Cleveland. A second party under the Reverend Seth Hart and Seth Pease completed the survey the next year.

The whole of Ohio had been contained in the County of Washington in 1788, with the seat at Marietta. In 1797 the eastern section of the Western Reserve belonged to Jefferson County, with its seat at Steubenville, and the western section, which included part of Michigan, belonged to Wayne County. In 1800 the whole of the Western Reserve formed the new Trumbull County, with its seat at Warren. In that year some 1,300 people were settled in 35 of the 135 townships east of the Cuyahoga and 700 miles of roads had been cut through the wilderness. They paid no taxes to the territorial government until the land titles they held from Connecticut were confirmed by Congress. New Englanders and Scots, Germans, and Irish from Western Pennsylvania set up a bulwark of Puritanism and Presbyterianism comparable to the first one in southern Ohio. Part of this Trumbull County became Geauga County in 1806; a further subdivision became Cuyahoga County in 1808.[2]

In Kentucky, south of Ohio and the Ohio River, Catholics were to be found among the pioneer settlers in 1774. Distinctly Catholic groups of immigrants from Maryland and from Ireland had increased their

[2] Cf. Samuel Orth, *History of Cleveland, Ohio*, 2 vols., Cleveland, 1910.

numbers to some 300 families in 1796. The first missionary to visit them was the Irish Franciscan, Father Charles Whelan, in 1787. Father William de Rohan built the first rude chapel there in 1790. They were without a priest for three years until Bishop Carroll in 1793 sent them the newly ordained Father Stephen Badin who labored, sometimes alone, on the great mission for about twenty-six years. He and the Belgian Father Charles Nerinckx, who arrived in 1805, are justly called the apostles of Kentucky. With far-reaching consequences for the Church in Ohio, Father Edward Dominic Fenwick in 1806 established the cradle of the Dominican Order in this country at St. Rose's Convent in Kentucky. In this he was directed by Bishop Carroll, who looked to the Fathers as future auxiliaries in the care of the immense territory assigned to him when he became the first Bishop of Baltimore in 1790.

The Holy See, at the petition of Bishop Carroll, divided his burden in 1808 when New York, Philadelphia, Boston, and Bardstown were made the seats of new dioceses. Bardstown, in Kentucky, was the first bishopric in the United States west of the Alleghenies and included in its jurisdiction not only the State in which it was situated but Tennessee and, for a time, the territory now occupied by Michigan, Ohio, Indiana, Illinois, Missouri, part of Arkansas, Wisconsin, and Iowa. The Sulpician, Benedict Joseph Flaget, who had at an earlier date labored on the western missions, was consecrated its first bishop in 1810. After a visitation in 1814, during which he confirmed 1,200 persons, he reported to the Holy See that he had ten priests to minister to approximately 10,000 souls, most of them in Kentucky. Tennessee had about twenty-five Catholics; in Indiana there were about 130 Catholic families around Vincennes; Illinois had three parishes and 120 Catholic families; Michigan had 2,000 Catholics not including the Indians; and in Ohio some fifty families were without a priest. He would need at least ten more priests, he said, to carry on the work amongst his scattered flock. In the Providence of God, before the good Bishop died in 1850, ten new dioceses had been formed out of the mother-diocese of the West, the seat of which was in 1841 transferred to Louisville.[3]

[3] *American Catholic Historical Society Researches*, I, 308.

❯❯❯ 4 ❮❮❮

FIRST CATHOLIC FAMILIES
IN OHIO

EVEN BEFORE THE ERECTION OF THE DIOCESE OF
Bardstown the Catholic families in Ohio had been eagerly asking that a priest be sent to bring the consolations of religion to
them. Jacob Dittoe, a German, and his family had settled near
Lancaster in 1802. In his piteous appeal to Bishop Carroll be
related that his "everyday's acquaintance" revealed to him that there
were "Catholics tossed about the country by the vicissitudes of fortune
who were very anxious for the establishment of the Church and who
were willing to contribute towards its support." In his own neighborhood there were then thirty souls, and two more families with others
from Conawego in Pennsylvania were expected to arrive soon thereafter. He asked the Bishop to direct any priest whom he would send
to Kentucky to interrupt his journey at Lancaster and to call upon the
Catholic family of the Boyles there, who would bring him to the Dittoe
farm. He had taken an option on a tract of land for a church site and
for the support of a priest. The Bishop was not able to help in the
purchase of the land but in accord with his instructions Father Edward
Fenwick, the future first Bishop of Cincinnati, visited the little community in 1808. He recognized the place by the sound of the axe fell-
ing the trees of the forest. He was welcomed as an angel from Heaven
by the Dittoe and Fink families, twenty of whom received the sacraments. This was the beginning of Father Fenwick's devoted missionary
work in Ohio and, although his time and energies were absorbed in
the establishment of his Order in Kentucky, he returned there as often
as possible. On land donated to the Dominican Fathers by Jacob Dittoe
the ten families in the neighborhood of Somerset built a rude convent
for the priests and a log house for a chapel. This, the mother-church
of the State, was dedicated to St. Joseph, December 6, 1818. Soon afterwards a second log church, dedicated to the Blessed Virgin, was erected
at Lancaster.

Another group of Catholics in Ohio was to be found at Cincinnati.
As early as 1811 a certain Jacob Fowlbe, aroused by the sudden death

15

of his wife without the last sacraments and her burial from the Methodist church, made an unsuccessful effort to organize a congregation. An advertisement in a local newspaper six years later, which recalled that liberty of conscience had been guaranteed by the Constitution of the United States, brought together sixteen adults and four children at a meeting in the home of Michael Scott, the host to Father Fenwick on his visits there. But it was not until after Bishop Flaget visited them in 1818 and urged and encouraged them, that the first simple chapel was built on the outskirts of Cincinnati. For this they had received some assistance from the Catholics of the East to whom they described themselves as the "lost sheep of the House of Israel, forlorn and forsaken, destitute of the means of exercising the duties of our holy religion, without guide, church, or pastor." Mass was first celebrated in the chapel on Easter Day, 1819, in the presence of some 100 persons. Michael Scott, Patrick Reilly, John Sherlock, Thomas Dugan, and Edward Lynch were named the trustees of the Christ Church Congregation incorporated as a religious society under an Act of the General Assembly of Ohio.

There were other smaller groups of Catholics in the southern part of the State who were visited at rare intervals by Bishop Flaget and Father Fenwick on their journeys to and from Baltimore. Still others, who had not seen a priest after their arrival in the wilderness, were forgetting their religion and were bringing up their children in complete ignorance of it. The Bishop grieved that he had no priest to send them even once a year. However, after the ordinations in Kentucky in 1816, Father Fenwick, who had reported that four priests were needed, was released to devote himself entirely to Ohio. Assisted later on by his nephew, Father Nicolas Young, O.P., he began to tour Ohio as an itinerant missioner. With the sacred vessels in his saddle-bags, he searched for the lost sheep living scattered about in the vast and trackless forests where, sometimes overtaken by darkness, he had to spend the night in the midst of the lurking dangers. In 1817 and 1818 he baptized 162 persons, both young and old, whose names and sponsors he could not recollect, while his nephew in the latter year baptized about 30.

Among those whom the valiant missionaries visited were the pioneer Catholics in northern Ohio who came from the seacoast, and from Europe—from Ireland, Germany, and France—and settled in the clearings along the road which led from Wellsville on the Ohio River to (New) Lisbon, to Hanover, to Paris, to Osnaburg, to Canton and Massillon, to Dalton, to Wooster, and then directly north to Cleveland. From Massillon another route led northwest to (Canal) Fulton and Chippewa (near Doylestown). The records of these visits have been lost and the details are therefore scanty. There is reason to believe that Father Fenwick called on the family of the Irish-born Daniel Shehy in Youngstown in 1815 or 1816. Shehy, one of the first settlers in the

Western Reserve and, according to family tradition, one of the surveying party of Moses Cleaveland,[1] in 1797 built a log-cabin home for himself and his wife, Jane McLain from Pittsburgh, on land purchased from John Young, the founder of Youngstown. This house served as a chapel for the few Catholics of the vicinity whenever a missionary visited them.

In 1817 Father Fenwick called upon the few Irish families who five years previously had begun to make a clearing in the dense forests of Columbiana County, at Hanover near Dungannon, about eight miles southwest of (New) Lisbon, a town laid out by the Reverend Louis Kinney, a Baptist minister, in 1802. Their joy was unbounded upon Father Fenwick's arrival. He was the first priest they had seen since they left Pittsburgh, whence they had journeyed eighty miles to the new settlement. Mass was offered and the sacraments dispensed by Father Fenwick in the log-cabin home of Daniel McAllister and his wife, who was the daughter of Daniel Shehy of Youngstown. Three years later the small congregation had built the first permanent church in northern Ohio, St. Paul's. It was 30 by 40 feet, very plain, as might be expected, but of brick.

On this same missionary journey of 1817 Father Fenwick followed the route to the west, visiting the few Catholics he found along the way until he came to Canton, which became the center of the missions in Stark and Wayne Counties. Here the pioneer Catholic was John Shorb, a German trader from Baltimore, who, after a short stay at Steubenville, had settled in Canton in 1807, with his wife and children. There he established a general store in a log cabin, one of the half-dozen in the clearing. He was soon followed by other Catholic families. Father Fenwick knew of this colony either from his own previous visit or from the visits of Shorb to Somerset. On this occasion Mass was celebrated in the open air, under the leafy branches of a great oak tree adjacent to the Shorb home, which itself was used as a chapel when the weather was inclement.

Not far from Canton, in Lawrence Township near the present Canal Fulton, Father Fenwick called upon a group of Irish Catholics who had settled there in 1812, and celebrated Holy Mass in the home of the pioneer, Matthew Patton. These families, together with those who lived in the Gallagher Settlement, afterwards formed the parish in Canal Fulton. The Gallagher Settlement has not been definitely identified but on the tombstones in an abandoned cemetery near Canal Fulton five of the names which were legible were of Gallaghers. One died in 1816; another, Anthony, died two years later, at the age of ninety-three. Other names were Kerr and McKinley. On one occasion Father Fenwick went a hundred miles out of his way to administer the sacraments to Edward Gallagher, Wooster's only Catholic, an Irishman by birth

---

[1] *Souvenir Booklet, Centennial Celebration of the Descendants of Daniel and Jane Shehy, 1796–1896,* privately printed.

and a successful merchant; his wife and large family were received into the Church.[2] At Louisville (Beechland) a few Baltimore relatives of Bishop Carroll settled in 1818 but they soon afterwards sought homes farther west. They were succeeded there by another group of Irish Catholics who traveled to Canton for the satisfaction of their religious needs.

Father Fenwick undoubtedly visited Cleveland on his journeys; he tells in a letter of 1818 that he had visited all the missions from "Kentucky to Cincinnati, Canton and on to Cleveland on Lake Erie." Whether or not he found or ministered to the few Catholics in this city at the time, we have no means of finding out. That there were at least a few we can assume. A card (a paid advertisement) in the Cleveland *Register,* August 3, 1819, inquired about a James Smith who came from Ireland; he was requested to communicate with his father of the same name then living at Stow in Portage County. John Smith, a veteran of the War of 1812, who died in 1813 at the age of thirty, was at first buried in the old Erie Street Cemetery before his body was transferred to St. Joseph's Cemetery.

[2] O'Daniel, *Op. cit.,* 325.

5

BISHOP FENWICK OF CINCINNATI

FROM HIS OWN EXPERIENCE AND THE REPORTS OF Fathers Fenwick and Young, Bishop Flaget was convinced that the appointment of a bishop in Ohio was necessary for the proper care of the growing Catholic population. Archbishop Maréchal of Baltimore forwarded his petition to the Congregation of the Propaganda in Rome and on June 19, 1821, the Diocese of Cincinnati was created by Pope Pius VII. The veteran missionary, Father Fenwick, was named its first bishop, with jurisdiction over the whole of Ohio. He was also given temporary charge of Michigan and the Northwest until another bishop could be provided for that district. He was out on the missions "in the woods of Ohio" when he received news of his elevation; only the counsels, admonitions, and the threats of his superiors induced him to accept.

The new Bishop was born, August 19, 1768, in St. Mary's County, Maryland. His parents were Ignatius, a large landholder, and Sarah Taney Fenwick, both of English ancestry. Sent to the English Dominican College of the Holy Cross in Bornheim, Belgium, to complete his education, he joined the order and was ordained priest at Ghent in 1793. His American citizenship did not save him from mistreatment at the hands of the French Revolutionary forces; he barely escaped with his life to his brethren in England. Together with Father Robert Angier he returned to the United States in 1804, with the intention of making the first foundation of his order in Maryland. He accepted, however, the counsel of Bishop Carroll, and with his paternal inheritance he built a convent and college and finally St. Rose's Church near Springfield in Kentucky. This accomplished, he resigned his position of superior, and labored as a missionary in Kentucky and Ohio for fourteen years before he became a bishop. He was consecrated, in the church he had built, January 13, 1822, by Bishop Flaget, who in virtue of a papal dispensation was assisted by Father Thomas Wilson, the Dominican Superior, and Father John Austin Hill, O.P., the future first resident pastor of St. John's in Canton.

It was a tremendous prospect which the new Bishop faced. There were an estimated 6,000 Catholics scattered among more than 580,000 people in the State, which had doubled its population in a decade. Most of his flock were poor: they had put all their money into the first payment on their land. Moreover, many of them—Germans, Irish, and Swiss—like so many others, had committed themselves as bond servants to defray the cost of coming to America. The southern part of the State had grown more rapidly in the beginning, but the development of industry and the opening of the canals later brought great prosperity to the northern section. A new wave of immigration, from Germany, France, and Ireland, substantially increased the number of Catholics. These workers, farmers, and artisans formed new Catholic centers in the north. The Erie Canal connecting the Great Lakes with the Atlantic Ocean was opened in 1825. The Ohio Canal from Cleveland to Portsmouth was not completed until 1831, but the section from Cleveland to Akron was in operation in July, 1827. A part of the Miami-Maumee Canal, which eventually was to connect Cincinnati with Toledo and the West, was also opened in that year. After the completion of these waterways the workers, many of whom were Catholics, settled in the towns along the course of construction or formed themselves into small farming communities.

Shortly after his consecration the Bishop ordained four Dominicans, in St. Rose's Church: Fathers Thomas H. Martin, John de Raymaecker, John H. McGrady, and John T. Hynes. All of them served in northern Ohio, except the last named who became Vicar Apostolic in British Guiana. Fathers Hill and Young at this time also labored in Ohio.

After a visitation which extended to Detroit Bishop Fenwick was more than ever impressed with the immensity of his task and he borrowed money to make a begging tour of Europe. In Rome he offered his resignation to the newly elected Pope Leo XII, who smilingly declined it and gave him money and one of the ten cases of church furniture which he sent back to America. The Bishop then asked that a prelate be appointed for Detroit and that he himself be given a coadjutor. He received considerable financial aid in several countries of Europe and the promise of an annual subsidy from the French Society for the Propagation of the Faith. Later he was also to receive contributions from a similar society, the Leopoldine Association of Austria, in the founding of which his agent, Father Frederick Rese, was instrumental. Upon his return, St. Peter's Cathedral was built, the most pretentious church structure in the area at the time; a college (the Athenaeum) and an ecclesiastical seminary were erected; and the first Catholic newspaper in the West, the *Telegraph*, made its appearance in 1831.

One of the happy results of the Bishop's European journey was to have secured the services of the above-mentioned Father Rese, who was to become the first Bishop of Detroit but who was then a student at the College of the Propaganda in Rome. Many German immigrants were falling away from the Faith because of the language difficulties. The young recruit had immediate success in reconciling with the Church thirty-three families in Cincinnati alone. When later he himself was sent back to Europe as the Bishop's vicar general, he induced two others, John M. Henni and Martin Kundig, Swiss students already well advanced in theology, to volunteer their services to the American mission, especially for work with the Germans. Bishop Fenwick ordained them in 1829. Father Henni became pastor at Canton in 1830 and was later promoted to be the first Bishop and afterwards Archbishop of Milwaukee.[1] Father Kundig labored on the Ohio missions, especially around Cincinnati, for a while before he went to Michigan and then to Wisconsin, where he helped to "set the foundations" of the Church.[2]

Bishop Fenwick's petition for the setting up of an episcopal see at Detroit for Michigan and the territory west of it was not answered until a year after his death. Meanwhile, in addition to his onerous duties in Ohio he had the care of that vast area and made four official visitations to it. At his earnest invitation the first band of Redemptorists established itself in Michigan to care for the German-speaking Catholics. Later these pioneer missionaries came to Ohio before going to Pennsylvania.[3]

The Indian missions fascinated the Bishop. He would have liked to devote himself entirely to that work but, as he could not, he sent others in his place. In 1822, in the first ceremony of its kind in Ohio, he ordained Father Francis Vincent Badin, the younger brother of the well-known missionary Father Stephen Theodore Badin, and sent him to help Father Richard in Detroit. From France, at the Bishop's invitation, came Fathers John Bellamy and Peter Dejean, to labor successfully among the Canadians and the Indians. Later, Father Peter Carabin and Father Samuel Mazzuchelli, the distinguished Spanish Dominican missionary, both ordained by the Bishop, were sent by him to the Northwest. In 1831 he personally escorted Father Frederick Baraga to his station among the Indians in Michigan, where in due time he became the first Bishop of Marquette. And in the last year of his life Bishop Fenwick made a difficult journey to Washington to secure for his beloved Indian schools some share in the funds which the United States Government had allocated for that purpose.

For the work in Ohio Bishop Fenwick depended almost entirely upon his fellow Dominicans but the temporary separation of Ohio from the Kentucky province for a while cut off that resource. In 1824 he ordained the Irish-born James Ignatius Mullon, the first secular priest to labor on the northern Ohio missions.[4] A little later, when Fathers Rese and Mullon were the only priests in the State who were not Dominicans, the Bishop proposed to Rome that Ohio be made a prefecture apostolic under the direction of the members of that Order. The Propaganda did not approve of this, but Bishop Fenwick was made

[1] Cf. George Paré, *The Catholic Church in Detroit, 1701 to 1888,* Detroit, 1951.

[2] Cf. Peter Leo Johnson, *Stuffed Saddlebags, the Life of Martin Kundig,* Milwaukee, 1942.

[3] Bernard Beck, *Goldenes Jubilaeum des Wirkens der Redemptoristen Vaters an der St. Philomena's Kirche in Pittsburgh und Umgegend nebst deren Ersten Missionen in der Vereinigten Staaten Nord Amerika's,* Pittsburgh, 1889.

[4] Cf. information on Fr. Burke given above.

Commissary General and Superior of the American Dominicans for life. In this way the transfer of priests to and from Kentucky was made dependent upon his decision.

Despite all his added responsibilities, the Bishop could never forget that he was a missionary. Accompanied by Father Mullon or Father Young or another Dominican and by one of the German-speaking priests, Fathers Rese, Henni, or Kundig, he toured Ohio from one end to the other. On these expeditions they had to be content with the poorest accommodations; sometimes their hosts were unfriendly to the Faith; sometimes they separated, lest the poor people go hungry themselves in furnishing food for several. Bishop Fenwick was often too exhausted to eat. They preached and talked and administered the sacraments in the open, in the taverns, in private houses, in public buildings, and even in non-Catholic churches, wherever they could gather people together. Questions and objections were answered and open discussions sometimes took place. But, as the Bishop reported, the consolations were in proportion to their labors. Many who had not seen a priest for a long time were reconciled with the Church. Many were baptized who were converted by their reading or from conversations with Catholic neighbors. One such consoling journey was the tour made with Father Mullon and Father Young in 1827 to give the people the opportunity of gaining the Jubilee indulgence.

During the time of the administration of Bishop Fenwick several new congregations of Catholics had been established in northern Ohio. From their headquarters at Somerset the Dominicans, Fathers Nicolas Young, John De Raymaecker, and Thomas Martin, called upon them regularly. At Canton the valiant John Shorb had used the money he had begged from his friends in Baltimore and Somerset to begin the brick Church of St. John Baptist, the second oldest brick church in northern Ohio, on land which he and the founder of the town, Bezaleel Wells, had donated. As it was nearing completion in 1824, a falling timber killed him. In 1826 Father John Hill was sent as resident pastor, with the additional charge of several other congregations.[5]

His was an interesting career. Born in England, he served in the English army in the Low Countries until his capture by the French. He became a Catholic upon his return to his native land. By mutual arrangement his wife went to live in a convent and he entered the Dominican Order. He was ordained in Rome in 1819, for service in Ohio. Father Hill was vicar general for Bishop Fenwick and Superior of the Dominicans in this State. He had great facility as a preacher and made many converts. The Bishop called him the best of his missionaries, learned, eloquent, zealous. At Canton, in 1828, he died of exhaustion and fever contracted on a two-month tour of the missions around Lake Erie, some of which had not seen a priest for three to four years previously. He had had charge of several congregations in the general vicinity of Canton, with supposedly 500 Catholic families in the whole

[5] O'Daniel, *Op. cit.*, 346, biographical note.

area. Bishop Fenwick himself had taken Father Hill's place for a while in the year before his death. Father De Raymaecker, who had been sent to ease the burden of his duties especially in taking care of the Germans, and Father William R. Tuite, one of the first Dominicans who came here from Belgium, took up the work after his death. They were succeeded by Father Henni, who became pastor in 1830.

Hardy French families from Alsace and Lorraine and Germans from Pennsylvania arrived in Louisville between 1824 and 1828. Father Hill was the first priest to call upon them in the clearing. The Irish, there previously, had traveled back and forth to Canton. At Lawrence Crossroads, two miles from Canal Fulton, a rough log chapel was built in 1831 under the direction of Father Henni. This had been one of the first missions of Bishop Fenwick in 1812, and he had returned there at a later date to administer confirmation in the house of Matthew Patton. There was another Catholic settlement near Canal Fulton, at Marshallville, in the early 1820's.

In Chippewa Township, Wayne County, at a point about a mile from the present Doylestown, George Whitman and his family settled in 1827. They had come from Pennsylvania and were soon followed by other families from Maryland and Pennsylvania. At least two of the men were veterans of the War of 1812. Father Francis Marshall, "a Pennsylvania Dutchman from Maryland," the newly ordained brother of one of the settlers, ministered to the small group in the summer of 1827 before returning to the East. A few months later Fathers Young and Mullon preached the Jubilee and administered the sacraments to the members of the fifteen families in the neighborhood, using as their chapel the log house of the pioneer, Whitman.

On this same tour in 1827 the Jubilee preachers visited a small congregation near Wooster, composed principally of Presbyterian converts. A chapel was being built by them. At Wooster itself one of the missioners preached in the Court House at the invitation of the Protestants. Father Henni in 1831 visited a small group of Hessians and Alsatians who had settled in Randolph Township, in Portage County, a few years earlier. He encouraged them to build a log combination church and school.

The oldest church building in northern Ohio, the Church of St. Paul, near Dungannon, had to be enlarged during this period because of the influx of new German families from Pennsylvania. The work was accomplished in 1827 under the direction of Father Thomas Martin, the Dominican.

It has been mentioned above that Bishop Fenwick had been in Cleveland at an early date. Bishop Flaget in his visitations in the north passed through here in 1818.[6] At that time, although there were less than 200 people living in the town, it was becoming an important center of travel. In 1820 stage-coach lines ran to Columbus, Norwalk, Pittsburgh,

[6] M. J. Spalding, *Benedict Joseph Flaget, First Bishop of Louisville*, Louisville, 1852.

and Buffalo. Schooners carried lake traffic to Detroit and Buffalo and other ports. The opening of the Erie Canal and the beginning of the Ohio Canal in 1825 brought an unprecedented increase in the population. From November, 1825, until July, 1827, up to 2,000 men were engaged in building the canal between Cleveland and Akron. A great number of these workers were Irish Catholics who came from New York and Canada. They lived under very simple and primitive conditions and moved their cabins with them as the work progressed. Some of them remained here, some returned to make their homes in this locality or in other places along the line.

The Dominicans from Somerset or from Canton undoubtedly called upon them, although the first recorded visit was made by Father Thomas Martin who came from Canton in the autumn of 1826. Father Hill in all probability visited them as well as those Catholics at what was to be Cuyahoga Falls and Peninsula. The town of Akron grew up around the hundred or more cabins of the canal workers. Friendly Indians carried news through the woods of the approaching priest, and here Mass was celebrated in the home of Mr. Dunn, or of Mr. McAllister, who was the contractor for the extension of the canal southward to Monroe Falls.

The Irish in Cleveland at this time were settled mainly at the mouth of the Cuyahoga River. In 1830 many German Catholic immigrants came here and made their homes along Lorain Avenue on the West Side and on the streets off Superior and Central Avenues on the East Side. Father John Henni had been commissioned by Bishop Fenwick to seek out the German Catholics. Perhaps he visited Cleveland regularly from the time of his appointment as pastor at Canton. Shortly before his own death Bishop Fenwick issued minute directions to Father Kundig who had succeeded Father Henni in the task of visiting the scattered Germans. In the summer of 1833 these two missionaries spent a few days with the Catholics of Cleveland, who were numerous enough to require the use of the Freemasons' Hall, in the Oviatt Block, at the northwest corner of Superior and West Ninth Streets, the "only place large enough at their disposal." It is presumed also that Father Stephen Badin on his journeys to the Northwest visited the first congregation in this city.

On his travels through Ohio and on his way into Michigan Bishop Fenwick visited other Catholic colonies west of Cleveland. At Tiffin a congregation grew up around the family of James Doherty who had settled there in 1823. The Bishop called on them in 1827. Father Mullon, who accompanied him, remained for a few days to administer the sacraments and to preach at the Court House, which was the common place of worship for several denominations. When he returned in 1829 the Bishop secured a plot of ground from the founder of the town upon which to build a Catholic church, and when he ordained Father Edmund Quinn (January 1, 1831) he sent him to Tiffin as the first resident pastor. In the next year a neat brick church was under roof.

In Peru Township, in Huron County, another group of Catholic families (from Lorraine in France) was to be found. The Bishop visited them in 1829 and 1830. He celebrated Mass in the cabin of Joseph Carabin, the father of the missionary, Peter Carabin. In 1831 Father Henni came from Canton to visit them and officiated in a log chapel built by the farmers on a plot of ground which had been donated by a Protestant named Taylor. In the following year a schoolhouse was erected. One of the three Redemptorists who had returned to Cincinnati from Michigan shortly before Bishop Fenwick's death, Father Francis X. Haetscher, who knew both French and German, was given charge of this congregation and the surrounding missions in 1832. Along the lake shore, at Port Clinton, a Protestant gentleman had given a lot upon which the Bishop hoped to build a church. At the time, the prospects for the development of that town were very bright.

It may not be amiss at this point to record the names of other Dominican Fathers who labored with those already mentioned in the establishment of the Church in northern Ohio. We include all up to the time of their entire withdrawal in 1842: Fathers Daniel J. O'Leary, Charles P. Montgomery, John G. Alleman, P. Fochenkress, Anthony Fahey, J. Meara, Theodore J. Van den Broek, Adrian Van de Weyer, P. Van Dromme, P. O'Bairne. All these at one time or another exercised the ministry at Canton or Dungannon, as did Father Richard Miles who became the first Bishop of Nashville, and Father Joseph S. Alemany who became Bishop of Monterey and Archbishop of San Francisco.

Such were the beginnings of the Church in northern Ohio, a few brick or log churches, a few others about to be started, a few centers of evangelization. From Dungannon and Canton the missioners traveled to other groups or settlements in the woods, on the farms, along the canals, in the towns. When Bishop Fenwick began his apostolic labors in this State there was no Catholic church edifice, no missioner but himself. At the end of his zealous career, in 1832, in the vast territory which then included Michigan there were twenty-four missioners and twenty-two church buildings, and several congregations without a meeting place of their own. Of these church buildings, however, there were but few in northern Ohio: at Canton, Dungannon, Randolph, Tiffin, and Canal Fulton (Lawrence Crossroads).

It was in northern Ohio, however, that the good bishop spent the last days of his life, the victim of his zeal for God and the Church. Not long after his return to Cincinnati from Washington, where he had obtained financial assistance for the Indian schools in Michigan, sick and enfeebled though he was he began what was to be the last visitation of his diocese.

He was in Canton on June 30, 1832, and from this center he visited the missions in the vicinity. The dreadful Asiatic cholera was claiming many victims. Nevertheless, he decided to pay a visit to Michigan. During the passage from Cleveland to Detroit a soldier died of the plague, and three persons, one of them a Catholic, died upon landing. The Bishop suffered from chills and fever, yet he persisted in his design. Upon his return to Detroit from the Indian missions, he found the aged Father Richard stricken with the scourge. Here he met the newly arrived Redemptorists, Fathers Simon Saenderl and Francis Xavier Haetscher, whom he hoped to see established in Detroit. On the return journey to Canton he visited Tiffin and Peru; and to keep his promise, though he was very sick, he made a diversion to administer Confirmation in the new brick church at Steubenville.

Business called him to Pittsburgh, but soon he was back again, to confirm a class in St. Paul's, near Dungannon. On September 23 he confirmed in St. John's Church in Canton, his last episcopal function. The news of the death of Father Richard in Detroit caused him to remark to Father Henni, "My son, I will soon follow him." A few days later he started for Cincinnati, intending to visit the missions on the way. His pitiable condition, "weak and dizzy" as he was, induced Miss Eliza Rose Powell, a convert of his who was teaching in Canton, to accompany him. Father Henni was kept at Canton by his duties to the cholera-stricken people.

On the road the Bishop became violently ill with the plague. Upon arrival in Wooster at sunset he was put to bed in Coulter's Hotel, which used to stand on the north side of West Liberty Street, midway between the Public Square and Walnut Street. Two physicians, Doctors Stephen F. Day and Samuel L. Bissell, were in attendance. Miss Powell and a Negro boy also did their utmost to care for his needs. The landlady's remark that "he had administered to many" but that in his extremity "no one was there to minister to him" caused particular sorrow to Miss Powell, left alone to watch him. The summons to Father Henni to bring the Holy Oils from Canton reached him too late. The Bishop after much suffering, but resigned to the Will of God, died at noon, September 26, 1832. For fear of the pestilence, the remains were buried hurriedly "under a little mound." Those concerned did not know that for the burial of Catholics in that neighborhood Father Henni had made "some arrangements with Mr. Gallagher and Chrismas." In the following February the body was transferred to the vault under the Cathedral in Cincinnati and later to St. Joseph's Cemetery in that city.

Thus passed the Apostle of Ohio, in circumstances not unlike those which attended the death of the great missioner, St. Francis Xavier. "No distance, no condition of weather or of primitive roads, no extremes of heat or cold dampened the ardor of the earnest ambassador of Christ." Bishop Spalding gives us a picture of Father Fenwick, the missionary priest, which is also characteristic of him as Bishop. He "lived on horseback. His zeal for the salvation of souls was as boundless as it was untiring and persevering. He possessed a peculiar tact for winning souls to Christ. His manners were of the most familiar, affable, winning kind. He could adapt himself to every emergency and to every description of character and temperament. Frank, open and sincere by nature, an American himself, he possessed an instinctive talent for dealing with Americans, whether Catholics or Protestants. Multitudes of the latter were converted to Catholicism through his agency."[7] The man chosen by Divine Providence to found the Church in Ohio died on the eve of its extraordinary development.

[7] John Henni to Fr. Rese, Wooster, Sept. 27, 1832, in Notre Dame Archives (abbreviated hereafter as N.D.A.); Lamotte, *Op. cit.*, 68; O'Daniel (*Op. cit.* 426); the last named authority identified the location of the Coulter Hotel.

6

BISHOP PURCELL OF CINCINNATI

FATHER FREDERICK RESE, THE VICAR GENERAL, ruled the Diocese of Cincinnati as apostolic administrator until his own consecration as the first Bishop of Detroit, October 6, 1832. Father John Baptist Purcell, President of St. Mary's College, Emmitsburg, Maryland, was the choice of the Holy See for Cincinnati. Born in Ireland at Mallow, County Cork, February 26, 1800, son of Edmund and Johanna O'Keefe Purcell, he came to America at the age of eighteen and was a private tutor for a while before he entered college at Emmitsburg. He studied in France also and was ordained, May 20, 1826, by Archbishop de Quelen of Paris. After two additional years of study with the Sulpicians he returned to America and in 1829 became the head of his old college. Archbishop James Whitfield consecrated him in Baltimore, October 13, 1833. He was installed in Bishop Fenwick's place on the following November 14.

In 1850 he became the first Archbishop of Cincinnati and presided over the First and Second Provincial Councils in 1855 and 1858. He was present at the Vatican Council in 1870 and with some of the other bishops had been given permission to return home before the formal definition of Papal Infallibility; he accepted the doctrine immediately and whole-heartedly. His last days were saddened by the well-known financial crisis in the diocese, for which he was in no way personally responsible. The famous decision in the case had far-reaching results in protecting the property of the Church. After his health began to fail he retired to the Brown County Convent of the Ursulines in 1879. From then until his death in 1883 the administration was in the hands of his coadjutor, Archbishop William Henry Elder.

Archbishop Purcell was looked upon as the champion of the Church in the West. An ardent advocate of Catholic education, he waged unceasing battle in defense of Catholic schools. The progress of the Church had aroused her enemies to scurrilous attacks upon her doctrines and motives. Lyman Beecher, the Cincinnati minister, the "ostentatious and virulent foe of Catholics" in his book, *The Plea for the West,* conjured up a supposed Catholic conspiracy to seize the Mississippi-Ohio Valley and he urged the strengthening of Protestantism against it. The book was popular and went through several editions. In 1837 the then Bishop Purcell engaged in an eight-day discussion with Alexander Campbell, the founder of the Campbellites or Disciples, an offshoot of the Baptists. The local newspapers were fair enough in reporting the debate and the results were better feeling towards Catholics, and many conversions.[1]

Like his predecessor, the Archbishop received material help from the Society for the Propagation of the Faith and from the Leopoldine Society of Vienna. The monumental new Cathedral was consecrated in 1845; and Mount St. Mary's Seminary of the West, which trained so many early missionaries, was opened in 1851. On his several visits to Europe the Archbishop found missioners for Ohio, including the future first Bishop of Cleveland. The Jesuit Fathers took over St. Francis Xavier College in 1840. The Sanguinists, the Franciscans, the Passionists, the Fathers of the Holy Ghost, the Brothers of Mary, and the Brothers of the Poor of St. Francis Seraph followed. And many new congregations of religious women took up residence in the diocese.

The northern section of Ohio grew and developed almost beyond recognition during the time of the administration of the second Bishop of Cincinnati. The steam railroads penetrated to those sections not already covered by the canals. Many German and Irish Catholic immigrants were among the thousands of workmen who built them and who after the completion of the work established homes and congregations along the route. The Monroeville and Sandusky City Railroad was chartered in 1835; another line joined Mansfield and Huron; connections were made then with Newark and Columbus. Still another line was opened in 1847 between Cincinnati and Springfield. Eventually the network covered the whole State. The district along Lake Erie began to rival the country around Cincinnati.

In his visitation of the northern part of his jurisdiction the new prelate generally traveled on horseback, though at times the early railroads eased the difficulty of travel. Willing hands, especially those of the Irish workers, propelled the small cars from one station to another. He visited the older missions as well as those which were springing up in the new towns and in the clearings made in the forests by the German farmers. He administered Confirmation and encouraged the building of churches and schools. He accepted many invitations given by the Protestants to speak in their churches. There and in the court houses he explained Catholic doctrine and practice and very often denounced the evils of intemperance.

From the accounts which the Bishop caused to be printed in the Cincinnati *Telegraph* it is possible to trace the progress of the Church in the northern section of the State.[2] In 1834 the Bishop visited the camp of the Irish workers who were engaged in the construction of the Sandy and Beaver Canal, which ran between Bolivar (near Massillon)

[1] Lamotte, *Op. cit.*, 78. A controversy with a certain Rev. Thomas Vickers was put in book form in a second edition, Cincinnati, 1868.

[2] In addition to the parish sketches, the pertinent extracts from the Cincinnati *Telegraph* are published in Houck, *Op. cit.*, I, 25-50.

on the Ohio Canal and the Little Beaver River at the Pennsylvania border. He was escorted to this camp, near Lisbon and Dungannon, by a Mr. De Long who claimed some seventy of his relatives and friends as converts. The project of a church building at Lisbon, however, had to be abandoned and the care of the canal workers devolved upon the pastor of nearby Dungannon. Father John McGrady, O.P., had been resident pastor there for four years. The mission received occasional visits from others also until in 1835 the Bishop appointed Father James Conlan, whom he had ordained the year before, resident pastor of Steubenville with the care of Dungannon and other places in the area. This pioneer priest accomplished untold good among the canal workers. Unfortunately many of them became victims of the fever and these he buried in St. Paul's Cemetery near Dungannon.

Father Conlan found a few Catholics at Wellsville and at East Liverpool in 1835. In the latter place, a new pottery town on the Ohio River, the Catholics were much beholden to John S. Blakely in whose house Mass was celebrated for years. Later, in 1837, Father Conlan built a brick church which was saved from the auction block and completed only after he had received a favorable response to a general appeal to the "Catholic Congregations of Ohio." A "mysterious" fire destroyed it eight years later. The good pastor in 1838 visited the group of Irish farmers who had settled at Summitville. There he celebrated Mass in the McAllister home. Then, in the next year, he remodeled a log cabin, sometimes called the McAllister church. Bishop Purcell laid the cornerstone of the present brick church in 1846; its completion was delayed by the "hard times" for several years.

The Catholics in Youngstown also claimed the attention of Father Conlan. They and missions in the vicinity had been visited by Father Edward T. Collins from Cincinnati in 1834. The congregation met in the homes of Daniel Sheehy, William Woods, and Neal Campbell. It was only after 1846, when coal was found to be a successful substitute for the charcoal previously used in the blast furnaces, that the towns in the Mahoning Valley developed into centers of steel and iron production. Bishop Purcell made the home of James Moore his headquarters on his visitation of 1847. He reported that Mayor Todd of Youngstown had donated a lot for the building of a church. St. Columba's (first frame church), however, was not completed for another six years. In nearby Warren Father Conlan cared for the Catholics there who had been visited for the first time, in 1835, by Father Patrick O'Dwyer who came to them from Cleveland. In 1842 Father Conlan moved his residence to Dungannon and began a new brick church in the town itself which was about a mile from the old location; before it was completed he was called to Cleveland by Bishop Rappe to be his vicar general and the first pastor of St. Patrick's.

Many of the Irish at this time spoke Gaelic and up to the turn of the century missions were given in that tongue in St. Columba's in Youngstown. There were also German-speaking priests, who came from Canton to Dungannon. According to the memoirs of the venerable Father Lindesmith, a native of the last-mentioned place, a German Catholic teacher kept a school at this time in the upper story of a log cabin. On one occasion Father Conlan helped and encouraged an old itinerant German missionary, whose name is not recorded, who celebrated Mass and preached to the Germans in a tavern near the town.[3]

To the west, in Canton and its vicinity, the congregations received considerable increase from the continued immigration. The missionaries resided at St. John's, which sometimes had two co-pastors, one of whom had particular charge of the German-speaking Catholics. Father Henni, who left in 1834, had been assisted by Father De Raymaecker. Father Saenderl, the Redemptorist, and Father O'Bairne, the Dominican, were there together for a period. Other Dominicans, with the occasional assistance of Father Stephen Badin, filled in the intervals until the appointment of Father F. S. Hoffman in 1837, when the Dominicans withdrew altogether from Canton. Fathers Michael McAleer and Ferdinand Kuehr helped Father Hoffman for a while before they became affiliated with other dioceses. Father Henry D. Juncker, destined to be the first Bishop of Alton, was stationed in Canton for a few months in 1840. Father Matthias Wuerz was the pastor for the following four years. During his time the German immigration increased the size of the congregation to the extent that St. John's Church was found to be uncomfortably small and the question arose about building a separate church for the Germans. When he resigned in 1844, he was succeeded by Father John J. Doherty with whom Father John Henry Luhr came to live. Before the latter was called to Cleveland, he organized the German Congregation of St. Peter and built the first church of that name, which was blessed by Bishop Purcell in 1847.

On this same journey the Bishop dedicated other churches in the vicinity of Canton. The Ohio Canal had brought great prosperity to Massillon. When the Bishop had visited the town six years before, he had been obliged to use a large public hall as a meeting place. Now he had the happiness of addressing the congregation of Irish and Germans in the stone Church of St. Mary, which had been constructed by Father Wuerz. At nearby Canal Fulton, which also derived its importance from the traffic on the canal, a frame church had been completed in 1845 by Father Maurice Howard, who was the resident pastor at Chippewa (Doylestown). On a previous visit the Bishop preached twice in the Methodist church. It was due to his encouragement that the Catholic congregation abandoned the log chapel at Lawrence Crossroads and moved the center of their religious activities into Canal Fulton.

About six miles from Canal Fulton, at Sugar Creek, the Bishop re-

---

[3] Fr. Lindesmith's reminiscences, in Cleveland Diocesan Archives (abbreviated hereafter as C.D.A.).

ported sixty communicants. His high hopes for the congregation of
Marylanders were, however, not to be fulfilled. The log chapel became
a sheep cote and even the cemetery was abandoned. The French-
speaking congregation at Louisville, in Stark County, had by 1840
grown to eighty families. Father Louis De Goesbriand, who arrived
from France in that year, enlarged the church and added a bell to the
tower before he was transferred to the Toledo area. A few brick
chapels were built in the German missions around Canton which were
attended by Father Luhr. There was one at North Canton, then known
as New Berlin, another at Navarre in 1844. Father Henni was responsible for the log chapel, in the last-named town, which upon completion of the new church was transformed into a school.

The Bishop on his visitation of 1847 was particularly impressed with
the congregation at Randolph (now St. Joseph). He commended
them for their temperance and love of education and their familiarity
with church music. Their school began in a log house in 1831. It was
moved into a frame building four years later. One of the oldest schools
in northern Ohio, it has had an uninterrupted existence. A separate
frame church, built in 1838 to replace their first log chapel, was
"mysteriously" burned down not long afterwards. Another frame
church was erected in 1845, when there were seventy-eight families
in the area, under the supervision of the Sanguinist, Father Van den
Broek. The Venerable John Nepomucene Neumann, afterwards the
Bishop of Philadelphia, passing through Randolph in 1842, distributed
Holy Communion to 100 persons.

The Church was growing commensurately in the section of the State
west of Cleveland. In June, 1834, the Bishop had established the Redemptorist Fathers in Peru, near Norwalk. They were given charge
of the many surrounding German missions and it was hoped that in
time they would be able to build a monastery and a college. But the
response to their efforts was not wholehearted nor generous and as
a result the Fathers withdrew in 1839. Fathers Peter Czakert, Simon
Saenderl, Francis Haetscher, Joseph Prost, and the Venerable John
Neumann, mentioned above, left their imprint upon the first foundations of the Church in the area. Father Francis Xavier Tschenhens returned for a while, at the instance of the Bishop, and together with
other priests of the vicinity attended the people until the coming of
the Sanguinist Fathers in January, 1844. The latter remained in Peru
for four years and then removed their headquarters to Thompson,
now Marywood, in Seneca County.

At an earlier period a section of the Peru parish, in contravention
of the orders of the Bishop who feared that a division of forces would
hurt the situation, built a frame church at Norwalk, three miles distant.
Ecclesiastical sanctions had to be used. Father Alig, a Redemptorist,
was brought in to adjust the difficulties. Through him the church was
finished and enlarged and a school for sixty pupils was opened in
1843. The title of the property was transferred by the trustees to the

proper authority. When Bishop Purcell visited Norwalk in 1846 to dedicate the church to St. Peter, he reported his great admiration for the faith of the people as displayed in the public procession of the Blessed Sacrament through the stately forest.

Father Edmund Quinn, the young priest who had been sent to Tiffin, the mission center for the country west of Peru, soon exhausted his energy and strength. His scattered flock included the men working on the Miami Canal and it was among them, at St. Mary, that he died of the Maumee fever, a victim of duty, in 1835. The Redemptorists assumed the responsibility until the appointment of Father Joseph McNamee in 1839. Although born in Ireland, he knew German and was able to minister in that language to many of the settlers in the newly opened northwestern section of Ohio. The German-speaking Sanguinist Fathers, however, had charge of most of the exclusively German missions. In a few cases secular priests came from Germany with their flocks. In the far northwest and along the canal French priests, among them Father Rappe who was destined to be Cleveland's first bishop, were Father McNamee's auxiliaries.

In the town of Tiffin itself immigration had so swelled the Catholic population that St. Mary's Church had to be enlarged to twice its former capacity. The Germans, moreover, under the direction of the Sanguinists built the brick Church of St. Joseph which Bishop Purcell dedicated in 1846. In the vicinity of Tiffin, at McCutchenville, a small mission church was built in 1840; an Arnold family from Maryland was host to the Bishop on his visit there. The village, however, did not develop according to expectations and the chapel was abandoned. In compensation for this disappointment the many settlements of German farmers in the area proved to be more permanent. The village of Glandorf in Putnam County was founded by Father William J. Horstmann and a group of his countrymen from Osnabrueck, Germany. While his people were clearing the land bought from the Government he built a simple log chapel in 1834 and a more substantial one in 1837. The hollowed-out trunk of a sycamore tree served as his rustic pulpit. He acted, also, as schoolmaster and, with what was rare justice in the mind of the Bishop, he received some help from the common school fund. In 1840 the community was composed of 140 families. Father Horstmann for a while attended another Catholic congregation at Fort Jennings, which was made up principally of men from Oldenberg, Germany, who settled on land bought from the Government in 1830 by the pioneer, J. F. Wellman. They shared with the non-Catholics the use of a log house for a school and church. Bishop Purcell urged them in 1845 to build their own church but for some time nothing could be done about it.

Hardy German settlers established a Catholic colony at New Riegel, then known as Wolf's Creek, near Tiffin, in 1833. Father McNamee and priests from Canton visited them, and Father Tschenhens, the Redemptorist, built a log chapel there in 1839. The Sanguinists were put in charge of the mission five years later but the new church which the Bishop urged the 145-family congregation to build was not begun for several years. Here it was that the first Sisters' convent in northern Ohio, a rude log construction, was opened in 1844. Sisters of the Most Precious Blood, devoted by rule to the Perpetual Adoration of the Blessed Sacrament, were installed in it by Father Francis De Sales Brunner, the American founder of the Sanguinists. They immediately began their work of educating young girls here and in the nearby village of Marywood. Father Tschenhens had visited Marywood in 1834, five years before a chapel was built. The Sanguinists were put in charge in 1844 and three years later Father Brunner became the first resident pastor. Here he constructed his monastery which was the mother-house of the Sanguinists and the center of widespread missionary activity in the several German settlements in the area.

At St. Sebastian (Bismarck), about five miles distant, a chapel of rough-hewn logs was built in 1846. In the same year a frame mission church at Liberty replaced the log chapel built by a small group of families who were first visited by Father Tschenhens in 1834. Father Brunner supervised the erection of a frame mission church at St. Stephen, Seneca County, in 1845, and a frame chapel at New Washington in the year following. Father Henni came from Canton in 1833 to visit the farming community at Bethlehem (Richland County), then called Shelby Settlement. The Redemptorists influenced this community to build a log chapel in 1837 and a log schoolhouse which was probably the first parochial school in that part of the State.

Not far from the western border of the State at Delphos, Allen County, in 1842 was to be found another community of German Catholic farmers. Two years after that date Father John Otto Bredeick arrived with another group from Westphalia, Germany, to join them. The log chapel built at that time had soon to be enlarged so that part of it could be used as a school. A second church of hewn timbers, which was started in 1846, was several years under construction.

>>> 7 <<<

TOLEDO AREA UNDER
BISHOP PURCELL'S JURISDICTION

THE DEVELOPMENT OF THE NORTHWESTERN section of the State was delayed by the nature of the country and to some extent by the dispute with Michigan about the boundary line with Ohio. The Black Swamp, a marshy area about 40 miles wide and 120 miles long, extended along the shore of Lake Erie between the Sandusky and Maumee Rivers. Wolves were not uncommon in the vicinity when the State built a road through it in 1827. In the wilderness of the Maumee Valley, through which the canal was under construction, there were no established settlements in 1834 between Defiance and the northern terminal at Toledo. In 1837 work was started on the Wabash and Erie Canal between Toledo and the Indiana border and it was finished in 1843. Two years later the canal coming up from Cincinnati was connected with it at Junction in Paulding County. Toledo was thus joined in 1849 with Cincinnati and the southern part of Ohio and with the State of Indiana by the renamed Miami-Erie Canal. The Black Swamp and the route of the canals were extremely unhealthful. Ague and fevers and even erysipelas were prevalent. Horses and men wore heavy coverings against the disease-bearing mosquitoes. The country literally "devoured its inhabitants; there was not one old man to be seen in the whole area; the Maumee fever destroyed whole families at a time." Irish Catholics were numerous among the workers who built these passages through the wilderness; their lot was not enviable.

To give them the opportunity to receive the sacraments the heroic Father Edmund Quinn, as we have seen above, called on them from his post in Tiffin. Father Emmanuel Thienpoint, the Belgian, visited them along the course of the canal from Cincinnati and took Father Quinn's place at Tiffin for a while. Father Edward T. Collins followed the same path up to Toledo in the next years. In 1839 Father McNamee took over this duty. Father Joseph P. Macheboeuf, the future first Bishop of Denver, and one of the five priests brought from France by Bishop Purcell in that year, was sent to assist him. The French-

35

Canadian settlements scattered in the northwest of the State were the particular object of the young priest's zeal but he also helped Father McNamee, whose health was not robust, in his other missions. In a few months he learned enough English from his pastor to "lisp it a little as they sat before the fire in Tiffin, recounting their experiences and resting a little to get breath for another run."

Sick calls and requests for Christian burial came from every direction: distance, bad weather, and bad roads were only obstacles to be overcome. They wore old clothes going into the woods but changed to frock coat and black cravat and collar upon arrival in the principal towns of the nine counties which they served. The equipment for Mass was carried in a long bag swung over the horse's saddle. Sometimes they used a four-wheeled open wagon "which was very comfortable and would not fatigue a person in a thirty or forty mile journey." Father Macheboeuf bought the horse and buggy of Father Tschenhens when the latter was recalled from the mission. In extremely cold weather the young priest kept warm by running alongside the horse; he was not surprised when on one occasion the horse ran away from him "because his own feet were cold." He heard the confessions of those who knew no French through an interpreter. Then he preached the "miserable little sermon" which he had prepared with much effort. At one Irish settlement all who were present at the Mass received the sacraments. The Irish laborers who were building the macadamized road through the Black Swamp between Fremont and Perrysburg persuaded him to stay with them over a Sunday; he preached in his halting English, and baptized some children. They were so pleased, he related, that they gave him enough money to pay for the Canadian pony he was riding.

After about a year Father Macheboeuf was sent to Sandusky as its first pastor and Father Louis Amadeus Rappe came to succeed him in the other missions, and to establish himself as the first resident pastor at Toledo. Father McNamee, despite his ill health, continued to care for the canal workers. He attended a group of 140 at Defiance, and there were more at Napoleon and other places along the route. Left alone, he asked Father McLaughlin to help him with the work around Tiffin, but the pastor of Cleveland had to care for his own missions. The Sanguinists, when they came, had relieved Father McNamee of much of the care of the Germans, in Findlay, for instance, and in Fostoria, where he was the first to celebrate Mass in 1839 and 1843 respectively. There were now five Catholic centers in northwestern Ohio: Father McNamee, at Tiffin, who might be called anywhere by the English-speaking Catholics; Father Rappe, at Toledo; Father Macheboeuf, at Sandusky; and the Sanguinists, at Peru and Marywood.

Father Rappe, like his predecessors, followed the line of the canal southward from Toledo. What he reported of his visit to the reservoir under construction in Paulding County is typical of his other experiences. In February, 1842, some 600 men attended his two Masses. He was impressed with the poverty and simple faith of the Irish workers, by their eagerness for instruction, and by their love of the sacraments. He recruited many for the Total Abstinence Society and asked Bishop Purcell to send him medals and pledge cards. The hardy son of France took the Total Abstinence pledge himself as an example to others. His methods were simple but thorough and he was indefatigable in teaching catechism to the children. The canal workers showed their appreciation in the monetary assistance they gave him for his other missions.[1]

As part of a speculative boom, Toledo, at the mouth of the Maumee River, was incorporated in 1836 and a few streets were laid out. It had been called a "mud hole on the banks of the Maumee surrounded by a few frame houses and log cabins, swampy, and full of fever." As the northern terminal of the canal, and a railroad center as well, it began to benefit from all the trade which passed through it. Bishop Purcell, there in 1837, was enthusiastic about the future of the town and of the "many Catholics from Ireland and Germany who had settled in the vicinity of the old Catholic Canadian French." He and the other missioners who had been there celebrated Mass in the cabins of the canal workers or of the few Canadians along the river. Father Macheboeuf visited the area (from Tiffin) in 1839 and offered the Holy Sacrifice "in the frame shanty of a poor Canadian who with his fellows had previously gone to Monroe, in Michigan, to receive the sacraments."

Only after the United States Congress had decided that the small tract of land around Toledo belonged to Ohio and not to Michigan was it definitely placed under the jurisdiction of Bishop Purcell. Father Macheboeuf thereupon rented a room over a drug store, improvised an altar, covered it with calico, and invited the Canadians as well as the others to come to Mass. Bishop Purcell and Father Henni visited the town again in 1841. The Bishop preached several times in the Court House to audiences which included some Protestants. A few of these signed the subscription intended to raise enough money to build a new church or to buy the one previously used by the Presbyterians, which was to be sold for a $2,800 debt. When Father Rappe arrived, he bought this former Presbyterian church, and established the first Catholic school in the excellent basement, which served also as his residence. The town officials, however, stopped the fee previously attached to the ringing of the bell which announced the hours to the citizens.

For his school and the academy he had in mind Father Rappe had hoped to secure the services of the Ursulines, who had come from his old home in France. They, however, established themselves in Brown

[1] Reminiscences of Bp. De Goesbriand and those of Bp. Macheboeuf, in Houck, *Op. cit.*, I, 51–60. W. J. Howlett, *The Life of the Rt. Rev. Joseph P. Macheboeuf*, Pueblo, 1908. Rappe-Purcell correspondence, in N.D.A.

County near Cincinnati. It was the Sisters of Notre Dame de Namur, whom he himself had escorted to America in 1841, that took charge. Five of them, after forty-eight hours on a canal boat, arrived from Cincinnati late in 1845, to find a house all ready and furnished. They were well received by the people and did much to dissipate prejudice in the town. In 1847 there were 7 Sisters teaching 105 girls, of whom 65 paid no tuition. A free school for about 40 boys was taught by a Robert Whantford. Bishop Purcell had praised the Sisters for braving the dangers of the Maumee fever in the interests of religion and education, but after the death of two Sisters they gave up the school and returned to Cincinnati in July, 1848.[2]

Up the river from Toledo were the older communities of Maumee and Perrysburg. At Maumee Father McNamee, with money given by the Irish Catholics engaged on the public works and by a few well-disposed Protestants, bought a neat frame church formerly used by the Episcopalians and converted it to Catholic worship. Bishop Purcell, who confirmed twenty-five persons on the occasion, dedicated it in 1841. Father Rappe took charge of it as a mission and completed the interior renovation. The few Canadian families across the river at Perrysburg attended it.

Further along the line, about twenty-six miles south of Toledo, at Providence, Father Rappe supervised the construction of a brick church in 1845 for the Irish Catholic canal workers who had settled there. This community was later destroyed by fire and never rebuilt. Still farther south, at Defiance, the canal workers furnished the means for the construction of a humble frame church in 1844. There were but two Catholic families living in the village itself and only fifteen families in the county. At The Bend (Delaware Bend) and Hicksville were small settlements of Catholics. In the latter place Father Rappe celebrated Mass in the home of Patrick Smith. In 1843 he visited for the first time the German Catholic farming community of New Bavaria (Poplar Ridge). Here the home of Francis Fleury was used as a temporary chapel until in the next year Father Louis De Goesbriand built a log house.

In January, 1846, Bishop Purcell sent this French priest from Louisville, where he had been pastor for several years, to the north to help Father Rappe, especially in the care of the Canadian communities along the lake shore and in the lower river valleys. Among these, the fishermen and trappers at Toussaints built a log chapel for themselves in 1845. Oak Harbor was another such station. The first Canadian Catholics along Sandusky Bay had been ordered inland by the British. They settled at Fremont (Lower Sandusky) and at La Prairie and were visited by Father Richard, who came to them from Detroit in 1823. There were twenty families at La Prairie when Bishop Purcell called there in 1841 to bless their log chapel. As the successor of Father Rappe in

2 Rappe-Purcell correspondence in N.D.A.

Toledo, Father De Goesbriand took charge of all his missions, and under his direction the German farmers at Marygrove (Raab) built a log chapel in 1847.

We have seen above that Father Macheboeuf had been made first pastor of Sandusky. This town, an important fur trading post in the earlier days which was laid out as Portland in 1817, had 600 inhabitants a dozen years later. Even after the completion of the canals, which naturally diverted some of their commerce, it was a popular port for travel between Lake Erie and the Ohio River. Situated at the far end of the Western Reserve, it had many settlers from New England. The first European Catholics arrived between 1826 and 1830. Father Macheboeuf estimated that in 1841 there were within a circle of ten miles about sixty families, "some Germans but mostly Irish, and none of them rich."

He used an upstairs room in the old Customs House as a temporary chapel. On lots donated by a Protestant landowner named Mills he began a stone church. Father McLaughlin, "his neighbor from Cleveland," laid the cornerstone and preached, October 13, 1841. His own people hauled the stone and prepared the timber. He paid the builders in kind, "with hams and other provisions." Money was scarce. Many of the Irish workers on the railroads and canals had lost their savings in the bank failures and were unable to give as generously as they would otherwise have given. The pastor had to borrow money to continue the building, but, as he wrote, "to be a true American one must be in debt." Bishop Purcell paid for the roof and, with the funds he himself collected in Canada and France, he completed the fine stone Church of the Holy Angels and a stone residence in 1845. In the next year, when Bishop Purcell dedicated the church, it was too small for the congregation of 200 families. In 1843, when part of the common school funds were allotted to him, the good pastor reopened the free school he had been obliged to discontinue. However, the $150 assigned to support the school teacher and his wife was considered to be insufficient, and it was difficult to find suitable class rooms for the many pupils.

Father Macheboeuf was not at first favorably disposed towards the Total Abstinence movement promoted by Bishop Purcell but for the sake of example he joined the Total Abstinence Society, and he enrolled 162 members in 1842. Moreover, he asked the assistance of the mayor of the town "in regulating the attitude of the grocery keepers."

The favorite mission of Father Macheboeuf was at Fremont, up the Sandusky River. As a rendezvous of the Indians it was not safe for a white man until in 1813 Colonel Croghan decisively defeated an English and Indian force near the town. Enterprising Canadians from Detroit, the Momenays and the Beaugrand families, soon established themselves there. Father Richard, as we have seen above, visited them as did other missioners. Bishop Purcell was there in 1836. Father Stephen Badin, who accompanied him, preached to a crowded audience

in the public schoolhouse. The Bishop returned ten years later to bless
the frame church which had been built with the help of the two
Protestant sons-in-law of Mr. Beaugrand. Father Macheboeuf had previously used Pease's Hall and a remodeled turner's shop for divine
services.

8

CLEVELAND UNDER BISHOP PURCELL'S JURISDICTION

THE PASTOR OF SANDUSKY REFERRED TO Father McLaughlin as his neighbor on Lake Erie at Cleveland. This city at the time, though "full of life and trade and business," was a commercial rather than an industrial center. The Ohio Canal to Portsmouth was opened in 1832 but the railroads were not in full operation through the town for another twenty years. Its geographical position, however, as a link between the coal beds of the interior and the iron and copper mines of the upper lakes, assured its future as one of the greatest manufacturing and industrial cities in the country. The population increased from 1,900 in 1833 to nearly 14,000 in 1848, of whom about one-half were born in the United States, the rest, for the most part, were from Germany, Ireland, and England. The Irish, almost exclusively, and a good proportion of the Germans were Catholics. The total number of Catholics in Cleveland in 1833 is difficult to estimate. Many who had helped to build the canals remained here after their completion. Others came directly from Europe. The first *Directory of Cleveland and Ohio City*, published in 1837, has many evidently Catholic names. At any rate they were numerous enough to come under the consideration of the Bishop as a congregation which deserved the regular attendance of a pastor.

Father Henni had been coming to Cleveland at intervals, and in 1834 he urged that a church be built here. At the end of the same year Father Tschenhens conducted the papal jubilee exercises for three weeks with great success and reported to Bishop Purcell that "the large number of German and Irish Catholics (estimated at nearly a thousand) required the services of a pastor and a church." He recommended that Father James Conlan be sent from Steubenville.[1]

The Bishop's choice, however, for the first pastor of Cleveland was Father John Dillon whom he had ordained with Father Conlan, September 20, 1834. Born at Drumcunny, County Limerick, Ireland, in

[1] Henni to Purcell, Jan. 29, 1834; Tschenhens to Purcell, Jan. 4, 1835; Nicolas Young to Purcell, May 6, 1835, all in N.D.A.

1807, he attended Longford College there. At the invitation of Bishop Purcell he finished his studies at the seminary in Cincinnati. He was in Canton when he received the Bishop's directions to proceed to Cleveland. He arrived early in 1835 and set to work immediately to organize the constantly increasing congregation, which the Bishop estimated at 300 families. The improvement in the position of local Catholics was soon observed and it elicited the high praise of the Bishop: "They were poor in this world's wealth but rich in faith."

Father Dillon at first held divine services in some of the larger homes. One of these in all probability was that of the Cahill family at the corner of Middle (East 2nd) and High Streets, where a visiting priest had once said Mass after his rescue by Daniel Fitzpatrick off a storm-tossed steamship in the harbor. Others were in Ohio City. Then he rented a small room on Spring Street (West 10th) which was the office of Doctor Samuel Underhill, a physician and justice-of-the-peace, the owner and editor of the short-lived Cleveland *Liberalist*, a journal apparently opposed to religion. The next meeting place was a room on Main Street Hill, opposite Union Lane (near West 10th Street). The subsequent move was to a large room (30 x 40 feet) in the upper story of the Merwin Square Building, at the northwest corner of Superior Avenue and West 9th Street. Sometimes used for theatrical performances, it was ambitiously called Shakespeare Hall.

Perhaps it was for this reason that Father Dillon rented a one-story frame cottage on the west side of Erie Street (East 9th) opposite the old cemetery. The large room in it was fitted up as a chapel, and the others were used as his living quarters. This building, later moved north on East 9th Street, survived until it was torn down in 1916. Because this location was too far out from the city and too distant from the Flats and the West Side, the pastor procured the use of a room in the newly built Farmers' Block, a merchandising center, at the northeast corner of Ontario and Prospect Avenues, the present site of a large department store. Here the Catholics of Cleveland met to assist at Mass until the opening of St. Mary's on the Flats in 1839. The pastor kept his residence at the cottage of East 9th Street, although the records seem to indicate that he sometimes stayed at a place on Euclid Avenue near that street.

A church building was a necessity. Bishop Purcell had urged it but the means were not at hand. Father Dillon, over the protests of his friends who knew that he had never been in robust health, went to New York and collected $1,000 with which to begin, but the effort and strain cost him his life. Shortly after his return he was taken down with a "bilious fever." Father Stephen Badin, on his way back from Detroit, found him very sick, but thought he would survive. Suddenly, however, he took a turn for the worse. Father Badin anointed him, and after two hours of great suffering Father Dillon died in the evening of Sunday, October 16, 1836. Father Badin conducted the funeral from the house on East 9th Street and the body was buried in the cemetery opposite. It was later transferred to the Cathedral crypt, and then to St. John's Cemetery, alongside the remains of his friend and colleague, Father James Conlan, who died in 1875.[2]

In an atmosphere which was not entirely friendly Father Dillon in a short time had won the respect of many who were not Catholics. Among his admirers was Harvey Rice, the local historian, who knew him well and characterized him as a cultivated and scholarly gentleman, polished and eloquent in speech, and zealous to the full capacity of his physical strength in looking after the spiritual welfare of his people. The newspapers in Cleveland had been making great sport of the Irish immigrants and of their exploitation by the "Yankees," often carrying on their front page anecdotes and "funny stories," ridiculing their religion and customs. The Holy Father and the Church were often the target of unwarranted criticism, although in one instance at least the Cleveland *Whig* acknowledged its error. These same newspapers now gave high praise to Father Dillon.

An editorial in the Cleveland *Weekly Advertiser*, October 20, 1836, carried the account of his funeral which was attended by many Protestant people and went on to say: "Mr. Dillon was an Irishman and one of the many Irish clergymen who left the luxuries and the society of the Old World to labor for religion among strangers, and in the midst of hardship and persecution; he was one of the finest scholars even of his own clergy who have ever stood foremost among the learned and able men of the world; as an orator he had few superiors; he labored without ostentation, yet in season and out of season he did his duty; the poor Irishman can testify whether this amiable and faithful man was not always at the bed of the invalid and the dying, administering the consolations of religion." The Cleveland *Advertiser* also referred to Cleveland's first Catholic pastor in similar complimentary terms. The first city *Directory* two years later recalled the universal respect in which he was held by all.

After the funeral, at a meeting of the heads of families, a petition was drawn up asking Bishop Purcell to appoint Father Badin in the place of Father Dillon. That sixty-eight-year-old missioner did stay until after All Souls' Day. He saw to it that the money collected by Father Dillon was safely deposited in the name of Bishop Purcell for the future church building, and he then left for Cincinnati "before the ice formed on the canal." Father Tschenhens was asked to take care of the vacant parish but he could not promise because he feared to "break" his missionaries who were already overworked.[3] As a result Cleveland had only the occasional visit of priests until the appointment in September, 1837, of Father Patrick O'Dwyer as the second resident pastor. He was born in Ireland, at Cashel, in 1802, and was ordained in Quebec, Canada, in 1830. He made his headquarters in a cottage at the

---

[2] Badin to Purcell, Oct. 13, 21, 23, 25, 1836, in N.D.A.
[3] Tschenhens to Purcell, Nov. 27, 1836, in N.D.A.

corner of Superior and East 12th (Muirson) Streets but continued to hold divine services in Farmers' Block.

The question of the location of the new church was much discussed. The majority of the parishioners lived in homes near the Cuyahoga River and wanted the church built near them. When Bishop Purcell was here in 1835, James S. Clark, a real estate promoter, and his associates offered him a lot in Brooklyn Village in the Lorain Avenue district just south of Ohio City. The locality was "connected with and almost identified with Cleveland by a bridge over the Cuyahoga." At the time the Bishop hoped that, through the exertion of the Catholics and the donations of the friendly and liberal Protestants, a church might be built there "so that the voyager on Lake Erie might soon be cheered in his approach to the city by the cross over it."

There was much rivalry at the time, between Cleveland on the east bank of the river and Ohio City on the west. Land speculators from the East were getting high prices for lots in the latter village. Clark and his company were developing Cleveland Center on the east bank. It comprised the peninsula formed by Ox Bow Bend, the first curve in the Cuyahoga River. Traffic coming in on the Wooster and Medina turnpikes was diverted from Ohio City and directed down Columbus Street and over the newly built "fixed" bridge to Cleveland Center and to Cleveland proper. Clark's company was responsible also for the Farmers' Block where Mass was celebrated on Sundays.

Father O'Dwyer apparently did not favor the project of building the new church at the top of Columbus Street hill. An advertisement in the Cleveland *Herald and Gazeteer*, shortly after his coming here, expressed the wishes of the Cleveland Catholics "to purchase a lot for the purpose of erecting a church and a glebe house thereon." The piece of land should be conveniently situated within the limits of the city and should have a frontage of 90 to 100 feet. What answers were received is not known but, when Bishop Purcell came here not long afterwards, he decided that what little money had been collected would be better spent on the actual construction of a church instead of on the purchase of a new lot. He accepted a new offer made by Clark of a lot in Cleveland Center, later known as the Flats.

The Bishop, who was already well known here through his public debate with the Reverend Campbell (printed and on sale at the Cleveland Book Store on Superior Lane near Shakespeare Hall), on the occasion of this visit lectured "by early candle-light" at the Court House in Cleveland. The land title to the new property at the corner of Columbus and Girard Streets, at the east end of the famous bridge, was made out to the Bishop "in trust for the Roman Catholic Society of Our Lady of the Lake of Cleveland," with the proviso that a church be built on it within four months and that it be used perpetually as a site for a church in active use. The land contract was made out, October 24, 1837, and the deed was transferred, November 21, 1842.

Cleveland had been spared the worst of the panic of 1837; yet the times were difficult. Father O'Dwyer, nevertheless, with the little means at his disposal managed within a few months to put up the walls and the roof of the first Catholic church in Cleveland but for want of sufficient funds he could not complete it. He returned to Canada probably in June, 1839. Bishop Purcell then came to the city with Father Henni. Through their exertions in the three weeks they were here the church was sufficiently completed to have the first Mass celebrated in it in October of that year. Probably Father Henni celebrated that first Mass for a First Communion class which had been instructed by the Bishop himself.[4] Before leaving the city the Bishop had given instructions to Andrew Golden, the builder, for the plastering and the completion of the interior and the building of an altar. The neat frame church building, measuring 81 by 53 feet, had a substantial gallery or organ loft and a "handsome ceiling." Four wooden Doric columns decorated the front which was topped by a squat square tower. The estimated cost was $3,000.

Returning from the Fourth Provincial Council of Baltimore, Bishop Purcell brought to Cleveland with him the renowned French prelate, Charles Auguste Marie Joseph, Count of Forbin-Janson, Bishop of Nancy, who had assisted at the council and was making a tour of America. He had helped to institute the "Missionaries of France" and was to found the Society of the Holy Childhood before his death. The prelates had a narrow escape from disaster in a storm which overtook their ship off Fairport. However, they made a safe landing in Cleveland at five o'clock on Sunday morning, June 7, 1840. On that day, nothing daunted by their experience, the French Bishop dedicated the newly completed St. Mary's Church and sang the High Mass, and Bishop Purcell preached before and after the ceremony.

The Cleveland Catholics now had a beautiful little white church of which they might well be proud. The Episcopalians had a church of similar proportions at St. Clair and West 2nd Streets since 1829. The Presbyterians had one of stone on the Public Square since 1834. The Baptists had one of brick, since 1835, at Champlain and West 3rd Streets. Bishop Purcell, however, had no priest to replace Father O'Dwyer until he ordained Father Peter McLaughlin, and sent him to St. Mary's in October, 1840. The new pastor, born in Ireland in 1805, had finished his studies at the seminary in Cincinnati. He put the finishing touches on the church. Mr. Golden donated six new candlesticks, his own special invention. Others gave paintings to beautify the walls. The funds of the building society, however, had to be diverted to pay for the pews. Although the parishioners were all hard-working people with few resources, the parish was out of debt in December, 1843. A reed organ, supposedly equal to the best in the city, was installed in June of the following year. A choir was organized, although it cost $4 a week, and singers were trained for Sunday vespers. There were four sets of

[4] Another account would have it that Father O'Dwyer said the first Mass in it on Christmas Day, 1840: *Catholic Knight,* Jan. 8, 1887.

vestments in the sacristy. Father McLaughlin reported his great emotion when the censer and ostensorium, sent by the Bishop, were used for the first time at Benediction of the Blessed Sacrament in January, 1845. He was grieved, however, a few months later, at the theft of some of the vestments and sacred vessels from the church.

After a few years it became evident that St. Mary's was not conveniently located. It was not easily accessible to the Catholics in Ohio City near the lake. They had to cross the river on the Center Street floating-bridge and follow the curving east bank to Columbus Street. Those who lived in Cleveland proper had to make their way down the hill into the valley and up again. From the beginning Father McLaughlin looked for the opportunity of bringing the church up out of the valley. He disliked the taunt, "the poor Irish of the Flats." He presented his arguments: the purpose of the Bishop in helping to build St. Mary's had been accomplished in the organization of the congregation, but, on the other hand, to command respect the center of Catholic activity would have to be moved into Cleveland proper. Bishop Henni, shortly after his consecration in Cincinnati, paid a visit to Cleveland at the end of March, 1844, and encouraged the project. In the following July Bishop Purcell came to administer the Sacrament of Confirmation. After exploring the situation further, he advised that new property be secured.

On January 22 of the next year (1845) Father McLaughlin in his own name signed a contract with Thomas May, a land agent, for the purchase of four lots at the northeast corner of East 9th (26 feet frontage) and Superior (132 feet frontage) Streets, the nucleus of the present Cathedral property. The consideration was $4,000; it had been sold in the previous April for $1,500. This was an illustration of the increasing value of land in what Father McLaughlin called the most beautiful part of the city. By September $1,300 had been paid on the purchase, and in January, 1846, the title of this fortunate acquisition was assigned in due legal form to Bishop Purcell.

The religious care of the German-speaking Catholics of the city was a source of anxiety to the Bishop. Their increasing numbers was put forward by Father McLaughlin as indicating the need of a larger church. He had learned enough of the language to administer the sacraments to them but he seemed disinclined to share St. Mary's with a resident German pastor, as was done in Canton. He would, however, allow Father Brunner, the Sanguinist, to hold special religious service for the Germans once a month. The latter felt that such occasional attendance was not sufficient, and he advised the formation of a separate congregation. The Bishop adopted this view and in response to their petition he publicly announced from the altar in St. Mary's that the new German parish would be in charge of the Sanguinist Fathers. Father McLaughlin began a German Catholic Society to raise money, and secured a site on Main Street for the proposed St. Peter's stone church. The option, however, was later abandoned.

Father McLaughlin, well versed in English and Latin literature, eloquent and energetic, was an outstanding figure in this community. He had hardly been settled here before he was asked to lecture in the Lyceum on the occasion of George Washington's Birthday. He discoursed on the subject of religious toleration. The Cleveland *Herald* answered the possible question about the choice of such a subject by asserting that political discourses were forbidden to Catholic priests. In accord with the request of the Government he conducted memorial services for the deceased President Harrison in St. Mary's Church.

It was especially his work in the temperance movement which made him prominent. The Protestant Temperance Society, organized in 1836, claimed to have 1,500 members in 1843, and to have reduced the number of licensed places for dispensing intoxicants. At mixed meetings for the promotion of temperance Father McLaughlin was nearly always one of the principal speakers. The Catholic Total Abstinence Society, which counted 400 members, marched as a body in public processions with other societies to celebrate not only St. Patrick's Day but other civic holidays, such as Independence Day, July 4. The German Catholics, also, took part in these public appearances, often led by John B. Wigman, who had helped to build St. Mary's Church and who regularly read the Gospel in German at Sunday Mass. These processions invariably began at the church or ended up there for religious service and a sermon. The banquets held in a public hall on St. Patrick's Day were attended by the leading officials of the town, and Father McLaughlin took this and every opportunity to emphasize Catholic loyalty to the republic.

He did not hesitate to use the columns of the local newspapers to defend the interests of Catholics and to controvert false charges made against them. He knew, as he wrote, that both the Whig and the Democratic press would willingly publish articles against the Catholic Church but they also rejoiced in publishing an answer. Cleveland was a Whig stronghold. The Democrats had a difficult time until the Cleveland *Advertiser* and its successor, the *Plain Dealer*, were able to present the arguments of that party, boasting that if enough subscriptions were secured the Western Reserve might be "redeemed" for the Democrats. Irishmen and their faith were caricatured and virulent attacks on the Church were reprinted from other newspapers. At the same time the editor claimed in a rather transparent subterfuge that he had nothing against Father McLaughlin or what he represented. He reserved the right, however, to publish what he wished, provided it were well written, without necessarily endorsing the attack.

Sometimes respectful enough accounts of Catholic events abroad were published but the Pope and the Jesuits rarely escaped criticism. Father McLaughlin's rejoinders were also printed. The local press manifested a strong interest in the progress of the Repeal movement in Ireland, which finally resulted in the restoration of civil rights to Catholics in that country. Prominence was given to the account of the trial and speeches of Daniel O'Connell and at a civic celebration of the Irish patriot's release from prison Father McLaughlin gave the principal address. Afterwards a group of citizens serenaded him in his home. The *Plain Dealer* warned him against the designs of the Whigs, who were accused of an alliance with the bigoted Native Americanism, the then current anti-Catholic movement, and of being interested in their local display only in the Catholic vote.

With the increase in Catholic influence Father McLaughlin sensed that the city was not as free from sectarian feeling as it had been previously, for "now that the Catholics have become a people, they must needs be abused and their religion suspected." Preachers who attacked the Church were brought in from the outside and the local ministers rallied around them. According to the pastor's report, however, the majority of Clevelanders were fair minded. Many non-Catholics came to listen to his lectures on Catholic doctrine. He counted several prominent converts: the lawyer Waldron and his wife and three children, Mrs. Oliver Johnson, the three sons of William Doubleday in Brighton, Doctor and Mrs. Griswold, James Convers who became a Jesuit, a Mr. Darwin of Oberlin College, and others whose names are not given. At the end of 1845 the career of Father McLaughlin in this city was drawing to a close.[5] On his way back here from Cincinnati in December of that year he was accompanied by an assistant, the Irish-born Father Michael Ambrose Byrne, whom Bishop Purcell had ordained in the previous month. From the canal terminal in Toledo, where Father McLaughlin preached in Father Rappe's church, they rode "two nags" to Cleveland. Father Byrne took charge of the parish on December 28. After regulating his affairs and seeing Father Byrne through a ten-day siege of the fever, the third pastor of Cleveland left the city in February, 1846; his dramatic leave-taking was reported in the local press. The *Herald* expressed the universal regret at his departure and recalled his self-sacrificing and tireless efforts to better the condition of his people; he was the Father Matthew of Cleveland and the Catholic citizens under his direction were an example of unobtrusive and respectful demeanor on public occasions and in political contests. He was given credit for preventing Nativism from obtaining much influence in this community. At the farewell exercises Father James Conlan came from Dungannon to summarize his accomplishments, especially in giving the Catholics a "standing" in the city. Father McLaughlin died on March 12, 1861, in Bath, Maine, where he was pastor.

Father Byrne in the few months he was here concerned himself particularly with the care of the German-speaking Catholics. He reported that the German immigrants who were flocking to the city were good Catholics, and recommended that they have their own pastor, especially on account of their children who might, otherwise, be lost to the Church. He knew enough of the language to hear confessions, and

[5] McLaughlin-Purcell correspondence in N.D.A. Files of Cleveland Newspapers, Western Reserve Historical Society library, Cleveland.

when it came time for him to leave the city the Germans begged him to stay because of the interest he had manifested in them; the fever, moreover, was raging and they wanted the consolation of the sacraments.[6] Father Byrne became a victim of the cholera and died in 1850 in Cincinnati.

Father Maurice Howard came to Cleveland as the pastor in February, 1846. Born in Ireland, he finished his studies at Cincinnati and was ordained by Bishop Purcell on October 23, 1842. He had spent the interval as pastor of Doylestown, with missions at Akron, Canal Fulton, Wooster, Mansfield, and Cuyahoga Falls. He had preached the St. Patrick's Day sermon in Cleveland in 1845. Taking up residence now with Father Byrne (until the latter's departure) at the American House on West Superior Street, he attacked the problem of a Catholic school. A few years before, Father McLaughlin had been offered a part of the town school money for a school, provided no religious exercises were held in it. The Cleveland Free School had been organized in 1830 by the Presbyterians in the basement of the Bethel Church near the foot of West Superior Street, presumably to "educate children of every denomination." It was supported by the city. Ohio City in 1837 maintained two district schools and another such Free School.

Catholic children, whom these apparently philanthropical institutions were designed to attract, stood in danger to their faith in attending them. Father Howard saw that catechism classes on Sunday alone would not counteract such influence. He obtained the approval of his people and of the Bishop for a school which would be built on the new lots at Superior and East 9th Streets. Father John J. Doherty came from Canton to preach at the St. Patrick's Day celebration at which the money was pledged for the project. The imminent division of the Cleveland territory from the Diocese of Cincinnati delayed action in the matter. For the same reason Father Howard hesitated to spend more money on St. Mary's Church building which he expected would be relocated by a new bishop. It developed that Cleveland's fourth pastor was sent to Tiffin shortly after the arrival of Bishop Rappe. After eighteen months he left the diocese and died in 1887 as the pastor of St. Francis de Sales Church, Keokuk, Iowa.[7]

Cleveland, like other towns in which a priest resided, became the center of many missions. One of the latter was at Laporte, then a stage-coach terminal with two hotels but now a crossroads, about midway between Grafton and Elyria. On the site of the present cemetery of the Grafton parish, a simple frame building dedicated to St. John of God, the first Catholic church which is still in use within the present boundaries of the Cleveland diocese, was opened in 1835. Eighteen years later it had to be enlarged and twelve years after that it was moved two miles to Grafton. There it served as a church, then as a school, and now, the arched ceiling still intact, it is used as a social hall.

[6] Byrne-Purcell correspondence in N.D.A.
[7] Howard-Purcell correspondence in N.D.A.

Father McLaughlin, as did the other pastors of Cleveland, visited the mission every month; he reported fifty-seven German and Irish Catholic farmers there. In 1846 Bishop Purcell confirmed sixteen persons in the little chapel and he delivered a lecture in the nearby Elyria Court House at the invitation of the sheriff. This and his speech in the Baptist Church in that very puritanical town helped to soften the previous hostile attitude towards the few Catholic families.

Father McLaughlin was the first priest to call upon the few German families who in 1833 had settled at Avon, in Lorain County. On March 21, 1841, he celebrated Mass in the log cabin of John Schwartz for the colony, which by that time had increased to eight families. Three years later when the congregation, including the newcomers who had settled at the western end of the township (French Creek), numbered more than fifty families the question of the site of a church divided them. Father McLaughlin, at the direction of the Bishop, favored the eastern section and offered the Holy Sacrifice at first in the home of Mr. Sheffield and then in a plain frame church which, though not finished in the interior for a few years, was opened for divine worship on November 21, 1844. In the same year the parishioners at the western end, under the supervision of the Sanguinist, Father Jacob Ringele, adapted a wagon shop for a meeting place, and five years later built a modest frame church. Upon the recommendation of Father Howard the Sanguinists were given charge, also, of the German farming community at nearby Sheffield, which had a log chapel in 1847. The Catholics at Dover and at North Ridgeville "went where they pleased."

On his journey south from Cleveland after the dedication of St. Mary's Church, in June, 1840, Bishop Purcell accompanied by Father O'Dwyer visited the two Catholic families at Strongsville. A deputation of German farmers met them there and escorted them to their settlement at Liverpool. Here the whole congregation turned out and went in procession to the cemetery, where the Bishop blessed a few graves and Father O'Dwyer celebrated Mass.

Because Rocky River at this point was so full at times as to make it difficult to ford, two log chapels were built in 1842, one at Abbeyville, which was soon replaced by a brick structure, and the other at Liverpool (now Valley City) on the other side of the river. Father McLaughlin was later assigned the task of composing the differences which arose over the cost of maintaining both chapels. He succeeded in obtaining from the trustees the deed of the brick church, which he favored as a more substantial building and as more accessible to the Irish at Medina and Grafton. The Bishop thought at the time that he would have to use severe measures to enforce this solution of the difficulty. Eventually (in 1849) a brick church was built on the site of the present church in Valley City. The Abbeyville chapel was abandoned about ten years afterwards. The Sanguinist Fathers had the spiritual care of these missions after 1844.

On this same visitation the horsemen who were escorting the Bishop lost their way and on that account it required nearly half a day to travel from Liverpool to Chippewa (near Doylestown), a distance of less than twenty-five miles. Here the Marshall and Whitman families had built a priest's house and a log chapel on a tract of some eighty acres which had been donated for the support of a priest. The construction of St. Francis Xavier Church, as it was called, 40 x 28 x 16 feet, and the first in Wayne County, was begun in 1836. Though unfinished, it was used for divine services in June of the following year. Upon its completion Bishop Purcell returned to dedicate it, November 14, 1841. He was enthusiastic in his praise of the Whitman and Marshall families and the other members of the congregation, declaring that "in no other part of the diocese had he witnessed more zeal, humility, and fervor than in this sequestered and delightful spot; surely the divine mercies are for such people." The Pennsylvania-born Father Basil A. Schorb had been sent in 1837, the year of his ordination, to become the first resident pastor of the place, with the charge of many missions which included Liverpool, Canal Fulton, Randolph, Massillon, Wooster, and a few farther west. When in 1842 he removed to the State of his birth (he was pastor at York when he died in 1871), Father Maurice Howard took his place and remained until his own appointment to Cleveland.

After the establishment of a residence in Chippewa, the pastors were given charge of the congregation in Akron, for which Father Schorb kept separate records from the beginning of his tenure. Father Howard in 1844 supervised the initial construction there of St. Vincent's Church, a frame building on Green Street, two blocks from the site of the present stone edifice. Father McLaughlin, who had visited the town in the interval between the two pastorates, blessed the foundations and preached. It was enlarged and completed by the Irish-born Father Cornelius Daly, who was appointed the first resident pastor of Akron in 1845, the year after his ordination. In the first ceremony of its kind in northern Ohio, Bishop Purcell in this little chapel on September 5, 1847, a few weeks before he consecrated the first Bishop of Cleveland, raised Father James Vincent Conlan to the priesthood. He had finished his studies at Cincinnati and after ordination was sent to assist his cousin, Father James Conlan, at Dungannon.

The Cleveland pastors and later the priests from Akron or Chippewa visited the Catholics in Cuyahoga Falls. Father McLaughlin thought that the town prospered more than Cleveland "though the people were coming and going." John O'Dunne built an addition to his house to serve as a chapel. It was his daughter, Mother Amadeus, who in later years helped to found the Ursulines in Montana. Bishop Purcell in 1835 contrasted the friendly attitude towards Catholics he found in Cleveland with the bitter feeling in this town. Some of the influential citizens of little or no religion were so chagrined at the calumnious attacks on the Church that they promised to help in building a Catholic church; there was no church building, however, for another fifty years. The few Catholics at Peninsula in the Cuyahoga River Valley often made the twenty-five-mile journey to Cleveland between the times of the infrequent visits of the priest to their village.

On the thickly wooded shores of Lake Erie the charcoal blast furnaces had attracted many Irish Catholic workmen. The Cleveland pastors called at the Vermilion Furnace every month when the men were busy there. Painesville, thirty miles east of Cleveland, in 1842, had a few Irishmen who worked at the Geauga Furnace in the vicinity. Father McLaughlin called his quarterly visit to them a lake trip. For Confirmation the candidates journeyed to Cleveland. Near Painesville, at (South) Thompson, the Sidley family in 1837 was the nucleus of an Irish farming settlement. Father McLaughlin called on them occasionally in 1844 and 1845.

In the preceding pages an attempt has been made to describe in outline the first framework of the Catholic Church organization in northern Ohio on the eve of the erection of the first Diocese of Cleveland. What Bishop Purcell wrote in 1841 after the visitation of that year was verified to a greater degree in every year which followed: "The rapid growth, the present urgent necessities, the prospects for the future would require the constant attention of two bishops and a hundred priests, patient, prudent, pious and learned men to preserve the faithful, to convert the erring, to found schools and to build the churches necessary."[8]

[8] *Catholic Telegraph*, Dec. 11, 1841, in Houck, *Op. cit.*, I, 47.

9

ERECTION OF THE DIOCESE OF CLEVELAND

THE SIXTH PROVINCIAL COUNCIL OF BALTImore, which opened its sessions, May 10, 1846, under the presidency of Archbishop Eccleston, at the petition of Bishop Purcell recommended to the Holy Father that Cleveland, Sandusky, or Toledo be made the seat of a new diocese in the northern part of Ohio, and that Father Louis Amadeus Rappe be made its first bishop. Pius IX, elected pope in 1846, accepted and approved the recommendations of the Council on February 7, 1847. The official papal documents formally establishing the Diocese of Cleveland as well as the Diocese of Albany and Buffalo in New York were issued at Rome, April 23, 1847, though the Bull of the same date appointing the "French priest, Louis Amadeus Rappe," did not arrive at Baltimore until the following August 25.[1]

Louis Amadeus Rappe was born, February 2, 1801, at Audrehem, near Ardes, District of St. Omer, Department of Pas-de-Calais at the northwestern tip of France, memorable in history because of the famous meeting of the Kings of England and France on the Field of the Cloth-of-Gold. His parents were farmers, Eloi and Marie Antoinette Noël Rappe, of whose five daughters and five sons, Amadeus was the youngest boy. Three brothers died in the wars of Napoleon and the other, unmarried, died when Father Rappe was a missioner in Toledo. Young Amadeus was of a naturally happy and generous disposition and a great favorite with the townspeople among whom, to all appearances, he was destined to spend his life. One day, however, his father expressed the regret that Amadeus' brother had not persevered in his studies for the priesthood. This remark made him decide to take that brother's place, and at the age of nineteen he began to study Latin under the direction of a relative, Father Noël, the pastor at Furnes not far away.

In October, 1820, he entered the nearby college at Boulogne-sur-

---

[1] Decretum "Cum in statu Ohio," Apr. 5, 1847; Breve Apostolicum, "Universalis Ecclesiae," Apr. 23, 1847; Purcell to Franzoni, shortly after Oct. 10, 1847; Rappe to Franzoni, Oct. 12, 1847; Propaganda to Purcell, Dec. 15, 1847, all in Propaganda Archives, Rome. Photostats of originals in C.D.A. Lamotte, *Op. cit.*, 99.

Mer. Because of his maturity he was put in charge of the younger students and he manifested a firmness and a strictness quite in contrast with his cordial if not exuberant character. Asked for an explanation of this, he was quoted as having said, "When vacation was over, I put all my mirth in a box which was not opened again until the next vacation." He brought his merriment as well as his seriousness to America, as we know from the testimony of his friends, Fathers Macheboef and De Goesbriand, at a later date. Going to visit him in Toledo, they broke through the ice on the lakeshore into what proved fortunately to be only five feet of water; when they reached their destination they reported that their "merry and amiable friend soon made them forget their mishap."

In 1821 the young man was ready for tonsure, and five years later he was accepted in the major seminary at Arras, the Cathedral town. He was a subdeacon in two years, and, finally, on March 14, 1829, he was ordained priest by his bishop, Hugo Robert John Charles Cardinal de la Tour d'Auvergne-Langereis. He began his ministry in the parish of Wismes, near Fauquembergues and the paternal home. Then in January, 1834, he was made chaplain and spiritual adviser to the Ursuline Nuns at their convent in Boulogne-sur-Mer. Here it was that he met Bishop Purcell who invited him to transfer his priestly activities to the missions in Ohio. He was already familiar with them through the accounts printed in the *Annals of the Society for the Propagation of the Faith.* Only his age and ignorance of the English language made him hesitate. But in February, 1840, he notified the Bishop of Cincinnati that after consulting wise and pious men his doubts had vanished and that he was ready to serve in Ohio or any other place. Bishop Purcell was only too well pleased to accept him. The Bishop of Arras gave his permission and after a short vacation at home he prepared to leave France.[2]

With a little band of religious women, Sisters of Notre Dame de Namur who later had charge of his first school in Toledo, he sailed from Antwerp, Belgium, September 10, 1840, and landed in New York, October 19. Bishop Purcell met them at the wharf in Cincinnati on November 1. Father Rappe was sent to Chilicothe, to the home of Major Marshall Anderson, a convert, who essayed to teach him English. "His memory, however, was not of the best; his ears could not catch the sound of words he had never heard before; he experienced serious difficulty in learning though he worked at it hard and long." In a few months, nevertheless, he could make himself understood, although his pronunciation always remained imperfect.

He was then sent to Toledo and the western missions, as we have seen above, where he labored courageously amid privation and difficulties with the hard-working and often fever-stricken canal workers. He suffered much from the fever himself. On one excursion to Detroit he was seriously sick with it but the Sisters of Charity and Bishop

2 Houck, *Op. cit.,* II, 11 sq., Rappe to Purcell, Feb. 27, 1840, in N.D.A.

Bishop Amadeus Rappe, first Bishop of Cleveland.

Bronze statue of Bishop Rappe.

Old St. Mary Seminary, group of professors and students.

Lefevre nursed him back to health. Returned home to Toledo, he rejoiced at the rest which was forced upon him in his convalescence. Father De Goesbriand, who was sent to assist him, reported that his amiable and genial example was enough to encourage and comfort any man in the midst of troubles.[3]

It was an open secret in 1846 that the Baltimore Council had proposed the name of Father Rappe. His friends, Fathers Macheboeuf and Lamy,[4] were wondering in August of that year about the delay in the announcement of his appointment. Fathers Byrne of Cleveland and Daly of Chippewa and Akron were prepared in September to return to Cincinnati. The good missioner himself prayed to know the will of God in the matter. He expressed the hope that the Pope would not be guided by the advice of the Council. However, sixteen months after the recommendation the official notification reached him at Maumee on his way to Fremont.

On the day chosen by himself, Sunday, October 10, 1847,[5] he was consecrated by Bishop Purcell in the Cathedral of Cincinnati. Bishop Richard Vincent Whelan, then of Richmond, Virginia, and Father Edward Purcell, vicar general and brother of the Bishop, were the assistants. Bishop Lefevre, upon whom he had counted, was prevented from attending. The sermon on the occasion described the new prelate's well-known zeal for the glory of God, his utter disregard for himself, his blameless life and fervent piety. On the third day after his consecration he was on his way to Cleveland and on October 17, assisted by Fathers Howard and Byrne, he took possession of St. Mary's, his pro-cathedral.

He addressed a very appreciative body of people, happy now to have a bishop in their midst. His sermon, according to the newspaper account, was "plain and practical and marked by good sense and deep religious fervor," urging as he did "the practice of charity and sobriety and Christian virtue and the avoidance at the same time of all noisy controversy." His fine musical voice made the service attractive; his language was "pleasing, terse and energetic but marred by the peculiar characteristics of the French when speaking English." Another local journal quoted with approval an excerpt to the effect that "a deserved honor was bestowed on an excellent man." Though the Cleveland editor did not "agree with his religious opinions," he admired, nevertheless, "his kindness and simplicity of demeanor" and remarked on his high reputation for "piety, ability, and usefulness." Bishop Rappe was greatly encouraged by the warm reception he received and so notified Bishop Purcell.

[3] De Goesbriand's reminiscences, in Houck, *Op. cit.*, I, 56 sq. Rappe to Purcell, Sept. 3, 1846, in N.D.A.

[4] Byrne to Purcell, Sept. 9; Lamy to Purcell, Aug. 24; Macheboeuf to Purcell, Nov. 23; Brunner, C.PP.S., to Purcell, Dec. 15; Kendrick (Philadelphia) to Purcell, Dec. 30, all in 1846, in N.D.A.; Rappe to Purcell, Jan. 26, July 10, Sept. 8, 10; Eccleston (Baltimore) to Purcell, Aug. 25, all in 1847, in N.D.A. Cincinnati *Telegraph*, Sept. 2, 1847.

[5] Attestation of consecrating prelate, in C.D.A.

His first pastoral letter was published in the Cincinnati *Telegraph* on October 10. In it, confident of the cooperation of the clergy, he promised to share in their labors and, while directing their activities, he hoped to be father and friend rather than superior. He called upon the people to stand fast in the unity of their faith despite differences of language and race; if it were necessary in certain parishes to have a priest who spoke a special language he would send one when he was able to do so; he, himself, was willing to go to missions for which he had no priest. He adjured all to give good example of holy living for the edification of those outside the Church. The reception of the sacraments, family prayer, the religious education of their children, all these were emphasized as part of the solemn duty of all Catholics.[6]

The new Bishop lived for a while, after his coming, in a rented house near the old Haymarket at the northern end of the (later) Central Viaduct. Soon he was able to purchase property at the corner of St. Clair and East 6th (Bond) Streets. The large brick house on it was fitted up as the episcopal residence and a few smaller frame buildings adjacent were remodeled to serve as a school and seminary. He gave his promissory note for $4,500 as the first payment on the original price of $8,000. The sale of parts of the property helped to pay for it. Soon the figure of the tall, wiry, sprightly Bishop was familiar on the streets of the city.

One of his first concerns was to clarify the extent of his jurisdiction. The division line with the mother-diocese had been fixed at forty degrees and forty-one minutes north latitude. It cut across some of the counties and left a few of the towns such as Bolivar and Mount Eaton in doubt. It was suggested that those counties the greater part of which was north of that line should belong to Cleveland and the others to Cincinnati. Bishop Rappe would "thank Divine Providence for tempering the burden to his forces," if the greater part of the disputed territory remained in the old diocese. Bishop Purcell agreed with the suggestion but he gave the administration of Holmes County, which would be doubtful still, to Cleveland for the lifetime of Bishop Rappe. The agreement was published in the Cincinnati *Telegraph* and was to be in force until Rome should give an official decision. Accordingly, the Counties of Mercer, Auglaize, Hardin, Marion, Morrow, Knox, Tuscarawas, Carroll, and Jefferson were considered to belong to the old diocese.[7] This arrangement of the bishops was ratified by Rome in 1868, when the Diocese of Columbus was erected, with this exception, that Holmes County was given to the new diocese.

The task confronting Bishop Rappe was tremendous. The popula-

    [6] Houck, *Op. cit.*, I, 76. Cleveland *Weekly Herald,* Sept. 15, 24, 29, Oct. 20, 1847. Cleveland *Evening Herald,* Oct. 18, 1847.

    [7] Rappe to Purcell, Sept. 25, 1847, Apr. 8, Nov. 14, Nov. 26, 1848, Jan. 2, 22, 1849; Purcell to Propaganda, Dec. 5, 1848; all in N.D.A. Cincinnati *Telegraph,* Jan. 14, 1849. Lamotte, *Op. cit.*, 99. Sr. M. Mildred Augustine, *Territorial Difficulties of the Early Dioceses of the Middle West, 1784–1860,* unpublished dissertation, Notre Dame University, 1937.

tion of Cuyahoga County was to grow from approximately 48,000 in 1850 to more than 132,000 in twenty years. Cleveland, which had 93,000 people in 1870, had become a bristling railroad center. The completion of the Sault Ste. Marie Canal in 1855 facilitated the shipment of the rich ores of the Lake Superior region to this city. From here they were transshipped to the Mahoning Valley and Pittsburgh, where they were worked in the furnaces which were fed by the coal mined in Pennsylvania and Ohio. But in 1870 Cleveland[8] had its own blast furnaces, rolling mills, forges, oil refineries, and shipyards. Toledo became one of the largest grain markets of the nation and the metropolis of northwestern Ohio; its population increased from nearly 4,000 to 31,554 in the twenty years after 1850. Sandusky, known for its fisheries and wine making, did not become a large manufacturing center. Akron had a population of some 10,000 in 1870, the year in which the rubber industry was started.

The men who settled the western lands, built the railroads and canals, and worked in the expanding industrial plants came in great part from Europe. It was the period of the great immigration from Ireland. Recurrent famine and pestilence drove them from their homeland: 1,250,-000 of them came to America between 1846 and 1855, although many of them died on the fever-laden ships or immediately upon landing. John Holland, who settled in Cleveland in 1848, reported that of the 225 passengers on his ship, coming from Ireland, 35 only survived. At one period, nevertheless, the Irish immigrants constituted forty-three per cent of the foreign-born population of the country. In 1848 nearly one-tenth of Cleveland's population were Irish. Most of them were Catholics. German immigrants came in more predominating numbers, many of them political refugees, and a good proportion of those who settled in northern Ohio were Catholics. Before the end of Bishop Rappe's administration the Slavs, Bohemians, Poles, Slovaks, and Hungarians began to make their presence apparent in the city, and most of them were Catholics.

Schools and churches had to be built by these Catholic newcomers. Institutions of Christian charity, orphanages and hospitals, were of pressing necessity and religious congregations of women had to be found to manage them. The new prelate needed priests to carry on the work of religion and a seminary to educate and train the men who would have to be able to cope with the problem of foreign languages in many of the parishes. And in the midst of his difficulties the Bishop had to meet the suspicious attitude of the first Puritan settlers.

He took up the life he had only interrupted to be consecrated—preaching, teaching, exhorting, hearing confessions. He was prepared, as he wrote to Bishop Purcell, to become a beggar in Ohio and in Europe for the help he needed to carry his additional burdens. The number of church buildings which were erected during the years of his incumbency is amazing, especially when it is remembered how

[8] *History of the State of Ohio*, as cited, IV, 24 sq.

little money the Catholics had and that it was out of this poverty they were built. That the foundations were well established we know from the subsequent history. His successors have developed and enlarged what he initiated, at the same time that they created new instruments for more modern necessities.

A few months after his arrival the Bishop brought his old companion, Father De Goesbriand, from Toledo and made him pastor of the Cathedral, succeeding Father Howard. Father Matthias Kreusch, the Sanguinist, served as assistant pastor for the Germans. St. Mary's had become too small for the accommodation of the 4,000 Catholics in Cleveland and many had to assist at Mass from a position outside the doors. It was, moreover, inconvenient of access and the neighborhood was filled with shops, foundries, and warehouses. As a temporary expedient to relieve the situation, the Bishop resolved to offer separate services to the German-speaking parishioners and to put Father Kreusch in charge of them, with the commission of "rescuing his countrymen from the kind of apostasy into which they had fallen because they had no German priest."[9] The good Father sang a High Mass and preached in German each Sunday at nine o'clock. The sermon at the High Mass at eleven o'clock was in English. The first Mass at seven o'clock was not sung.

In October, 1848, the Bishop confirmed the judgment of Father McLaughlin by securing five additional lots contiguous with and east of the original purchase on East 9th Street. The price, some $1,250, was paid to the same land agent, Thomas May. On one of these lots, the site of the present Cathedral House, the Church of the Nativity, a frame building, 30 by 60 feet, was opened for Mass on Christmas Day, 1849. Divine services were held in it thereafter at the same hours as at St. Mary's, except that the German sermon was given at the eleven o'clock Mass. During the week folding doors closed off the sanctuary of the little chapel and it was used for a school, the first parochial school building in the city. The teachers were the seminarists who lived with the Bishop, on East 6th Street. Into it was moved the Free School for Boys which the Bishop had started some six months previously in the Center Block near St. Mary's Church on the Flats. Plans, formed at the time, for a similar school for girls at St. Clair and East 6th Streets had to await the success of the Bishop in securing teachers from France.

Meanwhile, the plans for the new Cathedral were published in the Cleveland *Herald* (May, 1848) and an invitation was hopefully extended to the "well known liberality of the citizens to help in its construction."[10] The excavations were begun in the following summer. Mr. Delaney, who later became a Union officer[11] and died at the

[9] Rappe to Purcell, Nov. 8, 1847, Feb. 5, 1848, in N.D.A.
[10] Cleveland *Daily True Democrat*, Apr. 8, 1848: letter to editor quoting Cleveland *Herald*, Mar. 16, 1848.
[11] *C.U.*, Oct. 8, 1897.

Battle of Antietam, was sent to Canada to select the lumber. Bishop Rappe and his chief contractor, John B. Wigman, drew up most of the designs for the exterior of the building, after a visit of inspection to the cathedrals in Pittsburgh and Wheeling produced some misgivings about the ability of Cleveland Catholics to pay for a similar monument in this city. The talents of P. C. Keily, who had designed the fine Church of St. Patrick in Newark, New Jersey, and who was about to begin his long and brilliant career as a church architect, were enlisted to draw the plans for the interior.

The work progressed to such an extent that on October 22 the cornerstone was blessed with appropriate ceremony. Bishop Lefevre of Detroit preached at St. Mary's in the morning. In the afternoon an imposing procession marched up the hill to the new site. There were the Sunday School classes, the Ladies Society, and the Temperance Society, all with their striking banners, the three Bishops, the clergy, the seminarians, and the entire congregation. The men walked in Indian file, to the right and left of the line composed of women and children. The citizens were somewhat startled at hearing Catholic hymns sung in public but they were respectful enough. Bishop Timon of Buffalo laid the cornerstone and preached the sermon. Father John Henry Luhr, the pastor of St. Peter's in Canton, delivered an address in German. Fathers Macheboeuf and De Goesbriand, future bishops, assisted at the joyful celebration.

The foundations were completed late that year and the superstructure was begun in the following spring. The walls were up 25 feet in September but the roof was not put on until the next summer. The slate fastened with copper nails was imported from Wales. The financial stress, however, delayed the completion. The Bishop had not received all that he expected in France, on his visit there in 1849, and the money panic made it impossible to get the assistance he had hoped for in New York. He made another "begging tour" in Ohio and received some help from the congregations in Cincinnati.[12] In the interim the basement of the Cathedral was roofed over and used as a chapel in which three Sunday Masses were celebrated. The adjacent Nativity Chapel continued to be used for the Children's Mass at nine o'clock and for another at eleven.

The happy day for the dedication of the Cathedral of St. John the Evangelist finally came. On Sunday morning, November 7, 1852, in the presence of a thrilled and proud congregation, Archbishop Purcell (Metropolitan of the province since 1850) consecrated the building to the exclusive service of God. Bishop Rappe sang the Mass, Mozart's Twelfth Mass was rendered by Professor Adams and the Cecilian choir supported by Hecker's Band. Francis X. Byerley, who was the Bishop's secretary for a number of years, had installed the organ which was of

[12] De Goesbriand Reminiscences, *ut supra.* Cincinnati *Telegraph,* Dec. 6, 1851, quoted by Houck, *The Church in Northern Ohio,* 3rd ed., p. 296. Rappe to Purcell, Aug. 27, Oct. 12, 1851, in N.D.A.

exceptional quality. Bishop Martin J. Spalding, later Archbishop of Baltimore, in the absence of Bishop Timon of Buffalo who was delayed by a storm on the lake, preached the consecration sermon. In the afternoon Father Luhr presided at Vespers and preached in German.

In the evening the formal sermon was preached by Archbishop Purcell. Outlining the history of the Church in the United States, especially in the West and in northern Ohio, he spoke of the "benevolence and the warmheartedness of the Irish who labored on the railroads and who did so much to build our churches and to support our church system." He praised the self-sacrificing career of Bishop Rappe who had given up his home in sunny France to labor amongst the sons of toil on the missions in the then unhealthful Maumee River valley, and who had seen the Church in Cleveland increase from the humble band in Shakespeare Hall to the large congregation assembled in the great new Cathedral. The prelate called upon the faithful to continue to show their faith in the performance of good works and to make their hearts a pure inner temple corresponding to the material temple dedicated that day. Bishop Spalding closed the inspiring ceremonies with Benediction of the Blessed Sacrament.[13]

The Catholics of Cleveland might well be proud. The brick structure, 175 feet long, 75 feet wide, and 45 feet to the roof, was of the style called Ornamental Gothic; the interior was decorated in the style of the sixteenth century. The ceiling was beautifully arched and ornamented, the columns light and graceful. Fine stucco work covered the walls and arches. Beautiful stained-glass windows gave the proper reverential air to the whole building. The Gothic altar and the statues of the Blessed Virgin, splendid pieces of oak, were carved in France. The organ and the choir occupied the gallery at the west end of the building. The acoustics were considered to have been exceptionally good. A tower over the main entrance was added some years later.

[13] Cleveland *Herald*, Nov. 8, 1852. Cleveland *Plain Dealer*, Nov. 8, 1852. Cincinnati *Telegraph*, Nov. 13, 1852.

10

TOLEDO UNDER BISHOP RAPPE'S
JURISDICTION

THE MANY NEW CHAPELS, CHURCHES, SCHOOLS, convents, and other ecclesiastical buildings which under the direction of Bishop Rappe appeared all over the large diocese were visible evidence of his apostolic energy and palpable indication of the zealous cooperation and generosity of the clergy and faithful. For the sake of clarity the summary account of this development is divided into sections corresponding to the three present dioceses of Toledo, Youngstown, and Cleveland.

In the city of Toledo six new parishes were erected, two each for the English, German, and French language congregations. In the original parish of St. Francis de Sales Father Philip Foley, up to that time pastor of Massillon, took charge in 1848. Shortly afterwards he enlarged the frame church which Bishop Rappe had remodeled. A large new brick Gothic church, which was to be the Cathedral of Toledo for a while, was completed in 1870 under the direction of the Alsatian-born Father Felix M. Boff, the future vicar-general. The old church was then made over into additional school rooms. The first new English language parish, St. Patrick's, was organized in the southern part of the town in 1862 by Father Edward Hannin, later the administrator of the diocese. Soon a new brick church and a school building of the same material were erected. Part of St. Patrick's became the parish of the Immaculate Conception in 1867; Father John Quinn built a brick church at first, and then a frame church and a frame school in a new location.

The parish of St. Mary of the Assumption began when separate services for the Germans were held, first, in St. Francis' Church under the direction of Father Foley, and then (after 1856) in a new brick church of their own which had been erected by Father Charles Evrard, who came to America from Metz in France and had been pastor at Peru. Father Francis Xavier Weninger, the noted German Jesuit missionary, in the name of the Bishop dedicated the completed building which also enclosed a school operated by the Ursulines. In 1869 St. Mary's whole parish plant was given over to the Jesuit Fathers of the

German province. The second German parish in Toledo was authorized with the appointment in 1866 of Father Peter Dannenhofer, who
also came here from Metz to be ordained by Bishop Rappe; soon he
had a brick combination church and school in operation.

Father Evrard, mentioned above, organized the French congregation of St. Joseph and in 1854 built a small brick chapel on the
grounds bought by the Bishop as a site for the Ursuline convent. In
the eastern section of the city the brick Church of St. Louis was built
in 1871 for a second French congregation.

Nine miles south of the city of Toledo, at Maumee, the German-
born Father Flum in 1853 was obliged to enlarge the church because
of the growing congregation; Father Nicolas Roupp,[1] a native of
Lorraine in France, a few years later started a school which he put
in charge of James P. Molony who later became a priest and pastor
of St. Malachy's in Cleveland. At Perrysburg, across the Maumee
River, a Universalist meeting house was converted into a Catholic
church in 1862 and a few years later Father Charles Griss, an Alsatian,
established a school. Three miles from this town, at what was then
known as Roachton, a group of German farmers in 1856 erected a
frame chapel which unfortunately burned down twelve years later.
Along the railroad south of Perrysburg, at Custar, Bishop Rappe
blessed a frame chapel (built in 1864) and at nearby Wirtsburg, another such structure, which was afterwards abandoned. Immediately
west of Toledo, at Marygrove, a farming settlement, a frame church
in 1864 replaced a seventeen-year-old log chapel which thereupon
became a school. Another settlement of Irish, German, and French
farmers in the neighborhood at Assumption, first visited by Father
Foley from Toledo, was responsible for the erection of a frame church
in 1866.

Tiffin, one of the earliest mission centers, made great progress during this time: two large new churches were constructed and two
schools were established. Father Michael O'Sullivan supervised the
construction of the beautiful new brick Gothic Church of St. Mary
which was consecrated by Bishop Rappe in 1862. Father Michael
Healy, who had put the finishing touches to the new church, purchased a former public school building into which he moved the
parochial school that had been started by Father Molon some years
before. Also in 1862 the fine brick Gothic Church of St. Joseph in
the German parish of the same name was consecrated by Bishop Josue
Young of Erie, in the presence of the Bishop of Cleveland. The pastor, Father Joseph L. Bihn, converted the former temporary church
building into school rooms.

[1] Fr. Nicolas Roupp was appointed to the Cathedral staff to care for the German
Catholics in 1851; he prepared the building for its consecration. On instructions
from Bp. Rappe later he raised the main altar a few feet with beams and jacks. In
1898, writing to Houck from Europe, he remarked that "in America the face of
the earth changes at least three times in fifty years." Therefore he supposed that
the altar and everything else had been changed in the Cleveland Cathedral: C.D.A.

In the vicinity of Tiffin and under the direction of its pastors or of other priests several new churches and schools made their appearance. Father O'Sullivan (of Tiffin) in 1859 built the first church, a frame structure, at Findlay; Father John M. Roetzer, the first resident pastor, opened a school two years afterwards; fire destroyed the parish plant, but in 1868 Father Edward J. Vattman completed a large brick Gothic church to replace it. Father Dechant, another pastor of Findlay, built a frame mission chapel at Bluffton which the Bishop blessed in 1869. At Carey a small frame chapel was finished in 1870 under the supervision of Father Bihn of Tiffin. The first Mass was celebrated in Lima in 1846. Father O'Sullivan and the Sanguinists, Fathers Kreusch and Henneberry, attended the Catholics among the men who were building the railroad through that district. The brick Church of St. Rose was erected in 1858 under the direction of Father Kreusch; the first resident pastor, Father Edward J. Murphy, enlarged it and in 1865 opened the first parochial school in Allen County. Father Henneberry in 1864 opened a brick mission church at Bascom, where some Irish and German farmers had settled.

South of Tiffin, at New Riegel, Father Brunner directed the building of a large brick church which was dedicated by Bishop Rappe in 1849; the Canadian members of the parish were recognized as a separate congregation in 1856 and Father Molon built a brick church for them. At Alvada, another division of the original parish, the Bishop dedicated a frame church in 1859. At the other center of Sanguinist activities, Marywood (Thompson), a brick school was erected in 1847 and a brick church was completed two years later. Under the direction of the Sanguinists many other churches and schools appeared in the district. The frame chapel built by Father Brunner at New Washington in 1846 was replaced by Father Michael Becker, the first resident pastor, twenty-three years later with a large brick Gothic edifice; the parish school had been opened in 1855. At what was known as Crawfordville the log chapel of 1849 was replaced ten years later with a frame building. A plain wooden chapel was completed at Fostoria in 1851. At Upper Sandusky a brick church was put up in 1857, and at Kirby a frame chapel in 1864. At Reed a wooden chapel made its appearance in 1867. At New Cleveland, a division of the parish of Glandorf, the new separate congregation erected a frame church in 1861.

The growth of the Catholic population in the far western part of the diocese made it necessary for Bishop Rappe to establish a resident pastor at Defiance to care for the surrounding missions. Father Louis Filiere was there for a few years after 1850 and, although he continued to use the modest frame chapel in that town which had been erected by Bishop Rappe when it was one of his missions, he built a new log chapel at Archbold. The Sanguinists, who came after him at Defiance, opened a school. They were followed by Father Francis Westerholt, who in 1856 completed the new brick Church of St. John Evan-

gelist; he also built a log chapel at The Bend and a frame chapel at
Napoleon. In the last-named place Father John P. Carroll opened a
school in 1868. Father Aloysius Hoeffel, who succeeded Father Westerholt at Defiance, was responsible for frame chapels at Junction, St.
Michael Ridge, and Strycker and he converted a farm house in Marydale into a chapel.

In the general vicinity frame chapels were constructed at Blakeslee
and at Edgerton under the direction of Father Nicolas Kirsch, and
at Antwerp under that of Father Daniel O'Keefe. After Father Westerholt was transferred to Delphos (south of Defiance) in 1858, he completed the new church of hewn logs which had been started by Father
Bredeick and established a school; he also built frame chapels at Ottoville, Convoy, and Landeck. When he was called to Cleveland in 1868,
Father Hoeffel succeeded him at Delphos and built a large new schoolhouse. He also fashioned a church out of a frame residence at Antwerp.
At Fort Jennings in the same district Father George Boehne completed a brick church in 1854.

The growing town of Norwalk replaced Peru as the mission center
for the country east of Tiffin. Father Charles Evrard, later active in
Toledo, in 1847 built the stone Church of St. Alphonsus in Peru. Norwalk itself saw not only the development of St. Peter's but also the
establishment of the new parish of St. Mary for the English-speaking
Catholics. The new brick school of St. Peter's was built in 1859 under
the direction of Father Narcissus Ponchel, and nine years later the
new St. Peter's, combination church and school, at a new location in
the town was completed by Father Andrew Magenhann. Father Ponchel, at the Bishop's direction, began the erection of the brick Church
of St. Mary which Father John Quinn, the first resident pastor, completed. It was dedicated in 1861. Father Thomas P. Thorpe, the next
pastor, opened a brick school in 1865.

At nearby Bellevue in 1859 Father Ponchel, mentioned above, refashioned a warehouse for use as a church, and Father Timothy
Mahony, the first resident pastor, opened a school. At Monroeville, in
the vicinity, Father Francis X. Obermueller, pastor of St. Peter's, Norwalk, opened a school and converted a Methodist church to Catholic
usage in 1863. He built a frame chapel at Milan which Bishop Rappe
dedicated in 1866. At nearby St. Sebastian a brick church in 1857 replaced an eleven-year-old log chapel under the direction of Father
Kreusch, the Sanguinist. The brother of this missionary, Father John
Peter Kreusch, in 1853 completed a brick church at Bethlehem (Shelby
Settlement), south of Norwalk, and another center for smaller missions.

One of these latter was Mansfield where priests had called as early as
1834. The first church was a former Protestant church converted by
Bishop Rappe to Catholic use in 1849; a school was started in 1868
and two years later Father Magenhann completed a substantial brick
church. Father Joseph F. Gallagher, newly ordained and the first resident pastor of Mansfield, built a frame chapel at Crestline in 1861.

Father Jacob Kuhn, his successor, built a similar structure at Shelby in 1866. Another mission of Bethlehem was Bucyrus, which was first visited by Father Tschenhens, the Redemptorist, in 1835. It saw its first Catholic church, a converted Protestant building, in 1862. Galion was still another mission. Father John Peter Kreusch, mentioned above, erected the frame Church of St. Joseph there in 1855; the first resident pastor, Father John P. Puetz, replaced it with a combination church and school, and his successor, Father Joseph Gerardin, exchanged this property for a public school building which he remodeled to suit his purpose. The English-speaking Catholics of the town formed the separate congregation of St. Patrick and built a brick church in 1871, though they were served by the pastor of St. Joseph's until the end of the century.

North of here at Sandusky, on the lake, the increased Catholic population made it necessary for Father Macheboeuf to enlarge the Church of the Holy Angels. When he went to Colorado in 1851, he was succeeded by Father James Vincent Conlan who opened a brick school in a more central part of the town. When Father Alexis Caron came he replaced this building with another school and a chapel-of-ease on the same site. This was the beginning of a new congregation, and after eight years of construction the beautiful blue stone Gothic Church of Sts. Peter and Paul was completed by Father Robert A. Sidley in 1871. The German-speaking Catholics of Sandusky had formed a separate congregation in 1853. Father Felix M. Boff preached to them in Holy Angels' Church as a simple deacon for five months before his ordination to the priesthood. Father James Hamene, born in Lorraine, their second pastor, built the first small stone Church of St. Mary in 1855. In 1862 a stone schoolhouse replaced the original frame building.

Bishop Rappe, when he was pastor at Toledo, put the finishing touches to St. Ann's Church in Fremont, then known as Lower Sandusky. As bishop he appointed Father William L. Nightingale, a priest of English birth, the first resident pastor in 1848. During the tenure of Father Michael O'Neill (1862–1865) the church was considerably enlarged. Previous to this time, when the Bavarian-born Father John Roos was in charge (1856–1857), the German members of St. Ann's, without authorization of the Bishop and apparently with outside encouragement,[2] built the large brick Gothic Church of St. Joseph. Bishop Rappe withdrew the priest from the town but, after proper adjustments were made, Father Louis Molon was sent as their pastor with charge also of the original St. Ann's. A succession of French and Irish priests attended St. Joseph's until the long pastorate (1862–1911) of Father Seraphin Bauer, a native of France though of German an-

[2] Cf. Houck, *Op. cit.*, I, 418. Fr. F. X. Weninger, S.J., to Bp. Gilmour, no date, in C.D.A.

Franzoni to Purcell, Feb. 23, May 27, 1853; Purcell to Franzoni, Apr. 9, 1853; Franzoni to Rappe, May 27, 1853; Propaganda to Purcell, Dec. 17, 1859; all in Cincinnati Archdiocesan Archives.

cestry, who was one of the earliest promoters of the Forty Hours'
Devotion in the parishes. The school, which had been started at the
time of the completion of St. Joseph's Church, was continually improved.

Meanwhile the missions attached to the parishes of Fremont began
to build places of worship for themselves. At Toussaints, now in the
parish of Bono, a frame church replaced an earlier log chapel. At
Millersville the German farming community constructed a stone
church in 1858 and twelve years later started a school. At Prout Station, on a farm of 103 acres donated by Thomas Murphy, a stone mission church made its appearance in 1867. Father Thomas J. Walsh
(of Fremont) was the first to celebrate Mass at Clyde; Bishop Rappe
dedicated a frame church there in 1860. At Woodville, a farming
community, Father Michael O'Neill, mentioned above, built a brick
church in 1862. At Port Clinton, on the lake, Father Molon erected a
frame chapel in 1861. On Kelly's Island Father George Verlet (of
Port Clinton) built a stone church in 1863; the school was organized
a little later. In the stone quarries at Marblehead, where Catholics had
been living since 1842, Father John Koehn (also of Port Clinton)
superintended the erection of a small stone church in 1867.

YOUNGSTOWN UNDER BISHOP RAPPE'S JURISDICTION

I N THAT PART OF THE DIOCESE WHICH WAS TO BE-
come the Diocese of Youngstown a comparable growth was to
be observed, even though the industrialization of the Mahoning
Valley was not to come for another generation or so.

The Catholics of Youngstown itself continued to be visited
by the priests from Dungannon and other centers and many of them
went to St. James Chapel at New Bedford, a mile from the Ohio line
in Pennsylvania. They were said to have had some influence in having
this chapel brought so close to the state line. Father McGann, who
came to them from Akron, suggested that they build their own house
of worship and finally, through the exertions of William Woods, a
small frame church, the first St. Columba's, was completed in 1853.
Father William O'Connor, the first resident pastor, started a school in
1864, before he joined the Redemptorists. Father Eugene M. O'Callaghan, his successor, who is credited with the organization of the
Church in the Mahoning Valley, constructed a large brick Gothic
church in 1864 and transferred the school to the large basement under
it. A separate brick school made its appearance in 1871. At Brier Hill,
in the northeastern section of Youngstown, the parish of St. Ann was
organized in 1869 by Father Edward Murphy. He used a remodeled
store-room for church and school purposes. Father Patrick McCafferty, his successor, two years afterwards built a separate frame
church. Priests came from Randolph to minister to the German
Catholics of Youngstown until the appointment of a resident pastor,
Father Peter Becker, who in 1870 built the first brick Church of
St. Joseph.

The Catholics at Niles were attended by the priests of St. Columba's
for six years before Father O'Callaghan built a frame church for them
in 1864. Father Bernard B. Kelly, the pastor of Niles, four years later
opened a parochial school. At Warren Father O'Callaghan also in
1864 remodeled a former Protestant church for use as a Catholic
chapel. The first Catholics in Mantua were railroad workers, who were
first visited in 1864 by Father Jacob Kuhn who came to them from

Cleveland. A frame chapel was built there in 1871 under the direction of Father Edward J. Murphy.

In Columbiana County, south of Youngstown, the early missions were making considerable progress. In the village proper of Dungannon Father James Monahan completed a new brick church which Bishop Rappe in 1850 dedicated to St. Philip Neri; this replaced the original Church of St. Paul, just outside the town. For three years after 1855 Father Philip Flum personally taught school in a small frame building. At Summitville the church of hand-made bricks was finally completed in 1852. At East Liverpool the second frame church building was finished in 1851 under the supervision of Father Monahan and a school was opened a few years later by Father Dennis Tighe. At Wellsville in 1867 a brick church was completed under the direction of Father Patrick McGuire. The first Catholics in Leetonia were attended by Father Michael Prendergast from the mission center of Summitville. The first church, a frame building dedicated to St. Barbara, was opened for divine worship on Christmas Day, 1868, by the first resident pastor, Father Eli W. J. Lindesmith, who organized a school in the following year.

In the district around Canton several new churches and chapels made their appearance during this time. The stone Church of St. Mary at Massillon, which had been dedicated by Bishop Purcell a few weeks before the consecration of Bishop Rappe, was destroyed by fire in 1852 and had to be rebuilt by the pastor, Father Louis Molon. The parish school, begun in the basement of the church in 1849, moved into a separate brick building in the following year and finally, in 1870, into a two-story brick schoolhouse erected by the then pastor, Father Joseph Lais. Bishop Rappe authorized the English-speaking parishioners to form a separate congregation and appointed Father Alexis Campion (of Canton) to supervise the erection of the brick Church of St. Joseph which was completed in 1854. A most unusual development was the closing of this edifice for five years, because the property had been sold for debt at sheriff's auction four years after it was opened. When it was redeemed, the German-born Father Henry L. Theile was appointed the first resident pastor. The parish school, which was established in 1865, had to be considerably enlarged five years later.

At Navarre in 1851 a brick mission church erected under the direction of Father Molon (from Massillon) replaced the previous chapel. At Strassburg a brick mission church made its appearance in 1857 under the supervision of Father Louis Grevin and a brick school was built in 1870. At Harrisburg Father Casimir Mouret (pastor of St. Vincent's, Akron) presided at the opening of a brick chapel in 1848, erected by the French Catholics who had settled there about fifteen years before. A second brick church appeared there in 1876 under the direction of Father Louis Hoffer (of Louisville). A school, started in 1862, had a precarious existence. At Louisville in 1867 a brick school replaced a ten-year-old frame structure. Two years later Father Hoffer, pastor from 1861 to 1897, laid the foundations of the fine brick Church of St. Louis. At Robertsville, a small French settlement about eight miles from Louisville, Father Louis D'Arcy erected a frame chapel in 1857. He also personally maintained a small school there for a few years, hoping to attract other Catholics to the place, but it had finally to be abandoned.

The construction of the railroad brought some Catholic families to Alliance around 1850. Father Lindesmith came from Canton to visit the approximately thirty families there in 1859. Bishop Rappe celebrated the first Sunday Mass in a rented hall. Father Edward Hannin, who attended the mission from Cleveland for the next few years, had a small frame chapel erected. At North Canton Father John Luhr, coming from Canton, succeeded in having a brick church built in 1847.

A few more churches grew up around one of the oldest Catholic settlements at Randolph (St. Joseph), where in 1866 Bishop Rappe dedicated a new frame chapel, the third in the history of the parish. Father Patrick Brown was responsible for the brick church and the brick school which made their appearance in Ravenna in 1861 and 1862 respectively, to accommodate the Catholic railroad workers who settled there about five years previously. He also built a brick chapel in the nearby Kent, in 1867.

The few missions along the lake in Ashtabula County were attended by the pastors of Painesville. Father Charles Coquerelle contrived to have a small frame church built in the town of Ashtabula in 1860 and Father John Tracey opened a school in 1865. In the same year the same Father Tracey remodeled a large residence for use as a church in the neighboring town of Conneaut, where a few years before there were but two Catholic families. Inland from the lake, at Jefferson, in 1858 Mass was celebrated for the first time by Bishop Young of Erie in the home of his Protestant host for a group of seven Catholics. Ten years later Father Thomas P. Thorpe (then pastor of Thompson) built a frame chapel on a lot given by the villagers for the purpose. Unfortunately it was burned down by an incendiary two years afterwards.

12

CHURCH AND SCHOOL BUILDINGS IN CLEVELAND (1847-1871)

THE MOST REMARKABLE EXPANSION, HOWEVER, in the first years of the existence of the diocese took place in the city of Cleveland, in which sixteen new parishes were erected and nearly as many schools were started.

In the beginning Bishop Rappe was much opposed to what he considered to be a division of strength in the institution of a distinctly German parish.[1] The Germans, however, were tenacious of their language and preferred it as the medium of instruction. As we have seen above, he did allow separate services for them in St. Mary's and at the Cathedral, though he thought that catechism at least ought to be taught in English. Father Roupp, then stationed at the Cathedral, and the Sanguinists finally persuaded the Bishop that the division was necessary. As a result, Father John H. Luhr, who had organized St. Peter's in Canton, was brought to Cleveland and was given the exclusive use of old St. Mary's in February, 1853. In the autumn of the next year the center of their activities was moved to a two-story brick combination church and school which had been erected at the corner of Superior and East 17th Streets.

A few years later, on October 23, 1859, the Bishop dedicated the present brick Gothic Church of St. Peter, the third Catholic church on the east side of the Cuyahoga, which was described in the newspapers of the time as another cathedral. Father Luhr, because of the opposition of a small group of his parishioners, resigned from this pastorate in 1868. He was received by Archbishop Purcell and died four years afterwards in Cincinnati, where he was the pastor of St. Augustine's. Father Francis Westerholt had come from Delphos to replace him at St. Peter's and remained there until his own death in 1896.

The first daughter parish of St. Peter's was St. Joseph's. Many Germans had settled south of St. Peter's on Woodland Avenue and to accommodate them Father Luhr in September, 1855, opened a school in a few rented rooms on East 25th (Irving) Street. Two years later he had built a school at Orange and East 25th Street, and one of the rooms was used as a chapel. The separate congregation was organized in May, 1858, though it did not receive its own pastor until the appointment in 1862 of the Bohemian-born Father Anthony Krasney, who had been previously the assistant priest at St. Peter's. Bishop Rappe blessed the foundations of a frame church at the corner of Woodland and East 23rd Streets, which was completed in 1863, the year in which a new brick school building was opened. At the invitation of the Bishop, the Franciscans, Fathers Capistran Zwinge and Dominic Droessler, took charge of the parish in 1867 and built a monastery on Chapel Avenue at East 23rd Street. On the eve of his departure for Rome in 1869 the Bishop laid the cornerstone of the chapel connected with this monastery. Bishop Toebbe of Covington dedicated it the next year. On October 26, 1871, the same prelate returned to Cleveland to bless the foundation stone of the present magnificent brick Gothic Church of St. Joseph which replaced the original frame structure.

The village of Newburg, situated some six miles south of Cleveland and at one time more populous, was annexed to the city in 1873. Catholics were to be found there at a much earlier date. Bishop Rappe in 1854 gathered them together in the home of Thomas Byrne and celebrated Mass for them. Thereafter, the priests of the Cathedral visited them regularly, using private homes and the Town Hall as meeting places. It was through the good offices of Patrick Potts, in whose home Mass had often been said, that Father Eugene O'Callaghan, then an assistant at the Cathedral, purchased property at the corner of Miles Park and East 93rd Streets. The owners had publicly expressed their opposition to any Catholic edifice in the neighborhood. A stone church was begun on the site in 1862 and the roofed-over basement was used for Sunday Masses and for school purposes by the first resident pastor, Father Jacob A. Kuhn. The superstructure of the new Church of the Holy Rosary, as it was then called, was completed in 1867 by the second pastor, Father John Daudet, who converted a factory-building at the rear of the church into a school. Father Joseph F. Gallagher, who became pastor in 1871, enlarged the church itself by the addition of a frame sanctuary.

The new parish of the Immaculate Conception had its beginnings in the old Nativity Chapel, which the Bishop caused to be moved "out in the country" to the corner of Superior and East 41st Streets after the completion of the new Cathedral. At first the Ursulines used the low roofed-over frame building for teaching catechism. The priests from the seminary and the mother-church went there regularly for Sunday Masses. In 1865 Father Andrew Sauvadet, then recently arrived from Canada, was made the first resident pastor. He put up a large three-story brick building. The top floor was used for divine services, the lower floors for school purposes.

In between the Cathedral and the parish of the Immaculate Conception the congregation of St. Columbkille was organized in 1871 by Father James O'Reilly. It was intended for the convenience of the children and of the older people of the district. Activities centered around a frame building he erected at the southwest corner of Superior and East 26th Streets.

Another concentration of Catholic families was to be found around the present site of St. Bridget's Church on East 22nd Street, between Scovill and Woodland Avenues. Seminary and Cathedral priests celebrated Mass for the new congregation at first in the chapel of St. Mary's Home and then in a small brick church which was opened on Christmas Day of 1857. The first residential pastor, the Irish-born Father Dennis Tighe, took charge in 1864. He remodeled a frame building for use as the first schoolhouse.

The German and Irish Catholics who lived near the southern boundaries of St. Joseph's and St. Bridget's were gathered together in the chapel of St. Joseph's Orphanage on Woodland Avenue in July, 1863, by the German-born Father Anthony J. Abel. This was the beginning of the parish of St. Edward, then known as that of the Holy Family. Father Jacob Kuhn became their first pastor in 1871.

The Bohemians were the first of the Slav peoples who settled here in large numbers in the decade after 1860. The census of 1870 counted 786 persons who came to Cleveland from Bohemia and made their homes in the neighborhood of Broadway and East 55th Street. The French-born Father Anthony T. Martin, then a professor in the seminary, knew something of their language and held separate services for them in St. Peter's, in St. Joseph's and in the old Church of St. Mary on the Flats. In October, 1867, Father Anthony Krasney, the first pastor of St. Joseph's, was given charge of them. Bishop Rappe laid the cornerstone of their brick church on East 35th Place, near Woodland Avenue, in the same month. It was completed shortly afterwards and was dedicated to St. Wenceslas. Small but vocal groups among his countrymen opposed the pastor, who resigned after two years and was succeeded by Father Wenceslas Revis who remained for three years, until 1873.

On the west side of the river several new parishes were found to be necessary for the numerous Catholic body. Father James Conlan, the veteran missionary and one of Bishop Rappe's vicars general, after four years' service at the Cathedral, was in 1853 appointed the first pastor of St. Patrick's. This was at about the same time that the pastor of the Cathedral, Father De Goesbriand, became Bishop of Burlington. On January 8, 1854, a substantial brick church, seating 600 people, though unfinished was opened for divine services. It stood on the site of the present school building on Whitman Avenue. During the ten-month absence of Father Conlan in Burlington, where he acted as administrator of that diocese, Father Michael Kelly finished the structure,

St. Vincent first Catholic church in Akron.

St. John of the Cross Laporte (1835).

*Above Left:*Our Lady of the Lakes, Cleveland's first Catholic Church.

*Right:*Father Dillon's house on East 9th Street, the first pastoral residence.

*Below Left:*Log Cabin where Father McLaughlin offered the first Mass in Avon.

*Above Right:*Early Cleveland site of St. Mary Church.

*Below Right:*St. Francis Xavier log church, Chippewa, first in Wayne County.

*Above Left:*St. Mary Church, Painesville.

*Above Right:*St. Mary Church, West 30th Street.

*Left:*St. Mary Church, Brookpark Road.

*Right:*St. Patrick Church, Bridge Avenue.

*Far Right:*St. Peter Church, Superior Avenue.

which on November 27, 1857, was consecrated by Bishop Young of Erie. Bishop Rappe celebrated the Mass on the occasion and Archbishop Purcell preached the formal sermon. The cornerstone of the present beautiful stone Gothic church on Bridge Avenue was laid in August, 1871, by the same Archbishop of Cincinnati. Father Richard Gilmour, the future successor of Bishop Rappe, delivered the address. Financial stress, however, delayed the completion of St. Patrick's for another six years. The school, which began with the parish in a partitioned-off section of the first church, was continued in two brick schoolhouses on either side of the old church.

The first division of St. Patrick's was made in 1865 when St. Malachy's parish was formed in the section closer to the lake.[1] The Irish-born schoolmaster, Father James P. Molony, who had been ordained by Bishop Rappe and had labored on the missions in the western part of the diocese, was appointed the first pastor. He ministered to his people in old St. Mary's on Columbus Road until on Christmas Day, 1868, a large brick Gothic edifice was used for the first time. It was not dedicated, however, until March 5, 1871, when Archbishop Purcell officiated. A lighted cross on the pinnacle of the tower, which served as a beacon for the shipping on the lake, had at last fulfilled the hopes expressed by that prelate at an earlier date. Father Molony built the first schoolhouse in 1867 and four years later he remodeled a former public school building for parish use.

At the southern extremity of St. Patrick's parish, on the then fashionable University Heights, Bishop Rappe in 1861 built a small frame church at the corner of Tremont and Jefferson Streets, the first Church of St. Augustine. It was attended by priests from the Cathedral until the appointment in 1867 of Father Charles A. Grandmougin, a native of France, ordained by Bishop Rappe in that year. The young pastor died of smallpox, a martyr to duty, in 1871.

Between the territory of St. Malachy's and St. Augustine's the parish of St. Mary of the Annunciation was formed for the benefit of the French-speaking Catholics who lived scattered throughout the city. Father Andrew Sauvadet was changed from the parish of the Immaculate Conception in 1870 to be its first pastor. A frame combination church and school was opened in the autumn of that year.

The German-speaking Catholics who lived on the West Side considered St. Peter's on Superior Avenue too distant for their convenience. They were organized into a separate parish in 1854 and continued to use old St. Mary's on Columbus Road. Father John J. Kramer, ordained in Alsace, France, was their first pastor and built the first frame school. He was followed by Father Francis X. Obermueller (1855–1861) who was obliged to enlarge the school. The large brick Gothic Church of St. Mary of the Assumption, at the corner of Carroll and West 30th Streets, which Bishop Rappe dedicated, September 13, 1865, was constructed during the trying circumstances of the Civil War by

[1] William A. Manning, *History of St. Patrick's Parish, Cleveland*, Cleveland, 1903.

the German-born Father Stephen Falk. Looking to the future, Father Falk in 1869 built a brick combination chapel and school on West 54th Street, between Lorain and Bridge Avenues, for the accommodation of those who lived at the western boundary of St. Mary's. Father Casimir Reichlin, a native of Switzerland, ordained in 1870, was immediately appointed the first pastor of the new congregation of St. Stephen.

Bishop Rappe himself in 1848 first visited the Catholics settled at what was then Rockport but is now part of Cleveland. The Cathedral priests attended to them thereafter. A frame church on the present site of St. Patrick's Church plant was dedicated by the Bishop in 1854 and entrusted to the care of Father Louis J. Filiere, then pastor at Olmsted Falls. Not far to the east of St. Patrick's the small frame Church of St. Mary of the Assumption was built in 1860 by Father Andrew Krasney (from Cleveland) for the convenience of the German farmers in Rockport township. Father Michael Mueller, the first resident pastor, organized a school in 1867, and built a neat brick church which the Bishop dedicated in the following year.

The first Catholics in Olmsted Falls settled there after the construction of the railroad through the area. After 1849 they were visited regularly by the Cathedral clergy. The home of James Hickey and later an old log school were used as provisional chapels. Father Filiere, mentioned above, the first resident pastor, remodeled a large residence as a meeting place and then built a frame church in 1858. His successor, Father Edward J. Murphy, moved this building to a better location and enlarged it. The school which he started in a public school building had only a short existence. At the nearby Berea the few Catholics were visited after 1852 by Father Conlan and other priests from the Cathedral. Father Filiere (from Olmsted Falls) first remodeled a frame house as a chapel and then began the erection of the present stone Church of St. Mary which was finished in 1870. Here, too, the school started in 1860 did not last long. It was reopened, however, five years later with greater success.

West of Olmsted Falls, at Avon (then French Creek), the Sanguinist, Father Ringele, in 1849 built the frame Church of the Immaculate Conception. Father Andrew Gelaszewski, a native of Poland, was made the first resident pastor in the next year. When he left, the Sanguinists were again put in charge of the parish and started a school in 1854. At the other end of Avon Bishop Rappe in 1848 dedicated the first frame Church of the Holy Trinity, which had been built at an earlier date. Another frame church made its appearance in 1862 and, in the year after that, Father Nicolas Schmitz was appointed the first resident pastor. A frame building in 1860 replaced the original log schoolhouse. At Sheffield, in the neighborhood, a frame church built in 1853 under the direction of the Sanguinist, Father Van den Broek, replaced a six-year-old log chapel.

Just to the south of here, the few Catholic families in the thriving town of Elyria were attended by the Sanguinists and priests from the Cathedral. In 1853 the Bishop was able to send them Father Michael Healy, a native of Ireland whom he had ordained two years before. He built a small frame chapel in the following year. In 1859 the school was established and the chapel was enlarged by Father Robert A. Sidley. Several missions were attached to the parish in Elyria. Father Healy supervised the erection of a small frame church at Wellington in 1858, and the enlargement of the chapel at La Porte. Father Molon in 1868 built a small frame chapel at Amherst for the quarrymen.

Bishop Rappe established another mission center when in 1862 he appointed Father Thomas Halley, a native of Ireland whom he had ordained two years previously, resident pastor of Grafton. The chapel at La Porte, which had served the thirty-family congregation before, was moved two miles into Grafton itself. Father Halley, despite a "begging tour" to New York, was unable to complete the stone church he began in 1863. It remained for Father Alexander R. Sidley to do so seven years later. The fine edifice was dedicated in 1871 by the Apostolic Administrator, Father Edward Hannin, who had, meanwhile, transferred Father John Daudet from Holy Rosary in Cleveland to Grafton. A school was started in the old chapel. Father Halley had charge of the mission organized by Bishop Rappe in 1857 at what is now known as Broadview Heights. He remodeled a residence and then another frame building there for use as a chapel in 1864 and 1865. At Medina he refashioned a frame house into a chapel in 1864 for the few Catholics there. In the adjacent parish of St. Martin at Valley City (Liverpool) a brick church was built in 1849 under the direction of Father Peter A. Capeder, the Sanguinist. Another brick church made its appearance in 1861, built by another Sanguinist, Father Van den Broek. The school had been organized three years previous to that date.

At Wooster, in Wayne County, the brick church begun by Father Philip Foley in 1847 was completed a few years later during the tenure of Father Alexis Campion, who was there until 1852. One of his successors, Father Joseph F. Gallagher, opened a small brick schoolhouse in 1865 just before he was transferred to the Cathedral. At nearby Ashland Father Gallagher had remodeled a Presbyterian church for Catholic use in 1863. It was destroyed by fire six years later. Father Magenhann, then pastor of Mansfield, took charge of the mission and with the assistance of some friendly Protestant people and with other outside help began a brick church in 1870. It remained unfinished, however, for a long time. Father Magenhann was also responsible for the beginning of a brick church at Loudonville in that same year.

To the north, at Chippewa, one of the earliest settlements of Catholics within the confines of the present Diocese of Cleveland, the log chapel of St. Francis Xavier, finished in 1837, served the farming community of the district. Bishop Rappe persuaded the parishioners to build a brick church in the town proper of Doylestown, about a mile distant. This he dedicated under the new title of Sts. Peter and Paul in 1850, at the time that Father Alexis Campion (from Wooster) had charge of the mission. The school started by Father Joseph Lais, resident pastor from 1858 to 1862, had a fitful existence.

In the vicinity, at Marshallville, which had been visited by the Dominicans in the early 'twenties, a frame mission chapel was completed in 1849 under the direction of Father Luhr, then pastor at Canton.[2] Another group of French families a few miles away, at French Settlement (Rittman), formed a separate congregation. Father Lindesmith came from Doylestown to minister to them, and a small mission chapel was erected in 1858.

In Akron the Germans formed the separate congregation of St. Bernard in 1861. Father Henry L. Theile, the first pastor, held divine services in a public hall until the completion of a brick church in January, 1863. Father Peter Danenhofer opened a school in the autumn of that year. The native-born Father Matthew A. Scanlon was appointed pastor of the original parish of St. Vincent in 1859, shortly after his ordination. He directed the construction of the present great stone church, in the Classic style, which was first used in 1866. The old church was transformed into a schoolhouse.

North of Akron, at Hudson, the first few Catholics who had been employed in the construction of the railroad were attended by the pastors of St. Vincent's, Akron, and priests from the Cathedral. One of the latter, Father Eugene O'Callaghan, constructed a small frame chapel there in 1860 despite the spirited opposition of some of the townspeople. Closer to Cleveland, at Independence, the small community of farmers was visited by Father Roupp, another of the Cathedral priests, in 1851. He built a small stone church in the following year. The Franciscan Fathers of Cleveland, who had charge of the mission later on, succeeded in having a larger building erected in 1871.

The first Catholics in Euclid, about ten miles along the lake east of Cleveland, were men who worked on the construction of the railroad. Priests from the Cathedral visited them in 1860, and in the following year Father Edward Hannin built a frame chapel there. Father Anthony Martin, a seminary professor, became the first resident pastor in 1865. He opened a school in January, 1867. Railroad workers also were the first Catholics to settle in Willoughby, around 1850. Priests from Painesville attended them until in 1864 the Bishop gave their care to Father Martin. Various halls were used as meeting places until in 1869 he constructed a frame chapel on Vine Street. He had great difficulty in meeting his debts because, with the advent of coal-burning locomotives, many of his parishioners, who had gained their livelihood in cutting the wood previously used, lost their employment and moved to other parts. Father Martin was also responsible for the building of a small frame chapel in 1868 at Mentor, a few miles to the east.

Still farther to the east along the lake, at Painesville, the French

---

[2] Abandoned for a long time, it was sold during the administration of Abp. Schrembs.

priest, Father Peudeprat, who had been laboring among his countrymen here for the previous five years, was in 1850 appointed the first
resident pastor. He remodeled a carpenter shop for use as a chapel. On
his way to the Western missions to assist his friend, Bishop Lamy, he
fell a victim of the cholera at St. Louis in 1852. His successor in Painesville, Father Charles M. Coquerelle, who came from Bishop Rappe's
diocese in France, in 1857 erected a large brick church which, with
the several modifications since added to it, is still in use. He also opened
a school in a frame building in 1863. At his mission in Thompson a
frame chapel made its appearance in 1854.

13

CATHOLIC EDUCATION AND
RELIGIOUS TEACHERS

THE INFLUENCE OF THE PAROCHIAL SCHOOL in the earlier days, for education in general and for the preservation of the Faith of the Catholic children, cannot be overestimated. In the clearings in the forests as well as in the towns the almost invariable accompaniment of the church was the school building, the instructors, sometimes the priest himself or teachers who brought to their work the background of a good European education. The tone of the public schools was very often hostile to the Faith, and Catholic children were sometimes subjected to ridicule or abuse on account of their religion. The exception would be in those districts where Catholics were numerous enough to make their presence felt. The teachers were almost invariably Protestant, quite often Protestant ministers or former ministers, and the public schools themselves were operated in close cooperation with the local Protestant churches. Thus, in Cleveland in 1858 prayer meetings were held by a minister and the teacher in the school room after school hours. The State Teachers Association (Protestant) urged the daily use of the Bible in the class room.[1] The sole remedy at hand was to erect schools in which the children would be instructed in an atmosphere which was not unfriendly to the Faith.

Bishop Rappe assisted at the First Plenary Council of Baltimore in 1852 and signed the decrees in which an appeal was made for the establishment of a Catholic school in every parish. At the First Provincial Council of Cincinnati three years later he heartily agreed with the declaration that "the erection of Catholic schools is in many respects as important an object as the building of new churches." In the local synod of 1857 as well as in all such meetings of the clergy, the Bishop impressed upon the conscience of every pastor that he must erect a parochial school if it were at all possible. A decree of the Second Provincial Council of Cincinnati in 1858 imposed the same duty. Bishop Rappe had written to the Archbishop: "The Catholic Church and its schools must go together. The common schools from which religion

[1] *History of the State of Ohio*, as cited, IV, 176, 177.

is excluded form the man, more or less; the Catholic schools form the man and the Christian."[2] This same council commented upon the inequality and the injustice which Catholics had to suffer in the performance of their conscientious duty to give their children an education which included instruction in their religion. The bishops declared that the public or common schools, despite the name, effectively excluded Catholic children by excluding religious education; they contended that the school funds which were collected from all taxpayers should be used to support all schools and that Catholics should not be punished for their sincerity by having to pay out of their own pockets for religious liberty in education.

The first general school law of Ohio sanctioned but did not require local taxation for the support of the common schools. In 1825 the County Commissioners were compelled to assess a school tax; in 1853 the law imposed a general school tax and regulated its distribution. A special tax for school libraries was also imposed and the school term was set at seven months. An attempt to force through the legislature a law compelling all children to attend the common schools was defeated in 1853. Archbishop Purcell stood out against State monopoly of education. He was the spokesman for the Catholics who built their own schools and who thought that they should have some support for them out of the common school funds or at least that they should not be doubly taxed for their own and the common schools. To divert attention from the real issue the Archbishop was accused of opposing the use of the Bible in the common schools. He did oppose the exclusive use of the Protestant Bible.

In Cleveland the *Daily True Democrat* declined "to run with the herd" and reported the Catholic position as not opposed to the tax-supported common schools but as asking for public support for Catholic common schools. The editor favored this position if for no other reason than as an obstacle to despotism in education.[3] Because the editor of the *Plain Dealer* a few years later had a word of praise for the Catholics of this city because they erected and supported schools for their own children and paid for them as they went along in contrast with "the Protestant extravagant building," the editor of the local *Leader* took occasion to accuse the Catholic Church of fostering ignorance. He satirically called upon all Protestants to follow the editor of the *Plain Dealer* into the church.

The Catholics in the State and in the city, however, were in a minority and could be ignored in spite af a just claim. They were convinced, nevertheless, that at whatever the cost they should respect the rights of God and religion in the education of their children. And when

---

[2] *Pastoral Letter, First Provincial Council of Cincinnati, 1855.* Rappe to Purcell, July 7, 1857, Jan. 21, 1861, all in N.D.A. *Acta et Decreta 4 Conc. Prov. Cincinnati, 1855–1882,* p. 62. *Statuta Dioc. Cleve. lata in synodo dioc. hab. A.D. 1852 et in aliis synod. A.D. 1854 et 1857,* Cleveland 1863. *Rules and Directions . . . for the Diocese of Cleveland,* Cleveland 1863.

[3] *Annals of Cleveland,* Newspaper digest, 1853, p. 77. Lamotte, *Op. cit.,* 279.

Bishop Rappe returned from the sessions of the Second Plenary Council of Baltimore, which reiterated the Catholic position in regard to parish schools, its provisions were published in the Cleveland diocesan synod of 1868.

The Bishop had already shown in action his personal zeal for Catholic education, even in the primitive conditions of northern Ohio when as pastor of Toledo he established an academy in that town. At Cleveland the work on his new Cathedral was delayed until after the start of the first parochial school in the Nativity Chapel on the Cathedral grounds. Within six months of his installation as bishop he was trying to borrow money with which to build a girls' school in Cleveland. Soon he was on his way to France looking for teachers. It was through the trained teachers whom he brought from Europe that the Bishop made his great contribution to Catholic education. Accompanied by Bishop Lefevre of Detroit, he left Cleveland on September 12, 1849, and they were given a fishermen's reception on the French shore.[4] The Lyons Society for the Propagation of the Faith, alleging that Ohio was as rich as California, disappointed his expectations. The Bishop managed, however, to raise some money. One man loaned him 25,000 francs at five per cent interest. Before he left Cleveland the Bishop had confidently arranged for the purchase of the Cowles property on Euclid Avenue, the site of the present William Taylor Company department store. The raising of the money to make the payments gave Father De Goesbriand, the vicar general, some anxious moments. His commission had been to have the convent ready for the Ursulines expected from France.[5] At the convent in Boulogne-sur-Mer, where the Bishop had served as a chaplain for a while after his ordination, five brave and generous souls volunteered for the work in Cleveland: Mother Mary of the Annunciation (Mary Beaumont), the Superior; Mother Mary Charles (Victoria Bourdalier); Mother des Seraphin (Teresa Young); Sister Mary Benoit (Sylvia Piquot); and a young Englishwoman, Arabella Seymour, whom Bishop Rappe himself had received into the Church.

These, and two Sisters of Charity, four priests, and five students, and the Bishop were met by Archbishop Hughes when they landed in New York, August 6, 1850. While the other Sisters of the party went on to Cincinnati, the Ursulines came to Cleveland and were soon housed in their new home on Euclid Avenue. Father De Goesbriand celebrated Mass for them in their improvised chapel.[6] The first postulants to don

[4] *Blanc* (New Orleans) to Purcell, June 14, 1850; Rappe to Purcell, Mar. 16, 1848, Aug. 22, 1849, all in N.D.A.; Cincinnati *Telegraph*, Aug. 23, 1849. W.P.A., *Annals of Cleveland*, Sept. 17, 1849. De Goesbriand to Purcell, Feb. 4, May 22, 1850, in N.D.A.

[5] Mortgage deed, cleared in 1859, in C.D.A., *Annals of Cleveland*, Feb. 22, 1850.

[6] Cf. Sr. M. Michael Francis, O.S.U., *The Broad Highway, a History of the Ursuline Nuns in the Diocese of Cleveland, 1850 to 1950*, Cleveland, 1951.

the religious habit were the English convert, Arabella Seymour, who received the name of Sister Mary Austin, and Catherine Bissonnette, who became Sister Mary Ursula. The latter had distinguished herself in the heroic care of cholera victims in Sandusky and was destined to help Bishop Rappe in founding the Sisters of Charity of St. Augustine. Entering the convent on October 15, they received the novice's veil on December 26, 1850. By this time the work of education had already begun. In the previous September a free school and a tuitional school for girls were opened in two one-story brick buildings along the length of the property on Euclid Avenue. The Cathedral parochial school for girls started here and was moved into new quarters near the Cathedral itself only in 1867; the Ursulines, moreover, continued to be the teachers. Soon a boarding-school and academy was opened. "French, German, and singing were taught without extra charge." As other schools were opened in the city the need of Sisters to teach in them made it necessary for the Bishop to obtain a relaxation of the religious rule which would ordinarily forbid them to leave the cloister: thereafter they went back and forth to their duty in the several parishes in carriages with the shades drawn.

In October, 1853, they opened a school for girls in a building not far from St. Patrick's Church, in Franklin Circle, on a site now occupied by the Disciples Church; some 200 pupils were in attendance in 1856. When St. Patrick's established its own girls' school on the parish property in 1863, the Ursulines went there to teach and the distinction between paying and free pupils was abolished. Even before the appointment of the first pastor at the Immaculate Conception parish, the Ursulines as early as 1855 taught school there. They taught also in St. Bridget's before the appointment of a pastor. When St. Mary's School on West 30th Street was enlarged in 1859, they took charge of the girls' section. They organized the girls' department of St. Malachy's School in 1865.

Bishop Rappe in 1854, not long after the original Cleveland foundation, established the Ursulines at Toledo on a property he had prepared for them. Mother des Seraphin and her five companions soon had some 200 girls committed to their charge. In 1859 they built a three-story brick convent to replace the original frame structure. Not long afterwards they opened a boarding-school. The Tiffin foundation was made at the request of the pastors of that city in 1863. Mother Mary Joseph and two other Sisters arrived there in September of that year. Two years later they had constructed a two-story brick convent and school. A large square brick building crowned with a cupola was put up in 1870.

According to the *Catholic Directory* of 1869 there were at that time forty-eight professed Ursulines and thirteen novices living at the convent on Euclid Avenue. In their academy they had 225 pupils, at the Cathedral 460, at the Immaculate Conception School 225, at St. Patrick's 400, and at St. Mary's 345, making a total of 1,655 girls in their charge, not counting those at St. Bridget's. In Toledo they had 30 in their academy and 350 in the two schools of St. Francis de Sales and St. Louis. In Tiffin they had 505 pupils in the two parish schools.

The second community of religious teachers to come here at the invitation of Bishop Rappe were the Daughters of the Immaculate Heart of Mary, sometimes called the Ladies of the Immaculate Heart. Founded during the persecutions of the French Revolution, they did not wear a distinctive religious garb but were, nevertheless, devoted by vow to the works of religion and their own personal sanctification. Miss De Goesbriand, the French Superior and the aunt of Father De Goesbriand, had promised the Bishop in 1850 that she would send some of the Sisters to Cleveland. As the result of another appeal made by Father De Goesbriand himself on a visit to his homeland, the Mesdames Pance, Ferec, and Blehen arrived here in 1851 to make the first foundation of their congregation in this country. They taught in some of the earliest schools in the diocese.

In 1857 they had 100 pupils at Louisville and 200 at Sandusky. In 1860 they had the additional charge of the girls' school at St. Peter's, Cleveland, and of the girls' department at St. Joseph's on Woodland Avenue with its 300 students. At one time or another they have had charge of St. Patrick's School in Toledo, of St. John's in Canton, of St. Columba's in Youngstown, of St. Edward's and Holy Trinity and Holy Name in Cleveland, and of the schools in Lima and Massillon. Also entrusted to them was the domestic economy in the episcopal residence after 1855 and in the seminary after 1857; both charges were relinquished when Bishop Rappe resigned.

On June 18, 1864, Father John J. Begel landed in New York with the religious community he had founded in France ten years before, a group of some twenty persons, the original Sisters of the Holy Humility of Mary. They came at the invitation of Father Louis Hoffer who had been sent to Europe to find teachers for his school in Louisville. Sister Mary Ann (Anna Marie Tabourat) was the first superior in America. Sister Mary Joseph (Marie Gaillot) was the only other professed Sister among the first arrivals. Sister Mary Magdalen (Antoinette Poitier), the third professed Sister, died on the eve of departure and her patrimony was detained in France by her relatives.

After a short time at Louisville they were given a very difficult assignment at what is now their mother-house, at Villa Marie. Across the State line, near New Bedford, in Lawrence County, Pennsylvania, William Murrin, a pioneer Catholic of that district, had given Bishop O'Connor of Pittsburgh a farm of 247 acres on condition that it be used to support a Catholic orphanage. Shortly after 1847 the small Chapel of St. James was put up on this property and, as we saw above, the Catholics of Youngstown, some twenty miles away, had asked Bishop O'Connor to locate this chapel closer to them. A two-story brick building was erected to house the older orphan boys of Pittsburgh and the Franciscan Brothers of Loretto who had charge of them, but because of the distance from Pittsburgh and the ungrateful nature of the rugged land this experiment was abandoned. The restriction in the title against its use for any purpose other than the care of orphans induced the Bishop of Pittsburgh to give the place to Bishop Rappe in 1851 for the cost of the buildings on it. The Cleveland Sisters of Charity and the older orphan boys from St. Vincent's Asylum occupied it for several years before 1863. It was then assigned to the newly arrived French Sisters. They were at first dismayed at the task of developing the uncultivated land, but by dint of hard physical labor and with the assistance of the sympathetic people of Youngstown and the neighborhood they made it a successful farm.

These Sisters soon had the direction of many schools, especially in the smaller towns in the vicinity. They were the first teachers, too, at the parochial school in Newburg. They taught also at Louisville and Harrisburg. A special agreement between the ecclesiastical authorities of Cleveland and Pittsburgh arranged for the spiritual jurisdiction over the mother-house which was actually situated in Pennsylvania. Here in 1869 there were 18 Sisters, 17 orphans, and 8 other pupils living in the buildings which meanwhile had been doubled in size.

In the western part of the diocese the Sisters of the Most Precious Blood had expanded their activities and started a third convent at Glandorf in 1849. They had charge, also, of the Shrine of Our Lady of Sorrows[7] which had been erected in the midst of the forest near Marywood. In 1870 there were some 60 women in the entire community who cared for about 500 children.

The Sisters of the Third Order of St. Francis at Tiffin were founded in 1868 by Father Joseph L. Bihn, the pastor of St. Joseph's in that town, with the sanction of Bishop Rappe. They furnished teachers for the country schools of the district. The Sisters Servants of the Immaculate Heart of Mary were associated with the first parochial school in Painesville. Sisters Mary Josephine White, Mary Catherine Biry, and Mary Agnes McGovern came from their convent home in Monroe, Michigan, in 1862. They remained only a few years but at one time they had charge of some 200 pupils. Other communities, such as the Franciscan Sisters of La Crosse, of Minnesota, and of Joliet helped to staff the parochial schools.

The Sisters were generally forbidden by their rule to teach the older boys, and this task was assigned to laymen. In the larger parishes the boys' school and the girls' school were distinct institutions. It is to be observed that, in contrast with the few small schools in charge of the Sisters of the Most Precious Blood in 1847, there were 26 parish schools in 1870 taught by the women of religious communities, in some instances aided by laymen or by Brothers who instructed the boys.

Bishop Rappe was fortunate enough in 1856 to secure the services of

---

[7] Edmund Louis Binsfeld, C.PP.S., *The Shrine of the Sorrowful Mother*, Bellevue, 1950. This was the first shrine in the Middle West of the United States dedicated to the Blessed Mother.

the members of the Society of Mary for several of the Cleveland schools. This religious society, founded by the Venerable William Joseph Chaminade in France in 1817, was introduced into this country in 1849 by Father Leo Meyer, first at Cincinnati and then at Dayton. The Bishop and Father James Conlan, the pastor of St. Patrick's, were so well impressed with the work of the Brothers at the school opened by Father August J. Rollinet at Louisville that they invited them to take charge of the boys at St. Patrick's. The success of Brother John B. Stintzi with his pupils, who ranged from six to sixteen years of age and older, was remarkable and incited the admiration of the public school superintendent. With the assistance of Father Heitz, also a member of the community, he opened a night school which was eagerly attended.

In August, 1857, Brother Damian Litz took charge of the Cathedral Boys' School. He was succeeded there by his former pupil, the well-known Brother Thomas Mooney, an American member of the society. Soon afterwards the Brothers were able to take charge of the boys' departments at St. Mary's and at St. Peter's, so that by 1863 they had the responsibility for the boys in the four largest parochial schools in the city. According to the *Catholic Directory* they had in 1871 approximately 1,500 students. Bishop Rappe always remained a staunch friend of the society and was their protagonist at the meeting of the bishops.[8]

During the administration of Bishop Rappe the number of parochial schools had increased from 7 or 8 (not including the few country district schools in predominantly Catholic areas) to 87 Catholic schools of all types, but not including the academies and the orphanages. Of this total, 26 together with the academies of the Ursulines and of the Sisters of the Most Precious Blood and the orphanage school, made their appearance in the district which is now the Diocese of Toledo. In the present Diocese of Youngstown 22 together with the academy at Villa Marie had been started. And within the boundaries of the present Diocese of Cleveland 29 parish schools, several of them of considerable size, the Ursuline and Lourdes academies, and 2 orphan schools were operating in 1870.

It would be difficult to give the exact number of pupils in all these schools but the figures given in the *Catholic Directory* (1872) furnish the basis for an approximation. Cleveland (including Newburg) had 4,700 pupils in the parish schools alone; Sandusky had 750; Toledo, 1,600; Tiffin, 600; Massillon, 395; Youngstown, 450. In the other smaller schools the average attendance would vary from a dozen or so to 100 or more. It is to be noted, moreover, that the physical equipment was constantly improved: log cabins were as soon as possible replaced with frame structures and with buildings of brick or stone, most of them as modern as their time.

In accord with the desires of the people and of the pastors, religious

[8] Bro. John E. Garvin, *Centenary of the Society of Mary,* Dayton, 1917.

teachers were gradually taking over the instruction. Nevertheless, in most places outside the larger cities devoted Catholic laymen kept the school, and more often than not they were also the organists in the parish and presided over the singing at the solemn functions on Sunday. With few exceptions these schools, large or small, have had a continuous existence up to the present.

14

NATIVISM

BISHOP RAPPE IN 1855 ATTENDED THE FIRST PRO-
vincial Council of Cincinnati and had his part in drafting its
decrees. Three years previously Archbishop Purcell had been
made the head of the newly created Province of Cincinnati
which besides Cleveland included the Dioceses of Covington,
Louisville, Vincennes (Indianapolis), Detroit, and the Vicariate Apostolic of Upper Michigan. This meeting of the bishops was held at a
time when the Know Nothing attacks on the Church were most bitter.

Cleveland was spared the open violence but not the "unbloody persecution" incident to the general wave of intolerance. Perhaps typical
of conditions here was the remark of Father Howard when he was
putting up the first St. Vincent's Church in Akron: "They are burning
our churches in the East but we are building new ones out here."
Bishop Rappe's self-effacing devotion to duty and his public example
did much to modify the bitterness in Cleveland. In 1854 he wrote to
Archbishop Purcell that "things are sufficiently peaceful although for
a time there was a foment of bigotry." And a few years after his seventh visitation of the diocese, in a pastoral of 1856, he commended the
calmness and fortitude of the Catholics in the face of systematic persecution. The public lectures of the priests of the Cathedral also helped
to dissipate the latent prejudice.

Early Cleveland was not particularly religious-minded. The first
settlers threw off the puritanical restrictions of New England and they
resisted the compulsory support of the State Church, the Congregational. In time, however, a more friendly attitude developed towards
the Protestant church organizations. By 1853 Cleveland had three
Episcopalian, three Presbyterian, two Congregational, two Baptist, four
Methodist Episcopal, one Bethel, one Wesleyan, one German Episcopal
Methodist, one German Evangelical Lutheran, one German Evangelical
Protestant, one Associate Presbyterian, one German Evangelical Association, two Jewish, and one African Methodist church buildings, several of them finished in that year. In the next year there were in this
city several Catholic churches: old St. Mary's, the Cathedral, the
Nativity Chapel, St. Peter's, and St. Patrick's.

The freedom of religion guaranteed by the Constitution had resulted
in a great increase in the number of Catholic parishes in the State and

throughout the country and also in a country-wide suspicion and persecution of the Catholics who were coming here in ever-increasing force.
Only in Cincinnati, however, was the concentration of the foreign-
born sufficient to arouse violent persecution on the part of the Nativ-
ists. There one-half the population was of foreign birth, the Germans
(Catholics and non-Catholics) constituting three-fifths and the Irish
about one-fourth of the population. The native Protestant Americans
raised the cry of "America for the Americans," meaning of course for
the Protestants. This movement, a throwback to the persecuting spirit
of Colonial days, was called Nativism, and later developed into "Know
Nothingism." In Cincinnati Archbishop Bedini, the papal nuncio,
barely escaped with his life from the violence of the mob of foreign-
born revolutionaries who had been egged on by the American
fanatics. The invitation of Bishop Rappe to that distinguished prelate
to visit our city could not be accepted at the time.

In Cleveland Father McLaughlin had reported signs of ill-feeling
before 1847. The political parties, Democrats and Whigs, in an attempt
to influence the voters often appealed to race feeling and religious
prejudice. When the Whigs failed to gather in the "foreign vote," they
adopted a hostile attitude towards things Catholic, and the Republican
party in the beginning was identified with the Know Nothing movement and its anti-Catholic agitation.

Some notion of the feeling in Cleveland may be obtained from the
tone of the newspapers of the time. An advertisement in the Cleveland
Herald (Whig organ) invited the sympathetic, at twelve and one-half
cents a person, to attend a lecture in the Old Stone Church on Public
Square to be given by a supposed ex-monk on the subject of "Roman-
ism." Youth and ladies would be excluded from another lecture at
Empire Hall on "Popish Confession and Priestcraft." Curiously enough,
beneath this notice is another advertising to the public the first annual
ball given by the Cleveland Hibernian Guard.

The *Daily True Democrat* resented the Catholic support given to
the Holy Father in his difficulties with the Italians. It also gave space
to a certain Israel Brainard for an attack on the Pope. Catholics in
general were called foreigners who had emigrated to America to escape
the poverty and degradation of the working-classes in Europe and who
should be repressed in their building of churches and in the keeping
of their fasts and festivals. The same newspaper followed the "party
line" in attacking the Church at the time that the Hungarian Louis
Kossuth came to this country. As the victim of the Austrian monarchy
he served as a "convenient stick with which to beat the Pope." Brownson's remarks about Kossuth and particularly his lecture, "Protestantism Incompatible with Liberty," drew fierce fire. The defense of
the Church made by Archbishop Hughes of New York and Bishop
O'Connor of Pittsburgh was reported in invidious fashion and Catholic
newspapers were denounced for daring to attack her defamers.

Again, the *Daily True Democrat* warmly recommended the reading of a pamphlet, *Warning against Popery, or Our Country in Danger,* as a good preparation for the visit of the Italian apostate priest, Alessandro Gavizzi, who came to this country to annoy Archbishop Bedini, the papal representative. Gavizzi was given a hearing in Melodeon Hall and the usual calumnies were reported in the next issue of the newspaper. That all Clevelanders were not taken in might be gathered from the "mobbing down" reception given to a certain infamous Joe Barker who lectured here on the usual anti-Catholic subjects. The *Daily True Democrat* virtuously protested such treatment. The abuse of the Church and the hierarchy continued throughout the years. The accounts of the persecution of the Church in other parts of the country were given in detail and, by a curious logic, the Church and the bishops and the Irish Catholics were held responsible for their own ill-treatment. St. Patrick was burned in effigy at the corner of Cedar and Clinton Streets in 1854.[1]

The Cleveland *Leader* was more venemous still, stirring up the Protestant German Democrats already well known for their anti-Catholic feeling; the Pope was accused of political interference. An editorial in 1857 looked confidently for the dissolution of the Catholic Church "to which the lowest and most destitute people belong, kept that way by the exactions of the Church and whom honest men must support in times of depression." During the Civil War obviously the editor could not find fault with Catholic Clevelanders doing their full share in the defense of the Union. But diatribes against the Church were always in season with the dyspeptic editor. He had reluctantly to retract his statement that arms were stored in the Cathedral. St. Vincent's Charity Hospital, then the only general hospital in the city, was ignobly slandered by the editor, the devoted Sisters being falsely accused of interfering with the religion of their patients, and Protestants were urged to withhold their patronage.

Catholic bishops could not meet in council without the charge that they were conspiring against the country. The Council of the Vatican was a matter of much concern to the editor of the *Leader* in 1869 and 1870. At the same time that he offered his counsel to the bishops, he advised that every "good patriot and Protestant" should work to nullify the aspiration of the Church to make this a Catholic country. He gleefully announced that the Council was a failure, and when the Italian troops took Rome he was certain that the Catholic Church "had reached its end and was tottering to its fall." The doctrine of the Infallibility of the Pope was interpreted in his own fashion by the anxious publicist. He rejected Archbishop Purcell's explanation and defense of the doctrine, yet he printed a letter from a Catholic citizen which read: "We should have a rich faith indeed had we to accept newspaper definitions of our creed. We decline to receive definitions of our faith from Protestants." In another paid advertisement (card) the editor was taken to task for his easy acceptance of slanders about Catholic

[1] *Annals of Cleveland.*

clergymen and he was called upon to put an end to "those deadly insults to Catholic feeling." The campaign continued however: the public was urged to attend the public lectures of the "escaped nun" in Brainard's Hall; the editor was greatly pleased that the "terrible" Nast, the venal and talented cartoonist, had joined the "crusade against the Church" waged in *Harper's Weekly*. It would be hard to believe that the editor of the *Leader* represented the better elements of the city, but in any case he was well supported.

15

CHARITABLE INSTITUTIONS

(1847-1871)

A T THE FIRST PROVINCIAL COUNCIL OF CINCIN-
nati in 1855 attention was called to one of the results of
the then prevalent anti-Catholic agitation, namely, that
Catholic priests were effectively barred from entering
public institutions of charity, the orphanages, hospitals,
and homes for the deaf, dumb, and blind, to minister to the Catholics
in them. The Council saw no other solution of the problem at the time
than that Catholics themselves build and support institutions of the
kind, in which the faith of the unfortunate Catholic inmates would
be respected.

Bishop Rappe had anticipated the recommendation of the Council in
this matter. One of the most pressing problems he found in Cleveland
had been the care of the Catholic children who had been deprived of
their natural guardians by death or sickness and were an easy prey for
agencies willing enough to take care of them but at the sacrifice of
their religion. He had already had experience in this matter in Toledo
but he had no means to carry out his plan. He was to have better success in Cleveland. One of his first acts here was to form a society for
the preservation of unfortunate children. His next move was to secure
religious women to take up the work.

We have seen above that the first foundation in America of the
Daughters of the Immaculate Heart of Mary was made in Cleveland.
Bishop Rappe met the little band from France in New York on October 6, 1851, and escorted them to Cleveland where they were the
guests of the Ursuline Nuns on Euclid Avenue for a few weeks before
they went out to live with sympathetic families in order to learn the
English language. On December 6 of that year they took possession
of a home prepared for them on St. Clair Avenue at East 6th Street.
This was the first Catholic girls' orphanage in Cleveland; the first child
was admitted on Christmas Day of 1851. The Bishop, who lived almost
next door, did much to relieve the hardships of the new venture. The
first postulant came to them in the following August, when the number

of orphans had increased to twenty-five. These latter attended school at the Ursuline Convent until the arrival of two English Sisters, the Mesdames Williams and Smyth, who came by way of France with two other French Sisters.

A small addition to the original building accommodated the increased household until in October, 1853, Miss Deschargnes with five Sisters and twenty-six orphans took up residence in a new home, St. Mary's, on East 20th Street, which had been built with the family inheritance of Miss Pance, one of the pioneers. In 1863 Miss Morgan and twelve of the younger orphan girls took possession of the new St. Joseph's Orphanage, a large brick structure in a "country location" on Woodland Avenue near East 60th Street. Its chapel, finished three years later, was used as the first meeting place of the two new parishes of St. Edward and Holy Trinity and in later times by the new congregation of St. Elizabeth. In 1871 there were 30 Sisters in the Cleveland community and 160 girls in the orphanage. At least fifteen other foundations were made from Cleveland, including one among the Indians. The Buffalo house, established by Miss Nardin in 1857, became the headquarters twenty-three years later.

On the same ship with these Sisters coming out from France in the company of Father De Goesbriand were two Sisters of Charity, Sisters Bernardine (Caberet) and Françoise, and two novices, the Misses Louise Brouillot and Cornelia Muselet. They belonged to the community of Sisters who served as nurses in the Hospital of St. Louis at Boulogne-sur-Mer. Bishop Rappe, well acquainted with them and their work, on the visit to his homeland in the year before had requested them to assume the management of a hospital in his new diocese. They found their first welcome in Cleveland at the Ursuline Convent, where the two novices stayed until they received the white habit of their congregation from Bishop Rappe on December 8, 1851. Miss Brouillot took the name of Sister Mary Augustine, Miss Muselet that of Sister Mary Joseph. Not long afterwards the group took possession of a two-story frame house on an eight-acre plot at the corner of Monroe Avenue and Fulton Road which the Bishop had bought from the railroad; the sale of sand and gravel found on it helped to pay for the property.

Father James Conlan, of the Cathedral, headed a committee to raise funds for the new hospital; a well-advertised and well-patronized Public Fair held in Kelly's Hall on Superior Street produced the unusual sum of $1,300. With this, a one-and-one-half-story brick building was erected near the convent; it was dedicated as St. Joseph's Hospital, August 5, 1852. The first patient in the two-ward institution was admitted within the first week after that. For some reason or other, the two professed French Sisters returned to their native land in the following month. Sister des Seraphin of the Ursulines stayed with the little community for a short time until in October, 1852, on the day she made her profession at the Ursuline Convent, Sister Mary Ursula (Catherine

Bissonnette) was installed as the superior by the Bishop. Three other American young women had, meanwhile, joined the two French novices. Mother Ursula was especially devoted to the children and often relieved the mind of a stricken mother at the point of death by promising to care for her little ones.

The location of the hospital so far from the center of things proved not to be practical; St. Vincent's Orphanage (originally under the patronage of the Immaculate Conception) was more successful. In 1856, when there were 20 patients in the hospital and 50 in the orphanage, it was decided to use all the facilities for the work with the boys. St. Vincent's Orphan Asylum Society, which had 100 members in 1861, assisted the Sisters in various ways. When the Brothers of Mary took charge of St. Patrick's school, they also helped to teach the boys the useful arts of carpentry and tailoring. In successive years, in 1859, 1865, and 1867, the orphanage building was gradually completed. In 1865 there were 35 Sisters at St. Vincent's, which was also the mother-house; at this time 150 orphans found shelter there. The experiment of training the older boys at the "church farm" in New Bedford has been mentioned above in the account of the first foundation of Villa Marie.

The first Catholic hospital lost its identity in the orphanage; but the Bishop had plans as early as 1852 for establishing a hospital on the East Side of the city. In that year and in 1857 he bought land for the purpose at the present location of St. Vincent's Charity Hospital. Cleveland, a city of 43,417 in 1860, had no general hospital. Temporary pest houses or cholera wards had been set up in 1849 and 1850. The Marine Hospital for government personnel was opened in 1862. Cleveland City Hospital, the project of the medical men, functioned for a year before 1869. The Cleveland Homeopathic (later Huron Road) Hospital was organized in 1868.

The experience of the Civil War and the return of the crippled soldiers gave fresh force to the Bishop's arguments in favor of a refuge for the sick. In 1863, in the midst of the war, he offered to donate the site for a hospital and to furnish the nurses for it if Cleveland would contribute towards the cost of the building. A City Council committee of four and the Mayor conferred with the Bishop in May of that year. The appeal to the general public received a generous response. The industrialist and philanthropist, William J. Gordon, gave $10,000; the Bishop donated $1,000; the Cleveland parishes raised about $4,000; additional contributions increased the total to about $42,000. More property was bought and building operations began in that year. The Cleveland architect, J. M. Blackburn, designed the Franco-Italian style building, which had a normal capacity of 150 patients and in an emergency could care for 50 more. It was dedicated and opened to the public, October, 1865, in a grand ceremony in which the Bishop, ex-Governor Todd, H. B. Payne, Judge Tilden, and Surgeon General Barr participated. Six months later the Bishop thanked all the benefactors of the hospital but reminded them that of the original cost about one-half remained unpaid and upon that he was paying interest at the rate of seven per cent.[1]

The Sisters of Charity were as a matter of course given charge of the new St. Vincent's Charity Hospital. Doctor Gustav Weber, a retired army surgeon, headed the medical staff. The wards were used for the clinical instruction of the students in the college, which graduated its first class in 1865. Later the hospital became affiliated with the college at Wooster and finally with the Cleveland Medical College of Western Reserve University. By April, 1868, over 1,000 sick persons had been received into the hospital. The free patients far outnumbered those who were able to pay their expenses. The City Council for a short time, much to the annoyance of the editor of the Cleveland *Leader,* appropriated enough to pay for ten beds for the indigent. A great bazaar in 1868 brought in $6,500. The Sisters had on occasion to borrow money from the mother-house; but the long history of their heroic self-sacrificing devotion to the sick and unfortunate of Cleveland had begun.

At about this same time Bishop Rappe through Father Alexis Campion, the pastor of St. Francis de Sales, invited the Grey Nuns, the famed Sisters of Charity of Montreal, to begin their beneficent activities in Toledo. In 1855 they started under very primitive conditions in temporary quarters. Three years later the Sisters and forty-seven orphans (boys and girls) occupied their own building on Cherry Street; the third floor was used as a temporary hospital.

It was with the approval and blessing of Bishop Rappe that Father Joseph Bihn, the pastor of St. Joseph's in Tiffin, established St. Francis' Orphan Asylum and Home for the Aged on the outskirts of that city. On a fifty-eight-acre farm he installed the Sisters of the Third Order of St. Francis which he had founded. The widowed daughter of the principal benefactor, John Greifeldinger, and her own two daughters were among the first members. The unusual institution was incorporated as the Citizens Hospital and Orphan Asylum in 1869. The Sisters, the girl orphans, and the aged people who brought their own patrimony occupied a new building in 1871. The orphan boys and their supervisors, a kind of brotherhood who taught them farming and other trades, lived in separate quarters.

For the care of the aged and the destitute Bishop Rappe had invited the Little Sisters of the Poor, a congregation founded in France in 1839, to come to Cleveland. They began their work in a frame building on East 9th Street near the Cathedral in May, 1870. In the next year a large brick building on the site of the present home on East 22nd Street was remodeled to accommodate 150 elderly folk.

Another form of Christian charity was introduced into the diocese by Bishop Rappe with the coming of the Sisters of the Good Shepherd.

[1] Cleveland *Herald,* Feb. 9, 16, 1852. Warranty Deed, Philo Scoville to Bp. Rappe, Nov. 11, 1852, in C.D.A. Cleveland *Leader,* May 6, 12, 1863; Oct. 6, 1865; Apr. 7, 1866; June 20, 1867; Apr. 28, May 28, July 13, 1868.

He was personally acquainted with the French foundress of the community, Mother Mary St. Euphrasia Pelletier, and already in 1862 he had discussed a foundation in Cleveland with her. Seven years later, on July 19, four Sisters came from Cincinnati and took up residence in a frame building on Lake Street, east of the old St. Mary's Seminary location. A few weeks later they began their work for the reclamation of unfortunate women and the preservation of others in jeopardy. In 1870 the new convent and home on Carnegie Avenue at East 30th Street was started.

16

RECRUITMENT AND TRAINING
OF THE CLERGY

ONE OF THE EARLIEST PREOCCUPATIONS OF
Bishop Rappe was the recruitment and training of a diocesan clergy. When he came he had only about sixteen
priests, four of them Sanguinists, to assist him in the great
territory of northern Ohio. At the first opportunity he
began an ecclesiastical seminary in the episcopal residence on East 6th
Street. The frame buildings on the property previously used as stables
were fitted up as class rooms for the students themselves and for the
boys in the free school taught by the seminarians.

When the Bishop returned from France in September, 1850, with
some money, he bought what was then known as the Spring Cottage
and Bathing Establishment. It was a frame building on a plot of land,
255 feet square, between Lake and Hamilton Avenues east of East
17th Street, a site now occupied by the Cleveland Electric Illuminating
Company plant. An omnibus left Cleveland every hour to bring patrons
to what was described in the advertisement of the time as "Clifton Park
on Lake Erie, a summer retreat from the cares and the bustle of business."[1] A small stream ran through a gully on the property. The
three-story summer house, turned into an ecclesiastical college, with
chapel and class rooms, was soon afterwards occupied by the rector
and eighteen students. In the summer of 1853 a two-story brick
structure, 25 by 35 feet, was added to it. It cost about $12,000 and was
considered to be a "magnificent establishment." This was the one wing
attached to the entirely new brick main building, 30 by 70 feet, which
was finished for the fall term of 1860. The chapel occupied one of
the three floors. The dining room and kitchen were to be found in the
large basement under the older building.

Father Louis De Goesbriand, in addition to his other manifold duties,
taught theology and was the first Superior of St. Francis de Sales
Seminary and its ten students in 1848, as it was established on East
6th Street. In the autumn of the next year, when the name was changed
to St. Mary's Ecclesiastical Seminary, Father Alexis Caron, lately

[1] *Cleveland Directory*, 1837.

arrived from France where he had had a remarkable career as a member of a missionary society, the Fathers of Mercy, took charge and held that responsibility together with other duties for seven and one-half years. He was assisted by younger priests for shorter periods. Among them were: Father Peter Peudeprat; the Reverend Mr. Probst, a deacon who had but one arm; the Frenchman, Father John B. Maréchal, who was afterwards associated with the Abbé Migne in France in editing the works of the Fathers of the Church; the Irish-born Father William O'Connor, who after many years on the Cleveland missions joined the Redemptorist Fathers; the Frenchmen, Fathers John Edward Martin and Felix M. Boff.

Father John F. Salaun came from France in 1856 to become rector. He was assisted for a while by Father Louis Hoffer and by Father Anthony T. Martin, professor from 1857 to 1865. The Irish-born Father John Quinn, after some years on the missions, was appointed to succeed as rector in 1864. He was assisted by Fathers Julius Clement and Wilmott. In 1866 Bishop Rappe appointed Father James Stremler, D.D.,[2] rector. He was born in Lorraine in France and had been teaching at Quebec in Canada. When Bishop Rappe resigned in the summer of 1870, one of the first acts of the Apostolic Administrator, Father Hannin, was to appoint Father Nicolas A. Moes, a native of Luxembourg and pastor at Napoleon, Ohio, to succeed Father Stremler; he retained that position, in the last years as rector emeritus, until his death in 1908.

The number of seminarists varied with the years: 10 in 1848; 23 in 1856; 28 in 1866; 16 in 1870. Many of the students came from abroad and were already well advanced in the study of the classics and some also in theology; hence, they needed to remain in the local seminary only for a short time. The average course in philosophy and theology then required three years' residence but of the more than one hundred priests ordained in Bishop Rappe's time only about a third had to stay for that length of time. Many came here in answer to the appeal of the Bishop and of others in his name.

Quite naturally his first invitation was to his own countrymen; when he returned from France in 1850, he brought back five students and four priest volunteers. It is interesting to note from the correspondence that the hardships and dangers of the missionary life were alleged by others as reasons for not accepting the invitation. In preference and as a precaution against these difficulties, the superiors of the seminaries had advised the mission-minded students to join the religious congregations of missionaries. In later years the Bishop had to refuse permission to some of his priests to join religious communities because of his own pressing needs. A few exceptions were made as for Father William O'Connor, mentioned above, for Father Augustine Campion, who after he labored here from 1848 until in 1856 was allowed to join

[2] Author of *Traité des Peines Ecclésiastiques: de l'Appel et des Congrégations Romaines*, Paris, 1860.

the Sulpicians in Canada, and for Father John P. Dolweck, who became associated with the Benedictines.

An analysis of the origin of the seminarians who became priests during Bishop Rappe's administration may be of interest. Of the total number, nine were born in the United States; one in Canada; thirty-one in Ireland; twenty-eight in Germany; six in Alsace, and eight in Lorraine, both provinces in France in which French and German were spoken; five in Switzerland; and four in Luxembourg. Approximately twenty-five of all these after a few years in Cleveland became affiliated with another diocese.

The first diocesan priest ordained by Bishop Rappe was Father James Monahan, a native of Ireland, who had spent only a few months in the local seminary. Ordained with him, in the first class to receive Holy Orders in old St. Mary's Church, November 19, 1848, were two natives of Germany, Father August Berger, who shortly afterwards went to what is now the Diocese of Belleville, and Father John Peter Kreusch, who spent his last years in the Diocese of Wheeling. The Bishop in the previous February had ordained several Sanguinists in their monastery chapel: Fathers Maximilian Homburger, Andrew Kunkler, and Engelbert Ruff. Father Nicolas Roupp, who was born in Lorraine and made his studies there, after "a few months of self instruction amid various other occupations," was the first seminarian to undergo a solemn public examination before he was made a priest in St. Mary's, August 15, 1849, just before the Bishop set out for Europe. After fifteen years of service here he returned to his native land.

Of the priests who came here after their ordination and were received into the diocese by Bishop Rappe, twenty-one were Frenchmen in addition to three from Alsace and five from Lorraine; thirteen were from Germany; seven from Ireland; four from Switzerland; three from Bohemia; two from Austria; two from Belgium; one each from Holland and England; and one from Detroit. A Polish priest was in the diocese for a few months at Avon.

These statistics are of importance in understanding the Bishop's solution of the problems of language which existed in many parishes. There were many French-speaking Catholics in the western part of the diocese, along the lake shore, and around Louisville. German-speaking Catholics were to be found not only in the farming districts but also in the larger cities and towns, and in goodly numbers. At first the Bishop was of the opinion that, since everyone would have to speak the language of the country eventually, the sermons and instructions should be given in English. But as immigration increased it was brought home to him that, for a time at least, the Germans would have to have their own language as the medium of instruction. In the cities he gradually came to allow separate German parishes. This change of policy had its reflection in the method of recruiting the clergy.

The Bishop conceived the idea of adopting students from those parts of France (Alsace-Lorraine) where both German and French were spoken; coming here, they would naturally learn English and he would then have priests who spoke three languages. He believed that students born in this country, especially those of Irish ancestry, were not interested in learning German and for that reason he seemed to prefer European-born candidates in the seminary. It would seem to have been in accordance with this policy that Doctor Stremler was brought here from Laval University in Canada to head that institution in 1866. A good proportion of the native-born students, principally those of Irish descent, were released. This procedure, attested by all the documents available, served to trouble the feelings of the English-speaking priests (Irish and others as well), who advocated the formation of a native clergy as soon as possible.

Bishop Rappe denied any racial discrimination and insisted that his only guide in accepting students was the advantage of religion, and that it was only because of the needs of the diocese that he found it necessary to restrict the number of his (Irish) candidates. At the synod of 1868 an assessment of sixty cents per family was imposed for the support of the seminary. The Bishop felt called upon to explain the reason for the great preponderance of students of German origin over other nationalities in that institution, by the necessity of caring for the German-speaking Catholics, especially in the rural districts in which the pastor would have to be conversant with their language. The Bishop enforced this statute with appropriate sanctions.[3]

The instructions given in the seminary in the early days were necessarily practical and summary and adapted to the requirements of a pioneer age. As noted above, many of the students, however, had had a complete seminary course before they came here. The Bishop had great admiration for the discipline of the Seminary of St. Sulpice in France where Father De Goesbriand had studied and it was this spirit he strove to inspire in his first students. Father Caron, a seasoned veteran of the mission in France, worked to form the students in the same fashion. The Bishop himself drew up and gave authority to the rules of the local institution.[4]

In addition to the fundamental subjects of philosophy and theology, the study of languages was strictly imposed. In the beginning the ancient languages and other college subjects were taught in the seminary proper but in the autumn of 1854 a preparatory school was inaugurated with the opening of St. John's College, at Fulton Road and Carroll Avenue. Father Philip Flum, a native of Baden in Germany, was brought from Massillon to head it and a few of the older clerical

---

[3] Rappe to Purcell, Feb. 6, July 12, 1848, Aug. 14, 1850, Sept. 7, 1854, Jan. 9, 1862, Sept. 8, 1866, Oct. 2, 1869; Lamy (France), to Purcell, Aug. 27, 1848, all in N.D.A. Rappe to Spalding, in Baltimore Archdiocesan Archives. Warranty Deed to Trustees of St. John College, Jan. 11, 1855; Ankly to Houck, Sept. 3, 1887; Roupp to Houck, July 29, 1903; Bauer correspondence with Houck, all in C.D.A., *Annals of Cleveland,* 1855, p. 498. Cleveland *Daily Herald,* Oct. 18, 1848.

[4] Register of students and rule book, St. Mary's Seminary, Cleveland.

students, among them Seraphin Bauer, were the teachers. The principal instructions were in English and "then in German." The students who so desired were given the opportunity to study Latin. The venture failed, however, and the college was closed in 1856. Three years later the Brothers of Mary, from the nearby St. Patrick's school, made an attempt to use the building as a boarding and day school but they, also, found it to be impractical.

Destined to have more success was St. Mary's College which was operated on the grounds of the major seminary for the ten years following 1856. The Bishop had a large frame building, the former residence of a Doctor Miles on Euclid Avenue, moved to Lakeside Avenue and fitted up as a preparatory school. Sometimes it had its separate rector, as was the case under Father Anthony Martin; the older students of the major seminary acted as instructors. In 1859 there were twenty-eight students who were taught by three teachers. The combined student body of both schools, which met together in the chapel and dining room, sometimes numbered up to seventy.

In the meantime Father Louis Hoffer, a native of Lorraine, France, who had been teaching in the major seminary, was appointed pastor at Louisville where many of the French had settled at an early date. Here at the instance of the Bishop he built a substantial brick building with funds he had gathered in France and borrowed from his parishioners. It was called the College of St. Louis when it was opened in 1864. To insure for it a sufficiently large attendance, the twenty students of St. Mary's College were transferred to it two years later. Father Julius Clement, a French priest adopted by Bishop Rappe, was appointed rector; Father Bernard Quinn and three theological students who were too young for ordination went along with him as teachers.

In the next year the Basilian Fathers from Toronto in Canada took charge. Father Francis Hours, the president, was assisted at different times by Fathers Michael Mulcahey, Leo Cherrier, Joseph J. Aboulin, Michael Ferguson, and Francis Walsh, who was ordained by Bishop Rappe in the chapel at Louisville in 1867. There were twenty-eight students in 1869 and forty in 1872. Its out-of-the-way location, poor facilities, and the disappointment in the number of students were reasons given for closing the college in 1873. The Basilian teachers during their time at Louisville were of great help to the pastors in that section of the diocese.

17

LEGISLATION AND OTHER
INTERESTS OF BISHOP RAPPE

I N AN OFFICIAL REPORT TO THE HOLY SEE BISHOP
Rappe was able to say that in the first fifteen years of his tenure
he had made a more or less official annual visitation to every
parish. The knowledge derived in this way served him to good
purpose in establishing rules and regulations for the proper conduct of church affairs. These as well as the decrees of provincial and
national councils he published in the diocesan synods, which he held
usually after the spiritual retreat of the clergy. He presided over at
least six such synods in 1848, 1852, 1854, 1857, 1863, and 1868, and over
many other informal meetings of the clergy. After publishing the
fundamental statutes of the new diocese in the first synod, the Bishop
attended the Seventh Provincial Council of Baltimore in 1849 and made
the usual profession of faith required of a new prelate; he signed the
decrees which among other things petitioned the Holy See for the
definition of the dogma of the Immaculate Conception of the Blessed
Mother.

At the First Plenary Council of Baltimore in 1852, which asked
Rome to establish the metropolitan See of Cincinnati, Bishop Rappe
was accompanied by Fathers Caron and De Goesbriand. The decrees
of this council were formally published in the diocesan synod of the
same year. These regulations were principally concerned with the
gradual setting up of the machinery of ecclesiastical government in
our missionary country. One of them had to do with the method of
holding and protecting church property. Rules were established for
the election and conduct of the church committee[1] which with the
pastor had charge of the material side of parish affairs, and the obligation was imposed of making an annual report to the bishop. The
Cleveland diocese, owing to the prudence of Bishop Rappe, and of
Archbishop Purcell preceding him, was spared the troubles of Trustee-

---

[1] A lay committee, under the presidency of the pastor, had charge of the revenues
and made the report to the bishop. The members were chosen from a list of names
approved by the pastor and after their election were approved by the bishop. Rappe
to Purcell, Feb. 27, June 22, 1849, Feb. 29, 1856, in N.D.A. Cleveland *Daily True
Democrat*, May 10, 1852. Cleveland *Leader*, June 25, 1855.

ism, a system in which laymen were trustees of church property and had the opportunity of so abusing the confidence which had been placed in them as to defy ecclesiastical authority. The few instances of such violation of trust here were soon adjusted without much ado. The Baltimore Council in the powerful appeal made for parochial schools strengthened the plea of the Bishop to the local clergy in favor of them.

Instead of holding a synod in 1853, the Bishop issued a Lenten pastoral which prescribed the organization of the Society for the Propagation of the Faith. The next year's synod (1854) was occupied with a few local problems. At the First Provincial Council of Cincinnati (1855) Bishop Rappe, who was attended by Father Luers, took part in the sessions at which the province was dedicated to the Immaculate Conception of the Blessed Virgin. He also composed the customary letter of the bishops to the Lyons Society of the Propagation of the Faith to thank that organization for its benefactions. In his pastoral of the next year (1856), which Bishop Rappe published after his visitation to the diocese, he expressed his great joy at the progress of religion, manifested as it was in the increasing number of schools and religious institutions, and which he attributed to the great zeal of the faithful and clergy.[2]

At the local synod of 1857 the decrees of the previous Council of Cincinnati and those of all the preceding Councils of Baltimore (approved by the Holy See) were declared to be of binding force in this diocese. On this occasion, also, a plan[3] was devised by the Bishop to raise funds for the relief of infirm and disabled priests "to give them some measure of security and confidence should sickness or other disability overtake them in the performance of their duties." Father John Quinn of Toledo is mentioned in the records as treasurer, eleven years later.

To the Second Provincial Council of Cincinnati in 1858 the Bishop brought along Father James Conlan as his adviser. The pastoral letter which issued from this gathering of the bishops and was published in each diocese of the province called upon all to celebrate the Jubilee proclaimed by Pope Pius IX. It was appropriately observed in all the parishes of this diocese by the general reception of the sacraments. In this letter the people were again reminded of their obligation of seeing to the proper religious instruction of their children and of seconding to the best of their abilities the efforts of the pastors to set up schools and other Catholic institutions. A special plea was made for the encouragement of Catholic books and periodicals.

Fathers John F. Salaun and James Conlan accompanied the Bishop to the Third Provincial Council of Cincinnati in 1861. The assembled

---

[2] Cincinnati *Telegraph*, Feb. 2, 1856.

[3] Rappe to Purcell, July 7, 1857, Nov. 2, 1865, in N.D.A. Booklet, *Rules and Regulations of the Benevolent Society Established in the Diocese of Cleveland for the Support of Infirm and Disabled Priests,* Cleveland, 1866; the constitution was issued by Bp. Rappe, Dec. 18, 1865, C.D.A.

bishops expressed their deep sympathy with the Holy Father in the vexations he was made to suffer by the revolutionaries in Italy. The Fathers at the council also amicably settled a dispute about the line of division between the parishes of St. Francis de Sales and St. Mary in Toledo which had been referred to them. Another problem about which Bishop Rappe was concerned had to do with the method of supporting the churches in the larger towns, where the population was not as stable as in the country districts.

For the usual custom of quarterly pew rent the Bishop had substituted the practice of collecting a small seat fee at the entrance to the church on Sundays before the High Mass. Provision was made that no one would be excluded who could not pay the fee. It was hoped that, with the constant coming and going of transients, everyone in this way would have the opportunity of contributing his proper share for the support of the church buildings. The system was not liked by some, who denounced it. The council listened to the Bishop's explanation of the situation and seemed inclined to allow it in the circumstances but would restrict the practice to the "maritime cities" of Cleveland, Sandusky, and Toledo. The Congregation of the Propaganda in Rome, however, forbade it, and it was only after Bishop Rappe explained the case to the Holy Father himself that it was permitted for a time on account of the great financial needs.

The pastoral letter of this council, while glorying in the splendid progress of religion, showed anxiety about the dangers confronting the country in the impending Civil War which threatened to divide the citizens. The bishops appealed to the Catholic people to pray and to do penance that God might spare them the catastrophe. Acrimonious discussions had split the Protestant Churches on the issues involved. Catholics of all classes and grades were urged to be faithful in the discharge of the duties of their respective state in life and to keep as much as possible unity of spirit in the bond of peace. No one could doubt the attitude of the Catholic Church towards the institution of human slavery, which had been abolished long before in Catholic countries.

At the end of the war between the States, in 1866, Bishop Rappe with Fathers Caron and Conlan attended the Second Plenary Council of Baltimore, which was called together to devise ways and means to insure uniform ecclesiastical discipline throughout the reunited country. Its decrees as well as those of the Third Provincial Council of Cincinnati were formally promulgated at the diocesan synod of 1868.[4]

Bishop Rappe was well aware that legislation alone was not enough to produce the good envisioned in it. He made every effort to bring home to priests and people the importance of spontaneously making the truths of religion an intimate part of their daily lives in prayer,

[4] Cardinal Franzoni to Purcell, Dec. 4, 1858; Feb. 19, 1859; Jan. 27, Oct. 10, 1862, all in Cincinnati Archdiocesan Archives. Propaganda to Rappe, Dec. 4, 1858; Jan. 27, Oct 10, 1862 in N.D.A. Fr. F. X. Weninger, S.J., to Bp. Gilmour, undated, C.D.A. *Acta et Decreta 4 Conc. Prov. Cincinnati, 1855–1882.*

good living, and the practice of good works. He made much of the simple virtues of family life. He knew that even for those who were totally devoted to the salvation of souls it was necessary at times to withdraw from the busy world to meditate on the exigencies of their own salvation. As pastor of Toledo in 1843 he had directed a five-day spiritual retreat in his own home for the priests in his area. He had urged Father McLaughlin of Cleveland to take up such work. When he became bishop one of his favorite duties was to preside at the annual clergy retreats which were held at the seminary on Lakeside Avenue. His last official direction to the priests before his retirement was to summon them for the retreat of August, 1869.

He also encouraged missions and retreats for the laity as a powerful means of reviving their fervor and bringing them to the sacraments; the publication of the papal jubilee was a joy to him. He gave many missions himself and urged the pastors to exchange pulpits for that purpose. The famous German Jesuit, Father Francis X. Weninger, was invited by him to visit the diocese in the Lent of 1851. The well-known missioner worked with great fruit in the German communities and brought many back to the Church. At Sandusky, where he heard confessions during the whole night, the German atheistic societies attempted but in vain to interfere with the evangelization of his countrymen. From the Bishop's own letters it seems to have been his ambition to found a community of priests who would give missions throughout the year in the parishes and would in addition have the spiritual direction of the religious communities and the seminarists.

Bishop Rappe from his early days as a priest in the diocese was a staunch advocate of the Total Abstinence movement which he, like many others, considered to be the most effective cure for the habit of overindulgence in the use of alcoholic liquors. He had witnessed the terrible consequences of the abuse in his missionary days in western Ohio where, in following the lead of Bishop Purcell, the Total Abstinence pledge had been the instrument in his hands for the rehabilitation of many unfortunates. He became convinced that the progress of religion in many instances depended upon that remedy. The evils, of course were not confined to members of his flock. A similar movement was strongly favored by the non-Conformist religious bodies; some temperance societies had no connection with religious groups; some denominations forbade the use of intoxicants to all its members. Apparently, at times, the churches were quite indifferent if not hostile to the movement; some refused the use of their buildings for "temperance" meetings. The attitude in Cleveland, however, seemed favorable. In 1850 a "reformed drunkard" drew a large public audience to listen to his story.[5]

Bishop Rappe, of course, could not condemn the use of alcohol as an evil in itself; but for some he thought total abstinence to be their only salvation. He appealed to others to deny themselves for the sake

[5] *History of the State of Ohio,* as cited, III, 163.

of good example and to encourage the weak. In his zeal for the cause in Toledo he composed songs and ballads in denunciation of intoxicants, which were sung at the "temperance rallies" which he called together to listen to debates between the devil's advocate on the one side and the advocate of total abstinence on the other. Once established in Cleveland, the Bishop continued this endeavor and gave new life to the Catholic Total Abstinence Society which had already been started. The local newspapers commented favorably on this phase of the Bishop's activity: "The past efforts of the cold water laborers in laying the foundation of strict sobriety are as nothing in comparison with the six months' work of this stranger bishop."[6] Of course notice was also given of the efforts of non-Catholic ministers, "in turning thousands from their cups."

The high point in enthusiasm for total abstinence was reached when Theobald Matthew,[7] the Irish Capuchin, who was touring America in the interest of the movement, came to this city August 1, 1851, at the Bishop's urgent invitation. Two days later an estimated 2,000 persons, many of them not Catholics, assembled in the unfinished Cathedral to hear him. Bishop Rappe sang the High Mass. The frail Capuchin, introduced by the Bishop as the "joy of Israel and the honor of our people" and disclaiming any personal merit in the success of his work, urged the taking of the Total Abstinence pledge not only as a remedy but also as a protection. In his own peculiarly impressive manner he invited all to come forward. The example of the Bishop and of the clergy kneeling was followed by large groups of the people, who knelt or stood as they repeated the words of the promise with the zealous reformer, who afterwards greeted each individual with his cheery "God bless you."

On the next Sunday, also, the Bishop pontificated and Father Matthew preached from a temporary pulpit in the sanctuary. The Mayor and City Council and many others took the pledge on this occasion. On his way back to the Bishop's house Father Matthew was stopped by some who knelt in the street to take the pledge. Others visited him at the house itself. It was estimated that about 5,000 people were affected, many of whom for years afterwards treasured the certificate and medal he gave them as a constant reminder of their promise.

The organization of the "T-totalers" as they were called had other beneficial social effects. Their corporate appearance in the public parades in the city soon became familiar to the citizens. Father Matthew's visit gave new life and vigor to the "temperance society" which the Bishop had previously organized. In the set of rules he drew up for it the pledge was considered to be a solemn promise

[6] De Goesbriand to Purcell, Mar. 19, 1847, in N.D.A. Cleveland *Daily True Democrat*, Apr. 8, 15, 1848. Cleveland *Daily Herald*, Mar. 16, 1848.

[7] He arrived in America in 1849; he was an outspoken protagonist of the Church's attitude against human slavery. Cleveland *Plain Dealer*, July 7, Aug. 4, 8, Nov. 11, 1851. Cleveland *Herald*, Mar. 2, 1843; June 19, Aug. 2, 4, 6, 9, 12, 1851. *C.U.*, Jan. 21, Mar. 28, Apr. 18, 1889; Jan. 22, 1915.

*Left:*St. Paul Church, Euclid.

*Right:*St. Mary Church, Berea.

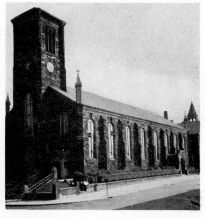

*Above Left:*Early St. John Cathedral and Cathedral School.

*Above Right:*St. Vincent Church, Akron.

*Left:*St. John Cathedral before reconstruction.

*Above:*Ursuline Convent and Academy, Euclid Avenue (1852).

*Right:*Old St. Vincent Orphanage.

*Left:*Old St. Joseph Hospital and first convent of the Sisters of Charity of St. Augustine.

Old St. Mary Seminary, Lakeside Avenue.   First St. Vincent Charity Hospital.

and not a vow made to God. The members met once a month for mutual encouragement and they approached the sacraments every three months. Roman approval of the society was granted, December 31, 1860, according to the formula of approval given to similar groups in Canada. The auditorium on the third floor of the Cathedral school building came to be known as Father Matthew Hall and in the course of time Temperance Halls used for all social gatherings were part of the equipment of many parishes. Father Matthew himself after a triumphal march through the United States, during which he gave the pledge to an estimated 500,000 persons, returned to Ireland a few months after his Cleveland visit.

It is to be understood that many even of the Catholic community did not favor total abstinence either on principle or for interested motives. Bishop Rappe, however, from what he saw, was so persuaded that the use of strong drink was almost equivalent to its abuse that in no uncertain terms he condemned, as did many others, everything connected with the liquor traffic. In a pastoral which was ordered read in all the churches he traced the ruin of virtue and the miseries of families to the frequentation of the "drinking shop, the sink wherein all that is good is buried."

"Groceries" which combined trade in food and intoxicants drew the special ire of the prelate because of the proximate occasion offered to patrons. As did many of the pastors, he appealed to Catholics in that business to give up their trade in liquor and counseled the people to refuse their patronage. "Frequenters of the groceries and the sellers of the vile poison would remain as it were under a kind of excommunication." Pastors were required to use every effort and influence to "put down these houses of scandal and ruin." He did not hesitate to offer suggestions to the proper civil authorities for the regulation and control of the "tavern grocery stores" especially on Sundays and holidays. It is on record that many men at great financial loss did give up their business in intoxicants at his and their pastor's suggestion. The Bishop became well known over the State for his indefatigable crusade against intemperance and for his uncompromising hostility to the means by which it was perpetuated in the community.[8]

[8] Cincinnati *Telegraph*, Apr. 5, 1851. Bp. Rappe to Arbp. Eccleston, Apr. 4, 1849, in Baltimore Archdiocesan Archives.

18

RESIGNATION AND LAST YEARS
OF BISHOP RAPPE

WHEN, TWO YEARS AFTER HIS CONSECRA-
tion, Bishop Rappe returned to Europe seeking
help and assistance for his diocese, it was his first
opportunity to personally thank the Holy Father
for the favor of his appointment and to pray at the
tomb of the Apostles. The particles of the True Cross and the relics
of the martyrs he asked for were later sent to him through the courtesy
of Bishop Timon of Buffalo. He was also advised that the Church in
America had its own calendar of feasts and need not borrow from that
of France. When he left Rome his chief preoccupation was with the
building of his Cathedral. He begged money from his friends and selected the altar, the statues, and other furnishings. Much of his time
was spent interviewing seminarians and young priests and persuading
them to volunteer for the American missions. During this time, too, as
we have seen, he arranged for the coming of the religious who were to
teach in the schools and work in the orphanages and hospital. He was
back with his flock in August of 1850.

He was again in Rome in July, 1860, with his decennial report,
printed in French. In it he told of fifteen students in the major and
twenty-five in the minor seminary; he praised the religious communities of men and women who were helping him and the clergy in their
work for the salvation of souls; he described the hundred churches
and chapels and the sixty schools and the thousands of pupils. He
lodged at the North American College, which had been opened a few
years before, and was impressed with its promise for the future. It was
on this visit that he presented to Pope Pius IX the petition of Bishop
O'Connor of Pittsburgh that the Church of St. James in Lawrence
County, Pennsylvania, with its adjacent territory be put under the
jurisdiction of the Bishop of Cleveland. Bishop O'Connor resigned his
see that year and nothing came of the petition.[1]

When Bishop Rappe was in Rome for the third time, in 1862, it
was at the personal invitation of the Holy Father to the American

---

[1] Propaganda (Rome) to Arbp. Kendrick, July 31, 1860, in Baltimore Archdiocesan Archives.

bishops to assist at the canonization of the Japanese Martyrs; he was officially granted honorary Roman citizenship. On his return to Cleveland he was solemnly escorted to his residence by the members of Father Matthew's Temperance Society and its band. Five years later he made his fourth visit to the Eternal City for the celebration of the 1800th anniversary of the martyrdom of St. Peter the Apostle. He also visited his native land and enlisted several advanced students for the seminary.

The call of Pope Pius to the Vatican Council brought Bishop Rappe to Rome for his fifth and last visit. With his old friend, Bishop De Goesbriand, he set out in October of 1869. They found the city thronged with dignitaries gathered from all over the world for the most numerously attended general council in the history of the Church. The learned discussions interested him very much. An "inopportunist" when he left America, nevertheless he was not long in Rome before he became a warm supporter of the definition of Papal Infallibility. He signed the petition for the closure of the general debates which were delaying the work of the council. He voted affirmatively both in the general congregation of July 13, 1870, and in the last solemn session in the presence of the Holy Father, five days later, when the dogma of Papal Infallibility was formally proclaimed.

Staying once more at the North American College, he found some diversion walking in the delightful villa placed at the disposal of the American bishops. But he suffered from a fever which was not allayed by the hot weather nor by the trouble he had with one of his eyes, the sight of which he eventually lost.[2] And he was much preoccupied with pressing matters.

As a pioneer bishop he had had many difficulties in clearing and planting the new vineyard of the Lord. The great immigration especially of German Catholics was one of his earliest problems, involving as it did the question of languages and getting priests who were conversant with them. His endeavors to meet the situation led to recriminations and it was said that he favored now the Irish, now the Germans, now the French. In the enforcement of the diocesan statutes the Bishop had had sometimes to use severe measures. The Church in the United States at this time was regulated by the rules for missionary countries and was under the immediate direction of the Sacred Congregation de Propaganda Fide. It was only after the Third Council of Baltimore in 1884 that to some extent the regular canon law of the Church was introduced. Parishes in the strictly canonical sense did not yet exist in the western dioceses and the tenure of the pastors was entirely and without formality at the discretion of the bishop. Bishop Rappe's administration in this regard had adversely affected a few of the pastors who referred the matter to the Congregation of the Propaganda.

[2] Rappe to Purcell, May 2, 1862, in N.D.A. Cleveland *Leader*, July 30, 1862. Fr. Anthony Martin's *Memoirs, St. Paul's Parish, Euclid, Ohio.* Mansi, *Sacra Concilia* (1927), LII, cols. 443, 1247, 1340. Quigley (Rome) to Hannin, Feb. 27, 1870, in C.D.A.

Bishop Rappe now, in Rome, was confronted with the necessity of making a great decision and a great sacrifice. Fatigued by his enormous labors in founding the diocese and fearful of his ability, in his declining age and infirmity, to cope further with the multiplying problems of that great diocese, he placed his resignation in the hands of the Holy See. Immediately after the proclamation of Papal Infallibility, and still suffering from the fever, he took ship with Archbishop Purcell for the United States. A committee went to Buffalo to greet him but missed him; he arrived in this city early in the morning of August 12. In the evening of the same day a great demonstration of Catholic societies conducted him from his house on East 6th Street to the Cathedral where a solemn Te Deum was sung for his safe return.

At St. Mary's Convent on East 20th Street he gave the final conferences in the spiritual retreat begun by a Jesuit Father and after the close he spent the morning talking about his early life as a missionary in the diocese and seemed to be as cheerful as ever. A few days later he was officially notified that the Holy Father had accepted and ratified his resignation and that Archbishop Purcell had appointed Father Edward Hannin, pastor of St. Patrick's in Toledo, the Apostolic Administrator in his place. Bishop Rappe thereupon, on August 25, retired to the hospital of the Grey Nuns in Toledo. Shortly after that date he paid his last visit to Cleveland, staying at St. Joseph's Orphanage on Woodland Avenue. Then accompanied by Father Stremler, the former rector of the seminary, he proceeded to the home of his former vicar general, Bishop De Goesbriand, in Burlington, Vermont; he never returned during his lifetime.[3]

Father Hannin, who had accepted his new responsibility with some misgivings on account of the distracted condition of affairs, arrived in Cleveland on August 27, 1870. Under the guidance of Archbishop Purcell he carried on the administration for nearly two years until the installation of Bishop Gilmour. He replaced the French priests who were pastors of Holy Name and the Immaculate Conception parishes.

Despite the appeal of Bishop Rappe himself and much to the chagrin and annoyance of the faithful, certain supposed partisans of his carried on a public discussion of the Bishop's resignation in the newspapers. The editor of the *Leader*, pretending to a neutrality which he did not possess, printed these letters and gave his own comment with such criticism of the Church as came to his mind. Father Hannin, by appealing for fair play and respect for the long services of the venerable Bishop, brought an end to the tiresome and factitious controversy. Another embarrassment for the Administrator was the attempt on the part of the pastor of St. Bridget's Church and his supporters to proceed with the construction of a new church building, which he had forbidden and which he considered to be more costly

[3] Bp. Rappe's first resignation "for the good of the diocese" was made in Rome shortly before July 29, 1870, the date of the letter from the Propaganda notifying Arbp. Purcell of the fact and telling him to appoint an administrator; the second definitive resignation was made in June, 1871, in Cincinnati Archdiocesan Archives.

than they could afford. He secured an injunction in the civil court which delayed further construction. Judge Paine who heard the case took occasion to refer in an irrelevant manner to Papal Infallibility. The case was settled when Father Bernard Kelly was appointed to replace the pastor, Father Monahan.[4]

The momentum of Bishop Rappe's work carried over during the administration of Father Hannin. Approximately ten new church buildings were erected and ten new parishes were started. It was during this time that Bishop John H. Luers of Fort Wayne, called in by the Administrator to ordain the students who had finished their studies, was struck down by apoplexy on his way to the railroad station, June 29, 1871. He was carried to the bishop's house nearby but expired in a few minutes. A delegation of the Cleveland clergy attended his funeral. An instance that gave public proof of Catholic unity during Father Hannin's administration was a great demonstration against the harsh treatment of Pope Pius IX at the hands of the Italian Government. A mile-long procession of some 1,800 persons marched to the Cathedral where appropriate ceremonies were held.[5]

Under the patronage of Bishop De Goesbriand the seventy-year-old Bishop Rappe took up the rough missionary life he had always loved. In Cleveland work and worry, the continual round of religious exercises and administrative duties, had absorbed all his time so that he had hardly any left, as he put it himself, in which to smoke a cigar. Outside the city he was the simple missionary. He took his place in the confessional like an ordinary priest. On one occasion the confessional was his resting-place for the night. This was on the episcopal visitation of 1868 when he arrived at Archbold, at the far western end of the diocese, at a very late hour. The pastor had given up hope of his coming that evening and returned home. No one was there at the station to meet him. Undaunted, the Bishop carried his heavy valise the two miles to the chapel and found shelter there.

When he left this diocese he carried with him the same devoted zeal of the pioneer missionary and now exercised it among the French-Canadian Catholics of Vermont. Bishop De Goesbriand, who had in 1869 issued a stirring appeal to Canada for help in tending his scattered flock, was very glad to have his services. The home of Father Zephyrin Druon,[6] vicar general and pastor of St. Albans, Vermont, who had

---

[4] Contemporaneous newspaper accounts; Hannin correspondence with Purcell, in N.D.A. Bp. Rappe to Arbp. Spalding and other communications from Cleveland to the archbishop in Baltimore Archdiocesan Archives. *Catholic Knight*, July 9, 1887.

[5] Cleveland *Leader*, Jan. 6, 7, 1871.

[6] Fr. Druon, born in 1830 near Bp. Rappe's home in France, was for a while in St. Mary's Seminary, Cleveland, but was ordained in 1853 in France after finishing his studies at St. Sulpice in Paris; he was at the Cathedral here for a few months before he affiliated with the new Diocese of Burlington in 1854; very active in the Franco-American movement, he helped to found the French newspaper, *Le Protecteur Canadien*. Cf. Mason Wade, "The French Parish and Survivance in Nineteenth-Century New England," in *Catholic Historical Review*, July, 1950; Gavin F. Moloney's pamphlet, *St. Rose of Lima, South Hero, Vt.*, Burlington, 1946.

served under him for a few months at the Cathedral in Cleveland, was assigned as his headquarters. He organized many Total Abstinence societies in Vermont and in Canada and was president of the one in St. Albans. At the close of a mission he gave in Montreal he administered the pledge to 3,000 men and 2,000 women and in other places to other thousands.

He built and helped to build several chapels; in each of them he used the sacristy for a class room and a tiny room above for his own quarters. This was the case at Alburg, Enosburg, and Isle LaMotte. In Swanton and St. Johnsburg he helped to build convents for the teaching Sisters. He encouraged the people to buy their own farms. Living the simple life of his neighbors, he often shared the fat pork and potatoes of his parishioners, among whom he was held in great admiration and respect.

It was while he was preaching a mission at Grand Isle in Lake Champlain that an old ailment (hernia) became seriously aggravated. He had to be transported to St. Albans where he was found to be somewhat incoherent in speech. Bishop De Goesbriand heard his confession. The attending physician thought he might recover even though he continued to be very restless and said that he wanted to return to the mission. He fell into a coma the next day and received the Last Sacraments at the hands of Father Druon, who quoted his last words: "I have prayed for my friends, I have prayed for my enemies, may God bless them all." He died peaceably in the Lord at nearly midnight, September 8, 1877.

The Bishop of Montreal, in whose Cathedral the dead prelate had preached a mission not long before, presided at the funeral service in St. Albans. Representatives of the clergy and people of Cleveland escorted the body here. A great crowd turned out to meet them at the Union Depot in the evening of September 13. The Catholic societies formed the funeral cortege; the orphan children followed close behind the hearse, which was drawn by six white horses. Flags at the City Hall and the Court House were flown at half-mast. The next day Bishop Dwenger of Fort Wayne celebrated the funeral Mass; Bishop Ryan of Buffalo preached the panegyric. The remains of the first Bishop of Cleveland were laid in a vault beneath the Cathedral he had built and in which he had officiated for so many years.

The local newspapers expressed the universal feeling of the city and the diocese in terms of high praise and appreciation; they recalled the "courteous, cultivated gentleman whose friends were to be found amongst people of all classes and religions." Bishop Gilmour, who could not be reached in time for the funeral, had given orders that his predecessor was to be buried here. At the Month's Mind Mass which he celebrated he gave a sympathetic description of the self-sacrificing and devoted prelate: "Seeking his people far and wide, preaching incessantly to them from the pulpit, patiently awaiting them in the confessional, consoling and exhorting the dying, guiding and protecting youth, the indefatigable Bishop knew no self but God. He came as a missionary and he persevered in that vocation."

Bishop Gilmour dwelt on the fact that it was not brilliant talent nor advantage of birth which distinguished him but his total devotion to the work of religion. Bishop McQuaid of Rochester could say of him at a later date that "his heart was as simple as his labors were complex and arduous." All agreed in admiration of the Bishop, who was so kind and approachable despite his erect, alert, and soldierly air. He was respected by those with whom he came in contact for his tolerance, affability, and good-will. His business ability was recognized by business men. He built the Cathedral, the seminary, and the hospital with very little money at his disposal. His love for the poor and unfortunate, particularly the orphans, was well known. Despite his French accent, he was a good and ready speaker, gifted in instruction and especially eloquent in the cause of Total Abstinence.

The celebration of the Golden Jubilee of the diocese in 1897 was devoted in great part to the memory of its first Bishop and his accomplishments. Bishop Gilmour through popular subscription had a marble bust and later a bronze statue made of his predecessor. The bust is preserved in the library of St. Mary's Seminary. The bronze, designed and cast in Rome by Varney Serrao, a Cleveland artist, stood at the corner of Superior Avenue and East 9th Street for many years until, to make way for the new Cathedral, it was moved to a place of eminence just north of the entrance.

It is evident from a perusal of the records (the correspondence of Bishop De Goesbriand with the Propaganda) that the Holy See, which had seen to his support after the resignation, was well pleased with his work on the missions in Vermont. There is evidence for the belief that the Holy Father was willing to bestow an honorary titular see upon him were the Bishop to so petition. Monsignor Roncetti, in the United States as the Ablegate of the Pope to bring the red biretta to Cardinal McCloskey in 1875, visited Bishop De Goesbriand in Burlington but he did not see Bishop Rappe, who was away on the mission. According to Bishop De Goesbriand's letter to Bishop Horstmann in 1884, the Ablegate intimated that he had been authorized to offer a diocese to Bishop Rappe.[7] His age and infirmity, however, would certainly have prevented him from taking up active duty as head of a diocese at that time, and up to the end he signed his correspondence as the ex-Bishop of Cleveland.

God in His Providence had chosen Bishop Rappe to found the Diocese of Cleveland. With the assistance of a self-sacrificing clergy, with the cooperation of the devoted members of the religious communities, and with the generous support of a faithful and God-fearing people, he laid the foundations deep and well. Under his immediate direction the body of the clergy, 16 priests (including the Fathers of the Precious Blood) in 1847, had grown to 117 in 1870, including

[7] Houck, *Op. cit.*, II, 18 sq.

not only the 7 Sanguinists but also 3 Franciscans in Cleveland and 5
Jesuits in Toledo. There were in addition a few Basilian Fathers teaching at the college in Louisville and Brothers of Mary teaching in
Cleveland. The 33 churches and chapels of all descriptions had been
replaced by some 160 church buildings, many like the Cathedral of a
substantial nature. A major seminary was training new priests.

Ninety parishes had their own schools. To teach in them the Bishop
had brought the Ursulines, the Daughters of the Immaculate Heart of
Mary, and the Sisters of the Holy Humility from France. He had
approved the organization of the Franciscan Sisters at Tiffin. Other
communities began educational work in the diocese under his auspices.
At his invitation the Sisters of Charity came from France to care for
the sick in the first general hospital in the city and the Grey Nuns
from Montreal started a similar project in Toledo. He sponsored the
inauguration of four orphanages and the beginning of the work of
the Sisters of the Good Shepherd and of the Little Sisters of the Poor.

God has blessed the work and upon this firm basis has been built the
magnificent superstructure we know today. Bishop Rappe was the cornerstone and merits well of the Church in northern Ohio, just as he
well merited the high praise given to him in later years by Cardinal
Simeoni, the Prefect of the Congregation of the Propaganda, when he
referred to him as "that holy and apostolic man."[8]

[8] Simeoni to Gilmour, May 8, 1885, in C.D.A.

19

APPOINTMENT OF
BISHOP GILMOUR

O N AUGUST 28, 1871, CARDINAL BARNABO, THE Prefect of the Congregation of the Propaganda, notified Archbishop Purcell to have the bishops of the province present the names of three priests, one of whom the Holy See would choose as the second Bishop of Cleveland. Apparently Father Francis S. Chatard, of the American College in Rome and later Bishop of Indianapolis, Bishop Stephen Ryan of Buffalo, and Father Richard Gilmour, pastor of St. Joseph's Church in Dayton, Ohio, were proposed for the vacant see. On February 15, 1872, Father Gilmour was appointed to Cleveland at the same time that Father Joseph G. Dwenger, C.PP.S., was made Bishop of Fort Wayne. In a letter of February 27 the Archbishop notified him of the choice though the official documents did not arrive for another month. On April 14, 1872, in St. Peter's Cathedral in Cincinnati Archbishop Purcell consecrated the two new prelates. Bishop William George McCloskey of Louisville and Bishop John Quinlan of Mobile were the assistant consecrators for Bishop Gilmour.[1]

Richard Gilmour was born in Glasgow, Scotland, September 28, 1824, the son of John and Marian Callender Gilmour, both staunch Presbyterians. His mother was of a family of farmers, his father was an artisan. In 1829 they brought young Richard to Nova Scotia where he spent a happy childhood in and near New Glasgow in the Pictou Province. Afterwards he was able to map out in his memory, "every foot of land along the brook between New Glasgow and the old red bridge."

Later, together with a small group of other Scotch families, the Gilmours immigrated into the United States and settled in Schuylkill County, Pennsylvania, in the village of Cumbola, where Richard attended school. The mother of Bernard Quinn, a fellow pupil, taught him his first Catholic prayers. The two young friends walked the five miles to Pottsville to attend Sunday Mass. At a Father Matthew rally

---

[1] Card. Barnabo to Purcell, Aug. 26, 1871, Feb. 6, 28, 1872; Perche (New Orleans) to Purcell, Dec. 27, 1871; both in N.D.A. Purcell to Gilmour, Feb. 27, Mar. 28, 1872; original Bulls; all in C.D.A.

in that town they took the Total Abstinence pledge from Father James Maginn, the first priest to whom young Richard ever spoke. He studied what he could of the Church secretly and resolved not only to become a Catholic but also a priest. Divine Providence opened the way.

In Fairmount, a suburb of Philadelphia, Father Patrick Rafferty, a veteran missionary and pastor of St. Francis' Church, kept a few promising boys in his house to teach them the fundamental knowledge necessary for their acceptance in an ecclesiastical seminary. Through the Quinns, Richard was introduced to him and was received into this primitive preparatory seminary. On August 15, 1842, in "a little room downstairs in St. Francis'," Father Rafferty baptized young Gilmour and a fellow student, Henry L. Wright, who also became a priest. The mother of Richard witnessed the ceremony. She and her husband were both received into the Church later on by Father Daniel Magorien, the pastor at Port Carbon, Pennsylvania, whose funeral sermon Bishop Gilmour preached a few years before his own demise. Other relatives in Ontario, Canada, seem to have been born Catholics.[2]

Father Rafferty was well known to the bishops in Pennsylvania. He had been ordained in Philadelphia in 1821 (or 1823); he did pioneer missionary work in and around Pittsburgh, Butler, Beaver, and York in Pennsylvania. With Brownsville as a center, he labored on the missions along the Beaver Canal, at McKeesport, and at Erie. He baptized the daughter of the Gillespie family who later became Mother Angela of the Sisters of the Holy Cross at Notre Dame, Indiana. Father Gilmour was, later on, a personal friend of the Gillespies and the Blaines at Brownsville.

On his way back from Rome the newly consecrated Bishop Michael O'Connor of Pittsburgh called at Father Rafferty's house. He adopted Richard Gilmour as his first ecclesiastical student in December, 1843, and in March of the next year the young student was attending classes in the short-lived St. Michael's Seminary in the Bishop's house at Smithfield and Virgin Alley, Pittsburgh. In November, 1844, the school was temporarily disbanded. Four of the students went to St. Xavier's College in Cincinnati, while young Gilmour and two others resumed their studies in the home of Father Hugh P. Gallagher, a

---

[2] Houck, *Op. cit.*, corrected a few details found in earlier editions. From Mrs. Elizabeth Farrington, the sister of his boyhood friend, Bernard Quinn, he learned that the Gilmour family never lived near Latrobe, Pennsylvania. They moved to Port Carbon after the ordination of their son, who with the help of Father Magorien, the pastor, later secured a place for them in Richmond, Indiana. When the father died, his mother after some time with Mrs. Farrington took up residence with Fr. Gilmour. Both parents were buried in St. Joseph's Cemetery, Cincinnati, Ohio. From Fr. Wright it was ascertained that young Gilmour's musical education began in Fr. Rafferty's house in Philadelphia. Farrington to Houck, Nov. 23, 1891; Wright to Houck, Nov. 20, 1891; Houck to Pfeil, Oct. 20, 1896; Gilmour to Elder, Apr. 12, 1885; to Fr. Jos. Hannon (Denny, Scotland), Sept. 27, 1889; to L. H. Lambert, Dec. 15, 1880; to Lambing, May 2, 1885; to N. J. Rosecrans, Oct. 5, 1884; to H. L. Wright, Aug. 15, 1889; all in C.D.A.

Bishop Richard Gilmour, second Bishop of Cleveland, 1872 to 1891.

Above, left to right:
Holy Name Church.
St. Joseph Franciscan Church.
St. Stephen Church.
St. Mary Church, Elyria.

Bishop Gilmour and group of professors and students at St. Mary Seminary, 1879.

Group of pioneer missionaries.

relative of one of the students, at Loretto, Pennsylvania.[3] Father
Gallagher and a Father A. Gibbs found time in the midst of their
missionary endeavors to instruct the collegians.

In September, 1846, Gilmour entered Mount St. Mary's College, at
Emmitsburg, Maryland. He earned his tuition as disciplinarian and
tutor and was a good student himself. A severe attack of pneumonia
forced him to return for a while to his old friend, Father Rafferty, who
coached him and helped him to learn French. Despite this interruption
he finished his studies at Mount St. Mary's in June, 1852. Meanwhile
he had been adopted by Archbishop Purcell of Cincinnati who ordained him a priest on August 30 of the same year. In the following
month he received his first appointment as "pastor of the Catholic
congregations in and around Portsmouth, Ironton, Wilkesville, Gallipolis, Aberdeen and at the furnaces in Lawrence and Scioto Counties."

At Portsmouth he built a church for the English-speaking portion
of the congregation and restored peace to a distracted community.
He "began religion" among the railroad workers at Ironton in a rough
shanty, enlarged with lumber salvaged from the river. A rude, unplaned
wooden cross proclaimed it as the first Catholic church in the town.
It was used as a school when a better church building was provided.
In addition to these places he had charge of all the missions from
Aberdeen on the Ohio River to Gallipolis, 150 miles up the river. He
served the Catholics in six Ohio counties and in one county in Kentucky and another in Virginia. In this same territory eventually many
parishes were started upon the foundations he laid. Horseback was his
usual method of transportation. He lived in shanties in the hills and
was often forced to seek hospitality of people very suspicious of a
Catholic priest. Once the small houseboat which sheltered him broke
loose from its moorings and carried him dangerously down the river.
He frequently risked his life in crossing the Sandy River in Kentucky.

In April, 1857, the traveling missionary was made pastor of St.
Patrick's in Cincinnati, succeeding Bishop Wood who went to Phila-
delphia. Here he built a model school in very trying circumstances.
He spent a scholastic year (1868–1869) as professor at St. Mary's
Seminary in the same city.

While he was in Cincinnati he translated from the French (itself a
version of a German original) and adapted for use in the schools what
became popularly known as Gilmour's *Illustrated Bible History*. It
was the only work of its kind in English for nearly sixty years, covering as it did both Testaments, and it is still a favorite. Published by
Benzinger Brothers in seven languages, it received the special commendation of Pope Leo XIII in 1880. Bishop Gilmour supervised the
new edition of that year and composed a condensation of the larger
book for the use of younger children. Before coming to Cleveland he

[3] Creedon, Lambert, Hay, and Gallagher went to St. Xavier's, Cincinnati; Rey-
nolds, McSweeney, and Gilmour to Loretto.

also edited a book of hymns called *School Recreation or Teachers' Companion.*

Encouraged by the immediate success of the *Bible History* he undertook in cooperation with Benzinger's to edit the *National Catholic Series of Readers* and he actually began the composition, and the selection of texts and illustrations, in Cincinnati. Various circumstances intervened to prevent the publication until after his consecration. The earliest school readers in the United States were calculated to teach not only reading and spelling but also to impart moral and religious instruction. Later series contained patriotic and moral reading selections with other various information, but omitted doctrinal implications almost entirely, intending to teach morality without insisting on any particular religious conviction. They sometimes misrepresented fundamental Catholic doctrine. Catholic readers appeared as an antidote for the use of Catholic pupils.

In the spring of 1874 he had his first manuscript ready. The many moral observations and the pictures and tone made the series distinctly Catholic. Five readers, a primer, and a spelling book were completed in 1877. A *Sixth Reader* was added four years later. The Bishop asserted that although others might have helped and counseled him, he himself was the only responsible author.

Several new editions were published and translations were made into other languages. At his suggestion a new series was issued in which the first five books were entirely replaced. For this work of revision he found time in the midst of his arduous duties, correcting the proofs and suggesting changes recommended by experienced teachers to whom he had submitted the manuscript. In June, 1889, a new *Primer* and a new *First Reader* came out under his name; in June of the next year the new *Second Reader* appeared; before his death, in 1891, he finished the final corrections on the *Third Reader*. He believed that the new school books ranked with "the best school literature." It was with his assistance that Benzinger brought out a small *History of the Church* in 1881. It is published even currently as an appendix in the *Bible History*. The Holy See took cognizance of his work and commended him for "his writing books of this character for the instruction of youth." The *Gilmour Readers* for more than forty years were the standard text in Catholic schools over the country.[4]

From Cincinnati Father Gilmour had been transferred to Dayton, where he was appointed pastor of the flourishing St. Joseph's parish. Here he built a school, and here it was that he received notice of his elevation to the episcopate in 1872.[5]

---

[4] Sr. M. Baptista McReynolds, *A Study of the Catholic National Series, The Gilmour Readers,* unpublished dissertation, St. John College, Cleveland, 1947; *C.U.,* Aug. 23, 1883; June 11, 1891. Voluminous correspondence with Benzinger's, in C.D.A.

[5] *C.U.,* May 5, 1881; Aug. 23, 1883. The young priest took out citizenship papers on Apr. 20, 1861 (C.D.A.).

Shortly after his consecration the new Bishop took possession of his Cathedral. His presence in Cleveland soon made itself felt. He was a man of commanding appearance five feet, ten inches in height, neither slender nor stout, erect with a slight inclination of the neck forward, with a high intellectual forehead, blue grey eyes, grey hair, compressed lips, oval face, and florid complexion.[6] He was eloquent in the pulpit and on the platform and his tongue had a "pleasant Scotch gilding" which gave his Angle-Saxon syllables a staccato emphasis and made him a pleasant and interesting speaker. He was described later as "a fearless member of the Church militant, a clear headed logician, a keen debater, a hard fighter and a courteous gentleman."[7]

[6] Passport, Aug. 11, 1875; Ireland (St. Paul) to Gilmour, Sept. 13, 1888; Walter Christie to Houck, May 8, 1886; all in C.D.A. *C.U.*, Apr. 15, 1886; June 9, 1887; Sept. 12, 1889.

[7] *C.U.*, quoting Cleveland *Plain Dealer*, Apr. 23, 1891.

20

THE BISHOP MEETS RELIGIOUS
ANTAGONISM

THE INDUSTRIAL REVOLUTION WHICH WAS
to bring unprecedented material prosperity and undreamed-
of increase in the population of Ohio began shortly before
the coming of Cleveland's second bishop. The glow of
the furnaces and rolling mills, the smoke of the factories,
the roar of the steam engines linking farm, village and city, the noisy
traffic on the newly paved streets, the bright clear light of the coal
oil lamps in the homes were all tokens of changing ways of life.[1]
The general character of the people remained what it was—the Germans, Catholic and Protestant, comprising nearly one-half of the foreign-born citizens of Ohio, Great Britain and Ireland sending the other
half, the majority of whom were Irish. The gigantic expansion of
industry attracted laborers and artisans, professional men, and youth
from the farms; but the new growth of the cities came principally
from new immigration.

The mighty industries of Cleveland and the area surrounding it absorbed a large proportion of the new arrivals. The capital of the Western Reserve was beginning to lose its peculiarly New England
character. The city population grew from nearly 93,000 in 1870 to
more than 160,000 in 1880 and to more than 263,000 in 1890. Bohemians
began to appear on this scene before 1870; they were the forerunners
of the Slavic and Near Eastern immigrants who were to find employment in the expanding industries. In 1870 there came to settle in this
city: 806 Germans, 393 Bohemians, 307 English, 268 Irish, 47 Hol-
landers, 81 Scots, and 2 Hungarians. It is estimated that in the same year
two out of every five persons in Cleveland were of foreign birth.

In the period between 1870 and 1895 there arrived here: 32,401 Germans, 16,844 Bohemians, 7,943 Irish, 7,000 Hungarians (including the
Slovaks), 6,457 English, 5,412 Poles, 2,452 Slovenes, and 1,528 Italians.
Most of the Poles, Irish, Hungarians, Slovaks, Slovenes, and Italians
and a good percentage of the Germans were Catholics. It was estimated in 1876 that nearly one-third of the people of Cleveland were

[1] *History of the State of Ohio*, as cited. Orth, *Op. cit.* Contemporaneous newspapers.

Catholics; later the number of Catholics in the city was proportionately greater.

The other large cities in the diocese experienced a comparable growth. Toledo, which with Cleveland had the largest proportion of foreign-born citizens in Ohio, increased its population from 31,584 to 81,434 in the twenty years after 1870. In the same period Akron's population increased from 10,000 to 27,601 and Youngstown's from 8,075 to 33,228. Canton had a population of 26,189 in 1890. The north-western counties were developed by the settlement of unoccupied lands. Although Sandusky doubled its population by fifty per cent during the Civil War period, it lacked the facilities and the desirable location for the industries and shipping which explained the growth of the other cities such as Cleveland and Youngstown, the leading centers in the production of iron. The great expansion continued up to the end of the century. Those who controlled the money became very wealthy but many others suffered in the periodical financial crises. In 1870 and in 1890 soup kitchens and relief stations and strikes were only too common.

It is difficult to estimate the number of Catholics in the whole diocese for the same period. According to the *Catholic Directory*, however, there were in round numbers: 100,000 in 1870; 125,000 in 1880; and 165,000 in 1883. Figures for the early part of the succeeding decade are not given for this diocese in the directories of the corresponding years.

Bishop Gilmour commented on the kindly welcome he received in Cleveland and throughout the diocese upon his first visitation. He was impressed with the great progress made in building churches, schools, and religious and charitable institutions. This he attributed under God to the common effort of Bishop Rappe, the clergy, and the generous laity. The local conditions which supposedly led up to the resignation of Bishop Rappe he felt had been very much exaggerated and he was determined from the beginning of his administration to "let the dead past bury its dead." He represented the priests and people as "earnest, zealous and self-sacrificing, hard workers, who needed rather to be restrained than to be encouraged." With such disposition in the clergy and faithful he had "great hopes of consolidating and building upon the foundation laid by his predecessor." That venerable prelate had sent his congratulations and the promise of his moral support and thanked God that "the diocese of his affection" had been entrusted to such worthy hands. Bishop Gilmour in answering him assured him that although he was far away no one would displace him in the hearts of the Catholics of Cleveland. "I fear," he continued, "that I do not have your power of building up, nor do I see how you created all you did."[2] The new Bishop was unconsciously underestimating his own abilities.

[2] Rappe (Rutland, Vt.) to Gilmour, May 6, 1872; Gilmour to Rappe, Apr. 30, 1873; Card. Barnabo (Propaganda) to Gilmour, Aug. 29, 1873; Gilmour to Bp. Quinlan, Nov. 1, 1873; Gilmour to Purcell, Oct. 19, 1872, all in C.D.A.

The rapidly growing diocese with its many nationalities needed an intrepid, fearless leader to keep them all in the unity of the Faith and to make them aware not only of their duties towards their adopted country but also of their rights under the Constitution. Bishop Gilmour, the new leader, proud of his Scotch Covenanter ancestry, said on one occasion, "I come of fighting stock; I was always a fighter," and he was prepared to do battle for those rights. After he had had time to study the local conditions he declared his position. In his first pastoral, February 26, 1873, he registered his solemn protest against the disparagement of Catholics and the disregard of their rights in a free country. The immediate occasion was an editorial in the Cleveland *Leader*, at the time when it was thought that the Holy Father would be forced out of Rome by the revolutionaries. The editor warned that Clevelanders should take measures to prevent the Pope from coming to this city and making of it another Rome.[3]

In his pastoral the Bishop reviewed the ordinary Catholic stand on the question of the relationship which should exist between the Church and civil government. Pointing to the persecution of the Church in Germany and Italy, he insisted on the rights of God and religion and conscience over which government had no control. The State, he repeated, existed for the benefit of the citizens, and not the citizens for the State. However, in everything not forbidden by God's law Catholics like all others owed unqualified obedience to the State. He denounced the abuse whereby rationalists and infidels use the authority of the State to impose an exclusively secular education on the children. He insisted that knowledge and secular education separated from morality and religion do not make virtuous citizens. He, thereupon, called upon the Catholic citizens here to forget petty national jealousies and to stand shoulder to shoulder in a bolder front in defense of their lawful rights. "Catholics," he wrote, "are too timid, thinking themselves well off when they are simply tolerated."

Returning to the school question, he gave it as his conviction that the ordinary honest American who believed in fair play, if he were made aware of the situation, would see the logic of the Catholic position; he would see the injustice of making Catholics suffer financially because of their conscientious scruples concerning the religious education of their children. It must not be forgotten that at that time the common schools were organized and managed in the interest of Protestantism. Taking the public schools for what they were, the Bishop told the parents that they could not send their children to them without endangering their faith. For that reason, if funds were insufficient for both, they must build a parochial school even before the church. Every parish was by the Bishop's express command ordered to establish and maintain such a school and all Catholic parents were in conscience bound to send their children to them, under penalty of denial of the

[3] Cleveland *Leader*, Feb. 15, 26, 1873; the pastoral itself was given in full.

sacraments except in cases where there existed a very serious reason to the contrary.

This first public statement of the Bishop gave considerable heart and encouragement to his flock but it was the occasion of lively controversy in the city. The editor of the *Leader* pretended to see in it an attempt on the sovereignty of the State, with but another step necessary for the introduction of the Inquisition. In a malicious vein he appealed to the Ohio constitutional convention then in session to make such laws as would restrict the bishop in the administration of the property of the Church.[4]

The perpetrator of such nonsense was Edward Cowles, one of the most influential men in the city's "boss politics." A bitter anti-slavery man, he was one of the earliest supporters of the Republican party. The charitable institutions of Bishop Rappe and his other public activities, as well as the part played by Catholics in the Civil War, had dissipated to some extent the prejudice against them. Nevertheless, after the war Cowles chose the Catholic Church as the particular target of his venomous pen. He supported the Order of the American Union, a secret society dedicated to the exclusion of Catholics from public office. Most of the Republican candidates here in 1877 belonged to this society and, if not actually chosen by Cowles, they were vigorously supported by him. He was still strong enough in 1883 to defeat Mark Hanna. This local situation reflected political conditions over the country. The Know Nothings formed part of the Republican party; they were in power and hoped to remain so. Catholics for the most part supported the Democratic party. However, this circumstance is only a partial explanation of the editor's bitter and uncompromising attack on Bishop Gilmour and what he represented.[5]

The Bishop was not slow in taking up the challenge. Alluding to his early training in the old fighting Scotch Presbyterian tradition, he asserted that he had a love for liberty as intense as that of the "intolerant Puritans" of Cleveland. Recalling the history of Catholic loyalty in the Civil War, he vindicated the rights of these same tax-paying citizens in time of peace. The same sentiments were expressed a few years later in more picturesque language: "Now that the war is over and they don't have to ask the bishops to intercede in Europe in favor of the North, and when Catholic soldiers and generals are no longer needed, the Know Nothing lodges are revived and lean cadaverous parsons begin to lecture, and sharp nosed Puritan tract peddlers are busy."[6]

Cowles at this time gave the appearance of fair play, allowing space in his newspaper to communications which defended the Bishop's position and even printing a long account of the Bishop's own defense of himself delivered in a sermon at the Cathedral. Much attention was

[4] Cleveland *Leader,* nearly every issue in March, 1873.
[5] Cowles as represented in *History of the State of Ohio* cited above.
[6] *C.U.,* June 5, 1875; Oct. 4, 1877.

also given to the letters and the account of the activities of the Unitarian minister, T. B. Forbush, who hired Case Hall for an anti-Catholic lecture. When the Cleveland *Herald* entered the list, the Bishop denounced its editor in very plain but vigorous language.[7]

The controversy in Cleveland had its echoes even in New York. *Harper's Weekly* carried a sordid cartoon by the well-known Thomas Nast who used his talents to vilify the Church. In it Bishop Gilmour was represented as occupying the papal throne and hurling bolts of excommunication against crouching Catholics who would send their children to the public school. An article accompanying it and highly approved by Cowles called for the establishment of "trusteeism" in the Catholic Church, for a rigorous system of compulsory education in the public schools, and for a clause in the Constitution proscribing "the appropriation of any public money for sectarian purposes."

The campaign of misrepresentation and vilification, and of what would ordinarily be considered libelous attacks, continued unabated from 1873 to 1874. When one of the graduates at the Central High School commencement delivered an offensive diatribe against the Catholic Church, the editor of the *Leader* approved, and found fault with the editor of the *Plain Dealer* for disagreeing. Everything was grist for Cowles's mill. He gleefully reported the "large crowd" at a lecture of a supposedly "escaped nun" who charged her gullible listeners fifty cents a head. He was consoled at the news that Bismarck in Germany was persecuting the Church and helping to bring about the fall of papal supremacy.

[7] Cleveland *Leader*, June 28, Nov. 19, 1873; June 10, July 6, 8, 10, 22, 25, 1874.

21

THE CATHOLIC PRESS

I N THESE CIRCUMSTANCES IT BECAME VERY EVI-
dent to Bishop Gilmour that he would have to have a Catholic
newspaper to defend the Catholic position and the Church in
general against irresponsible attack. He would not then have to
depend upon the favor of the local editors to publish his answers
to their attacks. The *Celtic Index*[1] founded as a Catholic newspaper
at an earlier date had done valiant service even though the *Leader*
ridiculed its efforts. It was, however, in financial distress. The Bishop
thought at first of reviving it; Fathers O'Callaghan and Sidley (of Sandusky) gave him their stock certificates. It was finally decided to buy
its list of subscribers and to begin an entirely new journal. An appeal
was made to the diocese with some measure of success.

Father Thomas P. Thorpe, who had been actively connected with
the *Celtic Index*, became the first editor of the *Catholic Universe*, the
first issue of which appeared on July 4, 1874. The masthead represented
the triumphant Christ with the motto "Veritas omnia vincit" (Truth
overcomes all things). The purpose of the weekly was proclaimed to
be "A Bold and Fearless Advocacy of Catholic Rights and Principles."
There was news from Europe and local news: of the dedication of the
Catholic University at Dublin; of the American pilgrimage to Rome;
of the convention of the Catholic Total Abstinence societies at Toledo;
of the dedication of St. Adelbert's Church in Berea; of the new chapel
at Parma; and of the three sermons, in German and English and Polish.
The directory it gave of Cleveland churches called St. Columbkille's
Church, St. Columba's. The editor had his comments to make on the
duties of citizens, on the Pope's situation in Rome, on total abstinence,
on the labor question, on the good behavior of the country in time of
panic despite the Communist attempt to stir up the people, and on the
absence of religious instruction in the public schools. He was already
advocating a combination of Catholic newspapers for the purpose of
securing accurate Catholic news.

It was a grave disappointment to the Bishop that he was confined to
a sick bed when the first copy of the *Universe* appeared. He had gone

[1] Gilmour to J. Walsh (Cincinnati), Dec. 23, 1873, Jan. 31, Feb. 21, 1874; Robert
Sidley to Gilmour, Sept. 24, 1879; E. M. O'Callaghan, transfer of stock, Aug. 27,
1872; same to Fr. Conlan, June 13, 1874; B. B. Kelly to Gilmour, May 13, 1874; S.
Bauer to Gilmour, July 10, 1874; all in C.D.A. Cleveland *Leader*, Dec. 13, 22, 1873.

to South Bend, Indiana, to deliver a commencement address and was taken ill immediately afterwards. Through his secretary he had ordered the appearance of the *Universe* on the day so significantly chosen and when he saw it he expressed himself as well pleased. Unfortunately, however, his recovery was delayed for two years and the *Universe* had to do without his personal and immediate guidance during that period.

Colonel Manly Tello, former editor of a St. Paul, Minnesota, journal, and a former officer in the Confederate Army, became editor in July, 1877. Bishop Gilmour after his return to duty kept him as editor apparently only after the prominent priests of the city petitioned him to that effect. In April of the next year Father Thomas F. Mahar, D. D., became associated with him as an editorial writer. He continued his able contribution even after he became pastor of St. Vincent's parish in Akron. Under the new editors the size of the paper was enlarged and the masthead simplified to "The Catholic Universe, God, Our Country and Our Rights."

Bishop Gilmour assumed personal responsibility for its debts and continuously had great difficulty in financing it. In 1882, with a weekly circulation of 7,560, there were some 2,060 unpaid subscriptions. In the next year the deficit ran between $1,400 and $1,500. In 1888 it was $2,500. In an effort to increase the circulation, the *Universe* was given the exclusive right to publish the official communications of the Bishop. Up to the time of his death, out of his personal resources which included the royalties from the sale of his publications, the Bishop had given more than $33,000 for the support of the paper.

Although the *Universe* was supposedly subject to the criticism and control of the Bishop, the editor followed his own devices except for an occasional signed editorial. He pursued a vigorous and aggressive policy but seemed to have the unhappy faculty of at times offending the feelings of the Germans and the Irish who naturally would be his best supporters. He had to be reminded that discussions about Jefferson Davis and the Confederacy were out of place and that he would have to be less political and partisan and more prudent and independent. His methods were often very embarrassing to the Bishop who kept a close eye on every issue. He did not hesitate to tell the editor that his editorials were too long or too heavy, that they should not be so quarrelsome, that there should be more news and less "scissoring." They remained on intimate terms until the end. During the sickness of Tello in 1880, Bishop Gilmour invited Francis Maurice Egan to take his place. The well-known writer and diplomat wrote that he would consider it an honor to be associated with Tello.

From the start, the *Universe* justified the judgment of its founder. Thereafter the Catholics of the city had the means of presenting their side of controverted questions. One of the first of these was the new Constitution for Ohio which was defeated by popular vote in August, 1874. Father Thorpe was jubilant at what he considered a victory over the editor of the *Leader* and his supporters. As far as Catholic schools were concerned, there was no change in the wording of the proposed new Constitution, namely, that "no religion or other sect shall have exclusive right or control of any part of the school funds of the state." Catholic schools had no support under either Constitution. But the Catholics were severely abused in the campaign for the adoption of the new one. Bishop Gilmour was taxed with ordering all Catholics to vote against it. He had indeed, sent a letter to the parishes advising against any change, which undoubtedly did influence the Catholic vote against it, but other causes helped to defeat the new draft of the Constitution. Chief of these was the campaign waged against it by the Temperance Crusaders and others who disliked the provisions which regulated the liquor traffic.

In the lively political campaign for the election of the Governor of Ohio the *Universe* ably defended the Catholic position in regard to Catholic schools. It reprimanded the Cleveland *Herald* for reprinting from *Harper's Weekly* cartoons insulting to Catholics, and the Akron *Argus* as well for its equally invidious tactics. The Republican candidate was Rutherford B. Hayes, the future President of the United States. He had been informed by his political advisers that the "Catholic Question" was especially important in the Western Reserve. The Catholic Question meant, of course, that Catholics had become very much aware that they should have equal rights with their fellow citizens; and, especially, it meant recognition of Catholic schools. He was cautioned to avoid the temperance issue so as to save the German vote for the party.

Thousands of Clevelanders stood in Monumental Park listening to Hayes while placards were paraded with such inscriptions as "Hayes and Free Schools," "The Book before the Priest," "No Geghan Bill for Us." The Geghan Bill had been passed in the previous Democratic Legislature to remedy the rather widespread practice of excluding Catholic priests from ministering to inmates in public institutions. The bill was considered to be the result of Catholic influence and, in an insulting caricature in *Harper's Weekly*, Archbishop Purcell was represented as ready to "deliver" the votes of all Catholics to the Democrats. It was repealed by the new Republican legislature under the pretext that it was unnecessary.[2]

On the local scene Father Thorpe in the *Universe* carried on a defensive campaign and drew down upon himself the personal invective of Editor Cowles. The Bishop, meanwhile, found a powerful auxiliary in his efforts to secure equal rights. This was the Catholic Central Association. At a meeting of the Irish societies gathered together for the purpose of arranging the St. Patrick's Day parade in 1874 he proposed his plan that five delegates from each parish and representatives of all the Catholic societies form a permanent committee which would be ready to assist him in all emergencies. The *Catholic Universe* announced that the projected union of Catholic societies would "watch

[2] *History of the State of Ohio*, as cited, V, 19, 20, 206. *C.U.*, Aug. 22, 1874. Cleveland *Leader*, Aug. 22, Nov. 25, 26, 1874.

and if necessary prosecute, and seek for legislation to punish and correct newspapers and editors who traduced the Catholic religion." The first meeting was held in Father Matthew's Temperance Hall behind the Cathedral, July 12, 1874. Bishop Gilmour explained to the delegates that he had no intention of interfering with the rights of others nor of asking any favors of those who differed from him, but he would "demand for the people whom God had committed to his care all that was guaranteed to them by the Bill of Rights." Through this organization the Catholic laity of all nationalities were enabled to present a common defense of their American privileges. The delegates from thirteen Catholic societies elected Mr. T. H. Graham president at their meeting in January of the next year. Charles McHannon was named vice-president, W. A. Manning secretary, William O'Connell treasurer, and Thomas Costello sergeant-at-arms. In 1878 the association was reorganized and a constitution was adopted.

On Easter Monday, 1879, the 300 members of the association were the guests of the Bishop at a dinner, thereafter called the "family banquet." The priests of the city as a matter of course cooperated in the work. Among the pioneer laymen, in addition to those mentioned above, were Patrick Reidy, Arthur Devine, John Koch, Henry Kramer, Martin Ehrbar, E. R. Brillon, James M. McNeill, John Lestrange, Marcus G. Monaghan, John Duggan, and Edward Hayes.

The association was active in the extension of religious liberty to the inmates of public institutions. A paid chaplain, never a priest, was supposedly sufficient provision for the religious needs of such institutions. The rule of the Superintendent of the Cleveland House of Correction (City Jail) effectively prevented any priest from ministering to the unfortunate Catholic inmates, who were, moreover, constrained to attend non-Catholic religious services. The prohibition of private conferences excluded the possibility of the Sacrament of Penance. The Catholic Central Association and its agent, Father Kuhn, the pastor of the neighboring parish of St. Edward, through the proper publicity, forced the Board of Directors to allow Catholic services. Shortly afterwards Mass was celebrated on Sunday mornings by a visiting priest and arrangements were made for religious instruction and the reception of the sacraments.

Father Houck, the chancellor, became a voluntary chaplain and was very active in the movement to separate youthful offenders from the others, a movement which culminated finally in the establishment of the Boys' Farm at Hudson. Bishop Gilmour to show his appreciation of the cooperation personally addressed the inmates of the Work House at a religious service in 1882. He had envisioned a Catholic Reform School on the property bought for the purpose by Bishop Rappe at Olmsted, but the financial straits of the time made such a thing impossible. The Catholic Central Association, however, continued its useful existence during the remainder of the Gilmour administration.[3]

[3] Cleveland *Leader*, May 11, 1874. *C.U.*, July 11, 1874; Apr. 14, 1887; July 11, 1910.

St. Bridget Church.   St. Edward Church.   St. Stanislas Church.

*Left:*St. Patrick
Church, Thompson.

*Right:*Sts. Peter and
Paul Church, Doyles-
town.

*Left:*Immaculate Concep-
tion Church, Grafton.

*Right:*St. Malachi Church
(original).

St. Alexis Hospital.

Old Notre Dame Convent and Academy, now the Catholic Young Women's Hall.

*Left:*Little Sisters of the Poor Home for the Aged.

*Below Left:*Immaculate Conception Church and School.

*Below Right:*Villa Angela Academy.

St. Ignatius College, now St. Ignatius High School.

(Good Shepherd Convent caption)

Good Shepherd Convent.

THE DEFENSE OF CATHOLIC SCHOOLS

ISHOP GILMOUR DESERVED HIS TRADITIONAL reputation as a great champion of Catholic schools. He had, moreover, definite notions about public education and was convinced that with the exclusion of religious training the child was only half-educated and had no effective basis for morality and good citizenship. Public as well as private education should be Christian and should rest on Christian principles. Purely secular education, especially when it established a State monopoly as against the right of the parents to supervise the education of their children, must inevitably lead to indifferentism in religion, if not to infidelity. He favored any system which would restore religious training in accord with the desires of the parents concerned. He suggested the possibility of confessional schools such as were to be found in Canada and Europe. His insistence was upon the religious training however it were given. "Morality, Religion, and God are essential for the well being of the State as well as for the good citizen—the child would be all the more loyal to the State if he were taught first to be loyal to God."

These same principles the Bishop expressed upon all possible occasions. At the national convention of the Irish Catholic Benevolent Union in 1876 and of the Catholic German Central Association in 1877 he obtained from the delegates a resolution condemning the exclusion of religion in the public school system. A lecture he delivered on the subject, together with those of two Anglican speakers at the annual meeting of the American Congress of Churches at the Music Hall in May, 1886, was printed in pamphlet form and widely distributed. The Cleveland *Press* opened its columns to the discussion of the subject. In the *Forum* magazine of New York the Bishop publicized his views in an article entitled, "What Shall the Public Schools Teach?"[1]

To prove that he was not opposed to State education as such, he offered to place the parochial schools of the city under the control of the local school board during schools hours when no religion would be taught, provided that freedom be allowed to impart religious in-

[1] *Forum*, Dec., 1887.

struction outside these hours, and that the city pay the salary of the
regular teachers. The system had been working with tolerable satisfaction in some districts in the State. Needless to say, the Bishop's
offer was not taken.[2]

Though no religion was taught in the public schools, they not only
favored Protestantism but in many instances were anti-Catholic. It
was well known that in most of them the Protestant translation of the
Holy Bible was read and that the prayers and hymns had a decidedly
Protestant bias. Some cases were brought to the attention of the
Bishop in which Catholic children attending the common school were
chastised and harassed for declining to take part in these activities and
were often forced to listen to unwarranted attack on their own religion.[3] This condition he considered to be a violation of religious
liberty and a step towards union of Church and State. The taxing of
Catholics for the support of the schools which they could not in conscience use, while they had at the same time to support their own
schools, he likened to a tax for the support of a State Church. He was
not sanguine about obtaining relief. Meanwhile, Catholic children had
to be educated and their faith preserved. "We must build Catholic
schools everywhere," he said, "and, at whatever cost, support and lift
them up until they are equal to the best."

In his pastoral of 1879 the Bishop expressed his satisfaction and his
joy that wherever there was a resident pastor there was to be found
a respectable Catholic school. Pastors (and finally the Bishop) were to
be the judges in cases where there might be doubt about the obligation
of the parents to send their children to these schools. The Bishop rigorously enforced the legislation in this matter and would not permit a
school once opened to be closed except in extreme circumstances.
Meanwhile, he carried on his defense of Catholic schools in general.
In Cleveland he challenged a comparison of the Catholic schools, grade
for grade, with the public schools at a time when up to one-half the
school children were in Catholic schools.

From the very beginning the Cleveland *Leader* and the group it
represented kept up a continual attack on the Catholic schools and
especially upon any claim for public support of them. In 1875 the
Leader complained about the number of Catholic members on the
Public School Board. By the State law of the time each ward elected
its representative to that body. Father Smythe, assistant pastor of St.
Malachy's, at one time was elected a member from the 8th Ward. He
was maliciously proclaimed as the spy of Bishop Gilmour when he
asked for an inquiry into the public support of the Industrial School
on Champlain Street. It was managed by a Protestant organization in

[2] *C.U.*, Sept. 23, 1876; May 19, 1877; May 27, 1886; May 31, 1888. Gilmour to
Elder, May 19, 1881; to A. W. Fenton, May 20, 1884; Gilmour correspondence with
Rev. Frank Clendennin, Frs. Hecker, C.P., Byrne (Boston), and Wm. McMahon, all
in C.D.A.
[3] Wheatley (Salinesville) correspondence with Gilmour, in C.D.A. Cleveland
Leader and Cleveland *Herald*, Feb. 13, 24, Mar. 3, May 2, Sept. 22, 1889.

connection with a "Ragged" school, a proselytizing agency. The managers were accused of taking poor Catholic boys and "steeping them in Protestant prejudice against the Catholic Church, the while they were taught some manual accomplishment such as making brooms."

Father Smythe questioned the right of the Board to award public funds to this privately owned institution at the same time that it denied aid to the Catholic orphanages which looked after many more neglected children than did this favored school. In the inquiry it was brought out that Protestant prayers and Bible reading were not uncommon in the Cleveland public schools. A resolution that such practice be prohibited was tabled. It was decided, however, that the teaching of the Protestant religion in the Industrial School would have to cease if public funds were to be used to pay the teachers. The editor of the *Leader* counted on Harvey Rice of the Board of Trustees of the Industrial School to "carry it through" as a Protestant institution.[4]

In later years a Doctor Campbell of the Public School Board introduced a resolution which would have the effect of excluding all those who had been educated in Catholic schools, no matter what their qualifications, from teaching in the public schools. The resolution was pigeonholed. Cowles of the *Leader* took the *Plain Dealer* to task for favoring the employment of Catholic teachers. In practice Catholic girls who aspired to be teachers had to spend the last few years of their preparation in the public institutions.

In answer to the continual attack on the Church in general, and to the charge that the Church was seeking to destroy the common school system, the Bishop delivered a public lecture at Case Hall in April, 1888. To a crowded audience he traced the history of "The Debt that America Owes to Catholicity." Among the Catholic influences for civilization in this country he pointed out that religious liberty is traceable to Catholic Maryland, which did not discriminate against any religion at a time when nearly all the other colonies denied full civil rights to Catholics. He pilloried the editor of the *Leader* as a public calumniator and a dishonest man. He called for the observance of justice towards Catholics in the light of their contribution to the country's welfare.[5]

To keep Cleveland aware of his determination to protect the parish schools he addressed a large meeting in St. Malachy's Hall which had been called to protest the closing of a French Catholic school in Massachusetts. The State courts there finally overruled the decision of the anti-Catholic crusaders.[6] That he needed to be on the alert, he and the Catholics of Cleveland had learned from their experience with those who would tax the Catholic school property. To add injury to injustice the local county auditor, L. D. Benedict, posted the Catholic school

---

[4] *C.U.*, Aug. 15, 1874; May 22, 1875. Cleveland *Leader*, Aug. 17, Dec. 30, 31, 1874.
[5] Pamphlet, in C.D.A.
[6] R. H. Lord, J. E. Sexton, and E. T. Harrington, *History of the Archdiocese of Boston*, New York, 1944, III, 126.

properties of the city as delinquent in paying taxes and put them up at public auction. This he did in spite of the decision of the Supreme Court of Ohio which had affirmed a decision of the Hamilton County Court of 1873 that declared against the taxation of church and school buildings. The State auditor expressed his surprise at the attitude of the local official who seems to have had his own purpose in defying the law. Monsignor Boff obtained an injunction, and the case was heard by Judge James M. Jones of the Court of Common Pleas in this city.

Bishop Gilmour, on the witness stand nearly two full successive days, was subjected to gross and disrespectful cross-examination by the attorney, J. E. Ingersoll, whose principal plea was to the effect that even though Catholic schools were institutions of public charity they were in his opinion hostile to the public policy of the State. He and the *Leader* made the most of their opportunity to misrepresent and malign the Church. Fathers James P. Molony, James V. Conlan, and Thomas Thorpe, as principals of three city parish schools, had to submit to the same humiliation on the witness stand. Attorney W. B. Sanders and Judge S. Burke argued the case for the Bishop. Judge Jones on July 5, 1877, decided for the exemption of the schools from taxation. He paid the penalty for his fairness by losing his position in the next elections; he was returned, however, in a subsequent division.

The District Court of three judges upheld the Jones decision, adding that the courts have no control over the religious faith of the people so long as they do not inculcate or practise any immorality or violation of the law of the land. On December 11, 1883, the Ohio Supreme Court upheld the verdict of the District Court. The Cleveland *Penny Press* severely censured the editor of the *Leader* for his unfair and unmanly tactics while the case was under appeal, and for his attempt to influence the Supreme Court. He was reminded of his complacent silence at the time of the then recent revelation of irregularities in the handling of public school books. "Cowles," it was said, "might just as well attack all private schools and preparatory departments. As for Bishop Gilmour [whom the *Leader* had personally berated], he could take care of himself well enough."[7]

After seven years of litigation the Catholic schools were saved from direct taxation, but the Bishop was justly incensed that it was necessary for Catholics to go to great expense to vindicate their legal rights whenever a local official thought it politic to deny them. During this same time a certain Covert, the candidate of the anti-Catholic faction

[7] *C.U.*, May 7, 15, Aug. 14, Oct. 2, 1875; July 5, 7, 14, 1877; Dec. 11, 1879; Jan. 22, Mar. 18, Apr. 14, 1880; Jan. 27, 1881; Nov. 22, Dec. 13, 20, 1883. Boff to Purcell, Jan. 13, 1876; Houck and Gilmour correspondence with State Auditor, Jan., 1879; Gilmour to Elder, Jan. 22, 1881; Gilmour to Chatard, Nov. 21, Dec. 24, 1883; Kleekamp to Houck, Aug., 1890; all in C.D.A. Cleveland *Leader*, Feb. 16, 1876. Cleveland *Penny Press*, Nov. 19, 1883. Gilmour's own account of the contest in Houck, *Op. cit.* The suit was carried to the Supreme Court of Ohio in the name of Frederick W. Pelton, County Treasurer: brochures with argumentation filed in the Supreme Court of Ohio, Oct. 29, 1880 and Nov. 14, 28, 1883, St. Mary Seminary Library.

and a creature of the *Leader*, unsuccessfully sponsored legislation to tax all church property and to require the vesting of it in church trustees.

The exclusion of benefits to Catholic school pupils induced the Bishop to oppose the several free school book bills introduced into the Ohio Assembly at this time also. Against one of them in 1885, with the cooperation of the Catholic Central Association, a monster protest was presented in the name of Catholic school children, the heads of the schools, and the whole Catholic population of the city.[8] There was a well-founded suspicion that it was not benevolence but more selfish and interested motives which inspired this and similar bills that were defeated at the time. Catholics, moreover, were not the only opponents. A local attempt in 1886 to furnish free text books, but exclusively to the pupils of the common schools, was vigorously and successfully protested in a mass meeting at Cathedral Hall which was addressed by the Bishop, who up to the time of his death looked upon such procedure as a blow aimed at the already overburdened Catholic schools.

Bishop Gilmour, also, like many individualists of his generation found fault with the compulsory school law of 1890 which compelled all children of school age and under fourteen years of age to attend school for a certain length of time each year. He looked upon this movement, which he had foreseen, as an invasion of individual liberty and of the rights of parents. What to his mind was more dangerous and insidious, it looked like an attempt to force secular education, divorced from moral and religious training, upon the growing generation. He opposed federal interference in education for the same reasons.

Father Patrick Quigley of St. Francis de Sales' parish in Toledo allowed himself to be arrested for not furnishing the list of pupils in his school to the truant officer, as a means of testing the compulsory school law. The Toledo *Commercial*, June 10, 1890, represented Doctor Quigley as commanding the sympathy of a large and intelligent body of American citizens; in testing the constitutionality of the law he was helping to solve a question of human rights and human liberty. It was also argued that if the State were to have the power to regulate private schools, the latter should share in the school fund for their support. The method adopted by Doctor Quigley, however, did not have the approbation of the Bishop nor of the other pastors in Toledo, who were advised by the Administrator, Monsignor Boff, to give the officials access to their lists. On appeal, the compulsory school law was found to be in accord with the Constitution of the State.[9]

---

[8] *C.U.*, Apr. 3, 1884; Feb. 19, 26, Mar. 19, 1885.

[9] *C.U.*, Nov. 28, 1874; Mar. 13, 1875; Mar. 24, 1877. Gilmour to Frs. O'Reilly and O'Brien, Dec., 1883; to Frs. Arnould, Barry, J. P. Carroll, and Kolasinski, in 1890; Circular, May 5, 1890; Hannin to Houck, June 12, 1890; Bauer to Gilmour, Sept. 12, 1890; Boff's Circular, May 27, 1891; all in C.D.A. Toledo *Commercial*, June 10, 1890. Judge Edward F. Dunne's pamphlet, *Compulsory Education*, St. Louis, 1891. *Compulsory Education in Ohio*, P. F. Quigley *vs.* State of Ohio, brief for the State by J. K. Richards, Columbus, 1891.

Having saved the right of the parochial schools to exist and to be exempt from crushing taxation, the Bishop continued his policy of insisting upon the erection of schools where they were needed and the improvement of those already in existence. The standards of all were to be raised so that parents might find no excuse for preferring the common schools.

To coordinate the work in Cleveland, the pastors organized the equivalent of a school board during the time that the Bishop was incapacitated; upon his return to duty in 1876 he gave it his full approval. These pastors had control only over the schools of which they were the respective pastors and principals. Twice a year the board held public oral and written examinations. At the end of the year the competitive examinations were attended by the Bishop and the public. The board also examined the lay teachers before accepting their services. A school board for the whole diocese was needed to supervise and regulate the entire system: to obtain uniformity in text books, in teacher requirements, and in grading.

The Cleveland Board of Education for the public schools had been started in 1853 and great progress was made especially after 1867. The many inducements offered in these schools in the 1880's had attracted many Catholic students. It was hoped that a similar board for the parochial schools would produce equally happy results. Finally on April 28, 1887, the new diocesan system was promulgated in the *Universe*. It followed the directives of the Third Council of Baltimore, which had been held a few years previously. The Bishop wrote the introduction to the *Rules and Regulations of the School Board,* which were published in a pamphlet composed principally by Father Bauer of Fremont, who was appointed the president of the Board. Father Mears of Youngstown was the secretary.

The first meeting of the Board was held in the episcopal residence May 9, 1887. In addition to the president and the secretary, Fathers Molony and Thorpe of Cleveland, Father Jung of Defiance, Father Hannin of Toledo, and Father Ankly of Wooster were appointed examiners in the seven school districts into which the diocese was divided. Father McMahon of St. Bridget's, Father Carroll of Holy Name, and Father O'Connor of St. Augustine's drew up a course of studies and made other recommendations, one of which was to the effect that fifty pupils ought to be the limit in one class room under one teacher. The Board was also empowered to judge the qualification of new teachers. Rules for the guidance of the district examiners were published in February, 1888.[10]

[10] Mackey to Houck and his reply, Mar. 7, 8, 1881; Gilmour to Benzinger's, Aug. 26, 1881; Gilmour to Bauer, Jan. 14, 1887; Molony to Gilmour, Mar. 22, 1883, June 22, 1886, July, 1890; Wm. McMahon to Gilmour, Sept. 25, 1889; John Heiland to Gilmour, May 20, 1884; Braschler to Gilmour, Oct., 1891; Houck to J. A. Burns, Aug. 7, 1882; all in C.D.A. *C.U.*, Apr. 28, 1881, Jan. 14, 1887. Pamphlet, *Constitution and By-Laws for the Government of the Parochial Schools of the Diocese of Cleveland,* Mar. 19, 1887. Pamphlet, *Rules and Regulations for Examinations and Reports by District Boards,* Dec. 13, 1887.

The school inspectors after their tours of the schools (133 of them) compared notes and made further recommendations as to methods and the grading of the schools. The scarcity of teachers often interfered with the execution of these desired improvements. One difficulty was the restriction of the Sisters to teaching boys under twelve years of age. The excellent system functioned for a few years. In 1890 Father Molony, himself a schoolmaster in his youth, called for the revival of the Board, to raise the standard and to win due recognition. The individual schools needed such coordination.

RELIGIOUS TEACHERS AND GROWTH OF CATHOLIC SCHOOLS

T HE BUILDING AND MAINTENANCE OF THESE schools depended entirely upon the generosity of the faithful Catholic people. The self-sacrificing labors of the Bishop, the priests, the religious communities of men and women, and the devoted lay teachers made it possible for them to succeed. In the smaller communities as before the teacher often had charge of the organ and the choir. In the western part of the diocese there were a few Catholic district schools, in such places as Delphos, Ottoville, Fort Jennings, Glandorf, and New Bavaria where the population was almost exclusively Catholic. Sometimes this arrangement led to difficulties and it became necessary to build a parish school.

In the interests of Catholic primary education Bishop Gilmour invited two new religious congregations of women to take up work here and for the higher education of young men the Fathers of the Society of Jesus came to Cleveland to begin the history of St. Ignatius College.

The Sisters of St. Joseph were first established in the United States at St. Louis in 1836. Mother St. George Bradley brought a few Sisters to the Diocese of Cleveland in August, 1872, and opened a house in Painesville. The Bishop gave the religious habit to two of their novices in St. Mary's Church on March 19, of the following year. St. Mary's school at the time had about seventy-five pupils. Their first Cleveland house was opened in the old Annunciation parish in 1875; the former St. John's College building on Fulton Road became the headquarters two years later. In 1880 a ten-acre plot was purchased on Starkweather Avenue in what was then known as University Heights, near the Cuyahoga River Valley. Eventually a two-story stone structure served as the mother-house and the first St. Joseph's Academy. Their community grew but not sufficiently to supply the demand for teachers. In 1891 there were 34 Sisters and they had 1,600 pupils in their charge in 8 parishes.

The Sisters of Notre Dame of Germany,[1] who traced their origin

---

[1] *Mother Mary Chrysostom* by Sisters Mary Aloysius and Patricia, New York, 1931.

to the Notre Dame Sisters of Namur, came to this country and to the diocese at the invitation of Bishop Gilmour, extended to them through Father Westerholt, the pastor of St. Peter's, Cleveland. Mother Mary Chrysostom Heck with eight Sisters left the mother-house at Coesfeld in Germany during the time of the persecution of the Church under the government of Prime Minister Bismarck. On July 6, 1874, they made their first foundation in this city. Cleveland was their headquarters from 1877 to 1887, when the mother-house was again established in Germany, at Muelhausen. The second foundation was made at Covington, Kentucky, the see city of Bishop Toebbe, the brother of Sister Modesta, the first provincial superior in Cleveland. Within four years after their arrival here 200 Sisters had come from Germany to the missions in Kentucky and Ohio. The mother-house (Notre Dame Academy), a very substantial brick structure at the corner of Superior Avenue and East 18th Street, was built in 1878. A school building and a chapel were added within a few years. In 1890 there were 101 of the Sisters teaching 6,407 pupils in 21 schools, principally in the German parishes. They were assisted in the instruction of the boys by 3 Brothers of Mary at St. Peter's and by 8 laymen in other schools.

The older communities experienced continual development. The Daughters of the Immaculate Heart of Mary in 1890 had 24 members teaching in 5 schools with a total of about 2,000 pupils. At the request of Bishop Gilmour the Sisters in 1873 opened a boarding-school for young women, St. Joseph's Academy, at Louisville, Ohio, in the building formerly used as St. Louis College. This venture was not successful; the average attendance was about eighteen boarders. The building was then used to house a school for deaf-mutes, from 1878 until 1883. A year later the Sisters moved their novitiate and normal school to their house in Buffalo.[2]

The Ursuline Nuns made great progress during Bishop Gilmour's administration. In Toledo a large new building was added to the original brick convent; the older buildings were enlarged and improved in 1872. Bishop Gilmour dedicated their new chapel two years later and conferred the first degrees granted under the State charter they had obtained in 1873. The Tiffin Ursulines became independent of the Cleveland convent in 1873, when the Cleveland Sisters returned home. They received their right to confer degrees under a State charter of 1878. A large wing was added to their establishment in 1887. A new foundation was made in Youngstown in 1874 by six professed Sisters from Cleveland, who took up residence in a small frame house adjoining St. Columba's School. The stringent financial conditions, following the panic of 1873, made it difficult for them to build. At the personal appeal of Bishop Gilmour seven Ursulines from Toledo went to their assistance in 1877 so that the community was able to take full charge

[2] Nardin to Gilmour, June 13, 1883; Gilmour to Masson, Dec. 17, 1888; Gilmour-Simeoni (Monaco) correspondence, Dec. 17, 1888, to Mar. 16, 1891; all in C.D.A.

of St. Columba's School, and to send a teacher to St. Joseph's School. St. Columba's parish helped them to purchase the title to their first property and subsequently a substantial brick convent was erected. Their academy was incorporated in 1882.

Meanwhile the Cleveland Ursuline Academy in 1871 obtained a State charter which raised it to the status of a college with powers to confer academic degrees. The growth of business in the downtown district crowded the convent on Euclid Avenue and induced the Sisters to accept the advice of Bishop Gilmour that they move their academy to a more favorable site. In May, 1874, they secured a plot of thirty-seven acres, the Gilbert property, on Lake Erie, east of the city, in Nottingham Village. In 1878 a boarding-school for girls was opened in a new brick building here and called Villa Angela Academy. A day-school was operated also for a few years. A hall used for graduation exercises and other public gatherings was erected. In 1886 twenty-seven acres contiguous with the original property were purchased. St. Joseph's Seminary for young boys was started in a renovated frame building on the ground; it served its purpose until a new building was finished in 1892.

It had been evident for some time that the mother-house on Euclid Avenue would also have to be moved and, when a suitable offer was made, the Bishop approved of the sale of the property in May, 1890. A stipulation in the contract allowed the Sisters to occupy the old buildings for three years. A new site was bought at the corner of Scovill and East 55th Streets and preparations were made for building.

To the community of Toledo principally belongs the credit for the foundation of the Ursuline missions amongst the Indians of Montana in the vast territory in which Jesuit missionaries, including the well-known Father Pierre de Smet, had been laboring. Father Eli W. J. Lindesmith, former pastor at Leetonia, Ohio, and regular chaplain in the United States Army from 1880 to 1891 with his headquarters at Fort Keough in Montana, in addition to his official duties had been ministering to the pioneer Catholics in the area. He acquainted Bishop Gilmour with the desperate need of Bishop John B. Brondel, the first head of the Diocese of Helena, for priests and Sisters. The Bishop of Cleveland placed the direct appeal of Bishop Brondel before the Ursulines for their consideration. The response was immediate and generous. Mother Amadeus, a former superior at Toledo, and five other Sisters accompanied by Father Joseph Eyler went out west in 1884.

Other volunteers, especially from Toledo, followed. There were, however, three Sisters from Cleveland, and representatives of the Tiffin and Youngstown convents, and one from Cincinnati. In September, 1887, Father Lindesmith as the delegate of Bishop Gilmour "gave the cap" to Mary O'Dunn, a young woman from Cuyahoga Falls, who was to have great influence in the growth of the community at a later date. In January, 1888, the new establishment numbered twenty-five members; a convent and an academy for the daughters of the white settlers were opened at Miles City, and the Sisters had charge of four Indian Mission schools. These religious women acknowledged Bishop Gilmour as the founder and "foster father" of their missions. Bishop Brondel expressed his warm appreciation "for all that he was doing for the poor Indians." The Montana Ursulines have made tremendous progress since those early days.[3]

In the Diocese of Cleveland in 1890, there were 85 Ursuline Nuns in charge of some 7,500 pupils in 20 parish schools. They were aided at the Cathedral by 5 Brothers of Mary and at St. Mary's by 4 others. In Toledo 2 Christian Brothers taught in the boys' department of St. Francis' School. In all about 25 lay teachers assisted them in their other schools.

The Sisters of the Holy Humility of Mary by dint of hard labor survived the primitive conditions in which they started at New Bedford (Villa Marie). In 1869 they had doubled the size of the original building on the property and in 1878 another addition was made. A brick chapel was built two years later. Villa Marie continued to be the mother-house. Here they also conducted a normal school for their teachers and still sheltered a number of orphan girls. Towards the end of Bishop Rappe's administration they opened the first Lourdes Academy in a large two-story brick residence, the former Colahan home, which still stands at 2016 Lorain Avenue, in the old parish of the Annunciation, in Cleveland. In 1890 these Sisters in 9 parochial schools had charge of 685 pupils. The flourishing community of the "Blue Sisters" at Davenport, Iowa, traces its origin to Villa Marie.

In the western part of the diocese by 1890 the Sisters of the Precious blood had built substantial convents at New Riegel, Marywood, and Glandorf. In the last-named village they taught in the Catholic district school, where 3 of them with 5 lay teachers had 353 pupils. Assisted by 5 lay teachers, 10 of them had 580 pupils in 5 other parishes.

The Franciscan Sisters of Tiffin were also of great value in the rural schools. In 1881 Bishop Gilmour dedicated a very beautiful Gothic chapel for them. In addition to their work with the orphans and old people, they had 26 members teaching 792 children in 10 schools of the diocese.

Other religious communities had representation in the parochial schools here in 1890. The Franciscan Sisters of Minnesota had 15 teachers in 3 schools and 1,342 pupils. The Sisters of Charity of Cincinnati had 13 children in 2 schools and 683 pupils. The Felician Sisters had 7 teachers in 2 schools and 486 pupils. The Franciscan Sisters of Joliet, Illinois, had 9 teachers in 3 schools and 415 pupils. The Dominican Sisters of New Jersey had 5 teachers in 2 schools and approximately 300 pupils.

When Bishop Gilmour came here there were according to the *Catholic Directory* 17,000 children in some 100 parish schools, and several

[3] Lindesmith-Gilmour correspondence, in C.D.A.

hundred more in the Catholic district schools. At the end of his administration there were 142 parish schools in the diocese including 9 which were partially district schools. The total enrollment in them was 27,579 pupils, of whom 26,896 were in strictly parochial schools, and there were nearly 600 children under instruction in Catholic welfare institutions. In the city of Cleveland there were 24 parish schools and some 7,500 enrolled in them. Toledo had 11 schools with nearly 3,500 pupils. Youngstown had 3 schools with nearly 1,600 pupils. In addition to these there were the several thousand students in the academies.

In the city of Cleveland the Cathedral School had the largest enrollment, some 1,000; St. Patrick's had 820; Holy Name, 816; St. Stanislas', 689; St. Stephen's, 670; Our Lady of Lourdes, 525; Immaculate Conception, 504; St. Mary's (Carroll Avenue), St. Michael's, St. Joseph's (Woodland Avenue), St. Malachy's, St. Wenceslas', each had between 400 and 500; St. Peter's, St. Procop's, St. Bridget's, St. Augustine's, St. Edward's, each had between 300 and 400; St. Colman's, Holy Trinity, Annunciation (Hurd Avenue), each had between 200 and 300; St. Francis' had 190; St. Adelbert's, 149; St. Ladislas', 89; Sacred Heart, 50.

HIGHER EDUCATION AND THE
DIOCESAN CLERGY

THE CLERICAL STUDENTS FROM ST. LOUIS COL-lege, Louisville, which for various reasons was closed at the end of the school term in 1873, were transferred to the preparatory seminary at Cincinnati in the autumn of that year. The Bishop was paying tuition for them three years later. A college and preparatory school were needed in Cleveland.

The Franciscan Fathers, under the direction of Father Kilian Schloesser, answered the Bishop's plea by opening St. Joseph's College in September, 1875. Two Franciscans and a priest of the diocese were the professors for the first twenty-four students. The classes were held in St. Joseph's school until in September, 1876, a new two-story building on Chapel Avenue was finished. The attendance, for the most part day students, increased to eighty in 1878 when the college received the State charter to confer degrees. The teaching staff was enlarged to six professors, three Franciscans, and three diocesan priests. But in the next year the college was closed; the Fathers were needed for other work. It was reopened again in 1893, this time for Franciscan students only. Anticipating the closing, the Bishop in a circular letter, January 20, 1878, asked his own clergy for suggestions about the foundation of a diocesan institution. In answer to inquiries made of them, the Fathers of the Holy Cross at Notre Dame University and the Jesuit Fathers of the Eastern Province pleaded that they had no teachers whom they could spare to begin a college here.

Already in 1878, however, Father Lessmann, the Superior of the Jesuit German Province of Buffalo, gave the Bishop reasons for hoping that he might establish a college in Cleveland.[1] On August 1, 1880, the Fathers of the Society, under Father Michael Zoeller, took charge of St. Mary's parish on West 30th Street with the purpose of observing at first hand whether conditions would warrant the establishment

[1] Gilmour to Lessmans, Nov. 12, Dec. 10, 1879, June 12, 1880, Nov. 9, Dec. 25, 1881, Feb. 27, 1882, Jan. 30, 1886; Gilmour to Zoeller, Apr. 24, 30, 1883; Gilmour to Sorin, Aug. 4, 1883, May 2, 1885; Lessmans to Gilmour, Mar. 26, 1878, Feb. 8, 13, 1882; all in C.D.A.

of a preparatory school. The project was delayed for a time especially
by the dearth of English-speaking professors. Under the new provincial,
Father Behrens, negotiations were completed and St. Ignatius College
opened its doors on September 6, 1886. Father John B. Neustich was
the first president. He supervised the erection of the first college building, a plain two-story frame structure, on property purchased by the
Fathers across the street from St. Mary's Church. Within two years
he had erected the north wing of a three-story brick building. He was
succeeded as president by Father Knappmeyer in 1888. The increase
in the number of students made it necessary to add the southern
wing, another three-story brick structure, in 1891. The college building now had a frontage of 200 feet on West 30th Street and 80 feet
on Carroll Avenue. It was incorporated under Ohio law in 1890 with
power to confer diplomas and degrees.

It was one of the best-appointed educational institutions in the city.
The effect on Catholic life in the diocese was soon felt as graduates
entered the business and professional world. Seventy-two per cent of
the graduates of the first ten years entered the diocesan seminary as
did a great majority of those of the next decade. In the regular session
of the first school year there were 76 students; this number was increased to 178 in the school year beginning in September, 1891, when
there were 14 Jesuits on the faculty. The regular course consisted of
three years of preparatory studies (academic, as distinguished from the
commercial course which was also given) and two years of college
work. Certificates were issued for the years of study which were completed.[2]

The need of a new diocesan seminary building on Lakeside Avenue
was brought home to the Bishop very forcibly when he held his first
diocesan synod there in 1872. No one had ever dreamed that the
"Spring Cottage" property would so soon be engulfed in the growing
city. In accord with the decisions of the synod, Bishop Gilmour contracted to pay $35,000 for a thirty-five-acre plot of land in Euclid
township, which came to be known as the Gilmour farm. It was only
with the greatest difficulty, because of the panic of 1873, that he was
able to carry the mortgage which finally was cleared off ten years
later. The seminary collection itself had to be diverted to pay for the
new Cathedral House.

Meanwhile, in 1882, a southern wing, a three-story brick building,
was built alongside the old seminary building and connected with it
by a glass-enclosed causeway. Thereafter most of the students had
their own rooms. Two years later the first floor of the main building
became the library and lecture room. The second floor was made
over into a chapel. The multi-colored oak beams in the open ceiling
and the stained-glass windows helped to give a brighter outlook in the
midst of the surrounding smoky atmosphere.

The priests of the diocese responded generously to the Bishop's

[2] *Golden Jubilee Book*, 1936.

appeal for assistance in building up the library, and many of the rare and valuable books in the present seminary were bought from European booksellers at that time. From France came great sets of the latest works in Holy Scripture, theology, philosophy, church history, canon law, and Catholic bibliography. The Bishop himself ordered the books or purchased them when he was in Europe. He was particularly interested in history and poetry, and Scotch, Irish, and English antiquities.

It is interesting to record that the Bishop entered into correspondence with Henry Lea, the author of a book on the Spanish Inquisition, suggesting that he was not writing a complete history of the subject as long as he sedulously avoided the treatment of the "Protestant Inquisition" in the British Isles and in America. Lea alleged the immensity of his subject.[3] Another interesting correspondence took place between the Bishop and William H. Brett, the well-known Cleveland librarian. He offered to supply a list of Catholic authors whose books he thought ought to be found on the shelves of the Cleveland Public Library. Mr. Brett accepted the offer and professed himself ready to refer the suggestions to the book committee; at the same time he expressed the hope that the better feeling which the Bishop foresaw might soon come. "Even now," he wrote, "the better day seems dawning clearly." Bishop Gilmour after the close of the Third Council of Baltimore subscribed to the plan endorsed by the bishops to subsidize the work of John Gilmary Shea in writing the history of the Church in the United States, and a few months before his death he sent money to the distinguished author to help him publish the third volume of his work.

The original course of studies in the major seminary, one year of philosophy and two years of theology, by the year 1885 had been lengthened by the Bishop to five and one-half years. It remained for his successor to add an additional half-year as was prescribed by the Third Council of Baltimore.

Bishop Gilmour declared definitely for a native clergy trained under his own eyes. The last group ordained by Bishop Rappe in 1869 had one American in it, two from Luxembourg, two from Ireland, and one from Lorraine. During the time of the Apostolic Administration visiting bishops ordained one American, three Germans, two from Switzerland, two from Ireland, and one from Austria. Ordained abroad but for this diocese during the same period were two more Swiss and three more Germans.

Father William McMahon, born in Ireland but educated in this country, was the first priest ordained by Bishop Gilmour. He and Fathers Wimar Mueller and Joseph Sproll, both natives of Germany, and Patrick O'Brien, a native of Ireland, were in the class raised to the priesthood in the Cathedral, July 21, 1872. Between 1872 and 1892, including both years, 122 young men were ordained for this

[3] Correspondence in C.D.A.

diocese, most of them by Bishop Gilmour. On occasion Bishop Fitzgerald of Little Rock, Bishop Mullen of Erie, and Bishop De Goesbriand were the ordaining prelates. In his last ordination, March 7, 1891,
not long before his death, Bishop Gilmour raised two to the priesthood; his successor ordained two more in the following June, and a
class of twelve in 1892.

Of these 122 young men fifty-five were born in the United States,
some twenty-seven of them within the boundaries of the diocese;
twenty-five were born in Ireland, most of them brought out to this
country at a tender age; fifteen were born in Germany, a few of them
reared here in the United States; eight were natives of Luxembourg;
seven, of Bohemia; four, of Switzerland; three, of Poland; two, of
France; and the others, of Lorraine, Lithuania (Russia), and Slovakia.
Most of these students spent on the average of three to four years in
the local seminary; about a dozen spent only a short time there before
ordination. In addition several were ordained in Europe, including
three in Rome. A goodly number of priests came to work in the diocese for a time but the French-born Father Louis Braire was the only
such priest ever incardinated after ordination by Bishop Gilmour.

One of the principal difficulties of the Bishop in regard to the diocesan clergy was to procure the services of priests who could minister
to the greatly increased Slav population in their own language. He
petitioned the Fathers of the Resurrection, a Polish religious congregation at Rome, for at least five priests to take charge of Polish and
Bohemian parishes. He expected to need more later on. To the Bishop
of Budweis in Bohemia he explained that there were some 2,000 Bohemian Catholic families in the diocese and only two Bohemian priests.
He begged for a priest or an advanced student who could finish his
studies here. In the same sense he wrote to the seminary in Olmutz,
to the Archbishop of Cracow, to the Jesuits at Innsbruck in Austria,
and to Hungary. The well-known Father Stephen Furdek, a native of
Slovakia, and then a student at Prague, in Bohemia, came out to this
diocese and after a short stay in the seminary was ordained by Bishop
Gilmour in 1882. His work for religion among the Slavic Catholics
was to have good and lasting effect. Sent to Europe by the Bishop
in 1890, he brought back several students who in due time were ordained here. Meanwhile, priests who belonged to other dioceses came
here for a time to help in the work of ministering to the newcomers.

Doctor Nicolas A. Moes continued during the administration of
Bishop Gilmour to preside over the seminary, which in 1890 had thirty-
four resident students. He was assisted by Father Michael Murphy
and Father John T. O'Connell. A bronze plaque in the old St. Mary's
Seminary commemorated the teaching career of Doctor Edward Hecht,
here during the time that the Cincinnati seminary was closed, from
1880 to 1887.

TOLEDO UNDER BISHOP
GILMOUR'S JURISDICTION

ESPITE THE DIFFICULT FINANCIAL CIRCUM-
stances of the period of Bishop Gilmour's administration, the material development of church and school
facilities proceeded apace. New missions and new parishes
were established in the growing cities, and in the older
parishes old buildings were replaced with new ones.

In what is now the Diocese of Toledo the seed planted by Bishop
Rappe had a marvelous growth. In the city itself four new parishes
were formed. Father Robert A. Byrne organized the new parish of
the Good Shepherd, a division of St. Francis de Sales's, and erected a
frame church-school building in 1873. Father John Thein founded the
parish of the Sacred Heart in territory previously belonging to St.
Mary's; he put up a brick combination church and school in 1883; his
successor, Father Anthony Eilert, erected a separate brick schoolhouse in 1889. Father Vincent Lewandowski organized the Poles, who
began to arrive in Toledo around 1870 in great numbers, into two
parishes. In 1876 he built the brick combination school and Church of
St. Hedwig which had to be reconstructed in 1886 (under the direction of Father Joseph Koudelka, the future bishop) after a disastrous
fire. In 1882 and 1883 he erected the frame school and frame Church
of St. Anthony.

New buildings made their appearance in the older parishes: in St.
Mary's, a three-story brick schoolhouse in 1873; in St. Patrick's, a four-
story brick structure opened by Father Hannin as a social center in
1874; in St. Joseph's, a new brick church, with school rooms attached,
in 1878 under the supervision of Father Andrew Sauvadet.

To the west of Toledo and in the vicinity, at Sylvania, the Jesuit
Fathers in charge of the mission put up a frame chapel in 1872. At
Marygrove (Raab) Father Wimar Mueller in 1878 finished a brick
church, replacing a frame building which had been destroyed by fire;
unfortunately the new church was hit by a cyclone two years later
and had to be entirely reconstructed. At nearby Assumption, Father
Thomas F. McGuire supervised the erection of a brick church which
was completed in 1890.

To the south of Toledo, at Maumee, Father John B. Mertes built a brick Romanesque church which was used for the first time on Christmas Day of 1889. Across the river, at Perrysburg, in the same year Bishop Gilmour laid the cornerstone of St. Rose's, the first stone church in the Maumee Valley; Father George Rieken finished this Gothic church in 1892.

The brick church put up by Bishop Rappe in 1845 at Providence, a few miles up the Maumee River, survived the destruction of the village by fire in 1850, as a mission center. At Deshler, one of these missions, Father Henry Best erected a frame chapel in 1875 and at Custar, another mission, he established a school in the same year. After Custar became a separate parish Father Michael Vollmayer in 1891 built a brick church there. A small frame chapel at Weston, five miles away, dating from 1877, was abandoned and the mission merged with Custar in 1887. Father Hyacinthe Kolopp (of Providence) supervised the erection of a brick church at Bowling Green in 1881.

East of Toledo, at Elmore, Father William McMahon in 1873 remodeled a frame building for use as a church. He built a frame mission chapel at nearby Genoa in the next year, and another frame chapel at Oak Harbor where Father Charles Griss opened a frame school in 1886. At Momeneetown Father John McMahon (of Toussaints) in 1883 constructed a modest frame chapel for the French-Canadians.

In the district around Defiance, in the far western section of the diocese, many fine new churches and chapels were constructed, in keeping with the development of the country. In Defiance itself the English-speaking members of the original St. John's parish formed the new congregation of Our Lady of Perpetual Help. Bishop Gilmour in 1878 dedicated their beautiful Gothic church which had been erected under the direction of Father Michael P. Kinkead, who eight years later added a brick schoolhouse. At Marydale (Mud Creek) Father Joseph Blaser in 1876 put up a frame chapel. At St. Michael Ridge Father Timothy P. McCarthy opened a school in 1877, five years before a new schoolhouse was built. At Blakeslee Bishop Gilmour in 1887 dedicated a brick church erected under the direction of Father John H. Kleekamp to replace a frame building which had been destroyed by fire.

At Bryan, in the vicinity, a frame chapel made its appearance in 1874 under the supervision of Father Polydore H. Delbaere; sixteen years later Father John H. Muehlenbeck replaced it with a brick edifice. At Wauseon in 1873 Father John G. Vogt remodeled a Methodist church building for Catholic use. At Napoleon, where a frame schoolhouse had been finished in 1878, Father Michael Peutz directed the building of a large brick Gothic church which Bishop Gilmour dedicated in 1883.

The successive pastors of Antwerp were responsible for frame mission chapels at Hicksville and at The Bend in 1880, at Payne in 1883, and at Latty in 1890. Bishop Gilmour in 1888 dedicated a new brick church at New Bavaria, which Father John A. Michenfeld had erected to replace one destroyed by fire. This same priest directed the building of frame chapels at North Creek and at Holgate. Another such chapel was erected in 1886 at Hamler.

At Delphos in 1881 Bishop Gilmour dedicated a magnificent brick Romanesque church which has a seating capacity of 1,800. Father Aloysius I. Hoeffel, the pastor, had also built a large brick schoolhouse. He was responsible, too, for a brick church at Van Wert (1874) and for a frame chapel, replacing a log house, at Spencerville (1876). East of here, at Lima, Father Alexander R. Sidley completed a substantial brick church in 1871. Father James O'Leary enlarged and remodeled it entirely, and in 1889 completed a large brick schoolhouse.

In the prosperous farming community of Ottoville Bishop Gilmour in 1888 dedicated a large imposing brick Gothic church which had been erected under the supervision of Father Michael Mueller, who was responsible also for a brick church at nearby Kalida (1878). At Fort Jennings a brick Gothic church made its appearance in 1884 under the direction of Father Jacob Heidigger. The pioneer Catholics at Glandorf built a great brick Gothic church which the Bishop dedicated in 1878; Father Dickman, C.PP.S., was the pastor. At Ottawa the Sanguinists erected a brick church in 1872 and fifteen years later a brick schoolhouse. At New Cleveland Father Henry Kaempker in 1876 erected a frame school to match the frame church put up fifteen years before. In the same year he built a frame chapel at Leipsic where a school was organized only in 1890. At Miller City, in the vicinity, a frame church was completed in 1888.

In the city of Sandusky Father Robert A. Sidley had completed the magnificent stone Gothic Church of Sts. Peter and Paul in 1871; Bishop Gilmour consecrated it in 1878. The Bishop also dedicated the large beautiful stone Gothic Church of St. Mary in the same city in 1880; Father Nicolas Moes, the pastor, erected a second stone schoolhouse seven years later. At Kelly's Island, off Sandusky, Father John B. Mertes entirely renewed the church building in 1883; the school had been reopened in 1879. At the adjacent Put-in-Bay Father Francis Metternich erected a frame chapel in 1877.

On the mainland, at Marblehead, Father Joseph Hoerstmann built a frame combination church and school building in 1889. To the east Father Ignatius Wonderly completed a frame church at Huron in 1890. South of here, at Fremont, Father Eugene O'Callaghan, the pastor of St. Ann's, built the first brick school in 1875; the great brick Gothic church which was dedicated in 1891 was erected under the direction of Fathers Alfred E. Manning and Thomas P. McCarthy, successive pastors. Near Fremont, at Millersville, Father Joseph Blaser entirely renovated the church which was rededicated by the Bishop in 1884; a frame school had been built there in 1873. Twelve miles away, at Kansas, Father Michael Dechant put up a frame chapel in 1890. Another frame chapel had been built at Bettsville, in the vicinity, in 1878.

To the east of Fremont, at Bellevue, Father William J. Gibbons supervised the erection of a new brick Gothic church in 1884; three years later a public school building was acquired for parish use. At Clyde in 1890 Bishop Gilmour dedicated a brick Gothic church, the last one he consecrated to the service of God. Father Alfred E. Manning had begun the construction which was finished by Father Francis T. Moran, his successor. At Green Springs a frame chapel made its appearance in 1872 under the direction of Father Joseph D. Bowles.

At Tiffin, to the south, Father Michael Healy of St. Mary's in 1884 adapted a public school building for parish use. Six miles away, at Bascom, Father Louis Heiland organized a school in 1872. At Fostoria, to the west, Father Matthias Arnoldi in 1879 superintended the building of a fine brick church which eleven years later had to be enlarged; a new brick school was opened in 1886. The church at Findlay was entirely reconstructed in 1889. At New Riegel, south of Tiffin, Bishop Gilmour in 1878 dedicated a magnificent brick church which had been constructed in the Roman style, under the supervision of the Sanguinists. At Berwick, in the immediate vicinity, Father Joseph P. Glodden put up a brick schoolhouse in 1872, and Father Arnoldi, mentioned above, a brick church which the Bishop dedicated in 1890.

Brick chapels were erected at Alvada in 1881 under the direction of Father Jacob Marte, C.PP.S., and at Liberty in 1889 under that of Father Ehrhard Glueck, another Sanguinist. At Kirby Father Francis L. Hultgen in 1891 completed a brick church. Father John G. Mizer, who had started a school in Kirby in 1880, finished a brick church at what was then known as Crawfordville in 1884. In the last-mentioned place Father Joseph R. Rosenberg in 1878 had opened a school.

Along the southern border of the diocese, at Upper Sandusky, a brick church made its appearance under the supervision of Father Charles Braschler; it was dedicated in 1880. At Bucyrus Father Hyacinth Kolopp reopened the parish school and in 1888 built a brick church. At Galion Father Kaempker in 1883 built the brick Church of St. Joseph; in the same town in 1876 St. Patrick's school was opened. In the vicinity, at Crestline, Father Clement Treiber was responsible for a brick Gothic church which was completed in 1890. At Mansfield, farther to the east, a public school building was purchased for parish use in 1874 by Father Andrew Magenhann who also finished a brick combination church and school in 1890 to replace the previous church which had been destroyed by fire.

At St. Stephen, in the north, a brick church was completed in 1887 by Father Philip Rist, C.PP.S. In the vicinity, at New Washington, Father Michael Becker in 1867 finished a brick Gothic church. At North Auburn a frame church put up in 1879 was reconciled with the Church authorities in the year following; Father Amadeus Dambach began a school there in 1883. In the adjacent Attica Father Aloysius Hutmacher in 1882 had a frame mission chapel built. At New London Father John Heiland in 1878 transformed a frame residence into a chapel.

To the north, at Norwalk, in St. Mary's parish, Father Thomas Halley put up a two-story brick schoolhouse in 1878, and Father Charles Chevraux in 1889 began the construction of the great Gothic stone church which was finished five years later. In St. Paul's, Father A. Eilert opened a brick combination church and school in 1876. In the vicinity of Norwalk at Peru, a brick school was put up by Father James Hamene in 1878, and Father Joseph Blaser in 1891 enlarged the church. Father John M. Puetz supervised the erection of a fine brick church at Monroeville in 1876 and of a frame mission chapel at Plymouth in 1872. At Milan a frame school was opened in 1872. At Wakeman Father Halley (from Norwalk) built a frame chapel in the same year. At Marywood Bishop Gilmour in 1886 dedicated a great Gothic brick church which was erected under the direction of Father Francis Griesmayer, C.PP.S.

26

YOUNGSTOWN UNDER BISHOP GILMOUR'S JURISDICTION

IN THE AREA OF WHAT IS NOW THE DIOCESE OF Youngstown a comparable expansion in church building took place during the same period.

The Catholic population of the city of Youngstown itself was increased considerably by those who came, after the panic years, in the last quarter of the nineteenth century. Father O'Callaghan, the pastor of St. Columba's, began a two-story brick school which was finished by his successor Father Walter Gibbons in 1872. Father Edward Mears, pastor from 1877 to 1923, in 1888 put up a six-room frame schoolhouse at the southern end of the parish for the accommodation of the children in that district. Father William J. Manning organized the parish of the Immaculate Conception, a division of St. Columba's, and in 1882 erected a frame combination church and school; the brick Gothic church was dedicated in 1891. Father George W. Leeming in his turn organized the parish of the Sacred Heart, a division of the Immaculate Conception parish, and built a frame church in 1888; the first school was opened in 1892 in a building formerly used as a public school. St. Joseph's congregation under the supervision of Father Charles Seltzer in 1882 put up a brick Gothic church; the old building was remodeled for use as a school.

Outside the city of Youngstown but in the vicinity, at Struthers, a frame chapel made its appearance in 1871. At Lowellville Father Nicolas Franche put up a brick mission chapel in 1884. Father John T. Schaffeld built a frame chapel at Vienna in 1873. He also completed the enlargement of the eight-year-old church at Hubbard which Bishop Gilmour dedicated in that year; the school had been started three years previously. At Niles the large brick Church of St. Stephen was completed in 1890 by Father Felix Scullen; the old church was made over into class rooms. At Mineral Ridge, nearby, a frame chapel made its appearance in 1872 under the direction of Father Francis J. Henry of St. Ann's, Youngstown.

In the district south of Youngstown, at East Liverpool, Father John P. Carroll reopened the school, and in 1889 completed a new brick church. Father Patrick McGuire supervised the erection of a frame church at Summitville in 1871, of a brick church at Salinesville in 1873, and the enlargement of the church at Wellsville in 1881. In the last-named place the school was not opened until 1891. At Lisbon Father John G. Vogt erected a brick church in 1887, but it was not dedicated for several years. At Leetonia Father William J. Fitzgerald finished the brick Church of St. Patrick in 1881; the old frame church, previously called St. Barbara's, was remodeled for use as a school. Father Clement H. Treiber put up a frame church at Salem in 1881 and a like building at East Palestine in the year following.

West of here, in Stark County, at Canton, the beautiful brick Gothic Church of St. John begun in 1870 by Father Francis Berthelet was dedicated by Bishop Gilmour in 1872; the school was reopened a few years later. The large brick Gothic Church of St. Peter in the same city, which under the supervision of Father Victor Arnould was five years in building, was dedicated by the Bishop in 1879; a large brick school was opened in 1890.

At Alliance a brick church erected under the supervision of Father James O'Leary was in 1881 dedicated by the Bishop; the old church was made over into class rooms. At Louisville the imposing brick Gothic church was finished by Father Hoffer in 1875. In the next year he completed a smaller brick church at Harrisburg. In 1870 he had erected a brick school at Maximo (Strassburg); in 1879 Father James O'Leary enlarged the church there.

At Navarre, to the south, a frame school was opened in 1872, and twelve years later Bishop Gilmour rededicated the brick church which had been enlarged by Father Francis Metternich. At Massillon the great stone Gothic Church of St. Mary begun by Father John Koehn in 1875 was completed five years later by Father Jacob Kuhn. At West Brookfield (now Massillon) a school was opened in 1871; Father Nicolas Kirsch in 1886 enlarged the nineteen-year-old Church of St. Barbara. At North Lawrence, near Canal Fulton, a frame public school building was refashioned into a chapel in 1889.

At Ravenna a frame schoolhouse had been opened in 1878 and the brick church was enlarged in 1888 by Father John T. Cahill. At nearby Kent Bishop Gilmour in 1872 dedicated the brick church which had been erected five years before by Father Patrick H. Brown; in 1881 a frame schoolhouse was opened by Father James Malloy. At Mantua the frame chapel was enlarged in that year.

To the north, along the lake shore, at Ashtabula, Father Edward J. Conway enlarged the original Church of St. Joseph in 1872; five years later he erected a brick schoolhouse. And in 1876 a frame church made its appearance at Jefferson under his supervision. Father Thomas M. Smyth was responsible for the erection of the first frame combination school and Church of Our Lady of Sorrows at Ashtabula (Harbor) which was dedicated in 1890. At nearby Conneaut Father Gilbert P. Jennings erected a brick church which in 1888 was dedicated by the Bishop.

27

CHURCH AND SCHOOL BUILDINGS
IN CLEVELAND (1872-1891)

WITHIN THE PRESENT LIMITS OF THE Diocese of Cleveland there was the same or greater expansion of material facilities. New churches and schools appeared to replace older ones and, of course, in the new parishes entirely new plants were constructed.

Shortly after his coming Bishop Gilmour made Father Felix Boff, previously pastor of St. Francis de Sales's in Toledo, his vicar general and pastor of the Cathedral, a duty which Bishop Rappe had reserved to himself. The old episcopal residence on East 6th Street, which became diocesan property in 1878 under the last will of the first Bishop of Cleveland, had proved to be inadaquate. One of Father Boff's first accomplishments was the construction of the three-story brick residence on the Cathedral property which housed not only the Cathedral priests but also the Bishop and the chancery. It was finished in March, 1875, and was so well built that it was readily adapted to remodeling seventy-five years later.

Father Thomas P. Thorpe, who became pastor in 1876, had the façade of the Cathedral made over and decorated with stone. The high steeple was completed in 1879. Five years later the interior was completely renovated: the sanctuary was enlarged and the main altar regilded; the new episcopal throne, other sanctuary furniture, and new frames for the Stations of the Cross were all of black walnut; the niches for the side altars were deepened and stained-glass windows were installed above the three altars; the walls were frescoed in oil; and a vestibule was added at the entrance. Two superb marble vases, ten feet high, which the Bishop had brought from Italy were placed on either side of the main altar; new statues were eventually put in place.

In 1888 Father Thorpe supervised the erection of the brick schoolhouse which had accommodations for nearly 1,000 pupils in its fifteen class rooms. On the ground floor was a spacious chapel; a meeting hall on the top floor was ready for use in 1889.

St. Columbkille's parish lost its independent status and became a chapel-of-ease attended by the priests of the Cathedral. In 1887 the original frame church was moved across East 26th Street to the present location of the school and was joined to a small brick church building which previously belonged to the Episcopalians. Just east of the Cathedral, in St. Peter's parish, a brick combination church and school was completed by Father Westerholt in 1874; ten years later the interior of the church was entirely renovated. Farther east, on Superior Avenue, the cornerstone of the great stone Gothic Church of the Immaculate Conception was laid by Bishop Gilmour, August 15, 1873; a temporary frame building housed the congregation until in 1882 the basement was roofed over. Father Robert A. Sidley finished the work which had been planned on a more pretentious scale by his predecessor, Father Thorpe. Monsignor Boff, in the absence of the Bishop, dedicated the monumental edifice, May 31, 1885. Still farther east, on Superior Avenue at East 71st Street, Father Westerholt in 1887 put up a frame combination church and school. This was the nucleus of the new parish of St. Francis of Assisi, of which Father Nicolas Kirsch was the first pastor; he had charge of the German-speaking Catholics of the northeastern section of the city.

South of the Cathedral, in St. Bridget's parish, the large brick Gothic church on East 22nd Street near Charity Hospital was dedicated by the Bishop, November 7, 1879. Father Bernard Kelly began the construction and Father William McMahon completed it. The latter also supervised the erection of a three-story modern brick schoolhouse and parish hall which was finished in 1886. A memorable event was the visit of Father "Tom" Burke, the celebrated Irish Dominican orator, the proceeds of whose lecture in the city were used to pay off a portion of the debt.

Near St. Bridget's, but closer to the Cathedral, the first Italian parish in the State of Ohio was erected under the patronage of St. Anthony. Father Pacifico Capitani, who had been ordained in Rome and had served in France and England, was appointed the first pastor. The survey he made indicated that about 680 of his countrymen lived in and around Cleveland, mostly Neapolitans; about the same number was to be found in the Youngstown area, and a few more at Ravenna, Navarre, and Wooster. It was decided on that account to build a church for them. The Bishop advanced enough money to transform Turner Hall, on Central Avenue near East 9th Street, into a church hall; it seated about 500. The Bishop dedicated it, May 8, 1887. Notice was taken of the event in Rome, in the *Osservatore Romano*. Cardinal Simeoni, the Prefect of the Congregation of the Propaganda, in the name of the Holy Father expressed his appreciation and, at the Bishop's request, he sent a mosaic picture of the Blessed Virgin and other precious objects for the Fair which was held in the interests of the parish. Father Capitani made periodic visits also to the Italians scattered in other parts of the diocese. The Bishop in an effort to secure another Italian priest for the Youngstown district corresponded with the Fathers of Mercy at Vineland, New Jersey, and with Bishop Scalabrini

of Piacenza in Italy who had been instructed by the Holy See to prepare priests for the American missions.

South of the Cathedral along Woodland Avenue, in St. Joseph's
parish, Father Schloesser brought the magnificent brick Gothic church
to completion and Bishop Gilmour dedicated it on October 5, 1873. Still
farther south on Woodland Avenue Father Jacob Kuhn, the pastor of
St. Edward's which was previously known as Holy Family, in 1873
erected a brick combination church and school. His successor, Father
Matthew A. Scanlon, supervised the construction of the imposing stone
Romanesque church which was dedicated by Bishop Gilmour, January
31, 1886. With its center a few blocks to the south on Woodland
Avenue, Father Peter Becker organized the German-speaking members
of St. Edward's into the new parish of the Holy Trinity; he erected a
frame school in 1880 and a frame church and a parish hall in the next
two years.

In the southern section of the city, along Broadway, there were
many new developments. Father Anthony Hynek, the pastor of St.
Wenceslas', remodeled a frame building for use as a school in 1886;
the church on the old site on East 35th Place was entirely renovated.
The third Bohemian parish in the diocese, that of Our Lady of Lourdes,
was organized with its center on East 55th Street near Broadway.
Father Stephen Furdek, appointed the first pastor in 1883, supervised
the construction of a frame combination church and school which
the Bishop dedicated in that same year. Soon new class rooms had to
be added and others were rented. The great brick Gothic church was
ready for use on Christmas Day, 1891, although much work remained
to be done in the interior. South of here the fourth Bohemian parish,
St. Adelbert's, was started by Father Hynek (of St. Wenceslas') when
he erected in 1883 a frame combination church and school on East
83rd Street near Quincy Avenue. Father John W. Malecha, the first
pastor, enlarged the school and completed the building which was
dedicated by Bishop Gilmour in 1888.

In the old Newburg area the industries, especially the steel mills, had
attracted numerous Catholic workers, many of them immigrants from
the Slavic countries in Europe. Father Joseph F. Gallagher, of Holy
Name parish then known as that of the Holy Rosary, moved the parish
center to its present site on Broadway near Harvard Avenue, and in
1874 he opened a modern brick school, the largest and best-equipped
in the diocese at the time. The cornerstone of the large brick Gothic
church was laid by the Bishop in May, 1881, but the strike in the steel
mills and the consequent financial difficulties prevented its completion.
The roofed-over basement, however, was used as a church from September, 1882, until the completion of the superstructure and its dedication, May 22, 1887. The establishment of the Holy Name Society
during a mission had suggested the change in the title of the parish.
Father Gallagher had been succeeded in 1886 by Father John T. Carroll,
who continued the splendid tradition of Catholic education.

Not far from Holy Name, with its center on Forman Avenue near Broadway, Bishop Gilmour organized the first Polish parish in the city, that of St. Stanislas, among the steel workers who had been coming to the city in increased numbers for several years. Father Victor Zareczny, pastor of St. Adelbert's in Berea, beginning in 1873 held services for the new congregation in old St. Mary's on Columbus Road; the charge was then given to Father John A. Marschal, the first Cleveland pastor. The Franciscan, Father Wolfgang Janietz, the new pastor in 1879, brought his little flock to the monastery chapel on Hazen Street for Mass on Sundays; in 1881 he erected a frame combination church and school on Forman Avenue. There were about 200 families in 1883 when Father Anthony Kolazewski, then recently ordained by Bishop Gilmour, was made the pastor; he enlarged the church. In 1886 the foundations were laid for the present great brick Gothic church which was finished and dedicated, November 15, 1891, by Monsignor Boff, the Administrator of the diocese.

The first division of St. Stanislas' became the new parish of the Sacred Heart of Jesus. Father Kolazewski in 1889 put up a frame combination church and school at East 71st and Kazimier Avenue. It was attended by priests from St. Stanislas until the appointment in 1891 of Father M. F. Orzechowski.

Magyar and Slovak Catholics who came from the old Austro-Hungarian Empire settled in the district along Buckeye Road in the southern part of the city. At the instance of Bishop Gilmour Father Furdek, who himself was of Slovak parentage, in 1885 organized St. Ladislas' parish for them with its center at East 92nd Street and Holton Avenue, just south of Buckeye Road. The first separate services were held for the new congregation at the Franciscan monastery on Woodland Avenue, and then in a frame church completed in December, 1888. Father John Martvon, a native of Hungary, the first pastor, erected a school building in 1891.

On the west side of the Cuyahoga River the building of the great stone Church of St. Patrick was delayed because of the "hard times" experienced by the people in the panic of 1873. Father Eugene O'Callaghan, however, was able finally to complete it to the extent that Mass was celebrated in it after May 1, 1877. Four years later, Father Timothy M. Mahony finished the interior. A modern brick school, accommodating 1,000 pupils and with a social hall on the top floor, was completed by Father Patrick O'Brien in 1891. The old Annunciation parish for the French, unable to meet its debts, was made a territorial parish and was given a section of St. Patrick's, so that the French-speaking members constituted only about one-third of the congregation; a frame school was opened there in 1872.

At the western end of St. Patrick's Father O'Callaghan organized the new parish of St. Colman with its center on West 65th Street near Lorain Avenue. Mass was first celebrated in a small rented house on Pear Avenue, many assisting in the open air; and, thereafter, in a small frame church erected in 1880 which had to be almost continuously enlarged. The school was started with the parish and it also had to be enlarged each year, until in 1885 a large frame schoolhouse with a hall in the upper story was completed.

In St. Stephen's German parish, Father Casimir Reichlin in 1873 began the construction of the magnificent stone Gothic church. Because of the financial stringency work was delayed and it was only on November 20, 1881, that it was ready for its dedication by Bishop Gilmour. The original schoolhouse was enlarged in 1885 and in 1890. The new German parish of St. Michael had its beginning in the frame schoolhouse erected in 1881 at Scranton Road and Clark Avenue by Father Michael Zoeller, S.J., the pastor of St. Mary's. Two years later Father Joseph M. Koudelka, the future bishop and the first pastor, put up a frame combination church and school on the same site. Bishop Gilmour in 1889 laid the cornerstone of the monumental stone Gothic church, which three years later was dedicated by his successor. In the neighboring parish of St. Augustine Father Edward Mears in 1877 enlarged the church and finished a large frame schoolhouse at Jefferson and Tremont Avenue.

In the southwestern section of the city St. Procop's, the second Bohemian parish, was organized in 1872. Father Anthony Hynek (of St. Wenceslas') held divine services for the congregation in old St. Mary's on Columbus Road until in 1874 he was able to put up a frame combination church and school on West 41st Street near Clark Avenue. Father Joseph Koudelka, who preached to the parishioners as a deacon, was appointed the first resident pastor in 1875, the year of his ordination. Shortly afterwards Bishop Gilmour gave him leave of absence to become editor of a St. Louis Catholic Bohemian journal but soon recalled him to remedy a situation which had arisen in the parish. Unable to restore peace, he was made pastor of St. Michael's. When Father Anthony Vlcek became pastor in 1885 normal conditions were restored.

On the southern outskirts of the city, at Brighton, "out in the wilderness of Brooklyn" (the present Broadview-West 25th Street section of Cleveland), Father Patrick Quigley, a professor at the seminary, when denied the use of the Town Hall held divine services in a cooper shop until a brick church dedicated to the Sacred Heart of Mary was finished in 1875. The failure of the district to develop according to popular expectations made it necessary for Father Quigley, who had in 1873 also built the frame church of the Holy Family in nearby Parma, to appeal for outside financial assistance. In the neighboring village of Rockport (now part of Cleveland) Father Patrick O'Brien in 1875 started St. Patrick's school. At Berea in 1873 the approximately 100 Polish families, members previously of St. Mary's, were organized in the parish of St. Adelbert, the first Polish parish in the diocese, by Father Victor Zareczny who finished a brick church in December of the next year. Under the direction of Father

Benedict Rosinski a brick schoolhouse made its appearance in 1891. Father John Hannin had completed St. Mary's brick schoolhouse in 1885.

In the nearby town of Avon Father George Peter in 1873 replaced the burned-out school in Holy Trinity parish with a brick structure. In the other parish of the Immaculate Conception (formerly French Creek) Father Stephen Falk in 1885 erected a new brick school. North Ridgeville became a separate parish in 1875; Father Jacob Heidigger put up a frame church that year. Eleven years afterwards Father Henry Best started a school which was housed a year later in a frame building that had been remodeled by Father Nicolas Pfeil. At Elyria, to the west, Father Louis Molon enlarged the old church and converted the old Town Hall into a schoolhouse. His successor, Father John T. Shaffeld, supervised the erection of the fine brick Gothic Church of St. Mary of the Assumption which Bishop Gilmour dedicated, June 13, 1886; the old church provided additional school space.

At Oberlin, in the vicinity, Father Shaffeld also built a brick church in 1890. At Amherst, to the north, the frame church was enlarged in 1873 and ten years later Father Joseph Roemer began a school. At Lorain, in the vicinity, Father Roemer in 1879 superintended the erection of the first frame Church of St. Mary; it was turned into a schoolhouse when the second frame church was put up in 1883. Five years afterwards a brick schoolhouse made its appearance under the direction of Father Wimar Mueller.

At Akron, south of Cleveland, St. Vincent's school, the original church building in that city, was considerably remodeled and enlarged; it served its purpose until in 1892 Father Thomas F. Mahar was able to complete a model brick schoolhouse. A few years earlier, in 1887, he had put up a brick combination church and school in the district which became the new parish of St. Mary. Father John Broun made a substantial addition to St. Bernard's Church in 1880; he was responsible also for the fine model schoolhouse which was in use in 1888.

Adjacent to Akron, at Cuyahoga Falls, Father Patrick Barry in 1884 erected a brick mission chapel; he had put up a frame chapel at Peninsula two years previously. At Doylestown Father Charles Seltzer erected a brick Gothic church which Bishop Gilmour dedicated, October 22, 1880. At Medina Father Francis X. Nunan put up a frame chapel which was blessed in 1878. At nearby Wadsworth Father Edward J. Vattman supervised the erection of its first frame church in 1886. At Wooster the schoolhouse was enlarged by Father Fridolin Ankly. At Loudenville Father Nicolas Schmitz in 1880 had the eight-year-old brick church dedicated by the Bishop.

In Collinwood (now Cleveland), on the eastern boundary of the city, Father Anthony Martin (of Euclid) in 1877 put up the frame Church of St. Joseph for the railroad workers; he was able to start a school three years later. The brick church at Madison, finally completed after sixteen years, was dedicated by Bishop Gilmour in 1884.

It is interesting to note in regard to new buildings that the Bishop had anticipated some of the regulations of modern building codes. The walls had to be of the thickness of two bricks; the doors of the larger churches were to open outwards; and proper attention was to be given to heating and ventilation. School rooms were to be at least twelve feet high, from floor to ceiling. Neither churches nor schools were to be located near a railroad, or factory, or other noisy place, nor near a public school or non-Catholic church.

»» 28 ««

DIOCESAN AFFAIRS UNDER
BISHOP GILMOUR

THE PIONEER STAGE IN THE DEVELOPMENT OF the diocese passed with the first administration. Bishop Gilmour's years, the formative period, were marked by definite steps taken for the introduction of the general laws of the Church with particular application to contemporary conditions and requirements. The Bishop presided over three diocesan synods, or formal sessions of the clergy with the head of the diocese who gave force of law to the statutes which issued from them. He was also an active participant in two provincial councils (of Cincinnati) and was prominent in the Third Plenary Council of Baltimore, the most important ecclesiastical legislative meeting in this country up to that time.

In his first synod held shortly after his coming, in November, 1872, the regulations formulated in the previous synods of Bishop Rappe and the decrees of the Councils of Baltimore were declared to be binding. Additional diocesan rules were issued from time to time to the clergy through circulars. The diocesan tax for the support of the bishop and the seminary and other diocesan institutions was established in 1873. The amount was computed according to the number of families in a parish and was subject to review by the Board of Revision every two years. A circular in 1876 forbade priests to wear a beard except by special permission; it also prescribed the recitation of the De Profundis prayer for the dead after the High Mass on Sundays. In another circular the Bishop announced the reorganization of the board which controlled the funds used to support sick and infirm priests.[1]

Eight dioceses were represented at the Provincial Council of Cincinnati which was held March 5–19, 1882: the three in Ohio, Louisville and Covington in Kentucky, Fort Wayne and Vincennes (Indianapolis) in Indiana, and Detroit in Michigan. Many new problems had arisen since the previous council of 1861, and the assembled priests gave their solution of them in eight titles or chapters which dealt with the Catholic Faith, ecclesiastical discipline, administration of

[1] Pamphlet, *Constitutiones Dioc. Cleve. 1873*, in C.D.A.

church property, marriage, Catholic and public schools, Catholic societies and confraternities, secret societies, and church music.

To Bishop Gilmour had been assigned the subject of the tenure of
church property. In his first pastoral (1873) he had taken a decided
stand in that matter against the dangers of trusteeism, since laymen
in control of the property of the church could, if so inclined, cause
trouble in the administration of it. It was made very clear that the
"bishop was the only trustee in the diocese" and that it was in his
name that church property was to be held. The pastoral letter of the
council, issued in the name of all the assisting prelates, was written
by Bishop Gilmour and was very much like his own pastoral of 1879.
It struck out against secularism, the exclusion of God from the direction of human affairs, and against false notions of liberty. The right
of workingmen to organize was recognized but violence and bloodshed
were severely condemned. The importance of Catholic newspapers was
pointed out and in general the evils of the day were stigmatized.
Appeal was made to the conscience of the faithful to follow the
Church's directions.

Upon his return to Cleveland after the publication of the pastoral,
which received considerable attention even in the East, the Bishop
in answer to the objections of the Cleveland *Herald* had to explain
again the Catholic doctrine on the origin and powers of the civil
government and to show that there need not be any conflict between
it and the Supremacy of God. The decrees of the council were
approved by the Holy See and were published later in pamphlet form
(1887) with a foreword by Bishop Gilmour giving them specific force
in this diocese. He called attention to the fact that the legislation was
in harmony with that of the Third Council of Baltimore and that of
the local synod.

Bishop Gilmour's second diocesan synod was held in the seminary
two months after the Council of Cincinnati, May 23–25, 1882. It was
the most important one in the history of the diocese. Present were 139
priests, of whom 12 belonged to religious communities; 14 others had
been excused from attending. The ordinances of the Councils of
Cincinnati and of Baltimore were recognized, and Bishop Gilmour by
his own decree gave force of diocesan law to 262 statutes. One hundred of these were printed in pamphlet form as the *Rules and Directions for the Administration of the Temporal and Spiritual Affairs.*
Given also was the manner of assisting at Mass, Vespers, and Benediction as prescribed by the provincial council.

The legislation concerning education was consistent with Bishop
Gilmour's firmly held principles, enforcing compulsory attendance of
Catholic children at Catholic schools and imposing a strict obligation
on pastors and people to build and support such schools. Sanctions
were to be applied in the denial of the sacraments to the parents who
were negligent and even to children themselves. The synod repeated
the obligation previously imposed by the Bishop that schools were to

be established in every parish and mission as soon as possible and they were to be under the immediate direction of the pastor.

The method of the control of the material affairs of the parishes was considerably modified and changed from that which was current in Bishop Rappe's time. Not trustees but councilmen were to be chosen by the congregations, not to rule but to guide and counsel the pastor in the conduct of parish finances. The electors should be Catholic men, twenty-one years of age at least, and known to frequent the sacraments and to be loyal upholders of the parochial schools. No debts could be contracted by the parish without the permission of the Bishop, and each parish was solely responsible for its own liabilities. Parishioners who were able to do so but who shirked their duty in refusing material aid to the parish (a minimum was set in a circular of 1876) could be denied the sacraments.

The ordinary revenues of the parish came from the renting of pews. An extraordinary means of raising money was to organize picnics or excursions. It was quite usual for people of neighboring parishes or even of distant ones to come together at the cornerstone laying or at the dedication of a new church and to celebrate with a picnic, making the event an occasion for helping the new congregation. A special speaker, and often the Bishop, would lecture or preach. If an outing to some resort or picnic grounds was for the benefit of the parish, written permission of the Bishop was required and other rules of order were imposed. If the affair was for the benefit of a private organization, permission was not easily granted. Another interesting regulation was one which prescribed the wearing of the Roman collar by all priests ordained after 1882.

Bishop Gilmour played an important role in the history of the Third Plenary Council of Baltimore (November 9 to December 7, 1884), the decrees of which were the fundamental ecclesiastical law for the Church in the United States while it remained a missionary country and until the appearance of the new Code of Canon Law in 1918. Out of the council came the Catholic University which has so largely fulfilled the great expectations of the Holy Father and of the prelates who took part in its foundation.

In preliminary meetings beginning in November, 1883, between representatives of the American bishops and the competent authorities in Rome the Prospectus, or catalogue of subjects, had been prepared for the council. The ecclesiastical legislation in England and Scotland was established as a model to follow. From the marking on the copy sent to him it appears that Bishop Gilmour was particularly interested in the chapters on the institution of bishop's consultors and irremovable rectors; the education of the clergy; the episcopal curia; the presumptive incardination of the clergy; the relation between bishops and the religious orders.

At the recommendation of Bishop Gilmour Father Nicolas Moes, the rector of the seminary, was chosen as a representative of this province to help to prepare the *Schemata,* the formulation of the anticipated decrees which were submitted to the Fathers at the council. He and Father Thomas P. Thorpe acted as advisers and theologians for the Bishop, who found quarters in Baltimore at the St. James Hotel in a room "with a fire." Preceding the opening of the council Bishop Gilmour preached on "The Necessity of Revelation."

His experiences in the Fourth Provincial Council of Cincinnati had prepared the Bishop for an active part in many of the discussions. He had very decided ideas on some of the subjects. He had previously on his visit to Rome advocated the establishment of an institution of higher learning for the clergy. As a member of the commission for Catholic schools he held for strictly compulsory attendance and severe sanctions for disobedience. He was on a special committee which studied the title of ownership of charitable institutions which were built with funds collected in a diocese; he held that the bishop should hold such title even though a religious congregation might have the perpetual administration of the work. He argued for the unrestricted right of the bishop to remove or to change pastors within his jurisdiction. In the institution of irremovable or permanent rectors as contemplated in the general law of the Church he advocated that only ten per cent of the pastors be so appointed. He opposed the presumptive incardination of priests who came to the diocese from the outside. He was against allowing any restraining authority to the diocesan consultors. The details of ecclesiastical trials were of great interest to him. He was eloquent in regard to the proposed establishment of missions among the Negroes and hoped that a religious congregation would take up that work.[2]

After the deliberations, the acts and decrees of the council were carried to Rome by Father Dennis O'Connell, future rector of the Catholic University and bishop. The council delegated Bishop Dwenger of Fort Wayne and Bishop Moore of St. Augustine also to go to the Eternal City, to explain what they had accomplished to the proper authorities, if necessary. When difficulties did arise, the future Cardinal Gibbons, who had presided at the council, and the other archbishops of the country chose Bishop Gilmour to assist these two bishops in their task. Hesitant, at first, he finally accepted the commission when Archbishop Gibbons wrote, "Your presence there would contribute much to the obtaining of the approbation of the decrees." His mission, according to his credentials, was to expose at Rome the reasons the council had for legislating as it did. He was said to be thoroughly acquainted with conditions in the United States and was familiar with

[2] Bishop Gilmour's marked copies of the *Prospectus* and of the *Schema decretorum.* Propaganda to Purcell, May 22, 1883; Purcell to Chatard, June 10, 1883; Gibbons to Gilmour, Mar. 26, Apr. 2, 1884; Gilmour to Gibbons, Mar. 28, Apr. 6, 28, July 9, 1884; Gilmour to Elder, Mar. 28, 1884; Moes to Gilmour, Oct. 16, 1884; all in C.D.A. *C.U.* Dec. 13, 1883; Nov. 6, 13, 1884. "Minutes of Roman Meeting Preparatory to the III Plenary Council of Baltimore," in the *Jurist,* beginning in issue of Jan., 1951. *Acta et Decreta Conc. Plen. III Balt., passim.* American Catholic Historical Review, XXXIV, 4.

its laws, civil and ecclesiastical. Because of this and his active part in the formulation of the decrees he was considered to be well qualified to give useful information to the authorities.[3]

He left New York on the S.S. Richmond, May 21, 1885. Though unwell and "trying to wear off the weariness," he preached to the passengers and recited the Rosary with them. The sunrise over Ireland on the morning of May 31 delighted him. After a stop at Queenstown the ship reached Liverpool on June 1. In London he held two conferences with Cardinal Manning on matters pertaining to the Baltimore Council. His boyhood friend, Father James Maginn, joined him at Modena in Italy and together they arrived in Rome on June 5. He immediately started upon the composition of the thirteen-page pamphlet or memorial[4] which Bishop Moore translated into Italian and which was presented on July 6 in the name of the three American bishops to the Congregation of the Propaganda.

It petitioned for the keeping of the decrees of the council in the form in which they had been passed in Baltimore and it alleged the special conditions in the United States as warrant for special legislation particularly in regard to pastoral permanency, the manner in which religious organizations held title to their institutions of charity, and the sanctions for compelling attendance at parochial schools. In the controversy over the competency of a bishop's consultors, Bishops Gilmour, Dwenger, and Moore went directly to the Holy Father himself to save the original wording of the decree of Baltimore, which restricted the powers of the consultors to a merely advisory capacity in the administration of a diocese.[5] The Holy Father on September 10 ordered that the decrees of the Baltimore Council be recognized and in the leave-taking audience of September 14 he told the American bishops that he had directed that the petition presented by them be granted.

In the pursuance of his mission Bishop Gilmour paid many visits to the cardinals of the Propaganda and to other prominent ecclesiastics, and much of his time was occupied in writing and consultation. Among others he asked the advice of the English Cardinal Edward Henry Howard (at Frascati) and of Bishop Vaughan (at the English College). He assisted at the ceremony of the consecration of Archbishop Walsh of Dublin and reported a conversation with Cardinal Moran of

[3] Credentials, *Memoriale* (in Italian); Gibbons to Gilmour, Feb. 10, 16, Apr. 3, 27, May 8, Aug. 18, 25, 1885; Corrigan (N.Y.) to Gilmour, Sept. 4, 1885; Gilmour to Gibbons, Mar. 25, Apr. 9, Oct. 3, 1885; Gilmour to McCloskey, May 10, Nov. 12, 1885; Gilmour to Simeoni, Apr. 25, 1885; Gilmour to McQuaid, Nov. 5, 1885; Gilmour to Elder, May 13, Oct. 31, 1885; O'Connell (Rome) to Gilmour, Nov. 24, 1885; Bp. Herbert Vaughan (Salsford, England) to Bp. O'Connor, Sept. 21, 1885; Gilmour (Glasgow) to Boff, Oct. 15, 1885; Boff to Gilmour, Oct. 23, 1885; Bp. Gilmour's Diary for 1885; Gilmour and Moore to Gibbons, Oct. 3, 1885; all in C.D.A. *C.U.,* Aug. 20, 1885; Mar. 18, Apr. 1, 1886.

[4] Copies were sent to the American prelates, Gibbons, Corrigan, McCloskey, McQuaid, and Elder.

[5] The general law of the Church would require not only the advice but also the consent of the consultors in certain matters of importance.

Australia. For the first two months of the period he lodged at the North American College and was present at the installation of Doctor Dennis O'Connell as rector. The latter was of invaluable assistance to him in his negotiations.

During the whole time the Bishop was not well and in seeking relief he moved his quarters to a residence on the Via Della Croce. For a total of nearly a month he was confined to his room by a fever and was visited by the English Nursing Sisters, among them the one who had attended Mrs. Pomeroy, the daughter of Cowles of the Cleveland *Leader.* He found time, nevertheless, to visit the churches and shrines of Rome and the immediate vicinity with Father Maginn. Several artistic pieces he found in the art shops of Rome were sent to Cleveland. And he granted several sittings for the marble bust which Mrs. Serrao Varney was making of him.

Wearied but confident that he had accomplished his purpose, the Bishop left Rome on October 7, going directly to London and then to his childhood home in Glasgow. He boarded the S.S. Ethiopia on October 15 and landed in New York on the 26th. There were very few Catholics among the passengers, but one of them became fatally ill and was prepared for death by the Bishop who presided at the burial at sea. After making a report on his mission to Archbishop Corrigan in New York and Archbishop Gibbons in Baltimore, he arrived in Cleveland on October 28, "tired but consoled."[6]

His colleagues in the episcopacy commended Bishop Gilmour on his success. The decrees of the council were officially recognized in a document issued by the Congregation of the Propaganda, September 21, 1885, and they were formally promulgated by Archbishop Gibbons on the following January 6. Bishop Gilmour, who upon his return home had to correct some of the mistaken notions about the council which had been published in the local newspapers, proclaimed them as binding in this diocese on March 31. Shortly afterwards he issued a pastoral recommending the use of the Baltimore Catechism about which he had been consulted on his Roman visit. The decree making the observance of the present six holy days of obligation uniform in the United States was also published.

In accord with the prescriptions of the council the Bishop appointed as diocesan consultors: Fathers Boff, Westerholt, Thorpe, Moes, Molony, and Bauer. These and other members of the diocesan curia were nominated in his last diocesan synod which was held on January 3, 1889. At the single session, which lasted one hour and forty minutes, 155 priests assisted. Nine pastors were named irremovable rectors: Father Westerholt of St. Peter's, Father Molony of St. Malachy's, Father Casimir Reichlin of St. Stephen's, all in Cleveland; Father Hannin of St. Patrick's in Toledo; Father Bauer of St. Joseph's in Fremont; Father R. A. Sidley of Sts. Peter and Paul in Sandusky; Father Hoeffel in Delphos; Father Mears of St. Columba's in Youngstown; and

[6] Bp. Gilmour's Dairy for 1885, in C.D.A.

Father J. M. Puetz of St. Joseph's in Tiffin. They were to have special rights and dignity and in ordinary circumstances would remain in their places for life.[7]

At the great council at Baltimore Bishop Gilmour made strenuous efforts to have the study of music, especially of sacred music, made mandatory in the parish schools. Although the story of his having been converted to the Church through the kindness of a Catholic organist, who supposedly taught him to play the organ, is not true, the Bishop was from his youth intensely interested in music. He had as a pastor edited a book of hymns and at a later date he was very happy to be able to recall that, through his encouragement, the number of pianos in his parish in Cincinnati had been greatly increased. The music often heard in the churches at the time bordered on the operatic and was far from devotional. It was not unusual to have a string band in the choir loft playing English hymns to the tune of "Home, Sweet Home."

Bishop Gilmour at the Fourth Provincial Council of Cincinnati was influential in having reform decreed in this matter; he strongly advocated the introduction of Gregorian chant. At the ninth general convention of the St. Cecilia Society held here in 1883 he spoke vigorously in favor of congregational singing. Any congregation, he said, could be taught to sing and it would be good for their souls. The song of the people was "the joyous shout of the heart." He appealed to the convention to simplify and to popularize the music of the Church: "Let us hear the shout of the people." In answer to this plea Father John B. Jung, pastor at Defiance, compiled the *Roman Hymnal* which was published by Pustet in 1884. A Vesperal made its appearance soon afterwards as did another hymnal, called *Laudate Pueri*, which was edited by the Notre Dame Sisters of Cleveland with the hearty approval of the Bishop.

He issued the official diocesan regulations for music some time later. Cecilian or Gregorian chant was to be used exclusively on Sundays; on the greater feast days figured music was allowed. The Introit, the Offertory, and the Post Communion prayers were to be sung by the choir. The same Mass was not to be repeated too often. These and other regulations were to be effective in March, 1888, in the parishes in Cleveland and in the larger cities. Some pastors asked for an extension of time but he insisted on the observance of the rules.

The Fifth Provincial Council of Cincinnati held its sessions from May 19–26, 1889. Bishop Gilmour was assigned the chapter on procedure in ecclesiastical trials. He had been expected to preach the opening sermon but he was occupied at the time in a Toledo court room and did not arrive until the fourth meeting on May 23. Eleven decrees were issued, in general, formally accepting the legislation of the Third Plenary Council of Baltimore. Religious communities subject to the bishop's jurisdiction were to hold their property in the

[7] *C.U.*, Dec. 20, 1888; Jan. 3, 10, 1889. *Statuta Dioc. Cleveland*, 3rd ed., 1908.

name of their incorporated society; charitable institutions, especially those supported by alms collected in a diocese, were to be subject to the bishop who also was to control the inauguration of new institutions of that nature. Various circumstances delayed the papal approbation of these decrees until July 3, 1893.[8]

[8] *C.U.*, Dec. 13, 1888; Jan. 24, May 9, 23, 30, 1889. *Acta et Decreta Conc. Cincinnati Prov. V.*, Cincinnati, 1893. Lamotte, *Op. cit.*

29

CHARITABLE INSTITUTIONS
(1872-1891)

THE ADMINISTRATION OF BISHOP GILMOUR saw the inauguration of new institutions of Catholic charity and the development of the older ones.

Charity Hospital under the watchful eyes of the Sisters of Charity continued its Christlike work for the sick in spite of serious financial difficulties. Without assistance except from the generosity of well-minded individuals the mortgage on the property was cleared off in 1873. The report for the year 1874 shows that the hospital took care of 555 patients, of whom 363 were free patients. During his episcopate Bishop Gilmour authorized the Sisters to spend some $50,000 for the general improvement of their facilities. Steam was introduced for heating and for the laundry; elevators were built and the entire main building was renovated. The addition of a clinic hall and modern operating room made the hospital the equal of any in the city.

In two rented frame houses on Central Avenue adjacent to the hospital Bishop Gilmour founded St. Ann's Infant Asylum and Maternity Home. A substantial three-story brick building was later erected in the rear of the hospital, facing Charity Avenue (then Marion Street). Opened January 27, 1876, it had all the then modern conveniences and a capacity of 40 patients and 50 foundlings. The cost estimated at $20,000 was paid by popular subscription in the city and in the Diocese of Cleveland. In its first twenty-seven years of existence, it annually took care of 150 infants and 100 adults. Foster homes were found for the children or they were placed when old enough in one of the orphanages. Western Reserve Medical School authorities continued to appoint the physicians and surgeons, subject to the approval of the Bishop and the Sisters.

The faithful zealous management of these two institutions followed the general principle of liberality towards the poor and unfortunate. Charity Hospital in the year 1891 gave its services to 818 patients. Very many of them, as was generally the case, were unable to pay for their treatment.

The second Catholic general hospital in the city was founded by the Poor Sisters of St. Francis Seraph of the Perpetual Adoration.[1] They came here from their headquarters at Lafayette, Indiana, at the invitation of the Bishop extended to them through Father Kilian Schloesser, O.F.M., of St. Joseph's. The Sisters, driven out of Germany during the time of the persecution of Bismarck (1875), found their first asylum in the Diocese of Fort Wayne. On July 16, 1884, Sister Leonarda and Sister Alexia and three postulants arrived here and began their work of mercy in a remodeled public school building on Broadway at McBride Avenue.

This building, which had been the first home of the Poor Clares, with the addition of a frame chapel became the first St. Alexis Hospital. Through the generosity of the Franciscan Fathers and of numerous benefactors it was equipped and made ready for its opening to the public on August 15, 1884. Doctors Sykora and Cook were the attending physicians. The five patients who were received within the first two weeks were treated gratis. Before the end of the year a frame addition to the building increased the capacity to 25. The Sisters, without charge, also visited the sick in their own homes. In 1887 there were 18 Sisters serving the hospital which had up to that time accommodated some 300 free patients. New property and other remodeled frame buildings (in 1891) afforded increased facilities for the work.

Bishop Gilmour had expected that St. Alexis Hospital would eventually be moved to the west side of the river. With that in mind the Catholic Central Association under his auspices sponsored a great Fair, and other appeals were made to the public to raise enough money for the purchase of a site. With the additional assistance of the well-known industrialist, William J. Gordon, who donated $5,000, the Bishop on September 6, 1890, secured the property now occupied by St. John's Hospital on Detroit Avenue. The architect had presented his plans in the previous year and the Bishop approved them but he did not live to see them accomplished. The frame building with its 60 beds was dedicated by Bishop Horstmann, May 12, 1892, under the patronage of St. John of God. St. Alexis Hospital was destined to remain on the East Side.

St. Vincent's Hospital in Toledo was built by the Grey Nuns of Montreal in the midst of great difficulties and financial embarrassment; it was opened to the public, July 19, 1876. The Sisters, who had an average of 100 orphans in their charge, won the admiration of the people of Toledo by their care of the pest house during the epidemic of 1876. With the alms they collected, under the authorization of the Bishop, the Sisters were able to complete the hospital building, which was considerably enlarged and modernized again in 1890.

The Sisters of the Holy Humility of Mary (the Blue Sisters) in 1879 built a small hospital on their grounds at New Bedford, for the

---

[1] Sr. M. Rosanna Peters, *History of the Poor Sisters of St. Francis Seraph of the Perpetual Adoration*, Lafayette, Ind., 1944.

benefit of the men who were constructing the railroad through that district. These Sisters also sheltered a small group of orphan girls.

The welfare of the orphans and the financial support of institutions for their care were a source of continuous anxiety for Bishop Gilmour. The Daughters of the Immaculate Heart of Mary had transferred the younger girls from St. Mary's Orphanage on East 20th Street to St. Joseph's on Woodland Avenue near East 65th Street, where in 1879 they erected a large three-story brick building. The older girls who remained at old St. Mary's were trained in the domestic arts.

The boys of St. Vincent's Orphanage on the West Side were crowding their quarters to such an extent that 50 of them were transferred in 1883 to the building at Louisville, used in the early days as a college. This was entirely remodeled to accommodate the 120 boys there in 1890.

There were a certain number of orphans at Tiffin who earned their own keep by working on the farm attached to the Citizens Hospital and Orphan Asylum which had been started by Father Bihn. The other orphanages, however, depended entirely upon the charity of the Catholic people to whom an appeal was made annually in the churches and in the "begging tours" of the Sisters themselves. In Cleveland and Toledo single parishes, and sometimes several of them together, held their annual Orphans' Fair, often a gala social event. The diocese outside the large cities was divided into districts which were assigned to the different sisterhoods as the field for their house-to-house visitation. In the country districts the farmers contributed food of one kind or another. An effort was made by the Bishop to prevent overlapping.

The total returns were never quite sufficient to pay for the cost of running the institutions. In 1881, for instance, through the Cleveland Orphans' Fair, $8,248 were collected. Of this amount St. Vincent's received about forty per cent to enable the Sisters to care for 185 boys in a year; St. Mary's and St. Joseph's were allowed about forty-four per cent to support their 195 girls. The rest was given to St. Ann's Infant Asylum. The deficit had to be collected by the Sisters. This precarious and inadequate method was as distasteful to the Bishop as it was to the pastors and the people. Regular contributions for the diocesan charities, he felt, would have been more desirable; he favored, moreover, a system which would house and train the orphans in usefulness on large farm lands. He approved also of the method practised by the Catholic orphan agency in New York; it was estimated that in 1883 their representative had "placed" some 200 orphans in foster homes in this diocese. The old system remained in practice here, however, for many years to come.

The Sisters of the Good Shepherd[2] and their charges moved into

---

[2] Sr. Mary of St. Teresita, *Social Work of the Sisters of the Good Shepherd,* Cleveland, 1938.

new quarters, a large brick structure on Carnegie Avenue at East 30th Street, on May 25, 1875. Although its foundations were laid in 1870, it was not until 1874 that the cornerstone was put in place by Bishop Gilmour who had made several public appeals in behalf of the Sisters. Mr. Gordon, mentioned above, donated $5,500 and twice that sum was gathered through Fairs to pay for the $40,000 building. It was dedicated by the Bishop on June 21, 1875.

The Little Sisters of the Poor soon found their new home on East 22nd Street too small for their work. On February 24, 1878, the Bishop dedicated a new three-story brick building at the same location. A chapel, another wing, and modern improvements were finished in 1890. Bishop Gilmour was one of the bishops who in 1879 and in 1886 gave official ecclesiastical approval to the religious community of the Little Sisters of the Poor.[3] A second house was opened in the diocese at Toledo when in June, 1885, four old people were received into their humble quarters; three years later a larger frame building was acquired which became the home of 40 elderly people and the 6 Sisters who cared for them.

It is fitting at this point to record that the Bishop was on friendly terms with Cleveland's wealthy philanthropist, William Gordon, whose benefactions were extended to Catholic institutions as well as to others. His only daughter, Georgiana, was a convert to the Catholic Church. In 1873 she married Viscount Alphonse Vilian XIV, secretary to the Belgian legation in Washington, in St. Peter's Church in Cleveland. After the death of his wife and daughter, Mr. Gordon gave their jewels to the Bishop for a precious miter which was rated at one time as one of the most valuable in the country. Other non-Catholics of the city could be named who were benefactors to Catholic charities.

The recurrent financial panics and consequent unemployment sometimes reduced the poor people of Cleveland, many of them Catholics, to a condition of great want. Catholic relief organizations, such as that of St. Vincent de Paul, and the pastors, who might be considered one-man relief agencies in themselves, often found the burden to be very heavy. Non-Catholic relief associations made no secret of their attempt to proselytize their Catholic clients; the editor of the *Leader* made capital of the sorry situation. This was especially true of the "Retreat," a home for unfortunate young women. In one instance the pastor, accompanied by the father of an inmate, went there to administer the last sacraments to her. Both were denied admittance and were told at the door that "the girl had confessed her sins to Jesus."

Bishop Rappe was successful to some extent in softening this attitude. His successor, disowning any unkindness towards anyone or any association that helped the poor and unfortunate, offered his own cooperation and that of the pastors for any work of relief, especially when assurance was given him that no interference would be made with the religious convictions of the clients. Better feeling did result and

[3] A. Helleu, tr. by Mary Agatha Gray, *Jeanne Jugan*, St. Louis, 1942.

many cases were referred to Bishop Gilmour for his advice. He was on the committee of the Cleveland Society for Organizing Charity. At an open meeting of the Bethel Associated Charities held in a public hall, November 15, 1887, he delivered an address on "The Duty of the Citizen towards the Poor." In this speech, which was well received by all, he recommended an organization which would anticipate what we know today as the Community Fund. It was publicly acknowledged that his endorsement of the Associated Charities of the time determined its success.[4]

[4] Gilmour to G. H. Ely, Jan. 15, 1878; Gilmour to H. N. Raymond, Oct. 22, 1887; H. N. Raymond to Gilmour, Dec. 12, 1883, May 29, 1888, Mar. 5, 1890; Gilmour to J. B. Perkins, June 8, 1881; all in C.D.A. *C.U.*, Oct. 27, Nov. 17, 1887. Cleveland *Leader*, Jan. 17, 19, 1874; Jan. 29, 1875; Nov. 22, 1876.

30

SOCIETIES AND ASSOCIATIONS DURING BISHOP GILMOUR'S EPISCOPATE

THE PERIOD AFTER THE CIVIL WAR WAS marked by a tremendous growth of organizations of every kind: literary, benevolent, social, insurance, and mutual aid societies. It was the age of secret fraternal orders. In one year (1883) 160 fraternal societies and benevolent associations were incorporated in the State of Ohio. The uniforms, the fantastic ritual, and the secrecy attracted many, the protection of insurance many more. The social and business advantages and the insurance were so many inducements to Catholic men also to join these societies. The Holy See in no uncertain terms had forbidden Catholics membership in the Free Masons or their affiliates; rules were given for identifying other forbidden secret societies which were not specifically named. The Catholic bishops, also, had warned the faithful that various secret societies tended to undermine revealed religion by their indifference to religious creeds and by the insistence on rationalistic instead of strictly Christian morality.

Many Catholic societies which appeared on the scene showed an inclination to imitate the secrecy of the other organizations. One of Bishop Gilmour's concerns was to regulate their relationship to Church authority. He encouraged Catholics to unite "in healthy societies" for beneficial purposes. However, he distinguished between a society composed exclusively of the faithful and a Catholic society as such. The latter when recognized officially by him enjoyed certain privileges, for instance, the right to assist in full regalia at the funeral of the members in the church. He laid down the conditions required to win his approval as a Catholic society: submission of their constitutions and rules; acceptance of a priest as their spiritual guide; and the promise to abide by diocesan regulations, which among other things restricted financial appeals to the general public. It was not long before the Catholic societies conformed. Other organizations called Catholic simply because of their exclusively Catholic membership the Bishop did not propose to regulate.

Secret societies, which were forbidden to Catholics, were much more numerous. These organizations admitted members without regard to their religious affiliation and, moreover, bound them by oath to absolute secrecy about their purpose and activities and to blind obedience to their officers, who might be involved as well as not in unlawful designs. Although it was thought prudent at the Third Plenary Council of Baltimore that no one bishop of his own authority should place the name of a specific society on the list of societies forbidden to Catholics, Bishop Gilmour, acting on the general principle that all bishops should warn their flocks against danger, forbade his people to join any secret oath-bound society even if it had not been specifically mentioned as forbidden to Catholics.

He proceeded, moreover, to name some of the latter, basing his stand on a letter from the Propaganda which was printed in the *Universe*: Free Masons, often condemned by Rome; Odd Fellows, condemned in the Fourth Provincial Council of Baltimore (1840) and by the bishops of the New Orleans Province; Knights of Pythias; Red Men; Grangers; Foresters; and secret labor organizations. If the character of a society were unknown, Catholics might retain membership in it or even join it provided they made the promise to give up membership should it be found to be objectionable. This was the formula recommended by the Bishop to pastors.

Because there was some sort of religious service connected with its meetings, the Bishop counselled Catholic veterans to avoid membership in the Grand Army of the Republic. If, however, they already belonged to the organization, they might wear a "button" in church but they would not receive recognition as a body. Nevertheless, in one instance he allowed another such society to attend religious service in a body, the Veteran Legion of the Army of the Rebellion. By the year 1889, however, after General Rosencrans, the brother of the Bishop of Columbus, had succeeded in having the objection to the G.A.R. removed, Bishop Gilmour recalled his disapproval.

Because the Ancient Order of United Workmen was a secret organization, the Bishop in 1879 counselled Catholics not to join it. The Sovereigns of Industry and the American Mechanics were likewise suspected though not condemned. After examining the constitutions of the Royal Arcanum, the Bishop forbade Catholics to join it. The Independent Order of Good Templars he marked as a secret society.[1]

The Fenian Brotherhood, a secret revolutionary Irish society, because of its appeal to violence was condemned by Rome. At the end of the American Civil War thousands of demobilized officers and men

[1] Fergus MacDonald, *The Catholic Church and the Secret Societies in the United States*, U. S. Catholic Historical Society, 1946. Gilmour to McCloskey, Feb. 20, 1882; to Fr. Kockerels, S.J., Feb. 20, 1884; to Mr. Dumoulin (Canton), Feb. 13, 1883; and to several other pastors; all in C.D.A.

were enlisted by the Brotherhood to fight in the war which was expected to develop because of the help given to the Confederates by the British. When this conflict was happily avoided, the Fenians conceived the idea of invading Canada and several scattered raids occurred in 1866 and the year following. Cleveland was one of the centers of this futile adventure.

The vast majority of Irish Catholics accepted the condemnation of the methods and practices of the society, but Bishop Gilmour suspected that the Fenians here hid their identity behind the curtain "of a large number of excellent men in the Irish Literary and Benevolent Society." His reasons were that that society had voted funds for a military company which had to be disbanded by the Federal Government and it had patronized a foreign lecturer who advocated "action circles" for the liberation of Ireland. He denounced the society from the pulpit of the Cathedral though he did not exclude the members from the sacraments. They marched with the St. Patrick's Benevolent Association, the Father Matthew Temperance Societies, and the Knights of Erin in the St. Patrick's Day parade of 1874; in the next year they were absent.

Bishop Gilmour had an important part in the final and favorable recognition of the Ancient Order of Hibernians. This was the most important Irish Catholic Society in America in the nineteenth century. It was descended from the secret societies in Ireland which were born of the "repeated frustration of all efforts to secure national freedom." Under the name of St. Patrick's Fraternal Society it came to America. Its constitution required that only Irish Roman Catholics of good moral character were to be members; these were forbidden, moreover, to belong to any secret society condemned by the Catholic Church. It was chartered in New York in 1853 under the name of the Ancient Order of Hibernians.

Common error blamed the Hibernians for the labor troubles in the coal fields of Pennsylvania, identifying them with the "Molly Maguires" whose excesses were rightfully condemned by the ecclesiastical authorities of that State in 1876. Later research has arrived at the conclusion that "the evidence does not show that the 'Molly Maguires' ever existed as an organization nor that the A.O.H. was to blame for the outrages allegedly committed by its members."[2] The A.O.H. denounced the "Molly Maguires" and disclaimed any sympathy for lawlessness on any ground. In 1878 its constitution was revised and submitted to the Church authorities for approval. The order would accept a Catholic chaplain and require its members to fulfill their religious obligations.

Bishop Gilmour's first attitude towards the A.O.H. is ascertained from the advice he gave to inquiring pastors. Although the Church had not condemned it, and its members were usually allowed to receive

[2] Walter J. Coleman, *Labor Disturbances in Pennsylvania, 1850 to 1880*, Catholic Univ. Press, Washington, 1936.

the sacraments, the pastor was by persuasion to discourage the organization in his parish.[3] This attitude must have been softened by the advice of Archbishop Purcell to encourage societies of Irish Catholics other than the Fenians. "Men would form some sort of aggregation and it would be better to have the Irish join the A.O.H. than the forbidden societies."[4] As long as the members were practical Catholics the Archbishop would be willing to allow them to come to church in their regalia. In Cincinnati they had asked for a priest chaplain. Bishop Domenec of Pittsburgh had allowed the Hibernians to appear in his Cathedral in a body. Shortly afterwards Bishop Gilmour approved of a branch of the order at Salineville when a document was submitted in which the promise was made to comply with the diocesan statutes.[5]

The Bishop himself explained that in the beginning he had unfavorable reports about the Hibernians. To test their loyalty towards the Church he asked them to make the yearly reception of the sacraments a requirement for membership, and to make their constitution conform to Catholic practice in all respects. When they did accept his proposals he accorded them the privileges of Catholic societies. Father Thorpe was appointed the chaplain of the Cleveland branch.

In his pastoral of 1879, however, Bishop Gilmour showed himself still suspicious of them, questioning their origin and challenging them to lay aside their secrecy and to reveal their aims. Despite their condemnation in some other dioceses, he would tolerate them even though full approval would require some changes in their constitution. They would have to sever any connection with the Board of Erin, a mysterious group in the British Isles which supposedly exercised remote control over the Hibernians here, and with any other suspected secret societies of "trickstering politicians and secret plotters." As a token of their good-will he called upon them to give up any patronage of the *Irish World*, a journal printed in New York, which he accused of habitual disrespect for Church authority. His condemnation of this newspaper was repeated in the pastoral of the Fourth Provincial Council of Cincinnati in 1882.

Nevertheless, he appeared before the national convention of the A.O.H. in Cleveland in 1884 and in a forthright speech he again called upon the order to cast off its secrecy and its affiliation with other suspected organizations. In response to this exhortation, the majority of the delegates voted to cut off any connection with the Board of Erin or the Clan-na-Gael, a mysterious secret society which seems to have been dominated by the suspected Fenians. Bishop Gilmour thought better of the Hibernians for taking such action: "They were too valuable a body to be rudely dealt with."

Because of this, at the Council of Baltimore in 1884, he sought for

---

[3] Gilmour to Schaffeld, Aug. 16, 1872; Healy (Lima) to Gilmour, Aug. 23, 1877; Mullen to Gilmour, Feb. 19, 1873; all in C.D.A.

[4] Purcell to Gilmour, Feb. 13, 1873; in C.D.A.

[5] Approbation dated Mar. 5, 1873; in C.D.A.

formal recognition of the parent organization, stripped of outside domination. Other bishops also strongly defended the order. The extraordinary and fervent speech of Archbishop Feehan of Chicago in its favor closed the debate, though no pronouncement was made. Bishop McQuaid of Rochester drew up a set of questions which were sent to the A.O.H. authorities asking them about the supposed outside domination of the order. The answers influenced the bishops of the New York Province in their meeting to declare that the Hibernians, especially those who expressed willingness to conform to Church regulations, were not to be considered as a forbidden society. The questionnaire had been submitted for approval to Bishop Gilmour.

The Bishop of Cleveland also suggested to Cardinal Gibbons that the leaders of the A.O.H. be invited to appear for direct questioning at the customary meeting of the archbishops of the country. Although this suggestion was not followed, the archbishops did not condemn the order. Moreover, ten of the twelve metropolitans favored the granting of a chaplain as a sign of approval to those branches of the Hibernians which requested one. Up to the last, Bishop Gilmour would not countenance those branches which recognized the control of officials in Ireland. His great friend, Bishop McQuaid, after long years of disapproval gave the Hibernians official recognition in his diocese in 1894.[6]

The universal indignation at the cruel coercive measures used by the British Government to suppress the movement for land reform in Ireland had its passing reflection in Cleveland. The great famine which lasted from 1845 to 1848, one of the worst in European history, brought on starvation, fever, and death. Of those who survived as many as could emigrated to America or to England, with the consequent loss of some 2,000,000 people to the country. By virtue of the Land Act of 1849, moreover, a third of the old landlords who had been ruined by the famine were replaced by new English and Scottish owners who, to improve their estates, used their irresponsible power to abuse the rights of their tenants. The result was that the country suffered further famine and disaster. Then followed agrarian disturbances on the part of the oppressed people, which were met with more coercion laws and the suspension of civil rights. The crisis came when the crops failed again (1877 to 1879); the small farmers were evicted wholesale to starve and die on the roadside.

Irish leaders founded the Land League[7] in 1879 for the purpose of

---

[6] Frederick J. Zwierlein, *Life and Letters of Bishop McQuaid*, Rochester, 1926, II, 378 sq. Gilmour to John Sullivan, Nov. 11, 1873; O'Branigan to Gilmour, Jan. 10, 1879; Gilmour to M. Scanlon, Jan. 13, 1879; Gilmour to Quigley, Dec., 1880; A.O.H. (East Toledo) to Gilmour, July 26, 1880; Gilmour to Tuigg, Aug. 1, 1881; Gilmour to O'Hara, Aug. 2, 1881; Gilmour to Gibbons, Jan. 18, 1885, Oct. 16, 1886; Gibbons' sec'y to Horstmann, Nov. 8, 1895; Gilmour to McQuaid, Mar. 30, 1886; Corrigan to Gilmour, Mar. 27, 1886; the Bishop's answer, Apr. 3, 1886; Gilmour to Elder, Oct. 4, 1886; approval of A.O.H. branch in Massillon, May 5, 1885, Molony to Boff, Nov. 9, 1891; all in C.D.A.

[7] Zwierlein, *Op. cit.*, *loc. cit.* Edmund Curtis, *A History of Ireland*, London, 1936. Gilmour to Daudet, Feb. 15, 1881; Houck to Molony, Aug. 24, 1881; both in C.D.A.

ending by constitutional means the evils of "rack rent," evictions, and landlord oppression. The ultimate object in mind was the ownership of the land by those who cultivated it, with a fair compensation for the extinction of the landlord's interest. Charles Stewart Parnell, the head of the Home Rule party which sought a parliament for Ireland separate from the English Parliament, was made the head of the Land League also. Gladstone, the Prime Minister of England, favored relief for the Irish and, with the help of Parnell, he carried through the English Parliament the Land Act of 1881. This guaranteed fair rent, fixity of tenure, free sale, and some protection against unjust eviction; the landlords' rights remained practically intact. The purpose of both men was to make the country a land of peasant proprietors.

Michael Davitt, the inspiration and the "father" of the Land League, had been a Fenian and the bishops of Ireland had condemned that organization; but they gave their approbation to the Land League, with a warning against the use of unlawful or violent means. A new complication arose when Parnell and others were imprisoned, under the operation of new coercion laws, for having advocated the boycotting of landlords who refused to accept reduced rents and of those also who increased their holdings at the expense of others who had been evicted. From their prison they issued a No Rent Manifesto (October, 1881) in which the tenants were advised to withhold all rent until the laws were revised. This proclamation produced a complete division of sentiment about the Land League. The Irish bishops denounced the manifesto as contrary to the law of God and the fundamental principles of private property. The No Rent campaign failed of its purpose and more rent was paid than ever before; more violence took place and evictions were multiplied over previous years. Effective relief came only in 1892.

In the United States an auxiliary Land League was organized in 1880 and a few of the bishops in the East approved of it, but like the Irish bishops they deprecated violence or unlawful measures. In Cleveland the Parnell Land League was started. The *Catholic Universe* adopted a none too friendly attitude towards it. Bishop Gilmour suspected that it was dominated by the members of the Clan-na-Gael. Cleveland, however, gave a rousing welcome to Parnell and his companion Dillon, when they visited here in January, 1880. To listen to their plea for help for Ireland, approximately 5,000 marched in the parade to the Tabernacle, a public auditorium at the southeast corner of Ontario Street and St. Clair Avenue. Meanwhile the news of the No Rent Manifesto, mentioned above, reached the city and the Irish bishops were criticized in the local newspapers for having condemned it; the *Universe* denied the right of the local critics to speak for the Irish-American body. Bishop Gilmour identified the Cleveland supporters of the No Rent campaign as members of the Clan-na-Gael and he declined their invitation to deliver an address on the subject under their auspices.

Lest this refusal be construed maliciously, and he be put falsely in an anti-Irish position, the Bishop called a meeting of the Irish societies and of the Catholic Central Association and proposed to them that he would deliver a lecture on the Land League in a public hall, the proceeds of which would be devoted to the relief of the Irish sufferers. Meanwhile he urged Bishop McQuaid of Rochester to delay his visit to Cleveland to avoid the inference that he was influenced by that prelate's recent attack on the Land League. The great lecture, which appeared later in a twenty-two-page pamphlet, was given on February 6, 1882, before an appreciative audience which taxed the capacity of the Tabernacle.

The Bishop reviewed in sympathetic strain the history of Ireland's wrongs and traced their origin in good part to the unjust system of land tenure, according to which "the native Irishman lived in hopeless poverty and on constant notice of being evicted from his poor home, if he were unable to pay the rent on land he could not buy and for the improvement of which he was unjustly taxed." He looked for some relief as a result of the progress of the Land League, but he denounced the No Rent Manifesto as unlawful and a danger to the final success of the league which advocated fair rent and eventual ownership by purchase. The speech did much to dissipate any notion that the Bishop was against any well-ordered aspirations of the Irish people. Archbishop Croke of Cashel in Ireland wrote to thank the Bishop, saying that he was "immensely pleased with the speech which did not come a bit too soon."[8]

Not long after the Bishop's lecture the Ladies Branch of the Parnell Land League was founded in the city. The original women's branch of the Land League had been organized in Ireland at the time that the coercion laws threatened to put all the leaders in prison; the women would carry on until the emergency passed. Bishop McQuaid in Rochester, at a protest meeting against the suspension of civil rights in Ireland, had spoken in great admiration of the courage of the Irish women.

In Cleveland, however, Bishop Gilmour saw in the local women's organization the survival of those who favored the No Rent Manifesto. He criticized them in a sermon at the Cathedral and published a condemnation of their society in the *Universe*. He accused the fomenters of opposition to his stand of using the women's branch for their own purpose. In the name of womanly modesty and "to prevent Catholic women from turning into brawling politicians," he issued a formal excommunication against membership in that society. There was no intention of criticizing the Ladies Land League in general, although it had been condemned in Ireland. The Bishop was supported in this action, and only twenty attended the meeting he had forbidden. The Ancient

[8] Gilmour to Elder, Jan. 11, 1882; in C.D.A. *C.U.*, Nov. 10, 1881; Jan. 5, 19, Feb. 9 (text of speech), 1882.

Order of Hibernians, which had some 1,000 members in the city, passed resolutions heartily approving the Bishop's position.[9]

During this time the vituperous campaign of Cowles of the *Leader* reached its height. The Bishop in a public speech had defended the loyalty of Catholic citizens to American institutions, after giving an outline of their contribution. He recalled that Catholics had discovered and explored the country and had a large share in its development. The Irish immigrant had cut the roads through the forests, dug the canals, and built the railroads; they and other Catholic immigrants—Germans, Bohemians, and Poles—had contributed to the wealth and population of Cleveland. He rehearsed the history of discrimination against Catholics, from the burning of the Ursuline Convent in Boston to the founding of the Order of the American Union with its headquarters in Cleveland and its "rampant organ," the Cleveland *Leader*, "which daily falsified the doctrine and purposes of the Church." The Bishop asked that the Church be allowed to share in the constitutional guarantees of liberty and to carry out her religious mission without having to defend herself at every turn against calumnious accusations. Editor Cowles attacked the Bishop's statements but refused to publish his rejoinder which, nevertheless, appeared in the *Universe*. In it Cowles was blamed for making Cleveland the "byword of bigotry"; and it was stated that, while he "constantly raved about intolerance and coercion of conscience," he strove to "disfranchise and harass Catholics simply on account of their religion."

When the Bishop condemned the local Ladies Land League Cowles found a fresh opportunity for attack, accusing him of oppressing consciences. The editor in turn was taxed with having tried to coerce his own daughter in matters of religion. Miss Cowles had found out from personal investigation that the statements made about Catholics by her father were not true; she was received into the Catholic Church in Rome. The local press carried articles about the Pope and the Jesuits and the Bishop conspiring to embarrass the editor. Mr. Cowles had gone to Europe, hoping to shake the determination of his daughter, but his attempts were unsuccessful; she was permitted to return to Cleveland on condition that she would have nothing to do with Catholics in the city. The Bishop knew of this and he sent his secretary, Father Houck, with a paid advertisement to the editor, containing the charge. This was published by the *Penny Press* when it was refused by Cowles, who wrote an abusive and insulting note to the Bishop in regard to it.

The controversy in print continued, the Bishop contending that the calling of harsh names was not a denial of the statement at issue; he, moreover, insinuated that such persecution was the cause of the poor

[9] Gilmour to Shaffeld, June 30, 1882; T. McCarthy to Gilmour, June 5, 1882; Gilmour to Corrigan, Aug. 8, 1882; Chatard to Gilmour, Jan. 24, 1882; all in C.D.A. *C.U.*, May 25, June 8, 15, 22, 1882.

health of Miss Cowles. Thereupon the editor entered suit in the Common Pleas Court against the Bishop, the *Universe*, and the *Penny Press*. The case dragged on for more than a year during which Cowles continued his tirades. Finally, in 1884, at the request of the plaintiff, the suits were dismissed. The Bishop withdrew that part of his charge touching the illness of the innocent occasion of the controversy but not that part which charged persecution. The costs were shared by the parties to the suit. Contrary to what was published in the *Leader*, the editor's daughter, who offered her life for the conversion of her husband, received the last sacraments devoutly before her death in Italy in 1884. The *Leader*, thereafter, lost none of its animus against things Catholic.[10]

Bishop Gilmour continued to support the cause of Irish freedom. In 1886, under the auspices of the Irish societies of the city he delivered a public lecture in Music Hall, Cleveland's then newest auditorium on Vincent Avenue, west of East 9th Street, for the benefit of the Gladstone-Parnell parliamentary fund which was used in seeking Home Rule for Ireland. He was one of the principal speakers at a similar meeting in Toledo in the same year. Later, with other prominent citizens, at a public meeting he raised his voice in protest against the further English mistreatment of the Irish. Father Thorpe acted as chairman at other mass meetings of Catholic societies to welcome and to help Irish patriots who came here.

In his last years, especially after the Roman condemnation of the No Rent Manifesto and the boycotting procedures, the Bishop hesitated to discuss the Irish question in public. Though he felt that the American people ought to be warned against demagogues, he wished to avoid being maneuvered into a false position in doing so.[11] He made a general appeal to the public in the *Universe*, and ordered collections taken up in all the parishes for the relief of the stricken people of Ireland. He was able to send more than $11,000 to the Irish bishops, especially to those in the west of Ireland.[12]

Needless to say the Bishop vigorously encouraged all organizations which were willing to observe Catholic norms in their operation. As might be expected, he approved the Total Abstinence societies with his usual heartiness. The National Catholic Temperance Union held one of its first meetings in this city in 1872. Upon his return from Europe in 1883 the Bishop gave an account of his travels and visit to Rome in a public lecture at the Tabernacle for the purpose of raising funds to pay the expenses of the convention of the Total Abstinence societies. He often preached on temperance, especially during the time

[10] Voluminous correspondence in C.D.A. and contemporaneous local newspaper accounts, including *C.U.* Houck, *Op. cit.*

[11] Michael Corcoran to Gilmour, Apr. 5, 1888; Carroll (Holy Name) to Gilmour, June, 1888; the Bishop's answer, June 10, 1888; all in C.D.A.

[12] Gilmour correspondence with Irish bishops, and with Mother Angela (Notre Dame), Dec. 15, 1879; Gilmour to editor of Cleveland *Plain Dealer*, Dec. 19, 1879; all in C.D.A. *C.U.*, July 25, 1874; Nov. 6, 1879; Jan. 5, 10, 1880; June 24, July 8, 15, 1886; Apr. 28, Dec. 15, 1887; Feb. 7, 1889.

that he was urging Catholics to be less reticent on questions of public interest. Speaking in 1886 on the subject of law and order, and calling for the closing of the saloons on Sundays and a stricter regulation of the liquor traffic, he addressed a mass meeting here at Music Hall and a similar gathering in Toledo.[13] In that same year the Total Abstinence Union of Ohio, with the Bishop's full approval, paraded in public to celebrate the birthday of Father Matthew. As late as 1889 he used his oratorical ability to denounce the abuse of intoxicating liquors in a sermon at the Cathedral, which was extensively quoted in the East.

Many other societies were mutual benefit or insurance societies which combined with their obvious purpose other good works, such as the establishment of libraries, social halls, and reading rooms for Catholics. The Emerald Beneficial Association, the Irish Catholic Benevolent Union, the many German organizations, and those of other nationalities were all favored by Bishop Gilmour when he found them to be Catholic in spirit. In 1886 he addressed the convention in Toledo of the Catholic Knights of Ohio, who met in conjunction with the German Roman Catholic Central Society of America. The Knights of St. John and the Catholic Mutual Benefit Association solicited and obtained his approval.[14] Worthy of mention also is the Edgerton Club, an exclusively social organization among the Catholic young men of the city, which was formed in 1872 and lasted some twenty years. We have already seen above that the Dominican Fathers organized the first Holy Name Society in the diocese with 250 members in 1880.[15]

[13] Cleveland *Leader*, Sept. 17, Oct. 2, 1872. *C.U.*, Feb. 26, 1876; Nov. 12, 1885; Apr. 1, 1886; Jan. 31, Aug. 1, 1889.

[14] Gilmour to Molony, Apr. 8, 1873; C.M.B.A. Grand Council to Gilmour, Jan., 1887, Aug., 1888; Gilmour to State Council, Catholic Knights of Ohio, Aug., 1886; all in C.D.A.

[15] *C.U.*, Feb. 5, Apr. 22, 1880.

31

LABOR, CATHOLIC LOYALTY,
AND THE JUBILEES

I N REGARD TO THE KNIGHTS OF LABOR,[1] THE FIRST
all-inclusive labor organization in the country, Bishop Gilmour
in the beginning followed a cautious policy. Their secrecy made
them suspect to him and their ritual was said to be similar in some
features to that of the Free Masons. It had been forbidden to
Catholics in Canada in 1870 but the condemnation was not extended
to this country. When Catholics here joined it in ever-increasing numbers the secrecy was modified, especially after the election of a Catholic, Terence Powderly,[2] as president in 1879.

The mind of Bishop Gilmour was manifested in his pastoral of that
same year. In it he vindicated the right of workingmen to band together for better wages and for their own protection, asserting that
the strong arm of the poor man was as much his capital in stock as was
gold the rich man's capital. Individualist that he was, however, the
Bishop was against any attempt to force men to join the unions, feeling that such action would be an attempt on a man's liberty. And he
warned Catholics against secret labor associations and against participating in any attempt to force or coerce others, as well as against
any overt act of violence against the rights or property of others.[3]

In the pastoral of the Fourth Provincial Council of Cincinnati, which
he composed, the same principles were restated, some of them quite in
advance of the times. "Capital must be liberal towards labor and share
justly and generously the joint profits which come from their common
efforts." Capital has no more right to undue reward than labor, nor
should capital be unduly protected at the expense of labor. Mutually
dependent, both should recognize their common interest. At the same

---

[1] The Ancient Order of United Workmen came under the ban of the Bishop in
an announcement in the *Catholic Universe*, Feb. 3, 1879; this decision was relaxed
however at a later period. Sauvadet (Toledo) to Gilmour, Feb., 1879; Gilmour to
Gibbons (Bellevue), May 10, 1884; both in C.D.A.

[2] Terence V. Powderly, *The Path I Trod* (his biography), New York, 1940.
Henry J. Browne, *The Catholic Church and the Knights of Labor*, Washington,
1949.

[3] Pastoral, 1879, pamphlet. Browne, *Op. cit.*, p. 29, contrasts the idea of Bp. Gilmour on wages, viz., that a man may work for any wage he can get, with later
papal teaching in the matter, which calls for a living wage.

time, in words almost identical with those found in the pastoral of 1879, warning was issued against the coercion of other workingmen and against violence or injury to persons or property.[4]

At first Bishop Gilmour found it difficult to obtain a copy of the constitution of the Knights to study it and to decide upon its merits from the Church's point of view, but in the course of time his attitude of suspicion was changed. The twelve members in West Brookfield who had left the order, when it was intimated to them that it had been "condemned for Catholics," hoped that with the modifications made in the ritual and the secrecy which made it less objectionable they might be allowed to join again, especially since Catholics in other parishes belonged to it. The pastor of Canal Fulton took it upon himself to publicly forbid his parishioners to join, yet the men of the town wrote to the Bishop that the Catholics in Akron and Massillon were not so restricted. The Bishop's answer was to the effect that he had never given authorization to anyone to join and, apparently moved by the report of the pastor, he did not approve of their joining. Yet in the same month the Bishop wrote to the pastor of Mansfield that the Knights were not a strictly secret society and Catholic men might be allowed to join in good faith and to receive the sacraments, provided they made the usual promise to give up membership if the order were later officially forbidden to them.[5]

As Catholics became more numerous in the order the necessity of defining a united attitude towards it became imperative. Bishop Gilmour had information from Rome[6] that the Archbishops of Chicago and of Baltimore, among others, had written to the Propaganda advising against the extension of the Quebec condemnation of the organization to the United States. In accordance with the procedure prescribed in the Third Council of Baltimore, the archbishops of the country in their meeting in November, 1886, studied and discussed the question and voted ten to two against the condemnation of the order. Bishop Gilmour in answer to the request of his metropolitan, Archbishop Elder, had given his advice against condemnation and urged the Archbishop to write to Rome in that sense.[7]

Since the decision of the prelates gathered together in Baltimore was not unanimous, the matter was then referred to the Propaganda. Archbishop Gibbons, in Rome in the early part of 1887 for the consistory in which he was made cardinal, presented a long memorandum in favor

[4] *Acta et Decreta, ut supra*, p. 246.

[5] Kleekamp (West Brookfield: Massillon) to Gilmour, Jan. 11, 1881; the Bishop's answer, Feb. 14, 1882; Magenhann (Mansfield) to Gilmour, July 25, 1883; the Bishop's answer, Mar. 16, 1886; Gilmour to Kockerels (Toledo) Feb. 20, 1884; Gilmour to Mr. Dumoulin (Canton) Feb. 13, 1883; Henry Mullen (North Lawrence) to Gilmour, Mar. 10, 1884; Fr. Vattmann (Canal Fulton) to Gilmour, Mar. 10, 1884; Gilmour's answer to John Murphy (Canal Fulton) Mar. 11, 1886; Rupert (S. Toledo) to Gilmour, Sept., 1884; all in C.D.A. Letters from Massillon, Canal Fulton, Alliance, and Salinesville to Powderly, in 1882, in Browne, *Op. cit.*, 83 sq.

[6] Ella B. Edes to Gilmour, Sept. 15, 1886, in C.D.A.

[7] Gilmour to Elder, Oct. 5, 1886, in C.D.A.

of the Knights. He pointed out that the order was not subversive, that blind obedience was not asked of the members, and that the secrecy demanded was for the sake of protection and involved nothing against a man's conscience. The document was intended for private circulation only but an enterprising newspaper man secured a copy and published it in a New York paper. As a result the full text was given to the public in the Journal, *Moniteur de Rome.*

Writing of this event from Rome to Bishop Gilmour, Archbishop Ireland of St. Paul announced confidently that the Knights would not be condemned.[8] The Bishop of Cleveland thereupon wrote to Archbishop Gibbons that he "would deem it a great misfortune if the Knights of Labor were condemned." And in their defense he continued: "They have substantial grievances. Let us seek to guide, not crush, and only when in principle they are wrong to condemn. The few illegalities so far committed only show the inner spirit of justice in the body. Be slow to condemn, say I." In sending on a copy of the memorandum he had presented to the Propaganda, Archbishop Gibbons expressed agreement, adding that a condemnation of the Knights would be a real calamity for the Church in America. After the latter had returned to the United States Bishop Gilmour wrote to thank him for his efforts in behalf of the Knights.[9]

Under date of June 20, 1888, Doctor O'Connell of Rome notified Bishop Gilmour, as he did others, that the final Roman decision on the question of the Knights of Labor was to the effect that they were not to be condemned (*tolerari possunt*). Not long afterwards, in a communication to Archbishop Elder, the Bishop gave further expression to his conviction that "capital was driving labor to the wall; labor had much on its side to complain of," and it was to be expected "that systematical combinations of capital were met by systematical combinations of labor." He deplored the fact that riots and violence seemed sometimes unavoidable.[10]

The decision about the Knights was officially issued by Cardinal Simeoni, August 29, 1888.[11] On the front page of the *Catholic Universe*, on December 13 following, the Bishop gave an explanation of the decree which permitted Catholics to join the Knights with a safe conscience. It was expected that whatever in the constitution was susceptible of a wrong interpretation, especially in the matter of the rights of man to private property, would be corrected. "The Holy See would not condemn in principle any attempt of labor to organize even if outside its own control" and that it was, "far from putting its strength at the service of capital against the claims of labor."[12] The organization had reached its peak in 1886 when it had some 730,000 members;

[8] Ireland to Gilmour, Rome, Feb. 6, 1887, in C.D.A.
[9] Gibbons to Gilmour, Mar. 2, 1887; Gilmour to Gibbons, Mar. 16, July 16, 1887; all in C.D.A.
[10] Gilmour to Elder, Aug. 14, 1887, in C.D.A.
[11] Zwierlein, *Op. cit.,* II, 459.
[12] Browne, *Op. cit.,* 325.

these were gradually absorbed in the newly formed American Federation of Labor.

During this same period, by a singular combination of circumstances, the discussion of Henry George's book, *Progress and Poverty*, and his peculiar theories of property including that of single tax[13] exercised the minds of several prelates. Doctor Edward McGlynn of New York espoused the cause and was suspended by his superior, Archbishop Corrigan of New York, for refusing to give up his public campaign in its favor. Cardinal Gibbons and many others of the hierarchy were against any public condemnation of the theories.

Bishop Gilmour expressed himself as favorable to a better distribution of capital and a better recognition of the rights of labor as against too much centralization and monopoly. He did not favor the theories of George but he thought that more ought to be said about the conditions of the poor who sometimes protest against their lot. "Now to condemn George's book," he wrote, "will be turned to look as if the Church sided with capital and was against labor." He wrote to the Propaganda and to Cardinal Gibbons against the public condemnation of the book. He thought that such a procedure would only serve to advertise it and to make a martyr of its author who symbolized its economic theories. He felt that the movement would settle itself without involving the Church.[14] He had no patience, however, with Doctor McGlynn. He denounced him to Rome when he came to Cleveland to address the Ladies Land League in favor of his theories on private property, although the Bishop later denied that it was on account of these theories that he did so.

On the local scene the editor of the *Catholic Universe* undoubtedly reflected the ideas of the Bishop in supporting the cause of the striking steel workers in the early eighties in Cleveland. In 1882 two-thirds of them, mostly of the English-speaking nations, lost their jobs. The editor blamed the American policy of high tariff as responsible for such a situation. In the strike of 1885 most of the men were from the Slav nations; they marched 2,500 strong to protest the reduction of their wages. The newspapers raised a cry against the "foreigners." The *Universe* defended them as thrifty Americans who owned their own homes and, while reprobating any violence, protested against the "pinching and robbing and extermination of the workers."[15]

Bishop Gilmour took advantage of every favorable occasion to impress the general public with the fact that Catholics were always loyal to the Republic and to all that it represented. He saw to it that the Catholics of the city under the auspices of the Central Association participated as citizens in the centenary celebration of the Declaration

---

[13] The tax levied on a single object, especially the land as the sole source of public revenue; an economic policy of the 18th century revived by Henry George.

[14] Gilmour to Gibbons, Apr. 16, 1888; Gilmour to Elder, Apr. 17, 1888; Gilmour to Simeoni, Apr. 19, 1888; all in C.D.A.

[15] C.U., editorial, July 16, Aug. 6, 1885. Oscar Townsend (Cleveland, Lorain and Wheeling R.R.) to Gilmour, Jan. 31, 1887, in C.D.A.

of Independence; and he prescribed a Mass of Thanksgiving in every parish.[16] In a public lecture in 1878 he recalled the loyalty of Catholics to the Union cause and their traditional dislike for human slavery.

At the time of the assassination of President Garfield he called attention to the Catholic teaching on the fundamental necessity of respect for constituted authority, and at the same time he directed that prayers be said in every parish for peace and for the protection of religion and virtue. At the sympathy meeting on Public Square, July 4, 1881, and at the great mass meeting in the Tabernacle he expressed the unswerving loyalty of his people; and in a pastoral he pointed out that respect for authority was based on respect for God who could not be excluded from public affairs without disastrous results. In the procession which escorted the remains of the deceased President from the great pavilion on Public Square to Lake View Cemetery, the Bishop rode at the head of the Catholic societies which all turned out for the sad event. Later, at the dedication of the Garfield monument in Lake View Cemetery, the Catholic societies paraded again with the other citizens and the Bishop was one of the speakers. Among those present ex-President Hayes and General Sherman were well known to the Bishop; and it was remarked that when he arose to speak President Harrison uncovered his head out of respect for the venerable prelate.[17]

The Bishop's fame as a patriotic speaker caused him to be invited to make one of the principal addresses at the centennial celebration of the establishment of civil government in the Northwest Territory, at Marietta in July, 1888; his subject was "Religion and Civil Government." While the Catholic citizens of Cleveland participated officially in the celebration of the centenary of the Constitution of the United States, the Bishop represented the diocese at the Catholic Day commemorating the same event in Columbus.[18]

In the promotion of the spiritual well-being of his people Bishop Gilmour urged them to avail themselves of the special opportunities for grace in the papal jubilees which were published during his episcopate. The long processions of the faithful visiting the churches were the source of great edification to others as well as a public profession of their own belief and a manifestation of their devotion to the Holy See. The Jubilee of 1877, commemorating the fortieth anniversary of the episcopal consecration of Pope Pius IX, was marked by a solemn pontifical Mass of Thanksgiving in the Cathedral on February 27 of that year. When the beloved Pontiff died the Cathedral bells were tolled every day for a week, Masses were offered for the Pope in every parish, and the Bishop celebrated a funeral Mass in his Cathedral.[19] The diocese officially kept the Jubilees of 1879 and 1881 with much spiritual

---

[16] Cleveland *Leader*, June 12, 1876. *C.U.*, June 17, 1876.

[17] *C.U.*, July 7, Sept. 22, 29, 1881; May 28, June 5, 1890.

[18] Centennial pamphlet. Cleveland *Leader-Morning Herald*, July 16, 1888. *C.U.*, July 12, 19, 26, Sept. 20, 1888. Gilmour to Butler, Sept. 2, 1888, in C.D.A.

[19] *C.U.*, Apr. 10, 1875; Apr. 21, 1877; Feb. 21, 1878; Mar. 27, 1879; Apr. 7, 1881; Feb. 18, 1886.

benefit. In Cleveland the Cathedral, St. Peter's, St. Malachy's, and St. Patrick's were the churches designated for the visits.

The Jubilee of 1886–1887, celebrating the fiftieth year in the priesthood of Pope Leo XIII, was kept with extraordinary solemnity here. All the faithful offered their prayers and received the sacraments in honor of it. A great mass meeting was held in Music Hall on December 30, 1886, and five-minute speeches were delivered in the various languages of the diocese in praise of the Holy Father. Father Thorpe spoke in English, Father Westerholt in German, Father Healy in Irish, Father Gerardin in French, Father Capitani in Italian, Father Furdek in Hungarian, John Girousek in Bohemian, and John Kniola in Polish. The Bishop addressed the great crowd and a cablegram was sent to the Pope from his devoted children. Father Joseph Koudelka drew up an elegantly illuminated manuscript for the occasion, which was sent to Rome. In Toledo the Bishop presided at a corresponding celebration in Memorial Hall. Eulogies were given in English by Mr. McDonald, in Italian by Father Quigley, in German by J. P. Mettler, in French by Father Braire, in Polish by Father Wiecorek, and in Irish by Father Hannin. The newspapers there, unfortunately, reflected the bad manners of the anti-Catholic element in the city.[20]

[20] *C.U.*, Nov. 24, Dec. 15, 1887; Jan. 5, 1888. Cleveland *Plain Dealer*, Dec. 31, 1887. Toledo *Bee*, Jan. 2, 1888.

32

SPECIAL ACTIVITIES OF

BISHOP GILMOUR

ISHOP GILMOUR BROUGHT NEW LIFE AND VIGOR
to the diocese. He was a "fighter for truth and justice, for
morality and good order." Yet for long years, ever since his
sickness at the seminary at Emmitsburg, he was hardly ever
without some physical pain.[1] He himself mentioned a sun-
stroke but did not specify the particular time when it happened. In
June, 1874, he collapsed at South Bend, Indiana. Although he arrived
there in an exhausted condition, he insisted upon giving the commencement address at St. Mary's Academy and as a result he was taken down
with "one of those periodic attacks of blood rushing to his head." He
said Mass the next morning, nevertheless, and was preparing to return
to Cleveland when the physician ordered him to bed for a complete
and extended rest.

He was fortunate in finding himself in the care of sympathetic
nurses; through the friend of his youth, Father Rafferty, he had become acquainted with Mother Angela Gillespie, the Superior of the
community of Sisters of the Holy Cross. To her and the other Sisters
he gave credit later on for "bringing him back from the brink of the
grave." It was through her that the Bishop kept the chancery informed
of his condition. It was by her pen that Father Conlan of the Cathedral
was authorized to expedite pressing diocesan business. In a few days
"the features of the congestion were under control," and the Bishop
was sufficiently recovered, on August 8, to ordain in the convent
chapel the five students who had been summoned there for the purpose: Fathers Charles Chevraux, Henry Dorner, James Hunt, John
Klute, and Nicolas Kolopp.

In the following December he was able in the company of his friend,
Bishop McCloskey of Louisville, to travel to Mobile, Alabama, for
the consecration of a bishop, but fatigue prevented him from taking
part in the ceremony. He remained in the South until his return to
Cleveland in May, 1875. Because the physicians here judged it would

[1] Gilmour to H. P. Gallagher, Mar. 13, 1880, to G. Keenan, Apr. 13, 1880; both in
C.D.A. Boston *Republic*, May 25, 1889, as quoted in *C.U.*, May 30, 1889.

be imprudent for him to take up his duties immediately, he arranged for Monsignor Boff to administer the diocese in his absence and for neighboring bishops to come for Confirmation and for ordinations, and he sailed for France, September 4, 1875, with Lourdes as his first objective.[2] In southern France his health slowly but surely returned.

In the spring of the next year he visited southern Italy and made his first *ad limina* visit to Rome, April 8, 1876. Before he went there his physician had advised him that he would have to follow a "less active and initiative life" than that which had marked his previous career, if he desired to conserve his strength. At Rome, in view of this report, the Bishop was given the promise of a coadjutor in case he were not able to go on with his work alone. He sailed from Liverpool without visiting his native Scotland, May 11, 1876, and arrived in New York on the 21st.

Great preparations had been made by the Catholic Central Association to give him a grand reception after his long absence of almost two years. On June 1, the uniformed societies and their bands met him at the Union Depot. The official cannon fired its salute of welcome; four white horses drew his carriage through the midst of thousands of people to the Cathedral, where he was officially welcomed by the clergy. A reception in the newly completed Cathedral House followed. He was presented with a horse and carriage in token of the satisfaction of all in his return.[3]

He dropped easily again into his usual round of duties. His visits to the schools and religious communities were turned into joyful receptions in which he entertained his listeners with the account of his travels. Bishop Dwenger found him in better health than he had anticipated.[4] All thought of resignation had vanished. Instead of asking for a coadjutor, he felt himself capable of continuing his work with the assistance only of a secretary and chancellor. Father Boff, worn out with the duties of administrator, was replaced as pastor of the Cathedral by Father Thorpe. Father Quigley had been considered for a position of chancellor and Father Mears actually served as secretary for a while; but finally in July, 1877, Father George Houck began his long career of usefulness in that capacity. A large vault was built in the Cathedral House for the chancery documents; a complete record was made of all parish property; lithograph copies were kept of all official correspondence; the record of historical happenings was made part of the annual report of the pastors. Soon the Cleveland chancery became a model of efficiency and accuracy and the Bishop was relieved of a great deal of the burden of official anxieties.

Nevertheless, his labors were interrupted very seldom. He spent the

[2] *C.U.*, Aug. 29, Dec. 19, 1874; Sept. 11, Oct. 23, 1875; Mar. 17, Apr. 22, 1876. Mother Angela's and Gilmour's correspondence with Conlan, in C.D.A.

[3] Cleveland *Leader*, May 15, June 2, 5, 10, Oct. 31, 1876. *C.U.*, Mar. 7, May 27, June 3, July 1, 1876.

[4] Dwenger to Purcell, Aug. 14, 1876, in N.D.A.

summer of 1880 in Nova Scotia seeking some relaxation with relatives
and the friends of his boyhood.[5] The routine was broken again two
years later when he made his *ad limina* visit to present his report to
the Holy Father for the first ten years of his administration. Written
in French with a summary account of the increase in the number of
churches and schools, it received the special approbation of Cardinal
Simeoni,[6] of the Congregation of the Propaganda. When he was preparing to leave Cleveland receptions were given him by the clergy,
in the Cathedral House, and by the Catholic Central Association, in
Cathedral Hall; he also was presented with a modest purse for the expenses of the journey. On this occasion he expressed his gratification
at the spirit of unity he observed among the people despite their different national origins; he hoped to be their shepherd for at least another ten years. As was the custom, the uniformed societies escorted
him to the depot.

He left New York, July 22, 1882, and after visiting England, Ireland,
and Scotland he reached the Eternal City on the Feast of All Saints.
He pontificated at the Scotch College on St. Andrew's Day. The Holy
Father received him in private audience on December 5, and graciously
accepted the crimson-lined buffalo skin which he presented for Father
Lindesmith in the name of the Indian children of the Ursuline missions
in Montana. The Pope was well pleased and sent his blessing to all concerned.[7] At the special request of the Holy Father both Bishop Gilmour and Bishop McQuaid of Rochester remained in Rome over the
Christmas holidays to give their views about the proposed Catholic
University[8] and about the other subjects which were to be treated in
the Third Plenary Council of Baltimore. This accomplished, the Bishop
left Rome and sailed out of Liverpool for home on January 13, 1883.

Thirty priests met him on the train at Ashtabula, on the boundary
of the diocese, and 5,000 enthusiastic people greeted him at the Union
Depot on the night of February 2. After the usual salute of twelve
guns the uniformed societies led him to the Cathedral; he was visibly
moved by this demonstration after his six months' absence. He spoke
feelingly of the Holy Father as the Prisoner of the Vatican and deprecated the confiscation of the property of the Church by the Italian
Government. The five mosaic pieces and an alabaster and a black
marble table which he brought from Rome for the Cathedral were put
on exhibition for a while in Ryder's show window on Euclid Avenue.

In the following summer the Bishop preached the retreat for the
priests of the Diocese of Brooklyn.[9] It is worthy of note that he was

[5] *C.U.*, Sept. 2, 1880.

[6] Simeoni to Gilmour, Mar, 29, 1883; *Rapport du Diocèse de Cleveland, 1882;* both
in C.D.A.

[7] *C.U.*, Apr. 20, 1882; Jan. 4, 18, 25, Feb. 8, 15, Mar. 22, 1883. Cleveland *Plain
Dealer*, Mar. 21, 1883. Cleveland *Herald*, Apr. 15, 1882.

[8] Hostlot (Rome) to Gilmour, Mar. 15, 1883, in C.D.A.

[9] *C.U.*, Aug. 16, 1883.

well liked as a retreat master. Other clergy retreats at which he presided were at St. Paul in 1872 and 1887 and at Baltimore in 1886.

Bishop Gilmour was to return to Rome sooner than he had anticipated. As we have seen, he spent May to October of 1885 in the Eternal City in the interests of the Third Plenary Council of Baltimore. One of the problems considered at the time was the way in which title to diocesan charitable institutions should be held; he had been busy with such a problem in Cleveland. Bishop Rappe had given the deed of the orphanage property on Monroe Street to a legal corporation, the "Hospital of St. Joseph," composed of certain members of the Sisters of Charity who were called trustees. According to the mind of Bishop Gilmour the title should be vested in the name of the bishop of the diocese. The trustees in question showed an inclination to demur and were penalized by the Bishop. The Cleveland *Leader* gave wide publicity to the affair in the Associated Press dispatches, exaggerating and distorting the story.

Rome referred the dispute to the Archbishop of Cincinnati who composed the matter. The deed was vested in the name of the Bishop of Cleveland, and the Sisters as a community were legally incorporated in 1884 as "The Sisters of Charity of St. Augustine," whose purpose was declared to be "the care and support of orphans and children abandoned by their parents or committed to the care of the corporation by their guardians or competent authority; nursing, supporting and the care of the sick, wounded and disabled, and friendless; and charity generally." The corporation was not for profit and had no capital stock.[10]

A similar case was that of St. Vincent's Orphanage in Toledo. It ran on for some years and was finally settled in 1888 by Cardinal Gibbons, acting as the papal delegate. The Grey Nuns, who were not a diocesan community, were left in possession of the property but were required to give an account of their administration of it to the Bishop. Cardinal Gibbons later gave credit to Bishop Gilmour for helping to bring about the solution of a disputed point in canon law.[11]

Another incident was associated with the Bishop's visit to Rome in 1885. He and Bishop Moore composed and presented to the Congregation of the Propaganda a "Memorial on the Condition of the German Catholics in the United States."[12] In this brochure of thirty-five pages in Italian the two bishops gave it as their opinion that Germanizing influences might make German influence a danger to the Church in this country and might also give occasion to her enemies to characterize the Church as a foreign institution. This supposed danger, they averred, was strongest in the West and the Northwest. In 1886 Father

[10] Incorporation papers, in C.D.A.
[11] Correspondence pertinent to the case, in C.D.A.
[12] Copies were sent to Bps. McQuaid of Rochester, McCloskey of Louisville, and O'Connor of Omaha. Bp. Gilmour's opinions are very clear in letters he wrote to Card. Franchi, Dec. 7, 1877, and to Arbp. Elder in Oct., 1880, in C.D.A.

Abbelen of Milwaukee appeared in Rome to secure a "declaration of the rights of the Germans."[13] He complained that the German Catholics were too dependent upon the pastors of the English-speaking parishes. One of the clauses in his memorial would require that all German-born Catholics as well as their children who were born here should be compelled to frequent the German churches exclusively. If the first or second generation of American-born Germans should elect to join the English-language parishes their choice would have to be formal and final.

Bishop Gilmour on the contrary was convinced that children of German parents when they came of age or when they married should have the free choice to attend the churches in which English was spoken. He was one of the many American prelates who disliked the enactment of special legislation to favor the German-speaking section of the Catholic Church, such as was advocated in a movement later called Cahenslyism.[14] He contended that other nationalities might also claim special privilege to the detriment of Church unity. In a letter intended for the inspection of the Prefect of the Propaganda he expressed deep displeasure with Father Abbelen's mission in Rome and told of his fears that special legislation for the Germans might arouse suspicion on the part of the general public and might even bring on a revival of persecution.

Bishop Ireland and Bishop Keane went to Rome, where they used the memorial of Bishop Gilmour and Bishop Moore in the presentation of the case against Father Abbelen's petition which itself was eventually set aside by the Propaganda.[15] The restrictions on the freedom of foreign-speaking Catholics to affiliate with the territorial or English-speaking parishes were not allowed. It was decided, however, that separate parishes might be erected for foreign-speaking groups.[16] In another dispute, with the editor of the St. Louis *Pastoral Blatt,* the

[13] *La Question Allemande dans l'Église aux États-Unis,* 25 pp., Rome, Dec. 6, 1886; D. J. O'Connell (Rome), to Gilmour, Nov. 8, 1886; Gilmour to D. J. O'Connell, Nov. 26, 1886; all in C.D.A. The correspondence of Msgr. D. J. O'Connell, rector of the North American College and agent of many American bishops, later rector of the Catholic University in Washington, and still later Bishop of Richmond, was discovered in 1946 in Richmond by Drs. John Tracy Ellis and Henry J. Browne. Microfilmed copies were placed at the disposition of scholars at the University of Notre Dame in Indiana and at the Catholic University in Washington. Fr. Colman Barry, O.S.B., who is preparing a volume, *The Germans and the Catholic Church in the United States,* recently discovered the correspondence of Abbot Bernard Smith, O.S.B., in Rome. A microfilmed copy of it is to be found in St. John's Abbey, Collegeville, Minn. Bp. Gilmour was one of his many correspondents. Cf. *Catholic Historical Review,* Apr., 1951.

[14] Cf. John J. Meng, "Cahenslyism," in *Catholic Historical Review,* Jan. and Oct., 1946. *Catholic Knight,* Dec. 21, 1889.

[15] In the C.D.A. is to be found voluminous correspondence in regard to the subject between Bp. Gilmour and the following: Card. Gibbons, Arbp. Elder, Arbp. Corrigan of New York, Bps. McQuaid, McCloskey, James O'Connor, Moore, Chatard, Watterson, Ireland, and Keane, Msgr. D. J. O'Connell, Abbot Smith, and E. B. Edes. The last three lived in Rome.

[16] The Propaganda Congregation declined to entertain certain other points, the settlement of which was left to the prudent judgment of the local bishops (C.D.A.).

Bishop declared himself "opposed to any attempt to foreignize American youth." He and the editor agreed in their purpose to save the foreign-born Catholics to the Church; they differed in their ideas as to how quickly the change in language should take place.[17]

In the autumn of 1889 the Bishop was considerably annoyed by the appearance in German and Italian of what purported to be a copy of his memorial. A German translation had been sent to the German priests. Much feeling was aroused; a few wrote to the Bishop expressing doubt about its authenticity.[18] The Bishop kept his patience in the face of some abusive letters. In a private letter he acknowledged his part in the original composition but added that his rule of practice had always been "to provide fully and generously for the wants of the German-speaking Catholics and to avoid discussion of nationality; but as against any attempt to nationalize the Catholic Church in America he would be a distinct opponent."

It was generally acknowledged in the diocese that this was true. He favored the gradual introduction of English in the predominantly German parishes, especially in the country districts where there was only one parish for all. He thought the early Masses at which English was spoken ought to be for the convenience of the children and of those who did not understand German. This was the answer he gave to pastors who reported that the children in such places did not know German. Public notice of this attitude was given at the pontifical Mass at the Cathedral for the third national convention of German societies in 1889. He congratulated the delegates for calling their meeting a Catholic instead of a German Congress, and that for the first time in Cleveland, "where so many healthy battle cries have had their start." He appealed for a broader outlook which would include all Catholic interests. At the public mass meeting in connection with the convention he again appealed for Catholic and American unity: "We shall in future have all nationalities, all tongues, and all races taking part in all celebrations just as our faith embraces all races, all colors, all nations, and all men."[19]

It has already been mentioned that Bishop Gilmour, even before the Third Council of Baltimore (1884), on his visit to Rome had spoken in favor of a school of higher theology, a *Seminarium Principale* for graduates of ecclesiastical seminaries, which would develop in the course of time into a Catholic University. He did not favor Washington as the site, however, but preferred the first choice of the com-

---

[17] Gilmour correspondence with Fr. N. Moes (Sandusky), Card. Gibbons, Arbp. Elder, Wm. Faeber, editor of the (St. Louis) *Pastoral Blatt,* and the editor of the *Wahrheits Freund* in C.D.A. Cf. also *C.U.,* Dec. 22, 1887; Jan. 12, 1888; *Catholic Progress* and *Catholic World,* Dec., 1887; *Pastoral Blatt,* Oct., 1887.

[18] Gilmour to Card. Simeoni, Dec. 14, 1889; Simeoni's answer, Jan. 9, 1890; Gilmour to Bps. John Ireland, McCloskey, and Dwenger and to Msgr. D. J. O'Connell; Dwenger to Gilmour; Rupert-Houck and Houck Meyer correspondence; Houck to Arthur Preuss of the *Fortnightly Review* in reference to the matter; all in C.D.A. Cf. Zwierlein, *Op. Cit.,* II, 41–44.

[19] Cleveland *Plain Dealer,* Nov. 4, 1889.

mittee chosen to find a site, namely, Seton Hall College in New Jersey. Later on, he seemed to favor Cincinnati for the proposed western branch and Emmitsburg for the one in the East. In the poll taken among the bishops, he chose Philadelphia. Finally, Washington was the choice approved by the Church authorities. Bishop Gilmour had received letters from his friend, Bishop McQuaid, who was not one of the supporters of the university; nevertheless, he published the appeal for funds to finance it and promised the rector, Bishop Keane, that he would always keep two students there.

Father William Kress was the first and Father Frederick Rupert was the second student from this diocese to study in Washington. The Bishop wrote that he could ill afford to spare them but that he wished on principle that the diocese be properly represented, "to uphold the new institution and to give it a fair start."[20] He consented to act as one of the first trustees of the university and it was he who gave the principal sermon at the dedication and the opening of the school of theology, invited to do so by Cardinal Gibbons and the rector. His subject was, "The necessity of the fulness of divine truth for the real advancement of learning and the true progress of our country."[21] In Baltimore a few days ahead of time he contracted a bad cold and had to go to the hospital. He went on to Washington, nevertheless, and there he left a sick bed at Providence Hospital to deliver his sermon at the university on November 13, 1889.

It was a very rainy day but there was a distinguished audience. The future Cardinal Satolli, the papal representative and later first apostolic delegate,[22] was the celebrant of the Mass. President Harrison and other members of the Government were there, as well as the American Hierarchy. Weakened by his sickness but inspired by his subject and the occasion, he had hardly begun to speak before "the old Scotch fire lighted up his countenance and gave glow to his words." He portrayed the long history of the Church as the educator of humanity. He asserted that the training of minds and of thinkers was to serve as a bulwark against the tendency of a prosperous country to make wealth the standard of excellence. True education should teach people to think and to lead them to God, the Source of all wisdom. During his sermon the sun broke through the clouds and lighted up the crimson robes of the new cardinals of Baltimore and Quebec, the purple of the archbishops and bishops, the many-colored garments of the clergy and of the others present.

In the midst of the general acclaim the Bishop returned to the hos-

[20] Gilmour to Elder, Mar. 25, 1885; Gilmour to Gibbons, June 18, 1887; Gibbons to Gilmour, Aug. 22, 1889; Gibbons' Circular, Nov. 11, 1887; Keane to Gilmour, Aug. 21, 1889; Gilmour to Keane, Oct. 2, 1889; all in C.D.A. Gilmour to Gibbons, Feb. 27, May 7, 1885, in Baltimore Archdiocesan Archives. *C.U.,* Sept. 10, 1885.
[21] Text in *C.U.,* Nov. 14, 1889.
[22] When Bp. Gilmour was in Rome in 1882 he counseled delay in the appointment of an apostolic delegate. This he averred in his correspondence between Feb. 24, 1883, and Nov., 1889, with Card. Gibbons, Arbp. Elder, and Bps. Shanahan and Moore, in C.D.A. Satolli was appointed in 1893.

pital, seriously ill. He notified Monsignor Boff to take charge of the urgent business of the diocese. Within ten days, however, he showed signs of improvement and at the end of the month he was back at his desk, "quite weak but rallying." He was able to pontificate in the Cathedral on Christmas Day. The exertion brought on a relapse and he was again confined to his room; the accustomed visit of the orphans had to be abandoned.[23]

The Bishop's illness in the East had prevented him from taking an active part (a few days previous to the Washington affair) in the centennial celebration in Baltimore of the beginning of the American Hierarchy in the person of Archbishop John Carroll. He had, however, approved of the plans for the Catholic Congress, as it was called, which were drawn up by Archbishop Ireland of St. Paul and Henry F. Brownson, the son of the famous convert and writer. As a member of the advisory committee he had helped to monitor the papers which were read by prominent Catholic laymen. Mr. Tello of the *Universe* and Mr. J. T. McDonnell of Toledo represented this diocese. Special tickets were distributed in the parishes and many other Clevelanders attended. It was stressed by all the speakers that the time had come for Catholic laymen to give public expression of their loyalty to the Church and of their interest in the questions of the day which affected the Church and society.

Bishop Gilmour had long been an admirer of Orestes A. Brownson, who died in 1876, and whose works have been published by his son in twenty volumes. It is believed by some that he better than many others understood the harmony which exists between the Catholic ideas of life and the institutions of the United States. The Bishop originated a movement for a Brownson Memorial in an article in the *Universe* in 1886; his subscription was matched by other prelates. The idea was adopted by the Catholic Young Men's National Union, which was responsible under the guidance of the younger Brownson for the notable success of the Catholic congress. In 1910 a bronze bust of his father was unveiled in New York City.[24]

[23] *C.U.*, Nov. 21, 28, 1889. Toledo *Blade*, Nov. 23, 1889. Houck to Pfeil, Nov. 30, 1889, in C.D.A.
[24] William H. Hughes, ed., *Souvenir Volume of the Centennial Celebration and Catholic Congress*, Detroit, 1889. *C.U.*, Mar. 18, 1886; Oct. 10, 17, 24, 1889; Nov. 4, 1910. *Catholic Universe-Bulletin* (hereafter abbreviated as *C.U.-B*), July 13, Aug. 31, 1928. Brownson to Gilmour, Mar., 1889; Gilmour to Gibbons, Aug. 3, 1889; both in C.D.A.

33

THE DEATH OF BISHOP GILMOUR

AT THE END OF JANUARY, 1890, THE BISHOP WAS able to go to Villa Angela in the country, at Nottingham, where Monsignor Boff was the chaplain of the Ursuline Sisters, for a few days of rest and quiet. He had been warned that any serious strain, mental or physical, would have fatal consequences. Nevertheless, from his retreat he continued to give detailed directions about planting trees and shrubs in the new cemetery in Toledo, and he attended to his more important appointments.[1] A few administrative problems which had caused him some concern reached their culminating point at this time. It will be remembered that his term of office covered the period of adjustment between the more fluid conditions of a missionary church and the more stable requirements of the general law of the Church. The regularity and smoothness of present diocesan administration are the result of that experience.

In the earlier days a pastor might be changed from one charge to another without much or any formality, and sometimes complaints arose. The formula for settling such complaints, a Board of Investigation prescribed by the Propaganda in 1878, was not set up by Bishop Gilmour until some time later.[2] The Third Council of Baltimore prescribed further concession to the general law of the church, for instance, in the establishment of some parishes as irremovable rectorates, though the appointment or removal of other pastors would still not require much formality. In the appeals made to Rome against some of his appointments the Propaganda in general upheld the Bishop's procedure.[3] Another point in law which he contested was the presumptive incardination or incorporation of a priest who would come from another diocese and work here for a certain period. At the end of his career two well-known cases transpired which are treated at great length in Houck's history. The perspective of time lessens the importance which they then had.

The one case was that of Father Patrick Quigley, the pastor of St.

[1] Gilmour to McQuaid, Feb. 3, to Fr. Braire, Feb. 18, and to Sr. Ignatia, Apr. 21, 1890, in C.D.A.
[2] Simeoni to Gilmour, Rome, Dec. 12, 1879, in C.D.A.
[3] Correspondence with Frs. Chas. Evrard, Wm. J. Gibbons, and John Quinn, in C.D.A.

Francis de Sales's in Toledo. The Bishop for reasons of his own relieved him of his parish and suspended him from the exercise of his office for a short period. The Congregation of the Propaganda reversed this action and, when the reasons for the procedure were not forthcoming, Father Quigley was reinstated. This was mid-year in 1889. The Toledo newspapers made much of the incident and published their own comment, tying up the matter with the transfer of other pastors in Toledo.

The other case was that of Father John B. Primeau who had come here from Canada and had been given temporary charge of St. Louis' French parish in Toledo. The assignment was recalled by the Bishop in November, 1888. Father Primeau declined to give up the parish residence. The Bishop appealed to the Toledo courts which heard the arguments for and against the presumptive incorporation of Father Primeau in the diocese because of his temporary appointment. The judge gave the opportunity to decide the case to the ecclesiastical court which in the end rendered a verdict supporting the Bishop's contention.[4]

It was during one of the sessions of the court in Toledo that the Bishop on the stand was constrained by the judge to read the contents of a letter which he had drawn out of his pocket by mistake. It was a private letter of his own, in which he had expressed some disappointment in the attitude of the Propaganda towards himself. A copy of the letter obtained surreptitiously was printed in the local newspapers and in other parts of the country. The *Catholic Knight*, a Cleveland weekly, was blamed for the publication of the letter. Fearful of what bad use might be made of the incident Bishop Gilmour in the *Universe*[5] published a courageous and forthright statement of his loyalty and devotion to Rome and the Holy Father, and a denial of any untoward interpretations which might be made of the letter by unfriendly persons.

The *Catholic Knight* was owned and edited by a Catholic layman who was not always respectful in his attitude towards the Bishop's conduct of affairs. In 1886 the journal was censured and its circulation curtailed; but after the publication of the above-mentioned letter and the bitter controversy which resulted the Bishop, in October, 1890, forbade the reading of it under ecclesiastical penalty. The Catholic Central Association and the Catholic public supported the Bishop's stand.[6]

Occupation with the Primeau trial in Toledo had made the Bishop late in attending the Fifth Provincial Council of Cincinnati in May, 1889. In the following July he was able to attend the meeting of the bishops of the province at Cincinnati. But when he returned to Cleve-

[4] The documents concerning these cases, in C.D.A.

[5] N. Y. *Herald*, Oct. 10, 16, 1890. *C.U.*, Oct. 16, 23, 1890. Gilmour to Simeoni, Nov. 8, 1890; Simeoni to Gilmour, Dec. 10, 1890; D. J. O'Connell to Gilmour, Nov. 15, 1890; all in C.D.A.

[6] *C.U.*, Sept. 16, 1876; Oct. 28, Nov. 11, 1886; Sept. 15, Oct. 13, 1887; Oct. 2 to 30, Nov. 6, 1890. *Catholic Knight*, Oct. 26, 1889. Greeves to Boff, July 27, 1891, in C.D.A.

land he was obliged to enter Charity Hospital for treatment; he was thought to be critically ill. He began to recover, however, and in September he was able to leave the hospital for short rides, visiting the office of the *Universe* and the episcopal residence, as well as several of the parishes. By the end of October he seemed quite well again and the Catholic Central Association passed resolutions of joy at his recovery and of loyalty to him as against the attitude of the *Catholic Knight.* On November 10 the final hearing in the Primeau case brought him to Cincinnati. He was back again at the end of the month at Charity Hospital, though he appeared on occasion at the chancery when the weather was favorable.

To assure the Bishop that he had the universal sympathy, love, and respect of his flock a giant parade and a mass meeting at Music Hall were arranged for December 5. A twenty-one-gun salute was fired in his honor. From the brilliantly lighted parlor window in the Cathedral House he reviewed a mile-long parade of 2,000 uniformed men. At the Music Hall nearly 5,000 persons assisted at the addresses of loyalty and affection made by representatives of the various nationalities. Doctor Perrier, a leading Cleveland physician, thanked the Bishop for fighting the battle for Catholic laymen and for having made the name of Catholic respected; he feelingly referred to the Bishop's devotion to the sick in the hospital during his own sickness. The Italian speaker recalled the statement of the Bishop at the dedication of St. Anthony's Church: "I am not an American, nor a French, nor an Italian bishop, I am a Catholic bishop." Mr. Randel spoke in German, Mr. J. S. Zybura in Polish, and Mr. C. M. LeBlond in French, all in praise of the accomplishments of their bishop. Obviously affected by this demonstration of enthusiasm, he appeared for a short time on the platform to thank them for their encouragement. He felt that he was not fully restored in health but he hoped that his epitaph would not be written for some time thereafter.[7]

The improvement, however, was only apparent. Yet he continued to carry on a vigorous correspondence with the Archbishop of Cincinnati about the condition of affairs in Toledo and he kept the reins of the administration in his own hands, though his residence was still at the hospital. As late as March, 1891, he conferred the priesthood on Fathers John W. Bell and James H. Halligan. Nevertheless, his physician, Doctor Vance, was convinced that for full recovery he would have to seek the warmer climate of the South. Monsignor Boff was again assigned the duties of administrator.

Leaving Cleveland on March 11, the Bishop was accompanied by two nurses from Charity Hospital, Sisters Mary Peter and Mary of the Sacred Heart. After short stays at Cincinnati and at Atlanta, Georgia, he reached St. Augustine, Florida, on March 19, tired and exhausted but cheerful, nevertheless, and hopeful. Quarters had been arranged in the finely situated mansion of a Captain Vogel overlooking the sea.

[7] *C.U.,* July to Dec., 1890.

After a week in bed, though he saw no reason for alarm, he sent for Father Houck who brought his ledger and other papers, including his last will and testament. He suffered an acute attack of pain in his left side and when his chancellor, and his confessor, Father Francis Camillus, O. F. M., arrived he told them that he was dying. He was anointed on April 7. As he dictated the last details of his will and signed other documents and letters his mind and memory remained clear and distinct.

Meanwhile Doctor Vance had come to consult with the local physicians who were much devoted to their distinguished patient. Bishop McCloskey of Louisville and Father Wright, both old friends, came for the final farewell. Though in great distress and very weak, the Bishop showed complete resignation to the Will of God: he was thankful for the pain; he knew that "his chapter would soon be finished. With all our weakness and failures God will find something to commend. He will forgive what human weakness failed to accomplish." The troubles he had were as nothing, he thought, compared to the great grace of his conversion and the consequent opportunity of serving God and religion in the diocese. Humbly he forgave all, as he hoped that God would forgive him. He had tried, as he said, "to do his honest best according to his lights and his talents."

Notice of the crisis reached Cleveland and public prayers were offered in all the churches. He rallied a little but remained perfectly helpless and gave up hope of recovery, though he was conscious to the last. At 7:15 in the evening of April 13, 1891, he rendered his brave soul to its Maker, a few days before the nineteenth anniversary of his installation as the second Bishop of Cleveland.[8] Doctor Vance had diagnosed the last illness as the result of the rupture of an ileocaecal abscess at the time that he preached at the dedication of the Catholic University at Washington.[9] This liver trouble was apparently of long standing; complications resulting from his exposure to the weather in a trip to the city from Villa Angela aggravated his condition. Even as early as 1854 he had asked to be relieved of his parish duties because of ill health. The complete breakdown, twenty years after that, required almost two years of rest and quiet. In his later years he suffered almost continuously with headaches.[10]

The mortal remains of the distinguished prelate were taken from the train at Cincinnati, where the Archbishop presided at a funeral Mass in the Bishop's old parish of St. Patrick. At Dayton, where he had also been pastor, a delegation respectfully viewed the body. At Galion the casket was removed to St. Joseph's Church. A delegation of priests and people from Cleveland accompanied it from there to the city. An immense crowd met the cortege at the Union Depot and escorted it to the

[8] Houck's account in *C.U.* Daily bulletins in Cleveland *Press* and Cleveland *Plain Dealer*.

[9] Cleveland *Plain Dealer*, Apr. 14, 1891. The transfer permit for the corpse mentioned cancer of the liver as the cause of death.

[10] Gilmour to Purcell, July 21, 1854, in C.D.A.

Cathedral House. The dead Bishop lay in state in the Cathedral from Sunday afternoon until the funeral service on Tuesday, April 25.

In the presence of Archbishop Ireland and twelve bishops and about 200 priests and of a great throng of the faithful, the Archbishop of Cincinnati celebrated the funeral Mass, and Bishop McQuaid of Rochester preached the sermon.[11] His old friend and confidant, who shared many of his ideas and with whom he has been compared in his general disposition, reviewed the career of the deceased as a missionary and as a prelate. He likened him to St. Paul, bold, brave, honest, sincere, with a clear mind and an indomitable will. Though his firmness was often misunderstood, he lived and died in the utmost simplicity, with no other purpose in life but the spread of the Kingdom of Christ on earth. After appropriate ceremonies the body which knew no rest while he lived found quiet and peace in the crypt beneath the high altar of the Cathedral.

At what was certainly a unique event in Cleveland over 5,000 people gathered together in Music Hall three weeks later to do honor to the memory of Bishop Gilmour as an outstanding citizen. His good friend, Mr. Gordon, was president of the meeting, which was attended by judges, lawyers, doctors, a Jewish Rabbi, a Presbyterian clergyman, and many other prominent Clevelanders. Speeches were made and letters were read recalling the excellent qualities and the public spirit of the departed prelate.[12]

In the press notices the tireless zeal of the Bishop in the promotion of Catholic education was always prominent. Recognized as the champion of religious education in the public schools, he fought for the right and emphasized the duty of Catholics to have their own schools for religion's sake. His first pastoral set the pattern for earnest and effective development of those schools. Everyone agreed about his naturally strong and fearless character. It was said he was "the fighting bishop, a publicist and controversalist, coming to Cleveland when a bold champion was needed; he would not compromise nor would he con- ciliate, but he gave battle for battle offered against the onslaughts of bitterness and ignorance. He was aggressive, bold, challenging, a fear- less member of the Church Militant in the cause of truth, justice, and religion." He had a somewhat severe exterior and his bluntness of man- ner was sometimes taken for harshness. At times stern and reserved, he was found upon closer acquaintance to be even tender-hearted, just, and without guile, a courteous gentleman. A lock of his mother's hair which he always carried with him betokened the softer side.

A man of action rather than a student of theories, Bishop Gilmour developed, enforced, and amplified the old without originating much that was new. He was on the defense to safeguard the disputed rights of the Church and Catholics. His ready wit and a quiet humor made him an interesting controversalist. His facile trenchant pen and a clear

[11] *C.U.*, Apr. 30, 1891. Houck, *Op. cit.*, II, 37.
[12] *C.U.*, May 7, 21, 1891.

concise style made him a forceful writer. One of the most zealous and active members of the hierarchy of his time, sometimes compared to the valiant Archbishop Hughes of New York, he merited much of the high praise he had given to Archbishop Purcell at that prelate's funeral in 1883: "From the beginning he identified himself with the destinies of his adopted country, claiming his rights as a citizen and refusing to admit that because he had become a priest he had ceased to be a patriot or part of his country."[13]

His last will and testament was filed in Probate Court soon after his death. He left no personal estate of any value. Souvenirs and pictures were distributed to friends. His library and books were given to the seminary. A curious rumor published in the local papers to the effect that Bishop Gilmour had been about to resign his see had no basis in fact and was officially denied by Archbishop Elder.[14]

The Catholics of Cleveland and the diocese cannot sufficiently appreciate the important benefits which accrued to them through the great leadership of Bishop Gilmour. The growth of the material facilities of the Church bespeaks his zeal and that of the clergy and people. During his administration the total number of churches had increased from 160 to 233, with over fifty stations where as yet there was no church. Many of the original 160 churches were replaced with larger and more substantial buildings. The number of schoolhouses increased from 90 in 1870 to 142 in 1891; it was especially true of these buildings that most of the older ones had been replaced or remodeled to accommodate the estimated 27,679 pupils who frequented them. In the cause of education Bishop Gilmour brought the Jesuit Fathers to Cleveland to begin their noble career. The Sisters of Notre Dame and the Sisters of St. Joseph came to the diocese, under his auspices, to aid other religions. Under his direction St. Alexis Hospital and St. John's and St. Ann's were started in Cleveland and St. Vincent's in Toledo. The orphanages were improved and the Sisters of Notre Dame began a girls' protectory. Under his patronage the Sisters of the Good Shepherd were able to finish their home and the Little Sisters of the Poor to expand their work.

Mention also must be made of the efforts of Bishop Gilmour to take good care of the newcomers from Europe who settled in the larger cities. He gave them their own churches and their own priests although he never tired in his endeavor to break down national divisions and to gather all together in the unity of the Church. Unfortunately undeserved importance has been given to the "troubles" of the Bishop. His energetic thought sometimes caused his language "to entrench on the sound form of words." Notwithstanding little flurries here and there, the Bishop ruled a very obedient and cooperative clergy, many

[13] Pamphlet, *Funeral Oration over Archbishop Purcell*, July 11, 1883. *C.U.* in issues from April 23 to July, 1891, quoted Catholic journals from different parts of the country. Arbp. Elder's sermon at the Month's Mind Mass, in *C.U.*, May 14, 1891.

[14] Msgr. D. J. O'Connell to Gilmour, Nov. 15, 1890; Elder to Boff, May 27, 1891; both in C.D.A. Cleveland *Plain Dealer*, May 30, 1891. *C.U.*, Jan. 28, 1892.

of whom he had ordained himself. His love of order and discipline explains what difficulties there were; his sickness in the last years explains much too. Shortly before the end he was assured by the Prefect of the Propaganda that his diocese was in excellent order. His devotion to the Holy Father was sincere and childlike; writing afterwards about an audience he had had with the Pope, he said that it was the happiest day in his life.

No one could doubt his purity and oneness of purpose. He accomplished his task to the best of his ability during very difficult times, namely, to carry the burden of the diocese from the pioneer days of Bishop Rappe to modern times and to give it the impetus for further development. As he had promised at the beginning of his administration, he made the name Catholic respected and Catholics conscious of their guaranteed rights and more appreciative of their rich heritage. Bishop Gilmour deserves well of the Church and the commonwealth.

34

THE THIRD BISHOP OF CLEVELAND

A T THE DEATH OF BISHOP GILMOUR, MONSIGNOR
Boff was again chosen as the interim administrator of the
diocese. He performed the duties of his office well and
without incident of great consequence. Meanwhile, in
accordance with the prescriptions of the Third Plenary
Council of Baltimore, the irremovable rectors and the consultors under
the presidency of the Archbishop of Cincinnati, May 13, 1891, drew
up a list of candidates whom they deemed worthy of the episcopate.
Two other unofficial committees made their recommendations, as did,
of course, the bishops of the province.[1]

In due time the Holy See designated the Reverend Doctor John
Frederick Ignatius Horstmann, chancellor of the Archdiocese of Philadelphia, the third Bishop of Cleveland. His was one of the names sent
to Rome at the time that Archbishop Wood was chosen for Philadelphia, and he had been popularly spoken of as the successor of Bishop
Keane of Richmond when the latter became rector of the Catholic
University at Washington.[2] The appointment, of which he had some
intimation earlier in the year, became official when the Holy Father
confirmed it in the consistory of November 29, 1891; the papal Bull of
appointment is dated December 14, 1891. Archbishop Elder in a letter
of November 29 officially notified Doctor Horstmann and Monsignor
Boff. The Bishop-elect formally accepted his appointment on January
26, 1892.[3]

Bishop Horstmann was born, December 16, 1840, in Philadelphia,
in the old district of Southwark, the third of the ten children of Frederick and Catherine Weber Horstmann. His parents had come to
America at an early age from the Grand Duchy of Oldenburg in
Germany and were married in Philadelphia. They were exemplary
Catholics and the family was very successful in business. John Frederick at first attended the school of Holy Trinity parish; he was then

[1] Molony Circular, Sept. 12, 1891; Westerholt Circular, Sept. 16, 1891; both in
C.D.A.
[2] John Tracy Ellis, *Formative Years of the Catholic University of America*, Washington, 1946, p. 344, note.
[3] Horstmann Diary, 1891; original Bull of appointment; Horstmann letter, July
8, 1891; Elder to Boff and to Horstmann, Dec. 11, 1891; Propaganda to Horstmann,
Feb. 15, 1892; all in C.D.A. *C.U.*, Dec. 17, 1891.

sent to the private school of a Madame Charrier. At thirteen he entered Mount Vernon Grammar School. Here he met the young Henry George, later the well-known exponent of the single tax theory, to whom he was able to explain many things about the Catholic Church. Next he attended Boys Central High School and graduated from it in 1857.

After two years at the Jesuit College of St. Joseph he entered the Seminary of St. Charles Borromeo, near Philadelphia. In 1860 he was sent, one of the first students from the archdiocese, to the North American College in Rome for his philosophy and theology. Among his colleagues were the future Archbishops Corrigan of New York and Riordan of San Francisco, and the Bishops Northrup of Charleston, Richter of Grand Rapids, and Byrne of Nashville. He was ordained priest, June 10, 1865, by Cardinal Patrizzi, the papal vicar. He received his doctor's degree in theology from the College of the Propaganda in the next year.

Returning home, he taught philosophy, German, and Hebrew in St. Charles Borromeo Seminary until in 1877 he became pastor of St. Mary's parish in Philadelphia. He published an edition of Potter's Catholic Bible and was the American editor of a book entitled *Catholic Doctrine as Defined by the Council of Trent*. He served as president of the American Catholic Historical Society and was assistant editor of the *American Catholic Quarterly Review*. A favorite lecturer and preacher, he was spiritual director of the Sisters of Notre Dame, of the Ladies of the Sacred Heart, of the members of the Catholic Club, and of several confraternities. He was a member of the Board of Trustees of the Roman Catholic High School of Philadelphia. In 1885 he was made chancellor of the archdiocese. His silver jubilee as a priest was celebrated with much ceremony at the Cathedral. The purse presented to him on this occasion he gave to St. Vincent Home for Orphans.[4]

Happy and encouraged by the many messages of loyalty and welcome upon his appointment as Bishop of Cleveland, the new prelate thanked all his well-wishers in a note in the *Universe*.[5] Some sixty priests from the diocese attended his consecration in the Cathedral at Philadelphia, February 25, 1892. Archbishop Elder, the consecrating prelate, was assisted by Bishop O'Hara of Scranton and Bishop Chatard of Vincennes. Archbishop Ryan of Philadelphia preached the formal sermon. A group of Cleveland priests met the Philadelphia delegation at Alliance, the railroad junction, and a special train brought the party to Cleveland in the evening of March 8. Although a heavy rain prevented a demonstration by the uniformed societies, the people under their umbrellas lined the streets from the Euclid Avenue station of the

[4] Philadelphia *Public Register,* Dec. 14, 1891. *C.U.,* Dec. 17, 1891. Houck, *Op. cit.,* II, 40. Horstmann to McCloskey, Mar. 27, 1893, in C.D.A.

[5] Boff to Horstmann, Dec. 16, 17, 1891; Thorpe to Horstmann, Dec. 16, 1891; Elder to Horstmann, "I believe you will find a great deal to encourage you in the diocese and very little to discourage or trouble you," Dec. 14, 1871; all in C.D.A.

Bishop Ignatius Frederick Horstmann, third Bishop of Cleveland, 1892 to 1908.

Holy Trinity Church.   St. Ladislas Church.

*Left:*St. Aloysius Church.

*Right:*St. Martin Church.

*Far Right:*St. Michael
Church.

Pennsylvania Railroad to the Cathedral House. The Mayor and other city officials participated in the reception there.

The next morning (March 9) Archbishop Elder formally installed Bishop Horstmann as the third head of this diocese. Bishop Foley of Detroit preached the sermon and Monsignor Boff, speaking for the clergy, welcomed him, and delivered over to him the administration of the diocese. In reply the new Bishop recalled his meeting with Bishop Rappe in Rome and with Bishop Gilmour here. Sent by the Holy Father to succeed them, he felt that he was no stranger among Catholics; he asked for the cooperation of all in working for the peace and prosperity of the Church. At Toledo he was welcomed by a public procession on May 1, when he went there for the blessing of the cornerstone of the Church of the Immaculate Conception.[6]

Back in Cleveland, his tall angular figure, for he was over six feet tall and of medium weight, made him a marked man in his regular walks through the busy streets. His friendly, easy manner, quite in accord with his scholarly disposition, won the respect and admiration of all classes of citizens.

Bishop Horstmann found a well-organized diocese at his coming. He was to develop and expand the work upon the foundations laid by his predecessors and to face new problems peculiar to his time. The immigration of Catholic peoples from new parts of Europe reached its peak during his administration. The population of Cleveland alone in 1892[7] was 309,243, and that of the other large cities had increased in proportion. No city in the State was more polyglot than this city and, according to a private survey made in 1900, Catholics made up about fifty per cent of those who attended religious services. It was the transition period for the earlier immigrants. In the German-speaking parishes the language of the country was gradually substituted, especially in the towns where there was but one parish; those who did not know German were not to be deprived of religious instruction in English. Although many[8] considered him the "defender of German conservative Catholicism," Bishop Horstmann favored the introduction of English whenever possible. There was to be a greater use of the English language in sermons and prayers, and in school. Pastors in the German parishes were advised to preach in English on alternate Sundays.

This policy in regard to the foreign-language problem was set by the Bishop in 1893.[9] It was to be followed until such time as a plenary

[6] *C.U.*, Feb. 4, 25, Mar. 3, 10, May 5, 1892. Houck, *Op. cit.*, II, 165.

[7] *Cleveland City Directory. History of the State of Ohio*, as cited V, 262. Cleveland *Plain Dealer*, Jan. 20, 1900.

[8] Horstmann to S. Falk, Feb. 14, 1893; to Kinkead, Feb. 16, 1893; to Hoeffel, Dec. 17, 1893; to Kirch, May 19, 1894; to Arnoldi, Oct. 17, 1896; to M. Schmidt, July 23, 1898; to Edmund Widmer, July 30, 1898; to Bauer, Feb. 23, 1900; to F. Schrantz, Nov. 3, 1900; to Lamb, Oct. 17, 1903; Treiber to Houck, May 16, 1902; John Schaffeld to Houck, Dec. 30, 1904; all in C.D.A. Toledo *Express*, Jan. 26, 1893. Sandusky *Demokrat*, Jan., 1893.

[9] Bishop's Council meeting, June 2, 23, 1893, in C.D.A.

council should decree otherwise. Non-English-speaking adult immigrants were to belong to the parish of their language; their children
at their majority were free to choose the parish to which they wished
to belong, such choice to be final; in cases in which one of the parents
spoke English, the family might belong to the territorial parish especially if the children had previously attended a school in which the
language used was English. The Bishop considered it his duty to protect the interests of the German parishes but not at the expense of the
children's welfare in an English-speaking country. To meet the need for
German-speaking priests the Bishop exhorted the aspirants to the sacred
ministry in the colleges to learn that language;[10] in the local seminary
its study was of obligation. And he wrote to other seminaries in search
of German-speaking students. For the newer immigrants from the
Slav countries it was considered to be more practical to allow them the
use of their native language in church and school, but the emphasis was
on the need of the children to learn English as soon as possible.[11]

The Holy See on May 12, 1897,[12] settled the difficulty with a directive issued by the Apostolic Delegation. The children of immigrants,
when they became independent of the family, were not obliged to
continue their affiliation with a foreign-language parish; the parents
themselves if they understood English, and so desired, might join the
territorial parish of the district in which they lived. The Cleveland
Plain Dealer published the decree not long afterwards and in an accompanying article Monsignor Thorpe showed that this policy had been
practiced in Cleveland for a long time.[13] Thereafter, the pastors in the
exclusively German parishes made more frequent use of the English
language in their Sunday sermons. One pastor was told that it was not
possible "to force people back to their mother parish church."[14]

The golden jubilee celebration of the Catholic Central Association
was the occasion of an official reception to Bishop Horstmann not long
after his arrival. Mr. Graham recalled the origins of the organization
and Mr. Ptak spoke of its success in uniting all the nationalities in the
bond of their Catholic Faith and of their common American citizenship.
The Bishop used the opportunity to sound the note which was to be
characteristic of his administration, namely, the preservation and extension of Catholic schools wherein the child's right to a Christian
education was recognized.[15]

From the beginning the Bishop acknowledged that it was the duty of
the Government to furnish the means and opportunity of education for
all children. He was not opposed in principle to the public schools but
he regretted the exclusion of religious and moral training. He would
prefer denominational schools in which religion might be taught ac-

---

[10] Horstmann to Magnier, Mar. 6, 1900, in C.D.A.
[11] Horstmann to Motulewski, Jan. 12, 1896, in C.D.A.
[12] Bouscaren, *Canon Law Digest*, II, 79.
[13] Horstmann to Martinelli (Washington), July 3, 1897, in C.D.A.
[14] Horstmann to Koudelka, Nov. 7, 1903, in C.D.A.
[15] *C.U.*, Apr. 21, 1892.

cording to the desire of the parents concerned; he was of the opinion, however, that State aid to the Catholic schools in the circumstances would not be granted. He objected, also, to the common practice of teaching some sort of Protestantism in the public schools.

A famous test case in Lowellville, Ohio, did not relieve his anxiety. John B. Nestle and other Catholics of that town sought an injunction against the local school board there which had ordered that a portion of the Bible (King James edition) be read in the public schools of the district as an opening exercise each morning. The complainants contended that such procedure was unauthorized by law and was an invasion of their constitutional right to liberty of conscience, since they were compelled by law to support the schools in question and to send their children to them. The Youngstown court held that according to Ohio law the Board of Education in each district had the full management and control of the common schools in it. It decided that the Lowellville Board of Education was within its rights when it prescribed the reading of the Bible.[16] A corollary of the decision would be that the Board could introduce any kind of text book no matter how offensive it might be to the constituents. The Protestant version of the Bible continued to be used there and Protestant hymns were sung as usual.

In Cleveland and throughout the diocese the same version of the Bible was read and commented upon in the public schools; Protestant prayers and hymns were used. This was particularly true at the normal school.[17] When Superintendent Jones defended the practice as in accord with the general custom, Bishop Horstmann in a letter to the *Plain Dealer* questioned its legality. The practice, however, suffered no interference, no more than did the other custom of holding school exercises in Protestant churches.[18]

The Catholic school was the particular target of the new anti-Catholic American Protective Association, especially in the country districts. The Bishop was not long in Cleveland before he became aware of the activities of the A.P.A. which had a large following in the Middle West. Founded in 1887, it was designed to keep Catholics out of political office and even out of positions in which they gained a livelihood. The *Universe* denounced them as an Orange Lodge imported from Canada for the purpose of excluding Catholics from office, shop, and school, of boycotting their business, and of encompassing their social and material ruin. In advertisements in the daily newspapers Catholics were notified that they would not be hired if they applied for a position; many Catholics lost their right to promotion and even their positions on account of the ill-feeling. Despite the fact that Catholics at the time composed a good proportion of the

---

[16] Youngstown *Daily Vindicator*, Apr. 4, 1894.

[17] *C.U.*, Apr. 8, 1893; Jan. 20, 1894.

[18] *C.U.*, Aug. 11, 1899; Mar. 2, 1900; Oct. 4, 1901; Jan. 17, 1902. Haupert to Horstmann, Mar. 2, 1900; Berthelot to Horstmann, July 6, 1906; both in C.D.A.

population of the city, the Church and her institutions were subjected to scurillous and irresponsible attacks.

At the raising of the flag over South Case public school in 1891 a speaker imported from a small town in Ohio gave public utterance to slander of this sort. A body of twenty Catholic citizens made representations to the local school board which contented itself with a half-hearted disapproval of such action.[19] The ex-priest Slattery, much to the delight of the Cleveland *Leader,* returned to the city to give his prurient lectures at Case Hall and "to defend the little red school house in danger." Other notorious lecturers, also, made that the theme of their tirades.[20] In the elections in Cleveland some of the non-Catholic candidates for office repudiated the endorsement of the A.P.A. President William McKinley had done so in no uncertain terms, but his name and that of others continued to be used as if they were friendly to the association. Bishop Horstmann appealed to the President to repeat his condemnation.[21]

The outbreak of intolerance was especially severe in Toledo where the A.P.A. was very successful in having its candidates elected to public office. One such individual was expelled by the school board for tampering with the examination papers of prospective teachers in an attempt to make certain that no Catholic would receive such a position. After a few more exposures and especially after a false encyclical of Pope Leo XIII was proved to be a hoax, the excitement began to cool off. As late as 1907, however, a commencement speaker at the Toledo normal school combined an attack on the Catholic priesthood with an attack upon the teaching of religion in the public schools. In Buffalo a preacher sponsored by the A.P.A. quoted a fictitious pastoral of Bishop Horstmann, and a false document attributed to the Pope calling for a general uprising against Protestants.[22]

For some time even after the elections the newspapers carried lurid stories about the Church. Dodgers were scattered in Cleveland with ridiculously incongruous warnings against the supposed plans of the Catholics to seize control of the country. After the elections, too, many successful candidates repudiated the support of the A.P.A. Some few, however, paid for their election by introducing bills in the Ohio Assembly calculated to harm the Church. One such measure, which was not passed, was intended to directly tax all non-State schools, Another, introduced by one Ashford of Columbiana County, provided for the State inspection of all private hospitals, convents, and seminaries. It was

[19] Horstmann to P. Walsh, Dec. 6, 1896, in C.D.A. Cleveland *Plain Dealer,* Oct. 6, 1891. *C.U.,* Oct. 8, 22, 1891.

[20] Cleveland *Daily Leader,* Apr. 25, 1892. *C.U.,* Mar. 31, July 9, 1892. Houck to Cleveland *Leader,* May 27, 1892, in C.D.A. Handbills. Others were the apostates, McNamara and Rudolph.

[21] Horstmann to McKinley, Sept., 1896; Horstmann to Sen. Hanna, Apr. 1, 1897; both in C.D.A.

[22] *C.U.,* Oct. 14, 21, 1893; Mar. 14, 1902; June 28, 1907; Apr. 24, 1908. Handbill, Mar. 29, 1896; Horstmann to Wieczorek, Apr. 19, 1894; J. Christophory to Horstmann, Aug. 11, 1893; all in C.D.A.

amended before it was passed to be effective for the houses of the Good Shepherd Sisters only.[23]

The movement to furnish free text books in the public schools was considered to be at least an indirect thrust at the parish schools and an additional burden on the shoulders of the Catholic tax payers who would receive no benefit from the measure. A general protest and remonstrance sent to Columbus against the Griffin Bill for free text books aroused the A.P.A. and similar societies in Toledo to a spurious campaign to rescue the public schools from "Romish rule." When the Cleveland School Board proposed to give free books in the local public schools, the Bishop protested in the *Universe* and suggested that free warm meals for the children who needed them would be more desirable. The German Catholic societies registered a solemn protest that the Catholics of the city, comprising at least a third of the population, should have to pay a disproportionate share in the cost of the free school books which would not, moreover, be available to them. A general protest meeting in Cathedral Hall denounced the project as unconstitutional and discriminatory. An injunction obtained at the time delayed the plan of the school director.[24] A few years later the Bishop was prepared to appear before the school committee in Columbus against the Wynne Bill for free school books. In 1908 he attacked the Pollock Bill of a similar nature, but this bill he found to be the least objectionable from the Catholic standpoint.[25]

The Bishop had advised obedience to the compulsory school law which was found to be constitutional on the appeal of Doctor Quigley of Toledo. But he voiced his opposition to the action of the Cleveland School Board which listed the pupils in the Catholic orphanages for the per capita school appropriation. It was like taking money under false pretences, to collect for children for whom the State did nothing. In spite of the apparent injustice he advised compliance with the ruling. The *Plain Dealer* in an editorial pointed out the strange character of the procedure according to which the county auditors collected taxes for the public schools and included in the total number of pupils those in the parochial schools.[26]

[23] *C.U.*, Jan., 1896.

[24] Toledo *Blade*, Mar. 28, 1892. A.P.A. handbill, Mar. 31, 1892. Cleveland *Leader*, Mar. 30, 1892. *C.U.*, Jan. 19, 1900; Feb. 17, May 24, Sept. 20, 1901.

[25] *C.U.*, Feb. 14, Mar. 6, Mar. 27, Apr. 10, 1908.

[26] Quigley to Horstmann, Apr. 27, May 23, 1892; Horstmann to Quigley, May 25, May 30, Sept. 16, 1892; all in C.D.A. Pamphlets with briefs in the case of 1891, in *Memorial Volume, 1893*. Horstmann's advertisement in Cleveland *Leader*, July 25, 1894. Bishop's Circular, Aug. 10, 1899. *C.U.*, Sept. 24, 1892; July 28, 1894.

35

THE CATHOLIC SCHOOL
QUESTION

S HORTLY BEFORE BISHOP HORSTMANN CAME TO
Cleveland he had been very interested in the much discussed
Catholic School Question. Archbishop Ireland of St. Paul,
in 1890, delivered an address in St. Paul before the National
Educational Council in which he seemed to favor compulsory education in State schools; at the same time he would guarantee
the natural right of parents to have their children instructed in other
schools of their own choice. The want of religious instruction was the
principal objection of Catholic parents. He suggested that to remedy
this defect the State should support denominational schools, as was
the case in England and Prussia. The speech raised a storm of protest
in the Catholic newspapers which opposed the Archbishop's policy.
The controversy became nation-wide. Doctor Thomas Bouquillon,
a professor at the Catholic University, supposedly at the request of
his superiors composed an article, "Education, to Whom Does It Belong?" in which he would allow a greater degree of State control in
education than was traditionally admitted. As associate editor of the
American Catholic Quarterly Review, Doctor Horstmann in Philadelphia declined to publish the article because he considered it "inop-
portune, imprudent and harmful." Thereupon it was given to the public
in pamphlet form, and provoked attack on the part of many Catholic
writers.[1]

A general public discussion about the limits of State control of
education ensued. Meanwhile, the well-known case of the schools in
Fairbault and Stillwater, towns in Minnesota in the jurisdiction of
Archbishop Ireland, had been referred to the Congregation of the
Propaganda in Rome. In these localities a temporary arrangement had
been made whereby the parochial schools received some support from
the local government; the teaching of religion was reserved to a time
outside the official school hours. On April 30, 1892, the Propaganda

---

[1] Pamphlets: Thos. Bouquillon, *Education, to Whom Does It Belong? A Rejoinder to the Civiltà Cattolica,* Baltimore, 1892; S. Brandi, S.J., *The School Question
in the United States,* New York, 1892; R. I. Holaind, S.J., *The Parent First,* New
York, 1891; James Conway, S.J., *A Study of Doctor Bouquillon's Pamphlet,* New
York, 1892. Articles in *American Ecclesiastical Review* in 1892.

gave the decision that in view of the particular circumstances in the case the situation might be tolerated but that the decrees of the Third Council of Baltimore concerning parochial schools remained in full force in all other circumstances: namely, that schools should be established in every parish, and constantly improved, unless the bishop in his diocese saw reasons for delay. The council, moreover, had ruled that a child or its parents were not to be denied the sacraments because the child attended the public school if proper precautions were taken to obviate the proximate dangers to the child's faith. The Holy Father had assured the bishops of the Province of New York that he desired to have these decrees constantly observed.[2]

To discuss ways and means for united action in settling the controversy, the archbishops of the country met in New York, November 17, 1892. Archbishop Satolli, the papal representative, presented to them the well-known fourteen propositions in which it was suggested that Catholic children attending the public schools were not to be denied the use of the sacraments if they had sufficient reason for doing so and proper provision were made for their religious instruction. The propositions which would seem to modify the strictly compulsory nature of the Catholic school legislation were considered to be confidential but a news dispatch carried notice of them all over the country.[3]

Another flurry of discussion and interpretation of the law followed. Archbishop Elder, upon his return from the meeting in New York, called the bishops of this province together to consider the fourteen points. All agreed that the decrees of the Baltimore Council relevant to the matter should be enforced. It was decided that a letter addressed to the Holy Father in their name should manifest this conviction and should suggest that any change might be dangerous. Bishop Horstmann, who helped to compose this letter, translated it into Latin. In the message it was pointed out that the Catholic schools in this province had been brought up to a high standard at the cost of much effort and sacrifice; they were the only practical safeguard of the children who attended them. It was the bishops' belief that to lift the sanctions for compelling attendance would endanger their existence.

The result of this and other communications was the request of the Holy Father for the personal opinion of the individual bishops of the country. Bishop Horstmann's letter, following the pattern of the provincial letter, described the situation in this diocese. Every parish with few exceptions, even those in the smallest towns, had its own school; in the larger cities these schools were comparable to the State schools. And this was the result of the lifetime efforts of his predecessor, Bishop Gilmour. Any interference in the compulsory nature of the school legislation he would consider dangerous for the future generation of

[2] Zwierlein, *Op. cit.*, III, 167 sq. *C.U.*, June 17, 1892.

[3] Francis Satolli's pamphlet, *For the Settling of the School Question and the Giving of Religious Education;* original pamphlet in Latin, with Bishop Horstmann's notation in pencil, in C.D.A. Cleveland *Plain Dealer*, Dec. 16, 1892. Toledo *Blade*, Jan. 16, 1893. *C.U.*, June 17, Aug. 12, 1893.

Catholics. Meanwhile, the Bishop continued, he would take what measures he could for the religious instruction of Catholic children who did attend the common schools.[4]

The *Catholic Universe* published the fourteen points and quoted an article from the *Michigan Catholic* in which it was stated that the propositions contained nothing new and that severe sanctions against the attendance of Catholic children at public schools were not in vogue in all the dioceses of the country. Many pastors in this diocese were much concerned about these various interpretations. An inspired editorial in the *Universe* ridiculed the idea that the Catholic schools would be abandoned; any such mistaken notion would have to be based on a palpable misunderstanding or misinterpretation of the documents which, it was hoped, would soon be officially corrected.[5]

The letter of Pope Leo XIII, May 31, 1893, to Cardinal Gibbons authoritatively ended the controversy.[6] The school legislation of the Third Council of Baltimore, supplemented by other directives, was to be strictly maintained; allowance was to be made for exceptional cases; the fourteen propositions, which would seem to have modified that legislation to some extent, were to be interpreted according to the intention of the Baltimore legislators.

Bishop Horstmann thanked the Pope for this letter and maintained that the great sacrifices required to support the Catholic schools would be repaid in the loyalty of the Catholic citizens who came out of them. He also made his own application of the papal letter in a pastoral issued in the autumn of 1893 in which he warned that Catholic parents were obliged in conscience to send their children to the parish schools unless he, for grave reasons, would allow an exception. He called upon all concerned to improve and perfect the schools according to the papal recommendation.[7] In his practical application the Bishop did make a few exceptions, in cases where the Sisters were not the teachers, and in others where the student had already received First Holy Communion and had been confirmed and desired to qualify for entrance into normal school, which at the time required previous attendance at a public school.[8]

After a new decree of the Propaganda in 1895 the pastors of the city of Cleveland drew up a set of resolutions based on it and on the diocesan statutes, which insisted upon the compulsory nature of attendance at the parochial school, with no exceptions but such as were allowed by the Bishop. It was to be understood, however, that if the Bishop did approve of an exception the sacraments were not to be denied the

---

[4] Minutes of the meeting, Aug. 31, 1892, original draft, in C.D.A.

[5] Horstmann to Sidley (Sandusky), Mar. 16, 1893; Rieken (Perryburgh) to Horstmann, Jan. 19, 1893; both in C.D.A. *C.U.*, Jan. 21, 1893.

[6] Zwierlein, *Op. cit.*, III, 196. *C.U.*, June 24, Dec. 9, 1893.

[7] Horstmann to Pope Leo XIII, Sept. 29, 1893; papal reply to letter of bishops of Cincinnati Province, Aug. 28, 1893; Pastoral, Aug. 28, 1893; all in C.D.A. *C.U.*, Sept. 2, 1893.

[8] Minutes of Council meeting, Sept. 5, 1893; Horstmann to Doerner, Feb. 14, 1894; to Lentsch, Nov. 2, 1905; all in C.D.A.

parents of the child concerned. One pastor from outside the city had notified the Bishop that he would take it upon himself to refuse to administer the sacraments to parents who were clearly bound to observe the law and did not do so.[9] As late as 1896 it was thought necessary to correct a false impression in this matter. Father Gilbert Jennings, pastor of St. Agnes' in Cleveland, had notices published in the local newspapers calling attention to the fact that it was the sole province of the Bishop to pass judgment on the reasons alleged in single instances for attendance at the public school.[10] The Bishop, moreover, required the submission of each case in writing. And even when permission was granted, unless proper precautions were taken for the religious instruction of the children involved, the parents were considered to be unworthy of the sacraments because of grave dereliction of their duty.

Pastors and people at the inspiration of the Bishop did all in their power to improve the schools. One pastor who had just finished a new church was admonished that a "parish without a parochial school is not a Catholic parish. The school must be the rock foundation and the soul of the future of every parish. Without the school the pastor's work is only half done." Another pastor was urged to postpone needed improvement in other church buildings so that he could begin the school immediately. Still another was told that Catholic children had a right to a Catholic education and that even if he had difficulty he should "keep his school." If through necessity a school had to be closed temporarily, the pastor was warned of his obligation to reopen it at the first opportunity and meanwhile to gather the children in the church several times a week for religious instruction. The Bishop kept a vigilant eye upon the school reports and made rigid inquiries about attendance.[11]

In an effort to secure uniformity of text books in the school system, the Bishop ordered that no change be made in these without his express permission and he asked the pastors of the city to solve the problem in the matter which arose for a child who had to transfer from one school to another. Although he had given a kind of tacit approval to the use of the series of *McBride Readers,* he strongly recommended the *Gilmour Readers* "out of respect and memory of the patron and defender of the parochial schools."[12] An indication of the high standard of the Cleveland schools was the fact that nine of them received awards for

[9] Sidley (Sandusky) to Horstmann, Sept. 22, 1897, in C.D.A.

[10] Resolutions addressed to Bp. Horstmann by Frs. Molony, Carroll, Scanlon, O'Leary, Sheppach, Farrell, Donahue, and Metternich, Aug. 13, 1896; Horstmann to Hutmacher, Nov. 6, 1899; all in C.D.A. Cleveland *Press,* Oct. 21, 1896.

[11] Horstmann to Frs. Meilinger, Berger, O'Brien, and Drohan in 1893; to Fr. McMahon in 1894; to Fr. Murphy in 1902; to Fr. Mische in 1904; to Fr. Kirby in 1905; all in C.D.A.

[12] Horstmann to Arbp. Moeller, Sept. 22, 1898; Resolutions of pastors' meeting, Aug. 13, 1896; Benzinger Bros. to Houck, Sept. 19, 1898; Houck to Messmer, Apr. 4, 1901; Horstmann to Broens and to Mahar, Sept., 1902; Jennings to Horstmann, Oct., 1902; Catholic Federation Resolutions, May 15, 1902; Lucas County Federation to Horstmann, Dec. 29, 1904; all in C.D.A. *C.U.,* Sept. 23, 1893; Oct. 5, 1897; Sept. 29, 1899; Jan. 5, 1900.

general excellence and others received commendation at the Chicago World's Fair in 1893.[13]

The supply of teachers was always a difficulty. Early in his administration the Bishop had taken steps to strengthen and extend the training of teachers. Each religious community had its own normal school, and institutes were introduced for the teachers during the vacations, when some professional educator informed the Sisters of the latest developments in their field. An increase in salary was intended to help in the better training of the teachers. The Bishop also urged them to prepare for the time when a State teaching certificate would be required in the parish schools.[14]

The task of finding religious teachers outside the diocese, when necessary, was left to the pastor, who was always considered to be the one responsible for his school. The expenses of each school were paid out of the general fund of the parish, and in the cities especially they constituted the heaviest drain on parish resources. Nevertheless, the Bishop forbade any special school assessment on the parents of the children actually in attendance. The entire parish was held to be responsible. Children unable to pay for their books were furnished them in one way or another. In a very few places, where the population was almost exclusively Catholic, especially in the western part of the diocese, district schools supported by general taxation were reluctantly accepted as supplying the need of a parish school. In most cases, however, the arrangement was found to be unsatisfactory and the Bishop urged the establishment of a strictly parochial school under the direction of the pastor. In one instance the State school was almost entirely abandoned when the children transferred to the new Catholic school. In another case the pastor found it quite unsatisfactory to use the parish school only during the few months when the State school was closed.[15]

In connection with the Catholic School Question it is interesting to recall that Bishop Horstmann vigorously defended Doctor Schroeder,[16] at the meetings of the University Board of Trustees and in the

[13] *C.U.,* June 16, 30, July 23, 1892; Dec. 2, 1893; June 19, 1896. *History of the Catholic Educational Exhibit,* Chicago, 1896.

[14] Horstmann to Superior, Jan. 16, 1893, in C.D.A. *C.U.,* July 27, 1900.

[15] Horstmann to Berger, Sept. 6, 1893; Horstmann to Hannin, Sept. 5, 1893; Hannin to Horstmann, Nov. 22, 1893; Horstmann to Braschler (Fort Jennings), Sept. 6, 1893, July 29, Aug. 3, 1898; Braschler to Horstmann, Aug. 30, 1893; Stenk (Delphos) to Boff, Sept. 28, 1894; Arnoldi to Horstmann, Feb. 11, 1905; all in C.D.A. *C.U.,* Apr. 30, June 30, 1892; July 20, 1906.

[16] Horstmann notes taken down at meetings of the University Board. Horstmann-Schroeder correspondence; Thos. Lee to Horstmann, Oct. 11, 1897; Horstmann to Thos. Lee, Apr. 5, 1902; Messmer (Grand Rapids) to Horstmann, Apr. 15, 1897; Horstmann to Messmer, Apr. 17, Sept. 9, 1897; to Fr. Litz, Sept. 28, 1897; to Fr. Le Halle, Dec. 26, 1897; copies of Schroeder correspondence with Card. Steinhaber, Sept. 1897; Horstmann to Card. Steinhaber, Nov. 13, 1897; all in C.D.A. Clevelanders contributed to the modest farewell purse presented to Dr. Schroeder: Horstmann's letter, Jan. 26, 1898; John Koerper to Horstmann, Jan. 28, 1898; both in C.D.A. The controversy was aired in the Washington *Herald* and the Philadelphia *Ledger,* Oct. 22, 1897. Bp. Horstmann did not favor the appointment of Msgr. D. J. O'Connell to

newspapers, in the dispute which followed over the latter's removal from the University staff because of his stand on this question. When Schroeder returned to Germany to become professor at the University of Muenster, the Bishop wrote to assure him of his confidence and friendship. As a member of the Board of Trustees of the Catholic University Bishop Horstmann was much concerned about its welfare. It was at his suggestion that Father Lindesmith established a burse, and when financial difficulties arose he pledged his assistance and ordered the annual collection in the parishes to relieve them.[17] He was active, too, in the councils of the German Catholic societies in the effort to establish a chair of German literature.[18] His name was prominently mentioned as the successor to the first rector in 1896.

---

the rectorship of the Catholic University in Washington because he considered him opposed to Dr. Schroeder's stand on the school question: Horstmann to Pope Leo XIII, Nov. 19, 1902, in C.D.A. O'Connell became rector in 1903.

[17] Rector of university to Horstmann, June 6, 1902; Card. Gibbons to Horstmann, Aug. 27, 1904; Horstmann to Turner, Mar. 12, 1908; Arbp. Ryan to Horstmann, Nov. 5, 1906; all in C.D.A. *C.U.*, Nov. 20, 1903; Nov. 18, 1904.

[18] Horstmann to Messmer, Oct. 7, 1896; Horstmann's notes about conditions to be attached to establishment of a German chair, Jan. 15, 1897; W. F. Faulhaber to Horstmann, Jan. 28, 1897; A. W. Walburg to Horstmann, July 26, 1898; all in C.D.A. *C.U.*, Jan. 17, 1908.

36

THE SCHOOLS AND RELIGIOUS COMMUNITIES

THE PROGRESS IN THE DEVELOPMENT OF THE parish schools during Bishop Horstmann's administration may be judged from an analysis of the substantially accurate figures given in the *Catholic Directory* for 1909. There were a few hundred more than 20,000 pupils in the Cleveland schools alone and a few less than 20,000 outside the city including the 1,400 in the 9 Catholic district schools in the country. The vast majority of the teachers were members of religious communities, although 56 laymen kept that number of small schools, and 31 laymen taught in the district schools.

Aiding the Sisters in Cleveland were 11 Brothers of Mary who had charge of the boys at the Cathedral, St. Patrick's, and St. Mary's and 5 Christian Brothers at St. Malachy's. In these and 21 other schools 109 Ursuline Nuns and 11 lay teachers had a total of over 9,500 pupils, boys and girls. In 1909 the Cleveland Ursuline community numbered approximately 171 members. Their mother-house and academy, a large brick and stone English Gothic building on East 55th Street near Scovill Avenue, was completed in the summer of 1893. Bishop Horstmann blessed it and its Chapel of St. Ursula on November 25. The Sisters also opened another academy, dedicated to the Sacred Heart, in East Cleveland; it served for a while as the parish school for St. Philomena's. The boarding academy at Villa Angela and the young boys' school on the grounds were in a flourishing condition.

The Tiffin Ursulines, who taught in the schools of that district, completed a three-story brick academy in 1898. In 1900 the Toledo Ursulines bought property on Collingwood Avenue where a new academy was started. The Youngstown Ursulines in February, 1897, occupied their new three-story brick convent.

Some 200 Sisters of Notre Dame assisted by 4 lay teachers taught 11,259 pupils in 32 schools in this diocese. At St. Stephen's and St. Peter's in Cleveland 7 Brothers of Mary had charge of the older boys. The Sisters conducted a flourishing academy near St. Peter's School, on Superior Avenue. A three-story brick convent was completed on

214

the same site in 1896. Mount St. Mary's Academy, on Buckeye Road, was also theirs. A new Notre Dame Academy, a four-story building, was opened in Toledo in 1904.

The Sisters of St. Joseph to the number of 74 aided by 4 lay teachers, had 4,172 pupils in 13 parish schools. Their mother-house and academy was moved from Starkweather Avenue to a new site, a fifty-acre tract of land on the east bank of Rocky River in old West Park, now a part of Cleveland. Bishop Horstmann dedicated a large frame building there in 1899.

Fourteen parish schools with an attendance of 2,545 were in charge of 55 Sisters of the Holy Humility of Mary. In September, 1897, the Sisters moved their academy from Lorain Street to a location on Franklin Avenue, where a new building with modern equipment was completed two years later. With a view to establishing their mother-house within the confines of the diocese, the Sisters occupied a sixty-three-acre site between Canton and Massillon. A boarding academy was opened there in 1905. A large five-story stone building (Mount Marie) was completed three years later.

Forty-nine Sisters of St. Dominic from Caldwell, New Jersey, had 16 schools and 2,357 pupils. The Dominican Sisters from Adrian, Michigan, had 2 schools and 675 pupils. In the 3 schools taught by the 29 Polish Franciscan Sisters there were 1,800 pupils. At St. Stanislas' School in Cleveland 19 Sisters of the Holy Family of Nazareth had charge of 1,510 children. Eighteen Daughters of the Immaculate Heart of Mary, aided by 11 lay teachers, had 1,492 pupils in 3 schools. Eighteen Sanguinist Sisters, together with 13 laymen, taught 1,220 pupils.

The Sisters of Charity of Cincinnati had 29 teachers and 1,205 pupils in 4 schools. Twenty-two Benedictine Sisters had charge of 6 schools and 1,118 pupils. The Franciscan Sisters of Joliet had 19 teachers and 1,010 pupils in 4 schools. Other religious communities with less than 500 pupils in this diocese were the Franciscan Sisters of Tiffin, the Sisters Servants of the Immaculate Heart of Mary, the Sisters of St. Agnes, the Sisters of Loretto, and the Sisters of Providence.

On June 14, 1906, Bishop Horstmann dedicated the new convent and chapel of the Poor Clare Nuns (Colettines) on Rocky River Drive not far from the Franciscan House of Studies. He had obtained from the Propaganda on January 14, 1905, the faculty for the erection of a religious house of the Second Order of St. Francis in Rockport, then a suburb of Cleveland. The Sisters took possession of their new home in the early part of 1906.[1]

The first permanent convent of the Poor Clares in this country was established, August 10, 1877, in a house on the property now occupied by St. Alexis Hospital at Broadway and McBride Avenue.

[1] Gilmour correspondence with Bishops Feehan and O'Connor in the matter: C.D.A. *C.U.,* June 1, 1900; Feb. 7, 1902; Sept. 1, 1905; Mar. 2, 1906; *C.U.-B.,* June 14, 1929; Feb. 3, 1933.

Mother Mary Magdalena Bentivoglio and her blood sister, Sister Mary Constance, said to be relatives of Pope Leo XIII, in August, 1875, came from Italy at the direction of Pope Pius IX to establish the Primitive Observance of the First Rule of St. Francis in Minnesota. Advised against going to the West, after several attempts to settle in the East they were finally welcomed by Archbishop Perche in New Orleans. Soon, however, in obedience to their religious superior, Father Gregory Janknecht, O.F.M., who was making a visitation of the Order, the Sisters and two postulants came to Cleveland to occupy for a few months the home prepared for them by Father Kilian Schloesser, the local Franciscan superior who had obtained Bishop Gilmour's authorization.

Shortly afterwards Mother Veronica and four other Poor Clares came from Germany; they followed the rule of St. Clare as it was revised by St. Colette. The difference in language and the slight difference in the rule induced Mother Magdalena and her sister in 1878 to accept the offer of John Creighton to found a convent in Omaha. There they endured many trials and misunderstandings. Sister Constance died in Omaha in 1902. Mother Magdalena, who founded the convent in Evansville, Indiana, died there in 1905; steps towards her beatification were taken in 1928.

The German Sisters who took over the Cleveland convent finished a three-story brick monastery on East 22nd Street north of St. Bridget's Church in December, 1881, and occupied it until their removal to Rockport. Mother Veronica, who founded their house in Chicago, died there in 1905. As is well known, the Poor Clares are strictly cloistered except for the "extern" Sisters who maintain contact with the public. Their day is spent in prayer, work, contemplation, and penance. The local community is also devoted to the perpetual adoration of Christ in the Blessed Sacrament.

St. Ignatius College continued to flourish under the benign patronage of Bishop Hortsmann, who never missed an opportunity to show his appreciation of the good work accomplished by the Fathers of the Society of Jesus. The average yearly enrollment in the college from 1892 to 1910 was 230 students with an average of 17 Jesuit teachers. In 1897 the distinct commercial school was discontinued and only classical and scientific courses were given. In 1902 the first American-born Jesuit of the Buffalo province, Father John I. Zahm, became president of St. Ignatius. He separated the high school from the college department and added a year of philosophy to the curriculum so that, thereafter, a bachelor's degree instead of a certificate was given to the graduates. Father Frederick L. Odenbach, a pioneer seismologist, in 1900 constructed his own instruments for locating earthquakes, and brought considerable prestige to the college. In 1907 Father George J. Pickel organized a fully equipped chemical and physics laboratory; thereafter, graduates were admitted, without difficulty, into medical school.

Loyola High School on Cedar Avenue at East 106th Street, a preparatory school, was opened by Father Pickel also in 1907. A remodeled residence and a one-story brick building housed the average enrollment of 100 students.

In Toledo the Jesuit Fathers at the request of the Bishop had started St. John's College in September, 1898, in a remodeled brick house with 33 students in the academic course. A new three-story brick college building was completed four years later. In 1909 there were 237 students who were taught by 19 Jesuits and a few lay teachers.

What had been known as the German Province of the Jesuit Fathers was absorbed in the American Missouri Province in 1907. Ten years before this the Cleveland Fathers had erected St. John Berchman's Hall, a two-story frame building, on a tract of land in Parma township. A three-story brick residence and a fine Gothic chapel were dedicated by Bishop Horstmann on May 31, 1900. It served as a novitiate and also as a retreat house for laymen.

The Bishop depended upon St. Ignatius College to prepare students for the seminary; although it was not technically a preparatory seminary most of the students, on completion of studies there, continued on to the priesthood. After the death of Bishop Gilmour Monsignor Boff started a campaign to raise money with which to build a residence hall for ecclesiastical students near St. Ignatius, and lots were actually bought on Carroll Avenue just west of St. Mary's Church. Bishop Hortsmann was not sanguine about the success of the project which was intended to be a memorial to his predecessor; times were hard and money was scarce. By 1903 the plan was abandoned and some of the funds were returned to the patrons at their request.[2]

Judging that the system as it existed was adequate for his purpose, the Bishop and others founded several scholarships for deserving students.[3] In his frequent visits to the college he pointed out the need for well-informed Catholic laymen but he also dwelt on the need of the diocese for priests to carry on the work of the Church. The few students in colleges outside the city were assisted to some extent by the Bishop who bequeathed much of his family fortune for the education of clerical students.

The old seminary on Lake Avenue, in down-town Cleveland, continued to function despite its severe physical handicaps. The cramped quarters were insufficient for the increasing number of vocations. Plans to buy a large building on a great tract of land on Euclid Avenue were thwarted when it became known that the Bishop wanted the property. As late as 1907 he was still hoping to build a new seminary on the Gilmour land in Euclid, Ohio, which previously had been considered to be too far out in the country. He had put aside a portion of his inheritance from his mother for that purpose. A story published

---

[2] List of donors: Horstmann to Kingsley, July 14, 1893; Houck to Vollmeyer, Dec. 12, 1894; all in C.D.A. *C.U.*, Jan. 7, 1892; Sept. 14, 1901.

[3] *C.U.*, June 23, 1899; Sept. 20, 1901; Aug. 29, 1902; May 12, 1905; May 15, 1908.

in the newspapers that the seminary was to be closed and the students sent to the provincial seminary in Cincinnati was officially denied by the chancellor.[4]

The capacity of the venerable institution was forty-one in 1908, much too small. When there were thirty-two students in 1893, many of the new applicants had to be sent to other seminaries. There was room for only one of the seven applicants in 1901; three years later only five of the sixteen who applied to enter could be accommodated.[5] The seminaries in Baltimore and Rochester absorbed the overflow. A few were sent to Cincinnati and a few to the North American College in Rome. Bishop Horstmann founded three burses at his old Alma Mater and at his recommendation Father Lindesmith founded another.

The great majority of the priests, however, finished their theological studies at the old school which began its existence with the diocese. In 1892 Bishop Horstmann ordained twelve priests, making the number of those who had completed their studies there since its opening approximately 250. From 1893 to 1908, inclusive, there were approximately 102 priests ordained for this diocese, more than seventy-five per cent of them born in the United States. Of the others nearly all were raised and educated here. Six came from Germany, five from Poland, four from Moravia (Bohemia), three from Slovenia, two from Ireland, two from Luxembourg, and one from Switzerland. Of the total number, eighty-two came out of the local seminary; three were educated in St. Bernard's Seminary in Rochester, New York; three in Rome; ten in Baltimore at St. Mary's Seminary; and one each in the seminaries in Niagara Falls, Yonkers (New York), and St. Paul (Minnesota) and in the American College, Louvain, Belgium. The Bishop was fortunate enough to obtain the services of other priests, ordained outside his jurisdiction, who were conversant with foreign languages.

[4] Horstmann to Martinelli, Feb. 6, 1897; to Elder, Mar. 20, 1899, Jan. 14, 1904; all in C.D.A. *C.U.*, June 23, 1899.

[5] N. A. Moes memorandum in C.D.A. N. Pfeil, "St. Mary's Seminary," in *American Ecclesiastical Review*, XIX, 272.

37

CHARITABLE INSTITUTIONS
(1891-1908)

T HE CHARITABLE INSTITUTIONS OF THE DIO-
cese continued to develop their resources under the guiding hand of Bishop Horstmann.

St. Vincent's Charity Hospital was expanded to meet
the demands for its services. Because most of the patients
could not pay their expenses, it was nearly always in debt. In 1898 the
two wings of the original hospital building were enlarged to make
room for 18 additional patients. In March, 1902, a three-story brick
wing facing Central Avenue was opened; it made room for another
50 patients and for the nurses. This unit, costing approximately $40,000
(raised by Doctor W. H. Humiston and his committee), gave the
hospital a capacity of 133 beds. The names of the principal donors
were registered on a bronze plaque. In 1907 another large brick building was erected to serve as a power-house and laundry. In 1902 about
half of the 1,350 patients and in the next year more than half of the
1,478 patients were unable to pay anything for their care. The free
dispensary which was started in 1894 took care of 7,800 cases in 1903,
and 18,000 in 1909. In this latter year, in the hospital itself, there were
1,036 free patients and 1,443 who were able to pay in full or in part
for the services they received.

At the urging of the Bishop a nurses' training school was begun in
1898; 17 nurses, 11 of them Sisters, finished the course in 1900. Some
years later Doctor Thwing, President of Western Reserve University, addressed the graduates. As previously, this university appointed
the physicians. In attendance at the hospital in 1909 there were 28
Sisters, 48 nurses, and 10 resident physicians.

St. Ann's Infant Asylum and Maternity Hospital in 1901 was moved
from its original location on the grounds of St. Vincent's to the remodeled Severance mansion on Woodland Avenue. It had developed
from an obscure institution into one of the most prominent in the
State. Doctor Hunter Powell, the chief of the medical staff for twenty-
five years, in 1906 might well have complimented the hospital for its
success and the reduction of the mortality rate to a very low percentage. The arrangements with the medical school of Western Reserve

University were the same as St. Vincent's. In the twenty years previous to 1903, 5,000 infants and 1,600 mothers had been treated. In the one year ending in July, 1904, shelter was given to 527 children, including those abandoned by their parents. In 1907, 200 of the 365 maternity cases were charity cases. In the last-mentioned year the building was already overcrowded and the Bishop authorized its expansion but it was not until 1910 that the new main building was erected and married women were admitted as patients.[1]

In 1901 Bishop Horstmann purchased a plot of land on Detroit Street, just west of St. John's Hospital, with the intention of remodeling the brick structure upon it for use as an extension of St. Ann's. This project of a nursery school for children three to five years of age, to be known as St. Catherine's Home in charge of the Sisters of Charity, was not carried out at the time. Most of the children for whom it was intended were taken by friends or relatives. Those for whom homes could not be found were kept at St. Ann's until they were old enough to enter one of the orphanages.[2]

The new Providence Hospital in Sandusky, which was dedicated by the Bishop in 1904, was entrusted to the care of the same Sisters of Charity,[3] as was the new Mercy Hospital in Canton. Mrs. Rose Lang Klorer purchased President McKinley's homestead in the latter city and donated it to the diocese. With a capacity of 40 patients it was opened to the public in September, 1908.[4]

The facilities of St. Alexis Hospital were taxed by the number of patients admitted through the great charity of the Franciscan Sisters and especially of Sister Leonarda, the Superior. In September, 1894, of the 118 patients, 105 were charity cases supported by the begging of the Sisters, by the proceeds of Fairs, and by other occasional donations. Nevertheless, the Sisters were able to build the north wing of the present hospital, which the Bishop dedicated on October 4, 1897. The 160 beds enabled the Sisters to care for about 1,200 patients a year. Six years later the main building facing on Broadway was ready for occupancy. On the occasion of its dedication, the well-known Doctor Crile, who had been an interne there, recalled that three-fourths of the 20,000 patients had been treated gratis. Worthy of recollection, also, is the fact that some of the Sisters from St. Alexis had volunteered at the Bishop's request to act as nurses at the two detention hospitals during the severe smallpox epidemic of 1902, after three other nurses had fallen victim to the disease.[5]

[1] Circular, Oct. 6, 1899; Horstmann to H. M. Hanna, Apr. 8, 1901; Charity Hospital to Supt. Bemis, Dec. 28, 1902; Powell to Horstmann, May 13, 1903; Horstmann to Sr. Peter, 1903, all in C.D.A. Printed appeal to the clergy, May 26, 1904. *C.U.*, Sept. 28, 1900; May 10, June 7, 22, Nov. 22, 1901; Feb. 19, 1904; Feb. 7, Oct. 16, 1908. Cleveland *Plain Dealer*, Oct. 16, 1908. *Souvenir Booklet of the Golden Jubilee*, 1917.

[2] Correspondence in C.D.A. *C.U.*, June 7, 1901.

[3] Sandusky *Register*, Sept. 20, 1902. *C.U.*, Apr. 8, 1904.

[4] Horstmann to Mrs. Klorer, Mar. 21, 1908 and other correspondence in C.D.A. *C.U.*, Apr. 24, Sept. 18, Oct. 16, 1908.

[5] Horstmann to Sr. Leonarda, Sept. 18; Sr. Leonarda to Horstmann, Sept. 14, 1894.

The original plan of Bishop Gilmour for the removal of St. Alexis Hospital to the West Side was abandoned in 1892 when Bishop Horstmann dedicated the new St. John's Hospital, a frame structure, on May 12 of that year. Seven years later the facilities were enlarged by the attachment to it of a large frame residence. Plans for a new building were approved in 1906 but the means for carrying them out were not available. The Franciscan Sisters had difficulty in meeting the running expenses of the institution.[6]

In Toledo St. Vincent's Hospital, which was in charge of the Grey Nuns of Montreal, was increased in size by the addition of two new wings which the Bishop dedicated in 1905. At that time 26 Sisters and 24 nurses served the hospital. The nurses' training school had graduated its first students in 1898. The Sisters cooperated with the Jesuit, Father Hiermann, to rescue many Catholic foundlings in the public institutions; they were kept at the hospital until they could be adopted or sent to the infant asylum the Sisters had in Detroit. Bishop Horstmann paid something for their support.[7]

In 1892, Father Bihn, the founder of the self-supporting home in Tiffin, bought a building, previously a hotel, in Lorain. It was used as an orphanage and home for the aged for two years and it then became the first St. Joseph's Hospital, where many accident cases from the steel mills were treated. A new wing, three stories high and of brick, was blessed in 1908. Two years previously the first students graduated from the hospital, which was then in charge of the Franciscan Sisters of Tiffin.[8]

In Youngstown two Sisters of Charity, former members of the Greensburg community, took charge of the small Mahoning Valley Hospital in 1897. The name was changed to St. Ignatius Hospital three years later in honor of the Bishop.[9]

For want of a better way Bishop Horstmann continued the old method of raising funds for the support of the orphanages. The diocese was divided into districts and to each was assigned the financing of one of the institutions. In the city each parish was given a quota which was generally raised in the Orphans' Fair. The Sisters made house-to-house collections themselves. The results were not adequate despite the generous donations of many and the Bishop thought of dividing the costs among all the parishes. He "blessed the day when the Sisters would not be obliged to go out begging for the institutions of which they had charge."[10]

1894; Crile to Horstmann, May 27, 1901, all in C.D.A. Sr. M. Rosanna Peters, *Op. cit. C.U.*, Oct. 1, 1892; Jan. 7, 1898; June 19, 1903; Dec. 17, 1909.

[6] Horstmann correspondence, in C.D.A. *C.U.*, Apr. 28, 1892; Feb. 16, 1906.

[7] Horstmann-Hiermann correspondence, in C.D.A. *C.U.*, Feb. 19, 1909.

[8] Bihn to Horstmann, Mar. 29, 1892, in C.D.A. *C.U.*, May. 15, 1908.

[9] Correspondence in C.D.A. *C.U.*, Nov. 15, 1901.

[10] Horstmann to Falconio, Mar. 22, 1905; Mar. 9, 1906; to Sr. Ambrose, Feb. 15, 1902; to Ankly, Nov. 29, 1895; J. T. O'Connell to Horstmann, Feb. 15, 1903; Houck to Baumgartner, Aug. 7, 1894; all in C.D.A. *C.U.*, Dec. 3, 1892; Jan. 9, 1903; Feb. 24, 1905.

The increased number of boys at St. Vincent's Orphanage on Monroe Avenue made it necessary in 1897 to add a three-story brick wing to the building. Three years later another structure housing the powerhouse and the laundry made its appearance. In 1906 the Bishop dedicated a new two-story brick schoolhouse. There were 287 boys in the institution on January 1, 1908, and another 114 in the old college building at Louisville where in 1901 the Bishop had dedicated a beautiful chapel which seated 250 persons.[11] The Sisters of Charity, who had charge of these boys and the several hospitals, moved their motherhouse and novitiate from Monroe Street to a very desirable site on Lake Avenue, in Lakewood, which had been purchased in 1885. The new three-story brick convent with its fine chapel was dedicated to St. Augustine by Bishop Horstmann, August 28, 1892. Soon afterwards a school for younger children was opened in connection with it.

At the direction of the Bishop all the girls of St. Mary's Orphanage on East 20th Street were moved to St. Joseph's on Woodland Avenue, where another three-story brick building had been put up in 1894. In 1908 there were 255 orphans in the institution. The Daughters of the Immaculate Heart of Mary, who had charge of them, remodeled the old building on East 20th Street and opened it as St. Mary's Home for working girls in 1895; it could accommodate 25 to 30.[12]

In 1907 the Bishop dedicated the large new $100,000 orphanage in Toledo which had been placed under the patronage of St. Anthony (at the suggestion of the Bishop) to distinguish it from the hospital which continued to use the name of St. Vincent. The Grey Nuns, who had some some 200 orphans, boys and girls, in their care, had transferred the title of the orphanage to the diocese.[13]

The Franciscan Sisters of Tiffin, who had about 115 orphans in their charge, erected a large four-story building which the Bishop blessed in 1906.[14]

The Marchant Bill introduced in the Ohio Legislature in 1900, which would authorize the State Board of Charities to control the children who were in the care of independently organized institutions, was successfully opposed by Bishop Horstmann and the authorities in charge of the Jewish and Protestant orphanages. The bill was considered to be an unnecessary interference of the State, since the children's rights were already well protected by the laws.[15]

[11] *C.U.*, June 8, 1906; Jan. 31, Feb. 21, 1908.
[12] *C.U.*, Jan. 4, July 26, 1895; July 28, 1899; Jan. 7, 1901; Jan. 31, 1908; Feb. 5, 1909.
[13] Correspondence in C.D.A. *C.U.*, Feb. 11, 1893; Dec. 22, 1899; Feb. 1, 1901.
[14] *C.U.*, Oct. 12, 1906.
[15] *C.U.*, Mar. 28, Apr. 6, 13, 1900.

38

SOCIETIES AND ASSOCIATIONS DURING BISHOP HORSTMANN'S EPISCOPATE

BISHOP HORSTMANN UPON HIS ARRIVAL HERE was well pleased to find the laity organized in the Catholic Central Association. In reorganizing this group he sought more thoroughly united action. "Clergy and laity working together for Church and Country would be the greatest bulwark against the dangers to peace, order and liberty." As a young priest, he recalled, he had admired the success of the united German Catholics against the persecutory tactics of the Bismarck Government. He was in no less admiration of the federated organization of the Catholic German societies in this country. He invited the Ohio Union of German Societies to hold its convention in Cleveland and he was enthusiastically received at the national conventions in Detroit and St. Paul. He was one of the principal speakers at the fiftieth anniversary of the Central Verein in Cincinnati.

The movement towards the general confederation of all Catholic societies in the country, without respect to their national origins, was started in Cleveland in 1889 at the convention of the Knights of St. John. Bishop Horstmann was looked upon as a promoter of such unity.[1] At a meeting held in Gray's Armory under the auspices of the German Catholic Union he and Bishop McFaul of Trenton, New Jersey, and Bishop Stang of Fall River, Massachusetts, urged the necessity of stronger organization to meet the threats against morality and religion.[2] At a meeting in Indianapolis held for the purpose of encouraging unity on a national scale Bishop Horstmann played a prominent role.

At home in the diocese the Cleveland Federation was formed in August, 1900. A standing committee, composed of two representatives from each parish in the city, stood ready to cooperate with the Bishop in any emergency. At the State convention of the federation

---

[1] McFall to Horstmann, Mar. 15, 1901, in C.D.A.
[2] C.U., June 15, 1906.

in the following year Bishop Horstmann celebrated the opening Mass. In his convention speech he cited the example of the exclusion of a priest from the public deaf-mute and blind asylums as a denial of religious liberty to those of the inmates who were Catholics. The Cleveland Federation became the Cuyahoga County Federation in 1906, at a time when the Catholics in the area constituted about one-third of the population. Separate units were formed in other large cities such as Youngstown and Lorain. The Canton Federation was responsible for the permission obtained to hold Catholic religious services in the county infirmary and the workhouse.

The Toledo Federation, also, had success in that city and it was active in procuring better public observance of Sunday. It sponsored a great meeting of protest against the persecution of the Church in France; at the corresponding gathering in Cleveland Bishop Horstmann contrasted this persecution with the religious liberty enjoyed in America.[3] At the suggestion of the Bishop the Lucas County (Toledo) Federation made a successful appeal to the general public for funds with which to establish the Sisters of the Good Shepherd and their work in Toledo. More than one-half of the donations were from non-Catholics, and a plot of a little more than twenty-three acres was purchased in January, 1906. At the end of the following August the buildings on the property were ready for the Sisters, and in October the first group of young women was admitted. The people of Toledo proved themselves very generous in furnishing the new institution and in providing food for the first winter.

The Bishop personally took an active part in the meetings of the local federation and he easily enlisted the active cooperation of the members in his many projects for civic and religious improvement. They helped him in his efforts to bring about a stricter observance of the Lord's Day in the closing of stores and taverns and other places of amusement. He publicly demanded the suppression of the wine rooms because of the danger in them for unsuspecting youth. He personally thanked the manager of a local theater for closing it on Good Friday. The Cleveland group also sponsored a series of lectures which were intended to point out the excellence of the kind of education imparted in the parish schools and to bring home to the public the great amount of money saved the tax payers in the schooling of some 23,000 children.

The Federation was called upon to find foster homes for dependent Catholic children. The Juvenile Court laws of the State required as far as possible that such children be placed in the homes of those who professed the same religion as the parents. Judge Adams cooperated in this city to the very best of his ability; there was, however, only one Catholic among the probation officers of the court, the widow of the first judge of the Juvenile Court, Thomas E. O'Callaghan. The latter had originated the volunteer probation officer system, according

[3] *C.U.*, Dec. 28, 1906; Jan. 4, 18, 1907.

to which a trusted individual supervised the conduct of a group of neglected young people. Mrs. O'Callaghan had the assistance of Daniel E. Lanigan in finding Catholic homes for some of the wards of the court; some few were sent to Father Baker's Home in Buffalo.[4] Cleveland had no such Catholic home. Bishop Rappe bought land in Olmsted and Bishop Gilmour was anxious to build an industrial school on it but circumstances were unfavorable. Bishop Horstmann, who was well acquainted with the work of St. Joseph's Home for boys in Philadelphia, preferred to establish a house in Cleveland to care for homeless boys when they left the orphanage. An industrial school for boys who needed special discipline would be another project.

A start was made when Father Eugene M. O'Callaghan of St. Colman's left his estate to the Bishop for that purpose. With this as a nucleus the Cleveland clergy collected a fund to enable the Bishop to carry out his plan. It was presented to him for the ruby jubilee of his priesthood. The feast was celebrated, June 15, 1905, with a Mass in the Cathedral and a dinner at the Ursuline Convent on East 55th Street. The general public gathered in the evening at the Chamber of Commerce Hall on Public Square to offer him their felicitations. Not long afterwards a large farm was purchased as the site for a boys' protectory. But, after trying unsuccessfully to obtain the services of the Holy Ghost Fathers who had charge of the home in Philadelphia, and those of the Salesian Fathers in Italy, the Bishop abandoned that project.

It was decided, however, to proceed with the home in the city for working boys. The buildings on a three-acre plot on Detroit Avenue at West 83rd Street were remodeled to accommodate some 40 young men, and on November 24, 1907, St. Anthony's Home was formally dedicated. Father Francis Hassler, who had been caring for the boys at Hudson Farm, a city institution, was put in charge as chaplain. The boys who had gainful occupation outside the home paid a nominal sum for their support, but it was returned to them when they left the institution.[5]

The Catholic Ladies Aid Society had been organized as the women's auxiliary of the Catholic Federation. They, also, responded to the Bishop's appeal to do something for the common good of the diocese. The members formed the St. Catherine Protective Association in 1900. It was responsible for the Catherine Horstmann Home for girls, who while temporarily out of employment might receive some training in the domestic arts. In 1909 a house which had accommodations for sixteen was opened at West 25th Street and Washington Avenue.

The Ladies Aid Society cooperated with the Sisters of the Good

[4] Correspondence in C.D.A. *C.U.*, Mar. 22, 1901; Mar. 17, June 16, July 14, 1905; Nov. 29, 1907. Circulars, Mar. 6, May 30, 1905.

[5] *C.U.*, Jan. 24, Apr. 3, 1908. *C.U.-B.*, July 17, 1942. Open letter of Msgr. Boff, Dec. 1, 1908. Correspondence in the matter including that between Bp. Horstmann and Fr. Rua in Turin, in C.D.A.

Shepherd in establishing in 1907 a detention home for girls who had been brought before the Juvenile Court. Through the combined efforts of the Sisters and the members in one period of eighteen months 109 young women found temporary shelter; this project later developed into an important organization for taking care of these charges. The Sisters of the Good Shepherd put an addition onto their building on Carnegie Avenue, which Bishop Horstmann dedicated to the Sacred Heart, May 8, 1895. Further expansion was necessary for the penitents in 1898. Later other improvements were made and a steam laundry was built. The Sisters despite the income from the latter source had to continue their appeals to the general public.[6]

The Ladies Aid Society was responsible also for the St. Catherine Labor Bureau, which helped unprotected young women to find suitable employment, and for the Catholic Travelers' Aid, which supported an agent at the Union Depot to look out for the welfare of incoming strangers. The first case cared for by the latter agency was a Mexican mother and her two children.[7]

The institution and development of settlement houses under non-Catholic auspices in the poorer districts of the city where many Catholics lived was a source of concern to the Bishop. Their representatives alleged that they were non-sectarian, but there was good reason to believe that the proselytizing motive was not always absent. However, a prominent Catholic, in the *Universe*, defended the settlement houses against that imputation.[8] In a few instances Catholic women were associated with the work. The Alta House on Mayfield Road, among the Italians, was opened in 1885; Goodrich House on St. Clair Avenue, in 1897; and the Hiram House on Orange Avenue, in 1906.[9] Day nursery services, recreational facilities, and other advantages were offered to all comers. Moreover, the Young Men's and Young Women's Christian Associations offered inducements which attracted Catholic youth and subjected them to Protestant influence.

The Bishop warned his flock against enjoying gifts which came from those who were unfriendly to the Faith. "Their literature was non-Catholic and their teaching contrary to the Catholic Faith."[10] As a counter-attraction he urged that clubs be organized which would interest the Catholic young people.[11] The Marquette Club of the Cathedral had been operating successfully with its library, showers, and meeting rooms. The Bishop was an honorary member of the Iroquois Club for young men. Father Francis T. Moran, of St. Patrick's, supervised the erection of the large fully equipped Catholic Club near

[6] *C.U.*, Jan. 5, 1900; Mar. 1, 1907; Nov. 6, 1908; Aug. 6, 1909; Apr. 8, 1910; Jan. 17, 1913.

[7] *C.U.*, June 22, Aug. 30, 1900; Apr. 17, 1908.

[8] M. A. Fanning in *C.U.*, Feb. 28, Apr. 17, 1908.

[9] Orth, *Op. cit.*, I, 406 sq.

[10] Horstmann to J. F. Imbs, Jan. 28, 1902, in C.D.A. *C.U.*, Jan. 6, 1905; Oct. 5, 1906. Toledo *Catholic Record*, Jan. 24, 1906.

[11] Horstmann to Mears, Dec. 6, 1898; to Braschler, Feb. 2, 1905; to Rupert, Jan. 10, 1904; all in C.D.A.

the church which cost over $50,000 and was called the Catholic Y.M.C.A. building. The Bishop opened it with proper ceremony in 1904. Similar centers were started at Toledo, Sandusky, and Lima. Youngstown had its Catholic Institute with reading and recreational rooms. In Cleveland clubs were started in several parishes with varying success. St. Mary's had its Young Men's Society since 1881. The Thorpe Club at the Immaculate Conception parish flourished for a long time. Meanwhile the Bishop envisioned an association which would unite all Catholic young men in a society comparable to the Y.M.C.A. Funds alone were lacking.

It was especially with the hope that the members might interest themselves in the young people that the Bishop published his desire to have a branch of the St. Vincent de Paul Society in every parish. He had been closely associated with this organization in Philadelphia and often lectured on the duties of Catholic laymen in modern life.[12]

Among the earliest social organizations of Catholics in Cleveland had been the Total Abstinence societies. The Bishop now called for the establishment of such societies in every parish. In his visitations throughout the diocese he always urged the "taking of the pledge" upon all children who would bind themselves to abstain from intoxicating beverages at least until they reached their majority. He assisted at the conventions of the societies to give his moral support. The fiftieth anniversary of Father Matthew's coming to America was celebrated in Cathedral Hall in 1899, and the 115th anniversary of his birth was kept in Akron by the Father Matthew Total Abstinence and Beneficial Society in 1905. By the year 1912, however, the uniformed Knights of Father Matthew alone represented such societies. The beneficial mutual aid organizations proved to be more attractive.

The Bishop gave his full approval to the Ancient Order of Hibernians, especially after their convention in 1898 in which they accepted the constitution adopted in Cleveland some fourteen years previously as the basis for the reunion of the separate branches. He also gave encouragement to societies and movements which were intended to help Ireland and the Irish.[13] The Knights of St. John were welcomed to Cleveland by the Bishop in 1899 for their twenty-first international convention; an entire issue of the *Universe*[14] was devoted to their aims and purposes. The Bishop served as grand spiritual adviser of the Catholic Mutual Benefit Association which was very popular in its day. He acted in the same capacity for the Catholic Order of Foresters, the Catholic Knights of Ohio, and the Catholic Ladies of Ohio.[15] The Ladies Catholic Beneficial Association received its first approval in Ohio from him.

[12] Philipps (Philadelphia) to Horstmann, Aug. 3, 1904, in C.D.A. *C.U.*, Oct. 16, 1908.

[13] Horstmann to J. P. Hannan, May 3, 1904, in C.D.A. *C.U.*, May 9, 1902; Mar. 6, June 3, 1903.

[14] *C.U.*, June 23, 1899.

[15] Voluminous correspondence in C.D.A.

The first council of the Knights of Columbus[16] in the Middle West was organized in Youngstown in 1897. A little suspicious of their secrecy in the beginning, the Bishop was soon convinced of their Catholicity and of their willingness to be of service to the Church. Their chaplain in Cleveland, Father Thomas C. O'Reilly, later Bishop of Scranton, in 1904 inaugurated the custom of the annual spiritual retreat at the Cathedral during the Lenten season. The little purple ribbon worn by the men during the time of the retreat was a source of much edification. The movement spread throughout the diocese and the country. The Bishop generally presided at the closing exercises, to show his approval and to express his satisfaction at seeing so many men approaching the sacraments together.

Cleveland at this time was one of the important centers for closed laymen's retreats. The Jesuit Fathers for this purpose at first used a small villa near Vermilion. When the novitiate of the province was moved to Missouri in 1908, their house at Parma was put at the disposition of week-end retreatants who came not only from this area but also from neighboring States.[17]

For some time after the coming of Bishop Horstmann the question of Catholic membership in other secret fraternal societies continued to be discussed. A Baltimore newspaper mistakenly carried the rumor that the Free Masons alone among them was forbidden to Catholics. To counteract the effect of such misunderstanding the Bishop had the pastoral of Archbishop Jannsens of New Orleans reprinted in the *Universe*.[18] In this the Odd Fellows and the Sons of Temperance were specifically mentioned and a warning was given against membership in the Knights of Pythias. In 1893 the Bishop had already taken it upon himself to forbid Catholics to join the last-mentioned society, anticipating the decision of the Propaganda, which when it came was published in the *Universe*. This forbade Catholic membership in any of the three.[19]

Apparently there were some few defections from the Church at this time.[20] In regard to other secret or quasi-secret organizations, especially those which had a religious exercise in connection with their ritual, the Bishop was cautious and warned his people to be cautious. He caused to be republished in the *Universe*[21] an article from the *American Ecclesiastical Review* which discouraged Catholics from joining such societies, even though they had not been specifically men-

[16] Horstmann to Specht, Apr. 3, 1900; Horstmann to Elder, July 13, 1901; both in C.D.A.

[17] *Records of American Catholic Historical Society*, XLI, 72, *C.U.*, Feb. 28, Mar. 6, 20, Aug. 14, Sept. 25, 1908.

[18] *C.U.*, June 16, 1892.

[19] Horstmann to Nogaret, Feb. 2, 1893; to Sidley, Dec. 11, 1893; to Satolli, Dec. 30, 1894; all in C.D.A. *C.U.*, Dec. 28, 1894; Jan. 11, 1895; Apr. 3, 1896.

[20] H. H. Schaefer to Horstmann, Mar. 9, 1895; H. Cook to Horstmann, June 26, 1892; both in C.D.A.

[21] *C.U.*, June 30, 1899.

tioned by the Church authorities. In sermons[22] on various occasions the Bishop repeated the warning that such associations led to indifference in religion and even in morality. He would be inclined to allow Catholics to belong to the society of farmers called the Grange if the religious ceremonies were eliminated. He gave a contribution to the Grand Army of the Republic which held an encampment here in 1901.[23] The Maccabees and the Woodmen and some other fraternal insurance societies were suspected on account of their ritual and their naturalistic tendencies.[24]

[22] For instance, at the dedication of the school in Elyria, May 17, 1900.
[23] *C.U.*, June 18, 1909.
[24] Horstmann to Burkel, Jan. 7, 1899; to Berthelet, Feb. 21, 1899; to Richter, Aug. 13, 1907; to J. B. Puetz, Sept. 22, 1900; to Vollmeyer, Aug., 1905; all in C.D.A.

39

SPREADING THE FAITH

A MEMORABLE ACHIEVEMENT OF BISHOP HORST-
mann's administration was the Cleveland Apostolate to
Non-Catholics. At the turn of the century many were
convinced that if the claims of the Catholic Church were
presented to the traditionally fair-minded Americans in
halls and public places they would receive a respectful hearing. On his
sickbed in Washington, in 1889, Bishop Gilmour had expressed the
hope of establishing a band of missionaries for that purpose. Archbishop Keane afterwards called the Apostolate to Non-Catholics, the
Gilmour idea. The Paulists of New York were particularly interested.
Father Walter Elliot, one of them and a Civil War veteran, presented
the plan before the bishops assembled at the Columbian Congress in
Chicago in 1893. Bishop Foley of Detroit authorized the experiment
in his diocese and for nine months Father Elliott preached and lectured
and answered the questions of the non-Catholics who came to listen
to him.

Meanwhile, Bishop Horstmann, who was much interested, encouraged a few young priests to prepare themselves for the work. Father
William Kress, pastor of Bowling Green, who knew the Paulists in
Washington as a student of the university, and Father Ignatius Wonderly, pastor at another small town, North Baltimore, began to give
missions and talks to the non-Catholics in their vicinity. In the villages
of Van Buren and Jerry City anti-Catholic lecturers had preceded them
and the questions asked by the people reflected this influence. The
people came to listen, nevertheless. A prayer meeting arranged to
counteract their meeting was abandoned, and the minister and the congregation went together to the G.A.R. Hall to hear the priests. In
fact, some of the non-Catholics cooperated in furnishing the choir and
the music.

After a conference with Father Elliott in 1894 the Bishop, despite
his great need of priests, decided to devote a few of them to this endeavor. He accepted Father Elliott's offer to train the missioners and
he approved the rules drawn up for their guidance.[1] They were to

[1] W. S. Kress to Horstmann, Mar. 1, 1894; Elliott to Horstmann and Horstmann
to Elliott, May, 1894; memorandum of agreement; Horstmann to Card. Vaughan,
Feb. 24, 1896, asking for a copy of the Rule of the Oblates of St. Charles; all in
C.D.A.

St. Theresa Church, Sheffield.

St. Patrick Church, Rocky River Drive.

Left: St. Columbkille Church.

Right: St. Procop Church.

Holy Rosary Church.

St. Thomas Aquinas Church.

St. Helena Church, first of
the Romanian Byzantine
rite in the United States.

Holy Trinity Church, Avon.

Our Lady of the Angels Church.

St. George Church, Warwick.

St. Mary Church, Collinwood.

support themselves by giving missions in Catholic parishes. Father Kress was appointed superior in November of that year. Fathers Edward P. Graham and Ignatius Wonderly were released from their parish duties to enable them to devote all their time to the venture. The pastors in the towns near the places of the missions gave full cooperation. Father Muehlenbeck of Archbold among others was especially helpful in the German neighborhoods. Fathers John Brennan and John Michaelis replaced the first missioners in 1899. Father Charles A. Martin served from 1901 to 1911. Others on the band at different times were Fathers John I. Moran, James Heffernan, and Stephen Wilson. Among those from outside the diocese, who received part of their training in Cleveland for the Apostolate in their own dioceses, were the future prelates, Bishops Swint of Wheeling and Noll of Fort Wayne.

After the formal organization of the Apostolate in 1894 Father Elliott, assisted by Fathers Kress and Muehlenbeck, began by giving a regular mission to the Catholic congregation in Bellevue. Then followed missions to non-Catholics in Green Springs and Clyde. There were many Seventh Day Adventists in the neighborhood who were not friendly to things Catholic. However, the Mayor of Green Springs, a fellow veteran of the Civil War, gave Father Elliott a warm welcome.[2] In the towns around Toledo anti-Catholic lecturers were got to follow in the traces of the missioners. In Toledo itself the Catholic Columbian Club sponsored a series of lectures which were given in Memorial Hall by Fathers Elliott and Kress as an antidote to the influence of the American Protective Association.

Father Elliott finished his work in this diocese in a great public mission held in Music Hall, Cleveland, from October 27 to November 1, 1895. The local newspapers gave much space to the subjects treated and to the questions answered by the veteran missionary.[3] The auditorium was generally filled and many who were not Catholic attended. Bishop Horstmann at the last meeting expressed his gratification at the results. He personally enjoyed the work and he often took part in the discussions and the answering of the questions which were put to him.

The method followed by the missioners in the country districts was simple enough. Their coming was advertised by the nearest Catholic pastor in the newspapers and in handbills. The city hall, the public school building, or the non-Catholic church building was used for the meetings. There was no disparagement of anyone's belief in the talks which were confined to positive exposition of Catholic doctrine and practice. After a hymn or song the missioners answered the questions which they found in the box set up to receive them. At the beginning of a mission it was found that these questions were the old stereotyped objections, often disrespectful, but they were answered

[2] *C.U.*, Oct. 19, Nov. 30, 1894, quoting Fr. Elliott's article in the *Catholic World*.
[3] Cleveland *Plain Dealer*, Oct. 28, Nov. 2, 1895. *C.U.*, Nov. 1, Dec. 13, 1895.

patiently. The audiences were, on the contrary, very respectful and sometimes invited the missioners to return. Pamphlets on Catholic subjects were freely distributed.

It would be hard to estimate how many converts were made for the Church but it is certain that these missions did much to dissipate prejudice and relieve the deep ignorance of things Catholic. In 1903 the Bishop estimated that in the previous ten years approximately 78,000 listeners had been reached in the 156 missions which had been given. In addition, the Apostolate had given 67 missions to Catholics and 11 to audiences composed of both Catholics and others.

When Father Kress was appointed pastor of St. Edward's in Cleveland in 1899, the large stone residence became the headquarters of the missionary band. Within a period of about eight years after that 265 converts had been instructed. Fathers Kress and Martin also made a name for themselves in widely publicized lectures and writings on the subject of Socialism. Father Martin, who made a grand missionary tour of the West and the South and who was one of the first to conduct a mission for the Colored, composed a 500-page book of apologetics entitled *The Catholic Religion,* which is still popular. Other booklets treated of Christian marriage and the Rosary. Father Kress remained head of the band until 1920, when he joined the Maryknoll Fathers.

The success of the Cleveland Plan as it was called, and which received the apostolic blessing of Pope Leo XIII in 1895, led to the formation of similar bands in other dioceses.[4] The Apostolic Mission House was established in Washington for the formation of young priests interested in the work. At its dedication in 1904 due credit was given to Bishop Horstmann for his pioneer activity in this field of endeavor. In the year after that twelve bands had been established and more soon followed. In 1906 the Cleveland Apostolate was renamed the Ohio Apostolate. Father Joseph H. Steinbrunner of Cincinnati lived at the Cleveland headquarters for five years. The exigencies of the First World War and the scarcity of priests brought an end to this noble experiment.[5]

The French translation of the *Life of Father Hecker* and especially the preface written by Abbé Klein, the editor, aroused a great controversy in France when it was published there. The missionary methods of Father Hecker, the convert founder of the Paulist Fathers, who proposed the conversion of America to the Catholic Faith, were presented to the French clergy for imitation. A group of French ecclesiastics made the charge that American missionaries in their efforts to make converts minimized and distorted Catholic doctrine and de-

[4] Horstmann to Propaganda (Ledochowski), June 5, 1895; Ledochowski to Horstmann, June 25, 1895; both in C.D.A. *C.U.,* Sept. 18, 1895 (Satolli's letter). *Universe* (Paris), Oct. 28, Nov. 23, 1895.

[5] The Scrap-Book of Fr. Kress with its newspaper clippings and handbills was found among his papers when he died in 1936.

preciated the virtues of obedience and humility, and religious vows, and ignored lawful authority and direction. These errors were gathered under the head of Americanism and were condemned by Pope Leo XIII, January, 1899, in a letter to Cardinal Gibbons.[6] The Holy Father was careful to point out that he did not find fault with the American system of political government, its laws and customs, nor any of the characteristic qualities which reflected honor on the American people. A small group of European liberal Catholics who had fostered these condemned ideas had taken certain incidentals of American Catholic life, certain tendencies and isolated events observable at the time, out of their context and "rationalized them into theological principles" which the Pope would necessarily have to condemn.[7]

Bishop Horstmann expressed surprise at the commotion raised in France over the *Life of Father Hecker*. The first American edition of the work had not caused any controversy, in fact, it was not very well known in the Middle West. The fundamental errors, however, to which his attention was called by Archbishop Ryan in the French version would, he believed, be condemned by the vast majority if not the totality of the American bishops and clergy, who gloried in the Faith of the Universal Church.[8] The *Catholic Universe* thanked the Holy Father for condemning the errors enumerated in the papal letter, which if allowed to go unchallenged would endanger the integrity of the Faith. The editor was of the opinion, however, that the formal heresy had little or no following in this country. He suspected a political basis for the discussion of the matter in France.[9]

Bishop Horstmann was one of the first American prelates officially to acknowledge the papal condemnation, although he too thought that very few Catholics in the country were affected by the errors. He assured the Holy Father that his own clergy were conservative and were not given to minimizing doctrine. He thought that something of the spirit of "Americanism" might be found in the opinions of so-called liberals who would favor a compromise with the State school system and who would allow Catholics to join secret societies on the pretext of diminishing prejudice. In Cleveland, on the contrary, Catholic schools were taken for granted and Catholic societies were numerous enough to satisfy the desire for organization. Everyone here thankfully accepted the papal pronouncement. The Holy Father through the Cardinal Prefect of the Propaganda acknowledged the Bishop's letter with satisfaction and in an audience shortly afterwards

[6] Joseph McSorley, *Outline History of the Church by Centuries*, St. Louis, 1944, p. 877; *Catholic Encyclopedia*, XIV, 537; J. Brugerette, *Le Prêtre Français et la Société Contemporaine*, Paris, 1938, III, 164 sq. Vincent F. Holden, "A Myth in L'Americanisme," Cath. Hist. Rev. July, 1945.

[7] Thomas V. McAvoy, "Americanism, Fact and Fiction," in *Catholic Historical Review*, July, 1945. Peter E. Hogan, "Americanism and the Catholic University of America," Cath. Hist. Rev., July, 1947.

[8] Horstmann to Abp. Ryan, Nov. 1, 1898, in C.D.A.

[9] *C.U.*, Mar. 3, 1899.

he made specific mention of the agreeable letters he had received from Cardinal Gibbons and Bishop Horstmann.[10]

The formal letter of acceptance on the part of the Province of Cincinnati was drawn up by Bishop Horstmann. In it the bishops thanked the Pope for his solicitous providence over the integrity of the Faith in the United States; they accepted the papal letter in the sense in which he wished them to accept it; they condemned what he condemned, such errors as would cause great harm to souls; they gloried in their country and its civil Constitution, but looked for the protection of their religion, faith, and morals and for spiritual progress to the Vicar of Christ; they asserted that the better Catholics they were the better Americans they were.[11]

The Bishop's first letter to Rome was quoted by some Catholic newspapers as authority for their contention that Americanism, or Heckerism, was unknown in this country. He felt called upon, therefore, to explain that in his first letter he referred only to the Diocese of Cleveland and that he had no intention to deny that the errors condemned by the Holy See were to be found in the *Life of Father Hecker*, nor that the condemnation was opportune. He wished now to have it known that he was opposed to the liberalism which threatened Catholicity in this country because of its attitude towards secret societies and public schools.[12] This second letter of the Bishop was quoted in the *Civiltà Cattolica* in Rome and in the French journal, *La Verité Française*,[13] to prove that Americanism did exist in America. Father Charles Maignen, the spearhead in France in the attack upon Heckerism, and Father George Peries, a former professor at the Catholic University in Washington, wrote to the Bishop to thank him for this second letter.[14] After the papal pronouncement the Bishop ordered the *Catholic Universe* to drop discussion of the subject.[15]

Especially in his earlier years here Bishop Horstmann took an active part in public civic celebrations. He was the principal figure in the local observance of the 400th anniversary of the discovery of America by Columbus which was kept at a great mass meeting in Music Hall, October 12, 1892. A special Mass was offered in every parish and many

[10] Horstmann to Pope Leo XIII, Mar. 7, 1899; Ledochowski to Horstmann, Mar. 29, 1899; Horstmann to Satolli, June 9, 1899; all in C.D.A. *C.U.*, May 5, 12, 1899.

[11] Original draft, May 16, 1899, in C.D.A. *C.U.*, Aug. 25, 1899.

[12] Horstmann to Satolli, June 9, 1899; to Fr. Brande, Aug. 18, 1899; both in C.D.A.

[13] Paris, June 19, 1899.

[14] Chas. Magnien, Paris, to Horstmann, June 22, 1899, in C.D.A. Bp. Horstmann was one of the Board of Trustees who desired to keep Peries on the teaching staff at the Catholic University when after the lapse of his three-year contract he retired to the Church of the Holy Trinity in Paris. Bp. John Ireland thought of him as the initiator of the anti-American campaign in France. His information supposedly influenced Card. Richard of Paris to oppose the congress of religions in France which was proposed in imitation of a similar gathering at the World's Fair in Chicago in 1893. Cf. Ireland's article in the London *New Era*, June 17, 1899. *The Catholic Citizen*, July 15, 1899. J. Brugerette, *Op. cit.*, III, 173. Horstmann's minutes of the meeting of the Board of Trustees; Horstmann to Schroeder, Dec. 12, 1901; to Thos. Lee, Apr. 5, 1902; all in C.D.A.

[15] Elder to Horstmann, Aug. 6, 1899, in C.D.A. *C.U.*, July 24, Aug. 25, 1899.

heeded the invitation to receive the sacraments in religious commemoration of the event. He was one of the principal speakers four years
later in the same hall at the celebration of the Cleveland Centennial,
when he reviewed the work of the Church in this area and spoke on
"The Influence of Religious Thought on the Social and Civil Life in
the Western Reserve." In a lecture on the city of Rome, which he
gave at Central High School, he imparted some homely advice to the
students.

The Bishop was a personal friend of William McKinley, the Presi-
dent of the United States, "a friend in all that the name implies."
Whenever he called on him at his home in Canton or at the White
House in Washington, he found him "kind, gentle, courteous, and
conservative in all his views."[16] The return of peace at the end of the
Spanish-American War was celebrated with solemn services at the
Cathedral. The Bishop then commended the patience and earnestness
of the President. When the latter lay dying of an assassin's bullet in
Buffalo the Bishop appeared in the pulpit of the Cathedral to ask
prayers for his recovery, and when the President died he presided in
the Cathedral at a memorial service.[17] The recitation of the Litany of
the Saints on four successive Sundays was prescribed in every parish
in addition to the Mass for Divine Guidance. And the Bishop was the
first speaker at a public sympathy meeting of the citizens in Central
Armory. Because of their friendship it was rumored that the Bishop
had ministered spiritually to the dying President, but he denied that
he had seen him at all during his last days.[18] He took official part in
the dedication of the McKinley Monument in Canton and gave the
benediction at the end of the ceremony, at which President Theodore
Roosevelt spoke.

His friendship with the President did not blind the Bishop to the
faults of the administration. The *Universe* was very frank in its criticism of the conduct of the American occupation troops in the Philippines after the war; it reported the mistreatment of priests and nuns
by the undisciplined soldiers, the abuse of the natives, and the dese-
cration of churches. The Bishop favored mass meetings of protest; one
such was held in St. Patrick's School. Here and at other gatherings
throughout the country resolutions were passed condemning the violation of Catholic conscience in the introducing of secular education.
Nevertheless, the Bishop in a circular sent to the clergy advised cooperation with the Government in an effort to obtain representative
Catholic teachers for the newly acquired territory; a few teachers
went from here at the time.[19]

[16] Horstmann to W. B. Kines, Oct. 5, 1901, in C.D.A.

[17] Horstmann to Mrs. Wm. McKinley and her answer, Sept. 25 and Oct. 7, 1901,
in C.D.A.

[18] W. B. Kines, editor of Baltimore *American*, to Horstmann, Oct. 5, 1901; Horstmann's answer, Oct. 15, 1901; both in C.D.A.

[19] Horstmann to Abp. Corrigan, Aug. 21, 1899, in C.D.A. *C.U.*, June 23, 1899;
Mar. 30, July 27, 1900; May 23, June 13, 26, Aug. 8, 1902; Jan. 6, 1903. Abp. Ireland's
Circular, May 5, 1903.

President Roosevelt later denied any knowledge of the arrangement whereby some 100 Philippine students were brought to this country and were placed exclusively in non-Catholic schools. Two of them at Oberlin College attracted attention to the matter. Later some students were sent to Catholic colleges through the efforts of Father Vattman, an army chaplain, who made a confidential report on the conditions he found in the Philippines. Father Vattman had been pastor at Canal Fulton and was often the host to President McKinley when he visited that town. At his suggestion, too, a few native students were brought to the United States to finish their studies in American seminaries.[20]

In a public address before the Builders' Exchange in Cleveland the Bishop took occasion to call attention to the papal encyclical on the "Condition of Labor." He criticized the system which "squeezed immense profits from the blood of the laboring man and only allowed him nine dollars a week to support his family; it was a crime which called to Heaven for vengeance." He asserted the right of the men to organize and said that the suppression of the unions would be a great misfortune. Both sides in the labor disputes of the day needed better mutual understanding; capital needed to have a better recognition of the dignity of the human person.[21] His sympathies were naturally with the workingmen who constituted the great bulk of his flock; but he was opposed to the use of violence and stood always for law and order.

He encouraged his clergy[22] to help the unions with their counsel and advice. Several priests of the diocese as a result acted as arbitrators in local labor troubles.[23] In the Cleveland street car strike of 1899 the Bishop made an earnest appeal to the strikers and to Catholics in general to avoid the mob violence which was damaging their cause. Public authority and city officials were to be upheld at all costs; he advocated compulsory arbitration of the differences. The Bishop's proclamation did much for the restoration of peace.[24]

In another instance Father Vaclav A. Chaloupka, the young pastor of Marblehead, had drawn attention to the semi-feudal conditions in which the Catholic quarrymen in his district lived. When Bishop Horstmann visited the area for the dedication of the Oriental Rite Church of the Assumption, there were 800 men on strike because of

[20] Fr. J. J. Wynne, S.J., to Houck, Oct. 14, 1904; Houck's answer; E. J. Vattman to Houck, Oct. 19, 1904; Vattman's description of the Philippines, Feb., 1903; all in C.D.A. *C.U.*, Oct. 6, 1905.

[21] *C.U.*, May 10, 1907. Peter Witt to Horstmann, May 10, 1907; H. S. Richards to Horstmann, May 10, 1907; both in C.D.A.

[22] Horstmann to Central Labor Union, Cleveland *Citizen*, Nov. 2, 1893.

[23] Fr. J. A. Kuhn in Massillon was chosen by the striking coal miners to represent them in negotiations with the owners. Fr. Joseph F. Schafield in Barberton helped to settle the strike in the match factory there. Cf. *C.U.*, May 26, Nov. 17, 1899. Isaac Barber to Horstmann, Dec. 5, 1895, in N.D.A. For Powderly's opinion of Horstmann's penchant for arbitration, cf. Browne, *Op. cit.*, 259.

[24] Horstmann to O'Leary, July, 1899, in C.D.A. *C.U.*, June 23, July 28, 1899. San Francisco *Monitor*, Aug. 18, 1899.

the reduction of their already low wages and also other grievances. He counseled them to avoid violence and the destruction of property and offered his services as an arbitrator. The tact, sagacity, and zeal of the Bishop brought about a temporary settlement, a compromise between the demands of the men and the claims of the company. Later when the promises made to him in favor of the men were not respected he withdrew from the case.[25] In another instance, not connected with a strike, however, it was in great measure due to the petition of the Bishop that the railroad shops were not moved out of Norwalk in 1900.[26]

The friendship between Bishop Horstmann and the wealthy Drexel family of Philadelphia extended over a long period. The daughters of one of these well-known bankers were particularly interested in the spiritual welfare of the Catholic Indians. One of them (Mother Katherine Drexel) in 1889 founded the religious community of the Sisters of the Blessed Sacrament for work among the Indians and Negroes of the United States. Out of their inheritance they had given more than $1,500,000 for building schools on the Indian reservations in the West. The United States Government had contracted beforehand to support these schools and others built by non-Catholic organizations in an effort to pacify and civilize the Indians. In 1895, influenced perhaps by the A.P.A. agitation as well as by other considerations, the Government began to curtail its subsidy and in 1901 it was announced that no more appropriations would be made for these "contract schools." In the so-called Browning Ruling the Indians were deprived of their right to choose the Catholic schools for their children even though they preferred them; then the rations which were due to all Indians were cut off from the Catholic school pupils. The very existence of these schools was threatened.

In this crisis Mother Katherine and the Catholic Indian Bureau, which had charge of Catholic interests in the matter, appealed to Bishop Horstmann to help them. In letters and personal interviews he pleaded the cause of the Catholic Indians. The *Universe* and other journals attacked the Indian policy of the Government as discriminatory. The Bishop put the case before his own people and the Society for the Preservation of the Faith among the Indians was established in every parish with happy results. The Browning Ruling was revoked and a few years later (1904) the Government rations were restored. The Bard Amendment, which would have denied the Indians any control over the tribal funds which they might wish to devote in part to the support of the Catholic schools, was defeated by the bold stand taken by President Roosevelt. As the result of this a few of the Catholic contract schools were benefited. Bishop Horstmann visited

[25] Horstmann, Chaloupka, Schoendorf, Houck, Caleb, and Gowan correspondence, 1904–1905, in C.D.A. *C.U.*, Feb. 12, 1904.

[26] Horstmann to Myron Herrick, Jan. 28, 1901; to W. H. Newman, Aug. 9, 1900, both in C.D.A.

the White House to thank the President for his sympathetic attitude. He had an appointment to see him again on the same subject, but before that time the Bishop had passed to his eternal reward.[27]

[27] A. T. Drexel to Horstmann, July 26, 1892; Horstmann to A. T. Drexel, July 29, 1902; Mother Katherine Drexel to Horstmann, July 28, 31, 1892; Horstmann to Mother Katherine Drexel, Feb. 25, July 9, 1902; to Pres. McKinley, July 1, 1899; to Sen. Hanna, Mar. 9, May 28, 1900; to Pres. T. Roosevelt, Aug. 7, 1906; other correspondence with the Bureau of Catholic Missions in Washington, D.C.; all in C.D.A. C.U., 1900 to 1908, *passim*.

40

DIOCESAN AFFAIRS UNDER
BISHOP HORSTMANN

THE PRECARIOUS FINANCIAL CONDITION OF the *Catholic Universe* was one of the earlier problems of Bishop Horstmann. He did not feel responsible for its debts since the question of ownership had not been definitely settled. The deficit at the time of his coming was about $2,500. Nevertheless, he confirmed the appointment of Father William McMahon, the pastor of St. Bridget's, who had been named its manager by the executors of the estate of Bishop Gilmour. Manly Tello, whose abilities were more literary than financial, wrote his last editorial on June 9, 1892. This intimate friend of Bishop Gilmour, declared by McMasters of the *Freeman's Journal* to have been the best-equipped Catholic editor of his time, died in Cleveland in 1905.

The Cleveland Universe Publishing Company, a stock company, was formed to assume charge of the new *Universe*, which announced that its policy would be to avoid political discussion, when religious interests were not concerned, and untoward dispute about nationalities. The old *Universe* in 1891 and 1892 had been very outspoken in its denunciation of what was called Cahenslyism in America.[1] The new journal was enlarged from forty-eight to fifty-six pages, and Thomas A. Connolly of Washington became the editor, July 9, 1892. The Bishop gave his approval and made it the medium of his official communications. Circulars were addressed to the pastors asking their cooperation and expressing his own concern in its success. At a convention of the Catholic Knights he spoke of the great mission of the Catholic press in safeguarding religious interests and recommended that every family subscribe to a Catholic newspaper.[2]

When Mr. Connolly left to become editor of the San Francisco *Monitor* in 1899, Father McMahon[3] took his place, assisted by Fathers Gilbert P. Jennings and John T. O'Connell. The well-known Anne O'Hare McCormick of the New York *Times* began her literary career

[1] Horstmann to Tello, Mar. 17, 1892; Elder to Horstmann, Apr. 2, 1892; both in C.D.A. *C.U.*, June 16, July 9, 1892.
[2] Bishop's Circular, Mar. 7, 1894.
[3] Author of a book describing his journey around the world.

with the *Universe* during this period. An edition of the New Testament was published by the *Universe* with the approval of the Bishop in 1905.[4]

The diocesan statutes which were formulated by his predecessor were confirmed by Bishop Horstmann and published in a second edition in 1892.[5] The third edition which appeared in 1908 contained additional statutes concerning marriage dispensations and other diocesan business.[6] Additional regulations were sent to the pastors in official circulars. The practice of ringing the De Profundis bell in the evening after the Angelus was prescribed in December, 1892.[7] In the same month certain powers of dispensation were withdrawn from the pastors. Sunday funerals, except in serious circumstances, were prohibited after January 1, 1898.[8] On February 21, 1905, the Bishop altered the previous regulations concerning the financial support of the clergy, and the relation between pastor and assistant pastors in that regard. The pastor became solely responsible for the domestic economy of the parish house and was allotted a share of the stipend of the assistant for that purpose.[9]

Plans were made for a diocesan synod in 1897. The committee in charge of it had gathered the materials together in one volume about seven years later but many things interfered and the synod was not held.[10] One of its problems would have been to find a more efficient method of supporting diocesan institutions. The apportionment of the diocesan assessment according to the number of families had proved inadequate and otherwise unsatisfactory. Another concerned the status of irremovable rectorates. The Bishop had been advised that he could give such rating to other parishes without interfering with those already established.[11]

After due investigation, the Bishop in 1906 sanctioned the formation of a diocesan fire insurance company on the model of those existing in several western dioceses. The rates of the "old line" companies were considered to be exorbitant. In the year of his death he urged the pastors to support the new company on the plea that any profits which might accrue would be used for diocesan charities. The company, however, had but a brief existence.[12]

Strict observance of the papal regulations on church music was imposed by the Bishop. He protested against such abuses as the mutila-

[4] *C.U.*, Aug. 25, 1905.

[5] *C.U.*, Jan. 13, 1893.

[6] *Stat. Dioces. Cleve.*, 3rd ed., 1908. *Rules and Directions for the Administration of Temporal and Spiritual Affairs*, reprint, 1908.

[7] Circular, Dec. 20, 1892.

[8] Circular, Dec. 23, 1897.

[9] Circular, Feb. 21, 1905.

[10] Horstmann to Elder, Aug. 8, 1898; Horstmann to Moeller, Apr. 11, 1908; Fr. Scanlon to Horstmann, May 12, 1892; J. N. Connolly to Houck, Jan., 1902; all in C.D.A. *C.U.*, Nov. 18, 1898.

[11] Horstmann to Falconio, Apr. 21, 1905, in C.D.A.

[12] Correspondence in the matter, Jan. 5, 1900, to Jan., 1908, in C.D.A. Circulars, Jan. 19, Feb. 17, 1906. *C.U.*, July 9, 1892; Apr. 29, May 5, 12, 1906.

tion of the words for the sake of the notes, and the protraction of the singing which delayed the progress of the Mass. He forbade any music or singing during the Consecration of the Mass. He had in mind to issue a list of Masses which he would officially approve. Father Ignatius Wilkins, O.F.M., dedicated a Mass to the Bishop because of his zeal for proper church music. It was in accord with the new regulations that the first exclusively male choir was started in the Cathedral in 1905.[13]

In the last year of Bishop Horstmann's administration the general law of the Church respecting the marriage of Catholics was introduced into the United States, Canada, Holland, and Great Britain. Previously, as in all mission countries under the immediate jurisdiction of the Congregation of the Propaganda, Catholic marriages were not subject to the law of clandestinity which required the presence of the priest as a necessary witness for their validity. As a result of the new legislation, after April 19, 1908, the presence of an authorized priest and two witnesses was essential for the validity of a marriage when Catholics were concerned.

This new regulation, which with a few modifications dated back to the Council of Trent in the sixteenth century, was officially promulgated in the Province of Cincinnati, February 13, 1908, in a letter signed by all the bishops of the province. It was read in all the churches three times before it went into effect. According to this decree of the bishops, all assistant pastors, administrators, and substitutes for the pastor (and, of course, the pastors) were vested with the "full and absolute power and authority to assist validly at marriages within the limits of their parish." The authority of the pastors was always to be respected. Catholics were, moreover, forbidden to assist as official witnesses at non-Catholic weddings without special permission, and none but Catholics were allowed to be formal witnesses at a Catholic wedding.[14]

For the promotion of piety among the people Bishop Horstmann encouraged the societies and sodalities which had that as their purpose. Every parish had its Sodality of the Blessed Virgin for the young women and the Sodality of St. Aloysius for the young men and a number of other organizations according to the taste and devotion of the people. In a pastoral in 1899 he urged the establishment of at least two confraternities of wider scope in each parish. He appointed Father Nicolas Pfeil diocesan director of the Association of the Holy Childhood to help that agency established for the rescue of abandoned children in pagan lands. The Christian Mothers Sodality of which he had been the spiritual director in Philadelphia received his special com-

---

[13] Minutes of Bishops' Meeting, Cincinnati, Sept., 1894; Fr. Wilkins, O.F.M., to Horstmann, May 6, 1897; Horstmann to TePas, May 28, 1897; all in C.D.A. *C.U.*, Feb. 10, 1905.

[14] *Ne Temere* decree of Congregation of the Propaganda, Aug. 2, 1907. Pastoral Letter on Betrothal and Marriage, Feb. 13, 1908, 12 pp. pamphlet and 3 pp. abstract of the new law. *C.U.*, Mar. 27, July 10, 1908.

mendation here, as did the Pious Association of the Holy Family which sponsored the common recitation of the Rosary in the home.

Following the direction of the Holy Father, a triduum of prayers was observed in every parish preceding the solemn and public consecration of mankind to the Sacred Heart in 1899, and in the succeeding years. In accord with the same directive, the Blessed Sacrament was exposed for public veneration on the first Friday of each month. The Bishop recommended all-day exposition with a sermon in the evening. His pastorals on this subject breathed the spirit of the love of Christ in the Holy Eucharist and they were much appreciated.

The *Universe* published the papal decree on Frequent Communion, March 30, 1906. Already in 1895 the bishops of the province in a pastoral had exhorted the people to greater devotion to the Real Presence and to a more frequent reception of the Blessed Sacrament. In the religious communities the Sisters received Holy Communion twice or three times and the professed Sisters as often as four times a week. After the papal decree the Bishop advised these communities to follow the directions given in the document. The practice of daily reception of the Sacrament was soon adopted outside the religious communities in the high schools and at St. Ignatius College. Sodalities now approached the Holy Table monthly instead of quarterly, and the general change was observable in the parishes. The great increase in the number of those who received the Blessed Sacrament weekly and oftener was soon noticeable especially among the children, and with the salutary effects intended by the Holy Father.[15]

Bishop Horstmann took every opportunity to show and to express his love and loyalty to the Holy See, and on one occasion the Pope sent an autographed letter to thank him for his generosity. The papal jubilee of 1893 celebrating the fiftieth anniversary of Leo XIII's consecration as an archbishop was kept in the diocese with a solemn triduum of prayers and the general reception of the sacraments. In 1895 Bishop Horstmann composed the common letter of the bishops of this province sent to the Pope to thank him for the encyclical, "Longinqua Oceani Spatia," and to express their hope for the restoration of the temporal power which had been suppressed by the Italian Government twenty-five years previously. Special religious services were held in all the parishes, which together with the various societies passed resolutions of sympathy with the Holy Father and condemned the demonstrations against him worked up at that time in Rome. These messages were bound together and sent to Rome.[16]

It was in obedience to the wishes of the Holy Father that the Bishop pontificated at midnight, December 31, 1899, in the Cathedral to solemnize the opening of the Holy Year which commemorated the end

[15] Papal decree, Dec. 20, 1905. Sisters of Notre Dame to Horstmann, Oct. 31, 1906, in C.D.A.

[16] Horstmann to Satolli, No. 16, 1895; Minutes of Bishops' Meeting, July 2, 1895; both in C.D.A. *C.U.*, Sept. 6, 1895.

of the nineteenth century. Like services in honor of Christ the Redeemer were held in every parish. At the end of the year he again pontificated at the Mass during which he consecrated the diocese to the King of Ages. When the Jubilee indulgences were made available to those who did not visit Rome, the Bishop's pastoral set forth the conditions for gaining them in this diocese. On the appointed Sundays the members of each city parish—men, women, and children—with their badges and banners, and with their priests in cassock and surplice at their head, marched through the streets in liturgical procession to certain designated churches. All converged at the Cathedral where section after section in turn crowded and vacated that structure late into the evening. On one Sunday there were 35,000 in the procession. Similar scenes of inspiring faith and devotion were to be found in Toledo and Youngstown and the other cities and towns of the diocese.

Religious services in all the parishes and pontifical Mass at the Cathedral celebrated the twenty-fifth anniversary of Pope Leo XIII's coronation. For the public civil observance of the same jubilee a great crowd gathered at Grays Armory on March 3, 1903, to do honor to the venerable Pontiff then in his ninety-third year. Addresses were given by the Bishop and thirteen priests who spoke in thirteen languages: Bohemian, French, Italian, German, Polish, Slovak, Hungarian, Slovenian, Lithuanian, Croatian, Syrian, Arabic, and English. At Toledo the rain did not dampen the enthusiasm of another such meeting. In the other towns and cities the unusual occasion was appropriately observed.

The tolling of the church bells announced the death of the beloved Head of the Church in the following July. Touching and sympathetic editorials and cartoons appeared in the local newspapers, indicative of the universal respect in which he was held even by those who were not of his flock. All the churches were draped in mourning and the Bishop's pastoral called for Masses and prayers. At the memorial service in the Cathedral Bishop Horstmann spoke feelingly and intimately of Leo XIII and his great accomplishments for the Church. The jubilee of 1904 proclaimed by the new Pope, Pius X, was appropriately kept here; and it was the Bishop's program which was followed four years later in another papal jubilee.[17]

In 1897 the observance of the Golden Jubilee of the establishment of this diocese was devoted principally, as might be expected, to the recollection of the life and labors of its first bishop and of the early missionaries, many of whom also became prelates. In a pastoral the Bishop happily described the splendid progress of the Church in this area and its thirty-fold growth in the previous fifty years. It was fitting that the first part of the celebration took place in St. Francis de Sales Church in Toledo, the first parish of Bishop Rappe. Bishop Horstmann pontificated and Father James F. Laughlin, a native of that parish but

[17] Horstmann to Ledochowski, Mar. 26, 1900, Mar. 7, 1902, in C.D.A. *C.U.*, Dec. 22, 1899; Jan. 5, Dec. 21, 1900; Apr. 26, June 7, July 12, 1901; Feb. 28, 1902; Feb., Mar., July, 1903.

then chancellor of the Archdiocese of Philadelphia, paid magnificent tribute to the pioneer prelate and gave due credit to him for inaugurating the system of parochial schools in the diocese.

At the official festival in Cleveland Bishop Horstmann again presided and Monsignor Thorpe drew a masterful delineation of the character and work of Bishop Rappe. At the public dinner in Cathedral Hall Archbishop Ryan of Philadelphia was the principal orator; he spoke of the difficulties inherent in the task of organizing a new diocese. A letter written by Bishop De Goesbriand of Burlington, whose eighty-one years were the reason for his absence, was read. In it this early associate of Bishop Rappe recounted some of the intimate history of his old friend. In the evening a grand parade of the Catholic societies was reviewed by the Bishop and his distinguished guests from a stand in front of the Cathedral House.[18]

In 1902, the year of the Golden Jubilee of the consecration of the Cathedral, Bishop Horstmann had definite plans for building a new one on Euclid Avenue at East 79th Street, the site of the present great Church of St. Agnes. He had, in fact, purchased property contiguous to the parish grounds for the purpose although he knew that the realization of his hopes "would not come for a long time." Meanwhile the Golden Jubilee was kept as Catholic Week from November 7 to November 9. The venerable structure was entirely renovated and new windows from Munich were installed. The three-day festivities included the pontifical Masses and the "home-coming" of the former pupils of the school and culminated in a vast parade, 15,000 strong, of the Catholic societies, which required sixty-five minutes to pass the reviewing stand. Several visiting prelates graced the liturgical procession to the Cathedral: Archbishop Ryan of Philadelphia, and Bishops Donahue of Wheeling, O'Donaghue of Indianapolis, Foley of Detroit, Richter of Grand Rapids, and McCloskey of Louisville. The venerable Bishop McQuaid of Rochester, who had known all the bishops of Cleveland, spoke at the unveiling of the bronze statue of Bishop Rappe.[19]

Very conscious of the needs of his great diocese, Bishop Horstmann was at times hard pressed to find priests for the foreign-language parishes in his jurisdiction. A few national groups in the country were asking for bishops of their nationality.[20] On his visit to Rome in 1904, with the approval of Cardinal Gibbons and other archbishops, he asked the Holy See to appoint as his auxiliary bishop for the Slav peoples of the diocese the Bohemian-born Father Joseph M. Koudelka, who had helped him to obtain priests from Europe and who was conversant with several languages. Complications arose to delay a decision. Father

---

[18] Horstmann to De Goesbriand, Sept. 6, 11, 18, 1897; De Goesbriand's answer, Sept. 8, 1897; both in C.D.A. *C.U.*, Oct. 1, 15, 1897. Houck, *Op. cit.*, I, 177, 178.

[19] Horstmann to Jennings, Feb. 1, 1902; Horstmann to Madigan, Apr. 16, 1906; Houck to *Catholic Columbian*, Aug. 9, 1894; all in C.D.A. *C.U.*, Nov. 14, 28, 1902.

[20] Minutes of Annual Meeting of Archbishops, Washington, 1901; Card. Gibbons to Horstmann, Apr. 10, 1902; both in C.D.A.

Seraphim Bauer of Freemont, unaware of the Bishop's particular request, suggested that only a German could be auxiliary bishop in Cleveland.[21] In 1906 Bishop Horstmann renewed his petition for Father Koudelka; he wanted him as an auxiliary and not as a coadjutor because he had "no desire to be responsible for his successor." At last his wish was granted and Bishop Doebbing, O.F.M., a former resident of Cleveland and for a short time a professor in the seminary but then Bishop of Nepi-Sutri in Italy, privately notified him of it.[22]

Joseph Marie Koudelka was born, December 8, 1852, in the village of Chilstova in Bohemia, the son of Markus and Anna Jazousshek Koudelka. He studied at the Imperial College at Klattan until at the age of sixteen he migrated with his family to Wisconsin. There he attended the preparatory seminary at Mount Calvary and then St. Francis Seminary, Milwaukee. Bishop Henni gave him minor orders. In 1874 at the request of Bishop Gilmour he came to St. Mary's Seminary, Cleveland. In the following year he was ordained subdeacon and deacon by Bishop Dwenger of Fort Wayne. As a deacon he already acted as the administrator of St. Procop's parish and after his ordination to the priesthood at the hands of Bishop Mullen of Erie, October 8, 1875, he took full charge of it. After seven years, during which he published three readers for the Bohemian schools, a short history of the Church in German, and several prayer books, with Bishop Gilmour's reluctant permission he became the editor of the St. Louis Bohemian journal, *Hlas*.

He was recalled to Cleveland, however, and after a short period again at St. Procop's he was made first pastor of the German parish of St. Michael. He was very useful to the Bishop also in starting new Slav parishes and in composing differences which sometimes occurred. His artistic ability was manifested in the lavish interior of the great Gothic Church of St. Michael which he built and in the model school which matched it. He was already a member of the Bishop's council and after his appointment as auxiliary bishop he was made vicar general for the Slavs, one of the first of four selected for that function in various dioceses. He was named Titular Bishop of Germanicopolis, November 29, 1907, although the official documents did not reach Cleveland until January 2, 1908.

In the first ceremony of its kind in this city, on February 25, 1908, he was consecrated[23] in St. Michael's Church by Bishop Horstmann who was assisted by Bishop Hartley of Columbus and Bishop Fox of Green Bay. The Archbishop of Cincinnati and nine other prelates

[21] Bauer to Horstmann, Aug. 6, 1904, in C.D.A.

[22] Horstmann to Houck, July 23, 1904; Koudelka to Houck, July 26, 1904; Koudelka to Horstmann, Aug. 28, 1904; Bauer to Houck, Mar. 9, 1906; Horstmann to Satolli, Apr. 18, 1906; to Doebbing, Apr. 19, 1906; to Gibbons, Dec. 12, 1906; to Moeller, Dec. 20, 1906; to Falconio, Jan. 3, 1908; Treiber to N. Pfeil, Jan. 5, 1908; Doebbing (Rome) to Horstmann, Dec. 4, 1907; all in C.D.A. *C.U.*, Jan. 10, 1908.

[23] *C.U.*, Feb. 21, 28, 1908. Joseph B. Code, *Dictionary of the American Hierarchy*, New York, 1939.

were present and some 180 priests. Bishop Richter of Grand Rapids preached in German, and Bishop Horstmann in English. The Bishop of Cleveland survived but a few months more; his Auxiliary continued the Confirmation tour of this diocese and also visited many of the larger cities of the country at the invitation of the bishops in the interest of the Slavs. Bishop Farrelly, when he came, felt that he did not need an auxiliary. So after twenty-eight years as pastor of St. Michael's, Bishop Koudelka on September 4, 1911, was transferred by the Holy See to Milwaukee as auxiliary bishop there. On August 6, 1913, he was named Bishop of Superior, Wisconsin. There he continued his apostolic labors and was especially active giving missions to the Slavs in many dioceses. He died at Superior, June 24, 1921, and was buried in the family plot at St. Mary's Cemetery, Cleveland.[24]

[24] Boff to Koudelka, May 29, 1908; Farrelly to Koudelka, June, 1909; both in C.D.A. *C.U.*, Sept. 25, 1908; Oct. 8, 1909; Sept. 8, Dec. 1, 1911; Aug. 8, 1913.

41

TOLEDO UNDER BISHOP HORSTMANN'S JURISDICTION

THE DEVELOPMENT OF THE PHYSICAL FACILI-
ties of the diocese, new parishes, new churches and schools,
followed its normal course during the eighteen years' administration of Bishop Horstmann. Again, for the sake of
clarity, this section is divided according to the present
status of the territory which is now distributed in three dioceses.

In the city of Toledo many fine new churches and schools made
their appearance in the older parishes, and in several new ones entirely
new plants were erected. The old Church of the Good Shepherd was
destroyed by fire; Father Patrick O'Brien replaced it with a magnificent stone Romanesque building, with a large dome and two towers,
which Bishop Horstmann dedicated in 1901. In the parish of the Immaculate Conception Father Timothy P. McCarthy superintended the
erection of the twin-steepled brick Gothic church which was dedicated by the Bishop in 1896. In the parish of the Sacred Heart of Jesus
Father Anthony Eilert was responsible for the great stone church with
its 185-foot spire which was used for the first time on Christmas Day,
1906; a school had been put up in 1895.

In the Polish parish of St. Hedwig the Bishop in 1893 blessed the
new stone Gothic church which was erected under the direction of
Father Simon J. Wieczorek; later, in 1904, a large schoolhouse of stone
was completed. In the daughter parish of St. Anthony the new brick
Gothic church, begun by Father Kolasinski and finished by Father
Felix X. Motulewski, was dedicated by Bishop Horstmann in 1894; a
new brick school made its appearance in 1901. St. Joseph's Church,
serving a French parish, was entirely remodeled in 1899. The Jesuit
Fathers in St. Mary's parish in 1903 put up a large brick combination
school and chapel.

In St. Patrick's parish, the former administrator of the diocese,
Father Edward Hannin, in 1901 completed a magnificent stone Gothic
church which has a seating capacity of some 1,400; Archbishop Ireland preached the sermon at the dedication, the Bishop of Cleveland
presided. In St. Peter's parish Father Gustav Rieken in 1904 put up a
large brick school and auditorium.

Ten new parishes were started in Toledo and its vicinity. At Rossford, on the outskirts, Father Louis Redmer in 1905 fashioned a combination church and school out of a frame building for the new Polish parish of St. Mary Magdalen. Holy Rosary parish for the Slovaks in the eastern section of Toledo was formed out of this two years later. St. Adelbert's was a division of St. Hedwig's Polish parish; Father John Wachowski put up a stone combination school and chapel which Bishop Rhode, Auxiliary Bishop of Chicago, blessed in 1910. St. Ann's parish, a division of St. Patrick's, was organized by Father John H. Muehlenbeck under whose direction a stone combination church and school made its appearance in 1900; a new church was put up after the separation of the diocese. Father Charles Herr was the founder of St. Charles's parish; in 1904 he erected a combination school and chapel.

At the eastern boundary of the city (Momeneetown) St. Ignatius' parish was formed and a brick combination school and chapel made its appearance in 1902 under the direction of Father Leo Broens. St. Michael's parish was organized in the northern section of the city by Father William A. Harks who put up a brick combination church and school in 1901. The Hungarian parish of St. Stephen in the eastern part of the city was founded by Father Robert Paulovitz; the frame church and frame school built in 1899 were destroyed by fire and had to be replaced in 1908. A second division of St. Hedwig's Polish parish became that of St. Stanislas Kostka; Father Joseph Kuta, appointed the first pastor in 1908, soon afterwards put up a parish plant.

In the larger towns outside the city of Toledo fine new churches superseded the original more modest structures. At Defiance the brick Romanesque Church of St. John built through the industry of Father Joseph P. Gloden was dedicated by the Bishop in 1896. At Findlay a brick school was completed by Father Henry Doerner in 1895. At Fremont the great brick Gothic Church of St. Joseph erected by Father Seraphim Bauer was blessed by Bishop Horstmann in 1893; a large brick school was opened in 1908. At Fostoria in 1902 the church was entirely remodeled and seven years later a new school made its appearance. At Galion in 1905 St. Patrick's new school was opened. At Lima the new parish of St. John was organized by Father Frederick Rupert and under his direction in 1901 a three-story brick combination church and school was completed. At Norwalk the Bishop dedicated two new churches in 1893; St. Paul's in stone and in the Romanesque style, put up by Father John A. Michenfelder; and St. Mary's likewise in stone but in the Gothic style, erected by Father Charles Chevraux.

At Sandusky Sts. Peter and Paul's School and auditorium, a memorial to Father Robert A. Sidley and erected by Father William F. Murphy, was dedicated by the Bishop in 1907. In the same city the Church of the Holy Angels enlarged by Father Thomas P. Lamb was rededicated in 1902. At Tiffin the great stone Church of St. Mary in the Roman

*Far Left:*St.
Ignatius Church.

*Left:*St Vitus
Church.

*Right:*St. Bernard
Church, Akron.

*Far Right:*Our Lady
of Lourdes Church.

*Far Left:*St. Francis
of Assisi Church,
Superior Avenue.

*Left:*St. Wenceslas
Church.

St. Paul Church, East 40th Street.

Immaculate Conception Church, Avon.

St. Joseph Church, Lorain.

Silver Jubilee of Monsignor Houck as Diocesan Chancellor, at Villa Angela, July 24, 1902. Reading from left to right starting at bottom:
ROW 1, H. Pfeil, P. O'Brien, H. Kirch, ?, J. F. McInerney, W. J. Horak, A. Hutmacher, P. Schritz, H. E. Boesken, S. F. Cappe, P. J. O'Connell, F. L. Hultgen, P. G. Scheondorf, F. J. Smith, F. Rupert, C. Herr, J. F. Haupert, J. A. Schaffeld, F. R. Forrer, J. F. Keubler, R. M. Mylott, J. W. Bell, ROW 2, ?, T. F. Mahon, G. H. Treiber, E. J. Murphy, J. G. Vogt, ?, ?, G. Vahey, Bishop Koudelka, N. A. Moes, S. Bauer, F. M. Boff, Bishop Horstmann, G. F. Houck, T. P. Thorpe, E. Mears, W. McMahon, A. Gerardin, N. J. Franche, C. Reichlin, ?, ?, N. Schmitz, S. Weber, G. H. Rieken, ROW 3, J. T. Stewart, C. Boehm, J. O'Connor, ?, F. F. Doppke, S. J. Zahm, H. Orlowski, C. Ruszkowski, E. J.

St. Philomena Church.

*Right:*Bishop Doebbing, O.F.M., and
Bishop Horstmann.

Conway, V. Szyrocki, A. J. Suplicki, V. Arnould, J. Johnston, C. V. Chevraux, J. P. McCloskey,
F. Schreiber, F. H. Hroch,, F. A. Malloy, A. Weber, ROW 4, ?, J. Thein, ?, J. J. Quinn, C. Andlauer,
B. Rosinski, J. H. Muehlenbeck, A. J. TePas, A. B. Stuber, T. P. Lamb, G. A. Branigan, J. W.
Malecka, P. Cwiakala, E. W. J. Lindesmith, J. P. Gloden, P. Quinn, J. S. Widmann, W. F. Murphy,
T. M. Smyth, K. P. Banks, ROW 5, J. O'Leary, P. Farral, ?, F. Houck, P. Barry, G. P. Jennings, C.
Martin, J. P. Michaelis, A. M. Seeholzer, Bishop Schwertner, J. Hoerstmann, A. Crehan, C. J. Mose-
ey, T. F. Fahey, T. F. Conlon, J. F. Collins, M. D. Leahy, ?, H. J. Gerhardstein, J. Gerz, L. J.
Plumanns, N. Drohan, N. A. Hassel, S. Furdek, F. Metternich, ?, ?, P. J. McGuire, ?, ?, T. F.
Mahar.

St. Wendelin Church and School.   Poor Clare Convent, Rocky River Drive.

Ursuline Convent, East 55th Street.

St. Augustine Convent, Lake Avenue.   Franciscan Monastery and Seminary, Rocky River Drive.

style, put up by Father Thomas F. Conlan, was blessed by the Bishop in 1906; Archbishop Glennon, later Cardinal, preached on the occasion.

Evidence of growth was to be found in the less populous towns and villages as well: new buildings reflected the generosity and self-sacrifice of the faithful. At Alvada a new school was opened in 1903 through the exertions of the Sanguinists. At Antwerp a brick church was built through the efforts of Father George A. Forst. At Archbold the brick church dedicated by Bishop Koudelka in 1908 had been erected by Father James Janssen. At Frenchtown (Berwick) the school was re-opened in 1900. At Bethlehem (Shelby Settlement) a large fine stone Gothic church put up under the supervision of Father Ferdinand Schreiber was dedicated by Bishop Horstmann in 1895; four years later Father Joseph F. Hopp remodeled the old church for school purposes.

At Blakeslee in 1907 a new church made its appearance under the direction of Father John Kiebel. At Bowling Green in 1894 the church was enlarged. At Carey the roofed-over basement of the great shrine Church of Our Lady of Consolation built through the exertion of Father John G. Mizer was blessed by Bishop Koudelka in 1909. At Deshler a brick mission church put up by Father J. P. Haupert was blessed by Bishop Horstmann in 1899. At Edgerton the church was enlarged in 1893 by Father Francis Pfyl. At Fort Jennings a brick schoolhouse was completed in 1908 by Father Matthias Arnoldi. At Kalida the church enlarged and completed by Father Chrysostom Hummer, C.PP.S., was rededicated by Bishop Horstmann in 1896; a new schoolhouse made its appearance in 1906.

At Kirby in 1907 a school and auditorium were fashioned out of the old church by Father Joseph Gerz. At Landeck in 1904 the new church erected under the direction of Father Dominic Zinsmayer was dedicated. At Leipsic a frame church put up by Father John Bertemes was blessed by Bishop Horstmann in 1893; six years later a brick school-house made its appearance. At Liberty a brick school was opened in 1900 by Father John R. Forrer. At Marblehead a frame school was opened in 1893 through the efforts of Father Francis J. Hroch; the church of the Ruthenian Rite was put up in 1904.

At Miller City a new brick church made its appearance in 1902 due to the exertions of Father Charles Wagner. At New London a frame mission church was put up in 1898 by Father John J. Powers. At New Washington a brick schoolhouse was opened in 1895 by Father John G. Vogt. At Payne a brick church erected by Father Joseph M. Paulus was dedicated in 1904. At Port Clinton a new stone church made its appearance in 1902 through the efforts of Father Francis Hroch. At Reed the brick church dedicated by Bishop Koudelka in 1908 had been erected by the Sanguinist Fathers. In Salem Township (Crawfordville) the brick church put up by Father John Mizer was blessed by the Bishop in 1896; the old one was destroyed by fire. At Strycker the church was completely remodeled in 1894. At Upper Sandusky a brick schoolhouse was opened by Father Aloysius Hutmacher in 1897; four years later he remodeled the church. At Vermilion the church was enlarged in 1893 by Father Ignatius J. Wonderly. At Wauseon the brick church dedicated by Bishop Horstmann in 1896 had been erected by Father John Muehlenbeck. At Williard the brick church put up by Father John P. Michaelis was blessed by the Bishop in 1897.

During this period a few small towns saw their first Catholic church. At Cloverdale a frame church was put up by Father Michael Mueller in 1898. At Continental a Protestant chapel was acquired for Catholic services in 1906. At Cygnet a store-room was fitted up by Father William Kress as a chapel for the oil workers in 1892; seven years later a brick church was completed. At Gibsonburg a Protestant church was remodeled for Catholic worship by Father Michael Dechant in 1892; it was changed into a schoolhouse in 1905 when a stone Gothic church was put up by Father John B. Wendling. At Luckey a Protestant chapel was taken over by Father Thomas F. McGuire in 1893; nine years later it was abandoned. At North Baltimore the frame church was erected through the exertions of Father Kress in 1892. At Paulding a hall was used for divine worship until in 1896 a frame chapel was finished by Father Matthew O'Brien. At Swanton a frame church was started by Father Thomas F. McGuire and was completed by Father John A. Schaffeld in 1893.

During this time also a few of the earlier mission chapels were abandoned. This was the case when the men who were engaged in the construction of the oil and gas wells or in the glass factories moved on to new locations. In other instances better transportation facilities made it more feasible to have the smaller communities come together in a common place of worship.

42

YOUNGSTOWN UNDER BISHOP HORSTMANN'S JURISDICTION

WITHIN THE LIMITS OF THE PRESENT Diocese of Youngstown, in the city itself St. Columba's massive monumental structure of Catskill granite, the roofed-over basement of which had been in use since 1893, was finally completed under the supervision of Father Edward Mears and was dedicated by Bishop Horstmann in 1903. The new brick school in the parish of the Immaculate Conception was opened in 1906 by Father Michael P. Kinkead. The large brick Church of St. Ann in the Norman style, under construction by Father John P. Barry for several years, was dedicated also in 1906. St. Joseph's School was much improved by Father John W. Klute in 1895.

The development of industry and the coming of the Slavs in greater numbers after 1880 made it necessary to erect several new parishes. The mother-church was that of Sts. Cyril and Methodius. The congregation was organized in 1898 by Father Aloysius Kollar who held divine services first in the old brick Church of St. Columba and then in the roofed-over basement of their own church; the superstructure of the fine brick Gothic church was completed in 1901. Six years later a brick school made its appearance through the efforts of Father John W. Becka. St. Anthony's was the first Italian parish in Youngstown. It was organized in 1898 by Father Anthony Petillo who used St. Ann's old frame church for divine services; the school, opened in 1903, lasted but a few years. The first Polish parish, that of St. Stanislas Kostka, was organized in 1902 by Father Charles Ruszkowski who used old St. Columba's Church. A frame church of their own was started by Father Ignatius Piotrowski and was in 1904 completed by Father L. Kuziusz; four years later a school was opened by Father Thomas Wilk. St. Casimir's, the second Polish parish, was given its first pastor in 1907 in the person of Father Thaddeus Siatecki; in the next year the first frame church was dedicated and a school opened.

At Alliance a schoolhouse was made of a large brick hall in 1900 by Father James J. Farrell. At Ashtabula the fine brick Romanesque

Church of St. Joseph, completed through the exertions of Father Matthew O'Brien, was in 1906 dedicated by Bishop Horstmann. At what was then known as Ashtabula Harbor, but now incorporated in Ashtabula itself, the stone Romanesque Church of Our Lady of Sorrows put up by Father Joseph F. Smith was blessed by the Bishop in 1900; the old church was converted into class rooms. The Italian-speaking members of this congregation were organized by Father Smith in the separate parish of Our Lady of Mount Carmel. A hall was used as a meeting place by the first pastor, Father Mirzan; a frame chapel was finished in 1903.

At Canton during this period four new parishes were inaugurated. In the southern section of the city the congregation of the Immaculate Conception (St. Mary) was organized by Father Clement Treiber who supervised the building of a brick combination church and school which was dedicated in 1900. In the western part of town St. Joseph's parish was founded also by Father Treiber; there he put up a brick combination church and school in 1903. The original Italian parish of St. Anthony used St. Peter's Church; a frame church of their own was erected in 1909 under the supervision of Father T. Adolph Cascianelli. In the southeastern section of the city St. Paul's parish was started by Father Joseph M. Paulus; in 1907 he refashioned a large barn into a chapel. In the oldest parish in the city, St. John's, a large new brick schoolhouse was put up in 1898 by Father Patrick J. McGuire to supplement the old school which he had enlarged several times.

At Conneaut a new brick school made its appearance in 1901 through the exertions of Father William F. Murphy. At Dungannon in 1899 the church was completely remodeled by Father Charles Andlauer. At Hubbard a brick Gothic church put up by Father Nicolas J. Drohan was dedicated in 1908. At Kent in 1904 the church was much enlarged by Father James B. Mooney. At Louisville in the same year the church was remodeled by Father Francis Senner. At Massillon the large brick Gothic Church of St. Joseph erected under the supervision of Father Thomas F. Mahon was dedicated in 1894; a brick school was opened in 1904 through the exertions of Father Francis Doherty. In St. Barbara's parish (then in West Brookfield, now Massillon) a frame schoolhouse was put up in 1894 by Father Peter L. Goebbels; the church was enlarged in 1893 and in 1896.

At Niles the Italian congregation of Our Lady of Mount Carmel was founded in 1906 by Father Vito Franco who gathered his people together in a large homestead. At St. Joseph (Randolph) a brick Romanesque church finished by Father John G. Vogt was dedicated in 1905 by Bishop Horstmann. At Salem the first brick schoolhouse made its appearance in 1904 as the result of the efforts of Father Thomas F. Conlan.

At Struthers in 1907 the new frame Church of St. Nicholas put up by Father Patrick Byrne replaced the previous one which was destroyed in a fire. In the same town and in the same year the Slovak parish of the Holy Trinity was founded by Father Melchior Fuerst who erected a frame chapel, and three years later a brick school (1910). At Warren the brick Church of St. Mary constructed through the exertions of Father Patrick C. N. Dwyer was dedicated in 1907. At Wellsville a large brick combination church and school was completed in 1904 under the supervision of Father James H. Halligan.

CHURCH AND SCHOOL
BUILDINGS IN CLEVELAND
(1891-1908)

I T WAS, HOWEVER, WITHIN THE CONFINES OF THE present Diocese of Cleveland that the greatest expansion took place. Great stone and brick churches replaced humbler structures. More modern school buildings were the rule, indicating the determination of the Catholic people to have their children educated in a religious atmosphere. Immigration from the Near East and the southern parts of Europe reached new heights; the newcomers settled in those sections of the city where they found their countrymen who had preceded them. New parishes had to be instituted and priests of their nationality had to be found to minister to them. Sometimes these parishes were organized before the Bishop had a priest to send to them. In some cases two or more nationalities joined together to form a parish until such time as they might maintain separate establishments. The problem of finding priests who were conversant with these languages was complicated by the overtures made by the Russian Orthodox Church to the Catholics of the Oriental rites to which some of the Slovaks and Hungarians belonged.

In 1904 Bishop Horstmann sent Father Joseph Koudelka to Europe to find the priests he needed. Fathers John Svozil and Ladislas Necid and several seminarians answered the invitation. Of the students Father Ulric Zlamal was ordained almost immediately by the Bishop; and Fathers Augustine Tomasek and Joseph Valka, after they had finished their studies here. All were conversant with Bohemian, Slovak, and German and were able to take Slovak as well as Bohemian parishes.

In Cleveland and its immediate vicinity, of the twenty East Side parishes which originated during the administration of Bishop Horstmann five were territorial; of the others the Poles, Slovaks, and Slovenians each had three, the Italians two, and the Hungarians, Croatians, Lithuanians, and Syrians each had one parish. On the west side of the river ten new parishes were started: three territorial, two Polish, two Slovak, one German, one Hungarian, and one Roumanian.

St. Agnes' was formed out of the territory on the eastern boundaries of the parishes of the Immaculate Conception and St. Edward. A large frame combination church and school on Euclid Avenue at East 79th Street, put up by the founder, Father Gilbert P. Jennings, was dedicated in 1893; a large modern stone schoolhouse and auditorium followed in 1904. Directly east of the Immaculate Conception parish Father Thomas F. Mahon organized St. Thomas' parish; a brick combination church and school on Superior Avenue near Ansel Road was dedicated in 1898; in 1905 Father Mahon had completed the present large stone Romanesque church with its distinctive cupola which was dedicated by Bishop Horstmann. In the district just east of St. Thomas', then known as Glenville, Father Joseph F. Smith founded the parish of St. Aloysius; for two years the congregation met in improvised quarters until in 1902 a three-story brick combination church and school made its appearance at St. Clair Avenue and Lakeview Road. South of here, in East Cleveland, Father Smith also organized St. Philomena's parish; under his supervision a stone Gothic church was erected on Wellesley Avenue near Euclid Avenue in 1902.

The first frame Church of St. Catherine on East 93rd Street at Heath Avenue was put up in 1898 by Father John T. Carroll to serve as a chapel-of-ease for the northeastern section of his parish of the Holy Name. Within a year because of a fire he had to replace it with the second frame structure, which Bishop Horstmann dedicated in November, 1899. It became a parish church with the appointment of Father James J. Quinn at the beginning of the next year; he opened a school in September.

For the accommodation of the Poles in the northeastern section of the city a brick combination church and school was built in 1892 at East 82nd Street and Sowinski Avenue under the supervision of Father Benedict Rosinski, the pastor of St. Adelbert's in Berea; Father Peter M. Cerveny became the first resident pastor of this the new parish of St. Casimir. In the southern part of the city St. Hyacinth's Polish parish, a division of St. Stanislas', was organized by Father Louis Redmer; late in 1907 he had finished a brick combination church and school at Francis Avenue and East 61st Street which in the next year was dedicated by Bishop Paul Rhode of Chicago. Another division of St. Stanislas', the parish of the Immaculate Heart of Mary, begun under inauspicious circumstances in 1894, used a frame combination church and school at Lansing Avenue and East 68th Street; the parish was recognized by the Bishop in 1908.

The northern section of St. Ladislas' Slovak parish was formed into the parish of St. Martin in 1893 when a frame Protestant church was taken over by Father Wenceslas A. Panuska; the great stone Gothic church on Scovill Avenue at East 23rd Street was completed in 1907 under the supervision of Father Wenceslas J. Horak. The northeastern part of St. Martin's was organized into the parish of St. Andrew by Father Emil E. Sloupsky; the brick combination church and school on

Superior Avenue at East 51st Street was dedicated in 1907 by Bishop Horstmann. The southern part of St. Ladislas' was taken to form the parish of the Nativity of the Blessed Virgin; a frame combination church and school on Aetna Road, dedicated in 1903, was erected by Father Joseph Ptasinski.

The thousand or more Slovenians in the district along St. Clair Avenue near East 55th Street were organized in the parish of St. Vitus in 1893 by Father Vitus Hribar, ordained in that year by Bishop Horstmann. The approximately 500 Gottscheers, who came from the same part of Europe as the Slovenians but who descended from an original German colony, were assimilated in the German parishes. Father Hribar finished a large frame church on Norwood Road near Glass Avenue in 1894 and a frame schoolhouse in 1902. The erection of the short-lived parish of Our Lady of Sorrows in 1906, with its center on East 55th Street near St. Clair Avenue, proved to have been unnecessary. St. Lawrence's parish for the Slovenians who lived south of Euclid Avenue was organized in 1901 by Father Francis L. Kerze; the congregation used the basement of Holy Name Church until the completion in the following year of a combination church and school on East 81st Street near Union Avenue. In the old Collinwood district the third Slovenian parish was instituted by Father Mark Parkiz who in 1906 put up a modest brick church on Holmes Avenue at East 156th Street.

St. Elizabeth's, the first exclusively Magyar parish in the United States, composed principally of those who previously shared St. Ladislas' Church with the Slovaks, received its first pastor in the person of Father Charles Boehm whom Bishop Horstmann had invited from Hungary for the purpose. A church begun in 1893 was dedicated two years later; the brick school finished in 1900 replaced one opened seven years previously. Father Boehm sought out the Magyar Catholics here and in other dioceses and was instrumental in starting parishes for them. He edited a Magyar prayer book and founded an influential newspaper in that language.

The parish of Our Lady of the Rosary (Holy Rosary) was established among the Italians who lived in the Mayfield Road district of East Cleveland, some miles from the original Church of St. Anthony. Father Joseph Strumia was the first pastor. The congregation used a small chapel, and then a frame church after 1892. Under the supervision of Father Anthony Ghibelli, like Father Strumia one of the Scalabrini Fathers, the construction of the present brick Romanesque church on Mayfield Road at East 121st Street was begun in 1905; it was not dedicated, however, until four years later. St. Marian's, the third Italian parish in the city, composed principally of immigrants from the Campo Basso district, originated in 1905; a small frame chapel was put up in that year on Petrarca Road near Fairhill Road by Father Angelico Idone.

The Croatians were organized in the parish of St. Paul with its center on East 40th Street near St. Clair Avenue; the present brick Gothic church was finished in 1904 under the supervision of Father Milan Sutlic. The Lithuanian parish of St. George was founded by Father Joseph Jankus; a frame combination church and school was put up in 1903 at Oregon Avenue and East 21st Street. The Syrian congregation of St. Elias was started by Father Basil Marsha in 1905; divine services in the Melkite Rite were held after 1908 in a frame church on Webster Avenue.

On the West Side of the city the northern section of St. Colman's was organized into the parish of St. Rose of Lima by Father Ignatius J. Wonderly; divine services were held in a hall until in 1900 a frame church on Detroit Avenue and West 114th Street was completed; school was started in a remodeled frame building. The southwestern part of St. Colman's was formed into the parish of St. Ignatius by Father Joseph Hoerstmann under whose supervision a brick combination church and school on Lorain Avenue near West Boulevard made its appearance in 1902. In the territory south of St. Patrick's, with its center on Fulton Road at Storer Avenue, the parish of the Blessed Sacrament was started by Father Thomas P. Lamb; in 1903 a frame church was completed and two years later a brick schoolhouse. The southern section of St. Stephen's was organized into the parish of St. Boniface by Father Adolph Seeholzer in 1904; a combination church and school on West 54th Street near Denison Avenue was put up principally through the generosity of the mother-parish; a separate schoolhouse which had to be continually enlarged was opened in 1906.

The parish of St. Wendelin, with its center on Columbus Road just east of West 25th Street, was organized among the Slovaks by Father Joseph M. Koudelka, then pastor of St. Michael's, who put up a frame church in 1903; a separate schoolhouse was erected through the exertions of Father Oldrich Zlamal in 1905. In 1903 also the Slovaks in Lakewood and the far western part of Cleveland were organized in the parish of Sts. Cyril and Methodius; the first Mass was celebrated in a remodeled frame building by Father Charles J. Ouimet; Father Koudelka and the Jesuit Fathers attended the parish until Father Zlamal of St. Wendelin's took charge and supervised the erection in 1905 of a combination church and school at Madison and Lakewood Avenues.

The Poles who lived in the territory of the parish of Sts. Cyril and Methodius formed the separate parish of St. Hedwig in 1906; the congregation came together in a refitted Protestant chapel, then in an annex to the Slovak church, and in a local theater until their own chapel was finished. Among the first priests to attend them on Sundays were Fathers Hippolit Orlowski and Albert Migdalski and the Franciscans. In 1905 St. Barbara's parish was established among the Poles who lived in the southwestern section of the city; a frame church was put up in the next year on Valley Road, in what was then known as South Brooklyn, through the efforts of Father Albert Migdalski who in 1909 also opened a school.

The parish of St. Emeric was established among the Magyars, with its center at Bridge Avenue and West 24th Street, by Father Stephen Soltesz who refashioned a few frame buildings for use as a church and school in 1904. The Roumanians who followed the Byzantine Rite in divine worship were organized in St. Helena's parish in 1905 by Father Epaminondas Lucaciu; under his direction in the next year the first Roumanian church in the country, a frame structure, was put up on West 65th Street just north of Detroit Avenue.

In the older parishes in the city many fine new churches and schools replaced the first temporary structures. In Holy Name a modern school was erected in 1906 by Father John T. Carroll. In Holy Trinity the fine stone Renaissance church dedicated in 1907 was put up through the efforts of Father Peter Becker. In the Immaculate Conception parish the great stone Gothic church, completed by Father Thomas P. Thorpe, was consecrated in 1904. The fine brick Church of Our Lady of Lourdes, dedicated in 1893, was the work of Father Furdek who was also responsible in 1907 for the erection of a sixteen-room school-house. In the Polish parish of the Sacred Heart of Jesus in 1908 a brick basement church was completed by Father Victor Szyrocki. In St. Adelbert's a frame school was put up in 1892 by Father John W. Malecha. The new brick Church of St. Anthony was completed in 1904 by Father Umberto Rocchi. The fine large brick Romanesque Church of St. Columbkille with its impressive cupola was finished, also in 1904, under the direction of Father George J. Vahey.

In St. Edward's a large brick schoolhouse was put up by Father William S. Kress in 1903. The monumental stone Romanesque Church of St. Francis of Assisi was completed in 1903 by Father Francis Metternich who nine years earlier had enlarged his school. In St. Joseph's (Woodland Avenue) the old monastery was transformed into class rooms in 1894. In St. Joseph's in old Collinwood a Norman-Gothic brick church raised by Father John Bell was dedicated by the Bishop in 1895. The fine brick Gothic Church of St. Ladislas erected under the guidance of Father John Svozil was dedicated in 1906. The Franciscan Fathers were given charge of the parish of St. Stanislas in 1906; in the next year a large brick schoolhouse was completed by Father Theobald Kalamaja. The great stone Gothic Church of St. Wenceslas erected through the exertions of Father Anthony Hynek was dedicated in 1902, three years after its completion.

On the West Side of the city the large brick Gothic Church of the Annunciation on West 22nd Street near Lorain Avenue was completed in 1898 by Father Augustine Gerardin. In the parish of Our Lady of Good Counsel, then known as that of the Sacred Heart of Mary in South Brooklyn, a frame school and auditorium was put up in 1893 by Father Augustine Steffen, S.J. A disastrous fire in 1907 destroyed the old church on Mechanic Road, corresponding to the present Broadview

Road; at a more central location, the present one, farther west on Pearl Road a combination church and school was raised to the second floor by Father Nicolas Weckel in the autumn of that year; it was completed in 1908 by Father Luke Rath, a member of the Sanguinist Fathers to whom Bishop Horstmann had given charge of the congregation.

A former Congregational church on West 14th Street at Starkweather Avenue became the new center of St. Augustine's parish in 1896 when it was adapted to Catholic worship by Father John O'Connor; a large brick school erected by Father Raymond Mylott completed the parish plant in 1907. In St. Colman's parish a modern brick school was put up in 1905 under the supervision of Father James O'-Leary. In St. Patrick's parish, in what was then known as West Park, a stone Gothic church on Rocky River Drive was completed by Father Joseph Hoerstmann in 1898. In 1893 he had put up the small brick school of St. Mary on Brookpark Road. In the parish of St. Michael the great stone Gothic church built under the direction of Father Joseph M. Koudelka was dedicated by Bishop Horstmann in 1892; eight years later the stone schoolhouse was brought to completion. The imposing Italo-Byzantine Church of St. Procop on West 41st Street, begun by Father Wenceslas A. Panuska, was completed in 1902 by Father Peter Cerveny; a large brick school and auditorium followed in 1908. In St. Stephen's parish a modern brick school was put up in 1897 through the exertions of Father Casimir Reichlin.

Outside the diocesan seat, in Akron, the massive brick and stone Romanesque Church of St. Bernard with its twin towers, completed under the guidance of Father John Broun, was dedicated in 1905. In St. Vincent's a large brick school made its appearance in 1892 and the church was much enlarged in 1893 through the efforts of Father Thomas Mahar; in St. Mary's, a division of his parish, he erected the first frame church in 1895. The Slovaks and Poles of Akron were organized in the parish of St. John Baptist in 1907; Father Melchior Fuerst held divine services in the basement of the new St. Bernard's Church until in 1908 the old church was acquired. In Avon the brick Gothic Church of the Immaculate Conception, constructed under the direction of Father Stephen Falk, was dedicated by Bishop Horstmann in 1895. In the same town the stone Gothic Church of the Holy Trinity was completed by Father Anthony Stuber in 1902.

At Barberton a frame chapel was put up in 1892 by Father Jacob F. Kuebler. St. Augustine's brick combination church and school was completed in 1902 by the first resident pastor, Father Joseph G. Schaffeld. The Slovaks of the town were organized in the parish of Sts. Cyril and Methodius and a frame chapel was erected under the direction of Father Augustine Tomasek in 1906. On Broadview Heights (Royalton) a granary was made over into a chapel in 1905 by Father Joseph Novak. At Doylestown a brick school was completed by Father Adam G. Hermann in 1908.

In Elyria St. Mary's new brick school was completed by Father John T. Schaffeld in 1901. In Fairport a frame church was put up in 1900 under the direction of Father Gerald I. Bergan of Willoughby; three years later the Magyars took over the parish when Father Anthony Hegyi was made their first pastor. At Grafton the Poles were gathered together in the parish of the Assumption; a frame church was put up by Father Stanislas Wozny in 1895; the school came five years later.

The establishment of the steel mills in Lorain at the end of the last century greatly increased the Catholic population of that town; several new parishes were required to care for their spiritual needs. In the original parish of St. Mary a fine brick Romanesque church in 1897 replaced, under the direction of Father Joseph Eyler, the frame structure destroyed in a fire two years before. Also in 1897 a large brick combination church and school was put up on Reid Avenue by Father Charles Reichlin, the first pastor of St. Joseph's German congregation. The Poles were organized in the parish of the Nativity of the Blessed Virgin in 1898 by Father Adolph Swierczynski who held divine services in St. Mary's school; St. Joseph's Hospital chapel was then used for a while until in 1900 a frame combination church and school was completed under the supervision of Father Charles Ruszkowski.

In the southern part of the city near the steel mills Father Thomas F. McGuire, the first pastor, put up the frame Church of St. John in 1900. It was shared for a while by several national groups. The Magyars were attended by Father Boehm and his assistants from Cleveland until the appointment in 1904 of their first pastor, Father Joseph N. Szabo, under whose guidance the reinforced concrete Romanesque Church of St. Ladislas was completed in 1907; the basement which had been used temporarily as a church was then made into class rooms. The Slovenians and Croatians, attended for a few months by Father Andrew Smerkar, were organized in a parish by their first pastor, Father Bartholomew Ponikvar, in 1906; St. John's Church was taken over by them and renamed in honor of Sts. Cyril and Methodius, and a school was inaugurated. The Slovaks were visited from Cleveland by Fathers Oldrich Zlamal and Wenceslas Horak who purchased land for the site of a church in 1903. The separate parish of the Holy Trinity was organized by Father Joseph Adamek, and under his direction a combination church and school was completed in 1907.

At Medina a stone Gothic church was put up under the supervision of Father John R. Kenny in 1908. At Sheffield (Lorain County) a brick Gothic church in 1907 through the efforts of Father Francis J. Pfyl replaced the frame structure which preceded it but was destroyed in a

fire. At Warwick a brick church made its appearance in 1908 under the
guidance of Father George Forst of nearby Canal Fulton. At Wellington in 1907 a brick structure previously used as a public school was
converted into a chapel through the efforts of Father Peter E. Dietz of
Oberlin.[1]

[1] Cfr. Henry J. Browne, "Peter E. Dietz, Pioneer Planner of Catholic Social
Action," Cath. Hist. Rev., Jan., 1948.

44

TRAVELS AND FINAL ILLNESS OF

BISHOP HORSTMANN

FROM THE TIME OF HIS COMING HERE BISHOP
Horstmann was troubled with asthma and hay fever. The
relief he found in confining himself to his room often gave
him the opportunity he liked to read and to write. He felt
himself sufficiently strong in November, 1894, after putting
Monsignor Houck in charge of the temporalities of the diocese, to
make his first *ad limina* visit to Rome. In an audience of nearly an
hour he found the Holy Father much interested in the development
of the higher grades in the parish schools here. On this occasion he
presented the photographs of all the ecclesiastical buildings in the diocese bound together in a single volume. After calling upon old Roman
friends he traveled to Switzerland and Germany, visiting Cloppenburg,
the birthplace of his parents. He was back in Cleveland for Christmas
Day.

The physicians now diagnosed the Bishop's sickness as organic heart
trouble.[1] He continued, nevertheless, to attend to his duties, but in
the summer of 1897, the year of the Golden Jubilee of the diocese, he
was obliged to take an extended vacation. In the autumn he had to can-
cel his Confirmation tour and was too ill to receive visitors. Three
years later, in July, 1900, he was forced to keep to his room as the result
of another attack; yet he was sufficiently recovered in August to pontificate at the Golden Jubilee celebration of the Ursulines and to act as
toastmaster at the dinner. However, he did not attend the bishops'
meeting in Cincinnati in the month following and was suffering with a
bronchial cough at the meeting of the board of Trustees of the
University in Washington a short time afterwards. In the spring of
the following year (1901) he made an extended visit through New
Mexico and California seeking relief. He preached in the Cathedral of
Los Angeles and again at the funeral of Senator White whom he had
prepared for death.

February and March of 1904 were spent, at the direction of his
physician, in the Southwest. He could not resist the temptation to

[1] Horstmann to Houck, Aug. 3, 1894; to Boff, Oct. 20, 1894; to Elder, Jan. 14, 1895;
all in C.D.A. *C.U.*, Dec. 14, 28, 1894.

preach in the Cathedral of San Antonio; an excursion into Mexico delighted him immensely. He returned to Cleveland for the Holy Week services. That summer, still wearing the bandages made necessary by an operation on his throat, he set out for Rome in the company of Doctor Patrick Farrell, the pastor of the Cathedral, on his second and last official visit to the Holy Father. They reached the Eternal City on June 15 and lodged at the North American College. In two lengthy audiences with the Pope, the Bishop was permitted the special privilege of keeping his episcopal cross exposed and was commended again for his interest in parochial schools and "for the good work of instructing the Catholic children in the public schools." His physical condition made it necessary to shorten his stay; he left Naples on July 1 and fifteen days later he was greeted in Alliance by a delegation of priests from this city.[2]

Inured to small but frequent attacks, he resumed his usual round of duties. Four years later, during his Mass for the First Communicants at the Cathedral in the early part of May, 1908, he suffered a slight heart attack; in spite of it he addressed the children in his usual captivating manner. The next day he began his Confirmation tour. He confirmed a class at the Immaculate Conception parish in Canton and preached a long and impressive sermon. The following day, Tuesday, he repeated this program at St. Peter's in the afternoon, and at St. John's in the evening. It was after his Mass at St. John's on Wednesday morning, in the parish house, that he suffered the first in the series of final attacks. Doctor Portman, the McKinley physician, administered stimulants, but a second onset left him very weak, though he still hoped to meet his engagements in a short time.

In the evening he recited the Rosary with his attendants and persuaded the physician to retire. Doctor Portman had scarcely left when the Bishop became suddenly worse. He had to be helped back to bed when he attempted to take a few steps in his room. In a few minutes a sharp pain caused him to cry out that it was the end; he gasped and fell back on the bed. Father Clement Treiber anointed him and gave him final absolution before he died at 9:20 P.M., Wednesday, May 13, 1908.

The tolling of the church bells announced the sad news. The people, who had gathered in the St. Paul Church where it was hoped he would confirm that evening, prayed for his soul. The death of the Bishop was a shock to Clevelanders and occasioned genuine regret to all who knew him, either as the tall loose-jointed figure who was familiar in the downtown streets, or as the great spiritual leader who defended every good cause and denounced every evil one, or as a public-spirited citizen devoted to the public good. The sorrow among the faithful was sincere

---

[2] Horstmann to Eilert, July 26, 1900; to Messmer, July 27, 1900; to Ryan (Philadelphia), Aug. 9, 1900; to Tiemann, Sept. 6, 1900; to McDonnell, Mar. 30, 1904; to Foley, May 20, 1904; to Houck, June 23, 1904; Farrell to Houck, June 26, 1904; Gotti (Propaganda) to Horstmann, July 7, 1904; all in C.D.A.

and deep. He had nobly upheld the dignity of the Church; he was the father of the poor and of the unfortunate; he was the guardian of the Faith.

The churches were dressed in mourning as the remains were brought to Cleveland on Thursday and were placed in the private chapel of the Cathedral House. On Sunday afternoon the body was laid out in state in the Cathedral itself. Mayor Johnson issued a proclamation of public sympathy and called for the suspension of business activity during the time of the funeral services. The courts and the City Hall were closed as a mark of respect and esteem for a leading citizen. The Funeral Mass was celebrated by Archbishop Moeller on Tuesday, May 19. Two other archbishops, eighteen bishops, some 400 priests, many non-Catholic clergymen, city and county officials, representative citizens, and an immense throng of the faithful crowded the sacred edifice. Significantly, among those present was Monsignor Joseph Schrembs of Grand Rapids. Bishop Koudelka preached the sermon in which he dramatically manifested his deep personal attachment. The body found its last resting-place in the Cathedral crypt.

Tributes to the dead prelate were published in all the local newspapers. The *Leader* recalled the usefulness of his career which broadened with the growth of a great city and the swift expansion of the Church. He had stood for morality and principle in public affairs; he did much to weld the great mass of newcomers to America into a great body of American citizens. The popular interest, the respect and affection for the Bishop, and the moving scenes at the funeral impressed the editor with the vitality of the Church and its influence in the lives of the people.

The *Universe* gave a more intimate picture, describing him as the shepherd who loved the little ones of the flock and who leaned always on the side of mercy and was at the call of the highest and the lowest. As an administrator he was a far-sighted organizer who encouraged the successful work of others for the development of the Church. As a priest he served the altar with a kind of passionate piety. As a bishop he bent to the burdens and rose to the majesty of his office. And yet with all his dignities and duties, great powers and great cares, he remained the simple, gentle, kindly man. Preeminently devoted to his duties, he seldom delegated his episcopal functions to others and "died in harness," dispensing his last day's strength in the great service of his Master.

Other tributes recalled his open and friendly disposition which might sometimes be mistaken for brusqueness; his love of peace and his dislike for the harsh use of authority; his unbounded charity for the needy and the afflicted, as was evidenced in his invariable rule at the end of every year to disburse any balance in his financial favor for their relief; his scholarship and learning and his patronage of Catholic education.[3]

[3] *C.U.*, May 15, 22, 29, 1908.

The devotion of the Bishop to his widowed mother was most edifying. He frequently visited her in Philadelphia; her appearances in Cleveland impressed everyone with her strongly religious endowment. She died at the age of eighty-four at her home, a few years after the consecration of her illustrious son. Much of the money he spent in charitable works came from her; in her name he founded free beds in the hospitals and burses at colleges. What remained of the considerable inheritance he had from her and from his father was left to the diocese at his own death. Gifts to churches were usual; he was especially generous to the Church of the Holy Rosary. He made a large donation to Bishop Doebbing in Italy to rescue a convent of indigent religious. The seminary in Cleveland inherited his magnificent library of rare and precious books which he gathered from many sources here and in Europe.

In the memory of the older priests his kindliness and spirit of Christian charity stood out above all his good qualities. To one young priest he gave the advice: "Your priestly charity will tell you what to do to gain souls." To another he wrote: "The quiet way is always the best way. Self must be nowhere and God everywhere in your personal priestly life." The Bishop's great love for children was manifested in the personal attention he gave to the little essays written by them. To a successful business man, not a Catholic, who had expressed his fears that he had lost his faith, the Bishop gave the homely advice "to go out into the world and try to relieve the distress of your fellow man; that will restore your faith and change your indifferent selfish character." The memory of Bishop Horstmann is still cherished in Cleveland.[4]

[4] Horstmann to F. A. Rupert, Mar. 18, 1892; to F. Doherty, June 25, 1892; to A. E. Manning, July 18, 1893; to A. Weber, June 11, 1894; to St. Vincent's orphans, Mar. 10, 1900; to E. H. Strauss, May 18, 1903; all in C.D.A. Reprint of an article in *Records of the American Catholic Historical Society*, Dec., 1935, written by E. M. E. Flick, "Ignatius F. Horstmann, 1840 to 1908." Bp. Horstmann was one of the founders of the A.C.H.S.

45

THE APPOINTMENT AND
JURISDICTION OF
BISHOP FARRELLY

MONSIGNOR BOFF SHORTLY AFTER THE DEATH of Bishop Horstmann was chosen by the consultors and the irremovable rectors as the administrator of the diocese. Vicar general since 1873, and domestic prelate in 1885, the seventy-seven-year-old priest, well known and respected by all, had served as temporary head of the diocese on six previous occasions.

The consultors (Bishop Koudelka, Monsignor Houck, Fathers James O'Leary, William McMahon, Anthony TePas, and Stephen Furdek) and the irremovable rectors[1] (Fathers Nicolas Pfeil, John McHale, Casimir Reichlin, Seraphin Bauer, William Murphy, Stephen Hultgen, James P. McCloskey, and Edward Mears) met in the Cathedral House under the presidency of Archbishop Elder, June 3, 1908. They chose the names of three candidates whom they suggested to the bishops of the province for the vacant see, namely, those of Bishop Koudelka, Monsignor Houck, and Doctor Thomas Mahar of Akron.[2] As was the rule in those days, the bishops gave consideration to these names in drawing up their own list of worthy men. However, negotiations over the boundary lines of the new Diocese of Toledo delayed the appointment for ten months until, finally, on March 16, 1909, the Holy See chose Monsignor John Patrick Farrelly whose name had been mentioned in the newspapers as the likely candidate, not long after the death of his predecessor.[3]

The fourth Bishop of Cleveland was born in Memphis, Tennessee, March 15, 1856, the only child of John Patrick and Martha Moore

---

[1] Aloysius Hoeffel was sick at Rome City.

[2] Houck to rectors and consultors, May 1; Boff to rectors and consultors, May 26; Moeller to Boff, May 29; Pfeil to Moeller, June 5, 12; Moeller to Pfeil, June 27; Pfeil and others to Falconio, June 23; Moeller to T. F. Moran, Aug. 17; Boff circular, July 13; Falconio to Wm. McMahon, July 7, all in 1908 and in the C.D.A. Pfeil papers in author's possession. *C.U.*, May 22, 29, Dec. 18, 1908; Feb, 12, 1909.

[3] Boff to Falconio, Mar. 19, 1909; Farrelly to Boff, Mar. 19, 1909, both in C.D.A. *C.U.*, Mar. 19, 26, 1909.

Bishop John Patrick Farrelly, fourth Bishop of Cleveland, 1909 to 1921.

*Right:*St. Adalbert
Church

*Far Right:*St. Casimir
Church.

*Far Left:*St.Colman
Church.

*Left:*Immaculate
Conception Church,
Wooster.

St. Elizabeth Church.

Immaculate Heart of Mary Church.

Clay Farrelly. His father, of Irish descent, was a cotton planter and an attorney at Memphis, having represented that city in the Tennessee "Long Parliament" and actively opposed secession before the Civil War. The Bishop's paternal grandfather, Terence, also an attorney, who lived for a time in Pittsburgh, Pennsylvania, helped to write the State Constitution of Arkansas. His mother, of fine culture and education, belonged to a Southern family which traced its origin in America to the early eighteenth century. Widowed at the outbreak of the Civil War, she brought her young son to his grandfather's large plantation in Arkansas. The war wasted her own property in that State. Gathering the remnants of her fortune she moved to Nashville, Tennessee. Thereafter, her life was devoted to the education of John Patrick. He attended primary schools in Tennessee, and St. Mary College, near Bardstown, Kentucky, where at the tender age of ten years he was received into the Catholic Church by Father Anthony Viala, the president of the college.[4] After some time spent at Georgetown University near Washington he went to Belgium to complete his preparatory course at the Jesuit College of Notre Dame de la Paix at Namur. In 1875 he was enrolled at the North American College in Rome and made his studies in philosophy and theology at the College of the Propaganda which awarded him the doctorate in theology. On May 22, 1880, Cardinal Raffaele Monaco La Valletta, Bishop of Albano, ordained him priest in the Lateran Basilica. His mother lived with him in Rome and died there.

After two years in the Holy Land and the Near East, in further studies, he returned to America in 1882 to become assistant pastor and then pastor of the Nashville Cathedral, and afterwards chancellor in Bishop Rademacher's administration. Five years later he went back to Rome as secretary to Bishop Dennis O'Connell, rector of the North American College, and after 1894 he served as spiritual director in the same institution. Confidential agent of several American bishops, he became a papal chamberlain in 1902 and made many visits to the United States. He had been in Cleveland itself not long before he became bishop.

On May 1, 1909, in the chapel of the North American College where he had celebrated his first Mass, he was consecrated bishop by Cardinal Girolamo Maria Gotti, Prefect of the Propaganda; Bishop John Morris of Little Rock, Arkansas, and Bishop Thomas F. Kennedy, rector of the college, were the co-consecrators.[5] The new Bishop, described in

[4] Monsignor Farrelly after twenty years revisited St. Mary's in 1885. "Every scene and spot was as fresh and vivid as if seen but yesterday." Father Viala who died in 1902 had been president of the college from 1865 to 1869. Though the record seems to have been lost Father Viala probably received young Farrelly's mother into the Church at the same time, *The Sentinel*, St. Mary College, St. Mary, Ky., Feb., 1902, Fall of 1951. Another more general source would have young Farrelly and his mother received into the Church in Arkansas.

[5] Notes in C.D.A. *C.U.*, Sept. 26, 1902; Jan. 1, 1904; May 7, 1909. Georgina P. Curtis, *American Catholic Who's Who*, St. Louis, 1910. Joseph B. Code, *Dictionary*

the dispatches as an accomplished scholar, and of impressive presence
and personal dignity, arrived in New York, June 8, with his secretary,
the newly ordained Doctor William A. Scullen. Early in the morning
of Sunday, June 13, they alighted from the train at the Euclid Avenue
Station of the Pennsylvania Railroad. After an informal welcome the
party proceeded immediately to the Cathedral where the Bishop
celebrated the installation Mass. In the presence of Archbishop Moeller
and four other bishops Monsignor Boff handed over the government of
the diocese to its new incumbent. The formal reading of the papal
documents was relieved by the expression of the Holy Father's warm
commendation. Father John T. O'Connell, of Toledo, made the formal
address of welcome in the name of the priests who filed up to the
episcopal throne to make their act of obeisance. Bishop Farrelly, after
paying high compliment to his predecessor and bidding adieu to all
his past associations, vowed himself to the service of the diocese in
words borrowed from the marriage ritual.

In the afternoon a great parade of some 15,000 persons, half of
them in special uniforms, representing all the parishes and nationalities,
passed the reviewing stand set up in front of the Cathedral House which
was occupied by the Bishop and his guests and the city officials. In the
evening the clergy tendered him a dinner in Cathedral Hall. Here,
inspired by a newspaperman's question, he announced that although he
had no immediate plans he did have principles which, with what he
learned by experience, would guide him in the conduct of affairs. On
Monday evening the Catholic Ladies Aid Society sponsored a public
reception at the Colonial Club. An estimated 6,000 persons lined up
through the Colonial Arcade and along Euclid Avenue for the opportunity of meeting the Bishop and extending a personal welcome.

The same enthusiasm marked the reception accorded by some 2,000
children in the Cathedral. Later in the Cathedral Hall each child received a medal which had been struck for the occasion; all took part
in the rendition of an especially composed song of greeting. The
Bishop was led to remark that "surely no bishop was so welcomed
before and encouraged to take up his work."[6] The priests of the
diocese in a special message thanked the Holy Father for sending
Bishop Farrelly to them.[7] Not long afterwards they presented him
with the title of a residence in Ambler Heights on the edge of the city.
Thereafter, the Bishop kept office hours at the chancery which still
occupied space in the Cathedral House.[8]

In the document appointing Bishop Farrelly the Holy Father reserved the right to divide the diocese if he saw fit to do so. Rumors of

of the American Hierarchy, is incorrect on date of ordination and the place of the
death of Bishop Farrelly.

[6] Bull of appointments. Boff to the Guardian Savings and Trust Co., Mar. 29, 1909;
both in C.D.A. *C.U.*, Apr. 2, 9, 16, May 21, June 18 (special installation edition),
June 25, Dec. 3, 1909.

[7] Merry del Val to Boff, May 7, 1909, in *American Ecclesiastical Review*, XLI, 348.

[8] *C.U.*, Aug. 27, Sept. 10, 1909. Other papers in C.D.A.

a new diocese with its seat at Toledo had been circulating for some time. In fact Bishop Rappe had envisioned such an event. During the administration of Bishop Gilmour, especially at the time that Doctor Quigley was restored to St. Francis de Sales's, the rumors took on new life and were exploited in the newspapers. Shortly after the coming of Bishop Horstmann the Toledo newspapers published reports of an impending division. In 1899 a petition was sent to the Propaganda in Rome asking for a redistribution of the ecclesiastical jurisdiction in the State; figures were published in the journals of the day to show how the Cleveland diocese might well dispense with part of its territory. A New York newspaper in the next year had it that Cleveland was to be an archdiocese including in its jurisdiction the new Diocese of Toledo and the dioceses in Michigan. In 1905 an anonymous petition in Latin addressed to the bishops of the province, which was circulated through the western part of the State, pleaded the great growth of Toledo as reason for its establishment as a separate diocese. Articles in the local newspapers embodied the same idea.

After the death of Bishop Horstmann discussion of the probable boundary lines occupied the authorities in Toledo and Cleveland. In September, 1908, the *Universe* announced that the bishops of the province favored the division of the Cleveland diocese and had made their recommendations to Rome. It was thought at the time, however, that the choice of bishops for Cleveland and Toledo would not be made until after November, 1908, when the decree withdrawing the Church in the United States from the jurisdiction of the Propaganda would become effective. The new prelates would be named under the newer dispensation. Bishop Farrelly was nominated in March, 1909, as we have seen above, but it was not until April 15, 1910, that the Holy Father approved of the creation of the See of Toledo within the limits recommended by the bishops of the province. By Apostolic Letter, April 20, 1910, Pope Pius X gave the new diocese official status and on May 5 following Bishop Farrelly received notice that he was to rule it as apostolic administrator until the appointment of another bishop.[9]

The new diocese comprised an area of 6,969 square miles, nearly one-half the territory of the old diocese: namely, all the counties in northwestern Ohio lying north of the southern limits of Crawford, Wyandot, Hancock, Allen, and Van Wert Counties and west of the eastern boundaries of Ottawa, Sandusky, Seneca, and Crawford Counties. Of the total population of some 600,000 in the area it was estimated

[9] Authentic copies of Bulls for the creation of the Diocese of Toledo; Horstmann to Hannin, Dec. 12, 1896; Hannin to Horstmann, Dec. 22, 1896; Bauer to Houck, Jan. 2, 1897; Nigsch to Houck, Oct. 25, 1905; F. A. Houck to Horstmann, Oct. 28, 1905; J. T. O'Connell to Horstmann, Dec. 9, 1905; Falconio to McMahon, July 8, 1908; Moeller to Boff, July 10, 1908; Boff to O'Brien, Aug. 3, 1908; Boff to McMahon, Sept. 3, 1908; Boff to Moeller, Aug. 13, 1908; Farrelly to Moeller, Oct. 9, 1909; Farrelly to Falconio, Nov. 20, 1909; all in C.D.A. *C.U.*, July 24, Oct. 30, 1908; Aug. 27, Sept. 3, 10, Dec. 10, 1909; May 6, 13, 1910. N. Y. *World*, Jan., Feb., 1903. Cleveland *Press* and Cleveland *Plain Dealer*, Oct. 27, 1905. *Stimme der Wahrheit*, Mar. 1, 1906.

that from 100,000 to 125,000 were Catholics, of whom about one-half lived in the city of Toledo with its twenty fully equipped parishes. The rest of the Catholics were scattered through sixteen counties which were principally rural. Serving them were 120 priests, of whom 31 were Jesuits, and Sanguinists. There were 111 churches with 86 resident pastors. In the educational institutions there were 12,500 pupils in 61 parochial schools; nearly 800 young women in the academies which were operated by the Ursulines, the Notre Dame Sisters, and the Sisters of the Precious Blood; and 272 students in St. John's College, belonging to the Jesuits. Three orphanages cared for 402 children. There were two homes for the aged, two hospitals, and a house of the Good Shepherd Sisters. Several other communities of religious women were occupied in the schools and in works of charity.

The old diocese retained seventeen counties and some 8,000 square miles in northeastern Ohio. Catholics were estimated to number 225,-000 to 280,000 in a total population of 1,200,000. They lived principally in the larger cities: Cleveland, Youngstown, Canton, Akron, Massillon, Warren, Lorain, and Sandusky. Attending them were 329 priests, including 71 Franciscans, Jesuits, and Sanguinists. Of the 205 churches 174 had resident pastors who maintained 132 parochial schools with their nearly 40,000 pupils. In the 12 academies there were nearly 2,500 young women. The Jesuit Fathers operated St. Ignatius College and Loyola High School for boys. The diocesan clergy taught in the major seminary. Cleveland retained four orphanages with their 750 children; one infant asylum with its 146 charges; a home for working boys and another for working girls; a home for dependent young women and a house of the Good Shepherd Sisters; and a home for the aged poor.

In September, 1910, the consultors and the irremovable rectors of the new diocese met with Archbishop Moeller to draw up a list of worthy candidates for the new bishopric. It was nearly a year, however, before the Holy See by Apostolic Letter, August 11, 1911, appointed Bishop Joseph Schrembs, Auxiliary Bishop of Grand Rapids, for the honor. He was installed in the pro-Cathedral of St. Francis de Sales on October 4 following. Monsignor Thomas C. O'Reilly, acting in the name of Bishop Farrelly who was present, gave up the jurisdiction of apostolic administrator.[10]

[10] Moeller to Farrelly, Sept. 4, 1910, in C.D.A. *C.U.*, Sept. 16, 1910.

46

CHURCH AND SCHOOL BUILDINGS DURING BISHOP FARRELLY'S ADMINISTRATION

URING THE SHORT PERIOD OF BISHOP FARREL-
ly's responsibility for the Diocese of Toledo he laid the
cornerstone for a new school at Bucyrus, in Crawford
County, in 1910, which was completed by Father Charles
Braschler. At Crestline, in the same county, Father Henry
Boesken put up a new school in the same year. At Junction, in Paulding
County, Father John B. Weis directed the construction of a brick
church which Bishop Farrelly dedicated in 1910. Three counties, Erie,
Huron, and Richland, which were later added to the Toledo diocese
remained attached to Cleveland during his lifetime. He had the pleasure
in 1917 of dedicating the fine Romanesque stone church at Mansfield,
in Richland County, which Father Ferdinand Schreiber had been constructing for the previous six years. At Shelby, also in Richland County,
a brick school made its appearance in 1910 under the auspices of
Father Andrew Crehan. In Erie County, at Sandusky, in the same
year the Bishop blessed St. Mary's large brick school and social center
which had been put up by Father Joseph S. Widman.

A summary account of the new parishes and of the improvements
in the old ones in the territory which belonged to Cleveland until the
erection of the Diocese of Youngstown may well be taken as an indication of the steady growth of the Church during the period and as
monumental evidence of the faith and self-sacrificing devotion of the
people who contributed the means for the development.

In the city of Youngstown eight new parishes were established: two
of them territorial, two for the Slovaks and one each for the Croatians,
Lithuanians, Italians, and Syrians. The northern section of St. Columba's was organized into the parish of St. Patrick by Father Charles A.
Martin in 1911; a concrete block church was completed in 1913 and a
brick school with accommodations for 600 children was opened in
the autumn of the next year. Another section of St. Columba's was
formed into the parish of St. Edward by Father Maurice F. Griffin

in 1916; the impressive white brick Romanesque combination church, auditorium, and ten-room schoolhouse was dedicated by Bishop Farrelly in 1918; it had been in use for some time previously.

At the western end of the city the Slovak parish of the Holy Name of Jesus began its separate existence with the appointment of the Croatian-born Father John A. Stepanovic in 1916 as its first pastor; he used a hall for divine services until he completed a basement church in December, 1917; his successor, Father Frank Dubosh, finished the superstructure of the brick Gothic church in the following year and started a school in the basement in 1920. The Slovaks in the southeastern part of the city were organized in the parish of St. Matthias by Father John M. Gerenda who in 1914 put up a frame church and started a school.

Father Michael G. Domladovac in 1912 organized his countrymen in the Croatian parish of Sts. Peter and Paul; a remodeled frame structure was used at first until he completed a large imposing brick Romanesque church which Bishop Farrelly dedicated in 1915; school had been started in the basement the year before. Father Vincent G. Vilkutaitis, assistant priest at St. Joseph's, was the first to minister to the Lithuanians of Youngstown in their own tongue; Father Felix Alinskas brought them together in the parish of St. Francis of Assisi, and completed a frame church in 1919. The parish of Our Lady of Mount Carmel, a division of the Italian parish of St. Anthony, was founded by Father Emmanuele Stabile who constructed a basement church in 1909; Father Vito Franco completed the superstructure of the brick Romanesque church which was dedicated in 1914. The Syrian parish of St. Maron was organized by Father Namatallah S. Beggiani who converted a Protestant frame church to Catholic usage in 1911.

The great Church of St. Columba was solemnly consecrated by Bishop Farrelly in 1919. The fine stone Romanesque Church of the Sacred Heart, completed by Father John I. Moran, he dedicated in 1912. The Magyar congregation of St. Stephen of Hungary, which had been using the old Church of St. Columba, moved into their own (frame) church in 1910. The Roumanian Catholics of the Oriental Rite were attended by priests from Cleveland for some time; among them were Father Alexander Nicolescu, later Archbishop of Alba Julia in Roumania, and Father Aurel Hatiegan who were responsible for the brick Church of St. Mary which was dedicated in 1909.

Outside the city of Youngstown, at Alliance, under the direction of the same Father Hatiegan a brick church previously used by a Protestant congregation was remodeled in 1914 for the use of the Roumanian Byzantine Rite congregation of St. Theodore. At Campbell the Polish parish of St. John the Baptist was founded by Father Joseph Rojewski who put up a frame church in 1919. In the same town the Slovak congregation of St. John the Baptist had without authorization constructed a brick church in 1917; it was recognized by Bishop Far-

St. Peter Church, North Ridgeville.

St. John Nepomucene
Church.

St. Vitus Church, Lorain.

St. John Cantius Church.

*Left:*St. Josaphat
Church.

*Right:*Our Lady of
Good Counsel Church.

St. Cecilia Church.

St. Peter Church, Akron.

St. Peter Church, Lorain.

St. Agnes Church, Elyria.

St. Mary Church, Chardon.

relly two years later. At Canton the Polish parish of the Holy Cross was founded in 1919; two years later a frame church was acquired at public auction and remodeled. The Roumanians were organized in the parish of St. George; a Protestant church was refitted for their use in 1912. In the Immaculate Conception parish the school was enlarged in 1909 through the exertions of Father Nicolas A. Hassel. In the parish of St. Joseph Father Clement Treiber in 1917 greatly enlarged the school; four years later he began the construction of a new basement church. The fine brick Church of St. Paul in the Basilica style was completed by Father John W. Schmitz in 1921; the old church was made over into class rooms.

At East Liverpool the parish of St. Ann, a division of St. Aloysius', was organized by Father Jerome J. Reidy who put up a frame church in 1918. At Girard a brick school made its appearance in 1910 under the supervision of Father Edward A. Kirby. At Hubbard a five-room brick school was erected by Father John F. Maloney in 1915. At North Canton the fine brick Romanesque Church of St. Paul through the efforts of Father Joseph Gerz was completed in 1911; eight years later the old brick church was remodeled into class rooms by Father Joseph J. Schmit. At Orville the first church, a frame structure, was put up by Father John McKeever in 1913. At Power Point a frame mission chapel made its appearance in 1920 under the direction of Father Clement Boeke of Lisbon. At Ravenna a brick school was put up in 1912 by Father Charles H. Gardner. At Rootstown in 1915 the frame church was enlarged by Father John McGoogan. At Sebring, organized as a parish in 1908, a frame chapel was put up by Father Thomas Hanrahan in 1911. At Struthers Father Emil Sloupsky supervised the erection of a brick school in 1910 and its enlargement in 1916; an auditorium was erected in 1919 by Father Joseph Zalibera.

In the city of Cleveland ten new parishes were erected of which six were territorial, two were for the Poles, and one each for the Bohemians and Roumanians. In the territory between St. Thomas' and St. Aloysius' Father John P. Brennan organized the parish of St. Philip Neri; he put up a frame church in 1914 on St. Clair Avenue at Ansel Road, and a ten-room brick schoolhouse in the next year. Farther east, in the northern section of St. Joseph's (Collinwood), Father Leo O. Hammer founded the parish of St. Jerome; in 1920 he completed a frame church on Lake Shore Boulevard at East 150th Street. The first parish on Cleveland Heights, St. Ann's, was organized by Father John M. Powers; under his direction an auditorium church of stone made its appearance in 1915; the school in provisional quarters was opened in the following year. To the south, on the border of Shaker Heights, Father James E. Cummins, a returned army chaplain, established the parish of Our Lady of Peace; he put up the first church at Buckingham Avenue and East 121st Street in 1920. Still farther south, in a territory of many nationalities, Father John T. Farrell organized the parish of St. Cecilia; the congregation used a storeroom on Kinsman Road until in 1916 a frame church was completed on the same avenue at East 152nd Street.

In the southeastern section of the city a division of the Polish parish of the Sacred Heart of Jesus was organized in the parish of Our Lady of Czestochowa by Father Victor Szyrocki; in 1914 he refashioned a frame building at Harvard Avenue and East 141st Street for use as a church; Father John Mlotkowski enlarged it, and put up a brick school in 1920. Near the downtown district the Polish parish of St. Josaphat was founded in 1908; the congregation met in the Cathedral chapel, until in 1917 Father Joseph P. Kocinski completed a brick Romanesque church and an eight-room schoolhouse on East 33rd Street north of Superior Avenue. Also in the downtown area St. Maron's (Syro-Maronite) parish was started by Father Peter Chelela; he converted a brick residence on East 22nd Street into a chapel which Bishop Farrelly blessed in 1916.

The eastern part of the Bohemian parish of Our Lady of Lourdes was separated from it and formed the parish of the Holy Family through the efforts of Father Stephen Furdek who put up a frame church there in 1911; Father Francis Faflik, the first pastor, and his successor, Father Joseph Kresina, were responsible for the L-shaped brick combination church, auditorium, and twelve-room schoolhouse on East 131st Street south of Union Avenue which was completed in 1922. The Roumanians of the Byzantine Rite who lived on the East Side were organized in the new parish of the Most Holy Trinity by Father Aurel Hatiegan; in 1915 he put up a brick chapel on East 93rd Street near Buckeye Road.

On the West Side of the city, in Lakewood, St. James's parish was established in July, 1908, during the administration of Monsignor Boff; Bishop Farrelly confirmed the appointment of Father Michael D. Leahy as the first pastor. Divine services were held in the O'Donnell Block on Detroit Avenue and in Miller Hall on Warren Road, and school was kept in an old roadhouse, until in 1914 a brick combination church and school on Detroit Avenue at Granger Avenue was ready for occupancy; the school needed to be considerably enlarged two years later.

In the older parishes in the city many new churches and schools supplanted the earlier buildings. On the east side of the river, in the Italian parish of the Holy Rosary, the brick Romanesque church was dedicated in 1909. In the parish of the Immaculate Conception an imposing brick and stone schoolhouse and social hall constructed under the supervision of Father George F. Murphy was blessed in 1916. In the Polish parish of the Immaculate Heart of Mary a temporary school was opened; the twin-towered brick Romanesque church put up under the direction of Father Marion J. Orzechowski was dedicated in 1915. In the Slovak parish of the Nativity of the Blessed Virgin Father Vaclav A. Chaloupka enlarged the school in 1909 and began the construction of a large new brick schoolhouse in 1915. In the Polish parish of the Sacred Heart of Jesus a large brick school made its appearance in 1917 through the efforts of Father John Czyzak. In the Bohemian parish of St. Adelbert a fine brick Romanesque church was completed by Father John W. Becka in 1912.

The outstanding monumental stone Romanesque Church of St. Agnes on Euclid Avenue raised through the exertions of Father Gilbert P. Jennings was dedicated by Bishop Farrelly in 1916. In the parish of St. Aloysius a brick church-auditorium was completed by Father Francis Malloy in 1913. In the Polish parish of St. Casimir in 1918 a great imposing brick Romanesque church was finished by Father Charles Ruzkowski who also enlarged the school. The fine brick Romanesque Church of St. Catherine was put up by Father James Quinn in 1915. In the Magyar parish of St. Elizabeth the great stone church in the Romanesque Baroque style was under construction by Father Julius Szepessy for four years before its dedication by Bishop Schrembs in 1922; a hall used temporarily as a church had made its appearance in 1917. In the parish of St. Francis of Assisi a large brick school and auditorium was put up in 1910 by Father Francis Metternich. In the Lithuanian parish of St. George a large brick combination church and school was erected in a new location at Superior Avenue and East 65th Street by Father Vincent G. Vilkutaitis in 1921.

In the Bohemian parish of St. John Nepomucene a fine twin-towered brick Romanesque church was dedicated by Bishop Farrelly in 1920; it was built under the direction of Father Francis J. Hroch who had increased the capacity of the school seven years earlier. In the Slovenian parish of St. Lawrence the school was enlarged in 1920 by Father John J. Oman. In the Slovenian parish of St. Mary (Collinwood) the school opened in 1913 by Father Paul Hribar had to be enlarged two years later. In the Croatian parish of St. Paul a brick school was opened by Father Nicolas Grskovic in 1910. In the parish of St. Philomena a four-room stone school was put up by Father Joseph Smith in 1911. In the parish of St. Thomas a wing seating 600 people was added to the church by Father Thomas Mahon in 1921. In the Slovenian parish of St. Vitus a large modern brick school with accommodations for nearly 2,000 pupils was completed by Father Bartholomew Ponikvar in 1913.

On the West Side of the city, in the parish of the Holy Family (Parma), a small brick church made its appearance in 1911 through the efforts of Father Albert Aust. In the parish of Our Lady of Good Counsel a basement church was completed by Father Luke Rath, C.PP.S., in 1918; the old church was converted into class rooms to supplement the capacity of the school which he had put up in 1915. In the parish of St. Boniface the church was enlarged in 1911 and a large brick school made its appearance six years later through the exertions of Father Adolph Seeholzer. In the parish of St. Colman the great monumental Italian Renaissance stone church with its exquisitely carved marble interior, under construction for four years, was completed in 1918 by Father James O'Leary. In the Slovak parish of Sts. Cyril and Methodius a brick school was put up in 1916 by Father Adelbert J. Masat. In the Magyar parish of St. Emeric in 1921 a frame school under the supervision of Father Joseph Hartel replaced one destroyed by fire.

In the Polish parish of St. Hedwig in Lakewood a frame church was put up by Father T. A. Czarkowski in 1914. In the parish of St. Ignatius an auditorium church was completed in 1914 and a brick school two years later under the direction of Father Joseph Hoerstmann. In the Polish parish of St. John Cantius a large brick combination church and school was opened in 1913 by Father Francis Doppke. The Church of St. Patrick on Bridge Avenue in 1913 was enlarged and completed by Father Francis T. Moran. In St. Patrick's parish in old West Park a new brick school was put up by Father Edward T. Calvey in 1916. In St. Rose's parish a brick school was completed by Father James J. Stewart in 1911. In St. Stephen's the brick school and auditorium was finished by Father Casimir Reichlin in 1916.

Outside the city a similar development was to be observed. In Akron seven new parishes were authorized, three of them English-language parishes, and one each for Polish, Magyar, Lithuanian, and Syrian Catholics. The eastern section of St. Vincent's was organized into the parish of the Annunciation in 1907 by Father Richard Dowed; in that year he put up a parish auditorium which was used for divine services until the completion of a cement stone church in 1913; a frame school was opened in 1911. Another part of St. Vincent's was taken to form the parish of St. Martha in 1919; Father John McKeever, the founder, remodeled a frame church structure which was used by the congregation until it moved into a combination brick school and church in 1924. St. Paul's parish in the Firestone Park district was founded by Father James Hanley, a returned army chaplain; he completed a brick Romanesque auditorium church in 1920.

The Poles were gathered together in the parish of St. Hedwig by Father Bernard Salomon who put up a frame church in 1913. The Magyars were organized in the separate parish of the Sacred Heart in 1915 by Father Oscar Selynos; the congregation used the chapel in St. Bernard's Church for the following ten years. St. Peter's congregation was formed for the benefit of the Lithuanians in 1917; two years later a brick church in the Mission style was put up under the direction of Father Felix Alinskas. St. Joseph's parish was organized among the Syrians by Father Malatios Haggar who in 1915 transformed a Protestant church edifice for the use of his Melkite rite congregation.

In the older parishes in Akron marked progress was made. The large brick high school in St. Vincent's parish was completed by Father John Scullen in 1918. The stone Church of St. Mary in the Roman basilica style was dedicated by Bishop Farrelly in 1916; Father Joseph

F. O'Keefe, the builder, in the next year also completed a twenty-six-room brick and stone schoolhouse. In Barberton three new parishes were established. The Magyars were organized in the parish of the Holy Trinity in 1911 and were attended by visiting priests who used a remodeled frame church building. The Poles under the supervision of Father Bernard Salomon put up the frame mission Church of the Immaculate Conception in 1912. The parish of the Sacred Heart was formed among the Slovenians in 1916; the congregation used the Polish church until in 1922 Father John A. Stepanic, the first resident pastor, erected a separate frame chapel.

At Bedford the first frame mission chapel was put up in 1910; the congregation was attended by the clergy of the adjacent Holy Name parish. At Chardon the first frame mission chapel was put up in 1910 under the direction of Father Julius M. Kitter and Father William A. Scullen. At Cuyahoga Falls a brick church in the English Gothic style made its appearance in 1912 through the exertions of Father John A. Nolan. In Elyria St. Agnes', a division of St. Mary's parish, was organized by Father James A. McFadden, later the first Bishop of Youngstown; he put up a brick school in 1915 and a brick church in the Italian Renaissance style which Bishop Farrelly dedicated in 1916. At Hudson the church was enlarged by Father James Nolan in 1909.

At Lorain, in the Polish parish of the Nativity of the Blessed Virgin, a large brick Gothic church was put up in 1915 and a two-story brick school in 1920 through the activity of Father Andrew A. Radecki. St. Basil's congregation was organized among the Roumanians of the Oriental Rite in 1918; a brick Gothic church was completed by Father Aurel Hatiegan in the following year. The brick Romanesque St. John's Church was completed by Father James Heffernan in 1909. St. Peter's parish was organized among the Italians in 1909 by Father John Salerno; the frame church which he began was finished through the efforts of Father Charles Reichlin of St. Joseph's in 1914, the year in which Father Damien Leone was appointed the first pastor. The Polish parish of St. Stanislas was organized by Father Thomas Tomecki in 1908; a brick combination church and school was put up the next year by Father John S. Zybura.

At North Ridgeville a brick schoolhouse made its appearance in 1910 through the efforts of Father Joseph Trapp. At Painesville a ten-room brick school was put up in 1920 by Father William J. Gallena. At Rittman a frame mission church was erected by Father Adam G. Hermann in 1909. At Wooster a brick and stone Romanesque church at a new location (the present one) in 1915 replaced the original church which was destroyed by fire; Father Edward C. Kramer, who supervised the construction, five years later increased the capacity of the school.

47

CHARITABLE INSTITUTIONS
(1909-1921)

SHORTLY AFTER HIS ARRIVAL IN CLEVELAND
Bishop Farrelly reorganized the diocesan curia. Monsignor
Houck who had so faithfully served Bishops Gilmour and
Horstmann, choosing not to engage in parish work, spent the
rest of his days as chaplain at St. Augustine's Convent in
Lakewood where he died in 1916. Doctor Thomas C. O'Reilly was
brought from the seminary and made pastor of the Cathedral and later
vicar general. Bishop Koudelka and Fathers TePas and O'Leary were
retained on the Bishop's council; Fathers O'Reilly, George F. Murphy,
and Gilbert P. Jennings were appointed new members. The Matrimonial Court and other episcopal agencies were established, and the
Building Commission was given control of all new constuction in the
diocese.

The founding of the Board of Charities in 1910 and the appointment
of Father Hubert LeBlond, later Bishop of St. Joseph, as the director
had far-reaching results.[1] The earlier bishops had, as we have seen,
expressed dissatisfaction with the old methods of raising funds for the
support of the welfare institutions. The Orphans' Fairs and the begging
tours of the Sisters had, moreover, proved to be inadequate. The
Bishop decided that he would have to resort to a more efficient system.
At a meeting of the Federation of Catholic Societies in October, 1909,
he spoke[2] in favor of a board of charities composed of priests and laymen who would study the situation and suggest remedies; the members
promised their full cooperation. At the end of the Knights of Columbus
retreat in March, 1910, he was able to publicly thank the Knights for
their pledge to do something substantial for the orphans. Finally on
April 1, 1911, the Board of Charities was established. The Board was
composed of city pastors: Fathers Doppke, Hroch, Jennings, Francis
Moran, Pfeil, John Powers, and Seeholzer.

In accord with its recommendations the cost of maintaining the
orphanages was distributed among all the parishes of the diocese.
Father LeBlond, who had been a member of the National Conference

[1] *C.U.*, July 2, Dec. 3, 10, 17, 1909; Oct. 14, Dec. 23, 1910; Jan. 6, 1911; Apr. 4, 1913.
[2] Dec. 6, 1911.

of Catholic Charities since its establishment in 1910, opened the first office of the local bureau, March, 1912, in the old O'Brien Building on Prospect Avenue near East 9th Street. His first task was to systematize the care of the orphans. Daniel Lanigan, coming from Juvenile Court, was put in charge of the investigation of their status. This office also controlled the Travelers' Aid agency in the Union Depot. In 1913 the first week of November was declared to be Orphans' Week during which the pastors were expected to raise their quota; the money and the envelopes containing it were sent to the central headquarters. In April, 1916, twenty-three delegates representing the welfare institutions and the Catholic societies formally inaugurated the Cleveland Conference of Catholic Charities and set up an executive board to coordinate all welfare activities. The bureau proved its worth from the beginning. A study made in 1910 showed that to support some 900 orphans only about one-fourth of what was necessary had been raised in the Orphans' Fairs, leaving the burden of the deficit on the Sisters. Most of the other charitable institutions were running at a loss and were also in debt. Again, according to the Bishop's circular,[3] in the year previous to October, 1913, it cost $60,000 to care for some 700 orphans; yet only $17,000 had been collected. Father LeBlond reported that under the new system nearly $42,000 was contributed in 1915; three years later the annual contribution amounted to $50,000.

During this same time the Cleveland Federation for Charity and Philanthropy was organized in the city. Its purpose was to combine all public appeals made for charitable institutions in one short intensive drive. The Community Chest would pay the deficit in the cost of maintaining the activities of member organizations. Catholic interests[4] were represented by Father LeBlond. In November, 1920, Catholic welfare institutions in Cuyahoga County benefited to the extent of nearly $500,000 in the distribution of funds. The Community Chest, however, did not furnish capital for the construction of new buildings.

This problem was solved by the organization of the Catholic Charities Corporation[5] in 1919. The original trustees, a group of prominent Catholic business men to whom Father LeBlond explained his difficulty, assumed the responsibility of collecting from the people in systematic drives enough money to build the necessary new buildings and to rehabilitate outmoded facilities. The pastors furnished the list of the prospective members of the corporation and appointed the solicitors who called on them during the drive. In April, 1920, Father LeBlond reported that approximately 8,000 members had been registered. Encouraged by so many pledges of an annual contribution, the trustees purchased a tract of 150 acres in Parma Township in that year. It was hoped that this would be the site of several welfare institutions. After Bishop Farrelly's unexpected death in the early part of 1921,

[3] *C.U.*, Oct. 15, 1909.
[4] Bishop's Circular, Oct. 27, 1911. *C.U.*, Nov. 3, 1911.
[5] *C.U.*, Jan. 23, 1914.

the campaign for funds was dedicated to his memory as the founder of the corporation.

With the hearty encouragement of Bishop Farrelly the hospital facilities of the diocese were greatly developed. He inspired the public appeal for the money with which the new St. John's Hospital on Detroit Avenue was erected.[6] A huge "thermometer" on the Public Square registered the daily progress of the successful drive in the early part of 1913. The four-story brick structure with modern equipment to care for 210 patients was opened, June 26, 1916. The Sisters of Charity had replaced the Franciscan Sisters in charge of it in 1915. The Bishop also had the satisfaction of dedicating a large addition to St. Vincent's Charity Hospital, a six-story surgical pavilion with its capacity of 150 beds, on April 15, 1917, the fiftieth anniversary of its foundation. The money was raised in a general appeal to the public made by a group of prominent citizens under the chairmanship of the well-known Charles E. Adams.[7]

St. Ann's Maternity Hospital, after the transfer of its location to Woodland Avenue in 1901, offered its facilities to private paying patients. The increased patronage made it necessary to build a modern building which the Bishop dedicated in 1910.[8] After an addition was made to the Loretto House in 1918 about forty-two per cent of the 130 beds were reserved for private patients and about seventy-seven per cent of the service provided in the infant asylum with its 140 children was gratis. A nursery school for children one to two years of age was started in July, 1921. In the fifty years previous to 1922 the Sisters of Charity had cared for more than 1,500 infants. In Cleveland in 1921 these same Sisters of Charity were caring for approximately 12,694 patients in their hospitals and 713 orphans.

In Sandusky a new two-story wing was added to Providence Hospital in 1909; a city-wide drive there made possible the erection of a new building in 1920. The Sisters of Charity who had charge of it were recalled to this diocese a few years later when Sandusky became part of the Toledo diocese. In Canton Mercy Hospital through the munificence of Mrs. Rose Klorer was considerably enlarged by the erection of a new building in 1909; a nurses' home was completed ten years later.

In Youngstown in 1910 the pastors of the city organized a public campaign for a larger Catholic hospital. As a result the new St. Elizabeth's Hospital was opened in December of the next year with accommodations for 30 patients. The provisional quarters in which it began were replaced by a six-story brick structure which Bishop Farrelly dedicated in 1915. He had given the administration of the new hospital to the Sisters of the Holy Humility of Mary.

Other new welfare institutions were inaugurated and old ones were

[6] *C.U.*, Nov. 14, 1919.
[7] *C.U.*, June 16, 1916.
[8] *C.U.*, Nov. 21, Dec. 12, 1913; Jan. 31, Oct. 16, 1914; Apr. 13, 1917.

Holy Trinity Church, Lorain.   St. Agnes Church.

*Left:*St. Catherine Church.

Annunciation Church, Akron.   St. George Church and School.

*Above Left:*St. Mary Church, Akron.

*Above Right:*Holy Cross Church, Elyria.

*Right:*St. Augustine Church, Barberton.

St. Paul Church, Akron.   St. Mary Church, Lorain.

expanded and improved. The Catholic Young Women's Hall for working girls was opened in 1917 in the old mother-house of the Notre Dame Sisters on Superior Avenue at East 18th Street. It replaced St. Mary's Home on East 22nd Street; the Sisters of Notre Dame, however, were in charge of it. The Catherine Horstmann Home, which at the time had 21 young women in residence and some 60 others under supervision in private homes, was moved to a larger and more commodious site on Rocky River Drive near St. Patrick's Church in 1918. Not far from here, on Puritan Avenue, the Home of the Holy Family was established in 1914 by Miss Ellen Donovan and a few other pious women whose purpose was to keep dependent brothers and sisters together in a homelike atmosphere. St. Anthony's Home for Working Boys moved into larger and more modern quarters in a brick building erected under the direction of Father LeBlond, who in 1911 had succeeded Father Haessler as chaplain there.

Under the auspices of the National Catholic Welfare Council and of the local branch of the Christ Child Society, Merrick House, named for Miss Mary V. Merrick, founder of the society, and Cleveland's first professional Catholic settlement house,[9] was opened in a frame building at the corner of Starkweather Avenue and West 11th Street in September, 1919, in one of the city's most densely populated areas. It had accommodations for about 50 children in its Day Nursery. The total attendance in all departments in 1920 was 13,700. Four trained social workers operated it with the assistance of voluntary helpers. For the fiscal year of 1921 the Community Chest allotted to it almost its entire budget of something more than $21,000.

Outside Cleveland, in Canton, a social center for young Catholics was opened in a four-story building in 1913 under the direction of the Catholic Community League.[10] In Youngstown the Guild of Catholic Women began its charitable endeavors in 1915. The Akron Catholic Service League[11] began its functions in 1920; a Catholic home for working girls had been started in the year previous.

The Federation of Catholic Societies was found to be ready for every good project. Bishop Farrelly gave it his full approval shortly after his coming. It supported in 1909 an agent who sought out foster homes for Catholic boys; three years later, in an understanding with Father LeBlond, Miss Margaret Kelly was appointed by the Humane Society of Cleveland to find such homes. In 1912 of the 76 children "placed" by the society in foster homes 33 were Catholics. The Bishop assigned the work of helping young people brought before Juvenile Court to the members of the St. Vincent de Paul Society; the expenses were met by the Catholic Charities Corporation. The Bishop expressed his desire that a branch of this society be established in every parish. The Cathedral Conference was organized in 1911 and the Particular

[9] *C.U.*, Feb. 11, 1910; Jan. 10, 1913.
[10] *C.U.*, Jan. 10, Sept. 5, 19, 1919.
[11] *C.U.*, Jan. 10, 1913; May 21, 1915; Apr. 23, 1920.

Council, composed of eleven conferences, in 1915. After the First World War it needed to be reorganized; in 1921 five new conferences were formed in a month.

To enable the Catholic deaf-mutes of the city to participate more intimately in the stream of Catholic life, despite their handicap, Bishop Farrelly in 1915 gave the care of their religious needs to Father Thomas Kirby, who was chaplain at Warrensville City Farm, and he pontificated at the first of the monthly Masses which were celebrated for them in the Cathedral. As early as 1895 Bishop Horstmann had found out upon investigation that there were 68 Catholic deaf-mutes in the city institutions. In 1900 Catholic children were about a third of the 63 pupils at a special school for them on East 55th Street. Father Ferdinand Moeller, S.J., the brother of the Archbishop, was interested in the work and was here in 1909 to give a retreat to the some 100 deaf-mutes in the city. He urged the establishment of a school for the children who were so affected.

The first Catholic books for the blind were placed in the Cleveland Public Library in 1903; they were loaned by the Xaverian Free Publication Society of Cincinnati.[12]

[12] *Catholic Bulletin Annual,* 1920.

SCHOOLS, THE SEMINARY,
AND RETREATS

ISHOP FARRELLY TOOK THE FIRST EFFECTIVE
steps towards the unification and standardization of the parish
schools and towards the uniformity of teacher training on
a diocesan scale. Bishop Horstmann, who was quite aware of
the need, had urged reorganization during the sessions of the
Catholic Educational Convention here in July, 1906; one result was
greater uniformity in the text books.[1]

Father William Kane,[2] already well trained in the work by Father
John Carroll of Holy Name who had the reputation of a skilled educator, was sent to the Catholic University in Washington and upon
his return was made superintendent of schools. Beginning in September, 1914, he introduced the so-called Shields System in the first grade.
In the previous summer 500 teachers were initiated in the new method
which limited the size of the classes, "worked down to the child," and
was subject to modification according to experience in the class room.
An advisory committee representing the teaching communities was
intended to recommend any changes in the system and to help the
superintendent in his work. A uniform calendar was prescribed for all
the schools which, moreover, were subjected to identical examination
questions sent to them from the central office.

The publication of an annual report in the *Universe* is the source of
information which shows the progress of the schools during Bishop
Farrelly's time. In the year previous to November, 1915, there were
41,769 pupils who were taught by 757 teachers in 122 schools. The
third report enters into more details: in the school year 1916–1917
there were 128 elementary schools (in 191 parishes), 47,597 pupils,
and 855 teachers of whom 68 were not religious. In addition there
were 771 students in the commercial high schools and 988 in other
high schools and academies. In the fourth year 1917–1918 there were
130 elementary schools (in 192 parishes), 49,000 pupils, and 898 teach-

[1] Horstmann to Supt. of Public Schools, Jan. 26, 1905, Aug. 5, 1907; Horstmann
to Wm. Raab, June 16, 1905; all in C.D.A. *C.U.*, July 13, 20, 1906; Feb. 25, Mar. 4,
1910.
[2] *C.U.*, Sept. 5, 1913.

ers of whom 71 were of the laity; there were 852 students in 18 commercial high schools, 10 of them in Cleveland; there were 1,120 students in other secondary schools. The report for the school year ending in June, 1922, shows a total enrollment of 55,984, an increase of 1,400 over the preceding year. An estimated one-half of the Catholic children of school age were attending the parish schools.[3]

It is interesting to note that nearly all the schools were in the hands of religious teachers. After the separation of the Toledo diocese there remained but one Catholic district school with its single teacher. In 1920 according to the *Catholic Directory* there were still 8 Brothers of Mary in 3 of the Cleveland elementary schools and some 71 lay teachers were helping the Sisters. A summary account of the activities of the several religious communities is taken from the same source.

The Sisters of Notre Dame had 230 members teaching 12,655 pupils in 25 schools; they had over 100 boarding students in St. Mary's Institute on Buckeye Road. Their imposing mother-house and novitiate, a brick structure on Ansel Road at Superior Avenue, was finished in 1914; the academy in the same building was attended by 674 girls. The Ursuline Nuns of Cleveland and Youngstown had 146 teachers in 20 schools and an approximate total of 7,914 pupils. In their academies were another 835 young women. The Youngstown community in 1919 acquired the old Andrews' homestead on Wick Avenue upon which they erected a large academy.

The Sisters of St. Joseph (of Cleveland) had 106 teachers in 12 parish schools and 8,291 pupils; their academy on Rocky River Drive had an enrollment of 300. The Sisters of the Holy Humility of Mary had about the same number of teachers and 5,820 pupils in 20 schools. At Lourdes Academy on Franklin Avenue they had 330 students, and at Mount Marie near Canton 163 boarders. The Sisters of St. Dominic of Adrian, Michigan, had 29 teachers and 1,748 pupils in 3 schools. Forty-five Dominican Sisters from Caldwell, New Jersey, had charge of 9 parish schools and 1,825 pupils; these Sisters also had 221 pupils in their academy built in 1914 near St. Bernard's Church in Akron.

The Polish Sisters of St. Joseph of the Third Order of St. Francis of South Bend, Indiana, had 48 teachers and 3,616 pupils in 5 schools. The Sisters of the Holy Family of Nazareth (of Pittsburgh) had 40 teachers and 2,317 pupils in 2 schools. The Franciscan Sisters of Blessed Kunegunda (of Chicago) had 41 Sisters teaching 2,240 pupils in 3 schools. The Sisters Servants of the Immaculate Heart of Mary (of Monroe, Michigan) had charge of 3 elementary and 3 parish high schools in which there were 33 teachers and 1,836 students. The Sisters of Charity (of Cincinnati) had 28 Sisters teaching in 2 elementary schools and 1 high school, with a total enrollment of 1,243 students.

Fifteen Sisters of St. Francis (of Tiffin) had charge of 2 schools and 786 pupils. Twenty-one Sisters of the Precious Blood had 924 pupils in 1 school. The Franciscan Sisters of Mary Immaculate (of

[3] Annual reports published in the *C.U.* by Dr. Kane.

Joliet, Illinois) had 17 teachers and 732 pupils in 1 school. The Franciscan Sisters of Our Lady of Perpetual Help had 11 members teaching 504 pupils in 2 schools. Other religious congregations which had less than 500 pupils in this diocese were the Felician Sisters (of Detroit), the Sisters of St. Francis of Christ the King (of Lemont, Illinois), the Sisters of Divine Providence, the Polish Franciscan School Sisters, the Benedictine Sisters, the Vincentian Sisters of St. Francis, and the Sisters of Loretto.

One of the greatest accomplishments of Bishop Farrelly was the Cathedral Latin School, a diocesan high school for boys. Doctor Edward A. Mooney, later Cardinal Archbishop of Detroit, then a professor at the seminary, was chosen to head the institution. In September, 1916, 160 young men in the first two years of high school began their classes in temporary quarters in the vicinity of the present structure. Ground was broken for the new building on August 13, 1917; Bishop Farrelly laid the cornerstone on the following October 7, a day described by himself as the happiest after his arrival in the city. Doctor John Cavanaugh, president of Notre Dame University and a native of Leetonia, then in this diocese, preached the formal sermon. On June 8, 1918, the Bishop dedicated the handsome structure. Bishop Shahan, of the Catholic University, was the speaker of the day.

The large tapestry brick building, on East 107th Street near Euclid Avenue, was designed in the Renaissance style by the well-known architect, Edward P. Graham of Boston, who had drawn the plans for several of the fine churches of the city. In it were twenty-one class rooms, laboratories, a small chapel, a gymnasium, and a large auditorium. This large hall was used for some of the conferences of the clergy and for a few ordinations.

The new school opened its doors to 387 boys in September, 1918. At the first graduation in 1920 among the 36 young men who received their diplomas were the future Bishop Begin and three others who became priests. The increased enrollment, 740, in the following September made it necessary to divide the school day into two full sessions, morning and afternoon. Eighty-seven graduated in 1922. Three priests of the diocese who taught the academic and 4 Brothers of Mary who taught the scientific subjects made up the first teaching staff. There were 12 diocesan priests (who also did parish work) and 22 or more Brothers teaching there in 1922 when Bishop Schrembs withdrew the clergy and gave complete charge to the Brothers who lived on the grounds. Eventually the system of parish support for the school was changed to that of individual tuition.

St. John's Cathedral College, a preparatory seminary, was opened in provisional quarters near the Latin School in September, 1920, with twelve students who had finished high school. Only one class was graduated; the remaining students finished their courses at St. Ignatius College or elsewhere.

A tuition-free diocesan Girls' High School was started in 1915 by

Doctor Kane in the Cathedral parish school building with 127 students. Sisters from the several religious communities were the teachers and support came from the personal exertions of Doctor Kane and the efforts of the Daughters of Isabella. Thirty-four young women graduated in 1920; two years later 410 were enrolled. The venture was discontinued not long afterwards.

The Girls' High School was a development of a previously existing commercial high school. Many of the parishes conducted a two-year commercial course which equipped the students for a career in the business world. A few parishes had a full four-year high school curriculum. Holy Name High School inaugurated by Father Patrick J. O'Connell, one of the first co-educational high schools in the city, was operated by the Sisters of Charity of Cincinnati. St. Vincent's and St. Mary's in Akron, and St. Mary's in Lorain supported full-scale high schools. The Sisters Servants of the Immaculate Heart of Mary were the teachers in charge of all three.

St. Ignatius College in 1911 celebrated the twenty-fifth anniversary of its foundation. Bishop Farrelly took the occasion to speak to the students of his need for more priests, saying that the diocese could use twenty new priests each year for twenty years thereafter. A fourth year was added to the college course in 1916 and, although many of the graduates entered medical school or law school or went directly into business, the majority of the students at this time left after the second year of college for the diocesan seminary. Some few joined the Society of Jesus or another religious order.

The attendance at the high school and college which still occupied the same campus broke all records. The great hall previously used as a chapel had to be divided into class rooms and laboratories. In 1914 a new brick gymnasium was put up on the campus. In 1921 there were 175 young men in the college department and 341 in the high school. They were taught by 25 Jesuits and 5 lay teachers. Loyola High School on Cedar Avenue had 170 students in 1916, 156 in 1918, and 106 in 1921, who were taught by 6 members of the Society of Jesus.

Bishop Farrelly had the plans already drawn[4] for a new St. Mary's Seminary when he was summoned by the Angel of Death. The antiquated buildings of old St. Mary's and their incongruous location in an industrial neighborhood had been calling for a remedy for some years. In his frequent visits to the seminary the new building was often the topic of conversation. Meanwhile he made life as comfortable as possible for the students and professors. As a temporary expedient a two-story brick residence hall with modern conveniences was put up in 1916 on the none too spacious grounds under the supervision of the rector, Monsignor James McFadden.

The people of the diocese itself were now offering their own sons

[4] Bishop's Council meeting, June 13, 1911; Apr. 16, 1915; Sept. 6, 1916; Mar. 5, 1919 (C.D.A.).

as students for the priesthood and the dreams of the earlier bishops were beginning to come true. The sons of the immigrants took the place of the generous self-sacrificing priests from Europe. In the interval after Bishop Horstmann's death Bishop Koudelka ordained eight priests; three were ordained in Baltimore by reason of a special mandate from Rome; three others were ordained in Cincinnati, three in Rome, and one in Rochester. On July 29, 1909, Bishop Farrelly raised his first class of young men to the priesthood. Among the ten was the future Bishop LeBlond. At the end of the year he ordained another Cleveland subject.

In 1910, on May 21, thirteen students assembled in the Cathedral for ordination when it was discovered that the mandate from Rome to ordain the Toledo subjects had not arrived. Bishop Farrelly conferred Holy Orders on the seven Cleveland students but the first group of new priests, which included the future Archbishop Alter of Cincinnati, to be ordained for the new Diocese of Toledo had to wait until June 4, pending the arrival of special Roman authorization. Altogether Bishop Farrelly ordained eighty-five priests for Cleveland, all except six natives of the country. During his administration eight, including the future Cardinal Mooney, were ordained in Rome and one each in Germany, Baltimore and Cincinnati. Archbishop Hurley of St. Augustine, Bishop Ready of Columbus, and Bishop Treacy of LaCrosse were made priests by Bishop Farrelly. In 1921 during the vacancy of the see Bishop Gannon of Erie ordained eleven Cleveland priests.

The old seminary buildings continued to be used for the annual spiritual retreats of the clergy although for want of space the priests were called in only every other year; two summer sessions could accommodate only half their number. During this time the lay retreat movement made great strides. The Bishop did all in his power to encourage the Knights of Columbus retreats at the Cathedral and when possible he addressed the men at the close of the exercises and suggested some good work for them to sponsor. The German Catholic League also held an annual retreat at St. Peter's or some other parish church and with remarkable success. Public retreats for women were inaugurated at the Cathedral and at the end of one of them, in 1916, 3,000 women received Holy Communion. Circumstances, however, favored closed retreats for women, in the hospitals or in religious houses. The closed retreats for men at St. Stanislas' in Parma were well patronized by Clevelanders and others who sometimes came a great distance to spend a few days in quiet contemplation.

49

NEW AMERICANS AND THE
FIRST WORLD WAR

THE PEAK OF IMMIGRATION HAD PASSED BE-
fore Bishop Farrelly's time but good numbers came into
the diocese up to the outbreak of the First World War.
At this period in the city of Cleveland it was estimated
that nearly seventy-five per cent of the population was of
foreign birth or of the first generation in this country. In the public
schools about sixty per cent of the 55,000 pupils were children of
immigrants. In the Catholic schools with their 15,000 the proportion
was probably higher.[1] The Bishop invited a few priests from Poland
and Hungary into the diocese to care for those who did not speak
English but for the most part he was dependent upon the sons of the
earlier immigrants who prepared themselves in the local seminary.
During the war an attempt was made to teach the clerical students
enough Hungarian and Italian to administer the sacraments in an
emergency.

Cleveland was the fourth largest city in the United States in the
number of Polish immigrants and their descendants and they constituted an important part of the Catholic population. In the diocese five
new parishes were erected for them by Bishop Farrelly; the older ones
put up new and imposing church and school buildings, as we have
seen above. The Bohemian Catholics had been well equipped with
church buildings; one new parish, however, was started in the city,
two new modern churches were built, and the equipment was improved in the older ones. New schools marked the progress of the
Slovaks in Cleveland, which is one of the large centers of Slovak influence[2]; outside the city three new parishes were inaugurated by
them.

In 1923 it was estimated that nearly fourteen per cent of the 220,000
Slovenians[3] in the nation lived here. St. Vitus' parish made many sacri-

---

[1] *C.U.*, May 13, 1904; Mar. 19, 1909.
[2] Farrelly to John Vincent Bonzano, Dec. 15, 1912, in C.D.A. *C.U.*, June 7, 1912;
July 21, 1925.
[3] *C.U.*, Sept. 28, 1923.

*Above Left:*St. Joseph Church and School, Collinwood.

*Above Right:*St. Cecilia School.

*Above:*St. Boniface School.

*Right:*St. Martha Church and School, Akron.

*Left:*St. Stanislas School.

*Right:*St. Hedwig Church, Akron.

*Left:*St. Joseph Academy, Rocky River Drive.

*Right:*St. Mary High School, Akron.

St. Ann School, Cleveland Heights.

Cathedral Latin School.

Notre Dame Academy and Motherhouse, Ansel Road.

fices for the great school which was put up; a new parish for them was started in Barberton. The oldest Magyar parish in the country, St. Elizabeth's, could well be proud of its great church; a new Magyar parish was erected in Cleveland, and three others in towns outside the city. The Croatians of Cleveland put up a school, and those of Youngstown a fine new church. The Lithuanians of the city built their first effective church plant at some distance from the crowded center of town; two new parishes for them were started outside the city.

It was in the Italian parish of the Holy Rosary that Bishop Farrelly administered the Sacrament of Confirmation for the first time in the diocese, in November, 1909, when he dedicated the new church. He sponsored Italian parishes in Lorain and in Youngstown. In 1911 two Ursuline Nuns and a group of Catholic women with the encouragement of the Bishop organized a confraternity to teach catechism to the children of Italian extraction who were attending the public schools. Cardinal Lauri, visiting Cleveland in the next year, celebrated Mass for these zealous catechists. St. Anthony's parish was the principal center; two others established on the West Side of the city opposite Protestant missions were the beginnings of future parishes.

For the Roumanians who followed the Greek Rite in the sacred liturgy five new missions, one of them on the East Side of Cleveland, were started during this time. As early as 1894 Monsignor Joseph Yazbek, who lived in Boston, came to Cleveland to minister to the few Syrian Catholics here. St. Elias' parish of the Melkite Rite served them all in 1908; those of the Maronite Rite built their own establishment in Bishop Farrelly's time; two new Syrian parishes were erected outside the city. Father Moses Nazarien for several years used the Cathedral chapel in which to gather the few Armenian Catholics together for religious services.

Many of the Slav peoples who came to the diocese in the last decade of the nineteenth century, from the old Austro-Hungarian Empire, from the Ukraine, Czechoslovakia, and Yugoslavia, belonged to the Oriental Ruthenian (Byzantine Slavonic) Rite[4] in which the old Slavonic language and to a limited extent the Magyar language were used in the celebration of the Holy Sacrifice. In the beginning they were subject like all other Oriental rites to the jurisdiction of the Bishop of Cleveland.

Because of the similarity of the liturgy they were sometimes the object of proselytism, as we have seen, on the part of the Russian Orthodox church officials. During a period in 1918 when there was no regularly appointed pastor in residence at St. John's Greek Catholic Church on Scovill Avenue near Charity Hospital, an Orthodox Greek priest insinuated himself into the good graces of the trustees of the parish and had the deed of the property transferred to the Russian Orthodox bishop. Previous attempts to have the title put in the name

[4] Voluminous correspondence in C.D.A.

of the Catholic bishop proved ineffective. A good minority of the parishioners opposed the change over to the Russian Orthodox religion.

The dispute was taken to court and was settled finally by the Cleveland Court of Appeals. Judges Washburn, Vickery, and Ingersoll on July 5, 1921, decided that an edifice erected and dedicated for the practice of a definite religious worship may not be legally diverted to the use of a different religious worship against the protest of even a small minority of the membership. The evidence clearly established that the congregation of St. John was Greek Catholic from the beginning. A change would be a real substantial departure from the trust, amounting almost to a perversion of it. The Court forbade anyone to officiate or to be pastor of the church under consideration except one appointed by the Greek Catholic bishop, appointed himself by the Pope. The title to the property as a result was restored to the Greek Catholic congregation and the schismatics were ejected.[5]

The first Ruthenian Rite priest to establish himself here was Father John Csurgovich who with the approval of his superior, Bishop Firczak of Munkacs, Hungary, and of the Congregation of the Propaganda in Rome organized the parish of St. John the Baptist in 1892. Bishop Horstmann, who had given him charge of all the Ruthenian Greek Catholics in the diocese, recognized it as a separate parish in 1895, after a frame church and parish house had been put up on Rawlings Avenue. A church on Buckeye Road near Ambler Street made its appearance in 1908. The congregation is composed principally of those of Hungarian descent.

The Rusins who belonged to the Ruthenian Rite began to hold separate religious services in 1898 in the Franciscan Chapel on East 23rd Street near Woodland Avenue. Afterwards they used an upper room in a building at Woodland Avenue and East 22nd Street. Under the direction of Father Keselak a church building at Scovill Avenue and East 22nd Street was acquired. The present fine brick church on the same site was erected in 1913; it was about this property that the Court of Appeals gave the decision mentioned above. The southwestern section of this parish was organized as the parish of the Holy Ghost; a brick edifice on Kenilworth Avenue at West 14th Street was put up in 1909.

St. Nicolas Greek Catholic Church for the Croatians, at the corner of Superior Avenue and East 36th Street, was dedicated in 1902; the building had been previously used by a Protestant congregation. Settlements of Ruthenian Rite Catholics at Lorain, Fairport, Ashtabula Harbor, Conneaut, and Kelly's Island were periodically visited by the Cleveland pastors. At Marblehead they had a church which was deeded to the Bishop of Cleveland in 1901. St. Michael's Church in Lorain put up in 1904 serves a Magyar congregation. St. Gregory's (Rusin) congregation was formed in Lakewood in 1905, and St. Michael's

[5] *C.U.*, July 15, 1921.

(Magyar) congregation, with its center on Bridge Avenue, a short time later.

Monsignor Andrew Hodobay came to the United States in 1902 in the interest of the Ruthenian Greek Catholics and acted as adviser to the local bishops in the conduct of their religious affairs until 1907. He then gave place to Bishop Soter Ortinsky, the first Ruthenian bishop consecrated specifically for service in this country. The new prelate was given charge of all the Ruthenian Rite churches in the United States, with his headquarters in Philadelphia. At first his exercise of authority depended upon the local bishops but in 1913 he was given independent jurisdiction. In 1924 the religious authority of the Apostolic Exarch of Philadelphia was restricted to the care of those who came from Galicia. The Ruthenians who came from Carpathian Ruthenia were made subject to the Apostolic Exarch whose headquarters were established at Homestead, Pennsylvania.

The shadow of the First World War fell across the middle years of Bishop Farrelly's administration. At the outbreak in August, 1914, the petition for peace was added to the Mass prayers, and in October the Bishop called upon his people to offer their devotions during the Month of the Rosary for the return of peace and for the welfare of the war victims. Passion Sunday of 1915, according to the desires of Pope Benedict XV who strove so ardently for world peace, was named as a day of supplication for it.[6] When on Good Friday of 1917 the United States entered the universal conflict, the Bishop reminded the faithful of the friendly relationship of the Government towards the Church and asked them to do all they could to assist in the crisis and to emulate what Catholics had done in the past. He pledged the allegiance of the Catholics of the diocese at a public service in the Cathedral which was attended by the Mayor and the city officials. Similar services were held in the other parishes.

The *Universe*, echoing the sentiments of the Bishop, stressed the bond between religion and patriotism and urged the immediate and vigorous support of the national effort. Catholic organizations took part in the patriotic parades and in the mass meetings of the citizens in Central Armory. They distinguished themselves as did the parish schools in the promotion of the sale of War Bonds, in conserving food, in the work of the Red Cross preparing clothes and bandages, and in everything else possible. The Catholic hospitals gave their full share of nurses for the care of the armed forces here and abroad. During the Lent of 1918 an estimated 300,000 of the faithful approached the sacraments in answer to the Bishop's appeal. In a solemn triduum of prayer, during which the Blessed Sacrament was publicly exposed, they begged divine aid and protection for the nation. Another General Communion was observed on May 30 after the declaration of the United States Congress that it was "the habit of our people to turn in

[6] *C.U.*, July 3, Aug. 7, Sept. 11, 30, Oct. 2, 1914. Circular, Mar. 10, 1915.

humble appeal to Almighty God for the protection of our cause and the restoration of peace." An open air Field Mass in Youngstown in Calvary Cemetery was another religious manifestation held in response to President Wilson's request.[7]

As had always been the case in times of national crisis the Catholics were well represented in the armed forces of the country. At this period they were estimated to be from eighteen to twenty per cent of the nation's population; yet Secretary of War Baker estimated that they constituted thirty-five per cent of the troops. Others also in touch with the situation would place the percentage at forty. An attempt to discover the number of those of this diocese in the First World War has been of little avail. According to the estimate of the *Universe,* however, there was a total of 12,468; and 458 of these died in the service.[8] These figures would seem to be incomplete. Each parish had its Honor Roll and its Service Flag, silver stars for the living, gold stars for the dead. Stanley Dobiez was the first Catholic of Cleveland to die in battle, Frank Reilly the first to die in the service. Patrick McMonigal of Youngstown was the first to receive the medal for extraordinary bravery.

At Loyola High School and Cathedral Latin School the students were given such military training as was possible. At St. Ignatius College[9] a Student Officers Training Corps was organized on the campus; two of these students died just as the war was halted. The college counted some 400 former students in the armed services, including many commissioned officers.

The pastors by mail and otherwise strove to keep the soldiers from their parishes conscious of their duty to God and religion. Some of the priests from Cleveland went to Camp Sherman in Chillicothe to help the overburdened chaplains.[10] The Government had entrusted the social welfare of the soldiers to voluntary non-governmental agencies. The National Catholic War Council was organized by the bishops to offer their assistance. Bishop Muldoon of Rockford, Bishop Schrembs of Toledo, Bishop Hayes of New York, Bishop Russell of Charleston, and the Sulpician, Father Fenlon, met with a committee of the National Federation of Catholic Societies to formulate plans for united effort. The Knights of Columbus were designated to carry out the program and they were principally responsible for having the first chaplains sent to the camps. The people of this diocese contributed liberally when the appeal was made for the funds which were used to support the first voluntary chaplains, and to build recreation halls and chapels on the military training grounds. From these funds also came the support of the K.O.C. secretaries who distinguished themselves overseas.

[7] *C.U.,* Apr. 13, 20, May 4, Sept. 28, Oct. 12, 1917; Feb. 15, Apr. 19, May 17, 24, 31, June 28, Sept. 27, Oct. 25. Nov. 8, 1918; Apr. 17, Nov. 7, 1919.

[8] *C.U.,* Apr. 12, 1918; June 16, 1920; Centenary special number.

[9] *C.U.,* May 17, 1917; Aug. 30. Sept. 13, 20, 27, 1918.

[10] *C.U.,* Aug. 17, Oct. 19, Nov. 30, 1917.

As the war continued the diocese was called upon to give its quota of chaplains, and this at a time when there was a scarcity of priests. The difficulty was met by "accelerating" the course of studies in the seminary and advancing the time of ordination. Father James M. Hanley, assistant priest at St. Bridget's, was the first to be allowed to go; he served with the 69th Regiment in France and was awarded the Distinguished Service Cross. Father Joseph N. Trainor, of the parish of the Immaculate Conception, was the second to receive his commission. Father James Cummins, of the Cathedral, was the fourteenth and the last. The others were Fathers Thomas McKenny, John Price, John Casey, Edward Gracey, Hilary Zwisler, George Koob, Anthony Sutter, Daniel Gallagher, Dominic Sweeney, Thomas Mulligan, and Leo Collins. Those of the chaplains who went overseas did not return until the summer of 1919.

Bishop Farrelly had been influential in having ministers of religion and divinity students exempted from inclusion in the Draft Bill passed at the beginning of the war which called for universal conscription.[11] Secretary Baker, a Cleveland man, was able to see that the country could not well dispense with the work of religion even in time of war.

The epidemic of influenza, which had claimed so many victims in the military camps, came to the city in the autumn of 1918. Cooperating with the health officials, Catholic churches and schools were closed for a short time in an effort to prevent the spread of the dread disease. In some of the parishes outdoor services were held; in one case the congregation assisted at Sunday Mass from the outside, looking through the windows of the basement church. During the emergency, when the hospitals were crowded, many victims had to be cared for in their homes. Some 400 Sisters of the various communities, at the appeal of the Bishop, distinguished themselves and reflected credit on the Church by tending the sick in the emergency hospitals and in their homes. In many instances the Sisters prepared the sick for the reception of the sacraments and did much to expedite the work of the hard-pressed priests. In November there were still 225 Sisters at their posts; although several contracted the sickness there were very few fatalities among them.[12]

As the hope of peace became brighter every priest offered his Mass on the Feast of St. Paul for the "return of charity and concord among nations." When the news of the Armistice reached Cleveland the Bishop instructed his people to make November 11 a day of special thanksgiving to God; he suggested that each anniversary be kept in the General Communion of all the faithful.

After the war, in 1919, at the invitation of Cardinal Gibbons all the bishops of the country gathered in Washington to devise ways and means for crystallizing the voice of the Church on pertinent public questions. This was the first time since the Third Plenary Council of

[11] *C.U.*, May 11, 1917.
[12] *C.U.*, Feb. 8, Mar. 1, Oct. 11, 18, 25, Nov. 1, Dec. 12, 1918.

Baltimore in 1884 that such a meeting was held. Bishop Farrelly, on his way to Rome, could not attend the sessions out of which came the famous pastoral letter on Reconstruction. He did attend the second meeting, however, in 1920 and he was one of the minority who were of the opinion that the National Catholic War Council had completed its purpose at the end of the war.[13]

Bishop Farrelly's relations with the civil authorities were friendly. However, the auditor of Lorain County had to be reminded that according to the State law the residences of the Sisters who taught in the schools were exempt from taxation.[14] Shortly before the arrival of the Bishop the Ohio Legislature had made a law which would legalize "meddling and prying" into Catholic institutions of correction. Protest was made against the manner of carrying out the law but the official visitation was allowed. The Prohibition Law, passed during the war, did not interfere materially with the supply of Mass wine, at least, not after the slight difficulty was adjusted, and the Bishop appointed a priest to supervise the distribution.

The flare-up of intolerance against the Church in Bishop Farrelly's time did not disturb the normal life of the Catholic community in Cleveland, although some disagreeable things happened in the smaller towns. The self-styled "Guardians of Liberty" were a pale recrudescence of the old A.P.A. and other societies of the kind. The infamous journal called the *Menace* served as their organ to vent their spleen and to publish the stereotyped calumnies about Catholics. An insulting article about the Shrine at Carey, Ohio, was carried in a local newspaper. On the other hand, a local Jewish newspaper refused an advertisement for the *Menace* and explained its proper attitude in an editorial. The *Catholic Universe*, also, printed and distributed pamphlets exposing the dishonest tactics of the scurrilous sheet. Judges, candidates for election in 1914, were queried by the Guardians about the manner in which they intended to use their office if they were successful. One small local journal reported the meeting at Gray's Armory at which a retired army officer attacked all Catholic candidates and even others who were inclined to show any toleration towards Catholics. The appeal of the Guardians, "invincible in peace and invisible in war," followed the usual line in reviving the old scare of the danger of the union of Church and State.[15]

As late as 1917 the Guardians were still pursuing their hateful tactics; but the approach of the time for the entrance of this country into the war put an end to the more open manifestations of this unfortunate but ever recurrent phenomenon.

[13] *C.U.*, Sept. 21, 1917; Feb. 1, Apr. 26, 1918; June 13, 1919; Feb. 13, Sept. 17, Oct. 1, 1920.

[14] *C.U.*, Feb. 28, 1908; Jan. 14, 1910. Decision, Nov. 19, 1907, *Ohio Law Bulletin, Supplement* (issue of Jan. 6, 1908), p. 11. Boff to Judge Adams, Dec. 10, 1908, in C.D.A.

[15] *C.U.*, Jan. 3, 10, Mar. 14, Apr. 11, July 25, 1913; Sept. 11, 18, 25, Oct. 9, 1914; Feb. 2, 1917. *Records of American Catholic Historical Society*, XLVIII, 210. Cleveland *Press*, Apr. 22, 1913. Cleveland *Leader* and Cleveland *Plain Dealer*, Jan. 22, 1917.

*Above Left:*St. James School, Lakewood.

*Above Right:*St. Catherine School.

*Right:*Ursuline Academy of the Sacred Heart, East Cleveland.

St. Vincent High School, Akron.   St. Mary High School, Lorain.

*Left:*Holy Family Church and School, East 131st Street.

*Right:*St. Vincent Charity Hospital Addition.

*Left:*St. John Hospital.

*Right:*St. Joseph Hospital, Lorain.

50

DIOCESAN AFFAIRS UNDER
BISHOP FARRELLY

URING BISHOP FARRELLY'S EPISCOPATE THE
papal letter on Frequent Communion, which was published in the *Universe* in September, 1910, was carried
into execution on a fuller scale. Many pastors had their
misgivings in the beginning about the age at which
children should be admitted to their First Holy Communion. They
feared that at least in some cases the child would be taken out of
the parish school once he had made his First Communion. The bishops
of the province, Bishop Farrelly among them, in a joint pastoral letter,
January 6, 1911, issued directions which were to dispel these hesitations
and to carry out the papal instructions.

The prelates were confident that the parish schools would still keep
the children. It was restated that Catholic parents were bound in conscience to send their children to them and that any exception would
have to have the sanction of the bishop. In places where there were no
parochial schools the parents were reminded that they were obligated
before God to send their children to the catechetical instructions which
were given twice a week by the pastor. The custom of the province
according to which First Communion was ordinarily deferred until the
child was twelve years of age was declared abolished.

Beginning with the Lent of that year children who had reached the
age of discretion and had the requisite knowledge and desire were to
make their "Easter duty." For that year the bishops advised that the
children be grouped in three divisions: those from seven to ten years,
those of eleven years, and those above that age. The pastor himself was
to see to the proper instruction of these children. When the younger
children had attained more mature years they were to receive several
days of instruction and preparation before the occasion of the General
First Communion when they would approach the Holy Table in a
body as was the custom previously. On April 28, 1912, Bishop Farrelly
personally distributed Holy Communion to the first such class in the
Cathedral. Time was to prove the wisdom of the Holy See and the
bishops in this matter as every priest who had the care of souls could
testify.

In March, 1916, it was announced that the Bishop had purchased a new site for his Cathedral. He had bought an L-shaped piece of land, 400 feet deep with a 270 foot frontage on the north side of Euclid Avenue just east of East Boulevard. In 1920, in preparation for the sale of the old Cathedral property, the so-called Schuster Building on the east side of East 12th Street north of Euclid Avenue was leased. It was to be used for the diocesan offices and a small chapel for Catholic business people in the downtown area. Death intervened, however, to change these plans.

The Bishop in 1913 introduced a new system of supporting the diocesan agencies and the seminary; the old one had long since become antiquated. Thereafter, a certain percentage of the ordinary income of the parishes was devoted to the purpose. For the more efficient support of the missions the various societies, some of them of a semi-private nature, were merged into a corporate unity called the Society for the Propagation of the Faith in Home and Foreign Missions. With the proceeds of the annual Mission Sunday collection taken up in all the churches help was not only sent to the missions abroad but the weaker parishes in the diocese were also afforded some assistance. An instance of the latter was the chapel in Chardon.

The love of the ancient music of the Church, which the Bishop had heard rendered so often in the Eternal City and which the Holy Father desired to see restored in all liturgical functions, induced him to bring out from Italy a professionally trained expert, Father Francis Clovis, who was made diocesan director of music. Soon the seminary choir had been trained in conformity with the papal directives and was able to give good account of itself at the pontifical celebrations at the Cathedral. Not long afterwards a choir of seventy laymen was prepared to sing at the Cathedral whenever necessary. Father Joseph N. Trainor, after his discharge from the army and after professional courses in Rome and the Isle of Wight, became musical director in 1921.

In the schools also every effort was made to inculcate the love of sacred music. Mrs. Justine Ward presided at the Teachers Institute in which she explained her method of "sight-reading" music. As a result the Catholic schools ranked very well in the Music Memory contests, sponsored by the Cleveland Orchestra in the interest of good music. The Bishop allowed his name to be used as a member of the Cleveland Irish Choral Society, which in its efforts to revive Celtic music brought the famous John McCormack to the city in 1911.

The deep personal devotion to the Holy See and the almost passionate attachment to Rome and things Roman, the result of his long residence there, remained with Bishop Farrelly to the end. His letters to the Holy Father breathe the spirit of humble submission and obedience to lawful authority. He took advantage of every occasion to propagate these sentiments in public and private conversation. In his first public address before the Chamber of Commerce, in 1910, Rome and the Pope and also his European experiences furnished the background of his plea for better understanding between nations. In obedience to the directions of the Holy Father, on December 27, 1910, he gathered his clergy together in the Cathedral and after the pontifical Mass he administered the oath of allegiance to the Pope and to Catholic doctrine in a denunciation of the heresy of Modernism which had just been formally condemned.

The papal jubilee of 1913, celebrating the 600th anniversary of the Emperor Constantine's decree emancipating the Church, was published and kept in this diocese, December 4–6, with a solemn triduum of prayers and thanksgiving in every parish. At the time of the death of Pope Pius X (August, 1914) the Bishop addressed a message to his people in which he mourned the passing of the one who had appointed him bishop, and at the pontifical Mass in the Cathedral on August 26 he was visibly moved as he spoke of his friendship with the dead Pontiff. All the churches were draped in the papal colors and prayers were offered for thirty days thereafter. A cartoon drawn by the well-known cartoonist of the Cleveland *Plain Dealer*, "Vic" Dohaney, depicting the Holy Father kneeling on a prie-dieu and contemplating the vision of the horrors of the war just begun, was much appreciated; it reflected the common feeling of sorrow and regret at the death of the Head of the Church who had done his utmost to prevent the tragedy. When in the first days of September Pope Benedict XV was elected, the Bishop celebrated a solemn Mass in the Cathedral. In response to his cablegram of congratulations the new Pope empowered him to authorize all the priests to bestow the apostolic benediction on their congregations.

51

LAST DAYS OF BISHOP

FARRELLY

AT THE MEETING OF THE BISHOPS OF THE COUN-
try in Washington in September, 1920, it was observed[1]
that Bishop Farrelly did not look well. No one suspected,
however, that he would not attend another such gathering. He had been accustomed to spend a few days periodically with old friends and relatives in Tennessee. On February 2,
1921, he set out from Cleveland on such a visit, intending to return in a
short time. A cold contracted while he was celebrating Mass there
developed into pneumonia. His secretary, Doctor Scullen, and his
personal physician, Doctor Merrick, summoned to Knoxville, found
him very sick. He received the last sacraments on February 11. Despite
heroic efforts to save him, he died peacefully on Saturday afternoon,
February 12, 1921. About an hour before his death he regained consciousness and expressed his resignation to the Will of God and tried
to console the sorrowing friends gathered around his bed. Doctor
Scullen quoted his last message to the priests of his diocese: "Tell the
boys that I love them."

A delegation of priests went to Cincinnati to escort the body of their
deceased superior to Cleveland. It lay in state in the Cathedral House
until its transfer to the Cathedral. The mourning faithful filed in end-
less procession past the catafalque to view the remains of their beloved
chief pastor. A special Funeral Mass was celebrated in the Cathedral for
the convenience of the school children who filled the sacred edifice.
Flags on public buildings were flown at half-mast; the churches were
draped in black. Archbishop Moeller of Cincinnati celebrated the
Funeral Mass. Ten bishops, about 400 priests, the Mayor, the city and
county officials, and a great throng of people crowded the Cathedral.
Bishop Morris of Little Rock, Arkansas, the friend of his youth,
preached the eulogy.[2]

With visible emotion and feeling he reviewed the career of his lifelong associate. He referred to his genuineness, his scholarly bearing, his

[1] Bp. Koudelka to N. Pfeil, no date, in author's possession.
[2] Bp. Morris' sermon, C.U., Feb. 18, 1921.

unfailing poise, his keen analytic mind, his knowledge of the world, his appreciation of the arts and sciences, his friendship with the rich as well as with the poor. He credited the dead prelate with having done more than anyone to dissipate intolerance towards Catholics in Tennessee. He recalled his love of country, his love for the Holy Father and for Rome. He characterized him as the high type of American of the old school, conservative, dignified, impatient of shams and fads. He took fond leave of his classmate in tones which moved the listeners to tears: "Farewell, Father, Brother, Friend."

The body of Cleveland's fourth bishop enclosed in a bronze casket was placed in the crypt under the high altar of the Cathedral. At the Month's Mind Mass[3] Father Thomas Mahon, who knew the Bishop intimately, declared that his reserved and apparently distant manner covered a gentle and forbearing disposition; he rarely gave commands, trusting that his confidence in them would produce the best results in clergy and people.

The sympathy of the whole community was expressed in the columns of the local newspapers. His pledge of whole-hearted service to all was recalled by them. Comments were made about his retiring disposition, his love for the clergy, his linguistic ability, his native conservatism bound up as it was with his approval of a venture, such as the Community Chest, once it had proved its worth and feasibility. Others remembered his love for fine literature, especially for the Italian poet, Dante, and for fine architecture, which he fostered in the diocese by his invitation to an Italian architect to establish himself in the city.

Bishop Farrelly was six feet tall and of average weight. Good portraits of him are to be found in the Cathedral House, in the Cathedral Latin School, and in several convents. The seminary library treasures a marble bust of him and of the other bishops, including his successor. Reserved and cautious when he came here from his secluded scholarly life in Rome, upon closer acquaintance with the clergy and people of this city he showed the genial, approachable, friendly side of his character. He could inspire confidence and enthusiasm; his plans for a new seminary were received by the clergy in conference at the Latin School with loud and prolonged cheers.

During his twelve years' administration the diocese, reduced in size as it was by the separation of Toledo, experienced great growth. The parish schools were not only multiplied but they were unified and modernized. The antiquated method of supporting the charities of the diocese was replaced by the Catholic Charities Corporation. Bishop Farrelly was one of the first bishops in the country to appoint a director of charities and to coordinate and strengthen the various social and welfare agencies. Thirty-six parishes were instituted and forty-seven new churches and schools were erected, among them several which are truly monumental. The diocesan finances were put on a modern and

[3] *C.U.*, Mar. 18, 1921.

efficient basis. The Bishop was justly proud of the Cathedral Latin School; he considered it his greatest accomplishment and he expected much from it in the development of an educated Catholic manhood.

The building of a new seminary and a new Cathedral was in the Providence of God reserved to his successors. The introduction of the practice of frequent Holy Communion in his time may well be taken as the symbol of the spiritual progress of the diocese under his leadership, the full accomplishment of which is known only to God. The diocese owes a great debt to the memory of Bishop Farrelly.

52

THE APPOINTMENT OF
BISHOP SCHREMBS

IMMEDIATELY AFTER THE DEATH OF BISHOP FAR-relly the consultors[1] chose as administrator Father William A. Scullen, who had been chancellor for six years. From February 14, 1921, until the installation of Bishop Joseph Schrembs on the following September 8 he directed the routine affairs of the diocese.

The fifth Bishop of Cleveland was born, March 12, 1866, at Wurzel-hofen, a suburb of Regensburg, in Bavaria, Germany, the son of George and Mary Gess Schrembs, his second spouse. Joseph was the second youngest of sixteen children and was baptized on the day of his birth in the parish church of nearby Sollern. He attended the primary school in Regensburg and sang in the famed boys' choir of that ancient cathedral town. When he was eleven years of age he came to America at the invitation of Bishop Rupert Seidenbusch, O.S.B., the newly consecrated Vicar Apostolic of Northern Minnesota, who visited the family.

At Latrobe in Pennsylvania he entered the Benedictine scholasticate of St. Vincent's Archabbey, where he met his older brother, Ignatius, then Father Rudicent, O.S.B., who died in 1908 at Johnstown, Pennsylvania, three years before Bishop Schrembs's consecration.[2] At the age of sixteen young Joseph left St. Vincent's, and taught school for two years at St. Martin's parish in Louisville, Kentucky, where another older brother, Jacob, who survived him, and a sister, Mrs. Elizabeth Sayer, lived. Adopted for the Diocese of Grand Rapids by Bishop Richter, he was sent to study philosophy and theology at the major seminary in Montreal, Canada; there he acquired remarkable facility in French. When he was a deacon he preached the Lenten sermons in the Cathedral of Grand Rapids, and on June 29, 1889, Bishop Richter raised him to the priesthood.

He made the difficult journey to Louisville, Kentucky, overnight to make it possible for his mother and relatives to assist at his First Mass on the following day, in St. Anthony's Church. His mother re-

---

[1] Minutes of the meeting in C.D.A. *C.U.*, Feb. 18, 1921.
[2] Fr. Peter Petz, O.S.B., was a cousin.

turned with him to Michigan.[3] After a short period at St. Mary's in Saginaw, he was appointed assistant and then pastor of St. Mary's in Bay City. In 1900 he was pastor of St. Mary's German parish in Grand Rapids, and three years later vicar general also.[4] In 1906 he led a pilgrimage to Rome and was made a domestic prelate to the Pope. On January 8, 1911, he was appointed Titular Bishop of Sophene and Auxiliary to Bishop Richter, who consecrated him in St. Andrew's Cathedral on the following February 22. Bishop Foley of Detroit and Bishop Maes of Covington were the co-consecrators. Archbishop Moeller of Cincinnati preached the sermon. Among the fourteen bishops who were present was Bishop Farrelly of Cleveland. Even as a pastor he had made a name for himself as an arbitrator in labor-management disputes in the furniture industry; he was also given credit for thwarting the insidious plans of the intolerant organization called the Ku Klux Klan in Grand Rapids.

He was appointed the first Bishop of Toledo, August 11, 1911, and on the next October 4 he took possession of his see. He spent ten years in organizing the new diocese. During his administration he ordained some sixty priests and instituted the annual seminary collection. At his invitation the Conventual Franciscan Fathers in 1912 took charge of the shrine at Carey, and the Redemptorists in 1916 made a foundation in Lima. The Mercy Sisters of Grand Rapids opened several hospitals: in 1912 at Tiffin, and in 1917 at Toledo and at Lima. The cloistered Visitation Sisters established themselves in the diocese in 1914, and the Franciscan Sisters of Rochester, Minnesota, started a provincial house at Sylvania. The Bishop induced the Ursuline Nuns of Tiffin and Toledo to unite in one community.

He inaugurated thirteen new parishes, nine of them in Toledo. In the older parishes more than twenty new church edifices were constructed. The plans for the massive Gothic Cathedral, drawn by the nationally known Comes of Pittsburgh, were carried into execution by Bishop Samuel Stritch, later Cardinal Archbishop of Chicago.

A zealous promotor of parochial education, he sponsored six new schools in Toledo and twenty-seven in the rest of the diocese. Father George Johnson coordinated the work in the schools and started the Teachers Institute in 1915. The Cathedral High School, begun in 1914 by Father John O'Connell, was made a central high school for the city. Doctor Karl J. Alter, later Bishop of Toledo and Archbishop of Cincinnati, organized the Catholic Charities Bureau in 1914. The Catholic Community House and St. Philomena's Home for working girls were opened, and a society for the religious care of the deaf-

---

[3] Bp. Schrembs to N. Pfeil (correcting a sketch of his life which was printed in *Der Grosse Herder*, X, 1170), Jan. 1, 1934, in the author's possession. *C.U.*, June 22, 1928. *C.U.-B.*, Mar. 1, 1929; June 29, 1934. Abp. McNicolas in 1936 recalled the then extant tradition in Grand Rapids about Fr. Schrembs's devotion to his mother, who died there, Aug. 19, 1905.

[4] His name was on the list of candidates for the vacant see of Columbus in 1903. *C.U.*, Dec. 18, 1903.

Archbishop Joseph Schrembs, fifth Bishop of Cleveland, 1921 to 1945.

Edward Cardinal Mooney, Archbishop of Detroit.

Archbishop Karl Alter of Cincinnati.

Archbishop Joseph Hurley, Bishop of St. Augustine.

Bishop Hubert LeBlond of St. Joseph, Missouri.

Bishop James McFadden of Youngstown.

Bishop Joseph Kouldelka of Superior.

Bishop August John Schwertner of Wichita.

Bishop Thomas O'Reilly of Scranton.

Right Reverend Stanislaus Gmuca O.S.B. First Abbot.

mutes was inaugurated. The work of the apostolate to non-Catholics was continued by Fathers Rupert, Goebel, and Sawkins.

In the persuasion that only a nationally united Catholic voice could command respect, Bishop Schrembs was much occupied in that endeavor. Long associated with the Catholic Men's Beneficial Association, he was one of its supreme trustees. At Toledo in 1912 he presided over the national convention of the German Catholic Union (D.R.K.C.V.) at which the Apostolic Delegate, Archbishop Bonzano, and nine other bishops were present. The National Federation of Catholic Societies held its convention under his auspices in 1915.

Toledo had had an unfortunate reputation for intolerance. Bishop Schrembs urged the Catholic societies there to make those who supported the outbreak of the Guardians of Liberty feel that they could not do so with impunity. He devoted a series of Lenten sermons, later published in a pamphlet,[5] to a refutation of the false charges made against the Church. In 1913, when he was in Rome at the head of a pilgrimage, his speech touching the temporal power and the freedom of the Holy Father attracted the attention of the Italian Government.[6]

During the First World War, as we have seen above, Bishop Schrembs was one of the four bishops on the administrative committee of the National Catholic War Council which acted in the name of the Catholic bishops and people in fulfillment of the pledge made to the Government "to do all that was possible for them to do for the preservation, the progress, and the triumph of our beloved country." Through this committee Catholics were given recognition and a hearing in matters affecting them and others. The distribution of funds gathered from the Catholic people for the benefit of the men in uniform was a very heavy responsibility. Its successful accomplishment merited the high praise given by the Government after the war.

The great majority of the bishops who met in Washington in 1920 were in favor of preserving the organization of the National Catholic War Council to deal with the problems of reconstruction in the postwar period. Bishop Schrembs was named one of the seven bishops who composed the permanent committee which supervised the various departments of Catholic activity. He had an important part in the elaboration of the well-known program of reconstruction which was issued in the name of the hierarchy. Many of its suggestions of legislation for the social betterment of the country were eventually followed by the Government. The energy, talent, and understanding displayed by Bishop Schrembs were responsible in good part for the institution and development of the National Council of Catholic Men and of the National Council of Catholic Women, in which Catholic societies were organized on a national scale. His ceaseless and untiring efforts in this regard merit well of the Church in America.[7]

[5] *Give Us a Hearing.*
[6] *C.U.*, Sept. 5, 1913.
[7] Bp. Ready in Golden Jubilee Number, *C.U.-B.*, 1939.

The news of his appointment to Cleveland was announced in the local newspapers on May 11, 1921, although the formal confirmation was not made in secret consistory by the Pope until June 16.[8] His fame had preceded him here; his past achievements gave reason to expect even greater things in Cleveland. In his first message he pledged himself to strive for the betterment and happiness of his new flock. "My door and my heart," he wrote, "shall ever be wide open to all my fellow citizens."

He arrived in Cleveland a few days before his installation. A group of priests and laymen including the city officials greeted him and the Toledo delegation at the old New York Central Depot on East 105th Street, and escorted them to Superior Avenue and East 30th Street. From this point he headed a grand procession of uniformed societies and of representatives of the city parishes and of the larger towns of the diocese until he reached the reviewing stand in front of the Cathedral House.

He was installed in the Cathedral on September 8 by Archbishop Moeller[9] who prayed that the noble qualities of his predecessors would be happily united in the new head of the diocese: "the zeal of Bishop Rappe, the wisdom and courage of Bishop Gilmour, the affable kindness of Bishop Horstmann, and the tempered firmness of Bishop Farrelly." Doctor Scullen in handing over his responsibility pledged the loyalty, obedience, and cooperation of priests and people, in the presence of twenty-eight archbishops and bishops, of mitered abbots and other dignitaries, and of the people who crowded the sacred edifice. The local clergy made their act of homage as they knelt before their new superior. The *Universe* expressed the conviction of all that he was a man of pleasing personality, of character, of courageous mind, who had the desire and the determination to devote all his energies to the work of God in his new field of endeavor.

At the dinner tendered him afterwards by the clergy, apparently in answer to a question, the Bishop announced that while he would urge the people of many national origins in Cleveland to cooperate with one another and take their rightful place in the great body of American citizens, he would also encourage them to cherish the language and customs of their European ancestors. In the evening of the same day a public reception was given him in the Knights of Columbus club rooms. The school children greeted him the next day in the Cathedral. His first appearance before a civic body at the City Club was the occasion for him to ask the business world to be more generous with the working man and thus enable him to raise his family in a Christian manner. The larger towns, including Youngstown where he presided at the close of the Knights of Columbus retreat, were given the opportunity to welcome him at a later date.

[8] Bull of appointment, in C.D.A. *C.U.,* May 13, June 3, July 15, 1921. J. R. Kenny to Pfeil, May 7, 1921, Pfeil papers, in author's possession. Cleveland *News*, Sept. 3, 1921.

[9] *C.U.*, Sept. 9, 16, Oct. 14, 21, 28, 1921.

Not long after his coming here Bishop Schrembs was notified that the Holy See by a decree of the Consistorial Congregation, June 1, 1922, had granted the request he had made as Bishop of Toledo, namely, that Erie, Richland, and Huron Counties be transferred from the jurisdiction of the Bishop of Cleveland to that of the Bishop of Toledo. Commissioned by the Apostolic Delegate to execute the decree, Bishop Schrembs in full pontificals, September 6, 1922, entered St. Peter's Church in Mansfield (Richland County) and took his seat on the temporary throne. The papal documents proclaiming the change were then read aloud. He thereupon divested himself of the robes of office and gave up the throne to Bishop Stritch. In the three counties were some sixteen parishes, including Sandusky, Norwalk, and the above-mentioned Mansfield. Nearly all the parishes had schools with an average total attendance of 2,400 pupils. Eighteen of the twenty-three priests concerned elected to remain in their places.[10]

[10] Original decree, Washington, July, 1922, Num. Prot. 5413f, in C.D.A. *C.U.*, July 14, Sept. 8, 1922.

53

DIOCESAN AFFAIRS UNDER
BISHOP SCHREMBS

THE EXPANSION AND MODERNIZATION OF THE diocesan offices, or episcopal curia, begun under his predecessor were continued by Bishop Schrembs. The number of consultors was increased from nine to eleven; the deaneries were divided to make eleven of them. At the beginning of 1923 the names of new officials were announced. Father Carl Frey became diocesan secretary; he was succeeded by Father George Habig and then by Father Floyd L. Begin. Father Patrick J. O'Connell, at an earlier date assistant to Monsignor Houck and then pastor of Holy Name, was brought back as chancellor in 1922; when he became pastor of St. Rose's in 1925, he was succeeded by Father James A. McFadden. As time went on, the Bishop entrusted more and more of the business of administration to his chancellor and his secretary. Monsignor Joseph F. Smith was made vicar general and later pastor of the Cathedral. Monsignor Thomas C. O'Reilly, his predecessor, was made the ecclesiastical superior of the religious women of the diocese; he afterwards became Bishop of Scranton.

The Church tribunal for marriage cases was reorganized and Doctor Scullen, who had been appointed pastor of Holy Name, was made the head of it in April, 1928. Then, years later, Doctor Begin assumed this responsibility; the court was again modernized according to more recent instructions from Rome. The full quota of pro-synodal judges was appointed and the work expedited; appeal cases were sent here from Cincinnati.

The building commission, reorganized by the Bishop, was given full control of all new construction and of all important alterations. In 1926 all the diocesan offices,[1] including the chancery with its archives, were gathered together in what is now known as the National Broadcasting Company Building on Superior Avenue near East 9th Street. The few rooms in the Cathedral House, used by the chancery since the early days of Bishop Gilmour, were relinquished to the parish.

In 1938 the Bishop again reorganized the diocesan agencies: all divisions of activity were placed under the supervision of one of the

[1] *C.U.*, Dec. 25, 1925.

older boards or under that of new ones; each department was given a director. The School Board was assigned the additional responsibility of supervising the high schools and academies, the Sisters' College, the Confraternity of Christian Doctrine, and the Newman Clubs. The Board of the Propagation of the Faith controlled all efforts made in the diocese in aid of home and foreign missions. In 1922 the Society for the Propagation of the Faith, founded by a humble Frenchwoman in Lyons, France, had been given pontifical recognition, and the headquarters were transferred to Rome. In the next year the Holy Father established the society in the United States attaching to membership in it the indulgences proper to it and the Society of the Holy Childhood. Accordingly Bishop Schrembs organized the Catholic Missionary Union and made Father James A. McFadden, until then rector of the seminary, the first diocesan director.

Beginning at the Cathedral in August, 1923, the latter launched a campaign for an increased enrollment of members; workers made a house-to-house canvass of the parishes. In its first year of existence the local society divided approximately $93,000 between the foreign and home missions and the struggling parishes of this diocese. The system of envelope collections in the churches on a designated Sunday in October was readopted in 1927 by Father Michael J. Ready, the new director. He had considerable success in interesting the school children who were responsible for nearly one-eighth of the $127,000 collected in 1929. The depression naturally restricted the ability of the people to help the missions.

When Father John Treacy became director in 1932 he introduced the Catholic Students Mission Crusade, an educational movement calculated to arouse the interest of young people in the missions. It was started at a meeting of several thousands who listened to addresses by Archbishop McNicolas, Archbishop Beckman of Dubuque, and Bishop Schrembs, all of whom inspired them with new zeal for the crusade. At the tenth national convention of the organization in Cleveland in 1937 the pontifical Masses in the Public Auditorium, pageants, special programs, and 150 missionary exhibits with attendant missioners brought home to the diocese the importance of mission endeavor. It is to be noted that the local office had helped to erect mission chapels in the South and in the West.[2]

The Board of Catholic Charities had, in addition to its obvious responsibilities, the direction of the St. Vincent de Paul Society, the Big Sisters, and the work with the Catholic nurses, the deaf-mutes, and the inmates of public institutions. In 1923 the Bishop assigned Father William L. Newton the duty of caring for the religious needs of the Catholic deaf-mutes; other priests were appointed for the same work in

---

[2] *Acta Apostolicae Sedis*, June 8, 1922. *C.U.*, June 28, 1922; July 20, Sept. 21, 1923; Sept. 19, 1924; Feb. 20, 1925. *C.U.-B.*, June 10, Sept. 30, 1927; May 25, 1928; Annual Review, 1929; Jan. 10, 24, 1930; Annual Review, 1930; Apr. 17, 1931; Annual Review, 1933; Aug. 20, 1937; Oct. 10, 1941.

the Akron, Canton, and Youngstown areas. The members of the local circle of the National Catholic Alumnae Association undertook to give their assistance. The Bishop himself gave First Holy Communion to twelve handicapped children who had been instructed at the Cathedral. Special arrangements were made for sending some children to Catholic institutions for deaf-mutes.

Father Eugene Gehl of Cincinnati and the Redemptorist, Father Higgins, were brought here for work with the adults. In 1933 the Church of St. Columbkille in the downtown district was made the headquarters for this special endeavor. Father Arthur Gallagher, the pastor and diocesan director, installed hearing devices in the church and in the confessionals. The Good Samaritan League, founded for the purpose of helping the deaf-mutes, was useful in many ways, especially in finding them employment. The Ursuline Nuns, who then lived in the old convent on East 55th Street not far from the school for the deaf,[3] were assisted by seminarists and others in the religious instruction of the Catholic children in that institution. Later St. Colman's Church became the center of such activity on the west side of the river.

Two new boards were those of Priestly Activities and Catholic Action; the Bishop's consultors were the official moderators though each department had its own individual director. Under the first heading came clerical conferences, the junior clergy examinations, church music, Eucharistic societies, the study of papal encyclicals and of church legislation, the vigilance committee, and the censorship of books. To the Board of Catholic Action were subject the departments having to do with the Catholic press and the local journal, the *Universe-Bulletin,* the local branches of the national councils of men and women, press and radio relations, youth activity, the Legion of Decency, the Apostleship of Prayer, the People's Eucharistic League, high school sodalities, rural life activities, and the study of papal encyclicals and of civil legislation affecting the Church.

At the beginning of the new administration, April 16, 1922, eighty-nine of the previously existing statutes of the diocese were reprinted in a pamphlet under the title of *Rules and Regulations of the Diocese of Cleveland.* They concerned the administration of the sacraments, the relation of pastor and people, finance, marriage, and funerals. The obligation of every parish to support a school is stressed as well as compulsory attendance at these schools or, in their absence, at catechetical instructions. Children who attained the use of reason were to be admitted to their First Holy Communion. There was to be no public celebration of marriages on Sunday, nor funerals on that day except in emergencies. These regulations were also printed on a large placard which was displayed in the vestibule of every parish church.

The question of relocating his Cathedral on Cleveland Heights or

[3] Alexander Graham Bell School for the deaf maintained by the Public School Board, opened in 1898.

on the property near University Circle, bought by his predecessor for the purpose, occupied the mind of Bishop Schrembs in the early days of his incumbency. In March, 1924, the property at Superior Avenue and East 9th Street was put up for sale. In 1926, however, it was found to be more advantageous to sell the University Circle property to Western Reserve University, and a few years later he publicly announced that the Cathedral would remain where it was as long as he was Bishop of Cleveland.[4]

Though the Cathedral had long since lost its original character as a prosperous parish church, it was supported by the city in general, by the transients who lived in the hotels, and by the many Catholics who worked in the stores and the business offices. The Bishop inaugurated the daily Mass at noon which was well attended particularly during Lent and the months dedicated to the Blessed Mother. The printers' Mass at two o'clock on Sunday morning was introduced in 1929. A Holy Hour was held every Thursday in the early evening. The priests of the Cathedral after 1931 celebrated Mass every Sunday in the county jail. The members of the so-called Service Clubs, postal employees, policemen, and firemen, found the Cathedral well suited for their annual common reception of the sacraments.

Monsignor Joseph Smith, the pastor, enlarged the sanctuary and renovated the interior of the venerable structure, and had the exterior painted gray to give it an attractive appearance. The steeple was removed in 1928. The chapel in the school building which had been used for week-day Masses and for hearing confessions was made over into a recreation hall in the year previous. What had been the residence of the Brothers, who had long since ceased to teach in the school, was adapted for use as a Community Center for meetings, for an information bureau, and for a while as the home of the Sisters who were taking a census of the parish, instructing the children, and preparing them for their First Holy Communion. An interesting episode was the baptism of the first Chinese convert in 1940; Father Martin Burke of the Maryknoll Fathers had converted him and several others in the Chinese colony which is within the boundaries of the Cathedral parish.

In the movement of the city population to more congenial surroundings in the suburbs were a proportionately great number of Catholics. To take care of their spiritual needs Bishop Schrembs established thirty new parishes in Greater Cleveland, sixteen of them territorial and one for the Colored. In the older parishes in the same area and during approximately the same period twenty-five new churches, twenty-seven new schools, and twenty-one new church-school combinations were erected and four buildings were adapted for divine worship. Outside Greater Cleveland but within the present boundaries of the diocese twelve new parishes were created, seven of them terri-

[4] Minutes of Bishop's Council meetings, May 5, Dec. 28, 1923; Mar. 12, 1926; all in C.D.A.

torial; in the earlier parishes twenty-one new churches, twenty-four new schools, and eight new church-school combinations made their appearance and four buildings were converted into churches.

In the area now comprised in the Diocese of Youngstown seventeen parishes were started, eleven of them territorial; in the older parishes thirty-three new churches, nineteen new schools, eight new church-school combinations were put up and six buildings were refitted for Catholic worship.

Of the parishes in the two dioceses in 1940 Bishop Schrembs had erected one-fourth, that is, forty-seven, and six missions were raised to the status of a parish. Of the 271 churches forty-seven per cent, and of the 180 elementary schools fifty-eight per cent, were built during this approximately twenty-year period. Moreover, several of the larger and more substantial churches were solemnly consecrated: in Cleveland, St. Agnes' and St. Thomas' in 1923, St. Philomena's and St. Aloysius (upon completion) in 1925, St. Colman's in 1928, St. Catherine's and St. Procop's in 1929, and St. Patrick's (Bridge Avenue) in 1931; in Canton, St. John Baptist's in 1924; in Massillon, St. Mary's in 1926.

In the interest of public devotion to the Blessed Mother Bishop Schrembs inaugurated several shrines, and encouraged the old Catholic custom of making pilgrimages to them. One of these was what he called the national Shrine of Our Lady of Lourdes, a replica of the grotto in France, on the property of the Sisters of the Good Shepherd at Providence Heights (Euclid Avenue near Chardon Road) which he dedicated in 1926 in the presence of thousands of people. In the next year he dedicated a similar shrine put up by Father Edward Spitzig in the town of St. Joseph (Randolph). A replica of the Shrine of Our Lady of Levocha was built, through the generosity of the women of St. Wendelin's parish, on the grounds of the Vincentian Sisters of Charity in Bedford in 1930.

Others are the Shrine of Our Lady of the Rosary on the property of the Sisters of the Incarnate Word in Parma which was blessed in 1936; the Shrine of Our Lady of Czestochowa in Garfield Heights on the property of the Franciscan Sisters of St. Joseph; and two dedicated to Our Lady of Perpetual Help, one at the Home for the Aged on Lander Road, the other in the church of the name on Neff Road. All these and a few others are very popular among the people who flock to them during the summer months.

54

YOUNGSTOWN UNDER BISHOP SCHREMBS'S JURISDICTION

A BRIEF NOTICE OF THE NEW BUILDINGS IN THE present Diocese of Cleveland and that of Youngstown will prove of interest.

In the city of Youngstown, at its western end, the parish of St. Brendan was organized by Father Andrew A. Crehan who completed a brick combination church and school in 1925; a mission chapel dependent upon this parish was opened in a remodeled frame building at North Jackson by Father Charles Mc-Donough in 1937. The Dominican Fathers returned to northern Ohio when Father Charles A. Haverty was appointed to organize the parish of St. Dominic in the southern section of the city; he put up a frame church in 1923 and completed a brick combination church-school in 1929. The Magyar parish of Our Lady of Hungary, a division of St. Stephen's, was inaugurated by Father Stephen Nyiri who directed the building of a brick basement church in 1929 and of a frame schoolhouse and hall shortly afterwards. The Slovak parish of St. Elizabeth was initiated by Father Joseph L. Kostik who in 1922 was responsible for a brick combination church and school.

In the older parishes in the same city much progress was to be recognized. In the Slovak parish of the Holy Name of Jesus a modern twelve-room school and auditorium put up under the supervision of Father Stephen Kocis was dedicated in 1927. In the parish of the Sacred Heart of Jesus a modern stone schoolhouse was completed by Father John I. Moran in 1923. St. Casimir's brick combination church and school put up by Father Ignatius L. Dembowski was dedicated by Bishop Schrembs in 1927. The frame Church of St. Francis of Assisi was completed in 1925 under the direction of Father Dominic Alinskas. The fine brick Romanesque Church of St. Matthias was finished by Father Francis Kozelek in 1926; the old frame church was converted into class rooms. The imposing stone Church of St. Patrick, in the Spanish Gothic style, put up under the direction of Father William A. Kane was dedicated by the Bishop in 1926; in the same year six class rooms and a gymnasium were added to the school. In the parish of Sts. Peter and Paul a modern two-story brick schoolhouse was completed by Father John A. Stipanovic in 1927. In the parish of St. Stanislas Kostka a brick combination church and school put up by Father John M. Zeglen was dedicated by the Bishop in 1925.

At Alliance (outside the city of Youngstown) the brick Romanesque Church of St. Joseph raised through the efforts of Father Alfred J. Manning was dedicated by Bishop McFadden in 1941. At Ashtabula St. Joseph's new school was completed by Father Matthew O'Brien in 1927; the frame Church of Our Lady of Mount Carmel was enlarged in 1928 by Father John J. Davidson. At Boardman the parish of St. Charles was started by Father Patrick Ferron in 1926; a frame chapel and small school was completed by Father John Crann two years later. At Brewster a parish was founded by Father Thaddeus Marchant who in 1928 put up a frame chapel. At Campbell the Italian parish of St. Lucy was organized by Father John Iammarino who transformed a hall into a church building in 1937. In the Slovak parish of St. John the Baptist a school was opened by Father John Krispinsky in 1926.

In the city of Canton Bishop Schrembs entrusted the founding of the new parish of St. Benedict to the Benedictine Fathers of Latrobe, Pennsylvania; Father James Spalding put up a frame church in 1923; Father Nicolas Seidl completed a brick combination church and school two years later. The Benedictines had charge also of the mission chapel at Waynesburg built in 1927. The new Slovak parish of the Sacred Heart was founded by Father John G. Hamrak who erected a frame church in 1923. In the Italian parish of St. Anthony a brick L-shaped combination church and school in the Spanish Mission style was finished by Father Joseph A. Riccardi in 1927. In the Roumanian parish of St. George a brick Romanesque church, sufficiently completed under the direction of Father Vamosiu in 1934 to be used by the congregation, was dedicated by Bishop McFadden in 1939. In the parish of St. John the Baptist the new hall and high school building put up by Father Edward P. Graham was dedicated in 1926. The fine stone Romanesque Church of St. Joseph completed by Father Clement Treiber was dedicated by Bishop Schrembs in 1932. In St. Paul's parish a new brick school made its appearance under the supervision of Father John A. Stepanic in 1928.

At Conneaut the brick church was enlarged by Father John Nolan in 1927. At East Palestine a brick Gothic church put up by Father Joseph M. Heid was dedicated in 1941. At Geneva a fine brick church in the Colonial style was completed in 1927 by Father Daniel J. Gallagher, the first resident pastor. At Girard a fine brick Gothic church erected under the guidance of Father Michael J. Coan was dedicated in 1942; a frame mission chapel improvised at McDonald in 1928 was attached to this parish. At Harrisburg a new brick school was opened in 1926 by Father John T. Kasinski. At Jefferson a brick Spanish Romanesque church put up by Father Edward Spitzig was dedicated in 1925. At Kent a modern brick school was completed through the exertions of Father James Nolan in 1924. At Leetonia a new brick schoolhouse was put up by Father Richard P. Gibbons in the same year.

At Lisbon, through the generosity of James Costello, Father Roman Bacher was able to erect a fine brick Gothic church which was dedicated by Bishop McFadden in 1938. At Louisville a modern brick schoolhouse made its appearance in 1922 under the direction of Father Nicolas Weckel who remodeled the church ten years later. At Lowellville the brick church was enlarged by Father Daniel B. Kirby in 1937. At Mantua the church was entirely remade by Father Edward Gracey in 1924.

In the city of Massillon Father John Casey, the pastor of St. Joseph's from 1922 to 1933, added four class rooms to the school and fashioned a parish hall in the basement of the church which itself was entirely remodeled. In St. Barbara's parish (West Brookfield) a modern brick school put up by Father Hilary Zwisler was dedicated in 1924. In St. Mary's parish a large brick school was completed by Father Nicolas Hassel in 1929. On the grounds of the State Hospital for the Insane the brick Gothic Chapel of St. Dympna made its appearance in the same year through the personal exertions of Father Austin W. Scully, the chaplain.

At Masury in 1934 a new parish was inaugurated by Father Joseph Bresnyak, who completed a brick Colonial church in 1940. At Maximo a brick schoolhouse was finished by Father Raymond Gorman in 1924. At Middlebranch a brick schoolhouse was transformed into a chapel in 1929 under the direction of Father Ralph Kotheimer; it was enlarged and improved by Father James Stevenson a little later. At Milton Lake a frame mission chapel was put up in 1927. At Newton Falls the concrete-block church in the new parish of St. Joseph was completed in 1923 under the supervision of Father Frank B. Tomanek. An independent Polish parish was reconciled with the Bishop under the title of Our Lady of Czestochowa in 1928; eleven years later a frame church was completed by Father Max J. Krajdzieski.

At Niles the brick Church of Our Lady of Mount Carmel was finished by Father Nicolas Santoro, C.PP.S., in 1924. St. Stephen's Church, which had been damaged by fire, was restored and remodeled by Father James M. McDonough, who in 1929 acquired a large building as a recreational center for the parish. At North Canton a large brick schoolhouse was put up by Father Ralph Kotheimer in 1927. At Orwell a frame schoolhouse was refashioned for use as a chapel by Father Anthony Suwalski in 1925. At Ravenna a fine brick Romanesque church put up under the supervision of Father James T. Daley was dedicated in 1927. At St. Joseph in 1923 a modern brick schoolhouse was opened by Father George Reber.

At Salem the beautiful stone Gothic Church of St. Paul reared under the supervision of Father Maurice Casey, who had previously enlarged and remodeled the school, was dedicated by Bishop Schrembs in 1931. At Sheffield Center Father Augustine A. Binna directed the conversion of a frame church to Catholic worship in 1937. At Struthers the brick school of St. Nicholas made its appearance in 1928 under the direction of Father Daniel O'Shea. At Vienna Father Richard Gaffney reorganized the parish and made a chapel out of a frame schoolhouse in 1934.

In the city of Warren the Slovak parish of Sts. Cyril and Methodius was organized by Father George Bobal in 1928; a frame schoolhouse was remodeled for use as a church by Father John M. Kandrac in 1933. The Polish parish of St. Joseph was founded by Father Adolph Bernas who put up a frame church in 1929. In the original parish of St. Mary a large brick school was erected by Father Emil Schaider in 1926. At Wellsville a large brick Gothic church was put up by Father Edward Gracey in 1927.

55

CHURCH AND SCHOOL BUILDINGS
IN CLEVELAND (1921-1943)

WITHIN THE LIMITS OF GREATER CLEVE-
land, on the east side of the Cuyahoga River,
Father Thomas P. Mulligan organized the eastern
section of Holy Name parish into that of St.
Timothy in 1923; he completed a brick combina-
tion church and school two years later. In the neighboring Garfield
Heights Father John W. Solinski founded the Polish parish of Sts.
Peter and Paul; in 1928 he put up a frame combination church and
school and ten years later a separate modern brick school. At the
southern end of Garfield Heights the parish of St. Theresa, the Little
Flower of Jesus, was organized by Father Richard P. Gibbons who
erected a brick combination church and school which was dedicated
in 1928. To the east of here, in Maple Heights, Father Joseph W.
Koudelka started the parish of St. Wenceslas; in 1923 he put up a brick
school and a year later a frame church.

In South Euclid, previously served by St. Ann's, the new parish
of St. Gregory the Great was founded by Father Maurice Riley in
1922; the frame church he put up was dedicated in 1925, when a frame
school also was opened. The eastern section of St. Ann's was used
to form the Gesu parish in University Heights; Father Francis J.
Rudden, S.J., improvised a frame church in 1927, and Father Benedict
J. Rodman, S.J., put up a brick combination church and school in
1940. The eastern section of St. Philomena's in East Cleveland was
organized into the parish of Christ the King by Father Thomas V.
Shannon in 1928; he used temporary quarters until the completion of
a brick combination church and school in 1930.

In Euclid, just east of Cleveland, the parish of the Holy Cross was
established in 1924 by Father Thomas A. Kirby who two years later
completed a brick combination church and school. The Slovenian
parish of St. Christine was founded by Father Joseph Czirbucz who
put up a frame combination church and school in 1926. The Lithuanian parish of Our Lady of Help was founded by Father Anthony M.
Karuziskis who remodeled a frame building for use as a church in 1930.

Between Euclid and Cleveland, in the old Collinwood district, the parish of the Holy Redeemer was organized among the Italians by Father Martino Compagno, of the Order of Our Lady of Mercy, who put up a frame chapel in 1925 and completed a brick combination school and auditorium three years later; the latter was remodeled for use as a church by Father Achilles P. Ferreri in 1940. The parish of Our Lady of Mount Carmel, a division of St. Marian's, was established among the Italians who lived along Woodland Avenue by Father William O'Donnell in 1936; the first basement church built in that year was abandoned for a site near East Boulevard and Woodland Avenue, where a brick Gothic church appeared in 1939. Just south of here the new parish of St. Benedict, a division of St. Ladislas', was entrusted to the Slovak Benedictine Fathers from Lille, Illinois; the brick combination church and school put up by Father Ladislas Necid, the pastor of St. Ladislas', was completed by the Benedictines and was dedicated by Bishop Schrembs in 1929. The southern section of St. Elizabeth's had been organized into the parish of St. Margaret by Father Ernest Richert who put up a frame church in 1922; eight years later Father Andrew Koller was responsible for a brick combination church and school.

Worthy of special notice was the establishment of the parish of Our Lady of the Blessed Sacrament for the Colored in 1922. With the substantial assistance of the family of Monsignor Joseph Smith the first pastor, Father Thomas McKenny, was enabled to construct a brick church on East 79th Street between Central and Quincy Avenues which was dedicated by Bishop Schrembs in the next year. Mother Drexel's Sisters of the Blessed Sacrament opened a school with forty-four pupils in a frame building which soon needed to be enlarged.

In the older parishes on the East Side of the city many new churches and schools appeared during this period. The Holy Name high school building was much enlarged by Father William A. Scullen in 1923. In the parish of the Holy Trinity an eleven-room brick school and gymnasium building was finished by Father Joseph M. Trapp in 1925. In the parish of the Immaculate Heart of Mary a sixteen-room brick school and auditorium was put up by Father Marion J. Orzechowski in 1926. The large imposing brick Romanesque Church of the Nativity of the Blessed Virgin was completed by Father Vaclav A. Chaloupka in 1927; three years later he had finished a fourteen-room brick school-house. In the parish of Our Lady of Czestochowa a brick combination church and school made its appearance under the direction of Father John Zeglen in 1930.

The Church of Our Lady of Lourdes was remodeled by Father Oldrich Zlamal in 1941. The brick combination school and church-auditorium in the parish of Our Lady of Peace was completed by Father James Cummins in 1923. The imposing brick Romanesque Church of St. Aloysius with its clerestory was completed by Father Francis Malloy in 1925. The brick combination church and school of

St. Andrew in the Spanish Mission style was put up by Father Stanislas Gmuca, O.S.B., (later abbot) in 1926. In St. Ann's parish the beautiful imposing stone schoolhouse with its twenty-one rooms made its appearance under the supervision of Father John M. Powers in 1925. St. Catherine's large brick school was completed by Father James Quinn in 1926. St. Cecilia's brick school was put up by Father Edward A. Kirby in 1925.

In the Syrian parish of St. Elias a non-Catholic church edifice was refashioned for Catholic worship by Father Malatios Mufleh in 1937. In the parish of St. Hyacinth a brick combination school and auditorium was put up by Father Joseph M. Sztucki in 1925. In St. Jerome's parish a twelve-room brick schoolhouse (enlarged by four rooms thirteen years later) made its appearance through the efforts of Father Leo Hammer in 1923. The fine brick Romanesque Church of St. Lawrence was completed by Father John J. Oman in 1940; the roofed-over basement had been in use as a church after 1924, permitting the previous old church to be made into class rooms. It was dedicated by Bishop McFadden on August 11, 1940. In the parish of St. Marian a seven-room frame school, the first Italian one in the diocese, was opened by Father Joseph Trivisonno in 1928.

In St. Mary's (Collinwood) a seven-room brick schoolhouse was put up and the church was enlarged under the direction of Father Vitus Hribar in 1928. The brick combination church and school of St. Paul in Euclid was erected in 1931 by Father Edward Gracey. In St. Philomena's in East Cleveland eight rooms were added to the stone schoolhouse in 1924 and the church was enlarged and remodeled in the next year by Monsignor Joseph F. Smith. The very large brick School of St. Stanislas, under construction for eleven years, was completed by Father Theobald Kalamaja, O.F.M., in 1934. In the parish of St. Thomas Aquinas a nineteen-room brick schoolhouse and auditorium was put up by Father Thomas F. Mahon in 1929. The fine imposing brick Church of St. Vitus, in the Lombardy Romanesque style with a clerestory and galleries, completed by Father Bartholomew Ponikvar, was dedicated by Bishop Schrembs in 1932.

The West Side of the city saw several new parishes. St. Rocco's Italian parish was established in 1922. In the beginning a small frame chapel put up by an independent congregation was reconciled and used for divine service by Father Alphonse de Maria and Father John Davidson. In 1926 a brick combination church and school made its appearance on Fulton Road under the supervision of Father Sante Gattuso, of the Order of Divine Mercy. In the same year this priest started the mission of Our Lady of Mount Carmel in the northern section of his parish; a hall was used for Mass until in 1933 a frame chapel on Detroit Avenue was improvised. The Slovak parish of Our Lady of Mercy was organized by Father Francis Dubosh in 1922. The small frame church on West 11th Street, previously used by an independent congregation, was acquired, and a small frame schoolhouse served its purpose until the erection of an eight-room brick schoolhouse and basement hall in 1926.

Farther out from the center of the city the western section of St. Ignatius' was organized into the parish of St. Vincent de Paul by Father Michael J. Flanagan. He supervised the construction of a brick L-shaped combination church and school on Lorain Avenue at West 134th Street which was ready for Christmas, 1922; the school section completed in 1924 had to be enlarged by eight rooms two years later. South of here the parish of the Annunciation (the title of the old French church which had been superseded by that of St. Emeric) was organized by Father Peter V. Hyland, who in 1925 put up a brick combination church and school on West 130th Street at Bennington Avenue. On the western boundary of the city, in what was formerly West Park, the parish of Our Lady of the Angels was organized by Father Columban Valentin, O.F.M. In 1923 he put up a brick schoolhouse which was enlarged by four rooms eight years later; the first church was the monastery chapel erected in 1904, which was much enlarged by Father Linus Koenemund, O.F.M. The latter was responsible for the exceptionally fine brick Romanesque church on Rocky River Drive which was dedicated December 8, 1941 by Bishop McFadden. Across Rocky River to the west, in Fairview Park, the parish of St. Angela de Merici was founded by Father Francis J. Stanton and a frame combination church and school on Lorain Road was completed in 1924; a modern brick school and auditorium was opened by Father Michael L. Stevenson in 1940.

North of here three new parishes were erected in territory previously belonging to St. Rose's and St. James's. The parish of St. Clement was founded by Father Joseph J. Schmit who in 1923 completed a brick church in the Basilica style at Madison and Lincoln Avenues in Lakewood; in the next year an eight-room brick school was opened which in 1927 was doubled in size and equipped with a gymnasium. The parish of St. Luke had as its founder Father John A. Nolan who put up a small frame chapel on Bunts Road near Clifton Boulevard in Lakewood in 1923; a modern brick school was opened by Father James Heffernan in 1927. St. Christopher's in the town of Rocky River was started by Father Richard Patterson who put up a frame church at Lakeview Avenue and Detroit Road in 1923; in the reconstruction of it after a fire a brick school and auditorium were added; in 1941 four more class rooms doubled the capacity of the school.

At the southern boundary of Cleveland, in Parma, the parish of St. Charles Borromeo was organized by Father Nicolas F. Monaghan, who in 1924 put up a frame church at Ridge Road and Charles Avenue and opened a school which in 1928 was housed in a modern brick building. The parish of St. Francis de Sales, also in Parma, was inaugurated by Father Francis J. McGlynn who built a frame church and hall on State Road at George Avenue in 1932; a frame school opened in 1935 had eight rooms four years later. The Polish parish of Corpus Christi was founded by Father Anthony B. Orlemanski who in 1935 put up a frame church on Stickney Avenue near the Parma boundary line.

Among the older parishes on the West Side, in that of the Blessed Sacrament the frame church was much enlarged in 1922 and the school also in 1930 by Father Stephen Wilson. The great brick and stone Church of Our Lady of Good Counsel in the Italian Renaissance style, with an imposing bell tower, completed by Father Sebastian Kremer, C.PP.S., was dedicated by Bishop Schrembs in 1930. In the parish of St. Barbara a one-story brick combination church and school on Denison Avenue was finished by Father John W. Solinski in 1925. St. Boniface's Church was enlarged by Father George Reber in 1932. In St. Colman's parish a twelve-unit brick school was put up by Father Charles Martin in 1924. In the parish of Sts. Cyril and Methodius in Lakewood the great brick and stone Romanesque church, with an impressive campanile, raised by Father Francis Dubosh was dedicated by Bishop Schrembs in 1931. St. Emeric's brick combination church and school on West 22nd Street was completed by Father Joseph Hartel in 1925.

The Church of St. Helena was enlarged and resurfaced with brick by Father George Babutiu in 1939. In St. Hedwig's parish in Lakewood a brick combination church and school made its appearance in 1926 under the direction of Father Michael Konwinski. The monumental stone Romanesque Church of St. Ignatius, with a high bell tower, which under the supervision of Father Thomas Hanrahan had been in construction for five years, was completed in 1930. Another monumental stone church, that of St. James in Lakewood, in the Sicilian Romanesque style, with its graceful towers and clerestory, was brought to completion by Father Michael D. Leahy in 1934; the roofed-over basement had served the congregation for the previous eight years. The fine brick Romanesque Church of St. John Cantius on Professor Street was erected by Father Joseph P. Kocinski in 1925; a parish hall appeared the next year.

St. Mary's Church on West 30th was resurfaced with cement by Father Augustine Hackert, S.J., in 1925. In St. Patrick's parish (in old West Park) a ten-room brick school and auditorium was put up by Father Edward T. Calvey in 1930; eight years later the stone church was remodeled by Father William Thorpe. In the parish of St. Rose a basement church was completed by Father Patrick J. O'Connell in 1928. In St. Stephen's parish a large auditorium was remodeled for use as a social center by Father Joseph Gerz in 1924. In St. Wendelin's a brick combination church and twelve-room school put up through the exertions of Father Augustine Tomasek was dedicated in 1925; ten years later a social hall (and gymnasium) was completed.

Outside Greater Cleveland, in the city of Akron, the parish of the Immaculate Conception was organized by Father John L. Waldeisen who put up a brick combination church and school in 1924. A part of St. Vincent's was formed into the parish of St. Sebastian by Father Hilary Zwisler who was responsible for a brick combination church and school in 1929. The Croatian parish of Christ the King was organized by Father Wenceslas Vukonic who refitted a non-Catholic church for Catholic worship in 1935; four years later it was enlarged and modernized by Father Michael G. Domladovac. The Italian parish of St. Anthony was founded by Father Salvatore Marino who constructed a basement church in 1934; the superstructure with its interesting marble mosaic interior was completed in 1941. The Syro-Maronite congregation of Our Lady of Mount Lebanon was responsible for a brick church and hall in 1937.

In the older Akron parishes there was considerable expansion. The Church of the Annunciation was enlarged and remodeled by Father Richard Dowed in 1924. In the parish of the Sacred Heart the brick Romanesque church and a hall made their appearance in 1925 under the direction of Father Ferdinand Pupinsky. In the parish of St. Hedwig a brick combination church and school was put up through the exertions of Father Francis Kozlowski in the same year. In the parish of St. John the Baptist a four-room brick school was constructed by Father George Novak in 1927. St. Martha's brick combination church and school was finished in 1924 by Father John McKeever. In St. Paul's parish a nine-room brick schoolhouse and gymnasium appeared in 1926 through the efforts of Father Clement H. Boeke who three years later was obliged to renovate entirely the original church building. In St. Vincent's a large brick gymnasium and an addition to the school were erected by Father John Scullen in 1927.

At Amherst a four-room stone school (and hall) was put up in 1924, and the church was enlarged in 1932 under the supervision of Father James Eischen. At Avon the modern brick School of the Holy Trinity made its appearance in 1925 under the supervision of Father Albert J. Aust, who had the additional task of rebuilding the great stone church which had been severely damaged in the tornado of 1924. At Barberton the fine brick and stone Romanesque Church of St. Augustine, with its rich marble interior, constructed under the direction of Father John Schmitz was dedicated in 1925. The brick Romanesque Church of the Holy Trinity and an auditorium were completed by Father Athanasius Kovacs, O.F.M., in 1933. In the parish of Sts. Cyril and Methodius a four-room brick schoolhouse (and gymnasium) was put up by Father Edward J. Stanko in 1926; five years later he had completed a fine brick church in the Byzantine style. In St. Mary's parish the church was enlarged and a hall fitted up in the basement by Father Joseph P. Napierkowski in 1933.

At Bedford a brick combination church and school was completed by Father George Stuber in 1928. In Berea the brick Romanesque Church of St. Adelbert was erected in 1938 under the supervision of Father Francis Duda. In the same town St. Mary's brick schoolhouse was completed by Father William Moseley in 1926. On Broadview Heights (Royalton) a brick Romanesque church, built by Father Michael F. Shannon with funds raised in a general appeal made to the diocese, was dedicated by Bishop Schrembs in 1931. At Chardon the frame church was entirely rebuilt and enlarged by Father Michael L. Stevenson in 1932. At Cuyahoga Falls a modern brick school made its appearance in 1923 through the efforts of Father John L. Lillis who eleven years later rebuilt and enlarged the church.

At Elyria in the Polish parish of the Holy Cross a brick Romanesque church, with school rooms in an annex, constructed under the supervision of Father Joseph L. Kuta was dedicated in 1924. The Magyar parish of the Sacred Heart was established in 1922 by Father Louis Unger; divine services were held in the basement of St. Mary's until in 1929 the rectangular brick Romanesque church completed by Father Joseph Peter was dedicated by Bishop Schrembs. St. Mary's, the parent church of the city, was remodeled and enlarged by Father James T. Dailey in 1932.

At Fairport St. Anthony's brick combination church-school-auditorium building was finished by Father Zoltan Demko in 1926. At Independence the church was enlarged by Father George Koob and the school by Father Francis Boehlein.

In the city of Lorain the Croatian parish of St. Vitus was organized in 1922 by Father Joseph Medin who two years later completed a brick Romanesque church with a fine bell tower. The parish of St. Anthony was founded by Father Isidore Rafferty, O.F.M., Conv., in 1923; improvised quarters were used for divine service until the completion in 1928 of a brick basement church and school. In the original parish of St. Mary a fourteen-room brick school made its appearance in 1923 under the supervision of Father John J. Johnston, who also, in 1931, completed a fine stone church in the Georgian style which replaced the brick church destroyed by the tornado of 1924. In the parish of the Holy Trinity a brick Romanesque church erected through the exertions of Father Wenceslas F. Novak was dedicated in 1927. The Spanish mission of Our Lady of Guadalupe was established in 1928 in a remodeled brick building near St. John's church; for four years it and St. John's parish were in charge of Spanish Franciscans. In St. Ladislas' parish a six-room brick school and basement hall was opened by Father Andrew Koller in 1926. The frame Church of St. Peter was enlarged in 1931 by Father Achilles P. Ferreri, who two years later converted a stone schoolhouse into a church at South Amherst for the congregation which he had organized there. The fine brick Romanesque Church of St. Stanislas was completed by Father Leo A. Rygwalski in 1940.

At Loudonville a pretty English Gothic church of Briar Hill stone begun by Father Lawrence E. Rockwell was completed by Father Edmund A. Kirby in 1939; the principal costs were borne by a wealthy family in the parish. At Mentor a brick church in the Colonial style was put up by Father William A. Thorpe in 1935. At North Ridgeville a brick Romanesque church completed by Father John Rhein was dedicated in 1923. At Painesville a large gymnasium was erected and an addition made to the school in 1939 under the supervision of Father William J. Gallena who in the next year remodeled and enlarged the church. At Parkman St. Edward's parish was organized by Father Edward Fasnacht (of Warren); in 1928 a Protestant church building was refitted for the use of the rural congregation.

The mission at Peninsula was given its first resident pastor in Father James William Fitzgerald who in 1935 enlarged the church. At Sheffield, in Lorain County, a room was added to the school in 1927 by Father Adam Senger. Solon received its first resident pastor in the person of Father Olderic Mazanec who built a frame church in 1930. At Thompson the church was enlarged in 1934. At Wadsworth a fine brick Romanesque church made its appearance in 1929 under the supervision of Father Carl J. Anthony. At Wickliffe a brick mission chapel was put up in 1923 by Father William Nash. At Willoughby a large brick combination church and school was erected by the same Father Nash in 1926.

St. Peter Church, Loudonville.   St. Anthony Church, Akron.

*Left:*Assumption Church,
Broadview Heights.

St. Mary Church, Mentor.   Our Lady of Mount Carmel Church,
Wickliffe.

*Left:*St. Lawrence
Church.

*Above Left:*Sacred Heart
Church, Wadsworth.

*Above Right:*Holy Trinity
Church, Barberton.

*Right:*Sts. Cyril and Methodius
Church, Lakewood.

56

IMMIGRATION INTO THE
DIOCESE

ALTHOUGH ON EVERY OCCASION WHICH OFFERED Bishop Schrembs urged the newcomers to the country and their descendants to adapt themselves to their new environment as soon as possible and to become citizens, he had a just regard for their ancestral language and their traditions. Following the example of his predecessors he insisted that there should be larger interracial contacts, all united in the common devotion to the Church. As a token of respect the Bishop acquired the ability to speak at least a few words to the various groups in their native tongue. English, French and German he knew very well. At a meeting of the foreign language pastors in Cleveland, speaking in favor of a project to inaugurate junior high schools, he recommended that the study of the language and culture of their European ancestors be made part of the curriculum even though English were the ordinary medium of instruction.

The descendants of the earlier Irish and German immigrants composed the bulk of the Catholic population of the diocese. Especially in the schools but also in the churches English replaced German in parishes previously known as German. Nevertheless, the Bishop encouraged the study of the language and culture of the land of his birth. He had always been an ardent promoter of the National Central Union of German Societies; he generally addressed their conventions in other cities and in 1925 he welcomed them in Cleveland. After the First World War he did much for the relief of the German war sufferers and in his pastorals he urged the general cooperation of the diocese in sending help to them and to the people of the Near East. He was chairman of the Schlachter Memorial Committee which had as its purpose the saving of the orphan children of Germany. On his visits to Europe he always visited his homeland except in the last years, after his forthright denunciation of totalitarianism. Here in the city he presided at a mass meeting and a dinner in honor of the heroic Cardinal von Faulhaber of Munich who came in 1923 to thank the people for their generosity.

The Bishop in the autumn of 1921 took part in a large mass meeting of Irish sympathizers who demanded that Ireland have its share in the benefits of freedom proclaimed in the Fourteen Points of President Wilson. The Association for the Recognition of the Irish Republic was very strong and active in this city, raising funds for that purpose. Eamon de Valera, the first President of the Irish Republic, was well received here shortly after the war; in subsequent visits in 1928 and 1930 he received some assistance for the foundation of his newspaper, the *Irish Press.*

Among the first of the Slavs to settle in Cleveland, the Bohemians had become prominent citizens, in the professions, and in the general life of the city. At a meeting of the Alliance of the Bohemian Clubs in Cleveland in 1931 the Bishop encouraged them to make their united influence more telling. One new Bohemian parish was started during this period: the new St. Wenceslas' at Maple Heights was composed principally of the people of the older parish of the same title who moved from the industrial district to the suburbs. With the exception of the latter all the seven Bohemian parishes in the city in 1940 had their full complement of parochial buildings.

The Polish Catholics of Cleveland were equally well organized, faithful to the Church, and prominent in civic life. It was at the invitation of Bishop Schrembs that the Polish Archbishop of Petrograd, Archbishop John Cieplak, came to America from the Soviet prison from which he had been released as a result of world-wide protest. The Bishop presided at the great mass meeting in Public Hall in his honor in 1925, and when the heroic prelate died in New York he accompanied the body back to Poland at the request of the Polish Government. The Bishop showed his sympathy for the liberty-loving Poles by pontificating in the Cathedral here at the tenth anniversary of the independence of their fatherland. And in the Church of the Immaculate Heart of Mary in the presence of the Polish Ambassador he protested his horror at the invasion and partition of Poland by the Russians and Germans; he ordered a special collection in the diocese for the relief of the stricken country. Of the twenty-six Polish parishes in the diocese in 1940 six of them were erected during this period; and seven of them helped to compose the new Diocese of Youngstown. In Cleveland their schools were among the largest and several new and more beautiful churches had been erected in the older parishes, monuments to the faith and self-sacrifice of priests and people.

The Slovak Catholics, also, prospered with the years, marking the progress with large new schools and fine churches. As manifest signs of their strength and of their devotion to the Church their powerful fraternal and beneficial societies filled the Public Auditorium for the pontifical Masses celebrating their anniversaries. The visit of Slovak prelates on their way home from the Eucharistic Congress in Chicago was another such occasion, when the patriot Monsignor Andrew Hlinka, the head of the Peoples party in Slovakia, spoke in the presence of Bishop Joseph Carsky of Kosice and Bishop Paul Jantauch of Trnava; Bishop Schrembs, as was his custom, read a message in the Slovak language. The Slovak Ladies Union which had important headquarters in the city joined with other societies in supporting the new Benedictine high school here; they also founded a bourse for the new seminary. Of the twenty Slovak parishes in this diocese in 1940, seven had been established by Bishop Schrembs and in 1943 nine were taken by the Diocese of Youngstown.

During the episcopate of Bishop Schrembs great strides were made in the religious care of the Italians, who to a great extent still continued to remain grouped together in certain sections of the city. Many, however, had become members of the territorial parishes. The Fathers of the Order of Mercy, the Sisters of the Most Holy Trinity, and the Filippini Sisters were invited into the diocese for work among their countrymen. The Mercedarian Fathers, as they were called, were given charge of St. Rocco's parish in the Fulton Road district in 1924 and of the mission attached to it, with its center on Detroit Avenue. They also began the parish of the Holy Redeemer in 1926 in the old Collinwood area, with its center on Kipling Avenue; but after fifteen years and some unpleasant experience it was given in charge to a priest of the diocese. Other parishes, one on the East Side, one in Akron and a mission in Wickliff, were also entrusted to secular priests. The first Italian parochial school in the diocese was opened in the parish of St. Marian in 1926; the Mercedarians began schools in St. Rocco's in 1927 and in Holy Redeemer in 1928. These schools served also as catechetical centers for the public school children. In St. Peter's, in Lorain, Father Vincent O'Dea contrived an effective system for the religious instruction of his young people who attended the public schools. The Ursuline Nuns were the first teachers in St. Marian's School (increased in size in 1928) and in that of the Holy Redeemer. In 1927 the Italian community of the Sisters of the Most Holy Trinity, whose headquarters after 1932 were in a stone residence on Mapleside Avenue, came to Cleveland and took charge of St. Rocco's School and eventually of that of St. Marian. They also taught catechism in the parish in which they lived, namely, that of Our Lady of Mount Carmel, and in the mission of the same title on the West Side.

Five Sisters of the Pontifical Institute of Religious Teachers Filippini took up residence in Holy Rosary parish, the largest Italian parish in the diocese, in 1936. Attempts to inaugurate a parochial school have been made; the relations with the public school authorities in the neighborhood continued to be very cordial. The Sisters organized clubs and sodalities, visited the people in their homes, and taught catechism every day after school hours. The same services were rendered by the Sisters in St. Anthony's parish in Akron. They took charge of the elementary school and the catechetical instruction in the parish of the Holy Redeemer, succeeding several other communities which had had that responsibility earlier.

Of particular interest was the amalgamation of the pioneer Italian parish of St. Anthony in Cleveland with the older territorial parish of St. Bridget, both of them in the downtown section of the city. Most of the people of St. Bridget's had moved out of the district, leaving the once very prosperous parish in a condition in which it barely survived the depression years. In a solemn ceremony in September, 1938, they were merged under one pastor, Father John Humensky; the Italian parishioners were thus given the advantage of a large parochial school which was under the direction of the Sisters of the Incarnate Word. St. Anthony's old church edifice on Carnegie Avenue was taken over by the Syrian congregation of St. Maron. An attempt at a similar amalgamation of St. Ann's and of St. Anthony's Italian parish in Youngstown was abandoned after a trial. In 1940 there were sixteen Italian parishes (including a mission station) in the diocese, of which seven were established during this period; the Youngstown diocese took six of them at the time of the division.

The Hungarian Catholics of the city were honored in 1926 by the visit of Cardinal John Csernoch, the Primate of Hungary, who had attended the Eucharistic Congress in Chicago. He came for the golden jubilee celebration of the ordination of Monsignor Charles Boehm, the pioneer Hungarian priest in this country and an old friend. In 1940 there were ten Hungarian parishes in this diocese, two of them erected during Bishop Schrembs' incumbency; two are now in the Youngstown diocese. Four Hungarian parishes of the Byzantine Rite were also to be found within the present limits of this diocese.

Archbishop John Saric of Sarajevo and Bishop Anton Jeglich of Ljubljana were feted by the Catholic Slovenians of Cleveland when they called here on their return from the Chicago congress mentioned above. The descendants of the original families have become prominent in business and professional pursuits. One of them was mayor of this city before he was thrice elected Governor of Ohio. In 1940 there were six Slovenian parishes in this diocese, one of them erected by Bishop Schrembs.

Archbishop Nicolas Dobrecic, the Primate of Serbia, was entertained at St. Paul's Croatian parish in 1926 on his way home to Europe from Chicago. In 1940 there were four Croatian parishes in the diocese; one in Akron had been established by Bishop Schrembs; one was of the Byzantine Ruthenian Rite; and in 1943 one became part of the Youngstown diocese.

Another distinguished visitor during the same summer was the Lithuanian prelate, Bishop Matulevicius of Vilna, who was respectfully received by the pastor and people of St. George's parish. Bishop Schrembs established a second parish of that nationality in the city in 1929. St. Peter's in Akron, however, was made a territorial parish in 1926 to insure its continuance. One parish was relinquished to the Youngstown diocese.

The vast majority of the Catholic immigrants had remained in the cities; they made their living in the various industries and generally raised their children in a parish of their own language. Their children, however, and grandchildren easily took their place with the children of the older immigration and sometimes they composed a good proportion of the territorial parishes. An interesting instance was the parish of the Annunciation in which were to be found Poles, Croatians, and Italians predominating the membership in a newly developed section of the city.

Some of the Slav immigrants, on the other hand, established themselves on small farms especially in the eastern part of the diocese. Many took to the land at the time of the depression; the early Connecticut settlers were abandoning their worn-out fields to the more enterprising immigrants. There were very few Catholic churches in these areas; the more hardy of the faithful made sacrifices to attend them and to see to the religious instruction of their children. The problem of transportation was a serious one and many grew careless. To remedy one situation, the mission of Parkman in the farming district was made into a regular parish with a resident pastor who was conversant with the Slav languages. A group of farmers around Sheffield Center in Ashtabula County, who had set up their own organization, through the good offices of the Polish Association of America were brought back to the Church in 1936; a refitted former Baptist church was renamed after St. Andrew Bobola and served as a center for the reclamation of many others.

57

CATHOLIC EDUCATION

THE ADMINISTRATION OF BISHOP SCHREMBS witnessed great expansion in the development of facilities for Catholic education: many new parish schools, high schools, and academies were started; two colleges for women and the Sisters' College were inaugurated; the Jesuit College was developed into John Carroll University; and a new diocesan seminary building made its appearance.

In 1922 a school board of five members was appointed and Doctor John R. Hagan replaced Doctor William Kane[1] as the superintendent of schools. The new director after special training here and abroad brought about the complete unification of the parish schools and their standardization at a high level. The Sisters' College[2] combined the efforts of the previous nine separate normal schools in which the teachers under episcopal direction received the latest and best scientific training for their important work. It was opened for the summer session of 1928 in the old Cathedral school which had housed the discontinued Girls' High School. In August of the following year 119 teachers, members of eight religious communities, received their certificates. In 1931 the charter was amended and a full four-year college course in accord with the requirement of the State Department of Education was inaugurated.

Bishop Schrembs had the happiness in June, 1933, of presenting 84 Sisters, the first graduates, with the degree of Bachelor of Science in Education and with teaching certificates recognized by the State. Previously 230 had received provisional teachers certificates. By the year 1936 ninety-six per cent of the instructors had State certificates. In that year priests and Sisters composed the staff of 34 teachers for the 143 full-time students and the 370 in the Saturday sessions. Three years later the college was empowered to grant the master's degree in education such as was required for high school teachers, principals, and supervisors. In 1939 through affiliation with St. John's and Charity

[1] Dr. Kane, later made a domestic prelate, was appointed pastor of St. Patrick's and dean in Youngstown, where he died in 1937.

[2] Incorporated and authorized by the Ohio Dept. of Education, 1928. In 1935 it was accredited to the American Association of Teachers Colleges. *C.U.-B.*, Mar. 8, 1935.

St. Andrew Church.

St. Adalbert Church, Berea.

Nativity of the Blessed Virgin Mary
Church.

St. James Church, Lakewood, Ohio.

St. Clement Church, Lakewood.

Our Lady of the Blessed Sacrament
Church.

Sts. Cyril and Methodius Church and School,
Barberton.

St. Emeric Church.

St. Stanislas Church, Lorain.

Nativity of the Blessed
Virgin Mary Church,
Lorain.

Hospitals the course in nursing education was started. The college was supported by the diocese.

The depression years brought on a grave financial crisis in the public schools which had depended principally upon the fruits of local taxation. The State government relieved the situation with the gasoline tax of 1933, the sales tax of 1935, and finally by guaranteeing minimum operation costs. It occurred to the managers of the Catholic schools that the State legislature might at least temporarily give some assistance to the equally hard-hit parochial school system. Bishop Alter of Toledo published a pamphlet to explain the plight: *Twenty-five Questions and Twenty-five Answers, a Thesis on the Question of State Aid for Parochial Schools.*

In an open letter to the Governor the plea was based on the acknowledged right of the parents according to the Supreme Court decision in the Oregon school case to choose the kind of school their children attended. Admitting the right of the State to set standards, the Church authorities pointed to the high rating and excellent experience of the teachers in the Catholic schools who were trained according to the requirement of State law. The four Catholic superintendents of schools in the State drew up the arguments supporting the request, showing that temporary relief would enable the Church schools to survive the crisis and to continue to save the tax payers the money which would otherwise have to be spent to replace them. It was estimated that $14,763,000 was the annual saving to the Ohio tax payers. In the Diocese of Cleveland alone there were approximately 76,441 pupils in the elementary schools who were receiving their education without cost to the general public; this cost, whether calculated at the ordinarily publicized rate of $103.18 per pupil, or at the per capita rate of $149.25 according to other estimates, represented a great amount of money.[3] In contrast with it, help was asked to the extent of $17 for each child in the parochial schools.

Sympathetic journals over the country applauded the efforts to obtain some relief from the double taxation imposed upon Catholics who desired to keep their schools open. The appeal, however, fell upon deaf ears. In 1932 the attorney general, whose previous attempt to deny the benefits of the "milk fund" to parochial school pupils had been overruled, now gave the official opinion that the bill introduced into the legislature to aid these schools was unconstitutional. Despite the rebuttal that such aid would be used exclusively for secular education, the bill was lost in the State Senate by one vote.

In the summer of 1933 Governor White asked the legislature for relief for all schools in the State. It was argued that parochial schools should benefit by the provisions of the State Constitution which called for "suitable laws to protect every religious denomination in the peaceful enjoyment of its mode of public worship, and to encourage schools and the means of instruction." Powerful interests, however, including

[3] *C.U.-B.*, June 30, Aug. 18, 1933.

the open opposition of the Citizens League of Cleveland[4] and the Junior Order of American Mechanics, blocked any concession in the matter; and the Goodwin and the Gunsett Bills were defeated. Bishop Schrembs could only say that no question would ever be settled until it was settled in the right way with justice.[5]

In the next spring the McNamee amendment, attached to the public school aid bill, was voted upon separately and was defeated by seven votes. It was still hoped that something might be done if the general public were kept informed of the true situation. The Cleveland *Plain Dealer* published an extended interview with Doctor Hagan in which he revealed the arguments for his case. The Cleveland *News* gave some notice of the controversy. The Cleveland *Press* and the two Youngstown newspapers came out in favor of temporary assistance. The Cleveland City Council passed a resolution recommending it. Radio talks asked for a "fair deal." The *Universe-Bulletin* published a series of articles written by Doctor Hagan to prove that "State aid" was neither unconstitutional nor unusual. Bishop Schrembs in an open letter to non-Catholic citizens asked for consideration of Catholic deserts and current needs.

The opposition was equally active. The Cleveland Ministers Union protested giving any aid to Catholic schools and the Ohio Council of Churches raised the hackneyed cry about the danger of the union of Church and State. Doctor Hagan had to point out, in answer to the spokesman for the Cleveland Federated Churches, that parochial schools were not Sunday Schools but were fully equipped institutions acknowledged already by the State as one means of carrying out the compulsory school legislation, which, moreover, did not require exclusively secular education.

Nevertheless, the Davis Bill, though it passed the Senate, failed in the House of Representatives by a vote of 86 to 42. In the electoral campaigns of 1934 and 1936 much was made of the question. In a last attempt at obtaining relief the Waldvogel Bill, which would allow a small monetary compensation to parents and guardians who were taxed because of their support of parochial schools, passed in the Senate by a vote of 25 to 11, but was defeated in the House. Other measures which would provide for free school books in parochial schools and for the use of public school buses by parochial school pupils, although seemingly favored by the Senate, were diverted to the hostile School Committee and were effectively "smothered."

With the coming of more prosperous times, undaunted Catholic citizens continued to carry the burden of double taxation and to make sacrifices for the expansion and perfection of the school system in which religion and morality had their rightful influence.

Despite all the efforts made in the Cleveland area, according to Doctor Hagan's report in the *Universe-Bulletin*, only a little better than

---

[4] *C.U.-B.*, Aug. 25, Sept. 1, 1933.
[5] *C.U.-B.*, Sept. 29, 1933.

one-half of the Catholic children of school age were attending the parochial schools. To assist in the religious instruction of these children Bishop Schrembs in 1922 admitted the Social Mission Sisters of the Holy Ghost into the diocese. Sisters Hildegard and Judith, coming from Hungary, with the help of Father Koller of St. Margaret's opened a mission house on East 116th Street near Buckeye Road, and by 1925 there were some 600 children under instruction. Successful catechetical centers were opened in St. Agnes' in 1931, and in the parish of the Immaculate Conception in 1938. To aid the Sisters the Social Mission Guild was organized in 1925; it held its meetings at the residence on Mapleside Avenue, and after 1932 in a large brick house on East Boulevard near Wade Park Avenue.

In the year 1946, when the community numbered eight Sisters and three novices, all young women born in this country, over 3,000 family visitations were made, and through the exertions of the Sisters 60 were baptized, 165 made their First Holy Communion, 265 were confirmed, 18 marriages were rectified, 87 adults were brought back to the sacraments, and 840 were registered for instruction. The Sisters made a religious census of several parishes and for a short time they had charge of the religious instruction of the children of the new parish of the Epiphany. In the same year the Sisters relinquished their work and under the direction of their first American Superior, Sister Julia Gutman, they established themselves in Arizona where they continued their endeavors among the Mexicans.

To train catechism teachers the Catholic Instruction League, founded in Chicago, was introduced here in 1926 with the appointment of Father Peter O'Brien, S.J., as director. Bishop Schrembs addressed meetings of high school and college students asking for cooperation. In 1930 the members, seminarians, teachers, and associates in the Parent-Teacher organization, to the number of 150, were instructing some 2,000 pupils in several centers: the Social Mission Sisters house on East 116th Street; the schools in the parishes of Holy Name, St. Colman, Our Lady of Good Counsel, St. Mary (West 30th Street), Blessed Sacrament, and a few others; and several public institutions such as Rainbow Hospital, Crippled Children's Hospital, and the Fresh Air Camp. Father Francis Zwilling, appointed by Bishop Schrembs, chaplain of the Social Mission Sisters and diocesan director of the Instruction League, was succeeded by Father George Dennerle in 1933 at a time when there were 23 different centers.

Six years later the Confraternity of Christian Doctrine had been organized in 56 parishes in the city; in other cities also the work had been systematized. In the country districts, around Painesville, for example, catechetical centers were established at various farm settlements, or arrangements were made to bring the children of several settlements together at one point for instructions on Saturdays and on Sundays.

Vacation schools were introduced in the summer of 1932. Seminarists and other volunteers taught and supervised the recreation of the children in some 60 centers. The purpose was not only to keep the young people in touch with the Church during the summer but also during the depression to supply food for the needy. Private funds furnished this assistance until the Cleveland Board of Education, at the solicitation of Doctor Hagan, extended the benefits of the State law, which provided food for about 15,000 children in the public schools, to approximately 6,500 in the Catholic schools and about 300 in the Lutheran parochial schools.[6]

Experience had led many educators to see the necessity of religious belief as the basis for moral living. The imparting of religious instruction in the ordinary administration of the public schools in the circumstances of the case would arouse much opposition. One plan to solve the difficulty was called "released time for religious education," according to which the public school buildings would be used for giving weekly instructions during the time of compulsory attendance to Catholic, Jewish, and Protestant children whose parents would so request; representatives of the various religious bodies would furnish the teachers. The attorney general of the State gave it as his opinion that such procedure was not against the law. The system was never tried in this city; an attempt in 1941 to introduce it in East Cleveland was effectively blocked. In the city of Youngstown, however, the plan had considerable success.

In January, 1941, classes in religion became "elective courses" in six public high schools. At East High School two Catholic priests began with approximately 347 senior students; in the next semester there were 600. In 1942 twenty-six priests were prepared to teach religion to all the Catholic students in all the grades above the first year of high school. The experiment seemed to prove the practicability of the system to some extent at least. It was dropped after the Supreme Court had declared that a similar arrangement in the West was unconstitutional.[7]

Previously an attempt to introduce compulsory Bible reading in the public schools was made by an interested group in an effort to inspire a sense of morality. Ohio is one of the States which favored the reading of an excerpt from the Sacred Scriptures at some time during the school hours; some States permitted it, others ordered it, three excluded it, and some had no policy in the matter. Bible reading without commentary was started in the Youngstown, Akron, and Lakewood schools by order of the public school authorities in 1924. A compulsory Bible reading bill had been introduced into the Ohio legislature in the previous year but it was defeated through the united opposition of Catholics, Jews, and Episcopalians and other Protestant representatives.

[6] *C.U.-B.,* May 6, Sept. 16, Oct. 21, 1932.
[7] *C.U.-B.,* Jan. 17, 24, 31, Feb. 14, Mar. 7, 21, 28, Apr. 18, June 5, Oct. 3, 1941; Sept 11, 1942; Aug. 13, 1943.

Two years later (1925) the Buchanan Bill, which prescribed that ten verses of the Bible be read every day in school and that children above the fourth grade be obliged to learn the Ten Commandments, passed the legislature under pressure from the "Ku Klux Klan bloc" but it was vetoed by the Governor. Although the bill exempted Catholics and others who were otherwise provided with the opportunity of religious instruction, Bishop Schrembs opposed it partly because of the bitter anti-Catholic feeling behind it and partly because it had the appearance of the State teaching religion. An injunction obtained by a citizen prevented the East Liverpool Board of Education from introducing Bible reading in the schools under its jurisdiction. The Weaver Bill sponsored by the Ku Klux Klan and the Junior Order of American Mechanics, another attempt at compulsory Bible reading, was lost in committee in 1929.[8]

According to the *Official Catholic Directory* in 1923 there were in the Cleveland diocese 132 elementary schools with approximately 55,000 pupils; an additional 1,900 students were to be found in other Catholic schools. The high point of registration was reached in 1929 when the total number of elementary school children was about 82,000; in 1934 there were only about 68,000. In the years which followed there was, as in the public schools, a marked decrease in attendance. In 1940 there were 1,762 less than in the previous year. It remained for the war years to restore the school population. The numbers in the high schools meanwhile had noticeably increased.

During the administration of Bishop Schrembs Catholic high school facilities were much expanded. In 1922 the enrollment at the Cathedral Latin School for Boys was approximately 700, of whom 210 were freshmen chosen out of 385 applicants.[9] In 1928 814 boys crowded the building beyond its normal capacity of 650. This situation was remedied by the addition of twenty-one class rooms and a gymnasium and other equipment in a three-story building blessed by Bishop Schrembs in 1930. An addition to the Brothers House in 1925 increased its capacity to thirty. There were 211 graduates in 1933. These and others who followed in their footsteps have given a good account of themselves in the various colleges and in the business world, and not a few have become priests of the diocese and members of the religious congregations.

Benedictine High School was started by the Slovak Benedictine Fathers, shortly after their coming to the diocese, in improvised quarters which served until the completion in 1940 of a fine large brick building on East Boulevard near Buckeye Road. Costing approximately $250,000, it had a machine shop in its equipment. It was quickly filled to capacity and had 571 students in 1942 who were taught by 20 Benedictines and 3 laymen.

[8] *C.U.*, Dec. 16, 1921; Mar. 23, 1923; Feb. 8, 1924; Mar. 13, 1925. *C.U.-B.*, May 28, 1926; Apr. 5, 1929.
[9] Minutes of Bishop's Council meeting, Apr. 13, 1922, in C.D.A.

The crowded conditions at St. Ignatius High School which made it impossible to accept all the applicants were relieved to some extent in 1935 when the college department was moved to University Heights. In 1942 there were 24 Jesuit Fathers and 10 scholastics teaching 725 students.

In the same year 657 young men and women were attending Holy Name High School; and the parish high schools in St. Vincent's and St. Mary's at Akron and in St. Mary's at Lorain had a combined enrollment of 755. The Sisters Servants of the Immaculate Heart of Mary had charge of these three, except that in more recent times they were succeeded by the Dominican Sisters in St. Vincent's. Several of the Cleveland parish commercial high schools expanded into a full four-year academic program. The Notre Dame Sisters staffed such schools in St. Boniface's, St. Francis', St. Michael's, St. Peter's, and St. Stephen's. The Ursuline Nuns had charge of the one in Holy Trinity parish.

The high school needs of the Catholics of Youngstown were met at least partially when the Ursulines in 1925 opened a new brick sixteen-room establishment for girls. Five years later it was changed over into a central co-educational high school after a public appeal brought in funds enough to enlarge and improve its facilities. Father Edward Conry, the principal, and other priests assisted with the teaching. With 700 students in 1943, it was a success from the beginning.

St. John's High School in Canton, which had been installed in a new building in 1926, at the invitation of Bishop Schrembs became a central high school for the boys of the city. Thirty-nine of them, the first graduates, received diplomas from his hand in 1930; twelve years later the Sisters Servants of the Immaculate Heart of Mary, in charge of the teaching, had some 180 students in their classes. Mount Marie Junior College and Academy in charge of the Sisters of the Holy Humility of Mary, which had 200 students in 1942, served as a central high school for the girls of the Canton-Massillon area.

New academies were opened by several religious communities during this period. The Sisters of Charity of St. Augustine, who had been devoting themselves almost exclusively to the care of the sick and the orphans, were induced by Bishop Schrembs to take charge of several parish schools. Also, on the grounds of the mother-house in Lakewood they opened an academy for girls in a fine new building in 1925; a new elementary school adjacent to it was put up four years later. The Sisters of St. Joseph in 1928 constructed a large new brick high school and academy on the property of the mother-house on Rocky River Drive near Lorain Avenue; more than 400 students were in attendance in 1941.

The Sisters of the Holy Humility of Mary started an academy on the former Coulby estate in Wickliff in 1930; it was, however, abandoned after a few years when the Sisters were obliged to give up the property. The Franciscan Sisters of St. Joseph in 1926 put up a large brick provincial convent in Garfield Heights; in connection with it they opened Marymount High School which in 1941 had 200 students. The Ursuline Nuns in East Cleveland erected a new brick building for their Academy of the Sacred Heart which was dedicated in 1924. The Dominican Sisters in Akron started their Academy of Our Lady of the Elms on the former Marks estate in 1929. Nevertheless, despite all this progress, according to the report of Doctor Hagan only 1,379 of the 5,272 graduates of the elementary parochial schools could find room in the Catholic high schools, which in 1940 had a total enrollment of approximately 7,000.

COLLEGES, THE SEMINARY, AND RETREATS

ST. IGNATIUS COLLEGE, WHICH HAD DONE SO much in the formation of the clerical body (more than two-thirds of the priests of the diocese had made their preparatory studies in it) and of the Catholic professional and business men of the diocese, was admitted into the North Central Association of Colleges in 1922. It is of interest that the rating officials who examined the situation considered the fact that the Jesuits taught without salary the equivalent of a million-dollar endowment. Plans were made for immediate expansion.

Early in 1923 forty-five acres were acquired in a new land development in University Heights, on Cleveland's eastern boundary. A State charter was obtained in the name of Cleveland University but this title was given up for that of John Carroll. A campaign of the same year to raise $3,000,000 for the first building unit was not very successful because of conflict with other drives. With the advent of Father Benedict Rodman in 1928 a campaign for $2,500,000 was inaugurated under the general management of John J. Bernet, the railroad financier. Bishop Schrembs gave it official approval and each parish did its share. In 1930 it was announced that that amount had been pledged, one-half of it by non-Catholics.

The cornerstones of two buildings were laid in July, 1931. The depression, however, made it difficult to collect what had been promised and the buildings remained in an unfinished state for several years. Another drive in 1935 resulted in the collection of enough money to make it possible to open the buildings for the first classes, which began in the fall of that year. The group of fine stone buildings was not completed, however, until 1937. The great auditorium in the main building is on occasion used as a chapel. Of great advantage to many who would not otherwise be able to finish their college studies were the evening courses which were started in old St. Ignatius in 1927; these college extension classes were later transferred to the new site. In 1940 there were more than 800 students attending the university; 28 Jesuits and 32 laymen were on the teaching staff.

Bishop Schrembs was not long in the diocese before two Catholic

336

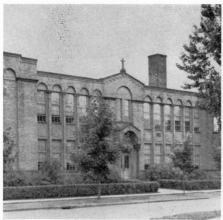

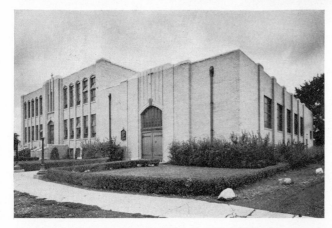

*Above Left:*St. Anthony Church, Fairport.

*Above Right:*Immaculate Conception Church and School, Willoughby.

*Left:*St. Paul Church and School, Euclid.

St. Vincent De Paul Church **and** School.

Christ the King Church and School, East Cleveland.

*Right:*St. Joseph School, Amherst.

*Left:*Holy Redeemer Church and School.

*Right:*St. Thomas Aquinas School.

*Left:*St. Clement School, Lakewood.

St. Mary School, Berea.

St. John Baptist School, Akron.

colleges for women were in operation. The Ursuline Nuns had had a college charter from the earliest days of the diocese but the needs of the elementary schools made it necessary for the Sisters after a few years to devote themselves exclusively to these. In the spring of 1922 they and the Sisters of Notre Dame were authorized by the Bishop to start separate colleges. The Ursulines began that year in a large brick building on Euclid Avenue on the site purchased by Bishop Farrelly for a cathedral. In the second semester of 1927 the college was moved to its present location on Cedar Avenue and Overlook Road, on the eastern edge of Cleveland, where two large residences had been remodeled for the purpose. Notre Dame College was opened in a large residence alongside the high school building on Ansel Road. In 1928 it was transferred to University Heights; the large new college building there was dedicated by Bishop Schrembs. Both colleges were fully equipped for their task; a few priests of the diocese and lay teachers completed the teaching staff of Sisters. They had their first graduation in 1925 and their first commencement exercises in the following year.

An interesting experiment was made in 1929 when the women's colleges, the diocesan seminary, and the nursing schools were all incorporated with John Carroll University which conferred the degrees. In June of the next year 303 received their diplomas at a mass graduation in Public Hall attended by some 13,000 people.[1] This colorful display of what the diocese was doing for higher education was repeated annually for a few years until some doubt was raised about the legal value of the diplomas awarded under such an arrangement. The separate colleges then fell back upon their own charters for authority to confer degrees and eventually each institution held its own commencement exercises. In 1936 John Carroll University and the Notre Dame and Ursuline Colleges held an open-air combined graduation exercise on the campus of the university to commemorate the fiftieth anniversary of the coming of the Jesuits to the diocese. Bishop Schrembs was awarded an honorary doctorate on the occasion.

What was undoubtedly one of the greatest achievements of Bishop Schrembs was the building of the Seminary of Our Lady of the Lake on Ansel Road near Superior Avenue. At a clergy conference in the Latin School in September, 1922, he announced that the old seminary was to be abandoned and that the advanced students for the priesthood were thereafter to be sent to the new provincial seminary in Cincinnati. The last class of theologians who finished their studies in the venerable institution, fifteen young men, had been ordained by the Bishop in the previous April; in the autumn thirty-two students went to Cincinnati.

Delay in the sale of the property on Lakeside Avenue induced the Bishop to repair and to use the old buildings for the beginning of a preparatory seminary. Thirty-two young men, twenty of them from St. Ignatius College and the largest class to enter the seminary, began

[1] *C.U.-B.*, June 6, 13, 1930.

their philosophy course in the fall of 1922. Father Edward F. Burke was appointed rector and three other priests were assigned to assist him. Before the first year was finished the property was sold to the Cleveland Electric Illuminating Company.

With a view to the convenience of day scholars the Bishop chose as a site for the new seminary a tract of land extending along Ansel Road which had been purchased by Doctor Scullen, the administrator, as a location for a new hospital. A small section of land on the west side of the street and a large residence were sold to St. Thomas' parish.[2] The Bishop broke ground on March 19, 1924, and on the following May 11 he laid the cornerstone. Bishop Gallagher of Detroit preached the formal sermon. The two-story (three stories in the rear) Spanish Mission type building, 800 by 200 feet, of buff-colored tapestry brick, with separate rooms for 155 students and suites for the professors, was sufficiently completed in the fall to accommodate the first two classes in philosophy. Bishop Schrembs celebrated the first Mass in an improvised chapel in one of the large class rooms, November 4, 1924.

The magnificent seminary chapel itself was solemnly dedicated by the Bishop on October 28, 1925. While the Bishop consecrated the main altar, his personal donation, Cardinal Samuel Stritch, then Bishop of Toledo, Archbishop John A. Floersch of Louisville, Bishop Gallagher of Detroit, and Bishop Muldoon of Rockford consecrated the other four marble altars. Archbishop Dowling of St. Paul preached an impressive sermon. Other prelates who assisted at the ceremonies included Archbishop Beckmann, then of Lincoln, Bishop Gannon of Erie, Bishop Hartley of Columbus, and Bishop Francis Howard of Covington.

The chapel, a separate wing between two enclosed monastic courts, is an especially fine piece of work. The travertine walls, the open ceiling and highly decorated beams, the glistening mosaic covering the apse, representing the Presentation of the Blessed Virgin in the Temple, the white marble altars, all add something to its beauty. The stained-glass windows, imported from Munich, picture the Fathers and Doctors of the Church. The Stations of the Cross, cast in bronze and imported from Europe, are each a work of art. The stalls face one another across the broad middle aisle, the whole a great sanctuary. A magnificent dome tops the front center of the building and under it is the library.

In the fall of 1925 first-year college students were accepted, some of whom boarded at the seminary, others returning to their homes each day after classes. At the same time 36 began the study of philosophy. The total enrollment was 85, of whom 62 were new students. A Brother of Mary came from the Latin School to teach chemistry and physics. The increased attendance made it necessary in 1927 to purchase all the property north of the seminary grounds to Dallas Road

[2] Minutes of Bishop's Council meetings, Apr. 14, June 3, 1921; Oct. 14, 25, Dec. 12, 1923; Jan. 7, 1924; all in C.D.A.

for a recreational field. For the sake of uniformity, and in accord with regulations governing the matter, all students in the next year were obliged to live at the seminary. With the appointment of Monsignor Francis T. Moran as rector in 1928, to succeed Doctor Burke who had unexpectedly died that year, Bishop Schrembs decided to return the seminary to the status of a major seminary.[3] Classes in theology began again in September, 1929, a few months previous to the death of Monsignor Moran, who was succeeded by Monsignor James M. McDonough.

In the interim the graduates of the minor seminary were sent for their theology to schools outside the city. Most of the 32 who finished in the first class from the new seminary went to Cincinnati for three years, and then to the Apostolic Mission House in Washington. A few went to St. Vincent's in Latrobe, and a few others were sent to Innsbruck, and to the American Colleges in Rome and in Louvain. After 1929 all the theological students, with the exception of a few who finished their studies in Rome, were kept in the Cleveland seminary. The first group, 30 young men, to make the complete course of theology in it were ordained by the Bishop, March 11, 1933.

Beginning with his first ordination in Cleveland (April, 1922) and including the class of 1940, Bishop Schrembs ordained 342 priests for the diocese. Altogether 419 were ordained during his administration. Twenty-two were ordained in Rome, 14 in Innsbruck, and 8 in Louvain and, in the last years, Auxiliary Bishop McFadden ordained 33, of whom a few were educated outside Cleveland. If we include 21 priests adopted into the diocese after their coming from Europe, it can be said that approximately sixty-eight per cent of the living clergy in 1942 had been recruited by Bishop Schrembs. It is to be noted also that with few exceptions the diocese was furnishing its own clergy. Through the petition of the Bishop many of the clergy and laity were honored by the Holy See: one was an apostolic prothonotary, fifty-eight were domestic prelates, and eight were papal chamberlains. Many laymen and laywomen, also, received recognition for special service to religion.

For the support of the seminary Bishop Schrembs had introduced the system of a special door-to-door collection in the month of October; the names of contributors were published in the *Universe*. Considerable monies for a new seminary had accumulated over the years but not nearly sufficient to pay for it. Hence the necessity of an intensive campaign, placed under the patronage of St. Theresa, the Little Flower, which was made during the construction of the new building. The need was brought home to the people in the parishes by chosen speakers, and in specially prepared articles in the diocesan journal. The priests pledged $150,000 for the chapel, and enough was collected from the people to pay for the construction and equipment of the seminary but not enough to endow it as had been hoped. Dur-

[3] Minutes of Bishop's Council meetings, June 26, 1928, and Feb. 4, 1929, in C.D.A.

ing the depression the seminary managed to survive only through the special generosity of the clergy and the indulgence of hard-pressed merchants. Finally in 1934 the Bishop was obliged to restore the annual collection for the seminary, to which in the next year was added the appeal for the Sisters' College as well.

Zealous as he was in fostering vocations to the priesthood, Bishop Schrembs was also much interested in the spiritual progress of his clergy. For the first three years after he came here the priests were gathered together for their annual retreat in the Hollenden Hotel; the conferences were given in the ball room which was transformed into a temporary chapel. He, personally, presided at the first retreat, led the meditations, and delivered the talks on pastoral subjects. This last-mentioned duty he kept for himself even when another retreat master was in charge. Beginning in 1926 the exercises were conducted in the new seminary building. The Bishop had had considerable experience; he had directed clergy retreats at least four times on the West Coast, and in Helena, Montana, in Milwaukee, Wisconsin, and in Baltimore, Maryland.

As had always been his practice, the Bishop inspired and encouraged spiritual retreats for the laity. He conducted the Knights of Columbus retreat here in 1923 and invariably attended the closing exercises in other years. St. Stanislas' House in Parma became the center of the Laymen's Retreat League organized in 1939 with the Bishop as honorary president. It was after a disastrous fire at St. Stanislas' in 1927 that the new and larger building was put up and the retreat movement took on new life. Up to 1937 5,103 men had made the closed retreat; during 1941 720 men attended. Closed retreats for women were inaugurated at the mother-house of the Sisters of the Holy Humility of Mary in 1932, with 22 from the Youngstown area in attendance; soon as many as 200 gathered there each summer. The Catholic Physicians' Guild began their annual closed retreat with one at the new seminary in 1936. The movement spread and closed retreats for special groups and one-day retreats for young people were a frequent occurrence.

59

RELIGIOUS COMMUNITIES

SEVERAL RELIGIOUS COMMUNITIES OF MEN AND of women accepted the invitation of Bishop Schrembs to make foundations in this diocese.

Father Stanislas Gmuca came here in 1922 from St. Procopius Abbey in Lisle, Illinois, near Chicago, to take charge of St. Andrew's parish, and to become superior of the first Benedictine priory, which counted four priests and three lay brothers. The new parish of St. Benedict was given to the order in perpetuity. In 1934 in the old Cathedral the Bishop solemnly blessed Father Gmuca as the abbot of the first Benedictine abbey in Ohio.

The Fathers of the Order of Mercy made their first foundation in Youngstown in 1922; two years later they were in Cleveland in charge of two Italian parishes. In 1942 the order acquired the old Leisy estate in Middleburg Heights near Berea where the provincial mother-house was established. Father Sante Gattuso remained still the Superior of the little missionary band.

The Fathers of the Blessed Sacrament, after the erection of the United States province as distinct from that of Canada, opened their first major seminary in a large remodeled residence on Euclid Avenue in Euclid, Ohio, in 1931. Bishop Schrembs dedicated their new chapel of perpetual adoration and the novitiate in October, 1935, when including the novices there were fifty-two in the community.

In 1929 a few members of the African Mission Society, called the White Fathers, established themselves in a remodeled residence, first on East 84th Street, and then on East 99th Street, near Superior Avenue. They were recalled by their superior in 1934.

In the old homestead of the O'Neill family in Akron the Maryknoll Fathers started a preparatory seminary for prospective candidates in September, 1937. The Bishop blessed their renovated quarters in the next year, when they had eleven students.

The Franciscan Fathers of the Order of Friars Minor Conventual came from Syracuse in 1923 to take charge of the new parish of St. Anthony in Lorain which was given to them in perpetuity. Sisters of the Third Order of Franciscan Conventuals began to teach in their school in 1925. The Dominican Fathers were likewise given the parish of St. Dominic in Youngstown in 1923.

The Fathers of the Most Precious Blood, who have labored in this district from the earliest days, established a new preparatory seminary on a 300-acre site at Brunnerdale, on the outskirts of Canton. Bishop Schrembs dedicated the large brick building in 1931 at a time when there were 125 students in residence. For a while after 1932 the headquarters of the Italian province of the same religious congregation were at Niles under the Superior, Father Nicolas Santoro.

The Missionary Servants of the Most Holy Trinity, a congregation founded by Father Thomas A. Judge, C.M., had charge of St. John's parish in Lorain from 1932 to 1937. In the previous four years this parish was the headquarters for the few Spanish Franciscans who had been driven out of Mexico by the persecution and had come here to minister to the Mexican immigrants who were to be found in several parts of the diocese.

Other victims of the same persecution were the Irish Sisters of the Incarnate Word who came here in 1927 to take charge of the school in the parish of the Annunciation. For a while the Sisters occupied a convent on St. Clair Avenue, near St. Aloysius' Church, previously used by the Carmelite Sisters. Then in 1940 they moved into a newly constructed mother-house and academy on Pearl Road, in Parma. The chapel is fashioned on the model of Cleveland's original Catholic church, St. Mary-of-the-Lake. The community, numbering about fifty, had charge of four parochial schools and of the catechetical instruction in several others.

In sympathy with the persecuted Catholics of Mexico the Bishop prescribed a triduum of prayers and all-day exposition of the Blessed Sacrament in all the parishes. His name was one of those attached to the pastoral issued by the American bishops in protest against the Mexican government's mistreatment of the Church; 10,000 copies were mailed to influential citizens in this city. The diocese also contributed its share in supporting the seminary for Mexican clerics which was established in New Mexico in 1937.

Several other religious communities of women made foundations here during this period. The Franciscan Nuns of the Blessed Sacrament came to the city in 1921. They were originally housed in one of the residences on Euclid Avenue, next door to the Ursuline College, on the property intended as a site for a cathedral, and their second convent was a large residence on East Boulevard, near Wade Park Avenue. In 1931 they moved into a new three-story brick convent which was attached to the Shrine Church of the Blessed Sacrament on Euclid Avenue at East 40th Street. The Sisters, who observe the strict cloister, are dedicated to the perpetual adoration of the Blessed Sacrament. Beginning with five members in 1921, the community numbered approximately fifty in 1942.

Six Discalced Carmelite Sisters from St. Louis founded the Carmel of the Holy Family in Cleveland in 1923. They lived first on Lakeview Road and then on St. Clair Avenue at East 112th Street. In 1935 seventeen Sisters took possession of the former Rollin White home at Fairmount and Lee Roads.

Early in 1926 a band of twelve Sisters of St. Joseph came here from St. Trudpert's Convent near Freiburg in Germany to take charge of the domestic economy in the new St. Mary's Seminary. They succeeded the Notre Dame Sisters, who were occupied for a while with that work, and the Sisters of the Holy Humility of Mary, who had served so long and so faithfully in the old seminary. Shortly afterwards the new arrivals were also entrusted with the home for elderly people at Louisville, Ohio. A small group which went to the preparatory seminary in Buffalo later returned to Germany. The Cleveland community, established as an independent American province in 1937 and affiliated with the mother-house (St. Mark) in Alsace, France, has its headquarters and novitiate on a thirty-acre city farm on Chardon Road, in Euclid, which was acquired in 1942.

The Vincentian Sisters of Charity of the Diocese of Cleveland owe their origin as a separate community to three Sisters who came here from the mother-house in Perrysville, Pennsylvania, in 1928 to establish a novitiate. In the next year they took possession of a large residence on a seventeen-acre plot of land in Bedford which had been donated to the diocese by Mrs. Sabina Schatzinger; a large brick convent was put up in 1932. The Sisters, who numbered more than 100 in 1942, taught in nine Slovak parochial schools and directed catechetical instructions in others.

In this diocese since 1893, the Sisters of St. Dominic of Akron in 1929 separated from the Caldwell, New Jersey, mother-house and established their own on the former Marks estate on West Market Street.[1]

In conclusion it is to be noted that Bishop Schrembs used every possible occasion to encourage young women to consecrate themselves to the service of the Church in one or other of the religious communities; and he urged his priests to cultivate vocations to the priesthood and to the sisterhoods.

[1] Sketches furnished by the religious communities.

60

CHARITIES AND SOCIAL WELFARE

ONE OF THE FIRST ADMINISTRATIVE ACTS OF Bishop Schrembs was to approve the Catholic Charities Corporation, which he considered "the greatest single asset in the diocese." He also confirmed Father LeBlond as its moderator and as the director of the Charities Bureau, the development of which was due in great measure to his ability and energy. When the latter became Bishop of St. Joseph, Missouri, in 1933, he was succeeded by Father Michael Moriarty, and then, in 1939, by Father Albert Murphy. Intensive campaigns each year sought to enlarge the membership in the Charities Corporation and to increase the amounts subscribed. Over $250,000 was pledged in the year that Parmadale was dedicated.

The group of cottages for the care of the orphans in Parma, at what came to be known as Parmadale, was the most outstanding accomplishment of the Charities Corporation; the total cost, half of which had to be borrowed, was put at $1,700,000. The first unit, which consisted of twelve two-story brick cottages each with accommodations for forty boys and two Sisters, a large administration building and schoolhouse, and a few other accessory buildings, was ready for occupancy in the summer of 1925. In September some 460 boys from old St. Vincent's, on Monroe Avenue, and from Louisville, together with the Sisters of Charity in charge of them, moved into their new home. Cardinal Hayes of New York, who called it "the most progressive departure in the institutional care of orphans," dedicated Parmadale, September 27, 1925. It was a gala day for the diocese and the rain failed to discourage the crowds who answered the Bishop's invitation to be present; they choked all the roads leading to the 180-acre plot which is eight miles from Public Square.

In the ensuing years the depression affected the ability of the people to contribute to charities. In 1930, when the budget of the eighteen Catholic social agencies in Cleveland, including hospitals, orphanages, and homes, was nearly $2,000,000, only $200,000 was subscribed. The Charities Corporation was hard pressed to make up the difference between what the Community Fund allocated and the actual deficit. The receipts, however, began to grow with the return of better times, increasing from $154,000 in 1933, and $248,000 (including several legacies) in 1939, to $424,000 in 1940. Owing to the many other demands made on the corporation, the debt on Parmadale was still $365,000 in the last-mentioned year. Among the published names of those who willed their estates to the Catholic Charities Corporation were John Gallagher, Patrick J. Finn, Bernard Kuhn, and Katherine Frady. The corporation benefited also from the last will of the Richman brothers of the well-known clothing firm, and from the Louis Beaumont Fund.

The Cleveland Charities Bureau expanded its activities through branch offices in other cities. The Catholic Service League of Youngstown was organized as the result of the appeal made by the Bishop to the Catholic Daughters of America to interest themselves in welfare work. St. Jean d'Arc Home for Girls with accommodations for twelve was dedicated in 1923. Anna Marie Receiving Home for children was established in the next year; in the first ten months of 1930 two-thirds of the 600 children cared for were restored to their homes or entrusted to foster mothers; in 1942 407 children were assisted and help was given to 318 families involving another 289 children. The league, staffed with a trained director and field workers, received support from the Community Fund of Youngstown.

The Catholic Community League of Canton, organized in 1920, operated a boarding-home for some thirty young women. A new community house was acquired in 1928. Through the league the welfare services of the other social agencies of the city were made available; a representative of the league cooperated with the Juvenile Court. The Gibbons Settlement House in the Italian neighborhood became the Guild House of the Little Flower in a new building in 1925. Partial support for the activity of the league is furnished by the Canton Welfare Foundation. To encourage another good work in that city, Father George Habig, pastor of St. Peter's, allocated $1,000 as the beginning of a fund to aid expectant mothers.

The Akron Catholic Service League, established in 1919, continued its functions with great success. A community house is the center of activities; fourteen social workers and a secretary in 1930 cooperated with other social agencies for the benefit of the Catholic population of Summit County. A community house for boys was inaugurated as a permanent institution, with a trained worker in charge, under the direction of Father John Scullen of St. Vincent's. The Akron Community Fund allotted nearly $80,000 to the Catholic Service League for the year 1931.

Other local offices were opened in Warren and Lorain in 1938 and in Ravenna, Lisbon, and East Liverpool in 1941, each with its trained social worker.

Catholic hospital facilities were widely developed under the direction of Bishop Schrembs. In 1923 he approved of the purchase of a seven-acre plot as a site for the first Catholic hospital in Akron, a city at the time with a population of about 308,000 in and around it. The campaign to raise money got under way in 1926. Michael O'Neill, of the General Tire Company, whose wife was the sister of Father Thomas Mahar (former pastor of St. Vincent's) for whom the hospital is named, pledged $100,000; the three other rubber companies in the city pledged $25,000 apiece. All subscriptions amounted to $500,-000. The additional $300,000 needed was raised by the parishes in Akron and its vicinity. St. Thomas' Hospital, a modern five-story brick structure, with the capacity to care for 142 patients, and accessory buildings, for the nurses and the Sisters of Charity who have charge of it, was blessed by Bishop Schrembs, September 24, 1928. A chapel on the second floor was the gift of Mrs. Michael O'Neill in memory of her husband. Miss Ellen Roche of Akron bequeathed $100,000 to the hospital in 1935. In its first year of operation approximately ten per cent of the patients were treated gratis.

Mercy Hospital in Canton increased its bed capacity from 60 to 200. A six-story brick structure costing approximately $500,000 was put up in 1929; Bishop Schrembs dedicated it on July 20 of the next year. Previously, on May 29, 1928, the Little Flower Hospital for Crippled Children was opened in the adjacent residence of Doctor H. M. Schuffel who had donated it; closed for a time, it was reopened in 1935 with seven child patients. Ten Sisters of Charity went from Cleveland to Columbia, South Carolina, in 1938 to staff Providence Hospital there which had been built with the help of the local mission office.

St. Vincent's Charity Hospital, Cleveland's oldest general hospital, kept its location in the downtown area when the other large hospitals moved to the eastern section of the city. It was hard put, therefore, to take care of the increased number of patients. As the result of an appeal to the general public $1,500,000 was subscribed; with this a new nurses' home and a surgical annex were built which Bishop Schrembs dedicated in June, 1928. A new Sisters' home, which enclosed a chapel, was put up in 1931. The free clinic continued to be operated with success and a medical social service department was organized. The facilities of St. John's Hospital were much increased when the nurses moved into a large new home; their quarters in the hospital proper were refitted for other purposes.

St. Alexis Hospital, operated by the Franciscan Sisters, was also greatly expanded. A four-story brick dwelling, named Leonarda Memorial in honor of the foundress, and costing some $360,000, increased the bed capacity by 25 and housed equipment and operating rooms. It was dedicated by the Bishop, December 20, 1925. Other improvements to the extent of $100,000 were made four years later. A five-story brick nurses' home which cost about $350,000 was completed in 1930.

The Sisters of the Holy Humility of Mary were given charge of two small hospitals, and their hospital in Youngstown was greatly enlarged. They succeeded the Franciscan Sisters (of Tiffin) in the control of St. Joseph's Hospital in Lorain in 1927; with a capacity of 125 beds, it cared for about 5,000 patients in 1942. Previously, in 1924, the same Sisters took over the management of St. Joseph's Riverside Hospital in Warren which had accommodations for 55 patients. The Grasselli Memorial Chapel in the building is another instance of the generosity of that family. St. Elizabeth's Hospital in Youngstown increased its capacity to 360 beds by the erection of the second large wing in 1929. The Stambough residence across the street from the hospital was refitted for use as a nurses' home.

From the time of the institution of the Community Fund the Catholic hospitals, as well as the others, have received considerable financial assistance from that source and are consequently subject to a certain amount of inspection and control. Bishop Schrembs took an important step in vesting the title of the hospitals in the name of the separate corporations of Sisters in charge of each of them.[1] He had obtained the approval of higher authorities for this departure from the traditional method of holding the property in the name of the diocese. St. Alexis had always belonged to the Sisters. In 1926 St. Vincent's Charity Hospital, St. John's, and St. Anne's Maternity Hospital in Cleveland and Mercy Hospital in Canton were transferred to the Sisters of Charity of Cleveland; St. Elizabeth's of Youngstown was transferred to the Sisters of the Holy Humility of Mary. The stipulation was made that such property would be used for hospital purposes forever.

On October 15, 1922, Bishop Schrembs dedicated a large residence on Euclid Avenue, in Euclid, as Rosemary Home for Crippled Children. It had been donated to the diocese as a memorial to his deceased wife, Johanna, by Caesar A. Grasselli. The Bishop three years later delivered a public address in the Hippodrome Theater to raise funds for this admirable institution in charge of the Sisters of the Holy Humility of Mary. The Home of the Holy Family, which shelters some 40 dependent children, was entrusted to the Sisters of the Incarnate Word when its founder, Miss Ellen Donovan, died in 1939. The Catherine Horstmann Home on Rocky River Drive, a haven for neglected and dependent young women, was put in charge of professional personnel.

Madonna Hall, a residence for professional and business women, was opened in 1926 in a large brick apartment house on East 82nd Street, near Euclid Avenue, by the Daughters of the Immaculate Heart of Mary; it replaced their St. Mary's Home of the earlier days of the diocese. The Catholic Young Women's Hall on Superior Avenue was thoroughly renovated and was taken over completely by the Sisters of Notre Dame; Bishop Schrembs rededicated it, December 12, 1928. The altar in the beautiful chapel came from old St. Mary's Seminary.

The Little Sisters of the Poor remodeled and enlarged their home on East 22nd Street to the extent that they could accommodate 200 elderly people. Monsignor Gilbert P. Jennings, the founder of St. Agnes' parish, made provisions in his last will for the building of a

[1] Minutes of Bishop's Council meetings, Apr. 8, and Aug. 17, 1925, in C.D.A. *C.U.-B.*, May 11, 1934.

home for elderly people who were not destitute. The Jennings Home for the Aged with accommodations for some fifty was dedicated in 1942. An unfortunate fire, however, destroyed it and claimed the lives of several of the old folks despite heroic efforts to save them. The chapel, a separate structure and a replica of old St. Mary on the Flats, and the convent of the Missionary Sisters of the Holy Ghost who have charge of the home were not harmed.

St. Joseph's Hospice for the Aged was opened in 1927 in the old college and orphanage building in Louisville which had been remodeled for its new purpose. Another small home for the aged on Lander Road was entrusted in 1939 to the Daughters of the Divine Redeemer, who had come to the diocese several years before to teach in St. Emeric's school. The Franciscan Sisters of Blessed Kunegunda in 1936 remodeled a large residence on Terrace Road in East Cleveland for use as a retreat center for the members of their congregation; it also sheltered a few elderly women.

Of great importance in the development of the social mission of the Church in this diocese was the inauguration of the Catholic Youth Organization, and the appointment of Father James O'Brien as diocesan director in 1937. In each parish one of the younger priests who was given charge of all the "youth activities" organized clubs of every kind, for study, for recreation, for athletics, among the young people, for the purpose of keeping them under the watchful eye of the Church in their formative years after they had left the parish schools. In most places existing facilities were remodeled for use as C.Y.O. club rooms; in some, however, as in St. Wendelin's parish, recreation centers were constructed at considerable cost. Young Catholics came to know one another better in inter-parish activities and in the diocesan athletic leagues.

The summer camps for adolescent boys were taken over by the new organization. The Knights of Columbus sponsored one at Lake Stafford near Ravenna for a few years following 1925 and two others near Canton and Akron. The Catholic Order of Foresters had a camp for boys near Wakeman. Father Kane's camp on a lake near Youngstown took care of 1,000 boys in a season. Father Chaloupka, of the parish of the Nativity of the Blessed Virgin in Cleveland, began a summer camp on Kelly's Island for the boys of his school in 1921; it was enlarged and made available to other groups some years later. Father Neil Gallagher, of St. Gregory's, operated a camp for the children of his parish.

The Bishop urged the organization of Catholic Boy Scouts in every parish. In 1937 about 1,000 boys, attached to 27 parish troops, assembled in the Cathedral for vespers and to hear a special sermon. They had distinguished themselves as pages and messengers during the Cleveland Eucharistic Congress.

For the specific purpose of assisting the Sisters of the Good Shepherd in the rehabilitation and protection of young people, the Catholic Collegiate Association was organized in 1924; many of the members belonged to the Catholic Daughters of America, a beneficial society, which financed their work. With Miss Mary O'Callaghan as president and Miss Catherine McNamee as secretary, the Big Sisters, as they were called, accomplished a great amount of good which has been recorded in a pamphlet written by Miss Anna King, the social service director of the institution at the time. Summer camp vacations were arranged for the girls and in 1929 the Little Flower Lodge for their exclusive use was opened on a site near Painesville. School-wage homes were secured for some of the young women who in general were encouraged and inspired to become useful members of the community. The Big Sisters, who in their first ten years assisted about 3,000 girls in one way or another, also assumed the task of teaching catechism to the young people temporarily confined in the County Detention Home on Cedar Avenue, and of procuring for them the opportunity of receiving the sacraments. Mass was celebrated there every Sunday after 1933.

61

THE KU KLUX KLAN, THE

CATHOLIC PRESS, AND RADIO

I N 1921 THE MAYOR AND THE CITY COUNCIL CON-
demned the Ku Klux Klan and its campaign of hate against Catholics, Jews, and Negroes. The "patriots" had raised the cry of
"Protestantism in danger" but they were disowned and denounced
by the better-informed citizens whatever their religion. In 1923
four Cleveland business men appeared unannounced at the Good Shepherd Convent and asked to make a tour of investigation. With them was
the author of the Hawkins Bill which was introduced into the Ohio
General Assembly and which would require the government inspection
of all privately owned institutions, religious houses, and schools. The
Bishop demurred at this unauthorized invasion of privacy but he conducted the party in a very thorough visit. The self-appointed inspectors
in a public statement reported the order and cleanliness of the institution and the contentment of the residents. As a result the bill, which
was a manifestation of the Ku Klux Klan agitation, was withdrawn.

The agitation carried over into the campaign preceding the presi-
dential election of 1928. The Democratic candidate, Alfred Smith, and
all Catholics had to suffer brutal, ignorant attacks upon their religion
and had to defend themselves against the usual false charge that they
could not be good Americans. These scurrilous accusations were circulated here as well as in the rest of the country. Father James M.
McDonough, then rector of the seminary, wrote two pamphlets in
defense of the loyalty of Alfred Smith and all Catholics, in answer to
the attack of a certain Charles Marshall. The dignity and forbearance
and good citizenship of the clergy and people under bitter provoca-
tion won the admiration of the better-minded non-Catholics. The
Cleveland district gave a majority of its votes in favor of Mr. Smith,
despite his Catholic religion.

Outside the city the Klan was able to exert more influence, especially in the smaller localities where Catholics were not numerous.
In Akron the Bishop took the occasion of a public celebration of the
Knights of Columbus to denounce the Klan in no uncertain terms; he
expressed his regret that the political parties did not do the same. Both

parties feared to lose the so-called Klan vote. However, the United States flag and the Bible, unwarranted symbols of the Klan, which one public high school principal had accepted, were returned upon instructions from the Akron School Board. In Massillon the Bishop and the Mayor in 1926 reviewed a parade of some 10,000 men which was intended as a protest against the anti-Catholic manifestations in the nearby small towns.

Despite the denunciations of the local newspapers, the Klansmen elected their candidates for mayor in Youngstown and Niles in 1923. In the autumn of the next year the Mayor of Niles issued a permit to the Klansmen to parade publicly in their distinctive disguise. He denied similar permission to an opposition group which called itself the Knights of the Flaming Circle, in contrast to the other organization which was sometimes called the Knights of the Flaming Cross from its custom of burning a cross at night as a warning to those with whom it disagreed. In the clash which attended the attempt of the Klansmen to parade some people were injured. The Governor of the State declared a kind of martial law, forbade the parade, and sent National Guardsmen to patrol the streets and to disperse the crowds.

In general the Bishop met the recrudescence of the spirit of intolerance which came after the First World War with the same vigor he had shown in Toledo against a similar movement. In the interest of general toleration he spoke before an assembly of the students of the University of Illinois; and he addressed a meeting of a prominent Jewish society in Cleveland on the subject of the principles of the American Constitution which guaranteed the liberty and equality of all citizens before the law. He approved the National League of Truth (founded by Protestants) and the American Unity League which were organized to combat the influence of the Klan. As late as 1933 he excoriated the self-constituted Citizens' League of Cleveland for its attempted exclusion of Catholics as such from the local board of education. He vindicated the right of Catholics as equal to that of other tax payers to examine the management of the public schools which they supported.

The *Catholic Universe* which had been doing valiant work for the Church since its foundation in 1874 was gradually losing its subscribers. A more lively journal, the *Catholic Bulletin*,[1] started in 1911 as the organ of the German Catholic societies, had grown to such an extent that it had local editions in Erie, Canton, Akron, and Youngstown, all issued by the Catholic Press Union. The Bishop approved of the amalgamation of the two in the *Universe-Bulletin*, which appeared in 1926 under the editorship of Linus Wey who had controlled the

---

[1] The *Bulletin* patronized study clubs under the inspiration of Fr. Francis Betten, S.J., who also promoted the St. Boniface Historical Society "to win for the history of the German nation the place due to it in English Catholic literature" (Betten's Circular).

old *Bulletin.* The stock of the privately owned weeklies was gradually acquired by the diocese for which the new one was the official organ.[2]

An intense effort to increase the circulation was made at the time that the plight of the parochial schools needed to be brought to the attention of the public. Bishop Schrembs and Monsignor McFadden, who was the president of the editorial board, and several of the younger clergy aroused the enthusiasm of the students of the upper grades and of the high schools gathered together in a large public hall. The youthful campaigners went from door to door in their neighborhoods canvassing for new subscriptions. Some 8,000 new subscribers were obtained in 1932; in the drive of 1938 34,549 paid subscriptions were announced. This unique advertising scheme, known as the Students Catholic Press Crusade, had an exhibit at the Catholic Press convention in Rome in 1936.

In the prelude to the Second World War when the totalitarian governments were using Spain as a testing ground for their weapons the Catholic press, including the *Universe-Bulletin,* in contrast with what looked like a conspiracy of silence on the part of the secular press, was the only reliable source of information about the fiendish persecution of religion by the Spanish Communists. At that time it was hard for Americans to believe the horrible accounts, and when a local newspaper did publish an article sent to it by a special reporter the Bishop had it reprinted in the *Universe-Bulletin* as confirmation of what the Catholic news service had been publishing. It was the time when an Ohio senator refused to withdraw his name from the list of some sixty public men who had signed a memorial of good-will towards the government of "Red Spain," but of whom at least one-half had signed a retraction. At this time, too, there was reason to suspect that pressure was brought to bear on our Government to send aid to the Communists in Spain. In a great petition the Catholics of the diocese under the direction of Monsignor Begin protested against the lifting of the embargo on sending arms to the distracted country.

Each year and on occasions of consequence the *Universe-Bulletin* has issued special editions in magazine form, such as those commemorating the anniversaries of the Bishop and of the diocese; those of 1934 and 1941 reproduced the pictures of many priests.

Bishop Schrembs was one of the earliest to realize the advantage which might accrue to religion from the use of the radio. The broadcasting of information about the Church and her teaching and practices, and about her position on individual and national problems, might lead to further inquiry or at least to a more understanding and sympathetic attitude on the part of those who were not Catholics. The National Broadcasting Company offered to the Catholic body, as it did to other religious organizations, the use of its facilities once a

[2] Minutes of Bishop's Council meeting, Feb. 17, 1926, in C.D.A. Bishop's letter in *Catholic Bulletin,* May 21, 1926.

*Left:*St. Hedwig Church and School, Lakewood.

*Right:*St. Margaret Church and School.

*Left:*St. Wenceslas Church and School, Maple Heights.

*Right:*St. Timothy Church and School.

*Left:*Gesu Church and School, University Heights.

St. Augustine Academy.

St. Joseph Seminary of the
Blessed Sacrament Fathers.

St. Luke School, Lakewood.

Benedictine High School.

St. Thomas Hospital, Akron.

St. Charles Borromeo School, Parma.

week on condition that incidental expenses be paid and a speaker be provided. Through Bishop Schrembs, the episcopal director, the National Council of Catholic Men took that responsibility. At a meeting of the American Federation of Catholic Societies, just before it became identified with the newer organization, the Bishop told the members that the Catholic Hour alone was sufficient reason to justify the existence of the National Council of Catholic Men.

The series was opened, March 2, 1930, from station WEAF in New York. Cardinal Hayes in dedicating the program to religion thanked the N.B.C. and the N.C.C.M. and introduced Bishop Schrembs as the one "whose wise counsel and apostolic leadership made the event possible." The Bishop's address, which was much appreciated for its earnestness and the kindliness of its language, was concerned with the value and need of religion, with special emphasis on the arguments from reason for the existence of God. The success and development of the Catholic Hour need no recounting here. Station WFJC of Akron canceled a regular broadcast to carry the first one to the Cleveland area.

On the local stations the Bishop was a frequent speaker. In August, 1926, he broadcast religious songs of his own composition from Public Hall at the invitation of a well-known local orchestra leader. He opened a series of broadcasts on a local network with a lecture on the necessity of religion for man's happiness. His subjects were generally of a religious nature but sometimes of social and civic interest. He spoke on the papal encyclicals, on the Pope's plea for peace, on mixed marriages. He appealed for the Community Fund and the Catholic Charities Corporation. On the Cleveland Community Religious Hour in 1930 he was the outstanding speaker. He gave the introductory talk to the broadcast of the Pope's voice at the request of a local station in 1931. Even before the Eucharistic Congress here, nearly every important Catholic "event" was put on the air as a matter of course. The twenty-seventh anniversary of the Bishop's consecration was celebrated in this way with a review of his career and the singing of a few of his hymns.

In later years Bishop McFadden and Monsignor Begin took his place before the microphone: the former opened a series of broadcasts sponsored by Father Joseph O'Keefe in Akron; the latter inaugurated another series of information broadcasts in Cleveland in 1937. At an earlier date Father Alfred Manning was the first priest in this area to use his private station in Salem and in Alliance for sermons and instructions. Father Edward Graham in 1925 was also using his own station to broadcast to the Canton district. In 1932 Father William Kane leased the facilities of Station WBKN for weekly talks on religion.

Mention was made above of the hymns composed by the Bishop. He brought to the diocese an interest in sacred music and liturgical singing which he had acquired as a choir-boy in Regensburg. Already the co-author of a text book for teaching Gregorian chant in the schools, at a meeting of music teachers in Baltimore in 1915 he outlined a plan for the reform of church music which was to begin with the children. At the meeting of the hierarchy in 1925 he was appointed episcopal chairman of a committee which in 1927 and 1928 brought out the two sections of the *Diocesan Hymnal.* This contained the words and music of hymns appropriate for congregational singing. A new edition appeared in 1932 with miscellaneous sacred songs which had been set to the tunes and airs which the Bishop had remembered from his youth. He was co-author, with the Benedictine Father Gregory, of the Catholic edition of the Progressive Music Series, and in the summer of 1927 the two of them taught the method to the music teachers of the diocese. For the strictly liturgical functions, however, he prescribed that only male choirs were to sing in church.

The Guild of Catholic Organists and Choir Directors was formed at the first diocesan Institute of Music held in St. Paul's Shrine of the Blessed Sacrament in 1931. Later the school for Catholic organists, established by Father Peter Schaeffers, the Cathedral organist, graduated eleven students in 1939. The members of the Boys' Singing Club, also trained by Father Schaeffers, received their certificates from the hand of the Bishop at an exhibition in Public Hall.

62

SOCIAL JUSTICE AND THE
NATIONAL CATHOLIC WELFARE
CONFERENCE

SOON AFTER HIS ARRIVAL HERE BISHOP SCHREMBS was given the opportunity of restating the principles already expressed with the other bishops in their program of reconstruction after the First World War. On the occasion of a local problem he upheld the fundamental right of laboring men to organize for the sake of collective bargaining with the employers. He considered the movement for an open-shop policy an attack on this right. Capital, more powerful and better organized, would have to remember that it as well as labor had made blunders and that both should in a spirit of cooperation find a solution for their difficulties. These ideas and other principles out of the papal encyclicals he stressed in his talks before the Industrial Association of Cleveland and the Builders' Exchange.

At the time of the steel strike in 1937 the Bishop expressed his deep sympathy with the working men, "who without the shadow of a doubt," he said, "had the right to set forth their grievances." Condemning violence and vandalism, and asserting the prior rights of the people in general to the preservation of peace and order, he did not hesitate to say that as the bishop of the diocese he considered it his privilege and duty to champion the cause of labor and to vindicate their right to a living wage and a sufficient competence for human existence. He appealed to both sides in the dispute to sit down at a conference table and find a solution.

Previously, at the Catholic Conferences on Industrial Problems held here in 1926 and 1931, Bishop Schrembs traced the evils of the industrial system to injustice and greed; he insisted that the laborer was not simply a cog in the machinery but that he should have an equitable share in the fruits of his labor; disregard of social justice would bring calamity on both sides. To do special honor to the Bishop on his golden jubilee, the second National Catholic Social Action Congress met in Cleveland and, while bishops and other prominent ecclesiastics and laymen discussed the Catholic answer to current industrial problems, proper and deserved compliment was paid to him for his lifelong efforts for the economic and social betterment of the working-man.

Not long after this the Cleveland chapter of the Association of Catholic Trade Unionists was inaugurated in the city for the purpose of instructing Catholic leaders in the various unions in economic morality. Steps were taken to organize the association on a national basis according to the plan outlined by Monsignor John Ryan, the well-known economist. In 1941 a Labor School was opened in St. Augustine's parish hall with competent teachers in history, ethics, and parliamentary procedure; sixty students, for the most part working-men, attended the lectures. As a symbol and a token of the deep interest which the Church has in the welfare of the working-man, directions were given to all the pastors to have a special Mass and sermon each year on Labor Day.

The Bishop at his coming had given his wholehearted approval of a minimum wage law in the State for the protection of women workers; the necessity of such provision became only too evident when some unscrupulous employers were paying starvation wages to women compelled to seek work outside their homes during the depression years. The Catholic people of the diocese were keenly affected by the great financial crisis which began in 1929. The failure of industry in the larger cities, where most of the Catholics lived, deprived thousands of family bread-winners of their means of livelihood and left other thousands without resources. People were evicted because they could not pay rent; mortgages on homes were foreclosed. Unrest and discontent were manifested in the march of 3,000 jobless men through the streets of Cleveland. Many children suffered from malnutrition and were insufficiently clothed. The Ohio legislature authorized local boards of education in 1931 to provide clothing and medical care for needy school children; this assistance was later extended to the Catholic schools.

Everyone is familiar with the direct and indirect relief afforded by the State and the Federal governments. Bishop Schrembs cooperated in the first tentative solutions of the problem. In his pastorals he urged employers to keep their men working even at a sacrifice; he commended the neighborhood plan to give work to one of the unemployed; he counseled his people to help in the movement to preserve food for the needy. Following the encyclical of the Holy Father he prescribed penance and prayers, asking God's help. And while he ordered collections to be taken up in the churches for the sufferers, he deplored the economic system which ignored social justice and "took better care of machines than it did of men." He was given credit among others for prodding the hesitant Ohio legislature into passing the necessary laws for the relief of the poor, reminding them that "empty stomachs do not reason." When the banking crisis came to Cleveland the Bishop tried to reassure the people and to restore confidence. He advocated a moratorium on the payment of debts. When some banks here failed to reopen after the "bank holiday" ordered by the Government, he and Bishop McFadden used all their influence in favor of the small depositors.

Meanwhile many pastors organized their own system of relief for the most needy cases; in this way many were tided over the worst moments of their troubles. In downtown Cleveland the pastor of the Cathedral, with food begged from the hotels and business houses, fed some 500 hungry men and women a day. Catholic organizations did what they could to help. In December, 1931, Father LeBlond at a meeting of the St. Vincent de Paul Society reported that up to 13,000 Catholic families were receiving relief from the Associated Charities. The Vincentians were called upon to exert themselves to the utmost to care for many others until such time as these could be helped by the organized relief agencies. They opened a clothing bureau in the Schuster building which by April, 1933, had distributed the wearing apparel gathered in a city-wide drive to some 27,000 persons. In 1938 about $59,000 was spent in assisting more than 20,000 persons. The Parent-Teacher groups and the Catholic Daughters of America distinguished themselves in helping to supply food and clothing for the needy children in the parochial schools.

During this time, as might be expected, the income for the support of the parishes reached a low level in many localities. A few could not pay the interest on their mortgages nor the salary of the Sisters who taught in the schools. This default was remedied in better times. A few parishes were saved when a composition was made with the administrators of the closed banks. In several parishes men out of work used their various skills in repairing church buildings and even in the construction of new ones. Despite all difficulties, the parishes survived to carry on the work of the Church with all the more vigor when the depression had passed.

Of peculiar importance was the rapid growth of the parish Credit Unions after 1936. These cooperative associations, common enough among the workers in the large industrial plants, loaned money to members at a minimum of interest, reminiscent as they were of the Monts-de-Piété encouraged by the Church in the Middle Ages. The first in this diocese was established in the parish of the Immaculate Conception whose people were mostly engaged in industry. Starting with a few dollars in 1936, this particular union in 1943 had made 842 loans amounting to over $100,000; the average interest charged was one per cent a month on unpaid balances. The *Universe-Bulletin* published the directions for organizing branches in the parishes. In September, 1941, there were twenty-one units, and sixteen of these formed the Cleveland Diocesan Credit Union Council. Two years later there were thirty-eight units, more than in any other diocese in the country.

In the words of the late Archbishop McNicolas of Cincinnati, Bishop Schrembs was the "second founder" of the National Catholic Welfare

Council, the peace-time extension of the National Catholic War Council with which also he had been intimately associated. In some quarters after the war misgivings had arisen and there were fears that the former organization might "assume some of the functions of a canonical plenary council contrary to the prescriptions of canon law." At "the definite request for its suppression by some American bishops" the Sacred Congregation of the Consistory by decree of February 22, 1922, dissolved it. This decision became public in articles published in the New York *Herald* and the Baltimore *Sun*. Bishop Schrembs, who had organized the laymen's societies on a national scale and who was well known for his activities in connection with the national organization of the German societies, was chosen by the general body of bishops to make a more complete presentation of the case to the Holy See.

On April 23, 1922, accompanied by Doctor James Ryan, later rector of the Catholic University and Bishop of Omaha, and ten priests of this diocese he set out for Rome. There he spent the greater part of two months explaining to the Holy Father and the cardinals of the various congregations that the N.C.W.C. was a "voluntary association, a clearing house and helpful agency for all episcopal proposals and that its recommendations imposed no legislative obligation on the bishops."[1] Additional information was also forwarded by the American bishops. Accordingly, the Congregation of the Consistory, following its meeting of June 22, 1922, decided that nothing was to be changed in regard to the organization but that there was to be a clear understanding that the resolutions of the bishops assembled voluntarily at their annual meetings had not the same force as conciliar legislation, and that there be no confusion of the hierarchy as such with the N.C.W.C. or any other standing committee.

Bishop Schrembs, in a news dispatch of July, notified the country of this decision and of the Holy Father's approbation of the annual meeting of the bishops. He reported about his mission to the bishops themselves at their meeting in the autumn. He explained that the laymen's organizations in which he was particularly interested were intended to coordinate and strengthen the local societies when united action was necessary. The bishops then approved and recommended the continuation of the national organization in each diocese under the control of the respective bishops. "Conference" was substituted for "Council" in the title of the organization. Bishop Schrembs, "making sacrifices which others would be unwilling to make," in his "utter forgetfulness of self, his whole hearted dedication to the cause for which he pleaded patiently, dramatically, rendered the most notable services to the Church in this country."[2]

The National Catholic Welfare Conference has proved its worth many times since. Among its many accomplishments were the assist-

[1] *C.U.-B.,* Feb. 23, 1940.
[2] *C.U.-B.,* Nov. 9, 1945.

ance given in the appeal of the Oregon School Bill to the Supreme Court of the United States which vindicated the right of private and parochial schools to exist, and in the help afforded for the abatement of the violent persecution of the Church in Mexico. The Popes have approved and justified the efforts of Bishop Schrembs in this regard. Pope Pius XI in a memorable message to the American bishops referred to the N.C.W.C. as not only a useful organization but a necessary one. The present gloriously reigning Pope Pius XII has been equally generous in his approbation.

The Cleveland diocesan units of the national organizations of men and women were inaugurated in January, 1924, at a meeting of some 200 delegates who adopted a constitution and elected James J. Murray as president of the men's, and Mrs. Martin B. Daley as president of the women's organization; Father Dominic Sweeney was appointed chaplain. The Youngstown deanery units were started in the next year.

In preparation for the sixth annual convention of the National Council of Catholic Men, which was held here in 1926, the local men's societies were reorganized in a rapid campaign which enrolled thirty societies (including eighteen councils of the Knights of Columbus) and 240 parish units (the Holy Name societies). The guest speaker, Archbishop McNicolas, characterized the N.C.C.M. as the "air squadron to meet any emergency; the swift athlete in the cause of Christ."[3]

Many of the Holy Name men were also members of the Knights of Columbus. Seven new councils of the latter had been founded during this period. The Cleveland Council in 1925 acquired a large auditorium which seated 1,200 and in which the Bishop for several years was tendered an annual reception to enable him to meet personally every Catholic in the city. At the forty-sixth annual convention of the Knights here in 1928 the Bishop made the formal address at the Mass celebrated in the Public Auditorium by Archbishop McNeil of Toronto; he complimented the Knights for their willingness to cooperate with him in all the works of Catholic Action.

The local unit of the National Council of Catholic Women was reorganized under the direction of Father LeBlond in 1927 to prepare for the annual convention held here in 1928. Archbishop McNicolas, again the principal orator, stressed the necessity for the various racial groups to unite their forces in a common effort for the protection of the Church and the general good of religion. For the occasion 1,000 young people arrayed in the traditional costumes of their European ancestors staged an interesting and inspiring Pageant of Nations in Public Hall as a vivid symbol of unity in diversity under the guidance of the Church.

It was the invariable practice for the Bishop to preside at the annual meeting of the N.C.C.W., when the delegates assembled to do him honor and to hear his message. In 1929, to celebrate his fortieth anni-

[3] *C.U.-B.*, Oct. 22, 1926.

versary as a priest, the women founded the Mary Gess scholarship in memory of his mother, at the National Catholic School of Social Service in Washington; this and another one established by Mrs. Martin Daley were intended for the education of young women from this area in social work.

Among the many objectives assigned to the women at these meetings (and to the Holy Name men as well) were: the promotion of the work of the Legion of Decency in "cleaning up" the moving pictures; the enforcement of the laws against the circulation of lewd books and pamphlets; cooperation with the courts in probation work; the promotion of the public observance of Good Friday; the moral support of the Interracial Federation in Cleveland; protest against the passage of laws considered to be inimical to good public morals. One committee helped newly arrived immigrants in adjusting themselves to their new environment; another occupied itself with teaching catechism to public school children. The Canton branch of the organization operated a Catholic circulating library. The Akron unit sponsored a series of lectures and radio broadcasts.

When in the autumn of 1922 Bishop Schrembs addressed the convention of the National Council of Catholic Women in Washington, and reported the enthusiasm of the Holy Father for their endeavors to preserve the Christian home and to solve other pressing problems, the organization represented 300 women's societies in twenty-nine states. In that year the National Council of Catholic Men represented 1,126 societies, local, state, and national, and forty-four diocesan units. When in 1934 the Bishop resigned from the administrative board of the National Catholic Welfare Council, under which these societies were organized, his vision of greater union and solidarity in the Catholic laity had been realized to the extent that nearly 4,000 units, representing millions of Catholic citizens, belonged to the national federation, all pledged to work for the welfare of the country and the good of religion under the high direction of the leaders of the Church. All freely acknowledged the great debt they owed Bishop Schrembs for this success; the assembled bishops expressed their gratitude for his unremitting apostolic labors in the promotion of national Catholic unity.[4]

[4] *C.U.-B.*, Oct. 12, Nov. 30, 1934; Golden Jubilee Number, 1939.

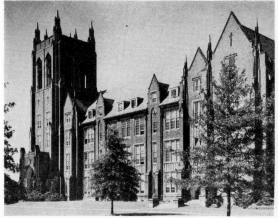

*Above Left:*Notre Dame College for Women.

*Above Right:*John Carroll University.

*Left:*Marymount High School for Girls.

Ursuline College for Women, Merici Hall.

St. Patrick School, Rocky River Drive.

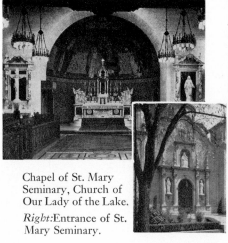

Chapel of St. Mary
Seminary, Church of
Our Lady of the Lake.

*Right:*Entrance of St.
Mary Seminary.

Our Lady of the Elms Academy,
Akron.

St. Sebastian Church and School,
Akron.

Villa San Bernardo, Motherhouse of
Vincentian Sisters of Charity.

Parmadale, view from the air.

63

EUCHARISTIC CONGRESSES

I N RECOGNITION OF HIS LONG ASSOCIATION WITH
such public demonstrations, the prelates assembled in Washington in 1934 honored Bishop Schrembs with the title of Episcopal Promotor of Eucharistic Congresses. One of his first official acts on coming to this diocese had been the establishment of the Shrine of Perpetual Adoration. On September 21, 1930, he dedicated to that purpose a former Protestant church, under the title of the Conversion of St. Paul. It became an important center for many devotions which included all-night vigil before the Blessed Sacrament kept by lay groups, and it was the headquarters for the People's Eucharistic League. It was the favorite repair of the Bishop. In 1928 perpetual adoration was inaugurated by papal rescript, also, in the convent of the Poor Clares on Rocky River Drive.

Under the inspiration of the Bishop many from this diocese attended the great International Eucharistic Congress which was held in Chicago in 1925; he prescribed prayers and public exposition of the Blessed Sacrament in every parish for its success. Many went by rail but the Bishop chartered a lake ship to carry himself and 600 pilgrims to Chicago, and to serve as their hotel. He was one of the principal speakers at the Coliseum on Women's Day, and he addressed several other meetings. As is well known, Bishop Hoban, then Auxiliary to Cardinal Mundelein, was the president of the congress, an outstanding event in the history of the Church in America, which was attended by Cardinal Bonzano as the personal representative of Pope Pius XI, and by other cardinals and prelates and by the clergy and faithful from every corner of the globe.

Meanwhile Bishop Schrembs had succeeded Bishop Maes as the head of the Priests' Eucharistic League. As such he was present at the Eucharistic Congress at Budapest in Hungary; on his return he conveyed the special blessing of the Holy Father to the national congress of the same league in Omaha in 1930. Two years later he led a large pilgrimage to the International Eucharistic Congress in Dublin, Ireland.

The high point, however, in the career of Bishop Schrembs as the promotor of the public recognition of the Real Presence of our Lord in the Blessed Sacrament was reached in the Seventh National Eucharistic Congress celebrated in Cleveland, September 23–26, 1935. The

Holy Father appointed Cardinal Hayes of New York his personal representative to preside over it. In his letter of August 20, 1935, Pope Pius XI gave his high approval to the congress as a practical means "to arouse and to accentuate the fervor and love of our Catholic people towards this august sacrament"; it would be a "solemn occasion when supreme honor would be paid to Our Heavenly King, hidden under the Eucharistic veils." He commended the theme of the congress, "The Holy Eucharist, the Source and Inspiration of Catholic Action," while he blessed every effort "to make the life work of the individual consonant with his Christian Faith" in order that "united Faith nourished by the Eucharist may be of great importance for the body politic." Monsignor Diego Venini, the Pope's private secretary, brought the gift of a beautiful chalice which was used at the principal functions, and Monsignor Carlo Grano came as master of ceremonies.

The whole diocese was thoroughly marshalled under the masterful direction of Monsignor Floyd Begin, the executive secretary, now Auxiliary Bishop; nearly every member of the clergy served in some capacity on committees appointed to take care of every phase of preparation. General headquarters were established in close proximity to the chancery. The publicity committee took effective steps to advertise the purpose of the congress and to arouse interest through articles published in magazines and newspapers, secular and religious, throughout the country. In the schools competitive essays, playlets, and pageants were arranged. Good use was made of the radio: Eucharistic programs were carried on national networks and regular broadcasts were made over the local stations during the months preceding September. A colorful shield dominated by a golden monstrance was adopted as the badge and souvenir of the congress. A special hymnal was published and great choirs of school children and adults spent much time in practice. Jubilee devotions were held in all the churches on three Sundays beginning with the last one in March; the official prayer for success was recited after every liturgical function. In the earlier part of September a triduum of prayers and the observance of National Communion Day by thousands of the faithful sought the blessing of Heaven on the momentous event.

Cleveland offered exceptional facilities for the immense throngs which gathered from all over the country and from foreign lands. The great Public Auditorium and the Stadium which were placed at the disposal of the congress by the city officials have few equals as meeting places. The main auditorium, which when combined with the adjoining Music Hall can seat 18,000 persons, was turned into a vast cathedral; the common stage between them with its altar, thrones, and canopies was the sanctuary for many of the great liturgical offices. The lower basement auditorium was transformed into the Hall of Altars: every diocese and vicariate within the jurisdiction of the United States, 128 in all, had its own altar identified by its heraldic shield and the résumé of its history. Here many Masses were celebrated every morning and the sacraments dispensed by priests assigned to that duty. One large adjoining hall was used for a missionary exhibit; missionaries of the various congregations presided at the many booths. Other rooms and halls were used for the sectional meetings of the clergy, of the different groups of professional men and women, and of other societies related in some way to Catholic Action.

The Municipal Stadium, a vast covered amphitheater on the shore of Lake Erie and within a short distance of the Auditorium, has a seating capacity of over 80,000; with people standing in the uncovered arena, it can enclose double that number and during the congress it was not ineptly called another Roman Coliseum.

On Monday morning, September 23, Cardinal Hayes and his official suite, which included Auxiliary Bishop Donahue of New York and Alfred E. Smith, America's most prominent Catholic layman, arrived at the Union Terminal on Public Square in a special train. Bishop Schrembs and Bishop McFadden, the honorary president of the congress, the Cleveland clergy, Governor Davey, Mayor Davis, other prominent citizens, and a great press of people which crowded the station and the square gave the party a New York welcome. The Cardinal and the bishops rode in open automobiles up Euclid Avenue to East 9th Street through a cheering multitude and then to the Cathedral, in overwhelming contrast to the reception which greeted the first little procession of pioneer Catholics from old St. Mary's in the Flats over the same route long years before.

The Cardinal in a gracious gesture greeted the great crowd which was unable to get into the Cathedral. Inside were the Apostolic Delegate, Archbishop Cicognani, Archbishop McNicolas, the Metropolitan, in all some forty-nine archbishops and bishops; other dignitaries and the clergy filled the sacred edifice. Bishop Schrembs officially and proudly extended the liturgical welcome to the Pope's personal Legate. On the way to the episcopal residence, shortly thereafter, all along Superior Avenue the school children assembled in front of the many parish churches waved an enthusiastic greeting.

In the evening of the same day people from all walks of life filled the Public Auditorium for the civic reception. Bishop McFadden, as chairman, introduced the Governor and the Mayor who again extended an official welcome to the Legate. James Farley, then Postmaster General and the personal representative of President Franklin D. Roosevelt, read the message of the Chief Executive in which he characterized conferences and religious assemblies such as the congress as vitally necessary for the welfare of the people and the nation. Quoting the words of George Washington, "that of all the dispositions and habits which lead to political prosperity, religion and morality are indispensable supports," he continued to say that without religion no nation can long endure, and he pointed out the significance of the fact that "from our beginnings to this day we have unfailingly championed its free exercise and encouraged it by the protection of our laws and our institutions." Judge Joy Hurd spoke for the laity and, after Bishop Schrembs's speech, the Cardinal in his most captivating manner had a word of praise for all.

The next morning in the crowded Auditorium the Legate celebrated the opening Mass which was sung by a massed choir of 3,000 voices; Archbishop McNicolas preached an inspiring sermon for the occasion. Thereafter, the Blessed Sacrament remained exposed in the great hall until the end of the festivities. At the only public social event of the congress the Cardinal and nearly 100 prelates were the guests of the diocese at a dinner after the Mass. In the evening an estimated 50,000 gathered in the Municipal Stadium, "on the shores of the new Gennesareth," to listen to Alfred Smith in his own inimitable way speak on the subject of Communism or Communionism, to Joseph Scott, the well known attorney from the West Coast, discourse on the Mass, and to Monsignor Fulton Sheen, now Bishop, the distinguished radio speaker, as he held the rapt attention of his vast audience with his talk on the Holy Eucharist and the Mystical Body of Christ. Bishop James McCloskey of Jaro in the Philippines took the occasion to extend an invitation to the International Eucharistic Congress which was held there two years later.

On Wednesday, the next morning, in the same great arena some 40,000 young people gathered for the pontifical Mass which was celebrated by the late Archbishop Beckman of Dubuque. The Cardinal addressed them before he went to speak to another large gathering of Catholics of the Oriental Rites in the Auditorium. Here Bishop Takach, Apostolic Exarch for the Ruthenians, celebrated the Mass in the presence of the Apostolic Delegate who had been a member of the Congregation for the Oriental Church in Rome. Father Theophile Zakovich gave the formal and instructive sermon on the unity of the Church. In the evening the Auditorium was filled again by a great crowd which included about 2,000 clerics who made the Holy Hour for Priests; the Cardinal presided and Bishop Schrembs led the meditations.

The most colorful and impressive spectacle of the congress took place that same evening in the Stadium, at the Holy Hour for men and the midnight Mass which followed. An estimated 175,000 participated, including those who could find no room inside the walls but followed the ceremony brought to them by the loud speakers. Originally scheduled to be held in Public Hall, this magnificent demonstration was transferred to the Stadium when notice was received that thousands of pilgrims were on their way from Pittsburgh. The present Archbishop Ritter of St. Louis presided; Archbishop Lucey of San Antonio led the prayers; the tremendous choir was directed by Fathers Joseph N. Trainor and Francis Johns; the Holy Name pledge was repeated by the multitude. The Apostolic Delegate, celebrant of the Mass, was brought with difficulty through the press of people to the glass-enclosed altar; the flood lamps were extinguished, and it was in the flickering light of thousands of candles that the Holy Sacrifice was offered. The awe-inspiring sight left an indelible impression on all who witnessed it. The plan to distribute Holy Communion at this Mass proved to be impracticable, but thousands satisfied their devotion in the parish churches, or in the Hall of Altars where hundreds of priests had been busy all night administering the sacrament of Penance. On Thursday, the last day of the congress, Archbishop Rummel of New Orleans celebrated the Mass in the Auditorium for the women of the diocese who themselves rendered the plain chant. Cardinal Glennon, late Archbishop of St. Louis, preached the sermon. Another Mass was offered in the Stadium for the "overflow" estimated at 50,000, including those who had already taken their places for the culminating point of the congress, the final ceremony in the afternoon. For this the Mayor proclaimed a holiday; the municipal offices were closed; Catholic employees in the business area were freed from their tasks. An immense mass of people converged on the Stadium from every part of the city; downtown Cleveland took on the appearance of a vast sanctuary.

The details of the public procession of the Blessed Sacrament had been admirably and meticulously arranged. At the sound of a cannon shot 20,000 uniformed marchers led by a company of policemen began to move towards the Stadium. The Knights of St. John and their women's auxiliaries, the Catholic Order of Foresters, the Catholic nurses, and other women's organizations in their variegated uniforms formed one division. Following them in another division were the Knights of Columbus, the policemen and firemen, and a delegation of the Irish American Civic Society. Then came various national groups in native costume, delegations from high schools and colleges in academic dress, uniformed parish societies, elementary school children in white blouses and dresses, shepherded by their teachers and city firemen, and altar boys in surplices and cassocks of varied hue.

The music of the many bands was replaced by the sound of muffled drums as the great line reached the Auditorium where it was joined by the ecclesiastics and then became a liturgical procession. First came the seminarians, the priests in chasubles and dalmatics, and the domestic prelates in white and golden copes, followed by a thousand little flower girls carrying their beautiful bouquets. Next followed the superiors of religious orders, including abbots in their distinctive habits and white miters. Immediately preceding the Cardinal walked over a hundred bishops and archbishops in full pontifical regalia. At the end came the Papal Legate, with his ministers in vestments of cloth-of-gold, carrying the Blessed Sacrament in a jeweled monstrance under a canopy of silk and gold brocade. In his suite and as a guard of honor marched the Knights of St. Gregory in their green military dress, delegations of laymen in formal attire, the torch-bearers, and prelates in purple cassocks.

The reverential silence of the great crowds which lined the streets was broken only by the continuous round of prayers and hymns directed through loud speakers from the Stadium which was already filled. According to a very ingenious and accurate plan, the marchers in the procession upon entering the grounds of the Stadium became part of an immense Living Monstrance which occupied the arena. When the Cardinal reached the center of this unique demonstration all joined in the Benediction hymns and the Divine Praises. Bishop Gallagher of Detroit led the acclamations, calling down God's blessing on all mankind. A profound silence was then observed in expectation of the voice of the Holy Father. The full sense of the devotion and love which the assembled multitude felt for the Father of Christendom was reflected in the hushed attention given to his words as they came by direct wire from Castel Gandolfo, intoning the apostolic blessing upon all America and especially upon those who participated in the congress.

Pope Pius XI indicated his desire to speak face to face and heart to heart with his own voice just as if he were present; he was joyful at the opportunity and praised the spirit of faith, love, and zeal of all who had assisted in preparing the magnificent banquet of Our Divine King; he prayed for the increase in faith and for the development of Catholic life and action in the struggle for moral uprightness, for modesty and decency; he deprecated the material and moral havoc brought on by wars and their dire aftermath of tears and sorrow; he prayed for peace and for "a less intolerable burden of life" for a world worn to exhaustion by the ravages of the great depression. With the final blessing of the Holy Father upon the country, its rulers, and upon all who were listening to him, the congress came to an end. The weather had proved to be ideal; the rain which threatened the last demonstration did not come until after the Cardinal Legate was well on his way home to New York.

Cardinal Hayes and Bishop Schrembs both made a full and detailed report and sent photographs of the principal events to the Holy Father.

In reply Cardinal Pacelli, then Secretary of State, now our gloriously reigning Pontiff, expressed in glowing terms the pleasure and satisfaction of Pope Pius XI and his own at its wonderful success: "The city of Cleveland accorded the Holy Eucharist a triumph which shall be written in golden letters upon the pages of history." He said further that "the congress was the moving portrayal of the primacy of the spiritual over the temporal," proclaiming as it did that "our hope and our strength and our salvation is from God and not from creatures." He invited all "to seek in Jesus Christ the grace to achieve the personal sanctification which must precede collective regeneration." He rejoiced at the magnificent tribute paid by the powerful and vigorous North America to Christ in the Eucharist, prelates and people adoring the veiled majesty of the Saviour and reflecting the vision of St. John, bowed down in reverence before His Almighty Power; and he prayed that moral cohesion and unanimity of purpose be preserved in the

Church in America as an example of the unity of the Church in the world, "even now sundered by hatred and contention."

The doctrinal theme of the congress, which was concerned with Catholic Action, was particularly pleasing to the Holy Father who saw in its development in lectures and conferences a special contribution to the Catholic cause. The Living Monstrance on the last day of the congress was for the Pope the visible and emblematic expression of Catholic Action: laymen aiding the hierarchy in the exercise of their apostolic functions for the purpose of restoring all things in Christ, everyone finding inspiration, greater fervor, and holiness of life in the Holy Eucharist and in turn distributing the talents of grace he had thus received. "Bishops and priests surrounding the altar as a halo, while the serried ranks of the faithful filled in the base, the stem, and the projecting rays of the monstrance." The aim and aspiration of Catholic Action, the Pope continued to say, "is that Jesus may be set before the world in all the splendor of His magnificence, and that the people who glory in His Name may cast aside error, rouse themselves from sloth and give themselves wholly to the Faith and the Law and the Grace of Christ in order to have life and have it more abundantly."

Catholic Action, however, cannot exist without charity and "the wellspring of charity is the Holy Eucharist, the source of the zeal, generosity, and sacrifice for the children of the Church in every land; this charity is the bond which joins us to God in submission, and to one another in mutual endeavor; and just as the grains of wheat and the single grapes are made into one bread and into one wine, and in the Mass become the Body of Christ, so the hosts of Catholic Action in their observance of the law of the Church and in their adherence to her doctrine will by common effort be united in thought and deed to the great advantage of the cause of religion."

Men of good-will in the world, the letter recalled, finding no satisfaction in what they have, often without realizing it reach out for the spiritual, and for the charity which should bind them all together, and for the truth which should give them light. The Pope prayed that this truth and charity would enrich all those who wage the battle for Christ under the banner of Catholic Action. In a closing paragraph he praised "his beloved children of North America" and especially those who deserved well for their part in the congress, the Cardinal Legate and the "most zealous Bishop of Cleveland." In a significant gesture he invoked prosperity and happiness upon those who, though unfortunately separated from the Catholic Church, yet by their kind and generous assistance helped to make the congress a success.[1]

Cardinal Pacelli, who three years afterwards was to be elected Pope Pius XII, visited Cleveland in 1936. Bishops Schrembs and McFadden and a delegation of priests and faithful greeted him and the future

[1] *Seventh National Eucharist Congress, Official Record*, 741 pp., Cleveland, 1936, reproduces the official documents and many fine photographs.

Cardinal Spellman at the airport when he graciously deigned to interrupt his journey through the United States.

Following the pattern of the Cleveland congress, but necessarily on a reduced scale, similar celebrations were held later in the different sections of the diocese. The first was in Youngstown in September, 1936, under the general direction of Father William Kane, the dean. The theme, "Christ in the Eucharist, the Source and Inspiration of Parish Life," was the subject of the conferences and lectures in the Stambaugh Auditorium which was the center of activities. In his pastoral inviting all to attend the Bishop suggested that the purpose of the congress be to console the Holy Father in his sorrow over the then current persecution of the Church in Spain. The Bishop presided at the midnight Mass celebrated at a gleaming stainless steel altar which symbolized so well the whole surrounding industrial country. In the closing ceremony he carried the Blessed Sacrament in public procession through the adjacent city park and bestowed the apostolic blessing upon the estimated 75,000 persons present. Out of the congress came the inspiration for a series of Holy Hours in the various city parish churches.[2]

The second diocesan congress, in Lorain in 1937, was under the supervision of the dean, Father James Daley.[3] The midnight Mass was celebrated in St. Mary's Church by Bishop McFadden; he and two Hungarian bishops were present at the public procession in Lakeview Park when Bishop Schrembs carried the Blessed Sacrament through a numerous and reverent throng of people.

The Akron congress[4] was held in May, 1938, under the management of the dean, Father Joseph O'Keefe. St. Bernard's Church was the center of devotions. An open air Mass was celebrated at Buchtel Field; some 14,000 marchers formed a Living Monstrance around the altar. About 50,000 people assisted at the ceremonies at which three bishops were present, Bishop McFadden, Bishop Takach of Pittsburgh, and Bishop Schrembs who presided. The keynote of the talks concerned industrial peace and it was thought that the congress had some effect in reducing the possibility of disturbance during the then current rubber strike.

The fourth congress was held in Canton[5] under the general direction of the dean, Father George Habig, in May, 1940. Unfortunately two days of rain interfered with the outdoor celebration but midnight Mass was offered in St. Peter's Church in the presence of a great crowd. Bishop McFadden carried the Blessed Sacrament in public procession through the Stadium under dripping skies; Bishop Schrembs presided at the closing and gave the apostolic benediction to several thousands who braved the weather to attend.

[2] *C.U.-B.*, Memorial Number, Oct. 2, 1936.
[3] *C.U.-B.*, Mar. 19, May 28, 1937.
[4] *C.U.-B.*, May 13, 1938.
[5] *C.U.-B.*, June 7, 1940.

Under the supervision of Father William A. Gallena, the dean, the fifth congress was held in Painesville in May, 1941. St. Mary's Church was the center of activities. Bishop McFadden carried the Blessed Sacrament through an estimated crowd of 10,000 assembled in Recreation Park; the Bishop of Cleveland gave the Benediction of the Blessed Sacrament and the apostolic blessing.

64

DIOCESAN CELEBRATIONS

PUBLIC DEMONSTRATIONS WERE DEAR TO THE heart of Bishop Schrembs and he rarely allowed an event of local or national importance to pass without one, convinced as he was that they were useful for religion and kept the people conscious of the fact that they were members of a living and active body.

In 1922 the seventy-fifth anniversary of the founding of the diocese was kept with a solemn triduum of devotions in every parish. The official celebration took place in the Cathedral on November 7, when the Bishop pontificated in the presence of Archbishop Moeller, the Metropolitan, and of seven other bishops. Bishop Schwertner of Wichita in his sermon sympathetically recalled the life and works of the early missionaries and bishops in this territory.

In the evening in the Public Auditorium some 20,000 people gathered to listen to Father John Cavanaugh of the University of Notre Dame deliver an eloquent speech in which he emphasized the fact that the Church in training her children in the virtues for citizenship on earth as well as for heaven makes an inestimable contribution to the common welfare of the country. He paid high compliment to the leaders of the Church in Cleveland. "Bishop Schrembs," he said, "was one whose voice was heard round the world, and whose energies overflowed his diocese to make his see more distinguished than ever." Bishop Rappe he called the "swift and substantial builder"; Bishop Gilmour, "the gladiator of God, the protector of his people, the fighting man and the writing man"; Bishop Horstmann, "the genial ruler on his throne, the learned scholar on his rostrum"; Bishop Farrelly, "the mitered recluse, except where duty called, the exquisite connoisseur, the inheritor of Old World culture."[1]

The Bishop of Arras in France sent his congratulations and recalled to mind that it was his diocese which sent the first Bishop and the first Sisters to Cleveland.[2] The Holy Father in special recognition of the event promised the precious relics of a Roman martyr, and three years later those of the Roman virgin and martyr, St. Christina, were

[1] C.U., Oct. 27, Nov. 10, Dec. 8, 1922.
[2] C.U., Mar. 16, 1923.

*Right:*Seventh Eucharistic Congress. Procession to the Cathedral: Cardinal Hayes, Archbishops Cicognani and Schrembs.

*Left:*Seventh Eucharistic Congress. Hall of Altars.

Seventh Eucharistic Congress. The Living Monstrance.

The first visit to Cleveland of Archbishop Cicognani, Apostolic Delegate.
Pictured from left to right: The Rt. Rev. Msgr. Charles A. Martin, L.L.D., the Rev.
Maurice F. Griffin, L.L.D., Bishop Schrembs, Bishop McFadden, the Rt. Rev. Msgr.
Gilbert P. Jennings, L.L.D., the Rt. Rev. Msgr. Nicholas Pfeil, D.D. In the rear: The
Rev. John R. Kenny, L.L.D., the Rev. Michael J. Ready, the Rev. Alphonse M. Schwitalla,
S.J., the Rev. Edward A. Reilly.

Pope Pius XII, then Cardinal
Pacelli, greeting Archbishop
Schrembs, 1936.

Seventh Eucharistic Congress.
Cardinal Hayes and Archbishop
Schrembs.

Seventh National Eucharistic Congress, 1935.
Cardinal Hayes, Papal Legate, and his official suite;
Seated, l. to r.: The Most Rev. Joseph Schrembs, The Most Rev. Amleto Giovanni
Cicognani, Patrick Cardinal Hayes, The Most Rev. John T. McNicholas, The Most Rev.
James A. McFadden. Standing: The Rt. Rev. Msgr. Carlo Grano, The Very Rev. John J.
Casey, Henry Coakley, Dr. Joseph Sullivan, Msgr. Michael J. Lavelle, Msgr. Diego
Venini, Marquis George MacDonald, Marquis Gerald Borden, Joseph Mulholland, Alfred
E. Smith.

enshrined in the Cathedral. The eightieth anniversary of the diocese was marked by the Achievement Edition of the *Universe-Bulletin*, which summarized the work of the Bishop and his predecessors.

In 1923 the Bishop went to Europe to recoup his energy in a visit to his old home in Bavaria, where he distributed monies which had been collected for the relief of the war sufferers. Two years later he led a Holy Year Pilgrimage to Rome and presented a substantial purse from the diocese to the Holy Father for his many and pressing charities. The Detroit pilgrimage led by Bishop Gallagher joined them in a special audience, in which Bishop Schrembs acted as interpreter and directed the singing of a hymn in honor of His Holiness. Through the generosity of an Akron merchant, Charles Byrider, he was able to offer the funds necessary for the construction of the Catacombs' Museum. After a four months absence a thanksgiving service in the Cathedral marked his happy return.

In the autumn of 1927, accompanied by Monsignor McFadden, he made his *ad limina* visit to the Tomb of the Apostles. He also went to Germany, and upon his return in February, 1928, before a crowded audience in the Cathedral he gave a graphic description of Theresa Neumann whom he had visited in Konnersreuth. Exhibiting a blood-stained head cloth as a relic of her having experienced the agonies of the Passion of Our Lord, he hoped that his recountal would arouse in his listeners a greater love of the Saviour. And while not anticipating the judgment of the Church in the case, he himself "felt as if he had been in the presence of the supernatural."

The same month witnessed the first episcopal consecration in the old Cathedral, that of the first native son of Cleveland to be so honored. Thomas Charles O'Reilly, the youngest son of Patrick and Delia Readdy O'Reilly, was born on February 22, 1873, in old St. Patrick's parish on the West Side and he attended its parochial school. After a course of studies in a business college he registered at St. Ignatius College on Carroll Avenue. He spent the scholastic year which began in September, 1893, at St. Mary's Seminary on Lakeside Avenue before going to Rome to the North American College to finish his clerical studies. He obtained his doctor's degree from the College of the Propaganda and was ordained priest, June 4, 1898, by the papal vicar, Archbishop Francesco Cassetta, later a cardinal.

He was at first appointed assistant priest at the Cathedral and then in 1901 professor at the seminary. Bishop Farrelly in 1909 made him chancellor and pastor of the Cathedral. Domestic prelate in 1914, he was vicar general from 1916 to 1921. In the administration of Bishop Schrembs he was diocesan consultor, head of the matrimonial court, and vicar general for religious women. He was prominent in civic as well as in ecclesiastical affairs. Chosen for the vacant See of Scranton, December 19, 1927, he was consecrated February 16, 1928, by Cardinal Dougherty of Philadelphia, his metropolitan, who was assisted by

Bishop Schrembs and Bishop Philip R. McDevitt of Harrisburg. In April, 1937, he was stricken with a heart attack; thus forced to retire to Florida, he died there, March 25, 1938.

The Golden Jubilee of Pope Pius XI in 1929 (and his recognition as an independent sovereign in the Lateran Pact) was published here, and the churches which were to be visited to gain the indulgences were designated, before the Bishop accompanied by many of the clergy and people again set out for Rome carrying with him a richly embossed book inscribed with the promises of many Masses and prayers. Cardinal Merry del Val received the group in the name of the Holy Father who himself at a later date gave the Bishop a special audience in honor of his fortieth year in the priesthood; the actual anniversary he had kept at Lourdes. Upon his return the Cleveland clergy feted him at a dinner in Hotel Cleveland and presented him with pledges for the amount necessary to build a chapel at Parmadale; in a fine gesture of approval he transferred the pledges to John Carroll University. He would, he said, await the celebration of his golden jubilee for the acceptance of any kind of memorial.

A great Holy Name Rally in September, 1931, marked the tenth year of the Bishop in Cleveland. An estimated 75,000 in the Stadium were there to honor him and to listen to addresses by Archbishop Joseph Rummel, then of Omaha, and to the well-known lecturer, Peter Collins of Boston. The Holy Name pledge was repeated by the great throng which joined in the adoration of the Blessed Sacrament, as a shower of roses was dropped from an autogyro flying overhead.

In 1932 the Bishop hurried home from the Dublin Eucharistic Congress to consecrate Monsignor McFadden his Auxiliary. James Augustine, one of the twelve children of Edward and Mary Cavanaugh McFadden, was born, December 24, 1880, in Holy Name parish in old Newburg. He attended the Cathedral school and, later, Holy Name school (for two years) before spending five years at St. Ignatius College. In September, 1899, he entered St. Mary's Seminary here and on June 17, 1905, he was ordained priest in the Cathedral by Bishop Horstmann. He was assistant priest at St. Agnes', Cleveland, until in 1914 he organized St. Agnes' parish in Elyria. Bishop Farrelly made him rector of the seminary in 1917, and in 1923 Bishop Schrembs made him the first diocesan director of the Society for the Propagation of the Faith. In 1925 he became chancellor and two years later a domestic prelate. He was the chairman of the successful campaigns which so greatly increased the circulation of the *Universe-Bulletin*, and was of incalculable assistance to the Bishop in other ways.

On May 13, 1932, the Holy See appointed him Titular Bishop of Bida and Auxiliary to Bishop Schrembs, who on September 8 following consecrated him in the Cathedral, with the assistance of Bishop O'Reilly of Scranton and Bishop Gallagher of Detroit. Present for the occasion were three archbishops and twenty-three other bishops, among them Bishop Hoban of Rockford. The clergy honored him with a dinner at Hotel Cleveland, the laity with a general reception in Public Hall. Until his transfer to Youngstown as its first bishop in 1943, he carried a large share in the burden of the administration of this diocese.

In the following year the Bishop had the privilege of consecrating another son of the diocese. This was Father LeBlond who had been chosen by the Holy See, July 21, 1933, to be Bishop of St. Joseph in Missouri. Charles Hubert, the only child of Anne Marie (Brennan) and Charles McGinley LeBlond, was born in Celina, Ohio, November 21, 1883. At the age of five he entered the Cathedral school; he received his secondary education at St. Ignatius College. He studied philosophy and theology at St. Mary's Seminary here and was ordained by Bishop Farrelly, June 29, 1909. He was assistant priest at the Cathedral until his appointment as diocesan director of charities and chaplain at St. Anthony's Home in 1911.

Above we have seen the prominent part he played in the organization of Catholic charities in this diocese. He was an original contributor to community welfare planning and to organized social work especially in the institutional care of children. He represented Cleveland at international gatherings of the leaders in such work in Peru, Germany, and France.

On September 21, 1933, Bishop Schrembs, assisted by Bishop McFadden and Bishop Thomas C. O'Reilly, conferred the dignity of the episcopacy upon him in the Cathedral in the presence of a great number of the hierarchy and of the priests of the diocese, whose guest he was at a dinner following the ceremony. Because of his intimate association with the public life of the city he was feted at many civic celebrations. Much attached to Cleveland, Bishop LeBlond was to be seen here at nearly every important ecclesiastical event.

Also in 1933 Catholic Day was observed by a great pageant in Public Hall; 800 participants portrayed scenes from the life of Our Lord. On June 17, 1934, the second such celebration was held in the Stadium under the sponsorship of the Holy Name Society; the Apostolic Delegate, Archbishop Cicognani, was the honored guest. Some 50,000 persons joined Governor White and Mayor Davis, Bishops Schrembs and McFadden, and the clergy in welcoming the representative of the Holy Father. Uniformed societies and other groups in academic dress formed a Living Cross around the altar from which the Benediction of the Blessed Sacrament was given; the great throng repeated the pledge of the Legion of Decency.

In this same year the Bishop made his *ad limina* visit to Rome. He was held in long audiences by the Holy Father, much of the conversation concerning the Cleveland Eucharistic Congress, the plans for which were already in the making. Upon his return the Bishop announced that the Pope had given him the special privilege of bestowing the apostolic blessing whenever the occasion demanded it. The next great public demonstration was for the twenty-fifth anniversary of the Bishop's consecration. In the Public Auditorium, April 27, 1936, he offered his Mass of Thanksgiving in the presence of fifteen members of the hierarchy, and of the faithful and clergy who crowded the large hall, and listened with attention and lawful pride to Archbishop McNicolas recount his accomplishments. According to custom the jubilarian and the visiting bishops were the guests of the local clergy at a dinner in Hotel Cleveland. In the evening at the civic reception Mayor Burton and Senator Bulkley were among the representatives of city, State, and nation who gave expression to the deep regard and admiration in which he was held.

65

ARCHBISHOP SCHREMBS

THE HIGH POINT IN THE CAREER OF THE
Bishop was reached when on the occasion of his golden
jubilee in the priesthood the newly elected Pope Pius XII
by decree of March 25, 1939, conferred upon him the
personal title of archbishop. The Apostolic Delegate in
making the announcement recalled that the jubilarian "had dedicated
every force and energy to the welfare of the Church and the salvation
of souls with the love and zeal of a true father and pastor." Mention
was made of his services to the Church in the National Catholic Welfare Council, of his efforts in the spread of public devotion to the
Blessed Sacrament, and of his "noble and inspired preaching." Thereafter, he was to be addressed as the Archbishop-Bishop of Cleveland.
The Holy Father, May 13, 1939, addressed a letter to him under the
new title.

President Franklin D. Roosevelt, in sending his official congratulations, recalled that the Archbishop was the last survivor of those who
drew up the Catholic bishops' program of social reconstruction which
called for readjustments, social, economic, and political, in the period
following the First World War. The ninety-third General Assembly of
the Ohio legislature also passed a resolution of congratulations to the
Archbishop whom they called a great churchman, counselor, and
leader.[1]

A colorful spectacle in the Municipal Stadium, June 11, 1939, gave
public expression to the general jubilation over the event. A great
throng of people who filled the seats of the amphitheater arose to their
feet as a striking procession filed into the arena. Teachers and professors from the higher schools of the diocese and of the nation and
representatives of foreign universities, all in cap and gown in all the
colors of the rainbow, walked in front of more than twenty bishops
and archbishops in full pontificals. Surrounded by this great academic
senate, the new Archbishop, himself a member of the Board of Trustees of the Catholic University, presented some 900 diplomas to representative graduates of that year from the schools and colleges of the
diocese. Governor Bricker and Mayor Burton represented the civil
government.

[1] C.U.-B., Mar. 25, 1939.

The principal speaker, the present Archbishop Karl Joseph Alter of Cincinnati, ably reviewed the life of the jubilarian and recalled his national leadership, his protection and support of the American Federation of Catholic Societies and of the Central Verein, and "his pleading the cause and rescuing the National Catholic Welfare Conference from oblivion." He credited the Archbishop with securing the recognition of President Wilson for the War Chest in the First World War. Archbishop McNicolas, then Metropolitan of this province, referred to the jubilarian as a public-spirited citizen, a champion of truth and righteousness, the apostle of peace, and the enemy of war. All agreed that he was the builder, the organizer, the great shepherd of souls, the warrior in the cause of social justice.

The distinctly liturgical celebration of the jubilee was held in the Cathedral on June 29, the actual anniversary of his ordination fifty years before. Assisted by the first and the last priest[2] whom he himself had ordained here, the Archbishop pontificated at Mass in the Cathedral in the presence of the clergy of the diocese who afterwards honored him with a dinner in Hotel Cleveland. There he surrounded himself with those of them who had already passed their fiftieth year in the ministry.[3]

To honor him still more the Holy Father, December 11, 1939, granted him the personal use of the pallium which Monsignor Joseph Hurley, later Archbishop-Bishop of St. Augustine, Florida, brought from Rome. On February 22, 1940, the twenty-ninth anniversary of his consecration, he was invested with it by Archbishop McNicolas who also preached the formal sermon. Nine other bishops and Archbishop Mooney of Detroit honored the occasion with their presence. The band of white wool with its black woolen crosses, which was fastened to the Mass vestments by three gemmed pins in the form of thorns, is worn by the Holy Father himself, and as a symbol of union with the Holy See is bestowed by him upon the archbishop of a province, and upon other prelates only by way of special privilege.[4]

This was the culmination of all his honors. He had been Assistant to the Pontifical Throne since 1920; the University of Freiburg in Germany had awarded him the doctorate in theology in 1923 in recognition of his generosity after the war; the University of Montreal in 1940 made him a doctor of the university because of "the diligence with which he cared for those of foreign nationality and language"; American universities gave him the honorary degree of Doctor of Laws. He was decorated twice by the Polish Government and by the governments of Italy, Czechoslovakia, and Hungary for his solicitude on behalf of their nationals.

The August of the year of his jubilee saw the seventy-three-year-

[2] Frs. Francis Brucker and William Winchester.
[3] *C.U.-B.*, June 16, 30, 1939; Golden Jubilee Number, 1939.
[4] *C.U.-B.*, June 9, Dec., 1939. Letter of Consistorial Congregation is dated May 5, 1939.

old prelate, with Monsignor Begin, again on his way to Rome for the last time to make his official report and to thank the Pope for the mark of his special favor. They were graciously received at the summer residence at Castel Gandolfo. The Holy Father expressed his great sorrow at the then recent fate of Poland which had so many times saved Europe from the invader. He was pleased to recall his short visit in 1936 at the airport in Cleveland. Forebodings of the war which was imminent were already in the air and it was only through the intervention of the American Ambassador Phillips that return passage was secured on the Italian steamship, Rex. Safely home, the Archbishop ordered that the oration for peace be said in the Mass, hoping that in the mercy of God the conflagration might be confined.[5]

Archbishop Schrembs was endowed by nature with an extraordinarily robust physical constitution. He referred on one occasion to his "hard-hitting blacksmith father" in explanation of his seemingly inexhaustible energy. It was not unusual for him in his best days to appear at three different public affairs and to preach an hour at least in his vigorous style at each of them. He was at the beck and call of every good cause. When a mass meeting was held in Public Hall in 1933 to protest the persecution of the Jews in Europe it was remarked that it was the "first time that Bishop Schrembs was not at a public meeting to raise his golden voice in behalf of suffering humanity." Towards the end of his life, however, he was forced to delegate a substitute; yet, on occasion, he would leave his sick bed at St. John's Hospital to make a public appearance when he considered it to be for the good of religion.

As early as the time of the Eucharistic Congress in 1935 his diabetic condition gave reason for anxiety about his health. His powers of recuperation were remarkable but thereafter he lived altogether at the hospital and much of the routine work of administration was performed by others. In March, 1942, he contracted pneumonia and was anointed; he hovered between life and death; his physician, Doctor Merrick, alone dared to predict his recovery. Yet he was able to celebrate Mass in his room in the following June, and attended by his nurses he took automobiles rides through the city. He suffered another crisis in September, was again anointed, and seemed to be at the point of death. He rallied, however, much to the surprise of his physicians. Although it was difficult for him to walk he appeared at the chancery on November 14; the visit was made one of jubilation and the newspapers carried the story of his recovery.

The appointment in the same month of the present head of the diocese, Bishop Edward Francis Hoban of Rockford, as his Coadjutor with the right of succession brought great relief to his mind. He expressed his gratitude to the Holy See for giving a favorable answer to his petition and dispatched a welcome message to Rockford. When Bishop Hoban a short time afterwards came to visit Cleveland, the

[5] *C.U.-B.*, Sept. 22, 1939.

venerable prelate accompanied his successor to his residence on the Heights. In December he was able to visit the Shrine of the Blessed Sacrament and to say a few words at the blessing of the Honor Roll of the soldiers. On January 13 of the new year, however, he fell into a coma and received the last sacraments; yet he regained consciousness the next day.

He had intended to assist at the installation of Bishop Hoban in the Cathedral on January 21 but his condition made that impossible. Bishop McFadden read the Archbishop's letter of welcome in which he reviewed his own career of service but recognized that his seventy-seven years and his sickness made it very difficult to continue, and he praised the wisdom of the Holy See in sending another to provide for the regular government of the diocese. He welcomed Bishop Hoban as the choice of the Holy Father and as one who came in the name of the Lord. He bestowed his blessing upon him and as an old bishop he prayed that his successor would bring peace and happiness, joy and consolation, to the priests and people of the diocese.

After Bishop Hoban took up permanent residence here, despite his onerous duties he found time to call at the hospital every day; the Archbishop looked forward to these daily visits which brought comfort and consolation to him. He celebrated his seventy-eighth birthday at the new episcopal residence on East 105th Street, but the next one found him quite unable to leave the hospital though he offered the Holy Sacrifice in his room and was able to receive the many visitors who came to see him. After July his strength gradually declined. In October he lapsed into his last coma and died at 3:25 on Friday afternoon, November 2, 1945. Bishop Hoban had given him final absolution; with him when he breathed his last were his nurses, his confessor, and the hospital chaplain.

The body of the deceased prelate was laid out in the chapel of St. Mary's Seminary and was guarded by the students in day and night vigil until on Wednesday Bishop Hoban, his consultors, and the professors escorted it to the Cathedral where it lay in state before the main altar. The children of the schools along the route stood at reverent attention as the cortege passed down Superior Avenue. In announcing the death of his predecessor Bishop Hoban referred to him as "father, friend, and counsellor" and he ordered that the church buildings of the diocese be draped in mourning for a month. Messages of condolence poured into the chancery. The Holy Father, Cardinal Pizzardo, and the Apostolic Delegate expressed the sympathy of the universal Church.

As a token of Catholic unity Vespers and Mass in the Byzantine Rite were celebrated in the Cathedral for his soul. At another Mass, attended by the members of the religious congregations of women for whom he had done so much, Monsignor McDonough, the vicar general, delivered the eulogy. He spoke of the singleness of purpose of the prelate whose work touched the lives of his people from every angle. Referring to the Eucharistic Congress in Cleveland as the climax of his career, the speaker recalled the "unabating enthusiasm and the elation of consecration" with which the deceased prelate was inspired even to his dying day. Leading business men of the city and representatives of the major religious groups joined in a memorial broadcast over Station WJW in which they extolled the virtues of the deceased. He was called an "eminent exponent of religious toleration so characteristic of Cleveland." A rabbi said of him that he "was another Joseph of the Old Testament; all mankind his brethren, fearless as he was in defense of principle."

Seven archbishops and fifteen bishops, many other prelates and priests, the Governor of the State of Ohio, the Mayor and the city officials, the British consul, representatives of the labor unions, and those of the faithful who could get into the building filled the Cathedral to capacity for the solemn pontifical Funeral Mass which was celebrated by Bishop Hoban on November 9, 1945. Archbishop McNicolas in his sermon spoke of the ceaseless journeyings, the preaching, the conferences, and the leadership in the diocese and the country which would have exhausted the physical stamina of any other man, and yet, in the last six years of his life, when he was removed from the sphere of this extreme activity and given time in the quiet and solitude of the sick room "to make his soul," his resignation and patience, his gratitude and cheerfulness, were marvelous sources of edification to all.

He recalled the Archbishop's love of every church function and of the sacred ritual, for sacred music and great public ecclesiastical demonstrations, of his skill as an apologist and his irresistible oratorical powers, and of his public-spirited interest in civic affairs when moral issues were involved. "Although he could be stern in voice and in the dramatics of a situation," he said, "in the presence of realities his emotional character softened and his heart was merciful. His zeal for the beauty of the Lord's House in the material expansion of church buildings was comparable only to that which he exercised in the encouragement of religious vocations to the priesthood and the religious communities of women. The bishops of the province owed him gratitude for his valuable advice and cooperation at their annual meetings; the hierarchy of the country, for the part he played in the restoration of the N.C.W.C. The cause he had advocated had been vindicated and approved by the Popes themselves."

The Archbishop was survived by his half-brother, Jacob Schrembs, by five nieces and two nephews and by his cousin, Theresa Gess, who had been his faithful housekeeper for many years. In his last will and testament he declared he held no ill-will towards anyone and, "for the love of God our merciful Father," he begged forgiveness of those he might have unintentionally offended. Believing that he was leaving the heritage of a consecrated life, he asked for prayers. After a few individual bequests to relatives and for Masses, "for his poor soul," he left his estate such as it was to Sisters' College which he had founded.

He was buried in the crypt under the Cathedral which he had taken care to have repaired and remodeled. Later the remains were transferred to the mortuary chapel in the new Cathedral edifice.[6]

Summoned by the Holy See to the high and responsible duties of the episcopacy, Archbishop Schrembs brought with him ability, foresight, and vision, tireless energy and contagious enthusiasm, and an irrepressible zeal for the spread of God's kingdom on earth. The Holy See recognized this and rewarded him for a lifelong unsparing and single-purposed consecration to that end. His achievement in the erection of churches and schools and in the training of priests and Sisters to carry on the work of the Church in them, his solicitude for the spiritual progress of his flock, his interest in the poor and the orphans, his fearless stand for the Christian solution of social and industrial problems, his unqualified condemnation of subversive agencies, his watchful promotion of lay organization and of Catholic Action, his interest in the Catholic press, in the youth movement, in the missionary activities of the Church—all these and many more accomplishments of which the Recording Angel has the account, proclaim him to have been a great man and a great bishop.

[6] *C.U.-B.,* Nov. 16, 1945.

➤➤➤ 66 ⇚⇚⇚

THE SIXTH BISHOP OF

CLEVELAND

LTHOUGH HE DID NOT SUCCEED TO THE TITLE
itself for nearly three years afterwards, Bishop Hoban
became the effective head of the Diocese of Cleveland
when he was installed as Coadjutor to Archbishop
Schrembs, January 21, 1943.

Edward Francis Hoban was born in Chicago, Illinois, June 27, 1878, the son of William and Bridget O'Malley Hoban, both of Irish origin. He had four sisters, Mrs. Cecilia Doherty, Mrs. Theresa Alcock, Mrs. Sara Dailey and Mary who died in childhood, and three brothers, Thomas J., William J., and Henry A. Hoban. Two of his nephews are priests of the Archdiocese of Chicago: Fathers Edward V. Dailey and Howard Doherty. Edward Francis was baptized, received his First Holy Communion, was confirmed, and attended the parochial school in St. Columbkille's parish, well known for the number of bishops who have been associated with it. He distinguished himself during his high school and college courses at the Jesuit College of St. Ignatius in his native city.

At old St. Mary's Seminary in Baltimore, where he made his studies in philosophy and theology, he was a favorite of Cardinal Gibbons who often called upon him to display his fine singing talent. He was ordained priest, July 11, 1903, by the newly appointed Archbishop James Edward Quigley in the Chicago Cathedral. For a short time he was assistant pastor at St. Agnes' in that city before he was sent to the Gregorian University in Rome, where he obtained the doctorate in philosophy and in theology.[1] Upon his return to this country he was made a professor at Quigley Preparatory College. In 1906 he became assistant to the chancellor, Doctor Edmund Michael Dunne, whose Mass he had often served at St. Columbkille's and whose place he took when the latter was promoted to the Diocese of Peoria in 1909.

Pope Benedict XV, who had made him papal chamberlain five years previously, in the secret consistory of November 21, 1921, announced his appointment as Titular Bishop of Colonia in Armenia and Auxiliary

[1] *C.U.*, Jan. 14, 1909; Nov. 18, 25, Dec. 30, 1921; Sept. 22, 1922; Feb. 22, May 16, 1924. *C.U.-B.*, Feb. 17, May 11, 25, 1928; rotogravure section, Nov. 22, 1946.

to the Archbishop of Chicago. In Holy Name Cathedral, where he had been ordained priest eighteen years before, Archbishop Mundelein, later Cardinal, assisted by Bishop Alexander McGavick of La-Crosse and Bishop Thomas Molloy of Brooklyn on December 21, 1921, raised him to the dignity of the episcopacy. His close friend, Bishop Dunne, preached the formal sermon on the occasion. Among the five archbishops and twenty bishops who attended the ceremony were the future cardinals, Stritch and Glennon, and two bishops whom he was to succeed, Bishops Muldoon and Schrembs. Among the hundreds of priests who attended were the future prelates, Archbishop Justin D. Simonds of Melbourne, Australia, and Bishop Thomas C. O'Reilly of Scranton.

The young Bishop, a man of personal charm, whose executive abilities and diplomacy had been well tested in the great metropolitan see, was tendered an extraordinary reception by the clergy and people of the city. In 1924 he took the place of Monsignor Michael Fitzsimmons as vicar general of the archdiocese. He was spiritual director also of the Archdiocesan Union of the Holy Name Societies. As the honorary president of the twenty-eighth International Eucharistic Congress he had visited Rome to obtain the appointment of Cardinal Bonzano as the papal legate to preside over it. As the head of the committees which prepared for the congress he had a great share in achieving its eminent success. As the confidant and "right hand" of the Cardinal he was proportionally responsible for the great spiritual and material development of the archdiocese, new parishes, new schools, and other institutions of learning such as the great Seminary of Our Lady of the Lake at Mundelein, the center of the magnificent procession of the Blessed Sacrament during the Eucharistic Congress.

On February 10, 1928, Pope Pius XI transferred him to Rockford to succeed Bishop Muldoon who died in the previous October. Archbishop Mundelein installed him in St. James pro-Cathedral on May 15, in a ceremony attended by twenty-eight archbishops and bishops. In the new sphere of activity he continued to merit the reputation of a builder and patron of education. In the see city he erected a large chancery building and episcopal residence and founded the parish of St. Edward; two new elementary schools were put up, and in two of the older parishes new churches; two other churches were completely remodeled and enlarged. The new St. Thomas High School for Boys was entrusted to the Augustinian Fathers and the new Bishop Muldoon High School for Girls to the Dominican Sisters of Adrian, Michigan. St. Anthony's Hospital was remodeled and enlarged. The monastery of the Colettine Nuns was made over.

Outside the city of Rockford four new parishes were established and new churches constructed in them; six other churches were extensively remodeled; one combination church-hall and four other auditoriums were newly constructed; five new elementary schools were put up and two others were enlarged.

Archbishop Edward F. Hoban, sixth Bishop of Cleveland, in his private chapel.

Inset:Archbishop Hoban (center) at his Silver Jubilee. Cardinals Mooney, Spellman and Stritch and Archbishop McNicholas.

Archbishop Hoban at celebration of his Silver Jubilee in St. Agnes Church.

Left:Archbishops Schrembs and Hoban examining the chalice sent by Pope Pius XI to the Eucharistic Congress in Cleveland in 1935.

Right:Archbishop Hoban and the Apostolic Delegate signing the Honor Roll of service personnel from the Diocese.

Cardinal Pacelli (Pope Pius XII) greeting Archbishop Hoban at the Chicago airport in 1936. Cardinal Spellman looking on.

Archbishop Hoban at the enlarged Parmadale.

At Aurora the new Marmion Military Academy was given in charge to the Benedictine Fathers, and Madonna High School was much enlarged and improved. At Elgin the new St. Edward's High School was started in 1941; the Servite Fathers opened a seminary, and the Missionaries of the Sacred Heart replaced theirs with a new building. At Freeport the Aquinas Community High School was enlarged, St. Joseph's Home for the Aged was modernized, and St. Vincent's Orphan Asylum was made the model institution of its kind in the Middle West. It was here at St. Vincent's that Bishop Hoban every year celebrated the Feast of the Immaculate Conception with the children for whom he had done so much. At St. Charles, Sterling, and Woodstock the high schools were enlarged to accommodate an increased enrollment. The Bishop left his first diocese with nearly sixty per cent of the parishes equipped with schools, and with one of the highest per capita parochial school attendances in the country.

In the diocese the Bureau of Catholic Charities was entirely reorganized and a new Social Center was opened at Oregon. Always an ardent supporter of the Catholic press, the Bishop founded the Rockford *Observer* in 1935. He led pilgrimages to Jerusalem, Manila, and Rome. On account of his interest in their nationals in his diocese, the Spanish and Italian governments bestowed high honors upon him.

Bishop Hoban was one of the bishops who greeted Pope Pius XII, then Cardinal Pacelli, when he visited this country in 1936. It was in obedience to the same Supreme Pontiff that he transferred his talents and activities to a new field in the Diocese of Cleveland. On November 14, 1942, the Holy Father confirmed his appointment as Titular Bishop of Lystra in Turkey and Coadjutor to Archbishop Schrembs with the right to succeed him in case of his death or resignation. The local newspapers, which expressed the satisfaction of all at the nomination, carried the announcement on November 17, the day the news was released by the Apostolic Delegate in Washington.

The latter in a decree[2] of January 6, 1943, authorized Bishop Hoban to take up his new duties without waiting for the arrival of the official papal documents which were necessarily delayed by the war conditions. Recalling that Archbishop Schrembs, "on account of his long standing ill health, and in order to provide adequately for the administration of the diocese," had asked the Pope for the appointment of a coadjutor bishop, Archbishop Cicognani reported the papal acquiescence. Bishop Hoban was the choice, and to him were given all the rights and powers needed for the direction and administration of the diocese.

After the public announcement, a flood of telegrams and letters assured the Bishop of a warm welcome and he came here on a quiet visit to arrange for his installation. At his Mass in the Rockford pro-Cathedral, January 14, 1943, he bade farewell and expressed his regret at

[2] Text of decree, in *C.U.-B.*, Jan. 22, 1943.

having to leave those who had given such generous support to his efforts for the advancement of religion and education.

Escorted by priests from Chicago and Rockford and a delegation of Clevelanders who had gone to meet him, he arrived in this city on January 20 and was met by Bishop McFadden and other officials at the Union Terminal. Much to the edification of all, even though the train was five hours late, he had kept his fast and celebrated his first Mass in the city at a temporary altar erected in Hotel Cleveland. At a dinner at the episcopal residence in the evening he was presented with a golden key as a token of welcome. The next morning (January 21) a colorful procession solemnly preceded him through the portals of the old Cathedral, already filled by the faithful eager to witness the installation of the first coadjutor bishop in the history of the diocese.

The Governor of Ohio, the Mayor of the city, and other officials were there to represent the civil authorities. Hundreds of priests, mitered abbots, and high prelates took their places to the triumphal peal of the organ: the Benedictine Abbots Neuzil and Gmuca, whom he knew in Chicago; Bishop Leo Binz, his former secretary; the prelates associated with him in the Catholic Extension Society: Bishops Eugene J. McGuinness, William O'Brien, and Bernard Sheil; the venerable missionary, Bishop Joseph Crimont, S.J., of Alaska; all the Ohio bishops; Archbishop Ritter of Indianapolis; Bishops Noll of Fort Wayne, Plagens of Grand Rapids, Schlarman of Peoria; the former Clevelanders, Bishops LeBlond and Hurley. At the end of the procession came the Archbishop of Chicago, the present Cardinal Stritch, and Bishop Hoban and last of all the Metropolitan of the province, Archbishop McNicolas.

Entering the sanctuary, Bishop Hoban was led to the episcopal throne on the Gospel side by the Archbishop who then took up his own position on a special throne prepared for him on the other side. The notary proclaimed the decree of the Apostolic Delegate and Bishop McFadden read the letter of welcome from Archbishop Schrembs. Bishop Hoban dramatically responded: "I am here, beloved Archbishop, in answer to your appeal to the Holy Father."

He pledged undying loyalty to the Holy See and unswerving fidelity to its commands and promised to the best of his ability to do his utmost to serve the Church in Cleveland. After gratefully acknowledging the warm welcome of the Archbishop and of Bishop McFadden, whom he commended for his generous cooperation, he addressed himself to the Cleveland clergy. Following the lesson for the Feast of the Epiphany, January 6, the date of the decree authorizing him to proceed to his new post, he asked for the gold of the obedience they had promised at ordination; for the frankincense of their Masses and prayers; and for the myrrh of personal sacrifice in the cause of Christ. He asked them to be his coadjutors, helpers, workers, servants, and sons; he would serve them, and serve with them. The churches, schools, and institutions of charity he had already observed in his tour of the city were for him monuments to the generous self-sacrifice of the laity. He had a word, too, for the men and women in the armed forces, and for the good account they were giving of their training in religion. Undoubtedly affected by the solemnity of the occasion, the Bishop called down the blessing of the Saviour upon all, and then proceeded to offer the installation Mass.

At the dinner in Hotel Cleveland tendered the Bishop and his friends, Archbishop McNicolas in welcoming him to the province spoke of his "episcopal maturity, of his kindness and mercy, and of the affectionate regard of the clergy gained in his fifteen years of administration in Rockford." He recalled that Cardinal Mundelein had told him that he was in great admiration of his discernment, and had acknowledged that a large share in the success of his administration in Chicago was due to the ceaseless labors and the apostolic zeal of his former chancellor and auxiliary bishop. Concluding, the Archbishop of Cincinnati said he looked forward to extraordinary accomplishments in the "most industrial and most populous section of the conservative Province of Cincinnati."

In response to this and other speeches, Bishop Hoban feelingly referred again to the overwhelming reception he had received here as something which he would forever treasure in his memory as a consolation for having had to sever his connections with the people of Rockford. He admired the wholehearted readiness of the people to accept him, a comparative stranger, because he came at the command of the Holy See. He asked the priests to act as his ambassadors of goodwill, and to pray that the grace of God direct and help him to fulfill the high hopes of the Supreme Shepherd of the Church. Characteristically he thanked all who were responsible for the success of the day, the local authorities, Archbishop Stritch and Archbishop McNicolas for their long years of friendship and kindness, the visiting prelates and priests for their significant presence. Though an ordinary man might well be exhausted by all these exertions, Bishop Hoban appeared alert and affable as he received the long line of men and women who came that evening to greet him in Hotel Cleveland; his first day as coadjutor bishop set the pace for the days to follow.[3] He became Bishop of Cleveland on November 2, 1945, and under date of July 23, 1951, he was notified that Pope Pius XII conferred upon him the personal title of archbishop.

Bishop Hoban was not long here before the Holy See by decree of May 15, 1943, created the Diocese of Youngstown.[4] This was not entirely unexpected. As early as 1902, when the great stone Church of St. Columba was completed, many were of the opinion that it was intended for a cathedral. In 1925, at the time of the death of Archbishop

[3] *C.U.-B.*, Installation Number, 1943.
[4] Text of decrees, in *C.U.-B.*, July 30, 1943. *Acta Apostolicae Sedis*, XXV, #12.

Moeller of Cincinnati, the newspapers carried the rumor of a new diocese in the Mahoning Valley.[5] When the Sisters of the Humility of Mary four years later took possession of what was thought to be a new mother-house in Cleveland, these rumors were revived and Bishop Schrembs felt called upon to issue a vigorous denial. Meanwhile, however, the district in and around Youngstown had grown very much in population and importance.

In announcing the institution of the new diocese Archbishop Mc-Nicolas publicly expressed the gratitude of Archbishop Schrembs that the Holy See had accepted his suggestion in the matter. In the papal document six counties in northeastern Ohio, Ashtabula, Mahoning, Trumbull, Columbiana, Stark, and Portage, comprising some 3,404 square miles and including such large cities as Youngstown, Warren, Canton, and Massillon, were separated from the Diocese of Cleveland. With this nearly one-half of the territory went approximately 143,929 Catholics, most of whom lived in the cities and constituted more than seventeen per cent of 812,908, the total population of the six counties. In the new diocese were 86 parishes and 10 missions which were served by 130 diocesan priests and a few members of religious orders; 49 parish schools with 11,500 pupils; a junior college for women and 3 high schools with another 1,000 students; and 3 hospitals.

In the eight counties left to this diocese there were an estimated 403,790 Catholics, a little more than twenty per cent of the total population of 1,861,834; in Cuyahoga County, which had a total population of 1,217,250, Catholics were generally estimated to be from forty to fifty per cent of the whole. This diocese retained 177 parishes and more than 500 diocesan and about 161 religious priests and some 25 Brothers of Mary; 143 parochial schools with an attendance of 45,030; nearly 30 high schools and academies with 8,280 students; 6 hospitals and 2 orphanages and 2 homes for the aged; 1 hospice for working boys and 2 for working women; a convent of the Good Shepherd Sisters and other welfare institutions. The diocesan seminary, the two women's colleges, and John Carroll University of course remained in the Cleveland diocese.

Pope Pius XII in the consistory of June 2, 1943, confirmed the nomination of Bishop McFadden as the first bishop of the new see. By his kindness, understanding, and devotion to the Archbishop, the Auxiliary Bishop of Cleveland had endeared himself to the clergy. He had confirmed more than 150,000 and had officiated at the dedication of many churches and schools. John Carroll University had awarded him the honorary degree of Doctor of Laws. For the farewell ceremony Bishop Hoban and the clergy assembled in the old Cathedral on July 20. Bishop McFadden pontificated and his lifelong friend, Monsignor McDonough, preached a touching sermon. At the dinner afterwards at St. Augustine's Convent, where he had made his home, the clergy pre-

[5] *C.U.*, Jan. 30, 1925.

sented him with a purse to assist him in meeting the expenses incidental to starting a new diocese.

Authorized by a decree of the Apostolic Delegate to do so, without waiting for the arrival of the papal documents from Europe, he took possession of St. Columba's Cathedral on July 22 in the presence of a numerous gathering of church dignitaries, priests, and people. The Metropolitan, Archbishop McNicolas, led him to the episcopal throne and presented him with the pastoral staff. Bishop Hoban, administrator of the new diocese for the short interval since its erection, transferred his jurisdiction and commended the generosity of Archbishop Schrembs and his great loyalty to the Pope in giving up a part of his diocese. After the Youngstown priests had made their act of homage Bishop McFadden proceeded to celebrate the installation Mass. Among the other sixteen prelates who assisted at the ceremony were Arch-Bishop Mooney, who had spent his boyhood in St. Columba's parish, and Bishop Emmet M. Walsh, who six years later became Coadjutor Bishop of Youngstown. At the installation dinner Bishop McFadden announced the names of his official family.

In the evening at Stambaugh Auditorium, where the mayors of the principal cities and the representatives of every parish had gathered, United States Congressman Kirwan in their name welcomed him and spoke of the great civic and spiritual advantages which were expected to come from the establishment of a bishop in their midst.

67

THE SECOND WORLD WAR

BISHOP HOBAN, WHO HAD BEEN VERY ACTIVE IN caring for the spiritual welfare of the soldiers in the camp near Rockford, came to Cleveland to find it like the rest of the country absorbed in general preoccupation with the Second World War. Catholics here as elsewhere had shared with their fellow citizens the anxieties which preceded our entrance into it. When it was thought hopefully but mistakenly that the Munich Conference might ward off a general European war, Bishop Schrembs in an Armistice Day broadcast and in a pastoral appealed to his people, "to talk and to act for peace and above all to pray for it." In the next year (1939) the diocese joined in the world-wide crusade of prayer to the Blessed Mother in her month of May for peace and concord among nations, and the Bishop urged the people to make family pilgrimages to the various shrines for that purpose.

After the outbreak of the war in Europe the prayers of the Catholic people supported wholeheartedly the proclamation of neutrality by our Government. Following the lead of the Holy Father, the Bishop appealed to his people to pray for world peace by receiving the sacraments and by keeping vigil before the Blessed Sacrament exposed in the churches. A great peace meeting at Kent, Ohio, was addressed by the well-known lecturer Father James Gillis, the Paulist. Nevertheless, when the war seemed imminent the Bishop advised his people that it was the duty and the business of the military authorities and of the Government to know the situation and to decide about the necessity of measures to protect the country, such as the universal conscription act; and it was the duty of the citizens to obey in such vital matters.

He fully concurred with the other bishops in their pledge of sincere loyalty to the American Government and to the basic ideals of the republic; they offered to give themselves unstintingly for its defense and for its lasting endurance and welfare. The National Catholic Community Service was organized to unify and supervise all Catholic activities and interests in national preparedness. War Emergency collections were taken up in all the churches to aid the Bishops' Relief Committee in its work of helping the war sufferers in Europe and in Mexico. When the attack on Pearl Harbor plunged this country into the momentous conflict, the hierarchy pledged all the spiritual forces at their command to safeguard the God-given blessings of freedom and they placed all the Catholic institutions and all the consecrated personnel of the Church at the disposition of the Government.[1]

As the young men and women were called to the service of their country by the Government, the Diocese of Cleveland did its noble share in sending many of the younger clergy to minister to them. Before the declaration of war some priests had already joined the Reserve Chaplains: Fathers Edward J. Gracey and John J. Price, who had been chaplains in the First World War, and Fathers Alphonse J. Konarski, John J. Kucia, John Tivenan, Paul Marceau, George E. Donnellon, Francis A. Masin, Paul P. Haren, Edward F. Kuczmarski, Edward F. Maher, Michael S. Ragan, Albert J. Klein, and Charles M. Logue. After the declaration of war the increasing need was met by an ever-increasing number of volunteers.

By January, 1942, the Archbishop had permitted seven more priests to leave: Fathers Edward M. Horning, Thomas J. Kelly, Joseph C. O'Neill, Lawrence M. Wolf, Charles A. Patrick, and Edward J. Murphy (navy). Soon four more followed them: Fathers William J. Buehner, Bernard P. DeCrane, Joseph D. Gorski, Edward J. Seward (navy). In August, 1942, Monsignor Howard Smith and other priests joined the ranks: Fathers Robert E. Murphy, Achilles F. Ferreri, Paul J. Hallinan, Henry Hofer, Joseph J. McGraw, Lawrence J. Andes and Hugh J. Gallagher; Fathers Howard E. Sammon and Edward C. Labbe went to the navy. Three months later Fathers John T. Murphy, John H. Archibald, and John I. Koch went to the chaplains' school and were followed, in January of 1943, by Fathers Carl C. Wernet and Francis Zwilling.

Fathers John J. Fleming, Martin E. Gallagher, James J. Moran, and William O'Boyle reported for duty in April; and Fathers H. Reginald McCormick, Stanislas B. Podbielski, and James A. Yavorsky (navy) in June. Six months later Fathers Raymond J. Gallagher and Walter A. Lectenberg went to the navy as did Father Harold E. Meade, in the following June of 1944, when Father Louis B. Baznik went to the army. Early in the next year four more joined the navy: Fathers James A. O'Neill, Edward M. Tulley, Bernard J. Tierney and Stanislas A. Mroczka. In June, Father John K. McNally joined the army chaplain corps. Shortly after the separation of the Youngstown diocese Father Robert E. Brentgartner and Leo A. Dempsey went to the navy and Father Colman J. Hynes to the army.

Many of the members of the religious communities who served as chaplains were natives of this diocese. Among them were: the Jesuit Fathers, Joseph F. Boggins, Paul Cavanaugh, George S. Chehayl, Francis T. Dietz, James S. McGinnis, Raymond Mooney, George L. Murphy, William T. Toomey, and John A. Weber; the Franciscan Fathers, Elwin J. Binna, Daniel L. Pfeilschifter, Arthur Jankowski, Leonard Paskert, Reyner Schwarz, and Ronald R. Zgodzinski; the

[1] *C.U.-B.*, Dec. 26, 1941; Jan. 2, 1942.

Benedictine Fathers, Bernard Slimak and Ernest J. Ziska; the Precious Blood Fathers, Robert J. Baird, Edward Charek, Bernard C. Schmitt, and Aloysius Selhorst; the Marist Fathers, Martin Barrett and Thomas J. Roshetko; the Holy Cross Father, Norman J. Johnson.

All the chaplains returned safely except two. Father Elwin Binna,[2] O.F.M., who had been an assistant priest at Our Lady of the Angels parish, died, while on duty, in an airplane crash, March 20, 1945. The other was Father Francis McManus,[3] who had served at St. Malachy's parish before he joined the navy as a regular chaplain before the war. He chose to remain with the other prisoners of the Japanese in the Philippines and distinguished himself in the relief of their suffering, but he lost his life in the sinking of the ship which was transporting the prisoners to Japan. The navy Silver Star and the Legion of Merit were awarded to him posthumously.

Several of the chaplains remained in the armed services after the war or served in the Veterans' Hospitals: Fathers Louis Baznik, Bernard DeCrane, George Donnellon, Hugh J. Gallagher, Joseph Gorski, John Koch, John Kucia, Harold Meade, James Moran, Stanislas Mroczka, Charles Patrick, Thomas F. Higgins, and Edward F. Maher.

The effects of the war as it progressed were felt in every parish. Honor Rolls with the names of the parishioners who had donned the uniform of the country were displayed in a prominent place in every church. Special Masses for the mothers of service men were well attended, and in every parish one of the Sunday Masses was offered for the welfare of the soldiers. In some parishes, as in that of the Holy Rosary, parents and relatives assembled nearly every evening for Benediction of the Blessed Sacrament and common prayers for the safe return of their loved ones. The "kneeling army" at home supported the fighting army abroad. Serious efforts were made to keep the soldiers conscious of this. One pastor[4] wrote individual messages to the 500 from his parish in the army in 1944. Other parishes sent religious articles and pamphlets and regular news sheets of local happenings as well as the local Catholic weekly. After the war every parish had its Memorial plaque inscribed with the names of those who had lost their lives.

The Catholics also did their full share in supporting the war effort at home, in the factories and in all other patriotic activities. They generously responded to the plea made to them by Bishop Hoban to give their blood for the Red Cross Blood Bank. The six hospitals trained their quota of nurses. The diocesan branch of the National Council of Catholic Women gave nine ambulances to the army in 1943;

[2] *C.U.-B.*, May 18, 1945.
[3] *C.U.-B.*, May 24, 1946.
[4] Fr. V. Chaloupka, of the Nativity of the B.V.M. parish; Cf. *C.U.-B.*, June 2, 1944. Msgr. Chas. Martin of St. Colman's parish edited a 4-page monthly publication called *The Jeep*, with news about his parishioners involved in the war and their photographs. The fourth souvenir album, Christmas, 1945, contains the story of the parish's contribution in personnel to world conflict.

other Catholic groups gave additional ones. Catholic societies and schools were very active in selling and in buying war stamps and war bonds. The Catholic Federation of Women's Clubs up to April, 1945, had sold more than $4,600,000 worth.[5]

The club rooms of the Knights of Columbus in the Hollenden Hotel were put at the disposal of the service men in February, 1942. The Cathedral Canteen in the old Cathedral Hall, opened by Monsignor Smith in November of that year, served an average of 19,000 free meals a month in its three and one-half years of existence. Bishop Hoban spoke in praise of it at the end of the Knights of Columbus retreat and gave charge of it to the Knights. An incidental result of the operation of the canteen was the conversion or return to the Church of 84 persons. Fifteen of these were members of the Star of the Sea Sodality organized among the women in service; they were confirmed by the Bishop together with more than 100 other adults on Pentecost Sunday, 1945. Catholic societies had charge of the official recreation centers (U.S.O.) at Kent and at Wooster. In Youngstown St. Columba's recreation hall was the Catholic service center for the soldiers of a neighboring camp.

The Government used the professors and the facilities of John Carroll University for the training of navy and air force cadets: there were 400 apprentice seamen, a good proportion of them Catholics, in residence in 1943. At the end of hostilities more than 2,000 students, 1,700 of them veterans, crowded the campus to complete their education. The spiritual care of these students was in the hands of the Jesuit Fathers. The Catholic military students at Western Reserve University, Fenn College, Kent State University, Akron University, and Wooster College were attended by the priests assigned to that task by the Bishop. By using the military facilities they offered ample opportunity to all to hear Mass on Sundays and to receive the sacraments. In keeping with the recommendations of the Government, St. Mary's Seminary and the two women's colleges followed an accelerated program of studies which eliminated the summer vacation periods.

In an effort to keep account of the Catholics of this area who served in the Second World War, the *Universe-Bulletin* sent an immense book, the Roll of Honor, on several tours of the diocese for the purpose of collecting the names. It is now sealed up in one of the altars of the Cathedral. A more recent attempt to ascertain exact figures failed of its purpose; complete statistics for the diocese were not available. For Greater Cleveland, however, which includes Lakewood, Rocky River, Fairview Park, East Cleveland, Euclid, South Euclid, Parma, and Cleveland, Garfield, University, Shaker, and Maple Heights, a reliable computation based on its own information and that of the local newspapers was made by the *Universe-Bulletin*. According to it, 53,000, nearly forty-one per cent of the total levy of 130,000 who served in the war, were Catholics.

[5] *C.U.-B.*, Apr. 20, 1945.

The total number of those of the same area who lost their lives in the war was 3,378; of these 1,483, or nearly forty-four per cent, were Catholics. The total for the present diocese of those who made the supreme sacrifice was 1,647. At least 82 Catholics of Greater Cleveland, including the dead, received special citation for heroic action.[6] The Congressional Medal of Honor, the highest decoration conferred by the Government, was awarded to: Frank J. Petrarca of St. Marian's parish, who at the expense of his own life went to the rescue of his comrades in New Georgia in the Pacific; John R. Towle of St. Agnes' parish, for sacrificing his life for his comrades in Holland; William A. Foster of St. Theresa's parish, for throwing himself upon a Japanese hand grenade to save his companions.[7]

On May 8, 1945, Victory in Europe Day, a continuous stream of devout and grateful people visited the churches in which the Blessed Sacrament was kept exposed. This was in accord with the advice of the Bishop who had called upon his flock to celebrate the day in a Christian manner, to pray for the souls of the fallen, for the comfort of the bereaved, and for the solace of the wounded, to ask for the reconciliation of nations and, especially, to beseech the Mother of Divine Wisdom to inspire those concerned to make a truly Christian peace. The Mass of Thanksgiving in the Cathedral the next day attracted a large assembly. The war in the Pacific was over on August 14, and August 15 was dedicated to the Blessed Mother in gratitude for the end of hostilities. The President of the United States had asked the country to pray for the return of Christian charity and the restoration of confidence and friendship among nations.

Bishop Hoban strongly urged the soldiers returned from the camps to associate themselves with the Catholic War Veterans Incorporated, an organization founded by Father E. J. Higgins in Astoria, New York, some years before. The pioneer post in this diocese was inaugurated by Monsignor Joseph O'Keefe in his parish of St. Mary in Akron[8] when in August, 1944, he fitted up comfortable club rooms in the basement of the schoolhouse; the Bishop blessed the flag in a special ceremony. The movement grew to such an extent that in 1947 there were thirty-two posts, and four divisions of the women's auxiliary, in Greater Cleveland, with a membership of some 2,000, which was fifty-seven per cent of the State enrollment; it has been growing gradually ever since.

The Bishop presided at the State convention in Akron in February, 1947, and at the twelfth national assembly in Cleveland in the following June, which he opened with a pontifical Mass in the Cathedral; Cardinal Spellman of New York and the former Ambassador of the United States to Yugoslavia, Mr. Patterson, addressed the delegates.[9]

[6] *C.U.-B.*, Nov. 17, 1944; Jan. 19, May 18, Aug. 17, 1945; Dec. 19, 1947.

[7] *C.U.-B.*, Dec. 27, 1943; Jan. 21, 1944; Mar. 9, 1945; Aug. 16, 1946; Jan. 28, Mar. 11, 1949.

[8] *C.U.-B.*, Sept. 15, 1944; Feb. 14, 1947.

[9] *C.U.-B.*, June 13, 1947.

*Left:*Bishop Floyd Lawrence Begin,
Auxiliary Bishop of Cleveland.

Abbot Theodore G. Kojis, O.S.B.

Bishop John Raphael Hagan, Auxiliary
Bishop of Cleveland.

Bishop Michael J. Ready of Columbus.   Bishop John F. Dearden of Pittsburgh.

Archbishop Amleto Cicognani, Apos-   Bishop John P. Treacy of LaCrosse.
tolic Delegate.

In 1950 over 1,000 attended the State convention in this city and 500 veterans marched to the Cathedral for the opening Mass celebrated by Bishop Begin.

Each parish unit had its priest chaplain as did the central organization, the Cuyahoga County Chapter. The Catholic Veterans use their united voice in the interests of religion, public morality, and decency. On May Day of 1949, they sponsored a memorial service for the dead soldiers in opposition to the Communist observance of the day. In the following year other veterans' societies joined them in this project. In their endeavor to counteract the same sinister influence they brought to Cleveland the moving picture, *Guilty of Treason*, the main theme of which was the persecution of Cardinal Mindszenty by the Hungarian Communists.

68

CHARITIES AT HOME AND
AID FOR EUROPE

THE CATHOLIC CHARITIES CORPORATION AND the works which it supports have enjoyed a marvelous development under the guiding genius of Bishop Hoban. Over the radio, in the *Universe-Bulletin*, and through the pastors he has explained that every Catholic shared his responsibility to care for those who are unable to care for themselves; that the exercise of practical Christian charity was the test of the love of God and of religion; that charity was the cornerstone of Christian society, the perfection of Christian living. In an effort to arouse interest, the people were invited to visit the charitable institutions of the diocese to see for themselves what good was accomplished through their generosity and they accepted the invitation in great numbers.

The response to the appeal for increased subscriptions broke all previous records. Including legacies and extraordinary gifts, $390,000 was collected in 1943. The goal of $450,000 set in 1945 was over-subscribed. In 1947 bequests amounting to $120,000 made a total of $506,000 collected, and made possible the reduction of the capital debt by $350,000. The goal of $500,000 set in 1948 and in 1949 was over-subscribed in both years. In 1950 the total of $573,000 was raised. In the campaign of the next year a total of $636,000 was pledged. In addition, the Charities Corporation was made the beneficiary of over $68,000 in the last wills and testaments of Martin J. Cartin of Alliance and Martin T. McCormick of Cleveland. One-half million dollars was paid off the capital indebtedness.[1]

The Catholic Charities Bureau has developed into a large modern social agency, and is staffed with a body of social workers technically trained for family and child welfare work, in religious and recreational guidance, and in the methods of child-placement in foster homes and institutions. The central office is to be found in the new chancery building on Cathedral Square. Branch offices at Akron, Barberton, and Lorain have been expanded. The Painesville branch office and a re-

[1] *C.U.-B.*, May 19, 1950; Oct. 14, 1949, in which it was announced that David Champion had given $65,000 to Parmadale; June 25, 1948, announcement that John E. Crew had willed over $150,000 to Catholic Charities Corporation.

ceiving home for the children of the area were opened in 1947. Another office was started at Wooster in February, 1950. The local bureau and the Children's Service, a non-sectarian agency, cooperate with one another when there is a question of Catholic children.

The bureau is responsible for the spiritual care of those confined in public institutions. At the county detention home near Charity Hospital more than twenty children each year make their First Holy Communion. The Franciscan Fathers have charge of the work at City Hospital and at the municipal penal and welfare institutions at Warrensville; they and a Sunday chaplain at Blossom Hill, a county institution for young women, receive assistance from the bureau. The increased volume of activity made it necessary for the Bishop to appoint three assistant directors: Father Michael B. Ivanko, who has particular charge of the homes for the aged and the works of the St. Vincent de Paul Society; Father Raymond J. Gallagher, who directs the Catholic Youth Service in the solution of juvenile problems; and Father Frederick B. Mohan, special director in the child-caring department, who succeeded Father Albert Murphy as diocesan director of charities in the spring of 1950.[2]

A new agency of the Catholic Charities Bureau, the Resettlement Advisory Council, was organized in 1948 to centralize and coordinate the diocesan efforts on behalf of the many displaced persons who were coming here especially from Eastern Europe, Lithuanians, Hungarians, Poles, and Slovenians. In cooperation with the pastors and others who were interested, money was raised for their transportation here and homes and positions were found for them. Several Cleveland societies, such as the Slovenian Catholic League and the Slovak League, were very active in aiding their countrymen here and in South America and Canada.

Bishop Rozman of Ljubljana in Yugoslavia, an exile from his native land, who has ordained a few of his countrymen priests in St. Lawrence's Church in anticipation of the day when they may return to their homeland, is often the guest of the Slovenian pastors. The latter and others give friendly assistance to the "refugee priests," several of whom have found a new field of endeavor in this and in other dioceses in the United States. The first group of "displaced persons" to arrive here under the auspices of the Council came in 1948; in the twenty-seven months which followed the council had sponsored more than 4,100 persons. The Akron Deanery Council was organized early in 1950 under the direction of Father Edward Wolf of St. Bernard's.[3]

Upon his return from Rome in the summer of 1949 Bishop Hoban reported the Holy Father's deep appreciation of the liberality of this diocese in helping to assuage the sufferings of the peoples of Europe. Each year since the war, at the exhortation of the Bishop, they have

[2] *C.U.-B.*, Mar. 10, 1950.

[3] *C.U.-B.*, Oct. 24, 1947; June 18, 25, Oct. 22, Nov. 5, 12, Dec. 3, 1948; Jan. 21, Mar. 25, Apr. 22, May 13, June 17, 23, July 29, Dec. 16, 1949; Jan. 13, Oct. 20, 1950.

contributed generously in the collection which is taken up in all the parishes in Laetare Sunday.[4] It is used to send clothing, food, and medicine to the homeless thousands of refugees from Russia and Communism in Europe and from the wars in Palestine and China. The fund is distributed under the supervision of the American bishops and much of it under the immediate direction of the Holy Father, who had appealed to America to enable him to alleviate the distress of his unfortunate children.

Cleveland school children have listened with grave attention and loving reverence to the voice of the Holy Father coming to them over the radio[5] and pleading in paternal tones for the homeless and stricken children who had benefited and hoped to benefit still from the fruits of the Lenten sacrifices and generosity of their more fortunate brethren in the United States. Their pennies and dimes had brought health, warmth, and happiness to children who would never know a parent's love.

Under the guidance and inspiration of the Bishop the diocese has been very active, too, in gathering together actual food and clothing for the war-stricken abroad. Catholics here have supported the general efforts to send food to Europe, and especially the distinctly Catholic drives directed by the Bishops' Overseas Relief Service under a diocesan supervisor. Every parish each year since 1945 was the center for the collection. In 1947 there were 148,200 pounds of canned foods contributed, and enough money to buy 100,000 pounds more. As the result of the 1949 Thanksgiving Drive tons of clothing, shoes, and soap were sent from here across the Atlantic. In the same year the Catholic Federation of Women's Clubs sent 25,000 articles of children's clothing and $1,000 to replenish the Pope's storehouse of such articles. In 1950 100 tons of wearing apparel were collected. Various national groups on their own responsibility have dispatched much more relief to the land of their ancestors.

Catholics here have also given their full moral support to the victims of Communist rule in Europe. One of the earliest of these was the first President of Lithuania, Antonas Smetona, who died in this city and was buried in Calvary Cemetery. Bishop Hoban pontificated at his funeral in the Cathedral, January 13, 1944, and expressed the sympathy of all people for that martyred nation.[6] The harrowing story of the persecution of the Church there was told by Bishop Vincent Brizgys who was here in 1948 at the invitation of Bishop Hoban.

On the anniversary of Polish independence, May 7, 1944, the Bishop of Cleveland pontificated in the Public Auditorium, and in the following September he presided at the convention of the League for Religious Assistance to Poland and expressed his sympathy for the fate of that Catholic country at the hands of the Russians. Since the execu-

   [4] *C.U.-B.*, Apr. 3, 1943; Mar. 9, 1945; Apr. 4, 1947; Feb. 27, 1948; Feb. 25, 1949; Mar. 10, 1950.
   [5] *C.U.-B.*, Feb. 13, 1948; Feb. 24, 1950.
   [6] *C.U.-B.*, Jan. 14, 1944.

tion of Father Tiso, the Slovak patriot, the Cleveland Slovak societies have kept the anniversary of his death; in sympathy with them the Bishop in 1947 pontificated at the memorial services held at the Shrine of Our Lady of Levocha in Bedford.

When the Communist Government of Czechoslovakia suppressed freedom of worship in that country and arrested Archbishop Beran of Prague, a mass meeting of citizens at Public Hall on June 27, 1949, registered vigorous protest. Addressed by Bishop Begin, Monsignor Zlamal, and Mayor Burke, the gathering passed resolutions expressing solidarity with the Holy Father and the Archbishop in the struggle against tyranny and for the rights of God and man. Copies of these were sent to the United States Department of State.

When the Yugoslav Communist Government of Joseph Broz (Tito) imprisoned Archbishop Stepinac because of his defense of the liberties of the Church, a flood of protests were sent from Cleveland to Congressmen in Washington. The *Universe-Bulletin* for a long time published each week a cartoon of the Archbishop hanging from a cross made of the hammer and sickle. At a great meeting in Public Hall Bishop Hoban and the exiled Bishop Gregory Rozman of Ljubljana paid high tribute to the constancy and righteousness of the imprisoned prelate and Father Edward Lodge Curran of New York lauded him as the symbol of religious liberty.

Cleveland also reflected the indignation of the world at the treatment of Cardinal Joseph Mindszenty, the Primate of Hungary, for his fearless defense of the rights of religion. On his return journey from the Marian Congress at Ottawa, Canada, in 1947 the Cardinal confided to his host in Cleveland, Monsignor Tanos of St. Elizabeth's, his determination to go back to Hungary and his willingness to die for the Church. A cartoon in the *Universe-Bulletin* pictured him as the proximate victim of Communist fury.[7] At the news of his arrest a public rally of American citizens of Hungarian birth or descent, which was addressed by Mayor Burke and other prominent citizens, protested in the name of humanity. Bishop Hoban expressed the feelings of all in a pastoral in which he prescribed that a novena of prayers be celebrated for the Cardinal and for Archbishop Stepinac and the thousands of others of the clergy and the faithful who were suffering for their faith under the Communist rule. February 6, 1949, was designated as Cardinal Mindszenty Day and the priests were directed to add to the prayers in the Mass the one for prisoners unjustly detained.[8]

When the news of the conviction of the Cardinal on trumped-up charges reached here, Cleveland added its force to the storm of protest and indignation which broke out in the civilized world. Catholics sent letters and giant petitions to the President of the United States calling for official protest; the Cleveland City Council condemned the miscarriage of justice; two diplomatic aides at the Hungarian consulate here

[7] *C.U.-B.*, July 4, 1947; Dec. 31, 1948; Jan. 7, 1949.
[8] Pastoral, Jan. 24, 1949.

resigned their positions and asked for asylum as political refugees. The celebration of St. Patrick's Day, which began with Bishop Hoban's Mass in the Cathedral, was dedicated as the protest of all nationalities against the outrage. Following the august example of the Holy Father and at his direction, the priests of the diocese offered a second Mass on Passion Sunday, for the remission of sins. The whole diocese felt the deepest sympathy with the Pope in his impassioned appeal to the great multitude assembled in St. Peter's Square in Rome asking them and the world to support his proclamation that there could be no understanding between the Church and atheistic Communism.

Cleveland's interest in saving Catholic Italy from Communist domination was brought to a point in 1947 by the appearance here in Public Hall of Cardinal Spellman of New York, Secretary of State Byrnes, and Alcide de Gasperi who discussed conditions in that country.[9] Before the popular elections of the following year Americans of Italian descent and others entered wholeheartedly into the plan devised by a Brooklyn lawyer to flood Italy with letters from America warning of the dangers of trusting in the deceitful promises of the Communists; thousands of letters were sent especially from the Italian parishes. Public prayers for the defeat of the Communists were held in the schools. All were gratified finally to learn that the attempt of the Communists to take over the government in the Pope's own country had been roundly defeated in the election of de Gasperi.[10]

In another country, however, in Roumania, the Byzantine Rite Catholic congregations were entirely suppressed by the Communists. The oldest parish of the rite in this country, St. Helena's, was visited in 1947 by Cardinal Eugene Tisserant, the head of the Congregation for the Oriental Church in Rome, which has the direction of the churches of that rite.[11]

After this digression incidental to the Catholic Resettlement Council, which is one department of the Catholic Charities Bureau, we turn to the Catholic Youth Organization, which is another such department. The Youth Service Bureau organized by Father Raymond Gallagher, after special university training in the work, offers professional assistance to young people, including the older school children, in the solution of their peculiar problems. The C.Y.O., as it is called, has been expanded; permanent and adaquate headquarters have been established at Madison-on-the-Lake. In 1945 the Bishop purchased and remodeled a group of buildings on a hundred-acre plot of land at North Madison, forty-two miles east of Cleveland, and a summer camp was opened in the next year. Holy Mass is celebrated every day during the season in the separate chapel. Approximately 800 boys and girls in different sessions were accommodated in the summer of 1949 and were supervised by trained workers and seminarians. Father James O'Brien was suc-

[9] *C.U.-B.*, Jan. 3, 17, 1947.
[10] *C.U.-B.*, Mar. 26, Apr. 16, 23, 1948.
[11] *C.U.-B.*, May 23, 30, 1947.

ceeded in 1950 by Father Thomas C. Corrigan as the director of the C.Y.O. and of this camp.

The great amount of time and energy devoted by the younger clergy to the purpose of making religion an integral part of the social, cultural, and recreational activities of the adolescent have been well rewarded in the results. Through them the C.Y.O. exercises its influence in the numerous parish and interparochial organizations. The Bishop has, moreover, encouraged each parish to have its own gymnasium and social and recreational center as a means of keeping the young people together in a Catholic atmosphere. Club rooms and "canteens" have been opened in new permanent quarters or in those newly accommodated to the purpose. St. Patrick's Youth Canteen was started in 1944 in the rooms of the old Catholic Club next to the church on Bridge Avenue. Other parishes improvised meeting places in the basement of the churches or in remodeled halls. The Akron branch of the C.Y.O. was organized in 1937 as a department of the Catholic Service League. In 1950 it was using thirty parish halls, twenty gymnasiums, and thirty-four playing fields for its activities; it also had two summer camps under its supervision. In 1952 an 80-acre plot of ground near the city was purchased as the site for a youth camp capable of caring for 90 children each week of the summer.

In the history of charity in the diocese, prominent place must be given to the St. Vincent de Paul Society[12] which had grown from the first few units in 1866 to some seventy-four conferences in Cleveland, and several others outside the city, in 1950. Bishop Hoban, who pontificated in St. Peter's Church in 1945 to commemorate the centenary of the introduction of the society into the United States, had always encouraged every parish to have its own conference; he presided at the quarterly meetings of the particular councils here and in Akron.

The annual report for the year ending in September, 1949, is a commendable record of much good accomplished. At that date there were 457 active and 169 honorary members in Cleveland. Through an expenditure of more than $51,000 assistance had been given to 907 indigent families; thousands of visits had been made to private homes, to hospitals, and to public institutions of relief or correction; thousands of religious articles and pieces of reading matter had been distributed; 55 irregular marriages had been rectified; 92 persons had been baptized, and 125 successfully encouraged to return to the practice of religion; over 400 children had been directed to religious instructions; 57 converts had been led into the Church.

The salvage bureau, which has several trucks at its disposal, collects old clothes and furniture which after reclamation are sold or distributed to the needy upon requisition from the parishes. Through its operation in 1949, $21,000 was contributed to the charitable works of the society. The bureau was moved from its location on Superior Ave-

[12] *C.U.-B.*, Oct. 15, Dec. 17, 1943; Oct. 19, 26, Dec. 14, 1945; Apr. 25, Dec. 19, 1947; Feb. 13, 1948; Dec. 16, 1949; Feb. 3, 1950.

nue near East 12th Street to a large brick building on the same avenue near East 55th Street.

The executive secretary coordinated the activities of the society. George H. Paskert, Knight of St. Gregory, resigned in 1949 after an enviable record of twenty-eight years of service in this office. He was succeeded by Alexander J. Wey, also a Knight of St. Gregory. In the previous year Monsignor Thomas V. Shannon was succeeded by Father Michael Ivanko as spiritual director.

At an earlier date the members had cooperated with the Juvenile Court in cases involving young delinquents. Free legal advice is now offered to the poor. After the late war, at the suggestion of the Bishop, the Vincentians helped veterans to find homes for themselves and their families. Another project is the decent burial of indigents who have died in public institutions. Still another is the procurement of high school scholarships for the young people at Parmadale.

In response to the appeal made by a sightless man at a Cleveland public hospital, the Catholic Club for the Blind was inaugurated in 1949 and Father James A. Slaminka was appointed their chaplain. Catholic reading matter in Braille and the *Universe-Bulletin* on records were made available to them. Assistance is offered to transport them to church for Mass on Sunday for a more intimate participation in the public religious life of the Church. Forty-five blind persons made a special pilgrimage of their own to the Shrine of Our Lady of Lourdes in Euclid.

For the deaf and the hard-of-hearing regular instruction classes in the sign language are given in St. Columbkille's Church and the missions held at regular intervals were well attended.

*Left:*New St. John Cathedral, Cathedral Square, Rectory and Chancery.

*Left:*New St. John Cathedral, the façade.

*Right:*New St. John Cathedral, south apse.

*Right:*Mass of Thanksgiving offered by Archbishop Cicognani in the new Cathedral.

St. Hyacinth Church.   St. Rocco Church.

Holy Cross Church, Euclid.

*Far Left:*Church of the Transfiguration.

*Left:*Church of the Conversion of St. Paul.

69

CHARITABLE INSTITUTIONS
(1945-1951)

A SUMMARY ACCOUNT OF THE EXTRAORDINARY
extension and expansion of the institutions of charity during the past few years will serve as an indication of what
the generosity of the people has enabled Bishop Hoban
to accomplish in this sphere of Catholic activity.

On February 18, 1945, the Bishop dedicated St. Joseph's Home for
the Aged on Woodland Avenue near St. Edward's Church. This solidly
built brick structure with its fine chapel was purchased by the diocese
from the Daughters of the Immaculate Heart of Mary who had been
operating a girls' orphanage in it for a long time. It was thoroughly
renovated and modernized for the accommodation of 110 aged men
and women and was entrusted to the care of the Franciscan Sisters of
Blessed Kunegunda.

The latter were also put in charge of a home for elderly women, the
renovated and enlarged Madonna Hall on East 82nd Street near Euclid
Avenue, which previously had also belonged to the Daughters of the
Immaculate Heart of Mary who had used it for about twenty years
as a home for business women. The four-story brick building, acquired
by the diocese in 1946, was extensively rebuilt to make accommodations for 105 women. An adjoining residence was made over into a
residence for the Sisters in charge of it. A separate chapel, a pretty
structure of brick and stone seating 125 persons, was dedicated to the
Immaculate Conception on June 26, 1948, by Bishop Hoban who had
enriched the walls with a precious painting of the Holy Family. On the
following day he blessed the residence hall itself, which is connected
with the chapel and the Sisters' house by a covered gallery. The dedication was the first event in the centennial celebration of the founding
of the diocese and the first institutional development in the beginning
of its second century.

The unfortunate destruction of Jennings Hall[1] for elderly people
had emphasized the need of homes for aged folk who, though they
commanded some financial resources, had difficulty in securing suitable
care in their enfeebled condition. Bishop Hoban decided upon its re-

[1] *C.U.-B.*, Feb. 8, Apr. 9, 1946; Oct. 10, 1947; Oct. 1, 1948; May 6, 13, 1949.

establishment. On the foundations of the original structure a fire-proof, two-story, T-shaped brick building in the Colonial style was started in the spring of 1948. Bishop Begin laid the cornerstone in October and, in the absence of Bishop Hoban in Europe, he opened it officially on May 8 of the following year. A beautiful painting of the Holy Family hanging over the altar in the chapel was a gift of Bishop Hoban. The home with accommodations for 106 persons, men and women, has all modern conveniences and is served by the Sisters of the Holy Ghost. The new building financed by the Catholic Charities Corporation, together with the chapel which survived the fatal fire, form an interesting and picturesque group on Granger Road near St. Theresa's Church in Garfield Heights.

In the three homes for which Bishop Hoban was responsible 321 aged people are housed; there is always a long list of others seeking admission. A start has been made to realize the Bishop's plans for a convalescent home for the aged on the grounds at Parmadale.[2] The Little Sisters of the Poor maintain the strict rule of receiving into their refuge none but those who are entirely without resources. They had some 200 guests in 1950. The home at Chagrin Falls operated by the Daughters of Divine Wisdom sheltered 35 in the same year.

Shortly after his coming Bishop Hoban accomplished the original plans for Parmadale, namely, to have brothers and sisters of the same family, who were dependent or orphaned, brought together in the same institution. As a temporary measure the 108 girls of St. Joseph's Orphanage were moved in March, 1944, to St. Joseph's-on-the-Lake, the former Cunningham Sanatorium on Lake Shore Boulevard near East 185th Street, which had been purchased by the diocese from the Timkin Foundation of Canton. It had been used for short time as the headquarters of the Catholic Youth Organization. The main building, a three-story brick structure, was remodeled into a home which was quite in contrast with the old institution on Woodland Avenue. An adjoining tract of nearly ten acres was given to the diocese by the trustees of the Louis D. Beaumont Foundation in 1945. This with another parcel of land purchased by the Bishop gave the diocese a plot of some twenty-seven acres in a very desirable location in the city.

Meanwhile, on March 17, 1945, the Bishop broke ground at Parmadale. On September 14, 1947, he dedicated three large two-and-one-half-story brick cottages which had been occupied by the girls transferred from St. Joseph's. The all-day program included a military Field Mass and a sermon by the Bishop in which he preached to the great crowd upon the necessity of religious education for the children. In the summer of 1952 a new convent and administration building was already under roof. The old administration building is to be converted into a home for the eighty children of pre-school age previously sheltered in St. Edward's and Holy Family Homes. The money bequeathed

[2] With a capacity for 143 persons it was completed at the end of 1952.

by the John E. Crew family and by Monsignor Nicolas Pfeil was devoted to this purpose. Bishop's Day at Parmadale has been kept on December 7 each year. At his morning Mass the younger children receive their First Holy Communion and in the afternoon Confirmation is administered. The 625 boys and girls between the ages of six and sixteen who find shelter there, under the care of the Sisters of Charity, entertain the Bishop with plays and songs they learn for the occasion.[3]

The Sisters of Charity have charge also of St. Edward's Home for the children who are too young to attend school. Opposite Parmadale on State Road, the two frame buildings previously used by the Sisters as a novitiate were purchased by the diocese and opened in January, 1946, for 42 children between the ages of two and six. It replaced St. Theresa's home which had been started three years before in the Delaney residence now incorporated in the home for crippled children. The same community of Sisters for a long time had been exercising their ministry of mercy and kindness in crowded and insufficient quarters at St. Ann's on Woodland Avenue. The Bishop approved of the plans for a new location and in April, 1947, the old Leisy estate at East Boulevard and Fairhill Road was purchased. The forty-room residence on the twenty-two-acre plot was remodeled to accommodate 100 babies and 40 mothers, and on February 22, 1948, the Loretto House, as it was called, was blessed by the Bishop. On September 3, 1950, he dedicated St. Ann's Maternity Hospital, a new brick building attached to the old mansion; its two and one-half stories were equipped with 58 beds and 5 incubators. Further plans call for the modernization of the old buildings on Woodland Avenue for the exclusive use of the mothers and children accommodated in the Loretto House. Hopes are high, too, for the expansion of the present new hospital into a six-story building; the help of the Cleveland Hospital Fund will be available for the purpose within a few years.[4]

One of the great achievements in the administration of Bishop Hoban was the interesting group of buildings known as Marycrest, in Wickliff, a suburb of the city. It is under the control and direction of the Sisters of the Good Shepherd. In the seventy-seven years previous to 1946 the Sisters had cared for and guided 5,000 young women, of whom 66 had joined the Magdalen Sisters, a strictly cloistered community dependent upon them. In the so-called preservation class, which in later years had been housed at Providence Heights in East Cleveland, 2,269 dependent or neglected young women had been cared for, and 37 of them had become members of various religious congregations.

In December, 1946, a fifty-acre tract of land at Euclid Avenue and Bishop Road had been purchased as the site. Ground was broken in the following March and Bishop Hoban dedicated the completed build-

[3] *C.U.-B.*, Sept. 21, 1945; Sept. 5, 1947; Dec. 8, 1949.
[4] *C.U.-B.*, May 29, 1942; May 6, 1949; Mar. 24, Sept. 1, 1950.

ings on August 29, 1948. The beautiful chapel, with its three naves, stands in the center of the nine units which occupy an area of nine acres. Included in these are three separate dormitories each accommodating 50 persons, a two-story high school building, an administration building, and two separate convents. Pictures and murals tell the story of the Good Shepherd congregation. An outside swimming pool was the gift of the Catholic Collegiate Association, the members of which continue to assist the Sisters. When Marycrest opened its doors in 1948 it sheltered 120 girls. The old convent on Carnegie Avenue was leased to the Ohio National Guard.[5]

In April, 1943, Bishop Hoban accepted a fifteen-room residence and the five and one-half acres of land upon which it stood from the widow of William J. Delaney as a memorial to her husband. The property borders on that of the Rosemary Home for Crippled Children. On December 21, 1947, the Bishop broke ground for the new one-and-one-half story brick fire-proof building which is flanked on one side by the Delaney residence, now used as a home for the hospital workers, and on the other side by the old Grasselli home, which is now the convent of the Sisters of the Holy Humility of Mary who have charge of it.

Estimated to have cost $300,000, the new home for crippled children can accommodate 50 patients, twice its previous capacity. The most modern equipment and the latest methods are used with remarkable success. Mirrored walls show the children the progress they make from day to day in learning to walk. In the new chapel, which was doubled in size, are two stained-glass windows from the private chapel of the late Archbishop Schrembs. Over the altar hangs a bas-relief of the Madonna and Child, the gift of Josephine Grasselli. Bishop Begin, who had been chaplain at the home, dedicated the completed buildings, May 15, 1949, during the absence of Bishop Hoban in Europe.[6]

The Catherine Horstmann Home was moved from its former location on Rocky River Drive to newly acquired quarters on Overlook Road in Cleveland Heights, which were blessed by Bishop Hoban on April 27, 1951. The Catholic Charities was responsible for the new property though the expenses for the upkeep are met by the Community Fund. Dedicated to the purpose of sheltering girls of school age from "broken" homes it gives them the opportunity of pursuing their education under more favorable circumstances.[7]

In recent years one entirely new general hospital was opened and the others were expanded or were preparing for additional improvement. Not long before the separation of the Youngstown diocese Archbishop Schrembs dedicated a new $500,000 nurses' home[8] which is

[5] *C.U.-B.,* Apr. 12, 1946; Aug. 6, 1948; Sept. 16, 1949.
[6] *C.U.-B.,* Dec. 26, 1947; May 13, 20, 1949. Cleveland *Plain Dealer,* May 12, 1949.
[7] *C.U.-B.,* Oct. 8, 1948; May 4, 1951.
[8] *C.U.-B.,* Oct. 30, 1942.

attached to Mercy Hospital in Canton, and at Warren St. Joseph's Riverside Hospital[9] with the assistance of Federal funds had erected a new wing.

St. Thomas' Hospital in Akron, also with Government subsidy, increased its facilities by the erection of a new wing which had a 52-bed capacity and was dedicated by Bishop Hoban on April 1, 1944. Nearly seven years later a drive for funds was successful and plans were drawn for another wing which when completed will make room for 265 beds, an increase of 60 over the present capacity. This institution was one of the first general hospitals to make special provision for the care of the victims of alcoholism.

In this connection it is worthy of note that with the approval of the Bishop one of the young priests of the diocese, Father Otis Winchester, in 1948 opened a refuge, appropriately called Stella Maris, for destitute and homeless victims who desire to rehabilitate themselves. An improvised shelter accommodated 35 men who were furnished the means of supporting themselves during the time of their treatment.[10] In its first seven months of existence 35 men were reclaimed for a better life.

Lenora Hall in Akron was started under the general direction of the Catholic Service League; a brick residence on North Portage Path was remodeled to accommodate 28 adolescent working girls. It was in charge of the Daughters of the Divine Redeemer who had been occupied with social work in the parish of Christ the King. A new community, they accepted their first novices here in November, 1950. Plans call for a ten-room addition to Lenora Hall which will serve as their headquarters in this section of the country.[11]

On August 27, 1950, Bishop Hoban blessed the three-story L-shaped additional wing of St. Joseph's Hospital in Lorain. This expansion, which was paid for by the Federal Government and the contributions of the city, increased the capacity by 125 beds. Other auxiliary buildings were completed not long afterwards and made 300 beds available in the institution, which was in charge of the Sisters of the Holy Humility of Mary.[12]

In Cleveland itself the industrialists and corporations combined in an effort to establish a fund of nearly $10,000,000 for the purpose of modernizing the fourteen voluntary hospitals already in existence and of building new ones in the areas where they were needed. Bishop Hoban in the name of the diocese donated $25,000 to the fund and in a pastoral urged his people to support the project in which Catholic hospitals would be benefited.

Among the latter is St. Alexis Hospital which started a maternity

[9] *C.U.-B.*, Mar. 27, 1942.
[10] *C.U.-B.*, May 6, Dec. 16, 1949; Jan. 13, 1950.
[11] *C.U.-B.*, Jan. 25, Apr. 12, Oct. 25, 1946; Nov. 24, 1950.
[12] *C.U.-B.*, Oct. 25, 1948; Oct. 28, Dec. 23, 1949; Sept. 1, 1950.

division in 1944. In the summer of 1952 the Sisters had raised three-quarters of the $1,000,000 they hoped for to enable them to construct a main building which will have a capacity of caring for 180 patients and serve also as an administration building.[13]

Plans for the expansion of St. John Hospital[14] were given to the public in 1949 and a start was made in 1951 towards their realization; two new wings and the remodeling of the interior will make room for 50 more patients.

The older buildings of St. Vincent Charity Hospital, one of them the original hospital of Bishop Rappe's time, stood in need of immediate replacement. The Cleveland Hospital Fund allotted about one-half of the $2,000,000 required; the rest was raised in a general appeal made to the public under the chairmanship of Judge James Connell. The razing of the old structures began in September, 1950. In the following Spring the Bishop broke ground for the erection of a new six-story building. In it are the most modern facilities and 102 beds, increasing the capacity to 321 patients. It was a very significant occasion when he dedicated the completed structure on August 3, 1952, the hundredth anniversary of the beginning of the work of the Sisters of Charity in old St. Joseph Hospital on the West Side.[15]

The new Marymount Hospital in Garfield Heights was built with the help of the Cleveland Hospital Foundation. The six-story brick structure, which cost more than $2,000,000, is beautifully situated on a fifty-acre plot in the southeastern section of the city; it has 100 beds and special equipment for several categories of the sick. Bishop Hoban dedicated the completed building in an all-day ceremony, October 30, 1949. He pontificated at the nearby Shrine of Our Lady of Czestochowa; Monsignor John Krol preached the formal sermon. A very large statue of Our Lady of Grace, carved in Italy, which adorns the entrance to the hospital was blessed at a later date by Bishop Begin who had laid the cornerstone. The Sisters of St. Joseph of the Third Order of St. Francis, who own and operate the hospital, have their provincial mother-house and Marymount Academy on the same grounds; they have plans for a nurses' home in the immediate vicinity.[16]

A great advance in nursing education was made in 1947 when the nursing schools in the hospitals became affiliated with St. John College and some 200 young women began to follow the academic and technical courses which lead to the degree of Bachelor of Science in Nursing. Monsignor Maurice F. Griffin, past president of the Catholic Hospital Association and very active in the national interests of Catholic hospitals, in 1949 gave up his position as diocesan director of hospitals to Father John Humensky. Soon after, a general code was issued under

[13] Plans for a large new modern building have already been made.
[14] *C.U.-B.*, May 27, 1949.
[15] *C.U.-B.*, Dec. 7, 1945; Feb. 6, 1948; Nov. 25, 1949; Feb. 17, 24, Mar. 3, 1950; Apr. 20, 1951. Cleveland *Plain Dealer* and Cleveland *Press*, Feb. 16, 1950.
[16] *C.U.-B.*, Sept. 17, 1948; Oct. 20, 28, Nov. 4, 1949; Jan. 27, 1950. Cleveland *Plain Dealer*, Oct. 25, 1949.

the authority of the Bishop prescribing the rules of medical ethics to be observed in the local hospitals.[17]

The Catholic hospitals of Cuyahoga County receive a good share of their support from the Cleveland Community Fund, of which Bishop Hoban has been from the beginning an active and enthusiastic promoter. As in previous years so at the opening of the thirty-second drive in 1949 he was one of the principal speakers, and his voice was carried to the people over the radio. He pointed out that the motive of Christian charity should have an important place in the care of the poor and unfortunate; that the laws of justice and charity required that those who had money, as stewards of this world's goods, should come to the assistance of the poor who are their brethren under God and oftentimes the innocent victims of social and economic conditions over which they had no control. He touched on some critical conditions in Cleveland which showed the necessity of exercising voluntary Christian charity to complete the work carried on in the tax-supported State institutions: the great number of aged and needy who had not the proper care and the number of the mentally deficient who were crowded into institutions not equipped to care for them. The Bishop's appeal was well received by the whole community.

In his pastorals the Bishop recalled to his own people the benefits which accrued to Catholic social agencies from the Community Fund, especially the hospitals and Parmadale; in 1949 about two-thirds of the running expenses of the last-mentioned institution were paid by it.[18]

Another beneficiary of the Fund to the extent of four-fifths of its budget for the same year was Merrick Settlement House. The original frame buildings had become inadequate for the work in a populous metropolitan area on the South Side. Under the direction of Bishop Hoban the Catholic Charities Corporation assumed the task of erecting new quarters at an estimated cost of $300,000. On April 30, 1950, he dedicated the three-story brick structure in a modified Colonial style of architecture at Starkweather Avenue and West 11th Street. The building has three "activity floors," where there are the gymnasium, the Little Theater, the day nursery, meeting rooms, and class rooms for adult education. A trained staff of social workers was assisted by a generous and willing group of volunteers. According to the report for 1949 there had been an enrollment of 1,459; 32,417 had attended the settlement house; and 8,595 calls had been made at the day nursery. A summer camp is maintained at Hinchley Lake for the children of the district.[19]

[17] *C.U.-B.*, Nov. 25, 1949; Apr. 25, 1947; Jan. 23, Sept. 17, 1948.

[18] *C.U.-B.*, Oct. 22, 1943; Oct. 17, 1947; Oct. 15, 1948; Oct. 7, 21, 1949. Cleveland *Plain Dealer*, Oct. 17, 1949.

[19] *C.U.-B.*, Dec. 8, 1944; Apr. 22, Oct. 14, Dec. 16, 1949. Cleveland *Plain Dealer*, May 5, 1950.

70

ERECTION OF NEW PARISHES

THE FOUNDING AND IMPROVEMENT OF HOS-
pitals and other welfare institutions did not exhaust the
energy and the zeal of Bishop Hoban in the accomplishment of an ambitious building program. New church
edifices and schoolhouses replaced the original structures
in older parishes and the many new parishes he created meant additional new churches, schools, rectories, and convents. In nearly every
new convent a new chapel was to be found. Well before the Second
World War the towns and villages on the outskirts of Cleveland had
experienced unusual growth. The depression, however, and then the
restrictions of war-time delayed the construction of parish plants.
Building material was difficult to obtain even for the repair of existing
facilities. As the war drew to a close, building campaigns were announced in many dioceses over the country as part of a general plan
to give employment to men made idle by the stoppage of war production.

The first new parish established here by Bishop Hoban was that of
St. Francis of Assisi in Gates Mills, the center of several rural com-
munities in the Mayfield Road area. Beginning in December, 1942,
Mass was offered by one of the Blessed Sacrament Fathers in the home
of Mrs. Charles Strong, a convert and benefactor of the parish. Father
William B. Gallagher was appointed the first pastor on August 18 of
the following year. The newly formed congregation made use of St.
Clare's Church on Mayfield Road to the west until their own brick
church in the Colonial style and seating 300 persons was completed.
It was dedicated by Bishop Hoban on October 3, 1948. Originally composed of only forty-eight families, the parish has enjoyed a continuous
growth.

The first new parish in the city of Cleveland in Bishop Hoban's
administration was organized by Father John A. Dunn who was appointed on the Feast of the Epiphany, January 6, 1944, in honor of
which feast the parish was named. One thousand persons who previously belonged to St. Cecilia's and St. Catherine's attended the first
Masses, which were celebrated in Novak's Hall in the thickly populated cosmopolitan neighborhood of Union Avenue and East 120th
Street. The new Briar Hill sandstone church, on East 120th Street just

south of Union Avenue, in the modern English Gothic style was started in September, 1946; it was dedicated by Bishop Hoban on April 4, 1948. The open, beamed ceiling and the solid limestone altar are pleasing characteristics of the church. Though it seats 700 people, six Masses are offered every Sunday to accommodate the congregation. An eight-room brick school was opened in September, 1950, for approximately 350 children (in six grades) who were taught by the Sisters of St. Joseph. Early in the next year two class rooms were added to the school and a rectory was completed; two unfinished class rooms were used as a parish hall.

In the densely peopled south end of the city the new Polish parish of the Transfiguration was formed out of parts of the parishes of the Immaculate Heart of Mary and St. Stanislas. A Protestant church edifice at Broadway and Fullerton Avenue was remodeled and enlarged, and was dedicated by the Bishop on February 6, 1944. It seats 950 people but five Masses are required on Sunday. Father Joseph F. Zabawa was made the first pastor. In 1949 a seven-room brick schoolhouse was opened; approximately 290 pupils were under the tutelage of the Sisters of St. Joseph of the Third Order of St. Francis.

In the southern part of the city but farther to the east in the rapidly developing district between St. Cecilia's and St. Timothy's parishes, Father John A. Hreha was appointed on October 1, 1946, to found the parish of St. Henry. First divine services were held in the auditorium of Beehive public school for the 400-family congregation. A brick combination church-auditorium and school was dedicated by Archbishop Hoban on May 25, 1952. The auditorium seats 700. The eight-room school section was opened in the fall of 1951 with an attendance of nearly 500 children. The Sisters of St. Dominic of Adrian, Michigan, whose convent adjoins the parish property on Harvard Avenue at East 185th Street, are the instructors.

In the northeastern section of the city proper three new parishes were created. Parts of St. Agnes', St. Thomas' and St. Philomena's were joined together in the new parish of St. Agatha by Father Stephen Towell who was appointed for that task on June 21, 1945. The congregation met in the beginning in Rosedale public school on East 115th Street. In the following August a large brick building at the intersection of Lakeview Road and Superior Avenue was purchased at auction and the basement was fitted up for divine service. Meanwhile the interior of the upper floors was remodeled. One floor was made into a very practical and well-furnished church which was filled six times every Sunday; the others were refashioned into eight class rooms. The Dominican Sisters of Akron had charge of 330 pupils. The basement was returned to use as a parish hall. The new parish plant was dedicated by the Bishop on October 10, 1948.

Closer to the Public Square some 600 families, formerly members of the parishes of St. Agnes' and the Immaculate Conception, were organized in the new congregation of Our Lady of Fatima. Father

Raymond Smith, appointed the first pastor, November 27, 1949, used the auditorium of Thomas Edison public school for six Sunday Masses until he remodeled a brick building on Lexington Avenue near East 68th Street, which seats 600 persons. Special buses were operated through the parish to bring the parishioners to Mass. The church, seating some 600, was dedicated by Archbishop Hoban on November 11, 1951.

Still closer to the Public Square, with the outlying parts of the parishes of the Immaculate Conception, St. Agnes', St. Bridget, and St. Edward, Bishop Hoban established the new parish of the Conversion of St. Paul in November, 1949; the shrine church at the corner of Euclid Avenue and East 40th Street, which can seat 900, was made the parish church and Father Jerome F. O'Hara was appointed the first pastor. Seven Masses were celebrated every Sunday for the congregation which includes many who are attracted by the special devotions held there, as formerly. The Franciscan Nuns of the Blessed Sacrament remained in the adjoining cloister.

In Euclid, on the eastern boundary of the city, the large new industrial plants attracted many Catholics who established homes in the vicinity. Seven hundred families in the eastern section of the original parish of the Holy Cross were organized in the new parish of St. William by Father John Fleming, a former army chaplain, who was appointed first pastor, May 26, 1946. Divine service was held at first in Upson public school and then in the Community Center Auditorium. On East 260th Street, north of Lake Shore Boulevard, an L-shaped combination church and school of Amherst sandstone was dedicated, September 11, 1949, by Bishop Begin. Six Masses were celebrated every Sunday in the auditorium which seats 700 people. Ursuline Nuns and laywomen taught the approximately 450 pupils in the eight-room school. Four class rooms were added in the summer of 1952.

In the territory between St. William's and Holy Cross parishes Father Charles J. McCann was appointed in October, 1950, to organize the parish of St. Robert Bellarmine. The first Masses were celebrated for the new congregation in a theater building on Lake Shore Boulevard at East 225th Street. Ground was broken in June, 1952, for the erection of a combination church and school on Lake Shore Boulevard at East 238th Street in Euclid.

On November 12, 1950, the Bishop established the parish of St. Felicitas in the area between St. Paul's parish in Euclid and Wickliff; it combines parts of Euclid and the village of Richmond Heights. Father John W. Lees, the first pastor, celebrated Mass for the new congregation at first in Veterans' Hall on Euclid Avenue at East 260th Street and then in the chapel of Marycrest High School in Wickliff. The Richmond Heights Village council[1] refused to relax the zoning regulations to allow the building of a combination church and school on the first property acquired in that town. Another site was secured

<hr />

[1] *C.U.-B.*, Jan. 5, June 8, 1951.

on Richmond Road near Euclid Avenue in the town of Euclid upon which a beginning was made in the summer of 1952 for the building of a church plant.

Along the lake shore east of Euclid, across the Cuyahoga County line, in the village of Willowick the parish of St. Mary Magdalen was founded by Father Harold A. Laubacher, January 27, 1949. It and a few other villages in the immediate vicinity had previously belonged to the parish in Willoughby. Divine services were held at first in Longfellow and then in Roosevelt public schools until in March, 1950, the church-hall of the brick combination church and school was ready for use. It seats 600 but three Masses were necessary on Sundays for the convenience of the 500 or more families who composed the new congregation. The eight-room school was opened in the autumn of 1949; Ursulines and laywomen had charge of 265 pupils in the next year. Bishop Hoban dedicated the completed structure, which has a unique façade, on September 17, 1950.

South of the lake and along the line of Mayfield Road, in addition to the parish of St. Francis of Assisi, mentioned above, at the eastern boundary of Cuyahoga County three more parishes were established. On September 18, 1944, the Bishop commissioned Father William Fitzgerald to organize the parish of St. Clare in the territory which included five communities that formerly belonged to the parish of St. Gregory the Great in South Euclid. A substantial building of frame and brick construction on Mayfield Road in the village of Lynd-hurst, previously used as a dance hall and restaurant, was remodeled for use as a church; although it accommodated 400 persons, four Masses were necessary on Sundays. A two-room school was also opened in the autumn of 1944. On a twelve-acre site across from the original property a brick school with eleven class rooms was completed in the early part of 1951. The 600 pupils were taught by the Ursuline Nuns who were assisted by lay teachers.

Closer to Cleveland and north of Mayfield Road, in a district which formerly belonged to the parishes of Christ the King and St. Gregory, Father Henry J. Hofer was authorized in June, 1948, to organize the parish of St. Margaret Mary. The congregation of some 350 families met for divine worship in the auditorium of Oxford public school until the completion of the brick L-shaped combination church and school at the corner of Belvoir Boulevard and Bluestone Road, on the border line between South Euclid and Cleveland Heights. The church-auditorium in the Colonial style, with high peaked roof, seats 600 and was used for the first time on Christmas Day in 1949. The school section was opened for 190 pupils in the previous September; the Sisters of St. Joseph assisted by a few laywomen were the teachers. Bishop Hoban dedicated the entire structure on October 22, 1950.

Still closer to Cleveland, in Cleveland Heights, the parish of St. Louis was officially erected December 14, 1947. Father Reginald Mc-Cormick, a former army chaplain, was the first pastor. He changed a large residence at Mayfield Road and Edindale Avenue into a parish center; the basement was remodeled into a chapel where the week-day Masses were celebrated. The congregation, composed of 600 families formerly belonging to the five contiguous parishes, met for Sunday Mass in the Center Mayfield Theater which had been put at its disposal gratis by the generous owner. On account of grave illness Father McCormick resigned and was succeeded by Father Leonard Klein, April 19, 1949. He began the construction of a new brick combination church and school on Taylor Road, just north of Mayfield Road, about a mile from the original property in October of that year. The eight-room school and social hall (the equivalent of four class rooms) was opened in January, 1951, for the approximately 200 pupils and the Felician Sisters who teach them. The church-auditorium section which seats 572, with additional room in the balcony, was used for the first time on June 3, 1951. Bishop Hoban dedicated the building on October 28 of the same year.

South of Cleveland Heights the first Catholic parish in Shaker Heights was erected in October, 1945. Father Edmund J. Ahern, the first pastor, resigned because of sickness and Father Roy J. Bourgeois took his place in January of the next year. Lomond public school auditorium was used at first by the 450-family congregation until the new St. Dominic's Church at South Moreland Boulevard and Norwood Road was ready for occupancy. Built of pink-colored brick, it is in the Colonial style, unique with its rounded corners, its four-pillared portico, and its ninety-foot tower and cross; it seats 750 people and five Masses were celebrated in it every Sunday. Bishop Hoban dedicated it on August 8, 1948. A ten-room school, adjoining the church, on Van Aken Boulevard was to be ready for the opening of the fall term of 1952.

Southeast of Shaker Heights, in the eastern section of Warrensville Heights, the Franciscan Fathers who ministered to the Catholics in the public welfare institutions in the neighborhood have had a residence for some time. Bishop Hoban, November 12, 1945, made it the center of the new parish of St. Jude. Father Roman Hasenstab, O.F.M., the first pastor, held divine service for the 200-family congregation at first in the friary and then in a public school building which he remodeled to seat 90 persons. On May 21, 1950, Bishop Hoban dedicated a new brick structure on Richmond Road; the parish hall served as the church for three Masses on Sundays; the wing comprising two class rooms is used as a social hall and catechetical center. Plans call for additional space which will be used for class rooms.

East of Warrensville Heights, on the boundary of Geauga County, in the town of Chagrin Falls, the mission parish of St. Joan of Arc was established in July, of 1947. Father Oldric Mazanec, the pastor of Solon, who founded the 130-family congregation and had charge of it, transformed a ten-room farmhouse on Washington Street into a chapel. The town council reluctantly and only with certain restrictions had given permission to build a church. The cornerstone of the pretty Colonial style brick edifice, which seats 235 persons, was laid on June 12, 1949. Bishop Hoban dedicated it on November 5, 1950.[2]

Early in March, 1952, the Archbishop instituted two new parishes in the district around Bedford, Garfield Heights and Maple Heights. Father Hugh J. Gallagher, a former army chaplain, was appointed the first pastor of St. Monica's parish, comprising parts of Maple Heights and Garfield Heights, with its center at Rockside Road and East 139th Street. The other parish named in honor of Blessed Pope Pius X was entrusted to the Marist Fathers who were invited into the diocese with the understanding that they would eventually set up a high school in conjunction with it. The center is a large tract of land between Warrensville Center and Northfield Roads near Berwyn Drive in Bedford. Father Joseph Buckley, a former army chaplain, was made the first pastor. Canonical boundaries were established between it and St. Wenceslas' parish which was officially declared to be territorial.

On the west side of the Cuyahoga River the development of parishes was equally extensive. Two new ones were erected in the old Brooklyn district in territory previously served by the parish of Our Lady of Good Counsel and four more in the area to the west of it and south of Madison Avenue. On June 14, 1945, Father James Downie was appointed to organize the parish of St. Mark with parts of the parishes of St. Clement and Our Lady of the Angels. Four Masses were celebrated on Sundays in Hayes public school until the completion of a two-story brick building on Montrose Avenue east of West 159th Street, just south of the Lakewood border. The auditorium, which seats 600 people, and the modern school, assembly hall, and Sisters' quarters, which occupy the rest of the space, were dedicated by Bishop Hoban, December 11, 1949. In the previous September classes had been started in eight rooms for the 225 pupils who were taught by the Sisters Servants of the Immaculate Heart of Mary assisted by several laywomen.

Father John T. Murphy, a former army chaplain, on November 12, 1945, was appointed to organize in the parish of St. Mel the 450 families in the district north of Lorain Avenue, between the parishes of St. Mark and St. Vincent de Paul. The auditorium of Riverside public school was used by the new congregation until in June, 1949, the new church at Triskett Road and Orchard Park Avenue was sufficiently completed for occupancy; it can seat 600 and the auditorium beneath it another 400. Four Masses were celebrated in it each Sunday. The four-room school in the brick L-shaped combination structure, which is in the modern Spanish style, was opened by the Sisters of Charity (of Cincinnati) in the autumn of the same year. Bishop Hoban dedicated the finished plant on April 23, 1950.

South of Lorain Avenue, the eastern section of St. Patrick's parish in old West Park became the new parish of the Ascension on June 26,

[2] *C.U.-B.,* Oct. 3, 1947; Oct. 1, 1948; Aug. 5, 1949.

1946. Father Martin E. Gallagher, who had also served as a chaplain in the army, was the first pastor of the congregation of some 700 families. In the beginning he held divine service in the auditorium of John Marshall public high school. The brick combination church and school which he erected on West 140th Street near Puritas Avenue was dedicated by Bishop Hoban, December 4, 1949. The church is on the first floor and has a capacity of 650 which can be increased to nearly 1,000 by raising a folding partition that separates it from the auditorium built in the rear of the sanctuary. It was used for the first time on Christmas Day, 1948. The school on the second floor with its eight class rooms and some 400 pupils was operated by the Sisters of Mercy aided by a few lay teachers. On December 4, 1949, the building was dedicated to the service of God by Bishop Hoban who on May 22, 1952, returned to bless a four-room addition to the school.

In the district northeast of Ascension parish approximately 1,000 families, who previously belonged to the parishes of St. Ignatius, the Annunciation, and St. Vincent de Paul, were organized in the new parish of Sts. Philip and James in April, 1950. Father James H. O'Brien, formerly director of the C.Y.O., was appointed the first pastor. He began by using the auditorium of Louis Agassiz public school as a meeting place for the congregation. At Bosworth Road and Adeline Avenue, on September 24, 1950, the cornerstone was laid for the T-shaped combination church and school the exterior of which is covered with gray Ohio sandstone. The Christmas Masses of that year were celebrated in the auditorium beneath the school section. In the ten-room school 280 pupils started classes under the direction of the Franciscan Sisters of Blessed Kunegunda in February, 1951. The attendance was 400 in the following year. On April 27, 1952, Archbishop Hoban dedicated the completed plant.

The northwestern section of the parish of Our Lady of Good Counsel, the Memphis Avenue district, was taken to form the new parish of St. Thomas More which was erected in March, 1946, when Monsignor Howard Smith, an army chaplain during the Second World War, was appointed the first pastor. Sunday Masses were offered in the Memphis Theater from that time until the new brick church-school combination at West 76th Street and Plainfield Avenue (in Brooklyn Village) was ready in December, 1949. In the contemporary style, the church-hall seats 670; the marble altars and remarkable statues in it were imported from Italy. The auditorium beneath is equipped as a social hall. The eight-room school with its 375 pupils in the lower grades was opened in September, 1949, by the Sisters of the Incarnate Word. The completed buildings, which served a rapidly growing congregation, were dedicated by Bishop Hoban on July 2, 1950.

In the populous Broadview-Schaff Road section of the parish of our Lady of Good Counsel Father Sylvester Lux, who was appointed on October 17, 1948, organized the new parish of St. Leo. For the first chapel Benjamin Franklin public school auditorium was used until a frame church seating 350 was put up in the next summer to accommodate the 800-family congregation. The brick combination church and school building was started in 1950 and in the autumn 400 pupils began their classes in a nine-room school under the direction of the Vincentian Sisters of Charity. The church-auditorium seating 750 was ready for the Christmas Masses of the same year. Bishop Hoban dedicated the new church plant, June 3, 1951.

In Bay Village, immediately west of the town of Rocky River, on August 28, 1946, the new parish of St. Raphael was formed and Father Francis G. Zwilling, a former army chaplain, was made the first pastor. For the members of the 350-family congregation, who previously attended the churches in Rocky River or in Avon, he held divine service at first in the local public high school auditorium; the permission to use it was obtained from the school board with some difficulty. The Zoning Board[3] refused to allow the building of a church plant on the originally chosen site at the corner of Dover Center Road and Wolf Boulevard but finally agreed that a seventeen-acre plot of ground farther south on Dover Center Road could be used for that purpose. On October 24, 1949, Bishop Hoban dedicated a brick L-shaped combination church and school at that site. The church-hall, which seats 280 persons, can easily be converted into class rooms when a new church is built. The four-room schoolhouse was opened in September, 1949, for the 190 pupils who were taught by the Sisters of the Holy Humility of Mary.

West of Bay Village, but in Lorain County, Father Carl F. Wernet, who had been an army chaplain, was commissioned April 20, 1949, to organize the 350 families in Avon Lake Village and the vicinity in the new parish of St. Joseph. The Avon Lake Theater was used for divine service on Sundays until the brick combination church and school on Lake Road was completed. On June 24, 1951, Bishop Hoban dedicated the finished structure. The church-hall, which seats some 450 people, is so built that it can be readily converted into class rooms. The Ursuline Nuns opened the four-room school in September, 1950. The parish now has its own school bus; the refusal of the local school board to permit the parochial school children to make use of the public school buses, even temporarily, received nation-wide notoriety. Ironically enough the father of one of the pupils who had been denied such transportation had written home, shortly before his death in the United States Army in Korea, that he was convinced that he was fighting for liberty of religion and education against those who would destroy them.[4]

Immediately south of Bay Village in the village of Westlake Father Joseph C. Dempsey was authorized in November, 1950, to found the parish of St. Bernadette. Four Masses were said each Sunday in the au-

---

[3] *C.U.-B.*, Nov. 1, 1946; Oct. 3, 1947.

[4] *C.U.-B.*, Sept. 8, 22, 29, Dec. 15, 1950; June 22, 1951.

ditorium of the village public school. In the summer of 1952 the walls were already up for the brick church-auditorium and school on Clague Road near Center Ridge Road. The five-class room school section was to be ready for the fall term. South of here in North Olmsted Father John P. Cullitan was commissioned in May, 1950, to organize the parish of St. Richard. He used the local public school auditorium for Sunday Masses until the completion of the brick church and school combination in the summer of 1952. The four-room school section was occupied already in the fall of 1951.

In the territory between Lorain and Elyria in the village of Vincent on State Route 254, the new parish of St. Vincent de Paul was canonically erected on November 27, 1949. Father Joseph P. Conlan, a former navy chaplain, was named to organize it. Divine services for the convenience of the approximately 200 families were held at first in the local public school, until the completion of a brick combination church and school building on North Ridge Road which Archbishop Hoban dedicated on July 20, 1952.

About 300 families on the east side of the city of Elyria were organized officially in the new parish of St. Jude on October 14, 1943, and Father John Carrabine was appointed the first pastor. The auditorium of Ely public school served as the first meeting place until a year later the Bishop offered the first Mass in a large residence on Cleveland Street at Abbey Road which had been remodeled to seat about 200. In 1948 the parish center was moved to a 21-acre plot adjoining the District High School site on Poplar Street. Ground was broken in the early part of 1950 for the erection of a brick T-shaped combination church-school and social hall. The church auditorium seating 528 was ready for use in March, 1951. The six-room school had been opened in September, 1950, by the Sisters of Notre Dame. Archbishop Hoban dedicated the completed plant on October 21, 1951.

In the village of Strongsville, just east of Elyria, but in Cuyahoga County, the new parish of St. Joseph was established, June 14, 1946. Father Joseph McGraw, who had served in the army as a chaplain, was made the first pastor of the 100-family congregation which had been previously attended as a mission of Berea. Fifty years before there were but three Catholic families in the whole township. Father McGraw used the Town Hall for Mass and catechetical instructions until Christmas Day of 1946 when the sheet-metal quonset type church was sufficiently completed; it seats 350 people and is situated on Wooster Pike at the northern approach to the town. Bishop Hoban dedicated the unique brick-faced structure on April 11, 1948. A four-room brick schoolhouse was opened in September, 1950, by the Sisters of St. Joseph. Here the local school board declined to honor the request that the parochial school pupils be allowed to use the public school buses.

In Summit County seven new parishes were established by Bishop Hoban, three of them in Akron. Three hundred families of the An-

St. Mary Magdalen Church
and School, Willowick.

Our Lady of Mount Carmel Church
and School (East Side).

St. Margaret Mary Church and
School, South Euclid.

Our Lady of Perpetual Help
Church.

St. Philip Neri Church.

Our Lady of Mount Carmel Chapel
(West Side).

St. Francis of Assisi Church, Gates Mills.　　　Annunciation Church.

*Left:*St. Joan of Arc Church,
Chagrin Falls.

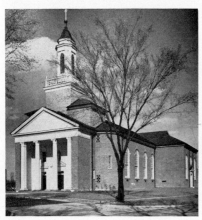

St. Dominic Church, Shaker Heights.　　　St. Edward Church, Ashland.

nunciation parish were taken to found the new parish of St. Matthew, August 18, 1943. Father Robert R. Wingerter gathered his people together in the Ellet public high school auditorium until he had finished the new Spanish Mission style church-hall on Canton Road, which seats 370 persons. Bishop Hoban dedicated it on November 3, 1946. A six-room schoolhouse in combination with the church was opened in the autumn of 1949; the Dominican Sisters (of Akron) had charge of the more than 200 pupils.

On the eastern boundary of Akron, in Tallmadge Village, Mass was offered in the Town Hall by one of the priests of St. Vincent's during the year 1943 for the convenience of approximately forty families. The mission was given the status of a parish when Father James M. Gallagher was appointed the first pastor, December 3, 1944. On March 3, 1946, Bishop Hoban dedicated the brick combination church and rectory building under the title of Our Lady of Victory. The church seats 220 persons.

In the southwestern part of Akron in the Portage Lake district the new parish of St. Francis de Sales was formed out of the territory previously served by St. Paul's. Father Francis H. Diederich, appointed the first pastor in May, 1948, began by holding divine service for the 300-family congregation in the Coventry Township High School Auditorium. The brick combination church (seating 850) and school building on Manchester Road was ready for full use on Easter Sunday, 1950. The four-room school beneath the church auditorium which itself will eventually be made into class rooms was opened with 175 pupils in the following September by the Sisters of St. Joseph. The three-level structure (there is a recreation hall in the English basement) was solemnly dedicated by Bishop Hoban on May 20, 1951.

The parish of St. Peter Claver for the Negroes of Akron was established in December, 1945. A brick building on West Bartges Street was transformed into a chapel and social hall. Father Anthony Kraff, C.PP.S., the first pastor, was soon succeeded by Father Vincent P. Haas who very effectively continued the work of the apostolate even after his appointment as chaplain at St. Thomas' Hospital.

Northeast of Akron the new parish of the Holy Family was erected in the village of Stow. Father Howard E. Sammon, a former navy chaplain, was appointed the first pastor in October, 1946. For divine service he gathered the members of his 165-family congregation (which included Silver Lake and Monroe Falls) in the auditorium of Stow public high school until on August 14, 1949, the brick L-shaped combination church-school building was used for the first time. The church-hall seats 300 persons. The four-room school section was ready in September following. The 150 pupils, brought by bus to the parish center on Route 5 near Stow's Corners, were taught by the Sisters of Charity of St. Augustine. The completed plant was dedicated by Bishop Hoban on May 30, 1950.

South of Akron, at Warwick, the mission of St. George was raised to the status of an independent parish on April 23, 1948, by the appointment of Father Paul F. Haren, a former army chaplain, as pastor. He entirely renovated the forty-two-year-old church. A bus was purchased to transport the children of the parish to the parochial school in nearby Doylestown.

West of Akron, in the village of Sherman (Summit County), in the district between Barberton and Wadsworth the new parish of St. Andrew the Apostle was established in May, 1951, by the appointment of Father Stephen J. Blasko as the first pastor of the 160-family rural congregation. The first Masses were said in a remodeled restaurant building in Western Star near the boundary line between Summit and Medina Counties. In the summer of 1952 divine services were held in the basement of the new church on a three-acre site at Johnson and Hametown Roads in Sherman.

Another rural community was organized in Wayne County in the Mission of St. Stephen at West Salem which is near the Ashland County boundary line. In the summer of 1952 a remodeled residence served as a chapel which was made dependent upon St. Edward parish in Ashland.

In Geauga County in Newbury Township southwest of Chardon a large barn was ingeniously converted into a neat and serviceable mission chapel named in honor of St. Helena for the use of the several hundred families in the rural area. Divine services were at first held in a club house by Father James E. Maher, the pastor of Chardon. On August 20, 1950, Bishop Hoban blessed the new chapel which had already been used in the preceding February. Some of the pews and two of the altars were brought from the old Cathedral. Father Maher in the spring of 1952 acquired a tract of 21 acres across the street from the church in Chardon. Plans for a new parish plant on this site call for the first parochial school in Geauga County. Provision for the children of Newbury is included in them.

71

NEW BUILDINGS IN OLDER PARISHES

THE ERECTION OF NEW PARISHES DID NOT prevent the earlier parishes, from which they had been formed, from putting up new and permanent churches and larger schools; many such structures were in contemplation, others were nearly completed in the autumn of 1952. Following the alphabetical listing, a short sketch of these improvements is given here.

On the East Side in the Gesu parish in Cleveland Heights, Father Seth S. Walker, S.J., in 1948 made an addition of six class rooms to the school which had been erected eight years previously. In the parish of the Holy Cross in Euclid, Archbishop Hoban in 1945 blessed the school which had been enlarged by Father Thomas Kirby; on September 3, 1950, Father Ralph McMonagle broke ground for the construction of an English Gothic stone church which is nearing completion. It will seat about 600. The old church-hall will be made into class rooms. In Holy Name parish in Cleveland, Father Charles W. McDonough purchased the old Broadway public school and remodeled it to accommodate 850 pupils and to house the Sisters who teach them; the Archbishop dedicated it in 1944.

In the Italian parish of Our Lady of Mount Carmel the brick English Gothic church near the intersection of Woodland Avenue and East Boulevard, erected at an earlier date under the supervision of Father William O'Donnell, was dedicated in 1948; in June, 1949, it was severely damaged by fire and this entailed considerable expense in its restoration; a new two-story ten-room brick schoolhouse was opened in September, 1950, with an attendance of 350 pupils who were taught by the Sisters of Notre Dame; the Archbishop rededicated the church, which seats 500 people, and blessed the school on October 29, 1950.

The strikingly beautiful new stone Church of Our Lady of Peace, seating 950, in the pure Greek Classical style of architecture, at Shaker Boulevard and East 126th Street, was begun by Monsignor Edward A. Reilly in the autumn of 1949. The graceful pillars in the portico and the marble interior fashioned by Italian sculptors make it one of the fine churches in the diocese. Father Reilly's funeral in September, 1951, was the first religious service held in the new edifice. Archbishop Hoban solemnly dedicated the building on the day chosen by the pastor, the 7th of the following month.

In the Lithuanian parish of Our Lady of Perpetual Help Father Joseph F. Angelaitis presided over the construction of the new brick Romanesque church on Neff Road which was dedicated by Archbishop Hoban on October 19, 1952; its 95-foot tower and marble interior are distinctive; its stained-glass windows were designed by a refugee Lithuanian artist who also painted the murals. In the Polish parish of the Sacred Heart of Jesus, the new imposing stone church in the Modern Gothic style with its unique façade, erected under the supervision of Father Stanislas S. Rybacki, was dedicated by the Archbishop May 6, 1951; built above the basement church at Kazimier Avenue and East 71st Street, it seats 1,000 persons; representations of Our Lord and Polish saints have been worked out admirably in the stained-glass windows. In St. Agnes' parish the old school and auditorium were completely renovated and modernized by Bishop Begin, the pastor.

The monumental Church of St. Ann on Cleveland Heights was dedicated by Archbishop Hoban on December 11, 1952. Father John M. Powers, the founder of the parish, superintended the construction. Of smooth Indiana limestone to match the schoolhouse it is in the Classical style. The Greek façade with its six great columns of stone, the clerestory supported by ten massive marble columns in the interior, the graceful 175-foot companile, and the separate Lady Chapel make it one of the most remarkable church edifices in the diocese.

On East Boulevard near Buckeye Road the imposing new Baroque Church of St. Benedict is nearing completion under the direction of Father Leo Rehak, O.S.B., the pastor. The great 60-foot dome covers the interior which can seat 1,000. The new St. Andrew's Abbey nearby with its 75 rooms and basement chapel and new facilities in the Benedictine High School adjoining were dedicated on August 6, 1952.

In the Polish parish of St. Casimir, the Archbishop on July 4, 1949, dedicated a modern eleven-room schoolhouse which had made its appearance under the direction of Monsignor Andrew Radecki. In the parish of St. Cecilia, Bishop McFadden, June 17, 1942, rededicated the church, which had been covered with brick and doubled in size (to accommodate 950 persons) by Monsignor John Ruffing; the latter five years later added four rooms to the school. In the parish of St. Christine in Euclid, which was given territorial status, Father Anthony L. Bombach on October 20, 1950, broke ground for the erection of a brick combination church and school on East 222nd Street. The church section with a seating capacity of 650 and the 12-room school section is now in use. In the parish of St. Gregory the Great in South Euclid, Father Paul Ferreri, a former army chaplain, directed the construction of a spacious 16-room schoolhouse which the Archbishop dedicated on April 23, 1950.

In the Polish parish of St. Hyacinth, the cornerstone of the new brick Romanesque church with a 60-foot stone tower and a seating capacity of 700 was laid by the pastor, Father Joseph M. Sztucki, on March 11, 1951. It replaced the church hall in the original combination structure and was dedicated by the Archbishop on June 22, 1952. In the parish of St. Jerome, Monsignor Leo Hammer, who founded it in 1919, broke ground on March 17, 1949, for a beautiful brick and stone church. In the English Gothic style of architecture it seats 850 persons and has a distinctively attractive façade and interior. It was dedicated by the Archbishop on May 11, 1952.

In the Italian parish of St. Marian the parishioners themselves under the direction of Father Angelo Trivisonno enlarged the church on Petrarca Road and covered it with a brick veneer; Bishop McFadden rededicated it on November 29, 1942. In the parish of St. Philip Neri, Father James P. Brennan supervised the erection of the fine new brick church at St. Clair Avenue and Ansel Road which the Archbishop dedicated, June 25, 1950; in an adapted Renaissance style, it has a beautiful rose window dominating the façade and a uniquely decorated interior; during its construction the roofed-over inside court of the schoolhouse served as a temporary church.

In the parish of St. Philomena in East Cleveland Monsignor Maurice Griffin put up a three-story stone addition to the schoolhouse, consisting of four class rooms, a basement hall, and a gymnasium, which the Archbishop blessed, November 5, 1950. In the parish of St. Theresa, the Little Flower, in Garfield Heights, Father Thaddeus T. Marchant enlarged the combination church and school: the church-hall was doubled in size to accommodate 750 persons; four units were added to the eight-room school to increase its capacity to 600 pupils. In a day-long ceremony the Archbishop on November 27, 1949, rededicated the plant which included a convent for the Ursuline Nuns.

On the west side of the Cuyahoga River in the parish of the Annunciation Archbishop Hoban on July 6, 1952, dedicated the new brick Colonial style church on West 130th Street at Bennington Avenue. It has an attractive tower at the side and four giant wooden pillars in front. It seats 750 people. The plans were drawn up under the supervision of Father Edmund A. Kirby. Father John Farrell, his successor, directed the construction of the edifice. The old church hall made room for more school space. In the parish of the Blessed Sacrament, ground was broken on October 12, 1952, for the erection of a new Romanesque church under the direction of Father Edward S. Hannon. In Corpus Christi parish, Father Anthony B. Orlemanski began the construction of a two-and-one-half-story brick schoolhouse on Stickney Road in the spring of 1952. This, the first school in the parish, will have eight class-rooms and rooms for other facilities. In the parish of the Holy Family in Parma, Father William J. Benesek put up the first school in its history, six rooms and a basement hall, in which 172 children began instructions under the tutelage of the Vincentian Sisters of Charity in September, 1950. The cornerstone for the church-auditorium, which has a seating capacity of 625, on York Road near Pleasant Valley Road was laid on June 17, 1951. The completed plant was dedicated October 12, 1952.

In the parish of Our Lady of Good Counsel six rooms were added to the school in the summer of 1952.

In the Slovak parish of Our Lady of Mercy, Father John W. Krispinsky supervised the erection of a fine new church on West 11th Street, which seats some 500. The style is described as Early Christian; the walls are of Crab Orchard stone; the interior has many striking features, including hand-carved wooden statues and a Shrine of St. Joseph the Workingman against a background of the history of the Slavs in America. The Archbishop dedicated the completed structure on October 23, 1949; the altar had been consecrated the day before by Bishop Begin.

In the Italian mission parish of Our Lady of Mount Carmel, Father Sante Gattuso, O.D.M., supervised the erection of the brick combination chapel and school at Detroit Avenue and West 70th Street which the Archbishop dedicated, July 17, 1949; the chapel accommodated 325; the four-room school with an enrollment of 70 in the first two grades was opened by the Sisters of the Most Holy Trinity in the following September. In the spring of 1952 ground was broken for the erection of a new church which will seat 600. In the parish of St. Angela Merici, Father Michael L. Stevenson completed the fine new church on Lorain Road in Fairview Park, which the Archbishop dedicated November 14, 1948; in the English Gothic parish church style, seating 700, and with a large social hall in the basement, it replaced the frame structure which was then made over into a residence and chapel for the Sisters of St. Joseph; in 1950 the pastor finished a sixteen-room brick schoolhouse accommodating 750 children, which had been constructed in successive stages.

In the Polish parish of St. Barbara, Father Joseph S. Jarosz broke ground on Denison Avenue at West 15th Street in July, 1950, for the construction of a new brick church in the Lombard round-arch style, capable of seating 650 people. Distinctive of the attractive structure is a 65-foot tower and the stained glass windows depicting the seven sacraments. Archbishop Hoban dedicated it July 13, 1952. In the parish of St. Charles Borromeo in Parma, Father Nicolas Monaghan in the summer of 1949 enlarged the school by the addition of five rooms and a gymnasium for the accommodation of the 600 children attending it. In the parish of St. Francis de Sales, also in Parma, Father Edward Kickel in 1948 put up a new brick schoolhouse and covered the old one with a brick veneer. In the summer of 1952 five more rooms were added for a total of nineteen rooms.

In St. Luke's parish in Lakewood, Monsignor James M. McDonough supervised the construction of a fine brick and stone church on Clifton Boulevard at Bunts Road. Designed by Father Peter Cherniss in a modified Romanesque style, it has a beautiful rose window in an impressive façade. The interior is dominated by an immense Crucifixion scene in the apse. The Stations of the Cross are in mosaic from Rome. Seating 750 people, it is air-conditioned and replaced the 27-year-old frame chapel which had been remodeled several times. Bishop Begin consecrated the main altar on May 3, 1952. On the next day the Archbishop solemnly dedicated the entire structure to the service of God. In the pioneer parish of St. Malachy, a disastrous fire a few days before Christmas, 1943, destroyed the venerable seventy-two-year-old church; the school auditorium was used as a chapel until the completion of a fine English Gothic church which seats 524 persons. For the first time in Cleveland Tennessee Crab Orchard stone was used to cover cement block construction; the seventy-foot bell tower is surmounted by an illuminated cross as was the tower of the old church when it served as a beacon to navigators on the lake. Attached to the rear of the edifice is an eighteen-room convent for the Ursulines who teach in the school. The Archbishop, who made the decision to make the new church a memorial of the Irish immigrants who had founded the parish, dedicated it, June 29, 1947. There was a generous response from those who were in any way associated with the old parish to the appeal of Father George F. Martin, the pastor.

In the old parish of St. Mary of the Assumption along Brookpark Road, Father Frederick I. Hitch completed a six-room cement block schoolhouse which was dedicated, September 11, 1949; the old school had been discontinued in 1940; the many new industrial plants in the vicinity had made it necessary to increase from 168 to 336 the seating capacity of the church building which the Archbishop rededicated, June 17, 1951. In St. Patrick's parish, the old stone church on Rocky River Drive and Puritas Road was dismantled in Easter Week of 1951 and divine services were held thereafter in the school hall; the enlarged church has a seating capacity of some 900, double that of the old building. Father William Thorpe, the pastor, expected the work to be finished in 1952. In the Italian parish of St. Rocco, Bishop Begin on September 3, 1950, laid the cornerstone of the new brick Romanesque church on Fulton Road; a beautiful representation of the patron saint in mosaic, brought from the Vatican, decorates the apse of the pillarless interior, and a graceful 105-foot bell tower sets off the exterior. It was erected under the immediate supervision of Father Sante Gattuso, O.D.M. Many of the parishioners personally worked on its construction. The Archbishop dedicated it on March 16, 1952. In St. Stephen's parish Monsignor Joseph Gerz completed a ten-room addition to the school in 1952.

Within the limits of Cuyahoga County, at Bedford, Father Peter H. Schaefers directed the construction of the new brick Church of St. Mary of the Immaculate Conception which was used for the first time on Easter Sunday, 1951; it is in the Classical style of architecture and seats 700 persons; the Archbishop dedicated the fine structure on

May 27, 1951; the old church was made into additional class rooms for the accommodation of the 450 pupils who were taught by the Vincentian Sisters of Charity. At Berea in St. Mary's parish Father Raymond A. Kathe in 1949 made a five-room addition to the four-room schoolhouse which had been constructed in 1926. At Olmsted Falls, Father Joseph P. Walsh put up a brick combination church and school which the Archbishop dedicated, May 7, 1950; the church-hall seats 380; the four-room school above it, in which the Sisters of St. Joseph were the teachers, was the first parochial school in the town; the old Church of St. Mary had been destroyed by fire in January, 1948.

In Solon, the Archbishop blessed the first parochial school in that locality on October 23, 1949; the two-story brick structure erected by the pastor, Father Oldric Mazanec, had been opened in the preceding month for the 190 pupils who were brought together in buses from the surrounding villages; part of the building was used provisionally as a chapel and a residence for the teachers, the Vincentian Sisters of Charity; the basement was fitted up as an auditorium. At Independence on June 10, 1951, the Archbishop dedicated the new school which had been opened in the previous autumn by the Sisters of Notre Dame for 255 pupils; the eight-room one-story stone veneer and concrete building put up by Father Francis Boehlein replaced the old building which was to be remodeled as a social hall.

In the city of Akron, Summit County, in the Slovak parish of St. John the Baptist a fine new church on Brown Street in the English Gothic style made its appearance under the supervision of Father Stephen J. Valko; constructed of Briar Hill stone, it seated 485 and was completed December 21, 1941; before that the Sunday Masses were celebrated in the auditorium of the brick school which was finished in 1928; a new auditorium and an addition to the school were completed in the early part of 1951. In the Syrian parish of St. Joseph, the Archbishop on May 22, 1948, dedicated the new brick church on West Exchange Street; put up under the direction of Monsignor Paul K. Malouf, and seating 250, it was combined with a rectory and a social hall, and replaced the church destroyed by a tornado in 1943. In the parish of the Immaculate Conception, Father John L. Waldeisen, the founder, directed the construction of a fine stone church which was nearing completion at the end of 1952. In the parish of St. Paul, Father Clement H. Boeke added nine class rooms and other auxiliary units to the schoolhouse to accommodate the more than 1,000 pupils, the largest parochial school attendance in the city, who were taught by the Dominican Sisters; the modern structure was dedicated by the Archbishop, October 12, 1947. In the summer of 1952, five more rooms were added. In St. Peter's parish, Father John J. Tivenan in 1950 completed a two-story eight-room brick schoolhouse, adjoining the church on Biruta Street; the 200 pupils were taught by the Sisters of St. Joseph of Cleveland. The Archbishop blessed the completed building on April 20, 1952. Ground was broken in the September following for the erec-

*Above Left:*Our Lady of Mercy Church.

*Above Right:*Sacred Heart of Jesus Church.

*Left:*St. Philip and James Church.

St. Malachi Church.

St. Jerome Church.

St. Benedict Church.   St. Ann Church, Cleveland Heights.

Our Lady of Peace Church.

St. Joseph Church, Akron.   St. Luke Church, Lakewood.

St. Helen Church, Newbury.

St. Peter Claver Chapel, Akron.

St. Vincent De Paul Church, Vincent.

Epiphany Church.

St. Clare Church, Lyndhurst.

St. Joseph Church, Strongsville.   Our Lady of Victory Church, Tallmadge.

Our Lady of Fatima Church.   Immaculate Conception Church, Akron.

St. Angela Church, Fairview.   St. Mary Church, Bedford.

tion of a new church. At Barberton, also in Summit County, in the Slovenian parish of the Sacred Heart, Father Matthias A. Juger directed the erection of an attractive brick English Gothic church, with a bell tower attached to it, which was dedicated by Bishop McFadden, August 9, 1942; seating 306 persons, it replaced a twenty-four-year-old frame building. In the parish of St. Augustine, Monsignor John W. Schmitz was responsible for a new three-story brick schoolhouse which the Archbishop dedicated on December 10, 1950; it has ten class rooms and other auxiliary units; the old school was used for a social hall and a gymnasium.

In Cuyahoga Falls, Father John F. Gallagher in 1947 added six rooms to the schoolhouse, and in February, 1951, began the construction of a new wing which, when it was completed in 1952 made a total of sixteen class rooms, and six specialized units including a chapel.

In Lorain County, at Amherst, Father James H. Smith modernized the schoolhouse in 1948 and was preparing to replace the church constructed in 1868. In Elyria in the parish of St. Mary, Monsignor William L. Newton in 1948 completed a modern seven-room brick school and an auditorium which seats 500. In the city of Lorain in the parish of St. Anthony, Father Anthony Aeschbacher, O.M.C., enlarged the school in 1949; four rooms were added in 1952; plans were made to finish the superstructure of the basement church. In the parish of Sts. Cyril and Methodius, Father Milan J. Slaje in the summer of 1952 began the construction of a new church. In the parish of St. Stanislas, Father Leo A. Rygwalski in 1950 added two rooms to the school. In Wellington, Father Charles J. McCann enlarged the seating capacity of the church from 70 to 175 and improvised a social hall in the basement; the Archbishop rededicated the remodeled structure on September 22, 1946. At North Ridgeville, a large addition was made to the school in the summer of 1952 under the direction of Father Francis A. Brucker.

In Medina, the first Catholic school in the town made its appearance under the supervision of Father William H. Randel. The ten-room brick building in the Early Colonial style was opened in the fall of 1951 by the Sisters of St. Dominic (Adrian, Mich.) with an enrollment of some 200. It was dedicated by the Archbishop on August 31, 1952. Plans call for the erection of a new church adjoining the school property which is at some distance from the old site. The first parochial school in Medina County was put up at Wadsworth by Father Oldric J. Korab and was dedicated by the Archbishop on April 30, 1950. The four-room building which has a social hall in the basement was opened in the previous September by the Vincentian Sisters of Charity with an enrollment of 115.

At Mentor, in Lake County, Monsignor George A. Whitehead opened the first parochial school in the town in the fall of 1952. Built of brick, on a one-floor plan it has eight class rooms, a kindergarten and other auxiliary space with accommodations for 225 pupils. Plans call for a parish hall in the near future. At Madison, in the same county, Father

John F. Mulholland in the late summer of 1952 broke ground on Hubbard Road for the building of a new church seating some 400. At Painesville, Monsignor William J. Gallena expanded St. Mary's ten-room school by the addition of eight rooms and a gymnasium in 1948. At Willoughby, in the same general area Father Brendan McNamara enlarged the school of the Immaculate Conception; the parish property became considerably more valuable by the donation of a contiguous piece of land and a residence as a memorial of the pioneer Catholic John Hill and his family.

At Ashland, in Ashland County, Father Vincent Jones reconstructed the eighty-year-old church edifice and doubled its seating capacity so as to seat nearly 300. The new Doric façade gave it an entirely new and attractive appearance. A social hall was contrived in the basement. The whole plant was rededicated by the Archbishop on May 30, 1951. The cornerstone of the first parochial school in the county was laid on June 1, 1952. The one-story four-class-room building with a complete basement was opened in September.

Up to the end of August, 1952, when Father Thomas D. McIntyre began the organization of the parish of the Immaculate Heart of Mary in Cuyahoga Falls, the Archbishop had inaugurated 28 new parishes in Cuyahoga County and a total of 41 in the diocese, including Warwick which had been only a mission. In addition, West Salem was given the status of a mission. Moreover, his substantial assistance enabled the pastors to begin immediately the construction of the parish plants. Most of these buildings were of the economical church-school-auditorium type which emphasized the fact that the parish was a social as well as a religious and educational center. In most instances the church halls can easily be converted into additional class rooms.

Moreover, in approximately twenty per cent of the older parishes in Greater Cleveland, new substantial church edifices were erected within the past ten years; and ten per cent had so completely remodeled and enlarged their churches as to make them the equivalent of new structures. During this same period many new chapels were inaugurated in the various educational and charitable institutions. In all the new parishes with but few exceptions, and in very many of the older parishes large new convents with their individual chapels made their appearance through the encouragement of Archbishop Hoban.

Of considerable interest in recent years because of the multiplication of parishes was the ruling of the Supreme Court of Ohio, in the early part of 1942, that the ban on the erection of church buildings in residential districts which was to be found in some zoning ordinances was unconstitutional, and was an unreasonable interference in the right of property. The test suit was brought by the Lutheran Synod of Ohio and the decision follows a similar one handed down by the Supreme Court of Nevada in a case brought before it by the Catholic Bishop of

Reno.[1] In this diocese a certain amount of opposition was encountered in the establishment of parishes in Chagrin Falls and in Bay Village.

In accord with the provisions of the Ohio General Code (section 7622) the Cleveland School Board has been allowing religious groups the temporary use of public school auditoriums upon the payment of the cost of opening them on Sundays. Most of the new Catholic parishes, just as other non-Catholic congregations, availed themselves of this convenience. The right was threatened momentarily by a veteran member of the Cleveland Board of Education who entered suit in the Court of Common Pleas to vacate the permission given by a majority of the board to a Lutheran group in August, 1945, to use a few rooms in a public school building. Whatever the motives in starting the suit, it was withdrawn because of the discussion it aroused. The *Universe-Bulletin* distinguished itself in the defense of the traditional and lawful custom. The other members of the board proposed that the local code be amended to conform with the Ohio General Code.[2]

[1] *C.U.-B.*, Feb. 6, 1942.
[2] *C.U.-B.*, Aug. 10, 17, 1945.

72

CATHOLIC SCHOOLS

URING THE ADMINISTRATION OF ARCHBISHOP Hoban up to the summer of 1952, thirty-three new elementary schools were opened in the diocese; others were prepared to open in the fall. In thirty-two of the older parishes entirely new schoolhouses were put up or the previous ones were remodeled and enlarged; others still were planning new ones. In most instances the buildings were crowded to capacity. Schools were opened for the first time in several of the established parishes: the two dedicated to Our Lady of Mt. Carmel and in that of Corpus Christi in Cleveland, Holy Family in Parma, St. Rita in Solon, St. Mary in Olmsted Falls, Sacred Heart in Wadsworth, St. Francis Xavier in Medina, St. Mary in Mentor and St. Mary in Chardon.

We have seen above that the separation of the Youngstown diocese in 1943 left approximately 45,000 pupils in the 128 schools of this diocese; despite the separation, in 1950 the attendance at the 154 Cleveland schools was well over 63,000 and on the way to equaling the number of pupils in the combined territory seven years before. Approximately one-third of the elementary school children in Greater Cleveland attended the parochial schools, though it was estimated that only one-third to one-half of the Catholic children of the same area were enrolled in parochial schools.[1]

The number of religious teachers in the parish schools has increased considerably but laywomen still perform an important duty in assisting them. In the fall of 1943 there were approximately 950 members of the religious congregations who were aided by 90 of the laity. In the autumn of 1950, there were 1,314 Sisters and 170 auxiliaries. The following summary is based upon the situation in the fall of 1950. Ursuline Nuns to the number of 216 aided by 40 laywomen had 11,986 pupils in 24 schools; 198 Sisters of St. Joseph aided by 48 lay teachers had 11,577 pupils in 23 schools; 178 Sisters of Notre Dame aided by 28 others had 9,089 pupils in 24 schools; 89 Sisters of the Holy Humility of Mary aided by 20 others had 4,671 pupils in 11 schools; 108 Sisters of St. Joseph of the Third Order of St. Francis aided by 5 others had 3,782 pupils in 12 schools; 68 Sisters of St.

[1] C.U.-B., June 5, 1951.

428

Dominic (of Akron) aided by 5 others had 3,242 pupils in 9 schools; 70 Vincentian Sisters of Charity had 2,712 pupils in 11 schools.

Forty Sisters of Charity of St. Augustine had 1,772 pupils in 5 schools; 30 Sisters of the Incarnate Word had 1,535 pupils in 4 schools; the Sisters of the Holy Family of Nazareth had 1,521 pupils in 2 schools; 22 Sisters of Charity of Cincinnati with the aid of 6 others had 1,344 pupils in 2 schools; 35 Daughters of the Divine Redeemer had 1,323 pupils in 5 schools; 22 Sisters Servants of the Immaculate Heart aided by three others had 1,152 pupils in 3 schools; 25 Sisters of St. Dominic of Adrian had 1,055 pupils in 3 schools; 20 Sisters of the Precious Blood aided by 4 others had 1,039 pupils in one school; 21 Franciscan Sisters of Joliet aided by 1 other had 933 pupils in 2 schools; 21 Franciscan Sisters of Blessed Kunegunda had 908 pupils in 2 schools; 11 Sisters of the Blessed Sacrament aided by 3 others had 616 pupils in 2 schools; 12 Franciscan Sisters of Lemont had 521 pupils in 2 schools; 17 Sisters of the Most Holy Trinity had 493 pupils in 3 schools; 6 Sisters of Mercy aided by 2 others had 449 pupils in 1 school; 7 Franciscan Sisters of Pittsburgh had 326 pupils in 1 school; 10 Felician Sisters had 313 pupils in 2 schools; 7 Franciscan Sisters of Syracuse had 280 pupils in 1 school; 4 Sisters of St. Basil had 207 pupils in 1 school; 4 Religious Teachers Filippini with the help of 1 other had 194 pupils in 1 school.

The outstanding ambition of the Archbishop in the educational field has been to offer the opportunity of a Catholic high school training to all the graduates of the parish schools. And although great progress was made in the first years of his administration, he launched a three-year drive in February, 1951, to double the capacity so as to be able to accommodate an additional 12,000 students. He called upon his people to make the necessary sacrifices, and instituted a monthly collection in the parishes to meet the costs of the buildings.

Early in 1946 he announced the plans for a district high school in Elyria which was to serve the surrounding towns of Oberlin, Grafton, North Ridgeville, and South Amherst; the campaign for funds made under the chairmanship of Monsignor Newton was very successful. On a thirty-two-acre plot at Gulf Road and Prospect Street, purchased from the Federal Government, a $600,000 three-story brick structure was erected, and the Archbishop had the satisfaction of dedicating it on November 20, 1949. It had eight class rooms, two science laboratories, study halls, a library, and chapel, and a gymnasium-auditorium with a seating capacity of 600. A large convent adjoining housed the Sisters of Notre Dame, the instructors. Father Joseph B. Lehane was named the director. The accommodations were already strained in the fall term of 1950 by the 375 students registered.[2]

For the convenience of the boys of the parishes on the west side of the Cuyahoga River, St. Edward's High School, at Detroit and Nichol-

[2] *C.U.-B.*, Feb. 8, 1946; Oct. 7, Nov. 18, 1949. Cleveland *Plain Dealer*, Nov. 19, 1949.

son Avenues, in Lakewood was established. Holy Cross Brothers from Notre Dame University in Indiana under Brother John W. Donoghue in September, 1949, started classes for 105 first-year students in the building previously occupied by St. Theresa's Academy. In the next year 417 boys were enrolled in the first and second-year classes, making it necessary to use the additional facilities of St. James' parish hall. Meanwhile the new building was completed. The T-shaped thirty-five-class-room brick structure, modern in every sense, has two floors in front and three in the rear. Three laboratories, the library, and other necessary facilities occupy the central section; one department teaches the industrial arts; the two-floor gymnasium-auditorium section seats 2,500; the faculty residence hall, with chapel, makes provision for thirty-five Brothers. In the spring of 1952, there were already 810 in attendance with the prospect of filling its capactity for 1300 students in the immediate future. Plans call for an immense athletic stadium. It was a happy day for the Archbishop when he dedicated the new building on April 26, 1952. Bishop Begin blessed the cornerstone and Archbishop O'Hara of Philadelphia gave the formal address in which he ably defended the right of the Church to have her own schools.[3]

The Holy Cross Brothers had already in 1946 established themselves in the diocese at Gates Mills. Many years ago Bishop Gilmour asked Father Sorin, the founder of Notre Dame University, to open a college here but it remained for the Brothers to come at the invitation of his successor. With Brother Theophane Schmitt as headmaster, they opened Gilmour Academy, a preparatory school for boys, at Cedar and SOM Center Roads on the 133-acre Drury Estate. The forty-room Tudor mansion and a new fifteen-room brick building were dedicated September 20, 1948. The original enrollment of 60 students grew to 140 in 1951, when there were 16 Brothers and 1 priest in the local community.[4]

St. Joseph High School, named in honor of Archbishop Schrembs, at Lake Shore Boulevard and East 185th Street near the Euclid boundary line, serves a rapidly growing section of Greater Cleveland. The Brothers of Mary who operate Cathedral Latin School have charge of it. Under the principal, Brother Louis J. Weismer, 120 boys in September, 1950, began classes in two large residences on the 27-acre plot adjoining the Diocesan Retreat House; in the following spring they moved into a few rooms in the new building. The three-story brick structure with its distinctive glass-brick façade can accommodate 2300 students. It has 60 class-rooms, a chapel seating 270, a library, laboratories, and other facilities in the main building. A separate one-story building is used to teach the industrial arts. A combination gymnasium-auditorium, seating 3,000, is to be found in a separate wing. The teachers have their residence in another building. A large stadium on the lake will complete the plans. On Memorial Day, May 30, 1952, the

[3] *C.U.-B.*, Aug. 12, Oct. 14, 1949; Jan. 20, 1950; Mar. 30, Apr. 20, 1951.
[4] *C.U.-B.*, July 13, 1945; Mar. 1, Sept. 6, 1946; Feb. 3, 1950.

Archbishop dedicated the great institution to Catholic education. Bishop Dearden of Pittsburgh congratulated him on the accomplishment and in his speech vindicated the right of Catholics to have their children educated under the watchful eye of religion. Boys were admitted into the third year in the fall of 1952 and the senior year will be added in 1953.

Another large district high school to serve the Catholic students of Akron and the wide area surrounding that city has been definitely planned by the Archbishop who is carrying on negotiations to secure the teachers to staff it. A forty-five-acre tract of land on Fifth Avenue was acquired by the diocese in 1949 as the most favorable location.

The Marist Fathers were admitted into the diocese in the early part of 1952. It is expected that within five years they will operate another high school for the boys of the southeastern section of the city.

Equal care has been expended in developing the opportunities for the Catholic young women. The Dominican Sisters of Adrian, Michigan, who for some time past have taught in several elementary schools in the city started Hoban Dominican High School for Girls on Harvard Avenue opposite Lee Heights Boulevard with 130 students in September, 1951. The three-story brick building with 21 class-rooms, laboratories, and other auxiliary rooms and accommodations for 1000 pupils was solemnly dedicated by the Apostolic Delegate, Archbishop Cicognani, on September 8, 1952.[5]

In 1942 the Ursuline Nuns acquired the large Painter estate of twenty-seven acres at Fairmount Boulevard and Lee Road in Cleveland Heights. The sixty-five-room mansion on it was remodeled and re-named Beaumont School for Girls in memory of one of the Ursuline founders. Dedicated on August 15 of the same year, it was opened in the following month with 112 students and 12 teachers; in 1949 the attendance had grown to 358 with 20 on the teaching staff.[6]

In February, 1951, the Sisters of Notre Dame announced their plans for the building of Regina High School for Girls on a section of their spacious fifty-acre grounds in South Euclid. Construction of the three-floor brick and stone building in the Colonial style with accommodations for 500 students began in November of 1952 and there are good reasons for hoping that it will be ready for occupancy in the fall of 1953.[7]

On April 16, 1950, the Archbishop dedicated the modern brick parish High School of St. John Cantius on Tremont Avenue on the south side of the city, which was erected by Monsignor Francis Duda. It has sixteen class-rooms, an auditorium, and other necessary equipment to accommodate 400 students. The Sisters of St. Joseph of the Third Order of St. Francis opened classes in September for the 108 who had registered.[8]

[5] *C.U.-B.*, Mar. 31, Apr. 28, July 7, Aug. 18, 1950; Feb. 23, 1951.
[6] *C.U.-B.*, Feb. 17, 1950; Apr. 6, May 4, 1951. Cleveland *Press*, Feb. 14, 1950.
[7] *C.U.-B.*, Feb. 16, 1951.
[8] *C.U.-B.*, Mar. 31, Apr. 21, 1950.

The high school in St. Edward's parish on Woodland Avenue was started by the Sisters of the Blessed Sacrament shortly after that parish plant was entrusted to the Fathers of the Precious Blood to enable them to expand their work with the Colored; 6 Sisters were teaching 63 pupils in 1950.

In many other parishes the ninth grade has already been added to the curriculum with a view to establishing the full four years' course.

All the older high schools and academies experienced remarkable growth. St. Ignatius High School was able to enroll more students by taking over the twelve class-rooms in St. Mary's parish school just across West 30th Street. The parish pupils were transferred to the school in the nearby St. Patrick's parish which in 1945 had been entrusted to the Fathers of the Society of Jesus. At St. Ignatius in 1943 there were 811 students and 35 Jesuits teaching them; in 1949 there were 937 students and 36 Jesuit and 13 lay instructors.[9]

In 1943, Cathedral Latin School (East 107th Street) had 860 boys in attendance, and 5 priests and 24 Brothers of the Society of Mary on the teaching staff; in 1949 the enrollment had increased to 1,134 and the teaching body to 48. In the last-mentioned year the school graduated 270, the largest class in its history.

Benedictine High School, which started in 1941, has developed into one of the largest in the diocese. In 1943 there were 571 students and a teaching staff of 25 Benedictines and 4 laymen; in 1949 there were 1,055 students and 33 Benedictines and 15 lay instructors. In the summer of 1951 it was announced that Abbot Kojis had agreed to expand the facilities of the school to accommodate 2,000 students.

The high school of Holy Name parish was enabled to accept more students by the transfer of part of the elementary grades to the public school building which had been purchased from the city. The attendance of 657 in 1943 was increased to 851 in 1949. In St. Mary's Parish in Akron at the suggestion of the Archbishop the high school was renamed St. Mary's Central High School for the opening of classes in September, 1950; Monsignor O'Keefe had finished and remodeled a large part of the grammar school for the purpose. The enrollment increased from 223 in 1943 to nearly 500 in 1950.

In St. Vincent's parish in Akron, the high school increased its registration from 418 in 1943 to 659 in 1950. The Dominican Sisters who operate St. Vincent's also have a private school, Our Lady of the Elms Academy, in connection with their convent and mother-house on West Market Street in Akron. Here they put up a modern gymnasium in 1945 and remodeled a fifteen-room house on an adjoining property for class-room use. In 1949 the Sisters had 87 girls in high school and 235 children in the elementary course; at their nursery school on West Exchange Street they had nearly 100 in their charge. In 1946, they sold their forty-three-year-old academy on property next

[9] *C.U.-B.*, July 13, Oct. 12, 1945.

*Right:*St. Thomas More Church and School.

*Left:*St. Joseph Church and School, Avon Lake.

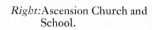

*Right:*Ascension Church and School.

*Left:*St. Leo Church and School.

*Right:*St. William Church and School.

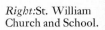

*Right:*St. Raphael Church and School, Bay Village.

*Left:*Holy Family Church and School, Parma.

*Right:*St. Francis De Sales Church and School, Akron.

*Left:*St. Henry Church and School.

*Right:*St. Louis Church and School, Cleveland Heights.

to St. Bernard's Church. In St. Mary's parish in Lorain, the high school increased its registration from 114 in 1943 to 270 in 1950.

Several of the older private academies enlarged their facilities and were able to accept more students. In 1944, the Sisters of the Holy Humility of Mary purchased a public school building at Bridge Avenue and Randall Road, which after a thorough renovation was dedicated as the new Lourdes Academy on November 28 of that year.[10] The old school on Franklin Avenue had an attendance of 204 in 1943; in the new quarters there were 475 students in 1949. In 1948, the same Sisters bought a sixty-five-acre plot of land on Center Ridge Road near Hilliard for future development.

In 1946, the Sisters of Charity of St. Augustine discontinued the elementary section of their academy on Lake Avenue, in which they had 140 girls, to make room for high school students; the high school enrollment increased on that account from 104 in 1943 to 285 in 1950. St. Joseph's Academy on Rocky River Drive in restricting itself to the older students made room for 502 in the secondary grades in 1950. The Ursuline Academy of the Sacred Heart in East Cleveland has had approximately the same number of students, 275, for several years. The Ursuline Academy of Villa Angela on Lake Shore Boulevard suffered considerable loss in 1946 when St. Joseph's Seminary for young boys was destroyed by fire; on the same grounds the girls' academy had 220 pupils in 1949. The Ursulines have charge also of the high school in Holy Trinity parish with its 120 students. Altogether, the same community in 1950 had 52 nuns aided by 13 laywomen teaching nearly 1,000 pupils in four high schools.

Marymount High School in Garfield Heights increased its attendance from 211 in 1943 to 382 in 1949. We have seen above that at Marycrest where the Angel Guardian Academy and Sacred Heart Vocational School were combined there where 88 pupils in 1950. The Sisters of the Incarnate Word began the construction of a new academy and Convent on Pearl Road in Parma Heights in the spring of 1952. Archbishop Hoban blessed the cornerstone on the following May 4th.

Notre Dame Academy on Ansel Road by the exclusion of the elementary grades increased the number of its students from 672 in 1943 to 833 in 1950. The Sisters of this community have charge of six parish high schools in the city which originally began with commercial courses but developed into regular four-year high schools. In 1949, St. Boniface's had 136 pupils, St. Francis' 149, St. Michael's 304, Our Lady of Lourdes 148, St. Peter's 206, St. Stephen's 355. In eight high schools, including the one in Elyria, nearly 100 Sisters aided by a few laywomen were teaching a total of nearly 2,500 pupils in 1950.

In the same year the high school in St. Procop's parish had 141 students who were under the tutelage of the Franciscan Sisters of Mary

[10] *C.U.-B.,* Nov. 24, 1944.

Immaculate; and in St. Stanislas' there were 275 pupils who were taught by the Sisters of the Holy Family of Nazareth. It will be observed that in 1943 in the eleven parish high schools there were approximately 2,276 students with less than 100 teachers, 80 of them religious. In 1950 there were fifteen such schools with an attendance of nearly 4,300, which was more than one-third of the total of 11,722 in all the Catholic high schools of the diocese, with 143 Sisters and 35 lay people teaching them.

In connection with Catholic schools it may be remarked that with few exceptions the attitude of non-Catholics towards the Church in Cleveland has been tolerant and friendly. As the successors of the earlier American Protective Association and the Ku Klux Klan, the organization calling itself the Protestant and Other Americans United for Separation of Church and State has similar objectives but more subtile methods.

The imminent passage in the United States Congress of the Barden Bill, which would exclude parochial school children from any of the benefits which would come from Federal aid to the schools of the country, excited the indignation of Catholics here as elswhere against the discrimination. Through thousands of post-cards, telegrams, and other forms of petition it was brought to the attention of the Ohio representatives that since no distinction of religion was made by the Government in time of war or in the collection of taxes, none should be made in the distribution of Federal assistance to its future soldiers and tax payers. The bill would ignore the existence of hundreds of thousands of children in the parochial schools and would deny them the auxiliary services only indirectly connected with their education such as bus transportation, medical supervision, and lunches. The country-wide protest at least delayed the passage of the measure.[11]

In the State of Ohio the educational director, despite the law which compels the local boards of education to provide transportation for pupils in elementary schools who live more than two miles from the schoolhouse, decided that the use of tax-supported buses by parochial school children was illegal. He based his decision on an opinion of an attorney general given in 1928. On the other side it was contended that this opinion did not have the force of law. With very few exceptions, however, the practice has been to discriminate.[12]

Although Catholic schools as such were not involved, the Ohio Supreme Court in recent years handed down decisions of interest to them. In denying the appeal of the Cleveland Rabbinical College against the local taxation of that institution the Court in the statement of Chief Justice William Hart (in 1948) defined a public college or academy or public institution of learning as one owned and operated by the State or by a political division of it in a governmental capacity. This seemed to contradict the precedent set by the decision of the

[11] *C.U.-B.*, June 24, July 1, 8, 1949.
[12] *C.U.-B.*, Feb. 23, 1940; Jan. 28, 1949.

same Court in the Gerke-Purcell case of 1874, which had to do with the taxation of the Cincinnati parochial schools and in which the word "public" was referred to the use and not to the ownership of the educational facilities. Upon the instance of the attorneys the Court admitted that public ownership was not necessary for tax exemption.

The traditional interpretation was further clarified in a four-to-three decision of the Court in April, 1949, which reversed a decision of the Cleveland authorities to tax the Cleveland Bible College. Justice Kingsley Taft who voted for the exemption recalled that an amendment of the Ohio Constitution, September 3, 1912, had changed the wording of the law on tax exemption from "institutions of purely public charity" to "institutions used exclusively for charitable purposes," and he held that if an institution were operated without any view to profit and were used entirely for lawful education or religion or both it meets the requirements for tax exemption whether open to the public or not. In further justification he quoted the well-known section 7 of the State Constitution which recommends the protection of religion and encourages schools and the means of instruction.[13]

Moreover, the attitude of the Cleveland courts in matters affecting Catholic interests has been generally fair and equitable. The local Probate Court Judge, at least on two occasions, upheld a "last will and testament" in deciding that a legacy left for Masses for the soul of the deceased was a valid charitable trust. The inheritance tax, however, is regularly charged against such bequests. In general, too, the courts have been careful of the right of a Catholic child to his religious faith in disputes about his legal custody. In November, 1943, a non-Catholic judge of the Court of Common Pleas ruled that a seven-year-old child of non-practising Catholics who were divorced, and had remarried at the time that the child was two and one-half years of age, would have to be afforded the opportunity to live as a Catholic.[14]

[13] *C.U.-B.*, Jan. 16, 1948; Apr. 15, 1949.
[14] *C.U.-B.*, Nov. 12, 1943; Apr. 8, 1949.

73

COLLEGES, TRADE UNIONS, AND CATHOLIC INSTRUCTION

G REAT ADVANCES HAVE BEEN MADE IN THE diocese in recent years in the field of university and college education. An outstanding accomplishment is the erection of St. John College on Cathedral Square.

The Cathedral parish was no longer a parish of homes and in 1943 there were only 66 children in the school; these were transferred to St. Peter's school which itself had an attendance of about 100. The Sisters' College then took over the entire building. Enlarged quarters, however, did not solve the problems of the college, and a new site was sought. The Bishop finally decided to put up a modern building near the Cathedral. Ground was broken at the eastern end of the property in October, 1945.

St. John College Auditorium, a separate building with its 1,000 opera seats on an incline looking down at a fully equipped stage, was finished in December, 1946. Its immediate use was as a temporary chapel during the interval while the Cathedral was in the process of rebuilding. All the activities of the parish and episcopal functions with few exceptions, thereafter, were held in it until the completion of the work on the Cathedral proper. The stage was readily adapted for use as a sanctuary; the well-lighted and artistically decorated hall filled the long-felt need of a meeting place for the clergy and for the Catholic public.

Connected with this hall by a corridor is St. John College, the new name adopted for Sisters' College in 1946. The beautiful three-story building, like the auditorium in the Tudor Gothic style of architecture, is constructed of Crab Orchard stone. It was ready for occupancy in May, 1947, when the first classes were held in it, though the formal opening did not take place until September. A small chapel on the second floor was dedicated on December 8. The increased attendance made it necessary to complete the third floor at the north end of the building in which are to be found additional classrooms and laboratories for the nurse students; at the same time the court in front of the college was enclosed within an ornamental fence into which is worked a beautiful outdoor shrine.

The college is fully equipped with the necessary facilities. The library of some 30,000 volumes occupies a separate wing which is connected with the hall and the other main unit by a corridor. Many rare and beautiful paintings, including some of the famous masters, statues, precious bronzes, and other works of art, the gift of the Archbishop, adorn the chapel, the reading room and library, and the corridors.

The teaching staff of the college is composed of specially trained priests and representatives of the teaching communities in the diocese; in 1949 there were 8 clergymen, 15 Sisters of seven different congregations, and 7 lay instructors. Improvement and advance in normal training are readily adopted after experimentation in the parish schools themselves. The latter are divided into four areas, each under its own supervisor and all subject to the control of the superintendent. At the Teachers Institutes held regularly in St. John Auditorium Archbishop Hoban is wont to address the Sisters on some special subject, insisting always on their primary duty to give religion its proper place in all education.

The college, which is affiliated with the Catholic University of America and belongs also to the American Association of Colleges for Teacher Education, confers the baccalaureate in nursing and educational science, and the degree of Master of Arts in Education upon graduate students, and is also empowered by the State of Ohio to give a provisional elementary teaching certificate. In 1947, there were 120 full-time students and 400 in the Saturday courses in the educational department, including, in the latter, 125 who were working for their master's degree. In the summer of that year 86 Sisters of the various communities attended a summer course in French and Spanish on the campus of Western Reserve University.[1]

There are generally more than 400 in the summer sessions at St. John's. In 1949 there were 290 students including the nurses in the regular courses and in the next year the total was 305. Eighty-two diplomas were issued in 1948 and 74 in the following year. The Archbishop, who is Chancellor, appointed Monsignor Robert B. Navin the president of the college and Monsignor Clarence E. Elwell superintendent of schools to succeed Bishop John Hagan who had held both offices, and for whom as its founder the college was named. Cardinal Stritch of Chicago presided at the public graduation in June, 1950, and gave their diplomas to 53 graduates, among whom were the first lay students to receive degrees.[2]

The facilities of St. John College are used by the Institute of Social Education, a school of adult education under the direction of Father Francis Carney. Evening courses are offered to the public for the pur-

[1] *C.U.-B.*, Aug. 15, 1947.
[2] *C.U.-B.*, June 9, 30, 1950.

pose of making them better acquainted with the moral teachings of the Church and its application to modern problems. Religious, ethical, and philosophical subjects are taught by priests and laymen. Over 1,000 persons followed the lectures in the fall term of 1949. The Institute also provides speakers for lecture courses in the parishes and it has brought prominent speakers to the city.[3] A digression is made here to record the Church's traditional attitude towards labor.

The Labor School, organized in 1941 under the auspices of the Association of Catholic Trade Unionists, was transferred to St. John's in 1945. Twice a week for nine weeks each year courses in parliamentary procedure, labor relations, ethics, and legislation affecting labor were given by competent teachers and were well attended. A free labor school was opened at John Carroll University in 1945 and another in St. Peter's parish in Akron in the next year.[4]

The Archbishop in September, 1945, at the opening Mass in the Cathedral for the meeting of the Catholic Conference on Industrial Relations, expressed his position in quoting the Holy Father and recalling that the Church is and must be the advocate, the mother, and the patron of working people. He vindicated the right of the Church as the guardian and teacher of Christian morality to speak authoritatively in matters affecting so many of her children: "The working-man should be restored to his place of dignity in the plan of Providence and be guaranteed the secure and stable position which other classes of society enjoy." These and similar convictions found expression also at the conventions in Cleveland of the Catholic Economic Association in 1946 and 1948.[5]

At the eleventh national convention of the Congress of Industrial Organizations here in 1949, which disavowed the Communist influence, the Archbishop addressed the delegates and encouraged them to repudiate all connections with the Communists whom he characterized as the enemies of God and of man who were attempting to divert unionism from its legitimate purpose. He complimented the unions for having defended the rights of labor to a living wage, to an honorable position in society, to economic security, and to a hearing in the courts of justice and the halls of the legislature; but he also reminded them of their duty to work for the rights of others, for their fellow men, their country, and their God.[6]

The 1950 regional conference of the Association of Catholic Trade Unionists was held in St. John Auditorium in April under the auspices of the Archbishop who celebrated the opening Mass. The Labor Day Mass in the Cathedral each year was well attended by the members of this association: 1,200 in 1949, and 1,400 in the next year, assembled to

[3] *C.U.-B.*, Jan. 16, Oct. 1, Dec. 3, 1948; Jan. 6, 13, 1950.
[4] *C.U.-B.*, Sept. 12, Nov. 7, 1941; Apr. 17, 1942; Jan. 15, Sept. 21, Oct. 5, 1945; Nov. 29, 1946; Jan. 10. Sept. 12, 1947.
[5] *C.U.-B.*, Sept. 14, 1945.
[6] *C.U.-B.*, Nov. 11, 1949.

beg the blessing of God upon their endeavor to find a Christian solution of their problems. The association, composed of labor union members but not intended to be a separate union nor a Catholic "bloc," was organized on a national basis for the purpose of furthering a Christian as opposed to a materialistic conception of human society. Locally, they have sponsored in successive years public meetings in which representatives of labor and management have discussed the principles laid down in the great papal encyclicals on labor. Father George Schneider, after a special course in the Catholic University at Washington, was appointed to succeed Father Aloysius Bartko, the first chaplain of the organization. The number of members is gradually increasing. Some of them attended their first closed retreat at the Diocesan Retreat House in 1949.[7]

Of interest in this regard was the organization of the Catholic Electric Guild[8] here in 1945; it is composed of employers and employees (300 in 1951) who work together for mutual assistance and in a spirit of Christian charity and understanding. Of considerable interest, too, is the growth of the Federal Credit Unions which have been established in many parishes for the relief of the small borrowers; in April, 1948, there were 186 units in the diocese and about 75,000 members. They have but a nominal connection with the parishes and are subject to regular government inspection.[9]

We return again to the educational institutions in the diocese. The Archbishop gave his full approbation to the two Catholic colleges for women in the city. Notre Dame College was one of the several in the country chosen to give special courses in social reconstruction work at the time that it was thought that young women trained in it might devote themselves to such endeavor in Poland after the last war. The college graduated 48 in 1948 and 66 in 1949; in the latter year there were 300 students and 43 instructors. In February, 1951, the Sisters announced their plans for a residence hall for 150 students.[10]

Ursuline College expanded its quarters in 1944 by the acquisition of the Sherwin estate in the immediate vicinity; a three-story Colonial style mansion was remodeled for the accommodation of 30 boarding students and was dedicated on November 28 of that year as Amadeus Hall, in memory of Cleveland's first bishop. Another two-story building, Brescia Hall, was remodeled for use as a gymnasium and for other college facilities. In 1948 there were 42 young women who received their diplomas and in 1950 there were 47; in the fall term of 1950, 231 students were enrolled and the faculty numbered 37.[11] The community

[7] *C.U.-B.*, Aug. 25, 1939; Sept. 6, 1940; Sept. 3, 1943; Sept. 9, 1949; Jan. 20, 1950. Cleveland *Plain Dealer*, Sept. 6, 1949. Pastoral, Apr. 18, 1949.
[8] *C.U.-B.*, Jan. 26, 1945; Feb. 16, 1951.
[9] *C.U.-B.*, Apr. 23, 1948; Feb. 10, 17, 24, 1950.
[10] *C.U.-B.*, July 28, 1944.
[11] *C.U.-B.*, Dec. 1, 1944.

announced in the summer of 1952 the plans for the erection of a group of college buildings on a 112-acre tract of land in the village of Pepper Pike on Lander Road at Fairmount Boulevard.

John Carroll University, which began in 1886 as St. Ignatius College, in the years of its existence up to 1947 had given instruction to nearly 9,000 persons including "part-time" students. In June, 1949, 240 graduated, making a total of 2,131 who had received academic degrees. The enrollment in the first year was 76; in 1948 it was 1,839, a figure which does not include the 446 in the evening classes nor the 875 in the summer school of that year. Among its alumni were four bishops and an archbishop, about 400 priests, over 100 attorneys, judges, and prosecutors, over 200 physicians and dentists, many teachers and business men, and others who have contributed to the general good of the community and the country.

During the First and Second World Wars its facilities were placed at the disposal of the Government for the training of officers in the armed forces. In September, 1948, returned veterans made up seventy per cent of the enrollment of 1,743, and they were fifty-six per cent of the 1,839 registered in the following year. In 1949 the student body numbered nearly 2,300. In recent years the courses of studies have been greatly expanded: degrees are granted in such subjects as labor relations and business administration and government. In these courses there were nearly 700 students in 1948; in the same year there were nearly 350 studying the social sciences and nearly 300 in the pre-medical and pre-dental courses; 221 were occupied with the natural sciences, 128 with engineering, and 113 with academic subjects.

It is interesting to note that beginning in 1936 the laymen of the teaching staff outnumbered the Jesuit teachers; in September, 1949, of the 99 professors 73 were laymen. Father Frederick Odenbach, one of the founders of the Jesuit Seismological Association who built his own instruments for the first earthquake observatory at St. Ignatius, had moved his equipment to the new John Carroll University in 1932, the year before his death. His scientific work was continued by Father Joseph Joliat, who published a monthly bulletin recording the findings he made with new instruments installed in 1947.

In 1949 Father Frederick Welfle, appointed rector in 1946, announced plans to raise up to $6,000,000 for further expansion. The present group of buildings, dominated by the collegiate Gothic tower, includes the administration building with a large auditorium, chapel, and library; the chemical and biology buildings which are connected by arcades; the faculty residence and students' dormitory; the gymnasium and power-house. During 1950 a large two-story barracks was built for the students of the officers training corps; military training became an integral part of college education. A three-story residence hall with accommodations for 218 students was completed in the summer of 1952. It was named Pacelli Hall in honor of Pope Pius XII and was dedicated by the Apostolic Delegate, Archbishop Cicognani, the following September 7th.[12]

It was estimated in 1949 that nearly one-fourth of the university and college students in Greater Cleveland were Catholics. To take care of their spiritual needs more efficiently the Archbishop reorganized the Newman Clubs, which had been previously established, and took the step of appointing Father Paul Hallinan, a returned army chaplain, diocesan director of all of them and resident chaplain on the campus of Western Reserve University. Assisting him were four non-resident priests assigned to the other large colleges in the area.

In 1947 two large residences on Abington Road near Euclid Avenue were remodeled to serve as the center for the six chapters of the Intercollegiate Newman Club, and as a dormitory for twenty students. They were blessed by the Archbishop who had donated the altar and the pews. A new two-story brick building containing a chapel and recreation hall was dedicated to St. Albert the Great on November 22, 1952. The Catholic students (610 in 1950) avail themselves of the services offered and participate enthusiastically in the social activities of the club; fraternization with the students of the Catholic colleges is also encouraged. The club issued a bulletin telling of its programs. Spiritual retreats were held at regular intervals in St. Agnes' Church; on one occasion Bishop Begin confirmed fifteen students, eleven of them converts.

Following the Mass celebrated for the combined Newman Clubs in the Cathedral in 1949, the Archbishop bestowed the apostolic blessing sent them by the Holy Father. It was at his invitation that the national convention of the Newman Club Federation met here in June, 1950; he pontificated at its opening in the Cathedral and stressed the necessity of bringing Christ to the college campus. He also presided at the two-day institute for Newman Club chaplains at the Diocesan Retreat House. It was at this convention that Bishop Kearny of Rochester presented the first Cardinal Newman Award to Myron Taylor, the personal representative of the President of the United States at the Vatican, who was among the 800 delegates present.

The Knights of Columbus of Ohio helped appreciably in the establishment of Newman Hall in Cleveland; they gave assistance also to a similar project in Akron. A part of St. Bernard's School in that city was dedicated as the center of Newman Club activities for the benefit of the estimated one-fifth of the 5,000 students attending Akron University; a priest was appointed there also to direct the work. In other college towns the priests of the parishes make every effort to keep in touch with the young people. The Archbishop in his pastoral of September 19, 1950, reminded all students attending non-Catholic colleges

---

[12] *C.U.-B.*, Jan. 3, Aug. 15, 1947; Jan. 30, Sept. 24, 1948; Sept. 16, Nov. 25, Dec. 23, 1949; Mar. 24, June 2, Sept. 22, Oct. 20, Nov. 1, 1950; Jan. 26, 1951. Memorandum furnished by Fr. Welfle, S. J., President of John Carroll University.

of their obligation to continue their religious education and of enrolling and participating in the activities of the Newman Clubs.[13]

In the same pastoral he admonished the Catholics in the public schools of their obligation in conscience to know and to study the truths of their religion, and the parents also of their corresponding duty to see to it that their children frequented the classes of religious instruction which were given in the parishes under the reorganized program of the Confraternity of Christian Doctrine. It was acknowledged that, although more than 65,000 children in the 130 elementary schools were receiving adequate care the many Catholics in the public schools were not, even though the pastors assisted by volunteers had been doing their best to meet the situation.

In the reorganization, the confraternity was established in every parish and a full schedule of classes was announced. The Archbishop, who had presided at the first regional congress of the confraternity, held in Columbus in 1948, upon his return appealed to the members of the National Council of Catholic Women in their diocesan meeting in Akron to give their services to the new program, which met with great success from the beginning. In Willoughby, through circulars addressed to them, 180 students in the local public high school enrolled themselves in the corresponding classes of the confraternity. In St. Joseph's parish in old Collinwood the first invitation was accepted by 125. In St. Theresa's parish in Garfield Heights the approximately 400 in the instruction classes used two private homes and the after-school facilities of two public schools. In St. Thomas' in Cleveland the children under instruction sit with the parochial school children during Sunday Mass and in this way learn the Catholic hymns.

Among the teachers of the confraternity are students of the Catholic high schools and colleges: the young women of Notre Dame and Ursuline Colleges devote their efforts principally to the children in the populous areas which do not as yet have a parochial school; some of the John Carroll University students spend nearly every Sunday morning with the young patients at Rainbow Hospital for Crippled Children. In September, 1949, it was announced that the confraternity had been successfully established in 164 parishes and that 629 teachers—priests, Sisters, and laity—were engaged in the work. In September, 1950, a full school-year program of instructions was published for the approximately 7,600 elementary and 4,700 high school pupils enrolled.

Another department of the confraternity was its Parent-Educator project: interested workers call upon the parents of younger children in their homes to distribute booklets which offer suggestions and indicate methods of imparting religious instruction to their children. The Archbishop was host, as was also Father Richard McHale who had succeeded Father Joseph Moriarty as diocesan director, to the fourteenth

[13] *C.U.-B.*, July 19, Nov. 29, 1946; Oct. 17, 1947; Feb. 27, Mar. 5, Dec. 17, 1948; Jan. 14, 21, Mar. 4, June 3, 24, Sept. 7, 23, 30, Nov. 5, Dec. 9, 16, 1949; June 2, 23, 1950.

annual meeting of such directors held here in September, 1950. The work gives every promise of accomplishing its purpose.[14]

In September, 1949, the Archbishop blessed and opened the Catholic Information Center established in rooms near the Cathedral. It is for the convenience of the general public but especially of those non-Catholics who are interested in the Church and its activities, but who hesitate to approach the parish house. It is staffed by members of the Legion of Mary under the supervision of Monsignor Richard Walsh, the rector of the Cathedral and diocesan director of this Catholic Action group which was introduced here in 1935. In 1949 it had 148 active and 700 auxiliary members, pledged to assist their pastors in teaching catechism, taking census, and reclaiming negligent Catholics. A Catholic book store and lending library is operated in connection with the Information Center, which also sponsors pilgrimages to the churches and shrines of the diocese; on the first tour in August, 1950, seventeen buses were necessary to transport the 631 persons concerned.

Many who visit the center are prospective converts to the Faith, and they are directed to one of the instruction classes which are held in every parish.[15] In many parishes, sign boards on the property invite inquirers and indicate the hours during which these instructions are given. Special provisions are made for individual cases, and groups, large or small, are always to be found preparing to enter the Church. The Inquiry Center of the parish of the Holy Family (Chapelside Avenue) in 1945 reported 100 converts in three years. The Religious Information Hour at the Cathedral has had remarkable success. Many Catholics as well as prospective converts attended the large classes and assisted at the Holy Hour to pray for conversions. During the annual novena for Church Unity the faithful are strongly urged to be solicitous especially for their friends and relatives who do not belong to the Church.

[14] *C.U.-B.*, Oct. 15, 1945; Oct. 15, 1947; Feb. 13, June 11, 25, Aug. 20, Sept. 17, Oct. 29, Nov. 26, Dec. 15, 1948; Feb. 11, 25, Apr. 15, 22, 29, Sept. 9, Nov. 11, 18, Dec. 30, 1949; Sept. 15, 22, 29, 1950. Pastorals, Aug. 10, Sept. 16, 1948.
[15] *C.U.-B.*, Apr. 5, Nov. 8, 1946; Jan. 10, Mar. 7, May 23, 1947; Mar. 12, Nov. 12, 19, 1948; Apr. 1, Sept, 16, 23, Oct. 14, 1949; Mar. 17, Aug. 11, Sept. 29, Nov. 17, 1950.

74

THE MISSIONS

THE UNEASY AND UNHAPPY CONDITION OF affairs in Europe in these later days transferred a great part of the burden of supporting the foreign missions to America. Mindful of the appeal of the Holy Father in this regard Archbishop Hoban uses every opportunity to ask help for the missionaries and to urge everyone to join the Society for the Propagation of the Faith.[1] The public veneration of the right arm of the great missionary, St. Francis Xavier, by some 80,000 persons in Cleveland did much to arouse interest in the foreign missions. The precious relic was brought to the city on its way back to Rome, after a triumphal tour of India and Japan and the western part of the United States. Escorted from the airport by an honor guard and the officials of the diocese, it was enshrined on the flower-banked altar in the Blessed Sacrament Chapel of the Cathedral. On the evening of October 21, 1949, Monsignor McDonough presided at the services; a pious throng listened to a description of the missionary career of the saint and the history of the relic. The next morning the Archbishop celebrated a solemn pontifical Mass. He recalled that years before on a pilgrimage to the Far East he had been prevented by the high seas from landing on the Island of Sancian where St. Francis died on his way to the Chinese mainland. On Sunday afternoon Bishop Begin presided at the veneration of the relic, and on Monday morning just before it was taken from the city Father Frederick Welfle, S.J., raised it in benediction over the people.[2]

A very useful auxiliary of the Society for the Propagation of the Faith are the so-called mission circles, small groups who meet at intervals in private homes to make their contributions and to hear the reports made by the individual missionary who is often a priest or Sister from the diocese and personally known in one way or another to the members. The Little Flower Mission Circles were formed to help the Jesuit missions, and in 1950 they numbered seventy. Monsignor Charles McBride, who succeeded Bishop Treacy as the director of diocesan missionary activity in 1945, adopted the method of the circles for the benefit of the missions in general, and in 1946 he instituted the St.

[1] Pastorals, May 9, 20, 1945; May 5, Oct. 13, 1948; Oct. 12, 1949. C.U.-B., Apr. 29, May 14, Sept. 9, Oct. 21, 1949; Oct. 20, 1950.
[2] C.U.-B., Oct. 14, 28, 1949. Cleveland Plain Dealer, Sept. 2, Oct. 22, 1949.

Francis Xavier Mission Association which was well received, and in June, 1950, counted 201 units.[3]

The diocese has not only given financial support to the missions but many of its young men and women have given themselves for the actual work of the missionary in the field. Many Clevelanders were and are to be found among the Jesuits in India, Central America, and on the Indian reservations in the West. Others were among the Franciscan missioners. The Archbishop gave mission crosses to those who went to Brazil in 1950. Bishop Espelage of New Mexico had presided at a similar ceremony five years previously. The Maryknoll Fathers had a school for missionaries in Akron from 1936 until 1951. Two of their Fathers, John Mihelko and Frederick Becka, recently driven out by the Chinese Communists are natives of this diocese. Early records recall George Schneider, a Brother of Mary, who taught in the high school in Nagasaki, Japan, several decades ago.

There has always been Cleveland representation in the religious communities of women who work on the missions. We recall the Ursulines who went to the Indian mission in Montana in the early days. The Sisters of St. Joseph established a mission school in California. The Sisters of Notre Dame had several schools among the Mexicans and the Colored, also in California, and in 1949 they sent six of their number to Jamulpur in the Patna area in India. This occasion was marked by the first such ceremony of its kind for Sisters in the diocese. In the Cathedral, on August 29, the Archbishop, acting for the Holy Father, blessed the missionary crosses and gave the white-robed young women their credentials. He compared their task to that of St. John the Baptist who prepared the way for the Divine Master. And he took the opportunity to appeal to the friends and relatives of the missioners who had assembled in goodly numbers to devote their lives to the works of religion on the missions, in the schools, and in the hospitals. Bishop Begin added his hearty approval. Accompanied by Monsignor McBride, who had just previously received an assistant in the person of Father James P. McIntyre, the Sisters started for India on the following September 15th. The school they opened shortly after their arrival met with immediate success.

The Carmelite Nuns of the local foundation in the summer of 1951 sent six of the community to Africa to reinforce the foundation there; and the Poor Clare Nuns at the same time were preparing to open a convent in Brazil.[4]

The work begun by his predecessor among the Colored has been greatly expanded by the Archbishop; in 1950 five Fathers of the Precious Blood, and sixteen Sisters of the Blessed Sacrament were engaged in two Colored parishes in this city, and one priest of the diocese in the Akron parish. Father Melchior Lochtefeld, in charge of the original parish in the East 79th Street area, in December, 1941, estab-

[3] Begun in 1930.
[4] *C.U.-B.*, Feb. 3, Oct. 27, 1950; July 6, 1951.

lished a mission center on East 21st Street near Central Avenue in a building previously used by the Syrian congregation of St. Maron. Convinced that the apostolate needed greater facilities, the Archbishop in August, 1942, gave the parish plant of St. Edward on Woodland Avenue to the Sanguinists for that purpose. The Sisters of the Blessed Sacrament occupied the large residence which was once the headquarters of the Cleveland Apostolate.

The schoolhouse, which was also a catechetical center for about 300 children, was soon crowded by 450 pupils (including those in the high school) who were not all Catholics. The summer school had an average attendance of 200. The number of conversions to the Faith was an encouragement to all concerned. Group baptisms were a common occurrence; and it was a great consolation to the Archbishop, aided by several priests, to pour the saving waters on the heads of these neophytes who in their turn acted as apostles for the conversion of others. On May 1, 1949, for instance, 100 including some infants were baptized. Since the establishment of St. Edward's in its new capacity up to 1951, 700, mostly grown boys and girls, have been baptized. In the pioneer parish (East 79th Street) in the ten years previous to May, 1947, 961 persons had been received into the Church.[5]

St. Peter Claver's parish for the Colored in Akron had its origin in the work of the members of the Third Order of St. Dominic who opened a mission center in a former tavern on Howard Street in 1944. In the following year the diocese acquired title to a two-story brick store-house on West Bartges Street which was made into a rude chapel with the reception room and the priest's quarters on the second floor.

Colored Catholics in other districts in Cleveland attend the church and the parochial school of their neighborhood. One of them, a successful business man and a member of St. Thomas' parish,[6] was awarded the James J. Hoey medal in 1949 by the Catholic Interracial Council. The editor of a local Negro weekly newspaper[7] who is not a Catholic, in reporting his audience with the Holy Father in 1946 during which he was reminded that all men are brothers in Christ, praised the Catholic Church in Cleveland for its efforts on behalf of the Colored; he cited the easy acceptance of them in the local Catholic colleges.

An interesting experiment was made in the summer of 1949 when a group of young people from the local high schools and academies, living the life of the missionaries under the direction of the Missionary Servants of the Most Holy Trinity, assisted in the erection of church buildings, in teaching catechism, and in simply advertising the Church among the young Negroes in and around Camden, Mississippi.[8]

[5] *C.U.-B.*, July 5, 1945; July 26, 1946; Dec. 31, 1948; Sept. 2, 30, Oct. 21, Nov. 25, Dec. 2, 1949; June 2, 16, Sept. 8, 1950. Cleveland *Plain Dealer*, Aug. 29, Oct. 22, 1949.

[6] *C.U.-B.*, Dec. 5, 1941; Mar. 19, Aug. 6, 20, 1943; May 19, 1944; May 4, July 20, 1945; May 17, 1946; Apr. 25, May 2, 9, 1947; May 6, 1949.

[7] Melchisedec C. Clarke. *C.U.-B.*, Aug. 5, 1949. Cleveland *Plain Dealer*, Aug. 5, 1949.

[8] *C.U.-B.*, May 31, 1946; Apr. 18, 1949.

The financial assistance given to the missions is collected in the churches of the diocese after the general appeal made to the people on Mission Sunday in October; the proceeds are divided between the home and foreign missions. In addition, priests representing the various missionary congregations make a personal appeal from the pulpit a few times a year, according to a schedule arranged by the chancery. The Pentecost collection is used for the support of the missions in the diocese. As the result of this, several small parishes have been established and others have been enabled to extend their activities to the more distant and less populous areas; many indifferent or "fallen away" Catholics have thus been brought back to the Church. The children are educated in the love of the missions throughout the year.

75

DIOCESAN AFFAIRS UNDER
ARCHBISHOP HOBAN

T HE ISSUE OF FREQUENT LETTERS OR PASTO-
rals which were published from the pulpit on Sunday and
in the *Universe-Bulletin* continued to be the ordinary mode
of communication used by Archbishop Hoban. With but
few exceptions he ratified the diocesan regulations he found
here upon his coming.

By virtue of powers received from the Holy See, in 1943 the people
were dispensed on account of war conditions from the observance of
the Lenten fast and abstinence laws except on Ash Wednesday and
Good Friday; the other Fridays of the year remained days of abstinence. The normal rules in this matter were restored in 1947, because
it was judged that the reasons for the dispensation had ceased to exist
in the diocese. Working-men and their families, however, were still
permitted to eat flesh meat at the principal meal throughout the year
except on Fridays, Ash Wednesday, the forenoon of Holy Saturday,
and the vigil of Christmas Day. In the Lenten pastoral of 1950, all
priests who had authority to hear confessions in the diocese were empowered to dispense in individual cases from the laws of fasting and
abstinence; at the same time it was also declared that the combined
quantity of the light meatless breakfast and lunch permitted under
the law on fast days was to be notably less than that of the principal
meal, and that those who were not obliged to fast should practice
some voluntary penance. In the Lenten regulations which were published on February 18, 1952, the Archbishop by reason of special
powers granted by the Holy See made further modifications. Complete
abstinence from flesh meat was to be observed on Fridays, Ash Wednesday, the vigils of the Feast of the Assumption and Christmas, and
on Holy Saturday morning. But in a departure from previous rule
even those who were obliged to observe the fast were allowed the
use of flesh meat at the principal meal on Ember Wednesdays and
Saturdays, and on the vigils of the Feast of Pentecost and All Saints'
Day and on all the days of Lent except on Fridays, Ash Wednesday,
and the forenoon of Holy Saturday. In the observance of the fast it

*Right:*St. Casimir School.

*Left:*St. Gregory School, South Euclid.

*Right:*Immaculate Heart of Mary School.

*Left:*St. Joseph High School.

*Right:*St. Mel Church and School.

*Above:*Hoban Domin-
ican High School for
Girls.

*Right:*Elyria District
Catholic High School.

*Left:*St. Edward High School.

St. John Cantius High School.

St. Peter School, Akron.

was also declared that liquids, including milk and fruit juices, were permissible.

During the Second World War, the Holy See had modified the strictness of the natural fast prescribed before Holy Communion for the benefit of the soldiers and of those who worked all night in the defense factories; they might approach the Holy Table if they abstained from solid food for four hours previously and from liquids for one hour. In 1946, the Archbishop extended the privilege to the Sisters who nursed the sick in the hospitals during the night; and the taking of medicine or liquid nourishment did not prevent the patients themselves from receiving the Blessed Sacrament. Individuals who habitually worked at night and certain others were able to procure this privilege through their pastors for use on Sundays and holy days of obligation and on one other day of the week. This dispensation with further restrictions was renewed for another three years in the pastoral of June 20, 1949, and June 16, 1952. The modified relaxation of the fasting law has increased the number especially in the hospitals of those who receive the Blessed Sacrament more frequently.

For the sake of uniformity the Bishop in August, 1943, issued instructions to the effect that the last Mass on Sundays and Holy Days in the parishes was not to begin later than twelve o'clock noon. This regulation, which became operative on September 1 following, modified the previous practice of starting Mass on Sundays as late as a few minutes before one o'clock. Permission could be obtained to begin Mass on week days during Lent at ten minutes after twelve o'clock for the convenience of the office workers.

A readjusted schedule of dates for the Forty Hours' Devotion in the diocese became effective in November, 1949; thereafter the devotion was held in all institutions, hospitals, colleges, and seminaries; and they began or ended on a Sunday.[1]

To make certain that the most important points of Catholic doctrine and practice were systematically treated in the pulpit, the Bishop in 1947 prescribed the subjects for the Sunday sermons in a series of booklets which have been issued each year since that time; the fourth one appeared on November 1, 1950. An officially approved text of the prayers to be said after a Low Mass was sent to all the parishes in April, 1949, with instructions about its exclusive use.

On March 1, 1951, the Bishop issued a brief summary of the papal directives regulating the church music in the diocese; this sixteen-page booklet gave the basic rules to be observed by choirs and organists in rendering sacred music, and a short list of Masses and of music magazines. Continual progress had been made in the improvement of liturgical music in the parishes. The Cathedral choir of men and boys, which drew its talent from the entire city, was a pattern for the others. On five Sundays during the summer of 1950 it was heard on the radio,

[1] *C.U.-B.*, Mar. 3, Aug. 13, 1943; Mar. 1, Sept. 13, 1946; Feb. 14, 21, 1947; Feb. 18, 1948; Apr. 18, Nov. 1, 1949; Feb. 15, 1950. Pastoral, June 20, 1949.

on the Catholic Hour, and each year it has been giving a public choral concert in the Cathedral under the direction of Matthew Lucas, to the great delight of music lovers.

Archbishop Hoban in 1944 opened the first diocesan music conference held under the auspices of the National Catholic Music Educators Association with pontifical Mass, at which he spoke in encouragement of their work. Charles Kissling, the local coordinator of the association, in the spring of 1950 began a series of seminars for pastors, choirmasters, organists, and music teachers; in the previous summer a special class in liturgical music at John Carroll University had been well attended. Church organists also followed a special course offered at St. John College where, too, the regular students received a thorough training in the most modern methods of teaching children to sing the music of the Church.[2]

One of the chief concerns of the Archbishop as for every head of a diocese has been the recruitment of his clergy; his efforts in that regard have been very successful. He introduced the system of the preparatory seminary in which boys and young men with the necessary qualifications and inclination may begin their studies leading to the priesthood at an early age. During the Second World War, bona-fide seminarists were excused from military service. After the war the Archbishop definitely adopted the practice of accepting boys as students for the diocese when they had finished the grammar grades or at any stage of their high school or college training. Depending upon circumstances, the preparants are responsible for the whole or part of their tuition but none are excluded for financial reasons.

To encourage vocations sermons are prescribed on the need of more priests for the expanding activities of the diocese and for the replacement of those who become incapacitated; pastors were urged to interest young men in talks and interviews; and in the schools during the week devoted to cultivating vocations the subject is discussed with the pupils.[3] An illustrated folder describing seminary life is given to likely candidates, to whom especially at graduation time an invitation is extended to consider their possible vocation to the priesthood.

The majority of the 147 aspirants in 1950 were to be found at St. Gregory's Seminary in Cincinnati; others were at St. Charles College in Maryland and at St. Meinrad's in Indiana. Many of them had attended Sacred Heart Seminary in Detroit. Approximately seventy-five per cent of the 105 students for the diocese in the local major Seminary of St. Mary in 1950 came from the minor seminaries to which they had been sent by the diocese; the others had attended other col-

---

[2] *C.U.-B.*, May 5, 1944; Mar. 25, May 6, July 29, 1949; Feb. 3, Nov. 17, 1950; Apr. 6, 1951. The Vatican decree on popular liturgical hymns was published in the *C.U.-B.*, June 2, 1950.

[3] Pastoral, Dec. 4, 1945, outlines program for observance of Vocation Week, during the octave of the Feast of the Immaculate Conception. *C.U.-B.*, Apr. 23, Dec. 1, 1948; Apr. 14, 28, Dec. 8, 1950.

leges. Late in 1952 the beautiful buildings of Marycrest in Wickliffe were acquired by the diocese. They will be remodeled to serve as the ecclesiastical preparatory seminary.

A great deal of effort has been expended in beautifying the grounds of the local seminary and in renovating the interior. The walls and rooms have been beautified by the donations of many fine paintings donated personally by the Archbishop. The library was thoroughly renovated and a modern system of cataloguing was introduced by an expert in the field. A large auxiliary section was built for the more precious volumes and to make room for the latest books. Another improvement was the complete restoration of the gymnasium.

In the period of eight and one-half years preceding June 30, 1951, 62 priests of the diocese died; about one-fourth of them had retired from active service. To replace them Bishop McFadden as the Auxiliary had ordained 10 priests in March, 1942. Bishop Hoban had ordained 140 priests for the diocese and has adopted more than a dozen "refugee" priests from Europe. He is responsible for about thirty per cent of the approximately 500 on the active list of parochial clergy. The class of 11 ordained by him in September, 1944, had received the diaconate at the hands of Archbishop Cicognani, the Apostolic Delegate, in the seminary chapel. During the time that the Cathedral was under construction the class of May, 1946, was ordained in St. Thomas' Church and the following year's class, in St. John Auditorium. Archbishop Hoban has also ordained many Benedictines and Fathers of the Blessed Sacrament and two Sulpicians, one in Wooster and the other in St. Sebastian's Church in Akron.[4]

St. Thomas' parish hall was used also for a while for the quarterly conferences of the clergy, which are now held in St. John Auditorium, where practical pastoral and clerical problems and the sacred sciences are treated in previously prepared essays and are discussed by the assembled priests. One such conference was given in 1949 by the chancellor of the Ruthenian Diocese of Homestead on the implications of the new Code of Canon Law for Orientals in relation to Catholics of the Roman Rite, especially in regard to the Sacrament of Matrimony.

Individual priests of the diocese according to the plan inaugurated by Bishop Begin, vicar general for the religious communities of women, have been acting as conference masters for these communities in the monthly instructions and exhortations given in each of the convents and institutions of the diocese.

At the Archbishop's instance the Holy See has conferred special honors on many of the clergy and laity of the diocese. The unusual distinction of prothonotary apostolic was bestowed upon Monsignors James M. McDonough, vicar general and pastor of St. Luke's; Maurice F. Griffin of St. Philomena's and Joseph J. Schmit of St. Clement's, both vicars forane; Charles A. Martin of St. Colman's; and Ferdinand A. Schreiber, pastor emeritus of St. Bernard's in Akron. Others were

[4] *C.U.-B.*, May 19, 1950.

made domestic prelates: Monsignors Richard J. Patterson, Thomas
V. Shannon, Wenceslas F. Novak, Leo O. Hammer, Thomas P. Mul-
ligan, George A. Whitehead, all six appointed diocesan consultors.
The number of this body was increased to ten in 1943. Still others who
were made domestic prelates were Monsignors Vincent B. Balmat,
John W. Becka, Edward B. Conry, Richard A. Dowed, Francis Duda,
Clarence E. Elwell, Richard P. Gibbons, Charles McBride, Joseph J.
Mullen, Albert J. Murphy, Robert B. Navin, John J. Oman, John T.
Ruffing, John W. Schmitz, Howard Teare, Augustine Tomasek, Rich-
ard P. Walsh, and Louis A. Wolf.

Others were made papal chamberlains: Monsignors John F. Dearden,
Kenneth Saunders, Francis P. Johns, John J. Krol, and Michael J.
Hynes. In a later promotion, the three last named and Monsignors
Daniel T. Gallagher, John M. Kandrac, Charles W. McDonough, Francis J. McGlynn, Frederick B. Mohan, and William A. O'Donnell were
announced as domestic prelates. In addition, thirteen women of the
diocese received the papal medal, *Pro Ecclesia et Pontifice*, and fourteen men were made papal knights.

At his installation the Archbishop had expressed the hope and the
desire of seeing thousands of men and women making an annual
"closed" retreat; he would broaden the existing facilities to allow
them to withdraw from the world for a few days of prayerful and
silent meditation on spiritual things. It was the fulfillment of a lifelong ambition when on February 17, 1948, he dedicated St. Joseph's
Diocesan Retreat House on Lake Shore Boulevard at East 185th Street.
On the previous day he had consecrated the main altar in the chapel
assisted by the first group of the clergy to make their annual retreat
there. The priests of the diocese had subscribed the cost of the building
as a commemoration of his silver jubilee, and as a memorial of the
centenary of the foundation of the diocese.

The three-story, forty-two room brick structure (just previously
used as St. Joseph's Orphanage) had been transformed into a year-
around house of retreats. The pump room was ingeniously adapted
to serve as a large well-equipped chapel; the twenty-one altars in it
made it convenient for the priests to say their daily Mass. The entrance
to the chapel required considerable architectural skill as did the lounge
and reading room which replaced the huge steel shell formerly a land-
mark in the neighborhood. Artistic masterpieces, gifts of the Archbishop, adorn the walls of the chapel, the parlors, and the connecting
corridors. The original accommodations for 84 adults were supplemented in 1950 by the addition of thirty rooms on a new fourth floor
which increased the capacity to 120; a new dining hall finished in monastic style seats 200 persons. A cottage was also remodeled as a residence for Monsignor Francis P. Johns, the director, and Father Robert
Knuff, his assistant. Well-paved walks wind through the wooded
grounds overlooking Lake Erie. The domestic department is in charge

of the Sisters of St. Joseph of St. Mark who succeeded the Notre Dame Sisters in that important office in August, 1949.[5]

Beginning in 1943 St. Stanislas House in Parma became available for week-end retreats for laymen during the entire year. Between that time and the opening of the diocesan institution the local clergy in groups of about forty made use of its facilities. The laymen who had made a closed retreat at St. Stanislas formed the Laymen's Retreat League; the Archbishop pontificated for the 700 members in the Cathedral in September, 1943. He also helped them celebrate the fiftieth anniversary of the first retreat at Parma with Mass in the Cathedral in June, 1947. Two years later the members were called upon for funds to enable the Jesuit Fathers to erect a three-story brick building which replaced the original house and which was dedicated by the Archbishop. It furnishes accommodations for 50 during the scholastic year week-ends, and for 100 during the summer months when the student priests are not in residence.[6]

The Diocesan Retreat House is open all the time and to groups of men and of women. The director and his assistant promote the movement among the people with moving pictures and lectures. The first retreat for women was held in November, 1947, under the auspices of the National Council of Catholic Women. Since then parish and society groups, groups of young people, the Catholic Physicians' Guild, the Nurses' Confraternity, groups of trade unionists (ACTU), of firemen and policemen, and many others go there for their retreat, or Day of Recollection. Exclusive of the clergy, some 3,000 persons made the retreat in 1949, and when in September of the next year the Archbishop offered Mass for them the membership of the Laymen's Retreat League had been greatly increased.

The opportunity of brief retirement from worldly distractions was not confined exclusively to these two houses. For instance, fourteen mothers who brought their children with them made a two-day retreat at a summer camp near Painesville in 1946; the C.Y.O. camp was also used for retreats by other groups; week-end retreats were held regularly in the Catholic Young Women's Hall on Superior Avenue.

In many parishes one-day Cana Conferences were held, a kind of retreat for married couples who rededicated themselves to the ideals of Christian marriage; and young people of marriageable age met in churches or parish halls for pre-Cana conferences, for instruction and indoctrination in the same ideals. A retreat for farmers in Grafton, so arranged as not to interfere with their necessary duties, attracted a good number. Days of Recollection for groups of all kinds were quite ordinary. Yet there was no falling off in the number of those who made the annual retreats of such societies as the Knights of Columbus.

[5] *C.U.-B.*, Nov. 14, 1947; Feb. 13, 20, 1948; Aug. 26, 1949.
[6] *C.U.-B.*, Dec. 11, 1942; May 28, Sept. 13, 1943; June 6, 1947; Oct. 1, 1948; Jan. 1, Sept. 30, 1949; June 12, 1951. Cleveland *Plain Dealer*, Sept. 26, 1949.

The "closed" retreat movement was gathering momentum and bade fair to realize the ambition of the Archbishop.

Every effort was made to encourage public and corporate devotion in the parishes. The novenas and triduums of prayer preceding the great feasts were well attended by the faithful as were also the great parish missions held every few years. Very popular were the year-around devotions in honor of the Blessed Virgin under her title of the Sorrowful Mother, and in association with the Miraculous Medal. When in 1942 the Holy Father in the midst of the war consecrated the world to the Immaculate Heart of Mary, and called upon all men to be converted from their sins and to enlist in a crusade of prayer in honor of Our Lady of Fatima for the return of peace, his children in this diocese readily hearkened to his appeal. As the war drew to a close in 1945 special devotions at which the Pope's own prayer of consecration was used were held every evening and afternoon during the month of May.[7] The great public demonstrations in the Stadium were dedicated to the same purpose and the same subject was the theme of many articles in the school journals. The Reparation Society of the Immaculate Heart of Mary[8] was introduced into the diocese in 1948 and was organized in more than fifty parishes. The members who received Holy Communion on the first Saturday of every month met later on in the day for a Holy Hour of Reparation in which they renewed their consecration, said the Rosary, and assisted at Benediction of the Blessed Sacrament.

The diocese proudly hailed the infallible papal definition of the Assumption of the Blessed Mother into Heaven. Recalling that he had consecrated the diocese to the Immaculate Heart, the Archbishop in a pastoral prescribed a triduum (October 29–31) of thanksgiving, and on the Feast of All Saints he celebrated a pontifical Mass in the Cathedral in honor of the Assumption and voiced the universal joy at the new token of homage offered to the Mother of God by her faithful children. Similar ceremonies took place in all the parish churches.

Popular enthusiasm for the public recitation of the Rosary has been remarkable in recent years. It was chosen as the keynote of preparation for the centennial of the diocese and all the pastors were called upon to make the devotion as attractive and as convenient as possible. Father Patrick Peyton, C.S.C., the well-known promoter of the Family Rosary, has spoken with good effect to large audiences here. Neighbors gathered in one another's houses for the Block Rosary, Catholic employees in shops and factories used part of their lunch hour for the same purpose; and groups in the downtown stores and banks and courts came together for the Rosary and for Mass in the Cathedral.

The first Cleveland radio broadcast of the Rosary was made by

[7] Pastoral, Apr. 25, 1945.
[8] *C.U.-B.*, Apr. 23, 1948; May 12, 1950.

the Archbishop from a chapel of the Cathedral, October 2, 1950;[9] continued by the Cathedral clergy, it proved to be very popular and by many was made the occasion of family prayer in their homes. Another broadcasting station carried a Sunday series based on the mysteries of the Rosary which was sponsored by the C.Y.O. In the Cathedral Square program, started in 1948, the Sunday High Mass and religious music were put on the air waves during the winter season. The Intercollegiate Newman Club in the same year presented thirteen weekly religious programs. Father Francis Fergus, diocesan radio director since 1946, supervised these and began the first regular weekly broadcast of "News and Views," a commentary on happenings affecting Catholics, which was supported by the Knights of Columbus. The Hour of St. Francis, a national program, received much assistance here from the members of the Third Order of St. Francis.[10]

Another very popular devotion in the diocese has been that of the Nine First Fridays in honor of the Sacred Heart of Jesus. As part of a world-wide movement, and in special commemoration of the centenary of the diocese, the Archbishop on June 4, 1948, the First Friday of that month and the Feast of the Sacred Heart, solemnly consecrated his diocese to the Divine Saviour in a specially composed prayer at pontifical Mass in St. John Auditorium. Corresponding ceremonies took place in every parish, and the Blessed Sacrament was exposed for all-day adoration, following a novena which had been held in preparation for the feast. Holy Hours were celebrated in the afternoon for the children and in the evening for the others. The pastors, united in spirit with Bishop Dearden who presided in St. John Auditorium, dedicated their flocks to the Sacred Heart in solemn ceremony. Later in the evening families in their homes gathered around a representation of the Sacred Heart to make the same act of consecration.

The diocese, ever loyal to the Holy See and to the person of the Holy Father, observed the silver jubilee of the episcopal consecration of Pope Pius XII in May, 1942, with a special Mass in the parishes and the general reception of the sacraments. Catholics here in sympathy with him joined in the universal protest at the bombing of Rome in July, 1943. To celebrate the fifth and the tenth anniversary of his coronation special prayers and Masses were offered for his safety in the midst of the dangers which threatened him because of his valiant defense of the Church against the evil forces of Communism. The *Universe-Bulletin*[11] published a picture of him addressing the vast throng in St. Peter's Square and denouncing the entrenched atheists of the Communist-dominated countries for their inhuman persecution and the attempted destruction of the Church and its leaders, in the person of Cardinal Mindszenty and other imprisoned prelates.

[9] *C.U.-B.*, Dec. 21, 1945; Sept. 29, 1950.
[10] *C.U.-B.*, Jan. 7, 1944; Nov. 1, 1946; Jan. 10, 1947; Oct. 5, 1948.
[11] *C.U.-B.*, Feb. 25, 1949.

When the Holy Father, weighed down by the anxiety over his children behind the "Iron Curtain," for the observance of his sacerdotal Golden Jubilee[12] in 1949 called upon the Catholic world to unite with him in prayer, in expiation for the crimes perpetrated by the enemies of God, the Archbishop, his clergy and his people offered a solemn pontifical Mass in the Cathedral on Passion Sunday for the Pope's intention; and every priest, in accord with the permission and desire of the Sovereign Pontiff, celebrated a second Mass of Reparation. The faithful in response to an episcopal letter cooperated in receiving the sacraments and by taking part in the crusade of penance and prayer for the Pope's intention. The children offered the spiritual bouquet of their prayers and good works, and others sent financial assistance.

For the official opening of the Holy Year of 1950, the Archbishop pontificated in the Cathedral on the Christmas Eve just preceding it, and special Masses were celebrated in the parishes with the same idea in mind. In his pastoral[13] all were exhorted to enter into the spirit of the Jubilee with multiplied acts of penance and charity and with more fervent prayers for Divine Mercy. The Pope's own prayer was recited every day in all the parishes. On a placard posted in the vestibule of the churches those who were not in a position to make the pilgrimage to Rome were informed of the conditions requisite for gaining the indulgence of the Holy Year here: the reception of the sacraments, four visits to a church where the Blessed Sacrament was reserved, and the prescribed prayers for the development of the Church, the dissipation of error, and the blessings of peace. Many parishes organized public pilgrimages to the four churches: for example, 600 members of the parish of the Epiphany under the leadership of the pastor made the visits in chartered buses; in the same spirit of faith and devotion the men of St. Agnes' parish walked over a six-mile route saying the Rosary in common. Before the year was over the Holy Name Society had organized such pilgrimages in each of the parishes.

Despite the unpredictable condition of affairs in Europe, many Clevelanders heeded the invitation of the Holy Father to make the pilgrimage to the Eternal City itself. They went individually or in groups such as those organized by the Third Order of St. Francis. The diocesan pilgrimage was put in personal charge of Father Edward Halloran, the director of the Holy Name Society; nearly 100 persons, including seven priests, visited other famous shrines on their way to Rome. For many it was the fulfillment of a lifelong ambition. They returned well satisfied that the fatigue of the travelling had been amply recompensed in the graces received and the unforgettable impressions of Rome and the Pope.

At the end of the year novenas were held in all the parishes and the people were called upon to intensify their prayers and to insistently implore the Babe of Bethlehem to give peace to a distracted humanity.

---

[12] *C.U.-B.,* Apr. 8, 1949.
[13] Pastoral, Dec. 15, 1949. *C.U.-B.,* Feb. 17, 1950.

*Left:*Sacred Heart School, Wadsworth.

*Right:*St. Jude Parish Center, Warrensville Heights.

*Left:*St. Christine Church.

St. Michael School, Independence.

Holy Family Church and School, Stow.

*Above:*St. Matthew Church and School, Akron.

*Left:*St. Therese (Little Flower) Church and School.

*Right:*St. Mark Church and School.

St. Paul Church and School, Akron.

St. Agatha Church and School.

When the privileges of the Jubilee Year were extended to the world outside Rome, a pastoral published in the *Universe-Bulletin*, January 26, 1951, laid down the conditions for gaining the indulgences: the reception of the sacraments, the prescribed prayers, and the four visits to the churches. After the winter began to break up, much to the edification of all, long lines of devout men and women were to be seen walking from sanctuary to sanctuary.

76

SOCIETIES AND ASSOCIATIONS DURING ARCHBISHOP HOBAN'S EPISCOPATE

IN 1947 THE ARCHBISHOP REORGANIZED THE HOLY Name Society through which the parishes were represented in the National Council of Catholic Men. Father Edward J. Halloran, who was appointed to succeed Father Sebastian Kremer, C.PP.S., as diocesan director, immediately began an intensive campaign to form new units and to reorganize the old ones. In January, 1949, at the convention over which the Archbishop presided, Father Henry Graham, O.P., the national director, gave the address. During the following year 60 more parish units came into existence, and 1,200 delegates attended the second convention. The work of reorganization continued with great success.[1]

Previously the Holy Name Society had sponsored several mass meetings in the city: under its auspices some 15,000 Catholics assembled at the Public Auditorium in January, 1942, to pray for peace and victory; at the same place, May 1, 1947, about 8,000 gathered to listen to the exhortation of Bishop Begin, to pray for the conversion of Russia and to reclaim May Day from the revolutionists.

The first great Holy Name Rally in fourteen years was held in the Public Stadium, May 22, 1949. Bishop Hoban sent his encouragement from Rome and the blessing of the Holy Father. A good crowd braved the rain to make public profession of their faith and to do honor to the Blessed Mother. Against the background of a thirty-six-foot oil painting of Our Lady of Fatima a great altar and above it a huge monstrance had been erected in the arena. In a mighty tribute to the Blessed Lady, Archbishop McNicolas spoke on the sanctity of the home; Monsignor (now Bishop) Fulton Sheen told the story of Our Lady of Fatima; the Holy Name pledge was repeated by the throng and prayers were offered for the soldiers who had died in the war. At the end of the ceremonies, shortened because of the pelting rain, Bishop Begin gave the Benediction of the Blessed Sacrament. It was a magnificent dis-

[1] *C.U.-B.*, Feb. 3, 1950.

play of faith and devotion: the clergy in their robes and the uniformed societies sitting or kneeling patiently despite the unfavorable weather; the faithful sheltered to some extent in the amphitheater; the thunder of voices answering the prayers and singing the Divine Praises. The unforgettable scene was relayed to the public by television.[2]

Under more propitious weather conditions the next rally was held in the Stadium on June 4, 1950. Again the great altar and the gilded monstrance were set up against a huge painting of the Temple of Jerusalem. The figure of the Blessed Mother was flanked by fifty-foot columns. The colorful procession of the prelates, Cardinal Stritch and Bishop William O'Brien of Chicago, the Archbishop of Cleveland and Bishop Begin, and of the clergy was led into the space before the altar by the uniformed Catholic War Veterans to the accompaniment of sacred music and of hymns sung by the great Holy Name choir which had been trained for the occasion. The Archbishop presented the Cardinal to the estimated 55,000 present and to the immense "invisible audience" as the principal speaker. That distinguished churchman traced the evils in the world and the suffering of the people to the prevalent disregard of God and the violation of His laws, and to the resultant manifestation of secularism; he spoke of Communism on the march attacking the Church which stands for freedom and for the rights of man as a child of God.

The Cardinal, in accord with the desire of the Holy Father, led those who listened to him in offering reparation, with Christ the Redeemer, to God for the sins of men, imploring Him in a miracle of mercy to pardon the offenses of mankind and to give peace to a distracted world. Then Bishop Begin recited the prayers of the Rosary. Three thousand high-school girls attired in white were marshalled on the field in such a way as to form a Living Rosary: 330 outlined the figure of the crucifix; the single beads were represented by smaller groups. By an ingenious arrangement as each prayer was begun the girls in each group turned upon themselves the vari-colored beams of the flash-lights they carried, leaving the others in comparative darkness, thus making a very striking impression. Father Lawrence Wolf repeated the prayers for the deceased soldiers and all recited the Holy Name pledge. In the subdued light of thousands of candles in the hands of the devout worshipers the Archbishop gave the Benediction of the Blessed Sacrament to close the exercises.[3]

The men of the Holy Name Society continued to show themselves ready to help in any endeavor for the betterment of the community; in recent times, for example, they have cooperated with the civil authorities in "cleaning up" the public magazine racks in the city. The Cleveland deanery Holy Name Union in 1950 had 15,000 members; the Akron Union which sent 700 to the demonstration in the Stadium in June, 1950, mentioned above, counted 21 units in that year.

[2] Cleveland *Press*, May 23, 1949.
[3] *C.U.-B.*, June 9, 1950.

Many of the Holy Name men belong to one or more of the several fraternal and beneficial societies. The numbers and influence of the Knights of Columbus had increased with the growth of the diocese. At the State convention in May, 1947, the Archbishop celebrated Mass in Music Hall and took the occasion to compliment them for their efforts against the spread of Communist strength; he also pontificated at their Field Mass in Parma and blessed a plaque, commemorating Cleveland's first Catholic church, which was donated by a particular group of the Knights, one of whose purposes is the preservation of Catholic historical monuments. He is always an honored guest at the annual public commemoration of Columbus Day.

Beginning in the spring of 1948 the Akron Knights joined the national movement to bring better knowledge of the Catholic Church to the attention of the general public by supporting paid advertisements in the Akron *Beacon Journal*. In 1949 there were in the diocese thirty regular councils of the Knights and three fourth-degree assemblies. The fifteen Daughters of Isabella guilds, the women's auxiliary of the Knights of Columbus, had a total membership of approximately 900 in the same year.

The Knights of St. John, a beneficial society which has flourished in Cleveland from an early date, had units or commanderies in many parishes; their military uniform lent color and dignity to ecclesiastical functions. The Archbishop pontificated at the opening of their national convention here in 1946; he and Bishop Kearney of Rochester, who addressed them, were among others chosen for the distinction of "Noble Knights of the Holy Cross." The women's auxiliary of the society had a membership of 800 in 1949. The Ancient Order of Hibernians, active in the diocese since 1865, continued to keep alive the memory of St. Patrick and of his ideals; together with the Irish Civic Association, organized in 1929, they celebrate their patron's feast in a public manner reminiscent of the earliest days of this city.

The Catholic Central Union (Central Verein), founded in St. Louis in 1877 as a fraternal insurance society and always interested in social reform, counted approximately 7,000 members in this diocese in 1949. The Catholic Order of Foresters, established in 1883, in 1949 had twenty-seven courts in the city. The Catholic Knights of Ohio, founded in 1891, had six branches in Cleveland in 1949 and a total membership of 7,000 in the State. The Archbishop presided at the opening of their convention in Cleveland in September, 1950; the society undertook to found scholarships in Catholic high schools for deserving young people.

Many other Catholic societies had large representation here in 1949: the Czech Catholic Union had a total membership of over 9,000; the District Alliance of Bohemian Catholics had 2,000 members; the First Catholic Slovak Union, the largest Slovak organization of its kind in the world, had 12,000 members here; the First Catholic Slovak Ladies

Union had 6,500 members in the diocese; the Catholic Slovak Federation of America, the purpose of which was to foster unity among the Slovak organizations, had eight parish branches; the Union of Poles in America had a membership of 10,622; the Association of Polish Women in the United States had 4,600 members. The Lithuanian Roman Catholic Alliance of America and the women's branch had a good proportion of their membership in the city. The Croatian Catholic Union and the Grand Carniolan Slovenian Union each had large representation here.

The exclusively women's societies were well organized. Among them were the beneficial societies such as the Ladies Catholic Beneficial Association, a branch of which was to be found in nearly every parish, the Catholic Daughters of America, which had nine courts in the diocese, and the Catholic Ladies of Columbia, with a membership of some 1,200.

Other societies were organized here for other specific social or charitable purposes. The Cleveland Diocesan Council of Nurses, founded in 1938, ten years later had some 2,000 members united in their own interests and for Catholic Action. The Catholic Collegiate Association of women with college degrees helped the Sisters of the Good Shepherd in their work. The Catholic Parent-Teacher League had fifty units in 1950; five prelates, including the Bishop of Cleveland, participated in their convention here in 1944. The Circle of Mercy had 250 members who met periodically to sew clothing for the needy. The Christ Child Society was especially active in the work at Merrick House. The Catholic Big Sisters operated a summer camp for underprivileged girls. The Catherine Horstmann Society was interested in the girls' home of that name, and the St. Anthony's Women's Guild gave assistance to the working boys' home. Every institution, hospital, school, or home had its supporting organization of friends.

The Cleveland unit of the National Council of Catholic Women is the coordinating agency for all the women's organizations, with an office and a permanent secretary in the chancery building on Cathedral Square. The Catholic Federation of Women's Clubs, composed of representatives of 130 affiliated societies with a total membership of about 20,000, is the Cleveland deanery unit. The Akron, Lorain, Painesville, and Wooster deanery units brought the total of affiliated societies to nearly 250. The Archbishop from the beginning had urged the women's societies to join the N.C.C.W., which he designated the official agency under himself for participation in the work of the Church.

Occupied as each branch is with its own special endeavor, the five deaneries meet at least once a year for mutual encouragement and inspiration. The Archbishop is the honored guest; the program for the year is discussed and a report is made about their accomplishments. The Council donated the furnishings of the Lady Chapel in the new

Cathedral. At present the organization is occupied in the foundation of study clubs in the parishes; in 1950, 184 had been started with the help of Father John H. Archibald, their adviser in the matter.

The Archbishop was honorary chairman and the host to the twenty-fifth biennial national convention of the N.C.C.W., in October, 1950, which he opened with Mass in the Cathedral. One thousand delegates from all over the country and a few from foreign countries, representing 6,300 affiliated organizations in 80 dioceses, held their public sessions in Music Hall. Present also were three archbishops and nine bishops and, among many distinguished laymen, John Chang, the Korean Ambassador to the United States. The Holy Father sent his blessing, "in recognition of past achievements in the field of Catholic Action and as a pledge of heavenly favor for the future program of the Council."

The President of the United States, Harry Truman, referring to the theme of the convention, "Peace in Our Day," commended the women for using their united moral strength in the service of the country: "In peace and in war, through evil days and good, the women of the N.C.C.W. have borne an honorable part in the activities of the nation." Among other resolutions passed at the convention, which spoke for 7,000,000 people, was one which pleaded that parish school children receive a "square deal" and be treated with justice and equity in the distribution of Federal aid to education.[4]

[4] *C.U.-B.*, May 7, 1943; May 12, 1944; May 3, 17, Sept. 20, 1946; Apr. 11, Oct. 17, 1947; May 14, 1948; Feb. 25, Sept. 2, 30, 1949; Sept. 1, 22, Oct. 13, 20, 1950; Mar. 23, 1951.

77

ECCLESIASTICAL CELEBRATIONS DURING ARCHBISHOP HOBAN'S EPISCOPATE

THE GREAT GOTHIC CHURCH OF ST. AGNES on Euclid Avenue, under the pastorate of the late Monsignor Richard P. Gibbons and during the time of the reconstruction of the Cathedral, was the scene of several memorable events of importance. Out of deference for Archbishop Schrembs, Archbishop Hoban had omitted the public observance of his previous anniversaries, but on November 21, 1946, a month in anticipation of the actual date, he celebrated his twenty-fifth year as a bishop in a splendid ecclesiastical ceremony seldom if ever equalled in the city.

Three princes of the Church, Cardinal Stritch of Chicago, Cardinal Mooney of Detroit, and Cardinal Spellman of New York, in all the magnificence of their red robes occupied individual thrones erected upon an elevated platform on the Gospel side of the richly decorated sanctuary. Archbishop McNicolas as the metropolitan used a throne on the Epistle side. Seven other archbishops and forty-one bishops in episcopal attire filled the sanctuary and the front seats in the transept. Hundreds of monsignors, priests, and religious, and the chosen ones of the faithful who could gain admittance to the crowded edifice, all gathered together to assist the Archbishop in thanking God for so many happy years in His service. Father Francis A. Ryan, his first secretary in Chicago, was the assistant priest; his two nephews, Fathers Daily and Doherty, were the other officiating priests. The Mass, on account of the presence of the cardinals, was celebrated from a faldstool at the foot of the altar.

Pope Pius XII had anticipated the celebration in a personal letter of October 28, in order as he said, "to lead the way for the jubilant rejoicing of the diocese." Addressing the Archbishop, he continued: "Your love of Us demands this mark of benevolence; your zeal exacts it for it was your zeal exercised so diligently in feeding the flocks committed to your pastoral care that earned for you eminent merits in the Church." Reviewing his career in Chicago, Rockford, and Cleveland

and mentioning especially the seminary in the first-named place, the Holy Father recalled that he had constantly focused his labor and effort on the furtherance of the glory of God and the salvation of his neighbor. He sent his apostolic blessing as a token of joy and invoked the benediction of God upon his future activity.

Cardinal Stritch, who himself had been consecrated in 1921, preached the formal sermon in St. Agnes' Church. He, too, sketched the varied and eventful career which began with his ordination forty-three years before. He spoke of him as the "mentor and faithful collaborator" of Cardinal Mundelein, his own predecessor in Chicago; of his "piety and zeal which had brought many parishes and schools into existence and had contributed so much to the building of the great seminary"; of his "gifts, his experience, the freshness of his enthusiasm, his creative imagination, his daring for God which had already won for him in Cleveland the cooperation of the priests and people for the arduous works of God." While speaking of his "kindliness, his disinterestedness and his priestliness," the Cardinal emphasized that it was as a bishop and witness of the Gospel that he was "the intrepid courageous dispenser of divine truth, the friend of the weak and the supporter of the strong" who relied not upon natural abilities but upon the grace of his office for the success of his labors. The glorious ceremony closed with the papal blessing which the Archbishop had been empowered to bestow.

At the dinner tendered the jubilarian in Hotel Cleveland, Archbishop McNicolas, speaking for the hierarchy, gave him high praise for his ability and accomplishments, with special reference to Cardinal Mundelein and Chicago; he also spoke of "his kindness and thoughtfulness, of his generosity and self-sacrifice." Monsignor Carl Frey of Akron in the name of the clergy, in presenting a silver trowel for the laying of the cornerstone of the Cathedral, assured the Bishop that all joined in "thanking God for the silver years which had passed and in asking His choicest blessings for the golden years to come." Monsignor James McDonough presented the spiritual bouquet made up of the good works and prayers of the school children and at the same time the offerings made by the clergy for the Diocesan Retreat House, the opening of which the Bishop was pleased to consider the crowning event of the celebration.

The various societies joined in paying high tribute to the chief shepherd in the diocese and offered also the spiritual bouquet of their prayers. The *Universe-Bulletin* issued a special rotogravure edition with excellent pictures of the jubilarian from the time of his childhood. The three local newspapers gave good notice to the principal events of the celebration and published editorials in honor "of Cleveland's first Catholic citizen who in a short time had demonstrated a spirit of leadership and religious zeal which enhanced his reputation for accomplishment; he had done much for the diocese and proposed to do more." On the day following the festivities the Archbishop went to Chicago to assist at the jubilee celebration of Cardinal Stritch and to offer the Holy Sacrifice in the Church of the Ascension for those of his many friends in that city and in Rockford who had been unable to come to Cleveland.[1]

Three of the four priests of the diocese who have been raised to the episcopacy in recent times were consecrated in St. Agnes' Church.

It was in the old Cathedral on October 2, 1945, that Monsignor John P. Treacy was consecrated by Archbishop Cicognani, the Apostolic Delegate, assisted by Archbishop Hoban and Bishop O'Brien of Chicago. The only child of John and Ann Margaret Kane Treacy, he was born in 1892 at Marlboro, Massachusetts. He attended Holy Cross College at Worcester and the Catholic University in Washington before entering St. John's Seminary in Boston. After a few months in St. Mary's Seminary here, he was ordained priest by Bishop Farrelly in the old Cathedral, December 8, 1918.

He served as assistant pastor at St. Mary's in Akron, and at St. Agnes' and St. Luke's in Cleveland, until in 1931 he was appointed to succeed Bishop Ready as diocesan director of the Society for the Propagation of the Faith. During the efficient administration of this office he was made a domestic prelate, and on August 22, 1945, he was nominated Titular Bishop of Metelis and Coadjutor Bishop with the right to succeed to the venerable Bishop Alexander McGavick of LaCrosse, Wisconsin. The clergy entertained the new prelate at a dinner in Hotel Cleveland. Soon after going to LaCrosse he became Apostolic Administrator and upon the death of Bishop McGavick, August 25, 1948, he succeeded to the full title. One of his first accomplishments was the erection of a diocesan seminary.[2]

The first episcopal consecration in St. Agnes' was that of Monsignor Hagan on May 28, 1946. The Archbishop officiated and he was assisted by Bishops McFadden of Youngstown and Treacy of LaCrosse. John Raphael Hagan, born in Pittsburgh, Pennsylvania, February 26, 1890, came to Cleveland with his parents, John and Catherine Foley Hagan, at the age of three years. He attended the school in the parish of the Immaculate Conception and St. Ignatius High School and College. Sent to the North American College in 1908, he completed his studies at the College of the Propaganda which conferred upon him the doctorate in theology and in philosophy; he was ordained priest, May 7, 1914, by Cardinal Pompili in the Lateran Basilica. Returning home, he was assistant pastor at St. Augustine's and at St. Patrick's in Cleveland, and during this time he wrote extensively on current subjects in the *Catholic Universe* and in the *American Ecclesiastical Review*.

After a short pastorate in Bedford he was appointed superintendent of schools, January 1, 1923. Advanced studies in educational methods here and in Europe, especially in Germany, won for him the degree of

[1] *C.U.-B.*, Oct. 25, Nov. 22 (special number), 29, 1946.
[2] *C.U.-B.*, Oct. 5, 1945.

Doctor in Educational Science from the Catholic University in Washington. He founded the Catholic Parent-Teacher Association in the diocese and was very active in civic as well as in educational affairs.

Made a domestic prelate in 1934, he was chosen by the Holy See as Titular Bishop of Limata and Auxiliary Bishop of Cleveland, April 27, 1946. After his consecration he was the guest of the clergy at a dinner in Hotel Cleveland. He exercised his episcopal functions but once when he confirmed at St. Mary's Church in Elyria, the pastor of which, Monsignor Newton, had preached his consecration sermon. Exactly four months a bishop, he died of undetermined causes at St. John's Hospital, Cleveland, September 28, 1946.

The body lay in state in St. Mary's Seminary, which for several years had been his home, until it was brought to St. Agnes' Church; and it was the sad duty of the Archbishop to perform the funeral rites for one whom he had so lately raised to the episcopate. Archbishop McNicolas paid high tribute to the educator-bishop upon whom great hopes had been built. "He was," the Archbishop said, "an ideal little priest wholly dedicated to his calling, enthusiastic, argumentative, crusading for the cause he espoused, industrious in an extraordinary manner in preparing himself for his tasks and faithful in performing the duties assigned to him." His remains rest in the tomb made ready for them in the Mortuary Chapel of the new Cathedral.[3]

Less than a year later, on May 1, 1947, and in St. Agnes' Church the Archbishop, assisted by Bishops McFadden and Joseph McGucken, then of Los Angeles, California, consecrated Monsignor Floyd Lawrence Begin who had been chosen by the Holy Father, Titular Bishop of Sala and Auxiliary Bishop of Cleveland. Four archbishops, twenty-eight bishops, three abbots, and many priests and laymen were present at the ceremony. An unusual circumstance was the presence of his parents, Peter H. and Stella McFarland Begin.

Born in Cleveland, February 25, 1902, he was the eldest of seven children, four of whom survived, among them a Sister of Notre Dame. He attended the schools in the parishes of St. Columbkille and St. Thomas, Loyola High School and Cathedral Latin School, and St. John's Preparatory College. For his philosophy and theology he was sent to Rome; residing at the North American College, he followed the courses at the College of the Propaganda which conferred upon him the doctorate in those subjects. He was ordained priest in Rome, July 31, 1927, by Bishop Ignatius Dubowski, Titular Bishop of Philippopolis. After a brief visit home he returned to the Eternal City to become vice rector of the North American College, and while there he won the doctorate in canon law from the Pontifical Seminary for Juridic Studies (Apollinare).

When he returned, Bishop Schrembs made him his secretary and vice chancellor. A papal chamberlain in 1934, he was largely respon-

[3] *C.U.-B.*, May 31, Oct. 4, 25, 1946. *C.U.*, June 9, 1916; Aug. 9, 1918.

*Right:*St. Rita School, Solon.

*Left:*Beaumont High School for Girls.

*Right:*St. Joseph School, Cuyahoga Falls.

St. Mary School, Elyria.   St. Augustine School, Barberton.

St. Stanislas Retreat House, Parma.

St. Mary Church and School, Olmsted Falls.

St. Francis Xavier School, Medina.

St. John College.

Lourdes Academy.

sible as general executive secretary for the success of the Cleveland National Eucharistic Congress; shortly afterwards he was made a domestic prelate. In 1938 he became *officialis,* the head of the diocesan tribunal, which he reorganized on a larger and more efficient scale. He was also director of the local unit of the National Council of Catholic Men. Archbishop Hoban appointed him vicar general over the religious communities of women in the diocese.

His elevation to the episcopacy was made public by a decree of the Consistorial Congregation on March 22, 1947. As was the custom, the new prelate was entertained by the clergy at a dinner in the Hollenden Hotel. He then was made vicar general for the diocese and pastor of St. Agnes'. In the summer of 1948, accompanied by his successor as *officialis,* Monsignor Louis Wolf, he paid his first visit to Rome as a bishop.[4]

The third priest to be consecrated in St. Agnes' was Monsignor John Francis Dearden, who by decree of the Consistorial Congregation, March 13, 1948, had been chosen Titular Bishop of Sarepta and Coadjutor with the right of succession to Bishop Boyle of Pittsburgh.

The eldest of the five children of John and Agnes Gregory Dearden, he was born, October 15, 1907, in Valley Falls, Rhode Island. He attended the parochial school in the adjacent Central Falls, and at the age of eleven he entered St. Philomena's School in East Cleveland. After four years at the Cathedral Latin School he spent another four at St. Mary's Seminary in this city to finish his study of philosophy. He made his theological studies at the College of the Propaganda and at the Pontifical Gregorian University in Rome, where he resided at the North American College, and after advanced studies he received the doctor's degree.

Ordained priest, December 8, 1932, by the Pope's vicar general, Cardinal Marchetti-Selvaggiani, he returned to this diocese and for three years was assistant pastor at St. Mary's in Painesville before he was appointed to teach philosophy in St. Mary's Seminary. The Archbishop made him rector of the seminary in 1944; in the following year he became a papal chamberlain. On May 18, 1948, Archbishop Cicognani, the Apostolic Delegate, assisted by Bishops Hoban and Begin, raised him to the episcopate. Twenty-three bishops, among them Bishop Boyle, three mitered abbots, many priests, including three hundred from Pittsburgh, and many of the laity, among them his mother, were present at the ceremony. Bishop Ready of Columbus preached the sermon. Afterwards, the new Bishop was tendered a dinner by the clergy in Hotel Cleveland.

On June 21, 1948, in a ceremony which also commemorated the golden jubilee of Bishop Boyle as a priest, he was installed in St. Paul's Cathedral in Pittsburgh in the presence of many prelates and a great

4 *C.U.-B.,* Mar. 28, May 2, 1947; July 9, 1948; Jan. 21, 1949.

gathering of priests who filled the sacred edifice. Upon the death of Bishop Boyle, December 22, 1950, he assumed the title of Bishop of Pittsburgh.[5]

[5] *C.U.-B.,* May 14, 21, 1948. Pittsburgh *Catholic Observer,* June 17, 1948.

78

THE NEW CATHEDRAL

AT THE TURN OF THE CENTURY BISHOP HORST-mann envisioned a new Cathedral on Euclid Avenue where the beautiful Church of St. Agnes now stands. Bishop Farrelly had planned it on the same thoroughfare, at University Circle adjacent to the present Severance Hall. Bishop Schrembs left the problem to the present Archbishop, who decided to use the old site in the heart of the city as a fitting tribute to the sterling faith of the pioneer Catholics, and to make the new Cathedral and the other buildings on Cathedral Square the lasting memorial of the centenary of the foundation of the diocese. The magnificent group in a permanent location, which has changed the face of that part of downtown Cleveland, was the result of his happy thought.

The new St. John College and the Auditorium were well under way when in December, 1945, it was announced that to match them all the old Cathedral buildings would be rebuilt, enlarged, and resurfaced with Tennessee Crab Orchard stone. It was hoped that the work would be finished in two years, but the shortage of material and the scarcity of workmen in the post-war period made that impossible.

The dismantlement of the venerable temple began immediately after the last Mass by the Archbishop. The sanctuary light was extinguished and the Blessed Sacrament was reserved, thereafter, in the chapel of the old school building which was used for the parish religious services until the completion of St. John Auditorium. The roof and the back wall were removed but the side walls, twenty-six inches thick and judged to be architecturally sound, were preserved and were the shell around which the new Cathedral was built.

In the midst of what looked like destruction, the stone masons and other craftsmen behind the high board fence were busily engaged in preparing the construction materials. In September, 1947, the scaffolding was removed from the façade to reveal the rich stone-carved Crucifixion group over the entrance. It was, however, March of the next year before the whole exterior was exposed for a complete view. The progress of the work in the interior kept pace with that on the outside. The last scaffolding was taken down and the resplendent new edifice, under construction for more than two years and complete

469

from crypt to spire, was ready for its consecration in the first week of September, 1948.

The beautiful and imposing French Gothic edifice is 75 feet wide, 208 feet long, and 50 feet high on the interior; the walls are 31 inches thick; the floor covers more than 15,000 square feet; and the seating capacity is 1,500, about double that of the old building. The new transepts give it the form of a cross. The high pointed roof is covered with vari-colored slate from Bangor, Maine.

The stately façade is topped with a stone cross and is flanked by two columns of masonry in which are set stone statues of Sts. Peter and Paul. A richly ornamented stone balustrade connects the columns. In a large arched recess above and behind the balustrade are three long, double-paneled, lancet stained-glass windows depicting a choir of angels on a rich field of red and blue. Above these under the arch is the heroic-sized Crucifixion group mentioned above. Three large oaken double doors are set in the three great arches of the front entrance and are decorated with shields and religious symbols worked into sixty stainless-steel panels. Just south of the main entrance and connected by a passageway with the front vestibule is a small octagonal-shaped baptistery which is lighted by three colorful stained-glass windows.

The side entrance on Superior Avenue is made through the base of the massive stone bell tower which adjoins the south transept. The armorial bearings of Pope Pius XII are carved in stone above the door. The copper-covered conical-shaped spire comes to a point to support a golden cross 185 feet in the air. The venerable bell of the old Cathedral, weighing well over a ton, was sent to the African missions of the Holy Ghost Fathers. Its place is taken in the new tower by a twenty-five-note carillon of electronic chimes, the equivalent through amplification of a great set of bells. A stone statue of the Blessed Mother surmounts the beautiful rose window in the south transept wall. The old statue of Bishop Rappe, which stood so long on the site of the present baptistery, was moved to the north of the Cathedral atop an ornamental stone wall which formed a kind of shrine for it.

The interior, especially that of the sanctuary and of the chapels, is lavishly decorated with many colored marbles and frescoes and contains rare and precious carved statues. The walls of the vestibule or narthex are wainscoted in marble and are painted a textured gray; the ornamental ceiling is in gold, red, and blue; hand-set Moravian tile covers the floor here as it does in the rest of the building except for the mastic tile under the oaken pews. Three double doors of oak, covered with leather and studded with bronze, lead into the nave through a wall embellished with stone tracery and stained-glass windows. Two other doors in the vestibule open the ascent to the large organ loft. The entrance to the baptistery is screened with a large ornamental iron gate through which may be seen the mural which depicts Christ and St. John the Baptist at the River Jordan.

The beautiful Gothic ceiling of the nave, reaching to the height of

50 feet, is carried into the sanctuary on sixteen graceful stone pillars. Stars and the figures of angels stand out on a background of blue. Over the side aisles and over the wings of the transept a profusion of fleurs-de-lis dot a field of Venetian red. The side walls, painted in tan and wainscoted in gray, are broken by eight large stained-glass windows, imported from Munich, which had been saved from the old Cathedral. The free-standing figures of the Stations of the Cross were fashioned from linden wood in three-quarters relief by Italian artists. Of the same material are the finely carved statues of the Sacred Heart and of the Blessed Virgin in their respective chapels in the transepts.

The sanctuary and the chapels are the glory of the new Cathedral. In the south transept is the Lady Chapel with its marble altar in an alcove recessed in the wall and lighted by two small stained-glass windows. Within the high arch above the altar is a richly colored rose window dominated by the dove, the symbol of the Holy Ghost. Reaching to the ceiling and surrounding the arch is the great Marian mural which covers nearly the entire back wall. It depicts the scenes of the Annunciation, the Nativity, and, high above, the Coronation of the Blessed Mother as Queen of Angels and of Saints. In this transept also are to be found the shrines of the Infant of Prague, St. Joseph, and St. Anne. On either side of the altar here as in the opposite transept are two confessionals built against the wall.

The great mural of the Apocalypse covers the back wall of the north transept. God the Father with the Great Book and the Seven Seals looks down on St. John on the Island of Patmos. In the background are the Seven Churches in Asia Minor and their angels or bishops; the Four Horsemen, representing the scourges of war, hunger, pestilence, and death; scenes portraying the conflict of the forces of good and evil, and the final victory of the new dispensation. At the top of the high arch and surrounded by the striking mural is another beautiful rose window in the center of which is the figure of the Hand of God. Beneath it is a representation of Christ and the New Jerusalem; and a miniature painting of the new Cathedral itself, in a decorative background, is behind the marble shrine of the Sacred Heart. In an adjacent alcove is the Shrine of the Sorrowful Mother and her Divine Son.

Immediately to the east, off this transept, a hand-wrought iron gate, over which are carved the armorial bearings of the Archbishop and his predecessor, opens into the Mortuary Chapel with its fourteen marble tombs centered around a marble altar, above which is painted the figure of the Risen Christ. Six of them are occupied by the mortal remains of Cleveland's former bishops, including those of Bishop Hagan.

The remarkable groined ceiling is covered with a large mosaic, 300 feet square, of vari-colored Venetian glass in a sunburst design of blue and gold stars. The walls are wainscoted in marble. A beautiful, double-paneled stained-glass window pictures a priest offering the Holy Sacrifice, and above in glory Christ receiving the soul released from Purgatory. Paintings of Sts. Peter and Paul decorate the north wall as do those of Aaron and Melchisedech the south wall of the chapel. An artistic iron screen covers an archway leading into the Tierce Chapel, the marble altar in which enshrines the relics of St. Christina. This chapel and the Blessed Sacrament Chapel with its marble altar and overhanging canopy on the corresponding south side of the main sanctuary, are separated from it by great hand-carved wooden screens set with statues of Sts. Augustine, Ambrose, Gregory, Patrick, Boniface, and Cyril and Methodius.

The focal point of the whole interior is the beautiful and impressive main altar and the **magnificent** hand-carved wooden screen on the wall behind it. The rise of a few steps leads through the Botticino marble communion-rail to the white, green-bordered marble platform of the sanctuary. The altar itself at the rear of the apse is a solid 1,400-pound block of Botticino marble ten feet long. The intricately carved pillars supporting it and the steps leading up to it are of the same material. Seen through the pillars beneath the altar is the figure of the pelican, the symbol of the Blessed Eucharist, on a background of red Moroccan marble, the material used for the wall which rises immediately behind the liturgical altar to form a support for the candelabra, and the flanking columns which are topped with adoring angels. The golden tabernacle safe rests on a stone shelf of colorful fleur-de-peche marble.

Behind the altar and covering nearly the entire back wall of the chancel hangs a great altar screen, 20 by 27 feet in size, in an intricate design composed of 850 pieces of hand-carved Appalachian oak, the most expensive article of furniture in the interior. In separate niches are carved wooden representations of St. John and the three other evangelists; just above the level of the altar is the place for the crucifix and for the monstrance when the Blessed Sacrament is exposed for adoration. Figures of angels, large and small, are to be found in profusion throughout the main piece as well as in the two intricately carved wings on either side of it.

Elaborately embellished with symbolical representations, the octagonal, crown-shaped, carved wooden canopy or baldachin, 9 feet in diameter, is suspended 25 feet above the altar. The pontifical throne of carved oak faces several rows of stalls on the opposite side of the sanctuary and is flanked by others. Choir stalls screened from the sanctuary occupy space to the right and to the left of the altar.

Looking out from the sanctuary, the spectator is impressed with the giant figure of Christ on the cross which dominates the intersection of the nave and the north transept.

Two lecterns, pillars of stone ornamented with the statues of St. Stephen and St. John the Baptist respectively, stand at the edge of the sanctuary; microphones carry the speaker's voice to amplifiers concealed in the chandeliers. The sound system is readily adjusted for broadcasting over the radio.

In the spacious gallery at the west of the nave is a new $35,000 organ with nearly 4,000 stops and three manuals; it is supplemented on occasion by a smaller two-manual instrument in the rear of the sanctuary. Rare and precious oil paintings and other artistic objects, the gift of the Archbishop, adorn the altars and the walls. A complete air-conditioning system makes the whole building both modern and comfortable.

79

THE CENTENNIAL CELEBRATION

THE HOLY FATHER, POPE PIUS XII, ON APRIL 22, 1948, wrote to the Archbishop: "It is particularly fitting that the solemn ceremony of the dedication of your newly enlarged Cathedral, the mother church of the diocese, should form the center, as it were, of your centenary celebration, for in this historic event the generous aspirations of your predecessors in the pastoral office, and of the devoted priests and faithful of past generations, find their fulfillment, and the accumulated labors of the past are merged with the beneficent activity of the present for the praise and honor of God."

In anticipation of the glad event, missions had been held in all the parishes; and public prayers of thanksgiving were offered in every church and chapel during the week of September 5. His Grace sounded the dominant note in his pastoral of August 31: expressing his appreciation of the loyalty and zeal of the clergy and the generous response of the faithful to his appeal for assistance in his undertakings, he called upon all to thank God for the one hundred years of divine blessing upon the successful cooperation of bishops, clergy, and faithful for the spread and upbuilding of His kingdom in this part of Ohio.

The week-long celebration began with the consecration of the Cathedral on September 6, 1948. Fourteen centuries before, Pope St. Gregory the Great had prescribed the ritual which was used. Early in the day the Archbishop with a few attendants circled the exterior of the building three times, blessing the outside walls; at his solemn summons the front doors were momentarily opened to him and then closed after he had entered. Then with his crozier he traced the Greek and Latin alphabets in the ashes in the middle aisle prepared for that purpose. Next, the inside walls and the doors were blessed with appropriate ceremony. With the Gregorian water containing the symbolical salt, ashes, and wine he blessed the main altar, circling it seven times. From the center of the edifice he then sprinkled this water in all directions to signify the universality of the Church. The twelve crosses on the inside walls distinctive of a consecrated church were anointed and the candles attached to them were lighted, to be relighted each

474

year on the anniversary day. The pillars inside the main entrance were anointed with holy chrism, after which the people waiting outside were admitted to witness the rest of the ceremony.

He then proceeded to the anointing and consecration of the main altar. The precious relics of the holy martyrs, Sts. Donatus and Felicitas, which had been brought in solemn procession through the main door, were sealed in the sepulcher hollowed out in the great table of stone, which was anointed with the holy oils and marked with burning incense as prescribed by the ritual.

Then, upon the newly consecrated altar the Bishop celebrated the first Mass just as he had celebrated the last one in the old Cathedral. Simultaneously four sons of the diocese said the first Mass upon the four altars they had consecrated: Bishop McFadden in the Lady Chapel; Bishop Treacy in the Blessed Sacrament Chapel; Bishop Begin in the Mortuary Chapel; and Bishop Dearden in that of Tierce.

On Tuesday morning, the Archbishop dedicated the Mortuary Chapel and blessed the tombs occupied by the remains of his predecessors. Later that morning, Cleveland's most illustrious son, Edward Cardinal Mooney, Archbishop of Detroit, offered the Mass for the living and the dead of the Cleveland Church. The colorful procession of the Prince of the Church in all the splendor of his office, the bishops, and clergy along Superior Avenue made a memorable and lasting impression. Bishop Begin, the preacher for the occasion, spoke with much feeling on the pertinent subject of the Communion of Saints and made special reference to the communities of religious women, hundreds of whom were present; he looked upon the new Cathedral as the symbol of the unity of the Mystical Body of Christ, representing, as it did, the combined efforts, hopes, and sacrifices of clergy and people.

On Wednesday morning Archbishop Cicognani, the personal representative of the Holy Father, celebrated the Mass of Thanksgiving, the formal Mass of the centennial. The special papal message was read by Monsignor Balmat, the chancellor, conferring the apostolic blessing upon all those present. A numerous and distinguished gathering of the hierarchy, including Cardinal Mooney, graced the occasion. Bishop LeBlond of St. Joseph, Missouri, whose family history and priestly career were bound up with the Cathedral parish, delivered the sermon. He spoke of the newly consecrated edifice as standing "unveiled in its queenly beauty like a prayer out of the hearts of a Catholic people"; it was "the crown of one hundred years of faith, sacrifice, and loyalty, a monument to the generation which built it, the lasting expression of a priest of God, building a House of Adoration for his Master, a fitting throne for his King provided by a bishop."

At the dinner in Hotel Statler tendered to the Apostolic Delegate and the high prelates of the Church, Archbishop Cicognani praised the Archbishop's zeal and enthusiasm, the result of which was manifested in new parishes, new schools and welfare institutions, and es-

pecially in the new Cathedral and the other monuments on Cathedral
Square. He warmly commended the generosity of the people of the
diocese in alleviating the sufferings of the victims of war in Europe
and of other unfortunates at home, a generosity adorned and completed by the happy celebration of the centennial of the diocese. And
he thanked Archbishop, clergy, and people who as a token of gratitude
to God and a further manifestation of brotherly love had made another substantial contribution to the work of papal relief.

On Thursday morning, Bishop Ready of Columbus celebrated the
Mass which was attended principally by the women of the diocese.
Archbishop Leo Binz of Dubuque, the preacher, pointed to the Blessed
Mother as the model for every walk in life. He challenged the women
to take their noble part in the spread of the Pentecostal fire upon the
earth and to give their wholehearted assistance to the Church in the
restoration of God in the family and in society, threatened as they were
by an unbelieving and secular-minded generation. He invited them to
dedicate themselves to personal holiness, to Catholic Action, and to the
Catholic apostolate. Moved by this stirring appeal and led by Archbishop Hoban, the women thereupon consecrated themselves and the
organizations they represented to the Immaculate Heart of Our Lady
of Fatima; on this occasion the Archbishop presented twelve papal
medals he had brought from Rome. In the evening Monsignor Griffin,
pastor of St. Philomena's and dean, presided at the Holy Hour at which
Father Reginald McCormick spoke of the Cathedral as the new and
better palace for Christ the King in the Holy Eucharist.

On Friday morning Bishop McFadden pontificated for the young
people who filled the sacred edifice. Bishop Treacy, who addressed
them, appealed to the rising generation in their youth and enthusiasm
to prove faithful to their Christian heritage especially in the field of
Catholic education. On Saturday morning the men of the diocese filled
every pew at the Mass celebrated by Bishop Begin, and they attentively
listened to Bishop Dearden recall to them their duty as loyal sons of the
Church to make their lives inspiring examples of Christian faith and
virtue.

The week of jubilee closed with the customary "home-coming"
Mass on Sunday morning for all those who in former times had been
members of the Cathedral parish. Monsignor Walsh, the pastor, gave
them a hearty welcome in a brief resumé of its history.

In addition to the strictly liturgical services, on Tuesday afternoon
and Wednesday evening concerts of sacred music were rendered
with the assistance of the new musical installations, which were attended by a large and appreciative audience. And outside the time of
religious service thousands of people, many of them non-Catholics,
passed through the aisles of the Cathedral for a closer inspection of its
beautiful details. Some 18,000 copies of a small souvenir booklet with
pictures and explanations, compiled by Father Caspar Heimann of the

Cathedral clergy, were passed out to visitors on the day of the consecration.[1]

A month before the consecration the four-story Cathedral rectory had been occupied by the clergy, who during the reconstruction had lived at some distance from downtown, in residences near the Retreat House. About one-quarter of the original width of the old rectory had been sacrificed for the lengthening of the Cathedral, the rear wall of which is nearly flush with the new house. The interior had been entirely remodeled. In the basement, entered through a door at street level, are the parish offices, a large sacristy for the altar boys, and other utility rooms. On the second floor are the sacristy for the priests, dining rooms, kitchen, and, facing Superior Avenue, a large reception parlor beautifully furnished and hung with many beautiful oil paintings. Living quarters for the Cathedral clergy occupy the upper floors. The Sisters responsible for the domestic economy are housed in a separate wing with their own chapel.

A finely carved stone bridge leads from the second floor of the rectory to the newly reconstructed chancery building, just east of it. This bridge spans the driveway between the two buildings and covers the side entrance to the rectory and it carries not only a passageway but also the chancellor's suite of rooms. In the chancery, a five-story structure, formerly the Cathedral school, are concentrated all the diocesan offices and those of the *Universe-Bulletin*. Those of the Archbishop, the chancellor, and of the matrimonial tribunal are worthy of special note. Over the entrance on Superior Avenue is to be found appropriately the heraldic shield of the Ordinary.

Time has amply vindicated the decision to keep the Cathedral in the center of the city and to restore it as the center of the religious life of the diocese. At the first anniversary of its consecration Monsignor Griffin recalled the unswerving determination of the Bishop, despite well-nigh unsurmountable difficulties incident to the postwar period, to establish Cathedral Square of which not only the faithful but all citizens were justly proud.[2]

In the spring the Archbishop made his first *ad limina* visit to Rome subsequent to his coming to Cleveland. On April 2, 1949, in the first ordination in the new Cathedral he raised twelve young men to the priesthood; the unusually early date was chosen to do honor to the fiftieth priestly anniversary of Pope Pius. Shortly afterwards, accompanied by Monsignor John Krol, he sailed from New York on the S.S. Queen Mary. Arrived in the Eternal City, he was received in private audience on May 3. The Holy Father was well pleased with the report of the swift progress of the Church in this diocese and with the general zeal for religion especially observable in the devotion to all works of Catholic Action. He empowered the Archbishop to bestow

[1] *C.U.-B.*, Centennial Supplement, Oct. 1, 1948.
[2] *C.U.-B.*, Sept. 16, 1949.

the apostolic blessing upon the diocese, and upon groups of people in it whenever the occasion demanded.

On the Feast of St. Catherine of Siena the Bishop celebrated Mass on her tomb in the Church of Santa Maria sopra Minerva, and on other days he offered the Holy Sacrifice at different historical shrines. At the canonization ceremony on May 15 of the French founder of the Daughters of Charity, Saint Jeanne de Lestonnac, the Archbishop in his rank as an Assistant at the Pontifical Throne occupied a prominent place in the immediate entourage of the Pope.

Leaving Rome on May 16, he journeyed through France to Boulogne-sur-Mer to visit the Basilica of Notre Dame which was in the process of restoration after the damage inflicted upon it in the war. It was in this town that Father Amadeus Rappe, spiritual director of the Ursulines, first met Bishop Purcell who invited him to the missions in Ohio, and it was to the same town Bishop Rappe returned begging alms for the building of Cleveland's first Cathedral. The Archbishop with funds gathered in a general collection in the diocese was able to pay a long-standing debt of gratitude.

After an interesting visit to Ireland he was in New York on June 2 and in Cleveland the next day. Eager and ready to resume his busy schedule, on June 4 he presided at the graduation exercises of St. John College. On Pentecost Sunday, June 5, he pontificated in the Cathedral, and confirmed a class of 160 adults in the early afternoon; he attended the graduation of Holy Name High School in the late afternoon, and that of St. Joseph's Academy in the evening in the Cathedral.[3] A busy Sunday was usual for the Archbishop even after the appointment of Bishop Begin to assist him. He might preside at the Cathedral sometimes twice on Sunday morning and later at three parishes confer the Sacrament of Confirmation, or dedicate a church or school. He keeps long hours in his office in the chancery, always at the disposition of his priests and others for the dispatch of diocesan affairs.

The above description of what he has accomplished in Cleveland may well explain why Pope Pius XII, in recognition of his ceaseless activity and the tireless expenditure of himself in the cause of religion, conferred upon him the personal dignity of an Archbishop with the title of Archbishop-Bishop of Cleveland. The diocese looked upon the well-merited distinction conferred upon its head not only as an acknowledgment of past accomplishments but also as a presage of future achievement.

[3] *C.U.-B.,* June 10, 1949.

Madonna Hall for the Aged.

Merrick House.

*Left:*Marycrest.

Gilmour Academy.

*Right:*Rosemary Home for Crippled Children.

*Left:*Diocesan Retreat House.

*Right:*Marymount Hospital.

*Left:*Jennings Hall for the Aged.

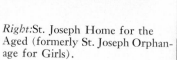

*Right:*St. Joseph Home for the Aged (formerly St. Joseph Orphanage for Girls).

CONCLUSION

U NDER THE GUIDANCE OF DIVINE PROVIDENCE the Church in northern Ohio has developed and expanded to a marvelous degree as the result of the faith, self-sacrifice, and zeal of bishops, priests, and people, working together in harmony for the glory of God and the salvation of souls. On the foundations set by the early missionaries and pioneer prelates their successors have built a structure of which they might well be proud.

Numbers and material construction do not give a complete picture of this great progress but they do indicate to some extent at least the result of the faith and self-sacrifice of those responsible for them. When Bishop Rappe took up the burden of his high office he found approximately 33 rude chapels scattered over the 33 counties in northern Ohio. He had some 16 priests to help him in his tremendous task. In this same territory in 1950, divided as it is into three flourishing dioceses with their complement of five bishops,[1] there were 466 well equipped parish plants, 9 mission churches and hundreds of chapels in which the Blessed Sacrament was reserved. The 1,281 priests included 322 who belonged to 18 orders and congregations. The 4,861 Sisters were members of 54 different religious communities. There were 108,803 children attending 304 elementary parochial schools and nearly 22,000 students in Catholic high schools, colleges, and a university; in all approximately 160,000 young people under Catholic instruction. There were 17 Catholic hospitals and 9 homes for the aged and scores of other Catholic welfare institutions.

If we confine ourselves to the 8 counties comprising the present Diocese of Cleveland the contrast with conditions at the beginning of its history is more striking still. The total population of the 8 counties in 1840 was about 160,000; in 1860 nearly 244,000; in 1880 nearly 1,290,000; in 1940 nearly 1,852,000. In 1940 more than seventy-five per cent of the total (1,564,648) lived in the metropolitan areas around the cities of Akron and Cleveland. About twenty per cent lived in towns of less than 2,500 population. By the year 1950 the total population of Greater Cleveland was approximately 1,453,556; that of Greater Akron was nearly 408,000. In and around the cities of Elyria and Lorain 146,501 were concentrated. It was in the cities that the estimated 544,518 Catholics were to be found. They made up more than twenty-five per cent of the total population of the 8 counties and, according to different estimates, thirty-seven to forty per cent of the population of Greater Cleveland.

It was estimated that Catholics made up from five to ten per cent

[1] Bishop McFadden died in Youngstown, Nov. 16, 1952.

of the population of the people of this area when Bishop Rappe arrived in Cleveland. In the 8 counties he had only St. Mary's Church in the city and small chapels at Akron and in Chippewa Township. To help him care for them and other stations he had two priests of the diocese and the occasional help of a few Sanguinist Fathers from Bethlehem. In 1950 in the same area there were 213 parishes of which 134 were in Greater Cleveland; all had fully equipped church plants. The two priests of the diocese had been replaced by 515 and the few religious by 209 members of 9 religious orders and congregations. A great company of more than 3,000 religious women belonging to 34 different congregations gave invaluable aid in the work of the Church. A total of nearly 64,000 in 158 elementary schools were enrolled in an educational system which rivaled the largest and most efficient in the State of Ohio. Nearly 12,000 young men and women attended 34 high schools and academies and 3,137 more the 3 colleges and the university. Bishop Rappe, were he to return to the city, would see the work of Charity Hospital supplemented by that of six other hospitals and a home for crippled children. He would find six institutions caring for the aged, and the St. Mary Benevolent Society he established replaced by the Catholic charities organization and its 32 social and welfare agencies. He would be pleased to see the hundreds of societies and organizations of all kinds which have replaced the total abstinence society he founded for the welfare of his people.

In the accomplishment of this great work of Christ's Church each generation, solving its own problems, made a distinctive contribution. Worthy prelates have succeeded one another in teaching, exhorting, and disciplining their people in the ways of God. Devoted priests have spent themselves in the service of religion. The generous faithful have contributed of their means and of their children to support the house of God at the same time that they have given splendid example of the practice of the other Christian virtues. All have carried the full burden of citizenship and in the one hundred or more years of the existence of the diocese they have contributed their full share in the upbuilding of the communities in which they lived. They have been good citizens in times of war and of peace. They cared for the orphans, the sick, and the unfortunate. They maintained their schools at great expenditure of money and at the cost of great self-sacrifice because they believed that religion and Christian morality were fundamental in education, and the community reaped the benefit. They have reflected credit upon their education and their Faith in all ranks and stations in life.

Archbishop Hoban who came to the diocese at the end of its first century to govern and guide it into the second has already established an enviable record of accomplishment. He has infused new life into all the departments of the Church's work. The new parishes, the new churches, schools, convents, and chapels and especially the new Cathedral with the beautiful group of buildings on Cathedral Square

are lasting monuments of his energy. The great high schools he established manifest his burning zeal for Catholic secondary education, and the inauguration of the system of the minor seminary his solicitude for the recruitment of the clerical body. Newman Hall and the Confraternity of Christian Doctrine indicate his paternal interest in those not enrolled in Catholic schools.

The unprecedented response to his personal appeal has enabled him to extend and to broaden the Church's work for the relief of the poor and unfortunate, the sick, the aged, the orphans, and for the protection of the Christian ideals of youth.

Interest in the foreign and especially the home missions has been stimulated to a high degree. He has enlisted his flock in crusades of generosity for the relief of the stricken areas in the world. He has encouraged every form of prayer and devotion and has provided a house for spiritual retreats. He has consulted the needs and the convenience of large sections of the city in the opening of new burial grounds. This record of the accomplishments of a few years is a happy augury of future achievement for God and Country in the second century of diocesan history. We cannot do better than to echo the prayer of Pope Pius XII, now gloriously reigning, that God in His bounty grant him in a long life every possible happiness and spiritual comfort.

APPENDIX A

CLEVELAND PRELATES

THE GRACIOUS and paternal letter of Pope Pius XII to Bishop Hoban on April 22, 1948, made reference to the number of Cleveland priests who had been raised to the dignity of the episcopate. Those who were consecrated in this city have been mentioned in the course of the history. A summary sketch of those who were consecrated elsewhere but who had labored for some time in this diocese will prove of interest.

The Holy Father pointed particularly to the most distinguished son of the diocese, Edward Cardinal Mooney, Archbishop of Detroit. The youngest child of Thomas and Sarah Heneghan Mooney, he was born, May 9, 1882, at Mount Savage in western Maryland. Five years later the family moved to Youngstown, Ohio, where he attended St. Columba's school and served as an altar boy. Through the good offices of Father Edward Mears, the pastor, he was sent to St. Charles College in Ellicott City, Maryland. After an enviable record there he made a brilliant course in philosophy at St. Mary's Seminary in Baltimore, Maryland; he and a few others of his class had been sent to the eastern seminary for want of room in the local St. Mary's.

The autumn of 1905 found him in residence at the North American College in Rome; he won his degrees with highest honors at the College of the Propaganda. The papal vicar, Cardinal Respighi, ordained him a priest, April 10, 1909, in the Lateran Basilica, and on July 25 following he celebrated his first solemn high Mass in St. Columba's, Youngstown. He was professor at St. Mary's Seminary in Cleveland for nine years until in 1918 Bishop Farrelly chose him to be the founder and first president of the Cathedral Latin School. In September, 1922, Bishop Schrembs made him pastor of St. Patrick's in Youngstown. Five months later he was back in Rome as spiritual director of his old Alma Mater, the North American College. He served on several commissions in the Eternal City, including the one which revised the catechism, and he was made a domestic prelate in 1925.

In January of the next year he was appointed resident Apostolic Delegate to India, the first native of the United States to be so honored. Cardinal Van Rossum, Prefect of the Congregation of the Propaganda, Archbishop Marchetti-Selvaggiani, later Cardinal Vicar of Rome, and Bishop Julius Serafini, Titular Bishop of Lampsacus, consecrated him Titular Archbishop of Irenopolis, January 31, 1926, in the chapel of the North American College. Four of his former colleagues from here attended the ceremony.

On his way to his mission in the East the young prelate was given a tremendous welcome in Cleveland and in Youngstown. After pontifical Mass in the old Cathedral here he was the guest of the priests of the diocese at a dinner in Hotel Cleveland. In Youngstown the entire business district was closed to traffic during the demonstration in his honor. While he was in India his aged mother died; Bishop Schrembs pontificated; Cardinal Stritch, then Bishop of Toledo, and a great crowd of clergy and people attended her funeral in St. Columba's. His mission in India successfully accomplished, he was transferred in February, 1931, to Japan.

Upon his return to the United States he was chosen for the vacant See of

Rochester, New York, and was installed there in October, 1933. Two years later he succeeded Archbishop Hanna as episcopal chairman of the administrative council of the National Catholic Welfare Conference. On May 31, 1937, he was chosen the first head of the newly erected metropolitan See of Detroit; he received the sacred pallium the following December. Created a cardinal by Pope Pius XII in December, 1945, he crossed the Atlantic by airplane for the investiture in Rome. His visit to his home parish in Youngstown on March 25 of the following year was in the nature of a triumph; he pontificated in St. Columba's Cathedral and was feted by the clergy and the people of the city. He has honored Cleveland by his presence on many occasions. His career in Detroit needs no retelling here.[1]

The first priest of the diocese to become a bishop was Father Louis Joseph Mary Theodore De Goesbriand, who was born, August 4, 1816, at St. Urbain, Finistere, France, of Marquis Henri and Emilie de Bergean De Goesbriand. He studied at the seminary in Quimper and then at St. Sulpice in Paris, where he was ordained priest, July 13, 1840, by Bishop Joseph Rosati of St. Louis, Missouri. He came to America the same year and was appointed pastor of St. Louis' Church in Louisville, Ohio, and remained there until in 1846 he became associated with Father Rappe, the future Bishop of Cleveland, on the Maumee missions near Toledo. Bishop Rappe brought him to Cleveland and made him the head of the seminary in 1848 and vicar general.

Chosen for the new See of Burlington, Vermont, he was consecrated in New York City, October 30, 1853, by Archbishop Cajetan Bedini, the special papal envoy, who was assisted by Bishop Rappe of Cleveland and Bishop John B. Fitzpatrick of Boston. Guided by his prudence and sagacity, the diocese "passed almost painlessly through the transition from French Canadian to Franco-American." He attended the Council of the Vatican with Bishop Rappe.

Bishop De Goesbriand visited Cleveland in 1885 to ordain four priests, at the request of Bishop Gilmour who was in Rome on the business of the Third Council of Baltimore. He resigned his see in 1898 but continued to live in Burlington until his death on November 3, 1899. He was the author of several pious works and books on history.

Bishop Joseph Projectus Macheboeuf labored in northern Ohio from August, 1839, to January, 1851, before he went to the assistance of his old colleague, Bishop John B. Lamy, the first Archbishop of Santa Fe, New Mexico. He was born in France at Riom, Puy-de-Dom, in the Diocese of Cleremont, August 11, 1812, the son of Michael Anthony and Gilberte Planc Macheboeuf. Educated in his native town and at the major seminary at Montferrand, he was ordained priest December 21, 1836, at Cleremont by Bishop Louis Charles Feron.

Coming to Ohio three years later, he worked with Father Joseph McNamee on the Tiffin and Maumee missions until he was appointed the first resident pastor of Sandusky in 1840. He built the first churches in Fremont and Sandusky. On his visits to France he acted as Bishop Rappe's agent in securing help for the diocese. He was a missionary and vicar general in New Mexico for about eighteen years when he was made Titular Bishop of Epiphania and vicar apostolic.

He was consecrated, August 16, 1868, in Cincinnati by Archbishop Purcell,

[1] *C.U.*, July 30, 1909; Dec. 15, 1922; Sept. 11, 1925. *Catholic Bulletin*, Feb. 26, 1926. *C.U.-B.*, Sept. 1, 1933; June 4, 1937; Dec. 28, 1945.

who was assisted by his old friends, Bishops Rappe and De Goesbriand. The Holy Father later declined his resignation of the vicariate and in 1887 made him the first Bishop of Denver, in which city he died, July 10, 1889, full of merit. Monsignor W. J. Howlett, his vicar general, in 1908 published an interesting life of the pioneer prelate, the Apostle of Colorado.

The first native of the diocese and alumnus of St. Mary's Seminary raised to the episcopate was August John Schwertner. He was born in Canton, Ohio, December 23, 1870, the son of Anthony and Christina Richard Schwertner. He attended St. Peter's School and Canton High School before going to Canisius College in Buffalo. He entered St. Mary's Seminary in Cleveland in September, 1891, and was ordained priest by Bishop Horstmann in St. John's Cathedral, June 12, 1897. He served as assistant pastor at St. Columba's in Youngstown, and then as pastor of St. Mary's and St. Patrick's in old West Park, in Milan, and in Lima. In 1913 Bishop Schrembs made him chancellor of the new Diocese of Toledo and in 1916 he became a domestic prelate. Elected to the vacant See of Wichita, Kansas, on March 10, 1921, he was consecrated on the following June 8 by Bishop Schrembs, who was assisted by Bishop Gallagher of Detroit and Bishop Tihen of Denver. After eighteen years of fruitful labor he died in Wichita on October 2, 1939.[2]

The first native of the diocese and alumnus of Cleveland's major seminary to become metropolitan of this province is Archbishop Karl Joseph Alter. Born in Toledo, Ohio, August 18, 1885, the son of John and Elizabeth Kuttner Alter, he attended St. Mary's School and St. John's College, Toledo, before entering St. Mary's Seminary in Cleveland in 1905. He was ordained on June 4, 1910, in St. John's Cathedral by Bishop Farrelly, then Apostolic Administrator of the Diocese of Toledo. He was an assistant pastor until in 1914 as the first director of the Catholic Charities he organized that department in the new diocese; he taught at Mary Manse College during the same period. He lived in Washington, D. C., as the director of the National School of Social Service (later absorbed by the University) for three years preceding his nomination, April 17, 1931, to be head of his native diocese.

On the following June 17 he was consecrated in Toledo by Archbishop McNicolas, who was assisted by Bishop Joseph H. Albers, Auxiliary Bishop of Cincinnati and later Bishop of Lansing, Michigan, and Bishop Schwertner of Wichita. He established the *Catholic Chronicle* in 1934 and founded De Sales College two years later. Expert in the science of social welfare, he was episcopal chairman of the Department of Social Action in the National Catholic Welfare Conference. He advocated social and labor reforms in accord with Christian principles and the papal encyclicals. He suggested the current method of using "fact-finding" boards for solving disputes between management and labor. Very active in the effort to obtain relief for the parochial schools during the depression, he wrote an enlightening brochure on the subject.

In June, 1950, he was promoted to the metropolitan See of Cincinnati to succeed Archbishop McNicolas. On the following September 26 he was solemnly installed in St. Monica's pro-Cathedral by Cardinal Stritch, Archbishop of Chicago, whom he had succeeded in the See of Toledo nineteen years previously. Shortly afterwards, on October 17, 1950, he returned to install his own successor in Toledo, Bishop George John Rehring, previously Auxiliary Bishop of Cincinnati.

[2] *C.U.*, Mar. 18, 1921. *C.U.-B.*, Oct. 6, 1939.

In August, 1949, Pope Pius XII in recognition of sixteen years in the diplomatic service of the Church bestowed the personal title of archbishop upon
another alumnus of old St. Mary's Seminary, the Bishop of St. Augustine,
Florida, Joseph Patrick Hurley. The son of Michael and Anna Durkin Hurley, he was born in Holy Name parish, Cleveland, January 21, 1894. After
finishing at the parish school he made his high school and college courses at
old St. Ignatius College. He spent a year in St. Bernard's Seminary in Rochester and completed his theological studies in St. Mary's Seminary, Cleveland.
He was ordained priest, May 29, 1919, by Bishop Farrelly in St. John's
Cathedral.

He served at St. Columba's in Youngstown, and at St. Philomena's and the
Immaculate Conception in Cleveland, before going abroad as the secretary
of Archbishop Mooney, the Apostolic Delegate; he was temporarily in charge
of the legation in Japan. Domestic Prelate in 1934, he was appointed special
attaché in the office of the papal secretary of state. Chosen for the vacant
Diocese of St. Augustine, Florida, he was consecrated, October 6, 1940, in
the chapel of the College of the Propaganda in Rome by Cardinal Luigi
Maglione, Prefect of the Congregation for Extraordinary Affairs, who was
assisted by Archbishop Celso Constantini, Secretary of the Propaganda, and
Archbishop Clement Micara, Nuncio Apostolic to Brussels.

He received a warm welcome in Cleveland, and many priests accompanied
him to Florida where he was installed on November 26, 1940. After the war,
in October, 1945, he was recalled to Rome and was made Regent *ad interim*
of the Apostolic Nunciature in Belgrade, Yugoslavia, which had been vacated
by the expulsion of the Nuncio by the Germans in 1941; here he was a witness of the infamous trial of Archbishop Stepinac.

Bishop Michael Joseph Ready, head of the Diocese of Columbus, Ohio,
was born in New Haven, Connecticut, April 9, 1893, the son of Michael
Thomas and Mary Ellis Ready. Brought to Ohio as a boy, he attended the
parochial schools in Mansfield and in Barberton. After his classical course
at St. Vincent's College in Latrobe, Pennsylvania, he spent two years in St.
Bernard's Seminary, Rochester, and finished his theological course in St.
Mary's Seminary, Cleveland. He was ordained by Bishop Farrelly in the
Cathedral, September 14, 1918.

He served as assistant priest at St. Mary's in Painesville for a few years
before coming to Cleveland to teach in the Cathedral Latin School, meanwhile acting as assistant at St. Philip Neri's and Holy Name parishes. He
succeeded Bishop McFadden as director of the Catholic Mission Union. In
1931 he became assistant to Monsignor Burke, and then his successor as General Secretary of the National Catholic Welfare Conference. He distinguished himself especially during the feverish war years as the Catholic representative on many boards in Washington, and he was very active in keeping
the theological seminaries functioning during the crisis. He had been a papal
chamberlain and in 1937 he became a domestic prelate.

Chosen for the Diocese of Columbus, he was consecrated, December 14,
1944, in St. Matthew's Cathedral in Washington by the Apostolic Delegate,
Archbishop Cicognani, who was assisted by the Archbishops Hoban and
McNicolas. Many high-ranking officials of the Government were present
at the ceremony. Cardinal Mooney, with whom he had been closely associated in his work, paid tribute to his tireless energy and tact in the pursuance
of the welfare of religion and society. On his visit here the new bishop pon-

tificated at the Cathedral and was the guest of the Cleveland clergy at a dinner in Hotel Statler on December 27. On the following January 4 he was installed in the Cathedral in Columbus.

Cleveland has been honored by the Holy See in the choice of Bishop Daniel Ivancho as Apostolic Exarch for the Catholics of the Byzantine Rite of Carpathian Ruthenia. He was born in the old Austro-Hungarian Empire in 1908 and came to America with his mother at the age of six. He was ordained priest in 1934 at McKeesport, Pennsylvania, and was pastor of St. Mary's Ruthenian parish in Parma when he was named coadjutor to Bishop Takach. On November 5, 1946, Archbishop Cicognani, the Apostolic Delegate, consecrated him bishop in St. Paul's Cathedral in Pittsburgh; prelates of the Byzantine Slavonic Rite acted as co-consecrators. He succeeded to the full title of Bishop of the Greek Rite Diocese of Pittsburgh upon the death of Bishop Takach in 1948. There are about fourteen parishes in this diocese subject to his jurisdiction.

Cleveland has some claim also to Bishop John Ward of Leavenworth, Kansas. The son of Joseph and Ellen McGrath Ward, he was born May 25, 1857, on a farm in Westview near Olmsted Falls, where he was a boyhood friend of Father William McMahon, later pastor of St. Bridget's. He was the brother of Mother Mary Patrick, for long years the Superior of the Sisters of the Holy Humility of Mary. He went to St. Meinrad's Seminary in Indiana and, after Bishop Gilmour had in 1881 released him from this diocese, he was ordained priest, July 17, 1884, by Bishop Fink of Leavenworth. He was appointed to succeed Bishop Fink and was consecrated by Archbishop Falconio, the Apostolic Delegate, February 22, 1911. He died in Kansas City, Kansas, April 20, 1929.[3]

Worthy of mention also is the fact that the Franciscan, Father Bernard Doebbing, who taught philosophy in old St. Mary's Seminary for approximately two years preceding July, 1881, became Bishop of Nepi-Sutri in Italy. He was born in Germany in 1855 and was ordained in St. Louis in 1879. Living at St. Joseph's Monastery, he was well known to the Cleveland priests and continued his correspondence with them even after he had established himself in Italy. He was consecrated bishop by Pope Leo XIII in 1900. He visited Cleveland in 1905.[4]

[3] Bp. Gilmour issued his permission to young Ward to transfer to the Leavenworth diocese on May 29, 1881 (C.D.A.).

[4] *C.U.*, Aug. 11, 1905.

APPENDIX B

CEMETERIES

THE OLDEST formal public burying ground in Cleveland was near an Indian mound on the east side of Ontario Street at the corner of Prospect Avenue, a site now occupied by great department stores. In 1826 Erie Street Cemetery on East 9th Street, then "out in the country," was opened and the bodies were transferred to it. The remains of Father John Dillon, Cleveland's first pastor, were buried here in 1836. The names of other Catholics interred before 1840, when the records were either lost or destroyed, were: William Delaney, Dennis Reardon, C. McShane, Stephen Monahan. Others between 1846 and 1850 were: Thomas Toole, Hugh Donahue, John Desmond, Frances and Ann Dunn, Patrick McCarthy, Mary A. Kramer, and members of the Detmer, Wagner, and Tulley families. Still other names were: Matthews, Alwell, Wamelink, Lawler, Smith, Fitzpatrick, Duffy, Golden, McCarthy, Byrne, Mulcahy. Most of these bodies were later removed to Catholic cemeteries.

The oldest Catholic cemetery in Cleveland is that of St. Joseph on Woodland Avenue at what is now East 79th Street. On January 22, 1849, Bishop Rappe purchased a plot of approximately sixteen acres at that site and dedicated four acres of level ground for burials; about three and one-half acres were sold to the railroad and to industrial companies. In 1878 Bishop Gilmour dedicated an additional eight acres and had a large granite cross and fountain erected at the entrance of what was called the new St. Joseph's Cemetery. In 1901 flood water backed up in Kingsbury Run which divided the two sections and did much damage, exposing some of the caskets and overturning the headstones. The small stream was then enclosed, retaining walls were built, and the filled-in land afforded room for another 250 lots.

The first interment in St. Joseph's Cemetery was probably that of the body of Michael Walsh, twenty years of age, who died on December 18, 1849. In the next year many bodies were brought from the Erie Street Cemetery. In addition to those mentioned above, among other early Catholic settlers buried in the new cemetery were members of the families of Gibbons, Wigman, Olwill, Logan, Brogan, McCann, L'Estrange, O'Neill, Hancape, Kaiser, Faust, Foertsch, Treiber, Van de Velde, and Farasey.

The difficulties which interfered with the use of the full acreage of St. Joseph's induced Bishop Rappe to purchase, May 4, 1855, a level tract of land on Woodland Avenue farther north, opposite to Woodland Cemetery and adjacent to the present St. Edward's Church. It was opened as St. John's Cemetery and the first burial in it took place on January 1, 1856, that of James Scully, twenty years of age. The first lot was sold, August 23, 1858, to the Moon family for six dollars. Many of the pioneer priests found their last resting place here: Father John Dillon, whose remains, brought from the crypt under the Cathedral, were placed in the same grave with those of his old friend, Father James Conlan (d. 1875); Father James Vincent Conlan (d. 1883), the first priest ordained within the confines of the diocese; Father Thomas J. Conlan (d. 1879), Bishop Gilmour's first secretary; Father Julian Bourgade (d. 1857), who came here from France in 1853; Father Charles

A. Grandmougin, (d. 1871), first pastor of St. Augustine's and a martyr to duty; Father Walter Gibbons (d. 1885), one of his successors; Father Alexis Caron (d. 1873), vicar general and rector of the seminary; Father James Monahan (d. 1884), the first priest ordained by Bishop Rappe; Father Francis Westerholt (d. 1896), missionary and pastor of St. Peter's; Father Alexander R. Sidley (d. 1893), pastor of the Immaculate Conception parish; Fathers John Daudet (d. 1892) and Joseph F. Gallagher (d. 1886), pastors of Holy Name; Father Eugene M. O'Callaghan (d. 1901), missionary and founder of St. Colman's; Father Timothy O'Mahony (d. 1889), pastor of St. Patrick's; Father Matthew Scanlon (d. 1899), pastor of St. Edward's; Fathers Andrew Sauvadet and Augustine Gerardin (d. 1903), pastors of the old French Church of the Annunciation; Father Edward J. Murphy (d. 1904), missionary and pioneer schoolman; Father Anthony Gibelli (d. 1907), pioneer Italian pastor.

The Franciscan Fathers have fifteen priests and lay brothers buried in St. John's. The early missionary Daughters of the Immaculate Heart of Mary, the Misses Pance, Ferec, and La Masson, have their tombs there. The Sisters of St. Joseph in the beginning also used this cemetery. Some of the earliest Catholics were interred there: the Wamelinks, Byerlys, Gallaghers, Smiths, Olwills, Wards, Duffys, Gibbons, Whelans, Brennans, Mahers, Haworths, Gormans, Sextons, Keegans, Byrnes, Quinlans. Interesting are the names of R. Adams, professor of music, and of Doctor J. J. Conlon (d. 1865), probably the first Catholic physician in this city. Most of the prominent families of St. Peter's bought lots in St. John's: the Beckmans, Hackmanns, Nerachers, Edams, Reifs, Schaabs, Kaisers, Grohs, Krizs (Cross), and many others.

The pioneer German and Bohemian Catholics on the West Side were buried in St. Mary's parish cemetery on West 41st Street near Clark Avenue in the vicinity of St. Procop's Church. The most illustrious tomb in the five-acre plot opened in 1861 is that of Bishop Koudelka.

By the year 1878 nearly all the lots in St. John's had been sold and then it was that Bishop Gilmour, as we have seen above, dedicated the previously unused section of St. Joseph's Cemetery. He was constrained to do this, instead of developing the farm he had purchased in Newburg for the purpose, by the continuation of the financial stringency. Years later the need of new burial grounds led to the investigation of several possible sites within a radius of fifteen miles of the city. Bishop Horstmann accepted the recommendation of a committee of city pastors and purchased in 1893 the Leland Farm and an adjoining five acres in Newburg, some six miles from the Public Square. Subsequent acquisitions increased the total acreage to 288.

About 105 acres were dedicated, November 26, 1893, as Calvary Cemetery. The first burial was that of a husband and wife, John and Catherine Hogan, on the following December 1. The first lot was sold to Vaclav Ausperk. Many bodies from the Erie Street Cemetery were reinterred here, among others those of Mrs. J. Smith (d. 1843), Miss A. Cahill (d. 1847), Mrs. Gannep (d. 1848), four McKinty children (d. 1844–1856), Thomas McMyler (d. 1858) and his children, Charles and Bridget. Twelve hundred bodies were transferred to Calvary Cemetery when part of St. Joseph's Cemetery was sold to the railroad company.

The remains of Father Dennis Tighe (d. 1866), the first pastor of St. Bridget's, were brought here from the crypt under the old Cathedral. Monsignor Felix Boff (d. 1912), vicar general and many times administrator of the diocese, is buried in the priests' plot as are the remains of most of the clergy since that time. The Franciscans have their own plot as do the Benedictines. Several of the older communities of women, which had their own private burying grounds in the earlier days, have transferred their dead to Calvary Cemetery: Mother Ursula (Catherine Bissonette), the founder with Bishop Rappe of the Sisters of Charity in Cleveland, and her pioneer companions; Mother Mary of the Annunciation (Mary Beaumont), the first Ursuline Superior, and her companions; Sister Leonarda, the foundress of St. Alexis Hospital. In their respective plots sixteen communities were represented.

In the beginning the regulation of the cemeteries was principally in the hands of the sexton. Father Thomas Walsh had charge of them from 1855 to 1856. For a period of from two to three years other priests of the Cathedral succeeded him in this duty: Fathers Edward Hannin, Thomas P. Thorpe, Thomas Carroll, Joseph F. Gallagher, Edward Mears, Thomas Conlon, Francis McGovern, and Thomas F. Maher. Father George F. Houck, the chancellor, also served as director of cemeteries from 1879 to 1904. He made many improvements and revised the system of keeping records; his idea of a funeral car was adopted by the street railway company to make the cemetery more easily accessible.

The development of new sections in Calvary Cemetery was continued under his successor, Father Patrick J. O'Connell, who was manager until his appointment to Holy Name parish in 1913. Father Martin O'Malley, the pastor of St. Columbkille's, was director for five years. He was succeeded in 1919 by Father Eugene F. Duffy who was also chaplain at Charity Hospital; during his time definite and effective measures were taken for the establishment of a fund sufficient for the "perpetual" care of the graves in the three diocesan cemeteries, two of which were already filled.

Father Francis Joyce succeeded him in 1937; Father Stanislas B. Podbielski was appointed his assistant. He made new improvements, the most noticeable of which was the beautiful new entrance to Calvary Cemetery which gave easy access to both the old and the new sections. In the year 1947 it was estimated that 155,000 persons were buried in Calvary. About seventy acres remained for future development.

In the environs of Cleveland there were still a few isolated cemeteries attached to parishes. St. Patrick's, alongside the church of that name on Puritas Avenue at Rocky River Drive, was filled, though St. Mary's on Brookpark Road was still used by the lot holders. St. Mary's in Olmsted Falls was still serving the immediate vicinity. Another old cemetery still in use was St. Paul's on Chardon Road in Euclid. In other towns each had its own burying ground in charge of the pastor, such as St. Mary's in Painesville.

In the Synod of 1882 Bishop Gilmour made "union" cemeteries of obligation in the larger communities of more than one parish and he ordered the gradual abandonment of the smaller burying grounds. The first Catholic cemetery in Toledo was that of St. Francis de Sales; three others were opened in the course of time. The bodies, however, were reinterred in the large Calvary Cemetery which Bishop Gilmour dedicated in 1887. He put a great deal of time and energy into the work of landscaping the fifty-one-acre plot.

The old Rose Hill Cemetery in Youngstown purchased by St. Columba's parish in 1856 was used by all the other parishes which were formed out of it except St. Joseph's. In 1884 Bishop Gilmour prevailed upon Father Edward Mears to purchase some eighteen acres of land at the western end of the city where Calvary Cemetery was started. He cleared and improved the grounds which were dedicated in the next year; it gradually supplanted the older burying grounds. Adjoining parcels of land were acquired and developed in the course of time to make it a beautiful and well-regulated burial ground.

Father John B. Buerkel, the retired pastor of St. Paul's in North Canton, who died on November 20, 1904, was the first to be buried in the large new Calvary Cemetery which served Canton and Massillon. In 1907 Bishop Horstmann felt called upon to appeal to the Catholics in the two towns to use this common cemetery; lots were not to be sold in the older cemeteries except to *bona-fide* parishioners of the parish to which they were attached.

Father Francis McGann, pastor of St. Vincent's in Akron from 1850 to 1855, purchased the land for the first Catholic cemetery in that town. Father Timothy M. Mahony added six acres to it in 1879. Fifty-one veterans of the Civil War were buried here. In 1912 Bishop Farrelly secured a large tract of land on the outskirts of the city on East Waterloo Road, which under the guidance of Father Richard Dowed, the pastor of Annunciation parish, was developed as Holy Cross Memorial Park.

Calvary Cemetery in Lorain was a union cemetery under the supervision of the pastor of St. Mary's, the original parish in the town. St. Mary's Cemetery in Elyria, though it belongs to the parish of that name, was used by the several parishes in the vicinity.

As early as 1888 Bishop Gilmour considered the feasibility of opening a cemetery on the West Side of the city. Bishop Horstmann preferred to develop the newly dedicated Calvary Cemetery in Newburg. Archbishop Hoban, however, purchased in May, 1945, a 277-acre plot of land in Brookpark Village at the southwestern boundary of Cleveland. Bounded by Hummel, Smith, and Settlement Roads, it has a 1500-foot frontage on Brookpark Road, a great public highway. Rolling knobs and slopes were formed to break the flat surface of the property; and an artificial lake was built to drain it.

At the entrance is a seventeen-foot granite cross against a great granite panel. The stone wall across the front was built with material taken from the abandoned Washington Bridge at East 49th Street. White marble statues representing the saints, the Blessed Mother and Our Lord, and mysteries of the Rosary each in its granite shrine or oratory dot the surface of the cemetery, in which all other monuments are flush with the ground. Near the priests' plot a gigantic granite canopy, 31 feet high and weighing 50 tons, covers an open-air altar and a great Carrara marble crucifixion group. The public address system for rendering sacred music during the time of burials and other equipment make the cemetery one of the most modern in this area. Costing approximately $1,500,000, it was two and one-half years in preparation.

On October 29, 1950, Archbishop Hoban duly consecrated it as Holy Cross Cemetery in the presence of a great crowd. In his pastoral especially inviting attendance he had emphasized the duty and the privilege of using only consecrated ground for Catholic burials. The seminary students assisted in the blessing of the five wooden crosses which signify the universality of death and the hope of resurrection, and in the consecration of the grounds. After the instructive sermon and the commemoration of all the dead in the observance of All Souls Day, the altar under the great baldachino was used for the first time for Benediction of the Blessed Sacrament.

Michael P. Curtin, two months old, on the day after the dedication, was the first to be buried in the forty-five acres which had been prepared for immediate use. Cornell J. Phillips, forty years of age, was the first adult interred, on November 2 following. The first plot was purchased, before the dedication, by Peter H. Begin, the father of the Bishop.

In the summer of 1952 the Archbishop announced the purchase of 202 acres of land at Kirtland and Chardon Roads in Chardon, 24 miles from the Public Square. When it is developed for cemetery purposes it will serve the eastern section of Greater Cleveland as well as Lake and Geauga Counties.

For their "perpetual" care the Catholic Cemeteries Association was formed to take charge of all the diocesan burying grounds: St. Joseph's and St. John's on Woodland Avenue, and St. Mary's on West 41st Street, which were already filled; Calvary and Holy Cross in Cleveland; Calvary Cemetery in Lorain and St. Mary's in Elyria. The diocese was well provided with consecrated ground for the burial of the dead for many years to come.[1]

[1] Houck, *Op. cit.*, II, 545 sq. Typewritten sketch written by Emil Kessler.

SELECT BIBLIOGRAPHY

Alerding, Herman J. *The Diocese of Fort Wayne, 1857–1907.* Fort Wayne, 1907.

Aloysius and Patricia, Sisters M., S.N.D. *Mother Mary Chrysostom.* New York, 1931.

Annales de la Propagation de la Foi. 37 v. Lyons, France, 1837–1865.

Annals of Cleveland. W.P.A., Cleveland Newspaper Digest.

Atwater, Caleb. *History of the State of Ohio.* Cincinnati, 1838.

Avery, E. M. *History of Cleveland.* Cleveland, 1918.

Balmat, Vincent (comp.). *Necrology of the Bishops and Priests of the Diocese of Cleveland, 1847–1949.* Pamphlet.

Beck, Bernard. *Goldenes Jubiläum des Wirkens der Redemptoristen Vaters an der St. Philomena Kirche in Pittsburgh und Umgegend nebst deren ersten Missionen in U.S.* Pittsburgh, 1889.

Billington, Ray. *The Protestant Crusade, 1800–1860.* New York, 1939.

Binsfeld, Edmund Louis, C.PP.S. *The Shrine of the Sorrowful Mother, Marywood.* Marywood, 1950.

Blied, Benjamin J. *Austrian Aid to American Catholics, 1830–1860.* Milwaukee, 1944.

Browne, Henry J. *The Catholic Church and the Knights of Labor.* Washington, 1949.

Burns, J. A. and Kohlbrenner, B. J. *History of Catholic Education in the United States.* New York, 1937.

Carrière, Victor. *Introduction aux Études d'Histoire Ecclésiastique Locale.* 3 v. Paris, 1934–1940.

Cather, Willa. *Death Comes to the Archbishop.* New York, 1927.

Clarke, Richard. *Lives of the Deceased Bishops of the Catholic Church in the United States.* 3 v. New York, 1888.

Cleveland, Sein Deutschtum. Cleveland, 1898 (?).

Code, Joseph B. *Dictionary of the American Hierarchy.* New York, 1939.

Coyne, James H. Tr. and ed. *The Journal of René de Bréhant de Galinée.* Toronto, 1903.

Curran, Francis X., S. J. *Major Trends in American Church History.* New York, 1946.

Curtis, Edmund A. *A History of Ireland.* London, 1936.

Curtis, Georgina Pell. *American Catholic Who's Who.* St. Louis, 1911–1931.

De Goesbriand, Louis. *Catholic Memoirs of Vermont and New Hampshire.* Burlington, 1886.

Dehey, Mrs. Elinor Tong. *Religious Orders of Women in the United States.* Hammond, 1930.

Egan, Maurice Francis. *Hierarchy of the Roman Catholic Church in the United States.* 2 v. Philadelphia, 1888.

Ellis, John Tracy. *The Formative Years of the Catholic University of America.* Washington, 1946.

——. *A Select Bibliography of the History of the Catholic Church in the United States.* New York, 1947.

Enzelberger, John. *Schematismus der Katholischer Geistlichkeit Deutscher Zunge in den Vereinigten Staaten Amerikas.* Milwaukee, 1892.

Eucharistic Congress, Seventh National, Official Record. Cleveland, 1936.

Fish, Carl Russell. *Guide to the Materials for American History in Roman and other Italian Archives.* Washington, 1911.

Gabel, Richard J. *Public Funds for Church and Private Schools.* Washington, 1937.

Garvin, John E. *Centenary of the Society of Mary.* Dayton, 1917.

Gonner, Nicolas. *Die Luxemburger in der Neuen Welt.* Dubuque, 1889.

Guilday, Peter. *Life and Times of John Carroll.* 2 v. New York, 1922.

——. *The National Pastorals of the American Hierarchy, 1791–1919.* Washington, 1923.

——. *History of the Councils of Baltimore, 1791–1884.* New York, 1932.

Haiman, Miecislaus. *The Polish Past in America, 1608–1865.* Chicago, 1939.

Helleu, A. *Jeanne Jugan.* tr. by Mary Agatha Gray. St. Louis, 1942.
——. *Lake Erie.* New York, 1945.

Heming, H. H. *The Catholic Church in Wisconsin.* Milwaukee, 1898.

Hickey, Edward J. *The Society for the Propagation of the Faith, 1822–1922.* Washington, 1922.

Houck, George F. and Michael W. Carr. *History of Catholicity in Northern Ohio and the Diocese of Cleveland, 1749 to 1900.* 2 v. Cleveland, 1903.

Howe, Henry. *Historical Collections of Ohio.* 2 v. Columbus, 1890–1891.

Johnson, C. *History of Cuyahoga County.* Cleveland, 1879.

Johnson, Peter Leo. *Stuffed Saddlebags, Life of Martin Kundig, 1805–1879.* Milwaukee, 1942.

Kelly, M. J. and J. M. Kirwin. *History of Mt. St. Mary's Seminary of the West.* Cincinnati, 1894.

Kennedy, James H. *History of the City of Cleveland, 1796 to 1896.* Cleveland, 1896.

Lambing, Andrew A. *History of the Catholic Church in the Diocese of Pittsburgh and Allegheny.* New York, 1880.

Lamott, John H. *History of the Archdiocese of Cincinnati, 1821 to 1921.* Cincinnati, 1921.
Hatcher, Harlan. *The Buckeye Country.* New York, 1940.

Lord, Robert H., John E. Sexton and Edward T. Harrington. *History of the Archdiocese of Boston in the Various Stages of Its Development, 1604 to 1943.* 3 v. New York, 1944.

Macdonald, Fergus, C. P. *The Catholic Church and the Secret Societies in the United States.* New York, 1946.

Manning, William A. *History of St. Patrick's Parish.* Cleveland, 1903.

Maynard, Theodore. *The Story of American Catholicism.* New York, 1941.

McAvoy, Thomas T., C.S.C. *The Catholic Church in Indiana, 1789–1834.* New York, 1940.

McCann, Sister Mary Agnes. *Archbishop Purcell and the Archdiocese of Cincinnati.* Washington, 1918.

McGee, John W. *The Catholic Church in the Grand River Valley, 1833–1950.* Grand Rapids, 1950.

Metzger, Charles H., S. J. *The Quebec Act.* New York, 1936.

Meyers, Gustavus. *History of Bigotry in the United States.* New York, 1943.

Michael Francis, O. S. U., Sister Mary. *The Broad Highway, A History of the Ursuline Nuns in the Diocese of Cleveland, 1850–1950.* Cleveland, 1951.

Monica, O.S.U., Sister. *The Cross in the Wilderness.* New York, 1930.

Nolan, Hugh J. *The Most Reverend Francis Patrick Kendrick.* Philadelphia, 1948.

Noll, John F. *The Diocese of Fort Wayne.* Vol. II. Fort Wayne, 1941.

O'Daniel, Victor F., O.P. *The Right Reverend Edward Dominic Fenwick, O.P.* Washington, (2 ed.) 1921.

O'Gorman, Thomas. *History of the Roman Catholic Church in the United States.* New York, 1900.

One Hundred Years, 1849–1949. History of the Church of the Holy Name. Chicago, 1949.

Orth, Samuel. *History of Cleveland, Ohio.* 2 v. Cleveland, 1910.

Paré, George. *The Catholic Church in Detroit, 1701–1888.* Detroit, 1951.

Parishes of the Catholic Church, Diocese of Cleveland, History and Records. Works Project Administration, Cleveland, 1942.

Peters, Sister M. Rosanna. *The History of the Poor Sisters of St. Francis Seraph of the Perpetual Adoration, 1875–1940.* Lafayette, 1945.

Powderly, Terence V. *The Path I Trod.* New York, 1940.

Precious Blood, A Sister of the. *Not With Silver or Gold. A History of the Sisters of the Congregation of the Precious Blood, Salem Heights, Dayton, Ohio, 1834–1944.* Dayton, 1945.

Purcell, John B. *The Vickers and Purcell Controversy.* Cincinnati, (2 ed.), 1868.

Reilly, Daniel F., O.P. *The School Controversy, 1891–1893.* Washington, 1944.

Robison, Scott, and James Cockett. *History of Cleveland.* Cleveland, 1887.

Rogers, Patrick. *Father Theobald Matthew, Apostle of Temperance.* New York, 1945.

Rose, William Ganson. *Cleveland, The Making of a City.* Cleveland, 1950.

Ryan, Daniel J. *American Catholic World War I Records.* Washington, 1941.

Shaw, Archer H. *The Plain Dealer—One Hundred Years in Cleveland*. New York, 1942.

Shea, John Gilmary. *The History of the Catholic Church in the United States.* 4 v. New York, 1886–1892.

Shearer, Donald C., O. M. Cap. *Pontificia Americana. A Documentary History of the Catholic Church in the United States (1784–1884)*. Washington, 1933.

Spalding, Martin J. *Sketches of the Life and Times and Character of Benedict Joseph Flaget*. Louisville, 1852.

Teresita, Sister Mary of St. *The Social Work of the Sisters of the Good Shepherd*. Cleveland, 1938.

Thwaites, Ruben G. (ed.) *Jesuit Relations and Allied Documents*. 78 v. Cleveland, 1896–1901.

Waring, George. *Catholic Chaplains in the World War*. New York, 1924.

Williams, Michael. *American Catholics in the War*. New York, 1921.

Wittke, Carl. *We Who Built America. The Saga of the Immigrant*. New York, 1939.

——. General editor. *History of Ohio*. 6 v. Columbus, 1941–1942.

Zwierlein, Frederick J. *Life and Letters of Bishop McQuaid*. 3 v. Rochester, 1927.

——. *Letters of Archbishop Corrigan to Bishop McQuaid and Allied Documents*. Rochester, 1946.

INDEX OF NAMES

508

Index of Names

Martin, Thomas, O.P., 20, 22–24
Martvan, J., 153
Maryknoll Fathers, 232, 309, 341, 444, 445
Masat, A. J., 276
Masin, Francis A., 389
Matthew, Theobald, Capuchin, 104, 105
Matulevicius, Bishop, 326
Mazanec, O., 322, 412, 424
Mazzuchelli, Samuel, O.P., 21
McAleer, M., 31
McAllister, Daniel, 17, 24, 30
McBride, Charles, 444, 445, 452
McCafferty, Patrick, 67
McCann, C. J., 410, 425
McCarthy, T. P., 144, 145, 247
McCloskey, Bishop James P., 364
McCloskey, James P., 266
McCloskey, Bishop W. G., 113, 186, 197
McCormick, Anne O'Hare, 239
McCormick, M. T., 394
McCormick, R., 389, 411, 412, 476
McDonald, M., 185
McDonnell, J. T., 193
McDonough, C. W., 311, 419, 452
McDonough, J. M., 313, 339, 350, 378, 386, 422, 444, 451, 464
McFadden, Bishop James Augustine; early days, 306 f.; consecration, 372; Bishop of Youngstown, 386; installation, 387; later life, 451 f.
McFaul, Bishop James A., 223
McGann, Francis, 67, 492
McGavick, Bishop Alex, 382, 465
McGinnis, J. S., 389
McGlynn, F. J., 318, 452
McGoogan, J., 273
McGovern, Francis, 491
McGovern, M. A., 83
McGrady, John H., O.P., 20, 30
McGraw, J. J., 389, 416
McGucken, Bishop Jos., 466
McGuiness, Bishop Eugene J., 384
McGuire, P., 68, 148, 252
McGuire, Thos. F., 143, 250, 260
McHale, Richard, 442
McHannon, Chas., 126
McIntyre, James P., 445
McIntyre, T. D., 426
McKeever, J., 273, 276, 320
McKenny, Th., 293, 316
McKinley, Wm., Pres., 235
McLain, J., 17
McLaughlin, Peter, 36, 39, 45–48, 50–52, 58, 87, 103
McMahon, J., 144
McMahon, Wm., 132, 141, 144, 239, 266
McManus, F., 390
McMonagle, R., 419
McMonigal, Patrick, 292

McNally, J. K., 389
McNamara, Brendan W., 426
McNamee, Hugh, 330
McNamee, Jos., 33–38
McNeil, Archbishop, 359
McNeill, Jas., 126
McNicolas, Archbishop John, 307, 359, 363, 364, 374, 376, 379, 384, 385, 386, 458, 463, 464, 466
McQuaid, Bishop Bernard J., 111, 174, 176, 188, 198, 244
Meade, H. E., 389, 390
Meare, J., O.P., 25
Mears, E., 132, 148, 154, 161, 187, 251, 266, 483, 491
Medin, J., 321
Mercy, Order of (Mercedarians), 151, 316, 317, 325, 341, 422, 423
Merrick, Dr., 298, 377
Merrick House, 281, 407
Mertes, J. B., 144, 145
Metternich, F., 145, 149, 258, 275
Mettler, J. P., 185
Meyer, Leo, 84
Michaelis, John, 231, 250
Michenfeld, J. A., 145
Migdalski, Albert, 257
Mihelko, John, 445
Miles, Bishop Rich., O.P., 25
Mindszenty, Cardinal, 393, 397, 455, 456
Mirzan, Rev., 252
Missionary Servants of the Most Holy Trinity, 342, 446
Mizer, J. G., 146, 249
Mlotkowski, J., 274
Modesta, Sister, 135
Moeller, Archbishop Henry, 264, 298, 304, 370
Moeller, Ferdinand, S.J., 282
Moes, Nicolas, 145
Moes, Nicholas A., 142, 159
Mohan, F. B., 395, 452
Molloy, Bishop Thomas, 382
Molon, L., 62, 63, 65, 66, 68, 75, 155
Molony, J. P., 62, 73, 130, 132, 161
Momenay family, 39
Monaghan, James, 68, 97, 109, 490
Monaghan, M. G., 126
Monaghan, N. F., 318, 422
Montgomery, C., O.P., 25
Mooney, Edw., Cardinal, 285, 376, 387, 463, 475, 483, 484
Mooney, James B., 252
Mooney, R., 389
Mooney, Thomas, S.M., 84
Moore, John Bishop, 161
Moore, Jos., 30
Moran, F. T., 146, 226, 276, 278, 339
Moran, John I., 231, 272, 311
Moran, J. J., 389, 390
Morgan, Mde., 91
Moriarty, Jos., 442